Laying Out a Report

The report layout window gives you a simple, visual method of creating a report form. The window begins with three bands, one for the page header, one for the page footer, and one for the detail line that is repeated for each record included in the report. You can add bands for a report title and report summary; you can also group data and include bands for each grouping.

The report layout window

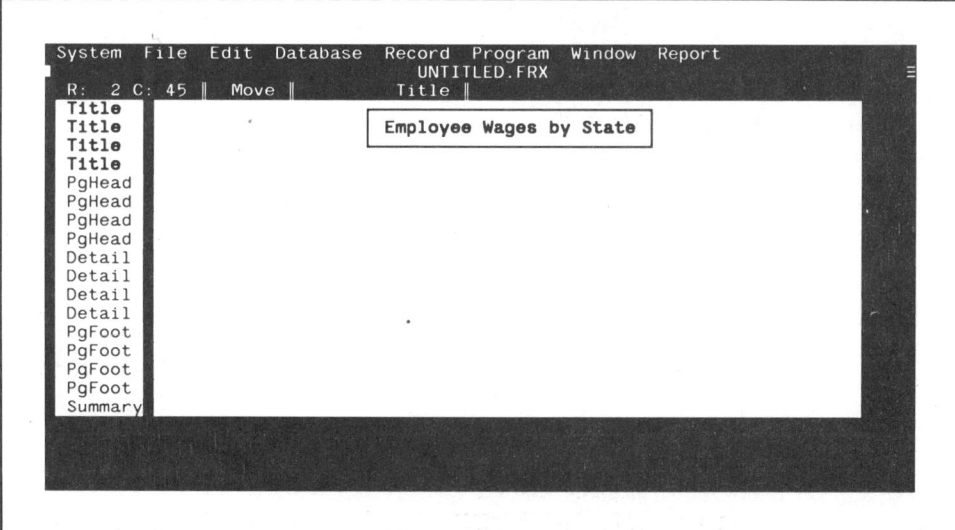

(continues on last page)

Computer users are not all alike.
Neither are SYBEX books.

We know our customers have a variety of needs. They've told us so. And because we've listened, we've developed several distinct types of books to meet the needs of each of our customers. What are you looking for in computer help?

If you're looking for the basics, try the **ABC's** series. You'll find short, unintimidating tutorials and helpful illustrations. For a more visual approach, select **Teach Yourself**, featuring screen-by-screen illustrations of how to use your latest software purchase.

Mastering and **Understanding** titles offer you a step-by-step introduction, plus an in-depth examination of intermediate-level features, to use as you progress.

Our **Up & Running** series is designed for computer-literate consumers who want a no-nonsense overview of new programs. Just 20 basic lessons, and you're on your way.

We also publish two types of reference books. Our **Instant References** provide quick access to each of a program's commands and functions. SYBEX **Encyclopedias** provide a *comprehensive reference* and explanation of all of the commands, features and functions of the subject software.

Sometimes a subject requires a special treatment that our standard series doesn't provide. So you'll find we have titles like **Advanced Techniques, Handbooks, Tips & Tricks**, and others that are specifically tailored to satisfy a unique need.

We carefully select our authors for their in-depth understanding of the software they're writing about, as well as their ability to write clearly and communicate effectively. Each manuscript is thoroughly reviewed by our technical staff to ensure its complete accuracy. Our production department makes sure it's easy to use. All of this adds up to the highest quality books available, consistently appearing on best-seller charts worldwide.

You'll find SYBEX publishes a variety of books on every popular software package. Looking for computer help? Help Yourself to SYBEX.

For a complete catalog of our publications:

SYBEX Inc.
2021 Challenger Drive, Alameda, CA 94501
Tel: (415) 523-8233/(800) 227-2346 Telex: 336311
Fax: (415) 523-2373

SYBEX is committed to using natural resources wisely to preserve and improve our environment. As a leader in the computer book publishing industry, we are aware that over 40% of America's solid waste is paper. This is why we have been printing the text of books like this one on recycled paper since 1982.

This year our use of recycled paper will result in the saving of more than 15,300 trees. We will lower air pollution effluents by 54,000 pounds, save 6,300,000 gallons of water, and reduce landfill by 2,700 cubic yards.

In choosing a SYBEX book you are not only making a choice for the best in skills and information, you are also choosing to enhance the quality of life for all of us.

Mastering FoxPro 2

Mastering FoxPro 2
Second Edition

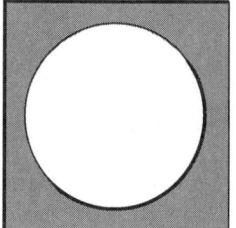

Charles Siegel

San Francisco • Paris • Düsseldorf • Soest

Acquisitions Editors: Dianne King and David Clark
Editor: Doug Robert
Technical Editor: Sheldon M. Dunn
Word Processors: Susan Trybull, Ann Dunn
Book Designer: Julie Bilski
Chapter Art: Charlotte Carter
Technical Art: Delia Brown
Screen Graphics: Cuong Le
Typesetter: Elizabeth Newman
Proofreader: Lisa Haden
Indexer: Anne Leach
Cover Designer: Thomas Ingalls + Associates
Cover Photographer: Mark Johann
Screen reproductions produced by XenoFont.

XenoFont is a trademark of XenoSoft.

SYBEX is a registered trademark of SYBEX, Inc.

TRADEMARKS: SYBEX has attempted throughout this book to distinguish proprietary trademarks from descriptive terms by following the capitalization style used by the manufacturer.

SYBEX is not affiliated with any manufacturer.

Every effort has been made to supply complete and accurate information. However, SYBEX assumes no responsibility for its use, nor for any infringement of the intellectual property rights of third parties which would result from such use.

First edition copyright ©1990 SYBEX Inc.

Copyright ©1991 SYBEX Inc., 2021 Challenger Drive, Alameda, CA 94501. World rights reserved. No part of this publication may be stored in a retrieval system, transmitted, or reproduced in any way, including but not limited to photocopy, photograph, magnetic or other record, without the prior agreement and written permission of the publisher.

Library of Congress Card Number: 91-65592
ISBN: 0-89588-808-4
Manufactured in the United States of America
10 9 8 7 6 5 4 3 2 1

Acknowledgments

I would like to thank all the people at SYBEX who have now taken this book through two editions, and thanks also to the people at Fox Software who have encouraged me and helped me, particularly Dave Fulton and Janet Walker, and also Gloria Pfief, whose technical advice was invaluable.

Contents at a Glance

Introduction — xvii

PART I — USING FOXPRO

Chapter 1	Getting Acquainted with FoxPro	3
Chapter 2	Creating a Database Structure	39
Chapter 3	Adding, Editing, and Viewing Data	73
Chapter 4	Understanding Indexes and Expressions	109
Chapter 5	Using Queries and Logical Expressions	159
Chapter 6	Generating Reports and Mailing Labels	207

PART II — ADDING POWER

Chapter 7	Using Relational Databases, the View Window, and RQBE	257
Chapter 8	Getting the Most from the Menu System	303
Chapter 9	Expanding Your Capabilities through Programming	341

PART III — PROGRAMMING WITH FOXPRO

Chapter 10	Understanding the Screen Builder	387
Chapter 11	Write Your Own Professional Menu Application	427
Chapter 12	Using the Menu Builder	487

APPENDICES

Appendix A	Installing FoxPro on Your PC	513
Appendix B	The FoxPro Utilities	521
Appendix C	Creating Applications and EXE Files	553

Index — 566

Table of Contents

Introduction	**xvii**
Versions Covered and Equipment Needed	xvii
How This Book Is Organized	xviii
Conventions Used in This Book	xix
Some Background Information on Databases	xx
Simple Databases	xx
Relational Databases	xxii
DBASE versus FoxPro	xxiv

PART I USING FOXPRO

Chapter 1	**Getting Acquainted with FoxPro**	**3**
	Introducing the FoxPro Menu Structure	4
	Making Menu Selections	6
	A Quick Tour of the Menu System	8
	Introducing FoxPro Dialog Boxes	15
	Dialog Box Controls	15
	Using Dialog Boxes	18
	Working with Windows	20
	Special Window Controls for Mouse Users	21
	Controlling Windows with the Keyboard	23
	How to Use the Editor	24
	The Edit Menu	27
	Working with the Command Window	28

	Other Features	31
	Getting Help	33
	Quitting	36
Chapter 2	**Creating a Database Structure**	**39**
	Creating a Sample Database File	40
	How to Create a New File	41
	How to Define the Structure of a Database	43
	Entering the Field Names and Types	50
	Saving the Database File	55
	The Database File in the Background	60
	Opening and Closing a Database File	61
	Copying and Modifying the Structure of a Database File	65
Chapter 3	**Adding, Editing, and Viewing Data**	**73**
	Appending Data	76
	Appending Data with the Change Display	78
	Appending Data with the Browse Display	84
	Changing (or Editing) Data	86
	Browsing through the Data	90
	Resizing and Changing the Order of Fields	91
	Partitioning the Window	93
	Deleting a Record	95
	Moving the Pointer	99
	Shortcuts Using the Command Window	102
Chapter 4	**Understanding Indexes and Expressions**	**109**
	Types of Indexes	110

	Using Some Simple Indexes	112
	Creating Simple Indexes Using the Index On Dialog Box	112
	Other Features of the Index On Dialog Box	116
	Indexing Commands	117
	Creating Simple Indexes Using the Structure Dialog Box	118
	Understanding Expressions	120
	Constants	122
	Functions and Operators	122
	Using Expressions in Indexes	140
	Using Indexes	147
	Selecting the Controlling Index	148
	Using Other Types of Indexes	149
	A Review of the Setup Dialog Box	153
	Sorting	155
Chapter 5	**Using Queries and Logical Expressions**	**159**
	Working with Logical Expressions	161
	Logical Functions	162
	Relational Operators	162
	Logical Operators	166
	To Index or Not to Index	170
	FOR and WHILE clauses	171
	Preparing to Use WHILE	172
	Rushmore Technology	173
	Making Queries for Single and Multiple Records	175
	Unindexed Queries for a Single Record	175
	Indexed Queries for a Single Record	180

	Queries for Multiple Records	182
	Querying with Other Data Types	188
	Dealing with Deleted Records	190
	Special Techniques	192
	Setting a Filter	192
	Building a Query into an Index	194
	Restricting the Query	197
	Scope	198
	Fields	200
	The Easiest Possible Report on a Query: LIST with Options	202
Chapter 6	**Generating Reports and Mailing Labels**	**207**
	Creating Reports	208
	The Report Layout Window	212
	The Report Menu	215
	A Sample Report	235
	Creating Mailing Labels	243
	Laying Out Labels	245
	What Next?	251

PART II ADDING POWER

Chapter 7	**Using Relational Databases, the View Window, and RQBE**	**257**
	Understanding Relational Databases	259
	Working with the View Window	261
	Setting Up a Relational Database	261
	Using a Relational Database	270
	Using Environment Settings	284

	Relational Query by Example and SQL	291
	The RQBE Window	291
	A Sample Query	296
	The Select Command	298
Chapter 8	**Getting the Most from the Menu System**	**303**
	Keyboard Macros	305
	Recording and Using a New Macro	307
	Working with Current and Saved Macros	312
	Advanced Editor Techniques	314
	Creating a Text or Program File	314
	Setting Up the Printer and Printing a File	315
	The Edit Menu	317
	Advanced Techniques for Manipulating Data	323
	Append From	324
	Total	326
	Calculations Using Memory Variables	328
	Replace	335
	Setting Colors	337
Chapter 9	**Expanding Your Capabilities through Programming**	**341**
	Structured Programming	343
	Some Preliminary Details	346
	Talking to the User: Input/Output	348
	Unformatted Input/Output	350
	Formatted Input/Output	357
	Control Flow	361
	Looping	361
	Selection	367

	EXIT and LOOP	372
	Procedures and Parameters	376
	The Scope of Variables and Passing Parameters	376
	User-Defined Functions	380

PART III   PROGRAMMING WITH FOXPRO

Chapter 10	**Understanding the Screen Builder**	**387**
	Creating Screens and Generating Code	388
	Manipulating Objects	391
	The Layout Dialog Box	391
	The DeskTop	391
	Windows	392
	Screen Code	395
	READ Clauses	396
	Adding Code Snippets	397
	Environment	398
	Boxes	398
	Fields	400
	Specifying the Field or Variable to Display	401
	Picture Templates and Functions	401
	Optional Clauses	405
	Other Features of the Field Dialog Box	408
	Text	408
	Controls	409
	Pushbuttons	409
	Radio Buttons	412
	Check Boxes	413

	Popup Controls	415
	Scrollable Lists	416
	Invisible Pushbuttons	417
	Controlling the Screen Design	419
	Quick Screen	420
	Generating Code	421
Chapter 11	**Write Your Own Professional Menu Application**	**427**
	Analysis	428
	Making a Structure Diagram	430
	The Main Menu	435
	Stub Testing	441
	Reports and Mailing Labels	444
	The Report Menu	444
	The Label Menu	452
	Exporting for Mail-Merge	458
	The Data Submenu	461
	Stubs for Testing	463
	The Edit Screen Program	464
	The LOOKUP Module	471
	The Append Screen Program	478
	Other Features of the Data Menu	484
Chapter 12	**Using the Menu Builder**	**487**
	The Menu Design Window	488
	Hot Keys	492
	The Options Check Box	493

The Menu Menu	494
General Options	495
Menu Options	496
Quick Menus	497
Generating Code	499
Menuing Commands	500
Defining a Menu	501
Using the Menu Builder to Create Non-System Menus	502
A Sample Menu System	503

APPENDICES

Appendix A	Installing FoxPro on Your PC	513
Appendix B	The FoxPro Utilities	521
Appendix C	Creating Applications and EXE Files	553
	Index	566

Introduction

WHETHER YOU ARE A BEGINNER TO USING COMPUTER database programs or a seasoned DBMS user, this book will give you a solid understanding of the latest version of the FoxPro database management system. Starting with the very basics—using the keyboard or a mouse to move through the on-screen menus and boxes—you will quickly progress through creating and using, by means of step-by-step tutorials, a sample database using all of the program's major features. The entire process is presented from the perspective of an experienced user/programmer, so you will be introduced to the rationale behind the best database techniques even as you learn the basics. After a thorough grounding in the use of databases, you can choose to continue with instructions on becoming a "power user" or progress to writing and customizing your own programs, using a structured programming approach, and the faster interactive programming tools that make the latest version of FoxPro so powerful.

VERSIONS COVERED AND EQUIPMENT NEEDED

FoxPro is distributed on high-density floppy disks, but if you have an older PC, Fox Software will provide you with a copy of the program that does not require a high-density disk drive for installation.

This book covers FoxPro version 2.0, released in mid-1991, which requires an IBM or compatible PC with at least 512K of RAM (640K recommended). To run the complete program with help files and utilities (which will allow you to take full advantage of the advice presented in this book), you should have at least four megabytes of free space on the hard disk. Because FoxPro creates temporary files while it is running, it is always better to have much more than the minimum available.

A color monitor is certainly useful, and the program enables you to select various color schemes to make the display more pleasing to the eye, but, unlike some packages designed to run on color monitors, FoxPro has no visibility problems on a monochrome monitor. A mouse is also quite useful, but hardly necessary. The book offers instructions for both keyboard and mouse.

This book does not offer specific instruction on installing or using the program over a network.

HOW THIS BOOK IS ORGANIZED

Throughout the course of this book you will run into many step-by-step procedures. Because the work you will be doing in these procedures will typically build upon work you will have done in earlier procedures, it would be best to start at the beginning of Part I and actually work through the examples. After Part I you can continue to Part II to learn more sophisticated techniques, or you can skip to Part III to learn about programming with FoxPro.

Part I of the book—the first six chapters—are meant to be tutorials on the features of FoxPro that are essential for ordinary business users. Unnecessary features of the program are put in later sections or in the appendices, so that they do not get in the way of your learning to use the program as quickly as possible. For example, the features of the menu system that are not essential are put off until Part II, so that they will not get in the way of your getting started with FoxPro quickly.

You can use Part I of this book and then get right down to work with FoxPro. You will have learned what you need to know to handle any simple database application—almost every application that you will come across in practice.

This book will also help you to become a power user of FoxPro. Part II teaches you all the features of the menu system. It will teach you, for example, to create keyboard macros that assign values to any of the function keys or to almost any combination of Ctrl, Alt, Shift and another key. It will also teach you to create and use relational databases.

Finally, this book is written to help you become a FoxPro programmer. Part III begins with a general discussion of the principles of computer programming, such as control flow and passing parameters, using FoxPro as an example. In the final chapters, you will write a complete mailing list program including windows, mouse support, and pop-up menus. FoxPro is powerful enough that you will be able to write programs of this quality by the time you finish this book, whether or not you have ever done any programming before. In fact, although this book does not cover all of FoxPro's advanced programming features, it serves as a thorough and valuable guide through the intermediate level, and will teach you to use the most important tools: the screen builder and the menu builder. In addition, a project builder is presented in one of the appendices.

If you are impatient to move on to programming, you may skip Part II of this book and go directly to Part III after you finish Part I. You will be able to follow all of the programs with Part I as a background. After you have learned programming, you can go back to Part II to learn additional FoxPro commands that will add more power to your programs.

The FoxPro language is so large that it is hard for anyone to learn it all. It includes all of the dBASE language plus much more. Even experienced programmers can browse through the reference manual and suddenly be surprised to learn new commands or functions that give them easier ways of doing things they have done for years. The FoxPro interface and the basic FoxPro commands that you need, on the other hand, are very simple to use. You can never finish learning FoxPro, but you should find it easy to begin.

> The Note icon points out additional information or reiterates the importance of a point made in the text.

> The Tip icon flags a different, faster, or easier way of doing something.

> The Special Alert icon will warn you of potential problems.

CONVENTIONS USED IN THIS BOOK

The margins of the pages will frequently contain special notes, tips, and special alerts, as shown to the left.

The text itself uses boldface type to denote commands and other words you are instructed to type at your keyboard. Command keywords (words that are part of the FoxPro language) are all uppercase; other words within commands reflect the way they would generally appear in the situation described. Descriptors identifying the type of information that should appear at that position in the command are shown in italics surrounded by angle brackets (less-than and greater-than signs); these words, and the brackets themselves, should be replaced by an actual value when you use the command. For example, if a command includes <*file name*>, you must type the name of an actual file.

SOME BACKGROUND INFORMATION ON DATABASES

When businesses began to computerize their recordkeeping during the 1960s, computer scientists developed theories about how to redesign the data that used to be kept in paper files so that it could be managed more efficiently on computer. In many cases, they simply used new terms in order to speak more precisely about the same sorts of things that people had always used when they used paper files. In other cases, though, they developed entirely new ways of handling data that had not been possible before computers were used.

SIMPLE DATABASES

A simple database is organized in pretty much the same way that data has generally been organized on paper.

A typical file in an old-fashioned office was made up of a collection of identical forms, each with blank spaces where information was supposed to be filled in. An example would be a list of names kept on a collection of index cards, each of which was printed to show you where to fill out the name, the address, the city, the state, the zip code, and the telephone number. Most data was kept on larger forms that went into file folders, but the basic principle was the same: a standard form would be preprinted to indicate the type of data that was needed, and there were blank spaces where you had to fill in the actual data needed on each form.

Simple databases are organized in the same way. All you need to learn are the new terms that are used to describe them once they have been computerized:

- **field:** Each blank space to be filled in is called a field. In the index-card database mentioned above, there is one field for the name, one field for the address, and so on.

- **record:** All the data that would appear on a single form is called a record. In our example, the name, address, and phone number of one person makes up one record.

- **file:** A collection of similar records that are used together is called a file. In our example, the box of index cards that holds all the names and addresses that you use together make up a file. Of course, you could also have another file with similar records—just as you could have another box of index cards where you keep another list of names and addresses.

These are the three basic terms that you will hear repeatedly whenever people are talking about databases. They are summarized in Figure I.1, which shows how database terminology would be used to describe the old-fashioned index-card file.

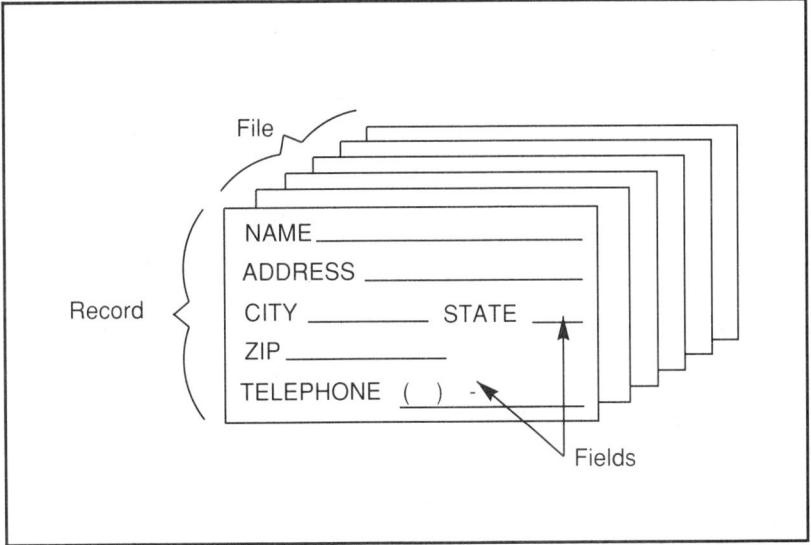

Figure I.1: Database terminology

It is often convenient to arrange this sort of data into a table. A computer, of course, lets you display your data both ways—as forms, with one form for each person, or as a table, with a column for the name, a column for the address, and so on, so that the data for each person can be listed on one line. When the data is arranged as a table, each column represents a field, each line represents a record, and the table as a whole represents the file.

RELATIONAL DATABASES

Some of the advantages of computerizing data are obvious. A computer can instantly look up the record you want—for example, if you are looking for the telephone number of a certain person. It can print out the data in different forms, saving you the trouble of copying it from the list in the form you need—for example, it can print out a list of names and phone numbers when you want to call people, and can print out labels when you want to do a mailing. It can instantly select only certain records from the file—for example, it can list the names and phone numbers of only the people who live in New York, or it can print out mailing labels for only the people who live in New Jersey. It lets you use the data in different orders—for example, you can effortlessly print out your mailing labels in zip code order and print out your list of names and phone numbers in alphabetical order.

In addition to these obvious advantages of computerizing data, early computer scientists found a more subtle advantage of computerization. They found that computers made it possible to avoid repetition.

In the days of the paper office a typical large business had dozens of different forms that included the name and address of each employee. The payroll department used a form with the name, address, and wages of each employee; the benefits department used a form with the name, address, and eligibility for benefits of each employee; the human resources development department used a form with the name and address and the training courses taken by each employee; and so on.

This repetition was obviously inefficient. The same name and address—and, of course, other basic information such as Social Security number and telephone number—had to be filled out over and over again. If an employee moved, a dozen different people in a dozen different departments would have to change the address on a dozen different forms.

Repetition could not be avoided in a paper office, but computer scientists quickly devised ways to let a business enter the names and addresses only once and to let each department use those names and addresses in combination with the specific data that it needed about wages, benefits, training courses, or whatever.

Early methods that were used for tying all this data together were very complex and unwieldy. There were hierarchically organized databases and databases organized as networks that were held together using pointers, both of which were so complicated that they could only be understood and used by programmers with training in database theory. Companies had to have teams of programmers just to retrieve information or to produce reports.

In 1970, E. F. Codd invented a new way of tying together this sort of data, which was called the *relational* database. His idea was to break down the data into separate files, which could be related using a common key field.

In the example we have been looking at, the business would probably use an employee number as a key field. Then it could have one file with each employee's employee number, name, address, and other basic data, another file with each employee's employee number and wages, another file with each employee's employee number and eligibility for benefits, and so on. Basic information such as the name and address would only have to appear once. Each department would have a program that used the employee number to relate the data it needed on wages or benefits to the basic data that everyone needed.

With relational databases, most of the work of relating the data was built into the database management program. You did not need programmers to create pointers to relate one record to another. You just had to enter the right employee number and wage in one file, and the database management system would do the work of relating that record to the record in another file that had the name and address for that employee number.

Codd analyzed the relational database using mathematical set theory and discovered ways to break down the data that minimized repetition. Because they were both powerful and simple to visualize and to use, relational databases quickly became the preferred method of handling complex data.

In simple databases—for example, the simple list of names and addresses that could be kept on index cards—there is no distinction between the database and the file: a simple database consists of only one file. Relational databases, though, consist of more than one file. We have to add one more term to those we already defined: in addition to field, record, and file, we now understand the term *database* itself. A database is made up of all the data used together in an application, whether it is kept in one file or in many.

DBASE VERSUS FOXPRO

When the IBM-PC and compatibles became popular during the 1980s, the program dBASE II, developed by Ashton-Tate, quickly emerged as the leading database management program. A couple of simpler programs had some brief popularity because they were so easy to use, but none of them let you manage more than a simple database, such as the basic list of names and addresses that you could keep on index cards. dBASE II was the most popular of the programs that let you work with either a simple or a relational database.

dBASE's interactive commands let business users create, edit, and print reports on databases. dBASE also included a programming language which was relatively easy to learn and to use, and programmers used it to create menu-driven custom applications for their clients. Business users who did not want to bother learning about dBASE could have programmers set their applications up for them, so they could just make choices from menus and edit data or print out exactly the reports they needed; it was quicker and easier to do this programming in dBASE than in other computer languages because dBASE was specifically designed for this sort of task.

Because of its power, dBASE was by far the most popular database management system for microcomputers. At the high point of its popularity, it was estimated that 80 to 85 percent of all database applications on IBM-PC compatible microcomputers used dBASE. dBASE became an industry standard. Even unrelated database programs were designed so that they could use dBASE data files.

dBASE II was followed by dBASE III and dBASE III+, both of which added to its power, but there were complaints about limitations.

Many users considered the various dBASE versions too difficult. Early versions of dBASE just presented the user with a dot prompt, and the user had to memorize all the commands that had to be entered at the prompt in order to manipulate the database. You had to enter exactly the right command to edit the data or to produce a report. Even if you were working with the simplest sort of database, you had to learn dozens of commands; if you spelled a command incorrectly or got its syntax slightly wrong, dBASE would display an error message and refuse to work.

Critics said that dBASE told the user less than any other program that existed: even DOS, which was notorious for being cryptic, at least displayed a prompt that told you what drive you were on, but dBASE just displayed a dot, the smallest, least informative prompt imaginable. Later versions of dBASE added an "Assistant" mode, which let you do some of the basics by using menus, but its capacity was limited.

Programmers had different complaints from users. There was grumbling about certain limitations of the dBASE language, such as its inability to create arrays, but the most common complaint by far was that dBASE did not include a *compiler*.

Most programming languages are compiled: the application program is written in an English-like language, and then the compiler translates it permanently into the sort of machine language that the computer uses. When programmers distribute the application, they can simply give the users the compiled program, which runs directly on their computers.

On the other hand, some more primitive programming languages (such as the early versions of BASIC) are *interpreted*. The program remains in the English-like language that it was written in. Each time it is run, the interpreter reads it one line at a time, interpreting each line into machine code. An interpreted program has two major disadvantages over a compiled program. First, it runs much more slowly: each line has to be interpreted before it is run, and that takes time. Second, the language program itself must be distributed along with the application: it cannot run by itself.

dBASE programmers complained about both of these problems. Everyone agreed that programs working on large data files ran too slowly. Some thought it was even worse that you had to own dBASE to run a program written in dBASE. If clients who did not already own dBASE hired a programmer to write a database management system for their business, they did not like the idea that they had to pay as much for a copy of dBASE to run the program as they had paid the programmer to write the program. Further, some programmers were beginning to use dBASE to write complete commercial applications, such as small business accounting programs, but they could not really distribute these programs commercially as long as users needed to own dBASE itself in order to run them.

In response to these complaints, a couple of companies that were not related to Ashton-Tate (which owns dBASE) came up with compilers and pseudo-compilers for the dBASE III and dBASE III +

languages—usually with enhancements and sometimes with slight incompatibilities compared with the original.

One of these was Fox Software, which developed FoxBase and then FoxBase+, dBASE-compatible development systems that include a *pseudo-compiler*. A pseudo-compiler does not translate programs into machine code that the computer can run directly. Instead, it does a sort of partial translation and creates something that is closer to machine code than the original English-like program and that runs much more quickly than an interpreted program would, but which still cannot run by itself; it must be distributed along with a *run-time module* that does some interpretation each time it runs.

FoxBase was widely considered one of the best of the dBASE compilers because its programs ran quickly and because it had a high-level of compatibility with dBASE itself. You could take programs written using dBASE and compile them using FoxBase, while other compilers usually required you to rewrite the program a bit before they could compile it.

You can see that different dialects of dBASE were emerging. Compilers not only enhanced the original dBASE language but sometimes also differed from it in minor ways. As more enhancements appeared, the dBASE standard became diffuse: Ashton-Tate could no longer define what the dBASE standard was, and dBASE IV has failed to establish itself as such. Programmers now commonly use the term xBase to refer to elements that are shared among the various database management programming languages.

When FoxPro, a major advance over FoxBase+, first came out, it was received quite well by many database users and programmers. With version 2, FoxPro now includes Fox's patented *Rushmore* technology, which tests have shown can make some queries over a hundred times faster than competing products. This is sure to make a difference for businesses running huge databases. FoxPro could now easily emerge as the new standard for database management systems.

As you will see, FoxPro is designed around a very powerful combination of a Macintosh-like user interface based on windows and pop-up menus (which can be used easily either from the keyboard or with a mouse) and a special Command window, where you can enter the type of procedural commands used at the dBASE dot prompt. As its most striking feature, this interface automatically generates commands in the Command window when you make the equivalent choices from the menu system, making it easy for users to get started with the program and to learn more and more about it as they go along.

For programmers, FoxPro includes a menu and screen builder that make it easy to create pop-up menus and screens with radio buttons, pushbuttons, and other advanced interface features. Now even intermediate-level programmers can create an impressive user interface with mouse support. Advanced programmers will want to take advantage of FoxPro's low-level file handling functions, which are similar to the file handling functions in the C language, and of its application builder, which lets you create standalone applications and .EXE files.

PART I

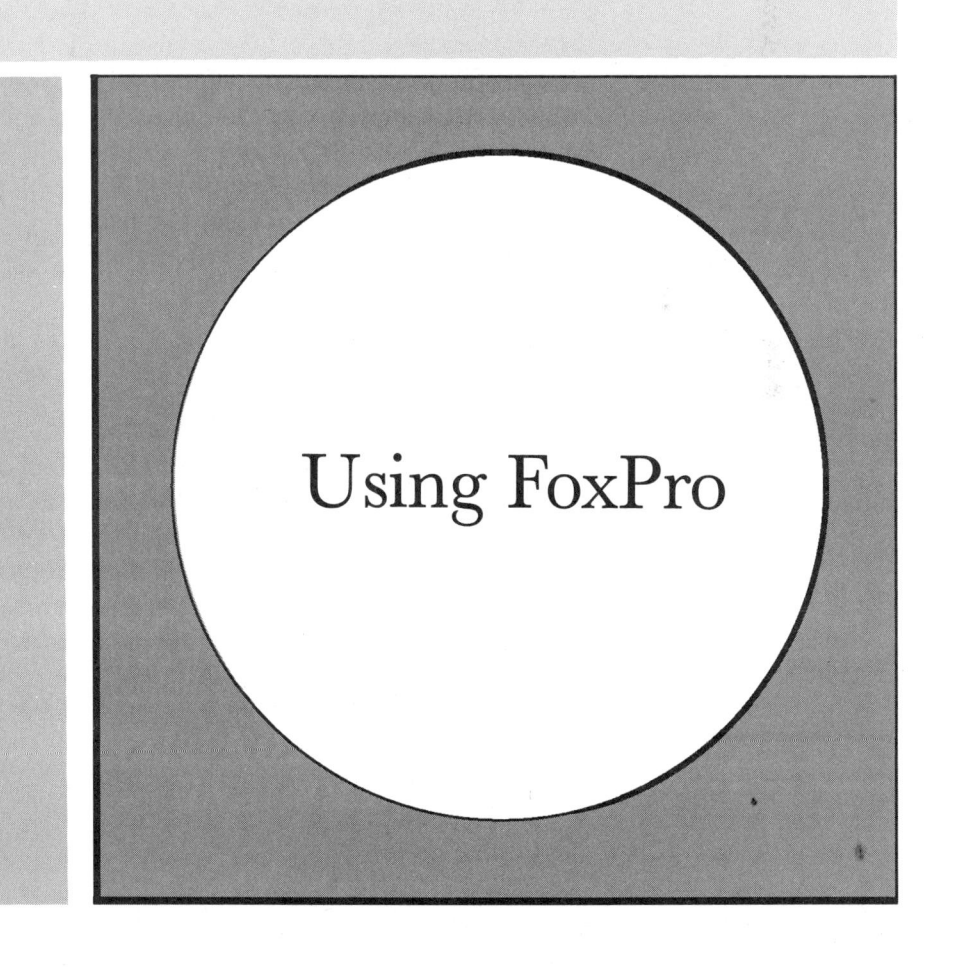

Using FoxPro

Chapter 1

Getting Acquainted with FoxPro

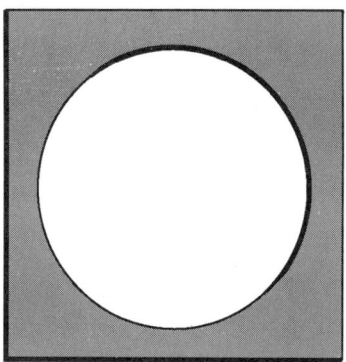

EVERYTHING YOU WILL DO WITH FOXPRO CENTERS around its interface of pop-up menus and windows. Beginners use this interface to perform simple menu-driven operations on their data. Advanced programmers use the same interface to write and compile their program files.

This chapter teaches you how to use the FoxPro interface and tries to make you comfortable with its basics before you go on to the rest of the book.

As you will see, FoxPro works well using either the keyboard or a mouse. With the keyboard, it often gives you several ways of doing the same thing. This lets you choose the method you find most convenient.

Because there are many ways of performing most operations, it will not be possible to list them all every time they are discussed. When later chapters give you step-by-step instructions on using FoxPro, they will simply tell you to make certain selections from the menu and from the dialog boxes. They will not detail all the ways that you can make these selections, because it would simply take too much time and would make the book difficult to read.

For this reason, it is very important for you to make good use of this first chapter. This chapter will detail all the ways of performing the basic FoxPro operations, the ones you will perform over and over again as you work with this book. Experiment with the different ways of doing things as you read. The rest of the book will be easier for you to use if you begin to become comfortable with one way of making selections from menus, one way of using dialog boxes, and one way of working with windows by the time you finish this chapter.

INTRODUCING THE FOXPRO MENU STRUCTURE

FoxPro combines an easy-to-use interface, based on choosing items from pop-up menus, with a Command window, where you can enter the sort of procedural commands that were used in early versions of dBASE. FoxPro's combination is unique in that when you make choices from the menu, the program displays the written command equivalent, which appears in the Command window.

In this section, you will learn to make selections from the FoxPro menu system and then will take a quick tour of the FoxPro menu structure. First, of course, you must start the program. If you have not yet installed FoxPro, see Appendix A for installation instructions before going on.

> The instructions in this book assume that you are using the basic, stand-alone version of FoxPro. If you are not, enter **FOXPROX** to start the extended version, **FOXPROL** to start FoxPro/LAN, or **FOXPROLX** to start the extended version of FoxPro/LAN.

1. Make sure you are in the FOXPRO 2 directory that was created when you installed the program.
2. At the DOS prompt, type **FOXPRO** and press Enter. You will see the initial FoxPro screen illustrated in Figure 1.1.

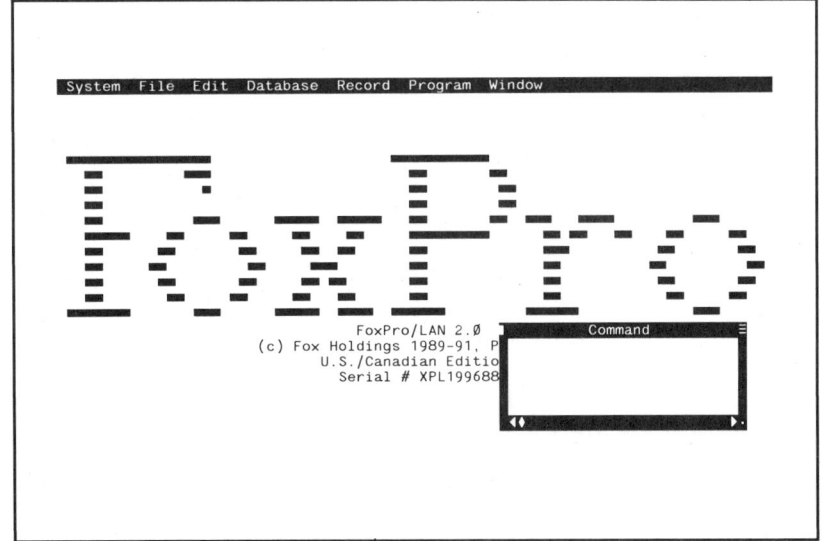

Figure 1.1: The initial FoxPro screen, with the menu and Command window

The main menu is at the top of the screen. Most of the screen is taken up by the FoxPro logo with the copyright notice under it, and the Command window is near the bottom of the screen. Notice that the cursor is in the Command window, ready for you to enter a procedural command. (Unfortunately, the cursor does not appear in the screen images used in the figures. When it is important to know where to find the cursor, the text will instruct you where to look.)

The highlighted menu across the top of the screen is called the *menu bar*. Each of the words written in the menu bar is called a *menu pad,* as in keypad. Think of each pad as a button. As you will see, when you select one of the menu pads, a *menu popup* will appear, containing a group or groups of choices called *menu options*.

When you perform certain operations with FoxPro, you will find that some of the menu pads that are no longer relevant to what you are doing will appear in a lighter color or disappear altogether from the menu bar. Sometimes, you will also find extra pads added to the right of the pads already on the menu bar. For example, when you are creating mailing labels, a Label pad will appear, permitting you to access additional options relevant to working with labels.

When you look through the menu popups, you will see that a single popup may be subdivided by lines to group related options.

You will also see that some menu options are dimmed, indicating that they cannot be chosen in the current situation. Some menu options have *Control-key shortcuts* next to them, a combination of the Ctrl key (indicated by the symbol ^) and some other key. You can use a Control-key combination to choose an option instantly without going through the menu system.

A menu option followed by an ellipsis (...) indicates that a *dialog box* will appear when you choose that option. Dialog boxes present more information and more choices relating to the option you have selected.

> Do not bother learning Control-key shortcuts when you are first starting with FoxPro. Because they appear next to the menu options, over time you will automatically learn the shortcuts for the options that you use frequently.

MAKING MENU SELECTIONS

If you are using a mouse, selecting options from the FoxPro menu system is simple and intuitive. If you are using the keyboard, selecting options from the menu is not as intuitive, but is still very easy to do once you are used to it.

USING A MOUSE

To make a selection from the menu using a mouse, simply point at the menu pad you want and then hold the mouse button down. This will make that pad's menu popup appear. Continue to hold down the mouse button and drag it downward until the menu option that you want is highlighted. Releasing the mouse button at that point selects that option. The menu popup will disappear, and FoxPro will do whatever your selection tells it to do.

Practice this technique by making each menu popup appear as you read the "Quick Tour of the Menu System" in the section following this presentation of techniques.

USING THE KEYBOARD

You can use the keyboard in several ways to make a selection from the menu. Choose the one that you like best.

First, you must make the right menu popup appear. You may either

- press the Alt key in combination with the highlighted letter of one of the menu pads to make that popup appear immediately, or

- press the Alt key by itself or the F10 key by itself to move the cursor to the menu bar. The cursor will land on the System menu pad initially, but the System menu popup will not appear. To select the menu pad that you want, use the left and right arrow keys to move the cursor to that menu pad; then make the menu popup appear by pressing any of the following: Enter, the space bar, the up or down arrow key, or any character key.

After you have made one menu popup appear, you can make others appear by moving the highlight left or right from one menu pad to another; however, only one menu popup can appear at a time. It is sometimes convenient to browse through the menu popups in this way.

Once the menu popup that you want has appeared, you can choose the menu option from within it in a couple of ways. Either

- press the highlighted letter of that menu option (usually the first letter), or

- use the up and down arrow keys to move the cursor to highlight the menu option you want. (You will notice that when the cursor is on the first option, the up arrow key moves the cursor to the *last* option as if you had reached the top and were starting over from the bottom.) Once you have

> The highlighting of the letter to press in order to select a menu option does not appear on some displays. Where this is the case, you may select options by using the up and down arrow keys and then pressing Enter or the space bar.

highlighted the option you want, select it by pressing Enter or the space bar.

After you select a menu option, the menu popup will disappear, and FoxPro will do whatever your selection has told it to do.

Try to become comfortable now with one or two of these methods of selecting menu options. Experiment with them by calling up the menu popups in different ways as you read the next sections that describe the popups. If you also practice selecting menu options in a few different ways, it will take you into the uncharted territory of windows and dialog boxes, but try it anyway. You can return to the menu system simply by pressing the Esc key repeatedly to "back up" until you reach the menu display.

A QUICK TOUR OF THE MENU SYSTEM

Some people find the organization of the FoxPro menu system a bit confusing at first, so when you begin with FoxPro, it is a good idea to look at each of the original menu popups in order to get an overall idea of how the menu is organized. Once you have a sense of its general structure, you will find it easy to work with the menu system.

THE SYSTEM POPUP

Use one of the techniques that you just learned to look at the System popup, illustrated in Figure 1.2. (The FoxPro logo and the Command window have been eliminated from the following illustrations to make them clearer.)

The utilities below the line—such as the Filer, the Calculator, the Calendar/Diary, and so on—are DOS and desktop utilities which can be handy, but they are not related to FoxPro's main functions. They are discussed in Appendix B of this book.

The utilities above the line are a bit more closely related to FoxPro's main functions. Macros will be discussed in Part II of this book, and Help will be discussed later in this chapter.

THE FILE POPUP

The File popup, shown in Figure 1.3, includes some of the most important options of the menu system.

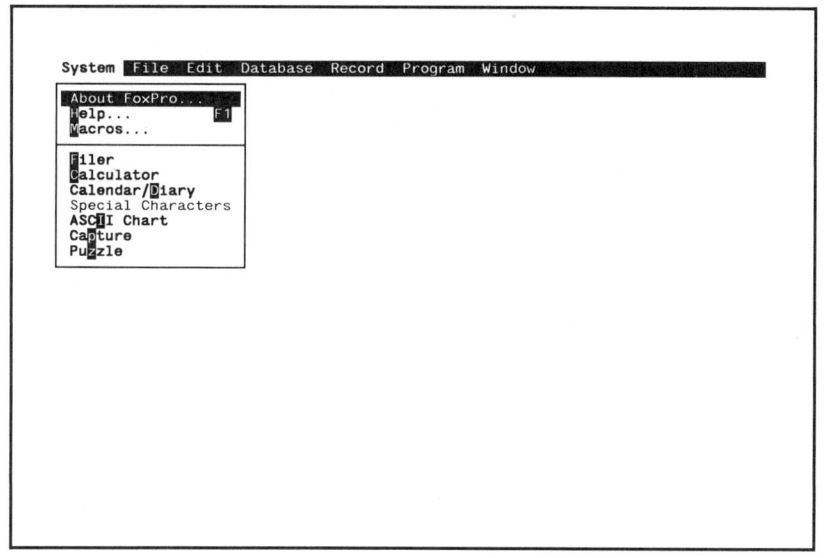

Figure 1.2: The System popup

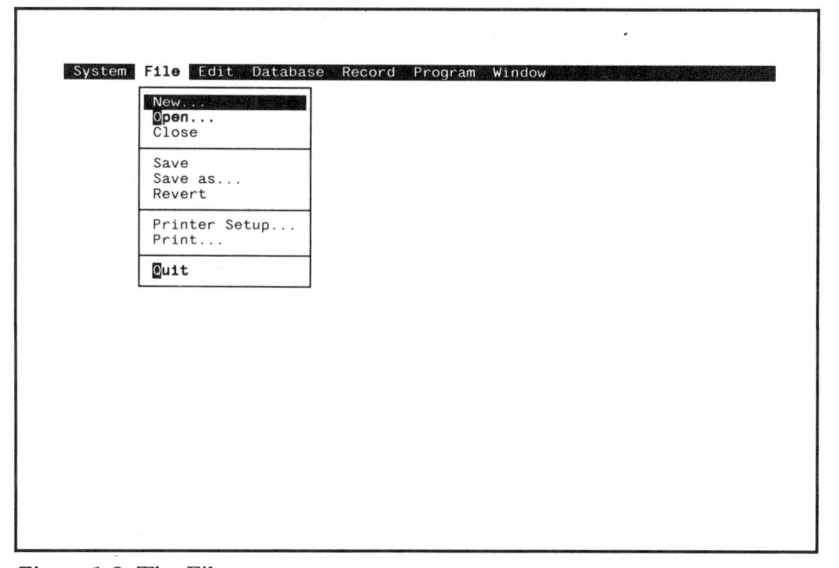

Figure 1.3: The File popup

The options above the first line let you create and use files—not only database files but also text files, program files, and the files that FoxPro uses for objects such as its indexes, reports, and mailing labels. New lets you create a new file; Open lets you open and use an existing one, and Close lets you close the one you are currently using. The next group of options is also for working on these files. Save lets you save the changes you have made, Save As lets you save them under another name, and Revert lets you cancel the changes that you made to a file since it was last saved.

As you work with FoxPro—creating objects such as database files, indexes, reports, and mailing labels—you will use these first two groups of menu options constantly.

The options in the third group let you print, and, finally, the Quit option lets you leave FoxPro and return to DOS.

THE EDIT POPUP

The Edit popup, shown in Figure 1.4, is useful mostly for advanced users who use the FoxPro editor to write and debug lengthy programs or text files.

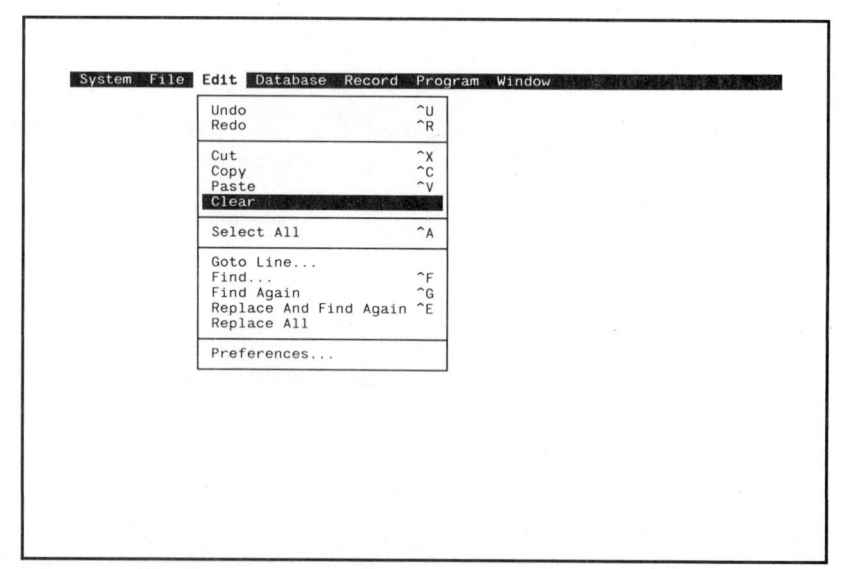

Figure 1.4: The Edit popup

The same editor is used throughout FoxPro for editing data in your databases and editing commands in the Command window as well as for editing programs and text. The editing that you will do in this book generally involves only the basic features of the editor, and not the advanced features that you access through the menu.

Notice that almost all of the advanced word-processing features on the Edit menu have Control-key shortcuts listed to their right. Once you become an advanced user of the editor, these shortcuts can make it a very powerful and fast word processor.

The basics of the editor and a couple of the most useful menu features, such as Copy and Paste, are discussed later in this chapter. Advanced features of the Edit menu are discussed in Chapter 8.

THE DATABASE POPUP

The Database popup, shown in Figure 1.5, is used to perform operations on an opened database. You will find it fundamental to the work you do with FoxPro.

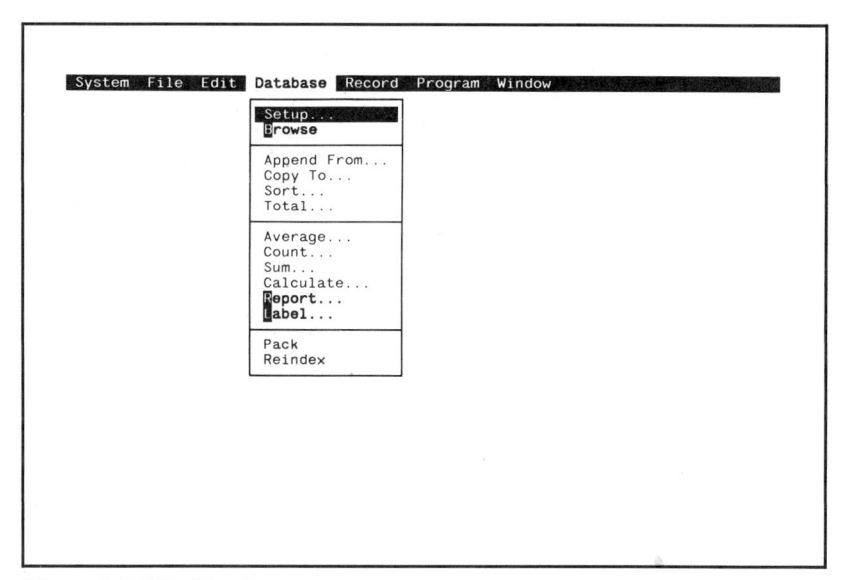

Figure 1.5: The Database popup

The two options in the first group let you do basic operations on the entire file. Setup lets you determine how the data in the file will be displayed. Browse lets you look at and edit data from the entire file.

The next group of options lets you perform operations that involve two separate files: appending the data in one file to another, copying from one file to another, sorting the records from one file into another, and totaling the numeric fields from one file into another.

The next group of options lets you work with one file, performing numeric operations or producing reports or labels.

The final group includes two utilities which let you finalize deletions and repair indexes.

THE RECORD POPUP

The Record popup, which lets you work with individual records of a database file, is not activated unless you have already opened a database file. On some screens, you can see that the Record pad is dimmer than the other pads. Since at this point you will not be able to bring forth the popup, you should look at the illustration of it in Figure 1.6 to follow the discussion of its options.

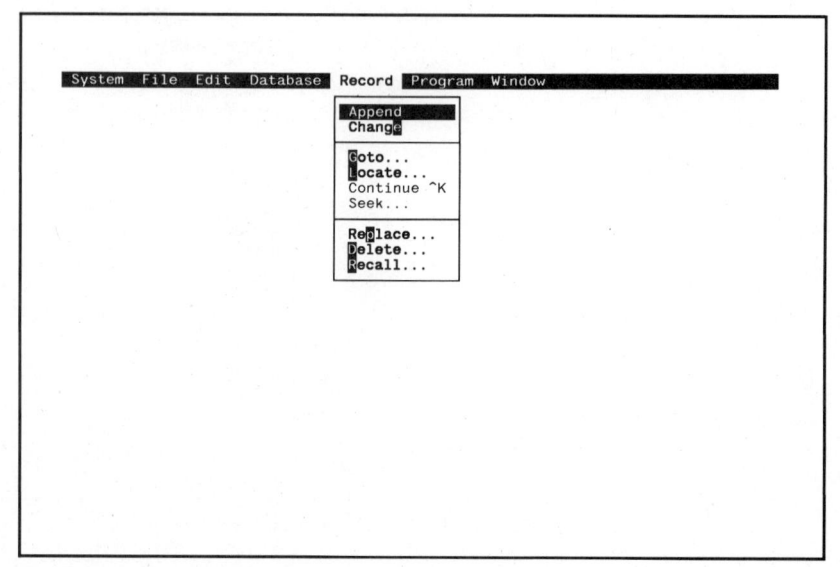

Figure 1.6: The Record popup

Like the Database popup, the Record popup is fundamental to the work you will do with FoxPro. The first two options, Append and Change, let you add a new record or edit an existing record. These options let you see only one record at a time, but they let you do much the same things that the Browse option on the Database popup lets you do.

The options in the next group let you move around the database to get to a record that you want to use. The options in the final group let you replace the values of records, delete records, or recall deleted records.

THE PROGRAM POPUP

The Program popup, as you may have guessed, includes options that are useful for writing FoxPro programs. It is illustrated in Figure 1.7.

The first option, Do, lets you run a program. The pair of options below Do let you stop running a program or resume running a program. The options in the following group are useful for debugging.

The options in the final group are utilities. Compile, predictably, lets you compile a program. Generate lets you generate programming code

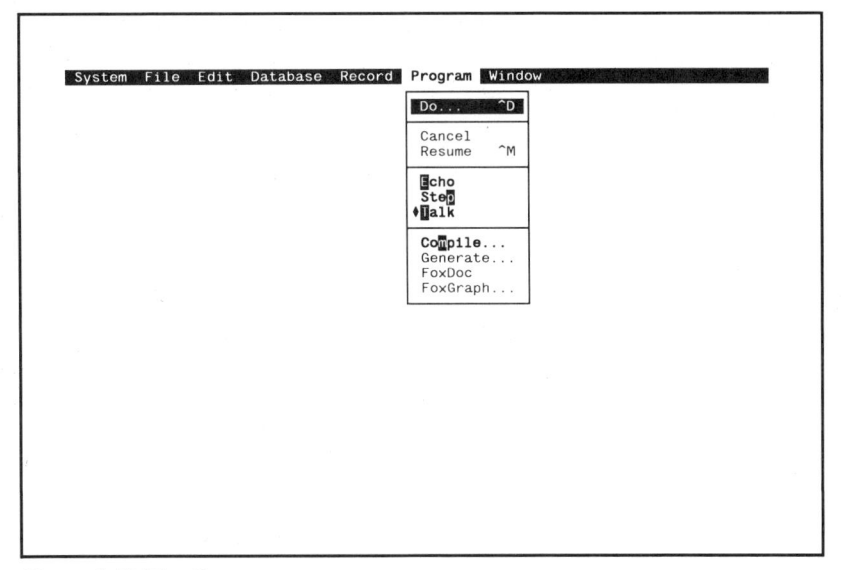

Figure 1.7: The Program popup

after you have designed a screen. FoxDoc is the documentation generator. FoxGraph lets you access a program to generate graphs of FoxPro data; this graphics program is not included with the FoxPro package and must be purchased separately.

THE WINDOW POPUP

The Window popup, illustrated in Figure 1.8, helps you use the window interface itself.

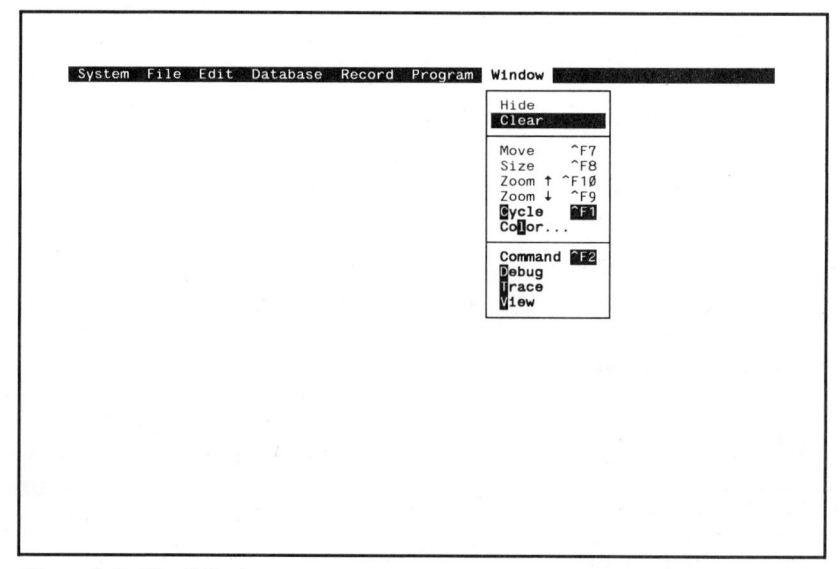

Figure 1.8: The Window popup

The first option, Hide, lets you hide a window and temporarily suspend use of it. The second option, Clear, clears the contents of a window. Both of these options will be discussed further later in this chapter, along with most of the options in the second group, which let you change the appearance of a window.

The options in the third group let you use special windows: the Command window (which you have already seen), the Debug and Trace windows (which are used in programming), and the powerful View window, discussed in Chapter 7.

SUMMARY OF THE MENU SYSTEM

Once you have this general overview of it, the FoxPro menu system is not difficult to understand. It offers so many options it can be confusing, but once you realize that only some of the options on a few of the popups are essential to using FoxPro, it becomes easy to understand.

Three of the popups are fundamental. The File popup is essential for creating and using the files that hold databases, indexes, reports, mailing labels, and so on. The Database popup is essential for working with whole database files, and the Record popup is essential for working with records and groups of records within files.

In addition to these, the Window popup, though it is not used for database management, is essential to working with the FoxPro interface itself.

The other three popups let you use utilities or advanced features, and you will not have to deal with them for some time.

With the general overview of it that you now have, you should not have any trouble finding your way around the menu system.

INTRODUCING FOXPRO DIALOG BOXES

> Dialog boxes are often called "dialogs" in other books about FoxPro. For clarity, however, this book uses the more precise term "dialog box."

As you have seen, many of FoxPro's menu options are followed by ellipses. If you choose one of these options, you will be presented with a *dialog box* asking you for more information. Within a dialog box, there are a number of different types of *controls,* which are used for different purposes. Some of these controls can also contain ellipses: choosing one of these controls will take you to another dialog box asking you to enter more information.

In this section, you will begin by looking at the different types of controls within dialog boxes, and then you will learn to use each of these controls with either a mouse or the keyboard.

DIALOG BOX CONTROLS

Figure 1.9 shows the dialog box that appears if you select Sort from the Database menu popup while you are working with a database file.

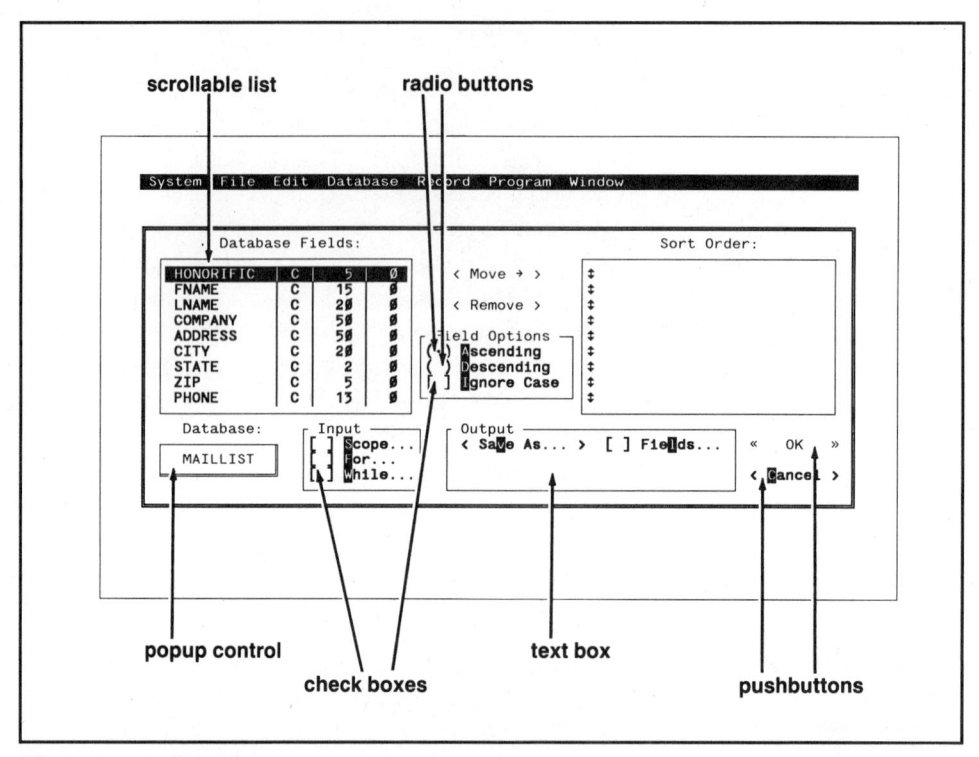

Figure 1.9: A dialog box

    This is a complex dialog box. In fact, it is used as an illustration because it is one of the only dialog boxes that is complex enough to use every type of control. You should not try, at this point, to understand fully how this dialog box works, though the discussion will sometimes mention sorting purely to clarify the functions of the different controls in this specific dialog box.

    There are six different types of controls. The use of these controls with the mouse and keyboard will be discussed in the next section. Their general functions are described here.

- **scrollable list:** A scrollable list is a boxed list with what is called a *scroll bar* on its right. A scroll bar is a vertical bar with an arrow at the top, an arrow at the bottom, and a diamond somewhere between to show you where in the list the cursor is. When it is activated, one of the items in the list is highlighted, and you move the highlight to make your selection. In this dialog box, the scrollable list lets you select database fields; in other dialog boxes, a scrollable list might let you select files or directories.

- **popup control:** A rectangle with double lines on its right and bottom edges is a popup control. If you select this control, a popup that is similar to a menu popup appears. In the example in the illustration, the popup control would display a list of available databases, enabling you to choose the database file to be sorted. After you choose one option from the popup, the popup disappears so it does not get in your way, and the name you chose appears within the control, as DEMO does now.

- **radio buttons:** Radio buttons are options with parentheses to their left. A dot in one of the parentheses shows which button is selected. These are used when you must choose one and only one option from a group of options: choosing one of the options automatically unselects whichever button was already selected. In this example, the set of radio buttons offers only two options—sorting in either ascending or descending order.

- **check boxes:** A pair of square brackets is a check box, representing an option that may be set on or off. An X appears in the check box when the option is on. Often several check boxes that perform associated functions appear as a list; unlike radio buttons, more than one check box may be chosen.

- **pushbuttons:** A word or two of text surrounded by angle brackets is a pushbutton. Some pushbuttons present you with yet more choices; others actually make something happen: after you have used the other controls to select all the options you want, you use a pushbutton to initiate or cancel the operation(s) as specified. Double angle brackets indicate the default pushbutton, the action which is most commonly performed. The example contains five pushbuttons, two of which are included in most dialog boxes: <Cancel> lets you leave the dialog box without initiating the operation, and <<OK>>, which is the default, initiates it as specified.

> In some FoxPro dialog boxes, only the position of the cursor lets you know that you can type text at that point.

- **text box:** The Output rectangle in this dialog box is a text box. You can type text into it, or you can have FoxPro display text resulting from your menu choices. In this example, you can either type the name of the file where you want the sorted output saved or select the Save As pushbutton within the text box to choose a file name, which will then appear next to (or often below) the pushbutton.

USING DIALOG BOXES

As with many other features of FoxPro, using dialog boxes with a mouse is very easy and intuitive, and using them with the keyboard is easy after you have gotten used to it. Though it is not hard to learn to work with the keyboard, you may want to refer back to this section a few times when you first use dialog boxes in later chapters. After a short time, dialog box techniques will become second nature to you.

> You can exit from the dialog box and cancel what you have done within it by choosing the Cancel pushbutton or simply by pressing Esc. You can execute the default choice by choosing the default pushbutton or by pressing Ctrl-Enter. These keyboard shortcuts (Esc and Ctrl-Enter) are useful regardless of whether you are using a mouse or the keyboard.

USING A MOUSE

Most controls in a dialog box can be selected by simply clicking them with the mouse. Click a pushbutton to perform that action. Click a check box to select it and an X will appear between the square brackets. (If an X is already there, clicking it will unselect the option and make the X disappear.) Click one of the buttons in a set of radio buttons and it will be selected, automatically unselecting any previously selected button in the set.

To make a selection from a scrollable list, you must move the cursor to the item you want within the list: once you have used the Tab key to make the list active, use the up or down arrow key to move the highlight. If the list is a long one, use the PgUp and PgDn keys to move the cursor more quickly. Once you have highlighted the item you want, press the space bar to select it.

or bottom of the scroll bar to move the list up and down, then click on the desired item to select it. (You can also drag the diamond at the center of the scroll bar to move quickly through the list.)

To use a text box, simply position the cursor in the box and type in the text, or select the pushbutton if there is one within or next to the box. The latter method will display another dialog box from which you can make choices that will automatically fill in the text box.

You can also reposition dialog boxes on the screen if they are in the way of something you want to see: just use your mouse to point to the dialog box's top border and drag to move it.

USING THE KEYBOARD

To use dialog boxes from the keyboard, you must first use the Tab key to activate the control that you want to use. Pressing Tab or Ctrl-Tab moves you from one control to another: generally, Tab moves the highlight "forward" through the controls, and Ctrl-Tab moves "backward." Once you have highlighted the control you want, you can use the arrow keys to move within it. For example, you would use the arrow keys to move to the different items in a scrollable list.

Once they are active (highlighted), most controls can be used simply by pressing the space bar. Press the space bar to use the pushbutton that is active. Press the space bar to place an X in a check box, or to remove the X from it if one is already there. Press the space bar to select the radio button that is currently active (and to automatically unselect any previously selected button in that group).

Sometimes one of the letters in a pushbutton is underlined or highlighted. When this is the case, you can use it by simply typing that letter, referred to as a *hot key,* without having to use the Tab key to select the control first.

To make a selection from a scrollable list, you must move the cursor to the item you want within the list: once you have used the Tab key to make the list active, use the up or down arrow key to move the highlight. If the list is a long one, use the PgUp and PgDn keys to move the cursor more quickly. Once you have highlighted the item you want, press the space bar to select it.

To use a popup control, you must first use the Tab key to make it active, then press the space bar to pop up the menu. Use the up and down arrow keys to highlight the option you want within the menu, then press the space bar to select that option.

To use a text box, simply tab until the text box is active, then type text into it or select the pushbutton if there is one within or next to it.

> Many controls can also be selected by pressing Enter—but not all of them. If you get in the habit of using Enter to select controls and then find that it does not work, remember you can press the space bar instead.

This latter method calls up another dialog box allowing you to make choices that will automatically fill in the text box.

When you are using the keyboard, it is particularly helpful to use shortcuts for the pushbuttons. Pressing Esc will cancel the dialog box. Pressing Ctrl-Enter will execute the default pushbutton, whether or not it is highlighted.

You can also reposition a dialog box if it is in the way of something you want to see. Press Ctrl-F7 and the border of the dialog box will begin to flash. Use the arrow keys to move it across the screen. (Pressing PgUp or PgDn will move it immediately to the top or bottom of the screen, and Home or End will move it immediately to the left or right edge of the screen.) Once the dialog box is where you want it, press Enter, and the border will stop flashing.

WORKING WITH WINDOWS

Most of your work with FoxPro will be done in windows. When you choose to browse, to add records, to use the Help facility, to write a program, to edit a text file, or to do most of the other things that the FoxPro menus and dialog boxes give you access to, FoxPro will open a window on the screen to let you do it.

You can open many windows at the same time. For example, if you want to look at two databases, write a program that uses them, and take notes on what you are doing, you can have all the windows that you are using visible on your screen at the same time.

A newly opened window will generally be in front of any windows that are already open. If a number of windows are visible, you can work on the frontmost window only. You can recognize the frontmost window because only it has the mouse controls along its borders. (These controls will be presented in the following section.) The mouse controls appear regardless of whether you are using a mouse. Of course, you can also recognize the frontmost windows because actions you perform occur within it.

If a window is in your way, you can hide it temporarily, without closing it, by selecting Hide from the Window menu. When you hide a window, its name is added to the bottom of the window popup; you can make it visible again simply by selecting its name from the popup.

> Hidden windows listed on the popup are numbered, beginning with zero. These numbers translate into hot keys that are particularly convenient for people using the keyboard. For example, to make the first hidden window on the list reappear, just press Alt-W to pop up the Window menu, then press 0 to unhide the window.

You can also get windows out of your way by bringing the window you want to work in to the front. If you are using a mouse, just click anywhere on a window to make it frontmost. If you are using the keyboard, select Cycle from the Window menu. This brings successive windows to the front: keep selecting Cycle until the window that you want to work in is frontmost.

There is also a shortcut that lets you hide or show all of your windows at once. Hold down Shift when you select the Window menu pad—either by pressing Shift-Alt-W or by pressing Shift when you make the selection with the mouse—and the Window menu popup will display the Hide All and Show All options instead of its Hide option. (Similarly, if you hold down Shift when you select the File menu pad, the popup will include a Close All option.)

If the frontmost window is in the way of your seeing something, you can also reduce it to the size of an icon by selecting Zoom ↓ from the Window menu. After you make this selection, only a small portion of the window's title bar, including its name, is displayed. Selecting Zoom ↑ from the Window menu restores the window to its original size.

SPECIAL WINDOW CONTROLS FOR MOUSE USERS

The descriptions of windows that you have read so far apply to both mouse and keyboard users. If you are a mouse user, FoxPro windows are particularly easy to manipulate, because of the special controls on their borders.

Figure 1.10 shows the Command window (looking a bit larger than usual) with the names of all the features that you find in window borders. The figure also shows the menu popup, for your convenience when you read the more general discussion of using windows.

Mouse users can control windows using the following features.

- **title:** You can move a window by putting the pointer on the title, holding the mouse button down, and dragging. When the window is where you want it, release the button.

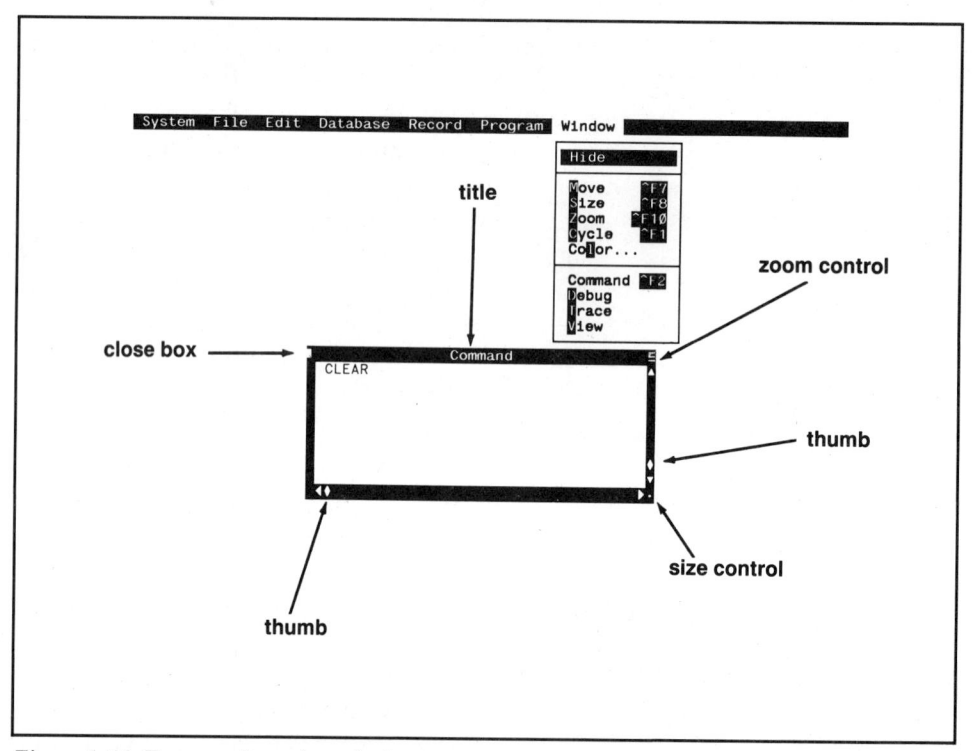

Figure 1.10: Features for using windows

- **close box:** Click the close box in the upper left corner to close a window. (You can also close a window by pressing Esc, which is sometimes easier than clicking the close box.)

- **zoom control:** Click the zoom control in the upper right corner to "zoom" a window—that is, to make it fill the entire screen. Click the zoom control again to return it to its previous size.

- **size control:** To change the size of a window, put the pointer on the size control in the lower right corner, hold down the mouse button, and drag. When the window is the size you want, release the mouse button.

- **scroll bar:** If the display is too long or too wide to fit in the window, a scroll bar made up of two arrows and a diamond appears. To move up or down through a file, click the up or down arrow on the right border of the window. The position of the diamond, called the *thumb,* indicates where in the file the cursor is. The closer the thumb is to the up or down arrow, the closer the cursor is to the beginning or end of the file. To move quickly through a file, use the mouse to drag the thumb. If the display is too wide for the window, a scroll bar also appears on the bottom border, and is used in the same way.

CONTROLLING WINDOWS WITH THE KEYBOARD

If you are using a keyboard, you can control windows by using the Window menu options, or the hot keys that appear next to some of the menu options. If you do something frequently enough, you will learn the hot keys without any effort, and then you will be able to work just about as quickly as someone with a mouse.

- **Move:** To change the location of a window on the screen, select Move from the Window menu. The window border flashes to show that it is ready to be moved. You can use the arrow keys to move it gradually across the screen, or use PgUp, PgDn, Home, or End to move it directly to the top, bottom, left, or right edge of the screen. When the window is where you want it, press Enter and the border will stop flashing.

- **Size:** To change the size of a window, select Size from the Window menu. The window border flashes to show that it is ready to be resized. You can use the arrow keys to adjust the bottom and right borders of the window and make it larger or smaller. When it is the size you want, press Enter and the border will stop flashing.

- **Zoom:** If you select Zoom ↑ from the Window menu, the window will expand to fill the entire screen. If a window has already been "zoomed" to fill the whole screen, selecting Zoom ↑ will return it to its previous size.

- **Scroll:** As long as the window's border is not flashing (from choosing an option from the Window menu), the arrow keys

> Since only the bottom and right borders of a window move when you are resizing it, the window is not always exactly where you want it after you resize it. It is best to resize the window first and then move it if you want to do both.

and the PgUp and PgDn keys will allow you to scroll through the contents of a window.

- **Close:** To close the currently active window, simply press Esc.

HOW TO USE THE EDITOR

The FoxPro editor is very elegantly designed, and its basic operations are very easy to learn.

Most keys are used in the ordinary way—the character keys to enter text, the Del key to delete the character the cursor is on, the Backspace key to delete the character to the left of the cursor, and so on.

The Ins key is used in the conventional way, to toggle back and forth from insert mode to type-over mode. When you begin typing, you are in insert mode: anything you type will be inserted to the left of the character that the cursor is on, and everything after that character will be pushed to the right to make room for it. If you press Ins to toggle into type-over mode, anything you type will write over and replace existing text, character by character. When you are in type-over mode, the cursor becomes large, a warning that existing text can be lost.

The cursor movement keys are also used conventionally. The arrow keys move one character to the left or right or one line up or down. The Home key moves the cursor to the beginning of the line it is on, and the End key moves it to the end of the line. PgUp and PgDn scroll up and down through text a window at a time. Of course, you might prefer to use the mouse to move through the text. Remember that the text will always be in a window, so you can use the scrolling techniques mentioned in the previous section.

All these ways of using the editor are very common. The uncommon thing about the FoxPro editor is the way it uses the cursor movement keys in combination with Ctrl and Shift. These key movements are summarized in Table 1.1. In general, Ctrl magnifies movements, and Shift marks text as you move.

Looking at the table, you can see that holding down Ctrl when you move the cursor makes it go further. For example, the right and left arrow keys by themselves move the cursor one character to the right

Table 1.1: Cursor Movement Using the FoxPro Editor

KEY	EFFECT
Home	moves to the beginning of the line
End	moves to the end of the line
Left Arrow	moves one character left
Right Arrow	moves one character right
Up Arrow	moves one line up
Down Arrow	moves one line down
PgUp	moves one window up
PgDn	moves one window down
Ctrl-Home	moves to the beginning of the text
Ctrl-End	moves to the end of the text
Ctrl-Left Arrow	moves one word left
Ctrl-Right Arrow	moves one word right

Any of these keys or key combinations can be used with Shift to mark text as you move the cursor.

Ctrl is not used with the up and down arrow keys, as PgUp and PgDn serve the same purpose.

If you decide after releasing the Shift key to continue to mark text, you can simply hold down the Shift key again and move the cursor further. Be sure you hold down Shift first, though, or else moving the cursor will unmark all the text you have already marked.

or left; Ctrl plus those keys makes it move a whole word to the right or left. Home and End by themselves move the cursor to the beginning or end of a line; Ctrl-Home and Ctrl-End move it to the beginning or end of the document.

In addition, since Backspace by itself deletes a character, Ctrl-Backspace deletes a word. However, Ctrl has no special effect with Del.

Holding down Shift when you move the cursor marks text, making it appear in reverse video; this is sometimes called selecting text. You can use Shift in combination with the arrow keys, Home, End, PgUp, or PgDn to mark text. You can also use Shift in combination with the extended cursor movements (those using the Ctrl key). For example, since Ctrl-End moves the cursor to the end of the document, Shift-Ctrl-End moves it to the end of the document and marks all the text along the way.

You can also mark text using a mouse. Position the pointer where you want the marking to begin, hold down the mouse button, and drag to mark the text; when you have marked all the text you want, release the mouse button. To unmark text, place the pointer anywhere outside the marked area but inside the window, and click. Apart from these simple mouse operations, there are other shortcuts for marking text with the mouse, shown in Table 1.2.

Table 1.2: Shortcuts for Marking Text with the Mouse

PURPOSE	METHOD
to mark a word	place the pointer on the word and double-click
to mark a line	place the pointer on the line and triple-click
to mark text word by word	double-click and drag
to mark text line by line	triple-click and drag
to mark a segment of text	shift-click the cursor then shift-click at another location to select all the text between
to unmark a segment of text	shift-click within the marked text at the point where you want the marking to end

After you have marked it, you can perform operations on the entire block of marked text. One of the notable consequences of this is that if you press Del or Backspace, the editor will delete *all* the marked text. The easy way to delete all the text from the cursor to the end of the line, then, is to press Shift-End to mark the text to the end of the line and then press Backspace to delete it. The easy way to delete all the text from the cursor to the end of the document, similarly, is to press Shift-Ctrl-End to mark the text and then press Backspace to delete it.

To unmark text, press any cursor movement key (Home, End, PgUp, PgDn, or one of the arrow keys) without holding down the

> Pressing the space bar or any character might also delete all marked text. If you mark text by mistake, be sure to unmark it by pressing a cursor movement key or by using the mouse before you resume typing. Fortunately, if you do delete text by mistake, you can recover it by selecting Undo, discussed below.

Shift key. The cursor will move and the marking of the text will disappear.

THE EDIT MENU

FoxPro enables you to perform more complicated editing operations by means of the Edit menu. Two of these operations, "cut and paste" and "copy and paste," take advantage of the marking techniques you just learned.

Cut and paste lets you take a block of text that you have marked, cut it out of the place where it is, and then put it wherever you want it. Copy and paste lets you leave the marked text where it is and also put a copy of it somewhere else.

To use these features of the editor, all you have to do is to select the Edit menu pad (using the mouse or the keyboard) when text is marked, and select either Cut or Copy from the Edit popup. Then you move the cursor to the place where you want the text to be placed, select the Edit menu pad again, and select Paste from the Edit popup. That's all there is to it. (As you get used to using FoxPro, you will naturally begin using the Ctrl shortcut keys to do these things, speeding up the operation even more.)

One other pair of features of the Edit popup that you will find very handy in circumstances that are not always possible to avoid are the Undo and Redo features. If you make an error, such as deleting a large block of text by mistake, select Undo from the Edit menu popup. This will undo the last editing action you made, restoring the text to the state it was in before you made the error.

You can continue to choose Undo to undo all the past editing actions that you made during the current work session, one at a time, starting from the most recent and working back to the first.

If you use Undo by mistake, then you can select Redo from the Edit menu popup to recover the editing action that you undid most recently.

You have now learned enough about the FoxPro editor to use it for most practical purposes. You will be using this editor throughout FoxPro for entering data, entering commands, writing programs, writing text files, and so on.

WORKING WITH THE COMMAND WINDOW

> Remember that the Command window behaves a bit differently from most FoxPro windows. You cannot close it by pressing Esc. In addition, it is not added to the list of active windows at the bottom of the Window menu popup when it is hidden. To unhide it, you simply reselect it from where it is always listed: in the Window menu's third group of options.

As you have seen, the Command window lets you enter the sort of procedural commands used in earlier dBASE compatible programs rather than having you work through the menu system. You also know that the procedural commands are generated in the Command window when you do use the menu system.

This sort of procedural command was the only thing available in the days of the dot prompt, but there are still reasons to use it in this era of the pop-up menu and mouse.

It is sometimes easier to enter commands than to make selections from the menu system—particularly when you are performing a repetitive task—since you can edit and reenter commands that you already used. A list of all the commands you have entered or generated by using menus remains available in the Command window throughout your work session. You can use the up arrow key (or the mouse) to move the cursor to earlier commands, even to those that have scrolled beyond the top of the window. Once you have found the command that you want, just press Enter to reuse it as is. At that point the command will be executed and the cursor will return to the bottom of the list, where a copy of that command will be added. If you want to use a variation on the command, you can edit it first, using any of the editing techniques you just learned, and then press Enter to execute it and add it to the list in its revised form.

Of course, if you ever want to do any programming, you must also *learn* these commands, since a program is, in large part, a list of these commands.

For these reasons, this book will begin by using the menu system to enter commands but will also mention the procedural commands that are generated in the Command window, so that you can learn both. For now, you should try entering a couple of procedural commands in the Command window, just to get an idea of how it works.

You may find the FoxPro command **RUN** very helpful in your work: this is a utility that lets you use any DOS command directly from within FoxPro. In the example, you will use the command

RUN DIR

to get a DOS directory from within FoxPro. Of course, you can also use **RUN** with other DOS commands—for example,

RUN FORMAT A:

to format the disk in the A drive. You will also use the FoxPro command **CLEAR**, which, like Clear from the Window menu, clears the screen or the contents of the current output window. You will notice, when you enter these commands, that they do not apply to the Command window itself.

1. You should already have started FoxPro, and the cursor should be in its initial position in the Command window. If it is not, press Esc until you have gotten out of the menu system and returned to the Command window. If, for some reason, the Command window is no longer on the screen, select Command from the Window menu to make it reappear.

2. Type **RUN DIR** and press Enter. FoxPro will display a DOS directory similar to the one illustrated in Figure 1.11. (Of course, your directory may not be exactly like the illustration.)

> While it runs, Fox-Pro sometimes creates and uses temporary files whose names are made up of random numbers and letters and which have the extension TMP; you can see three in the illustration of the directory listing. *Do not delete these files while you are in FoxPro.* Most will be deleted automatically when you quit FoxPro; if any are left, you may delete them while FoxPro is not running.

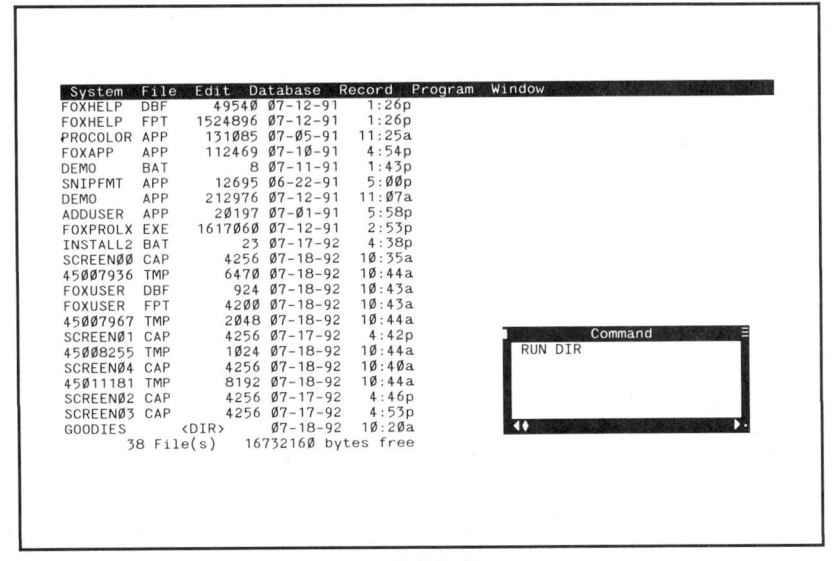

Figure 1.11: Using FoxPro to get a DOS directory

3. Type **CLEAR** and press Enter to clear the screen.

4. Now, try getting a directory of just program files with the extension .EXE by using the DOS command

   DIR *.EXE

   Rather than typing the entire command

   RUN DIR *.EXE

   edit the earlier **RUN DIR** command, using the editing techniques you just learned: press the up arrow key twice to move up to the line where the earlier directory command is; press End to move to the end of the line; then type a space and ***.EXE** and press Enter.

Notice that the command, in its edited form, is added to the end of the list of commands in the window and that the new DOS directory appears, as in Figure 1.12: again, the files in your directory may be different from these.

You can imagine how valuable the ability to edit and reuse commands can be if, for example, you are copying a large number of files with slightly different names. There are many cases where it is easier

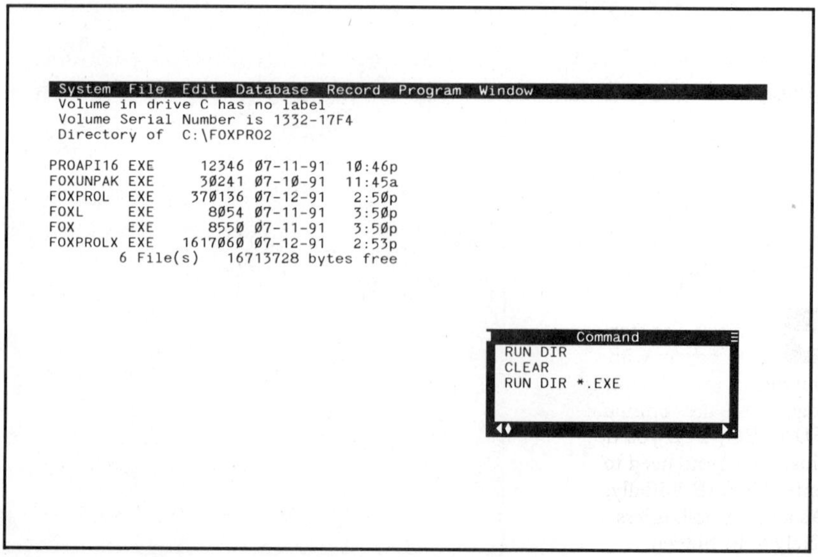

```
┌─System──File──Edit──Database──Record──Program──Window─────────┐
 Volume in drive C has no label
 Volume Serial Number is 1332-17F4
 Directory of  C:\FOXPRO2

PROAPI16 EXE      12346 07-11-91  10:46p
FOXUNPAK EXE      30241 07-10-91  11:45a
FOXPROL  EXE     370136 07-12-91   2:50p
FOXL     EXE       8054 07-11-91   3:50p
FOX      EXE       8550 07-11-91   3:50p
FOXPROLX EXE    1617060 07-12-91   2:53p
        6 File(s)   16713728 bytes free


                                          ┌──────Command──────┐
                                           RUN DIR
                                           CLEAR
                                           RUN DIR *.EXE
                                          └───────────────────┘
```

Figure 1.12: Editing the earlier directory command

to use and reuse commands than to repeat the same series of menu choices over and over again.

OTHER FEATURES

That takes care of all the major features of the FoxPro interface, but there are a few smaller ones that you should know about.

- **Esc:** Pressing the Esc key interrupts any FoxPro command or program (except for commands that could destroy data if they were interrupted). After you press Esc, FoxPro will give you the choices Cancel, Suspend, and Ignore. Choosing Cancel, which is the default option, stops execution of the command or program completely. Choosing Suspend stops execution of the command or program temporarily, but lets you start it again by selecting Resume from the Program menu or by entering **RESUME** in the Command window; this choice is only useful when you are debugging programs. Choosing Ignore makes FoxPro ignore the fact the Esc was pressed; thus FoxPro continues executing the command or program.
- **"talk":** When you make certain menu choices or use certain commands, what is called "talk" appears on the left side of the screen. For example, if you use certain commands to move around the database, the talk will serve as a status reporter telling you the number of the record you are currently on. However, if there is a window covering the area at the left of the screen where the talk appears, you will not be able to see it until you close the window.

  Ordinarily, talk appears at the lower left of the screen, where it is not likely to be hidden by a window. If you enter **CLEAR**, though, talk will appear at the upper left, where it is more likely to be hidden. In general, though, talk is not as important now as it was in the days of the dot prompt, when it was often the only way of knowing what was happening; now there is rarely any *need* to see it, but it can be helpful.

You can also start the program without displaying the FoxPro logo, using the command **FOXPRO -T**. If you do this, there is no need to enter **CLEAR** initially. As a result, talk is less likely to be hidden.

- **alerts:** An alert may appear on the screen if you tell FoxPro to do something that is impossible or that will destroy data. The alert is in a large box that is impossible to ignore, and its message is generally self-explanatory. Heed its advice if you consider it to be relevant. To make the alert disappear, click the mouse button or press any key except for a function key, Shift, Ctrl, or Alt. Then continue what you were doing.

- **system messages:** Like an alert, a system message is a box that gives you information about an action you have performed. Unlike an alert, it is not a warning or error message. For example, in Chapter 4, you will learn to check if an expression that you are using is valid. The box that tells you it is valid is a system message rather than an alert. Alerts actually interrupt what you are doing, since it could be destructive, and you must remove them explicitly, by clicking the mouse or pressing a key, as you just saw. A system message does not interrupt you. If you go on with what you were doing, it will disappear.

The preceding information on the Esc key and on "talk" tells you what FoxPro does by default. As you will see in Chapter 7, it is possible to disable either of these features by using the View window or by entering the command

    SET ESCAPE OFF

or

    SET TALK OFF

and it is possible to enable them again by using the View window or the commands

    SET ESCAPE ON

or

    SET TALK ON

In general, though, you should not disable these features unless you are a programmer setting up foolproof systems for end users. When you are using FoxPro yourself, it is always best to have escape on and talk on, as they are by default.

GETTING HELP

> Help will not be available to the extent described here if when installing the program you elected to save disk space by not installing the Help file.

FoxPro lets you get help in two different ways. You can get context-sensitive help for the window or dialog box you are currently using, or you can look through a list of topics to get help on any aspect of FoxPro that you want to look up.

To get context-sensitive help for the current (frontmost) window or dialog box, press F1. If you are using a mouse, you can hold down the Alt key and click on the desired window, dialog box, or menu option. In either case, FoxPro opens the Help window and displays information on that item.

To get help for any FoxPro topic, do either of the following:

- Select Help from the System menu
- Enter **HELP** in the Command window

When you do any of these, FoxPro opens the Help window and displays a list of topics.

There are three types of help topics, identified by style of "bullet," as listed below:

triangular bullet	General topic
square bullet	Interface item
no bullet	Command, function, or system variable

Figure 1.13 shows part of the list of topics. This screen happens to list mainly FoxPro functions.

You can move among the topics in the same way that you would scroll through lists—by using the cursor keys with the keyboard or the scroll bar with the mouse. You can also type the initial letter of the topic you want to find: the highlight will move immediately to the next topic that begins with that letter.

Once you have moved the highlight to the topic you want, use the <<Help>> pushbutton to get more detailed help on that topic. Figure 1.14 shows the detailed help for the command **CLEAR**.

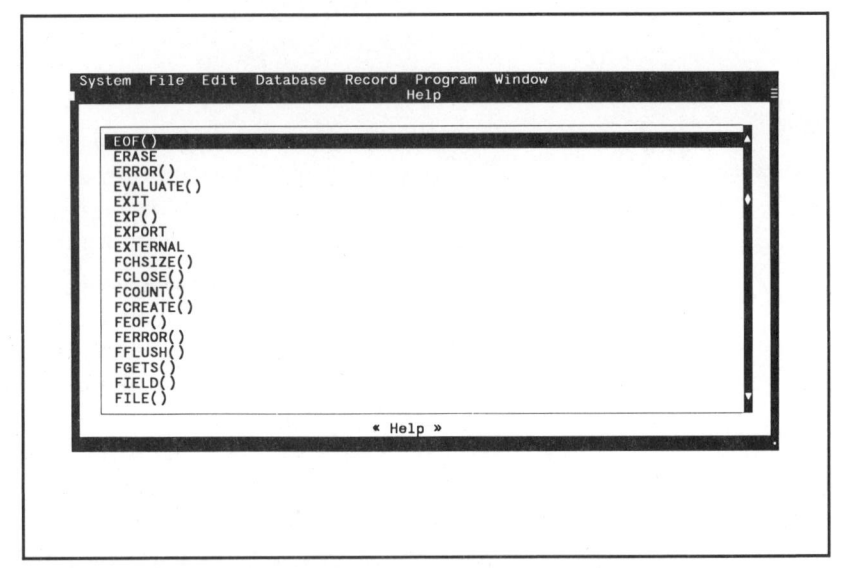

Figure 1.13: A list of help topics

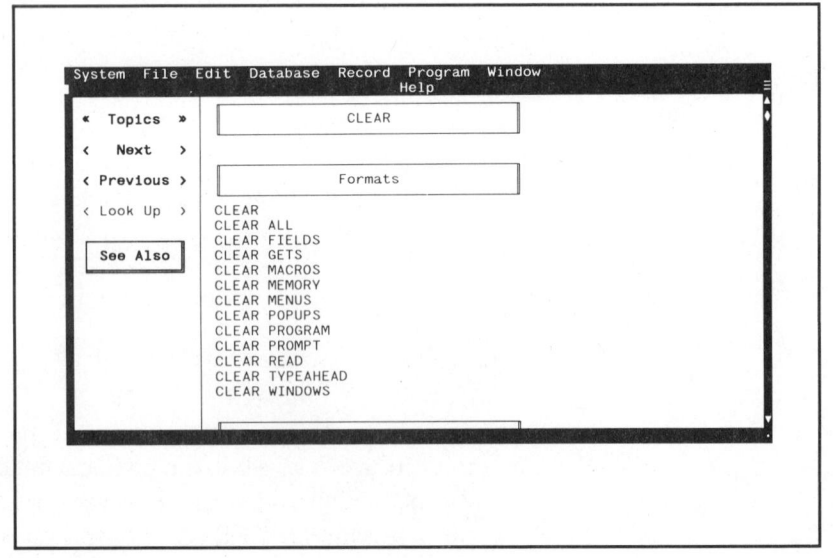

Figure 1.14: Detailed help for the command CLEAR

Notice that the detailed help screen is made up of two panels. The large panel displays the help, and the smaller panel (to the left) contains pushbuttons and a popup control that let you navigate through the Help system.

The way the first three of these work is more or less obvious. Selecting <<Topics>> returns you to the list of general topics. Selecting <Next> or <Previous> lets you see the topic that follows or precedes the current topic on the list.

The <Look Up> pushbutton gives you information about key words in the explanation of the current command. Mark the word you want to look up (using one of the methods that you learned for marking text when you read about the editor above), then select <Look Up>.

The See Also popup control displays a list of topics related to the current topic. As you can see, Look Up and See Also provide links among the topics in the Help window. It is very useful to use them to browse through related topics when you are learning about FoxPro, particularly when you are investigating programming with FoxPro.

One remarkable feature of FoxPro is that you can use the editor to copy commands out of the Help window and then paste them into the Command window. This feature is particularly useful when you are working with a complex command whose exact syntax is difficult to remember. You should try a simple example now to see how it works. In the following exercise, you will copy the **CLEAR** command out of the Help window and use it to clear the screen again.

1. Press F1 to use the Help window. A list of topics will appear. Notice that the command **HELP** was generated in the Command window when you pressed the Help key. Of course, you could have typed **HELP** directly into the Command window.

2. Zoom the window (by clicking the zoom control or selecting the Zoom ↑ option from the Window menu popup) so you can see more of the topic list.

3. Type **C** to move the highlight to the first topic beginning with C. Then press the down arrow to move the highlight to the command **CLEAR**. To get help with that command, select

the default pushbutton (Help) either by clicking it with the mouse or by pressing Ctrl-Enter.

4. For now, you just want to use the editor to copy the simplest form of this command. Move the cursor to the word **CLEAR** in the Formats list. Then hold down Shift and press End to mark the word. Select Copy from the Edit menu to copy the marked text. Then Press Esc to close the Help window (or click the close control with the mouse).

5. When the Help window disappears, the cursor should be on a blank line in the Command window, under the command **HELP**. Select Paste from the Edit menu, and the word **CLEAR**, which you just copied, will appear there.

6. Press Enter to execute this command. It will clear the screen of the directory listing that was there.

QUITTING

To quit FoxPro and return to DOS, simply select Quit from the File menu. Notice that the command **QUIT** appears in the Command window before FoxPro terminates. Of course, you can also type **QUIT** directly into the Command window to leave FoxPro.

> Always quit FoxPro when you are done with a session. If you simply turn off the computer without quitting first, you can lose data.

Chapter 2

Creating a Database Structure

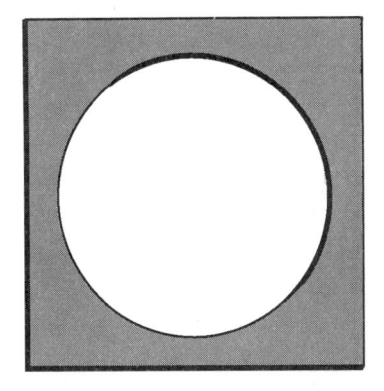

BEFORE YOU CAN WORK WITH A DATABASE FILE, YOU must define its *structure*. You have to decide exactly what fields you want to include in the file.

Defining the structure of a database is a bit like designing the preprinted form that you would use if you were working with paper files. You would have to decide, for example, that your index cards would have blank spaces for name, address, phone number, and so on.

When you are working with a computerized database, you do not have to decide on only one arrangement for your data. For example, in Chapter 3, you will look at the same data arranged in two different ways: first with one field above another, and then as a table, with the fields arranged from left to right. (You will also learn in Chapter 9 to create custom data screens, so that you will be able to arrange the fields of a database in any way you want.)

On the other hand, you do have to define, or specify, in advance exactly what fields will be in your database file, and here you must be even more precise than you are when you work with paper files. Since you cannot write with small letters to squeeze in a long name when you are working on a computer, you have to define the maximum number of characters for each field. You must also define what sort of data can be entered in each field, since some fields (as you will see) can hold only numbers, logical values, or dates.

In this chapter, you will define the structure of a database file that will be used as an example throughout this book and which will illustrate the different data types that are available in FoxPro.

CREATING A SAMPLE DATABASE FILE

The sample database that you will work with in this book is a list of employees. This database will be a bit like the database file that any small business might use, but it will be simplified to save you data entry; for example, it will not include Social Security numbers. The fields that are in the database will be chosen to illustrate FoxPro's capabilities, rather than as an example of an actual business application.

HOW TO CREATE A NEW FILE

Before you create the database file itself, you should create a DOS subdirectory for the work that you do in this book. Later in this chapter, you will use FoxPro to navigate your way through the subdirectory system and choose the directory where you want to save your database file. It is best to create the subdirectory in advance, so at this point there will be a brief discussion of how DOS subdirectories are organized. If you do not know how to use DOS subdirectories, simply copy the following commands to create the subdirectory.

We will work from the Command window to manipulate files, using the **RUN** utility plus DOS commands. Many people prefer using these ordinary DOS commands, but if you do not know DOS, or if you prefer a menu-driven operation, just follow these instructions without trying to learn the DOS commands. You can study the section on the Filer (in Appendix B) later.

> The FoxPro Filer (which is on the System menu popup) provides a menu-driven utility that lets you perform operations needed to manipulate DOS files.

1. If necessary, start FoxPro: first make sure you are in the FoxPro directory (if you are not, enter **CD\FOXPRO**), then enter **FOXPRO** (or **FOXPRO-T**) to start the program.

2. The cursor should be in the Command window; if it is not, press Esc until you get back into the Command window. If necessary, enter **CLEAR** (or select Clear from the Window menu) to clear the screen.

3. To create a new subdirectory for the exercises in this book, enter

   RUN MD \LEARNFOX

   (Do not forget to include the space and the backslash before the directory name.) The FoxPro **RUN** utility lets you use the usual DOS command for creating a new directory. The screen will become blank for a moment while the new directory is being created and then will reappear.

4. To create your new database file, select New from the File menu. FoxPro will display a dialog box with radio buttons to let you choose what type of file to create, as shown in Figure 2.1. The dot in the parentheses next to the word Database shows that it is the default file type.

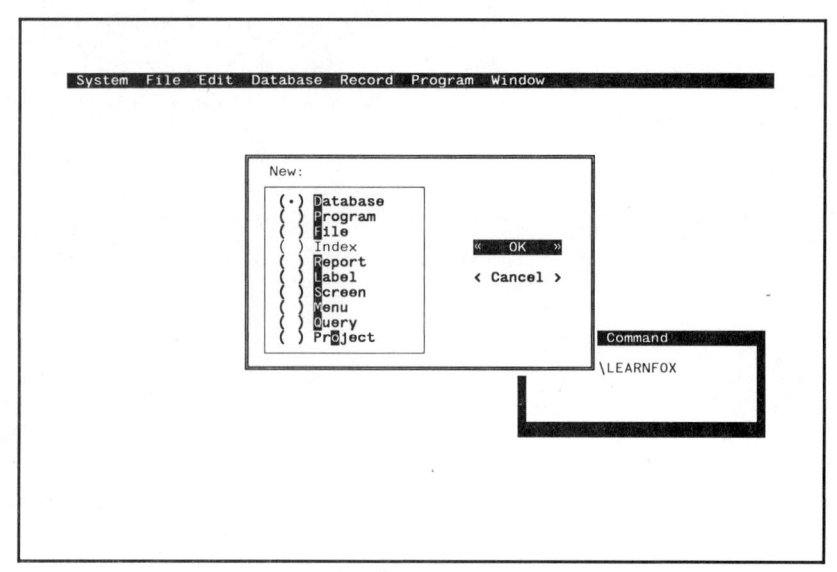

```
         System  File  Edit  Database  Record  Program  Window

               New:
               ( • ) Database
               (   ) Program
               (   ) File
               (   ) Index                 «   OK   »
               (   ) Report
               (   ) Label              < Cancel >
               (   ) Screen
               (   ) Menu
               (   ) Query                              Command
               (   ) Project
                                                \LEARNFOX
```

Figure 2.1: Creating a new database file.

5. Select the default text button, OK, to create a database file. Remember that you can select the default text button from anywhere on the screen simply by pressing Ctrl-Enter. (In later chapters, you will use this same dialog box to create reports, mailing labels, and other types of files simply by choosing the different radio buttons.)

The Structure dialog box appears, as illustrated in Figure 2.2, to let you define a new database.

Notice that this dialog box has the heading "Structure: Untitled" in its upper left corner. Though the Command window is partly covered now, you will notice later that the command **CREATE Untitled** has been generated.

If you were working from the Command window, you could have created a new database file simply by entering **CREATE** plus the name you want the database to have. When you work from the menu system, however, the file initially has the name Untitled, and you give it an actual name only when you save it. The command **CREATE** <*file name*> is used only to create database files. When you enter a new file name in this manner, the program automatically adds the extension .DBF to the name you give the file.

> Discussions of Fox-Pro commands usually use angle brackets to indicate words that must be filled in. **CREATE** <*file name*>, for example, indicates that you would enter the word **CREATE** followed by whatever name you use for the file. Do not type the brackets themselves.

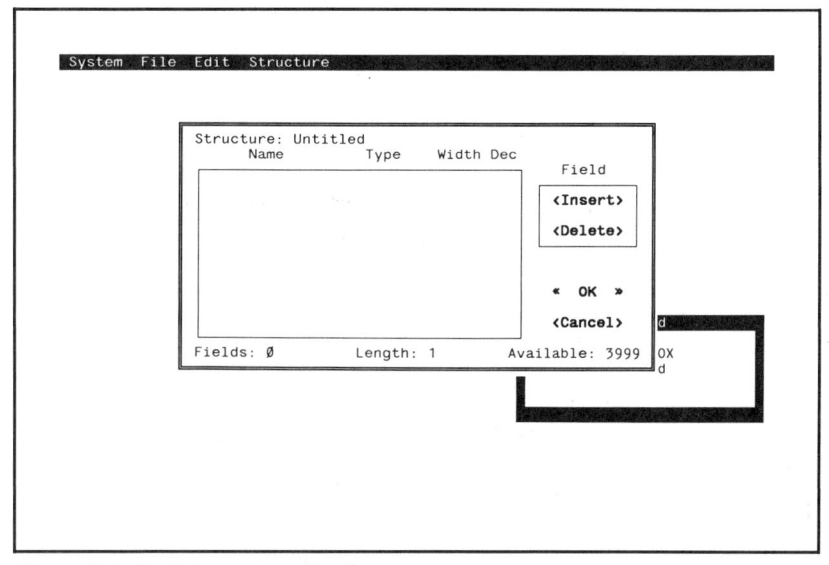

```
┌─────────────────────────────────────────────────┐
│ System  File  Edit  Structure                   │
│                                                 │
│   ┌──────────────────────────────────────┐      │
│   │ Structure: Untitled                  │      │
│   │   Name        Type    Width  Dec     │      │
│   │ ┌──────────────────────────┐ Field   │      │
│   │ │                          │<Insert> │      │
│   │ │                          │<Delete> │      │
│   │ │                          │         │      │
│   │ │                          │ « OK »  │      │
│   │ │                          │<Cancel> │  ┌─┐ │
│   │ └──────────────────────────┘         │d │ │
│   │ Fields: 0    Length: 1  Available: 3999│OX│ │
│   └──────────────────────────────────────┘  │d │
│                                              └──┘
└─────────────────────────────────────────────────┘
```

Figure 2.2: Defining a new database structure

You should also notice that the menu bar has changed. Only the menu pads for System, File, and Edit are left from the original menu bar, and a new menu pad for Structure is added to their right.

HOW TO DEFINE THE STRUCTURE OF A DATABASE

As you can see, the Structure dialog box has columns headed Name, Type, Width, and Dec (for number of decimal places). To define the database structure, you simply fill them in for each of the fields in your database file. The first line describes the first field in each record, the second line describes the second field, and so on.

Normally, you simply fill out the field definitions in sequence, from the first in each record to the last, but it is possible to move among the fields—for instance, to make changes in a definition before saving it. To do this from the keyboard, use Tab to move one column to the right (or, if you are in the last column, to the first column of the next line), or Shift-Tab to move one column to the left. Use the up and down arrow keys to move up and down the list. Of course, you can also use the mouse to move the cursor.

You can use the Insert pushbutton in the dialog box to insert a new field or the Delete pushbutton to eliminate a field you already typed. You can also insert or delete fields via the Structure menu popup. In fact, if you select the Structure menu pad, you will see that the only two options on the Structure popup are Insert Field and Delete Field, as shown in Figure 2.3. (These options offer the hot keys Ctrl-I and Ctrl-D; for keyboard users, this is faster than using the pushbuttons.) You will use the Structure menu popup later in this chapter when you are modifying the structure of a database.

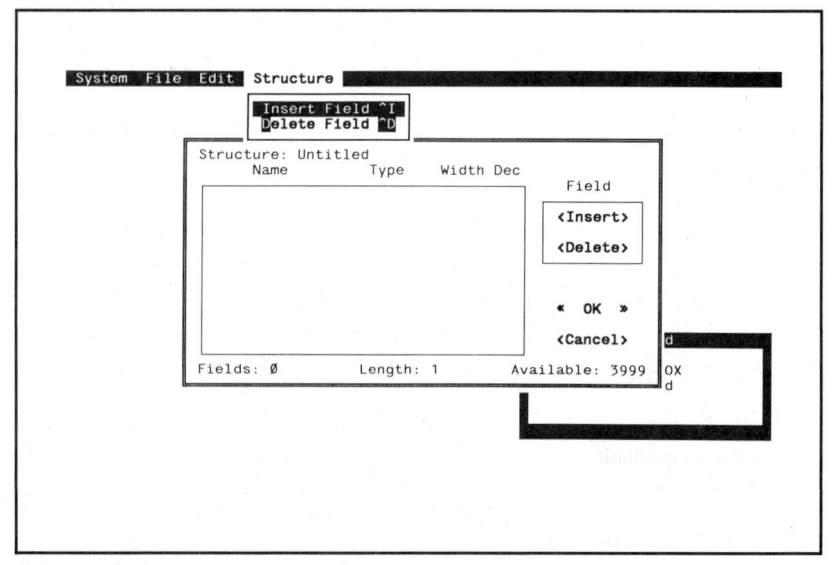

Figure 2.3: The Structure menu with the Structure dialog box.

> A field name cannot include any spaces. For this reason, if you have a field name made up of more than one word, it is a good idea to use the underscore character (_) to separate words, which makes them easier to read.

A field name may have up to ten characters: these characters may include the letters from A to Z, whole numbers, and the underscore character (_), but the field must begin with a letter. Field names do not distinguish between upper and lowercase letters, so FoxPro automatically capitalizes the name when you enter it. Of course, you cannot use two fields with the same name in the same file. Table 2.1 gives examples of a few valid and invalid field names, to illustrate these rules. You should note that a field name's validity is not of itself sufficient to ensure its usefulness. A useful field name will also tell you about the contents of that field.

Table 2.1: Valid and Invalid Field Names

FIELD NAME(S)	VALID OR INVALID?
Z	valid
2	invalid because it begins with a number
UP_DOWN	valid
_NAME	invalid because it begins with an underscore
CITY_STATE_ZIP	invalid: more than ten characters
ADDRESS_1 ADDRESS_2	both valid and may be used in same file
NOTES notes	may not be used in same file, as both have the same name (case differences—i.e., lowercase, uppercase—are ignored)

When you begin to enter a field name, Character and 10 are automatically filled in under Type and Width respectively. You can change the type by using a popup; the width changes automatically depending on the type you select. The data types and their default widths are summarized in Table 2.2.

A seventh data type, Picture, available with the Macintosh version of FoxPro, is not implemented in the current PC version.

Table 2.2: Data Types and Their Defaults

DATA TYPE	DEFAULT WIDTH	DEFAULT DECIMAL PLACES	CHANGE DEFAULTS?
Character	10	n/a	yes
Numeric	8	0	yes
Float	8	0	yes
Date	8	n/a	no
Logical	1	n/a	no
Memo	10 in .DBF file	n/a	no

DATA TYPES

The Type column must contain one of FoxPro's six data types. The data type you choose determines what you can enter into the field.

- **Character:** may contain any of the characters on the keyboard, including letters, numbers, and special characters (such as & or *). DOS also includes an extended set of special characters, including box-drawing characters and foreign characters with accent marks; character fields can hold any of these. FoxPro character data may include any eight-bit value, including the null character (ASCII character 0); thus advanced users can use character fields to store virtually any data, including binary data. The maximum width of a character field is 254 characters.

- **Numeric:** may contain numbers and a decimal point, and may also begin with a + or – sign. The maximum width of a numeric field is 20 characters. The decimal point and + or – sign each take up one place, so you must take them into account when you define the field width. If you want a field to hold amounts of money less than one thousand dollars, for example, it must be six places wide: three for the dollar amounts, one for the decimal point, and two for the cents. Add an extra place if you want to indicate + or – amounts. Note that a field that has a decimal point and a leading + or – sign can hold a maximum of 18 numeric digits (20 maximum minus 2).

- **Float:** like numeric, may contain numbers, a decimal point, and a leading + or – sign, and can hold up to 20 characters. The float data type is designed for scientific calculations, since it stores more significant digits internally. It is not commonly used.

- **Logical:** may contain only the values T or F, to indicate true or false. However, when you are entering data you may enter Y (for yes) or N (for no) as well as T or F, and the entry will be read as a logical true or false. Furthermore, any of these

> FoxPro uses only 16 significant digits internally and rounds numeric data wider than this. Though these are more than enough significant digits for most business uses, there are many scientific or statistical calculations where rounding might create errors. When in doubt about potential rounding errors, use the Float type.

characters may be entered as upper or lowercase letters. This type, then, makes it easy to enter true and false or yes and no responses.

- **Date:** includes date numbers and the slash character to separate them—for example, 10/02/91. The date field itself is always eight characters wide, though it can be *displayed* with a four-character year—for example, as 10/02/1991. Dates can also be displayed and managed in European format (with the day first) or in ASCII format (with the year first). In Chapter 4, you will learn about special functions that let you print the contents of date fields in character form—for example, to print out the name of the month.

- **Memo:** may contain any amount and type of data. The only limit to the length of a memo field is the amount of disk space you have. Like a character field, a memo field may include the null character and binary data; thus advanced users can use FoxPro memo fields to hold types of data that could never before be manipulated with database management programs, such as scanned images or digitized sound. In ordinary uses, memo fields act as variable-length character fields, and they can be manipulated using any of the functions that are used to manipulate character fields.

For every field you define, there is space taken up on the disk for the entire width you specify, even if there is little or no data in the field. Certain fields have unalterable widths: the logical type will always be one character wide, and the date type will always be eight characters wide. Memo fields, though they can hold any amount of data, are automatically defined as ten characters wide. The ten spaces reserved for it in the database file are just used to point to the location in a separate, variable-length file where the actual data for that field is kept. When you are entering data, the memo field at first appears to be only ten spaces long, but if you press Ctrl-PgDn when the cursor is on that field, you open a special memo window, as illustrated in Figure 2.4, to allow you to enter any amount of text (or other data); closing the memo window returns you to ordinary data entry.

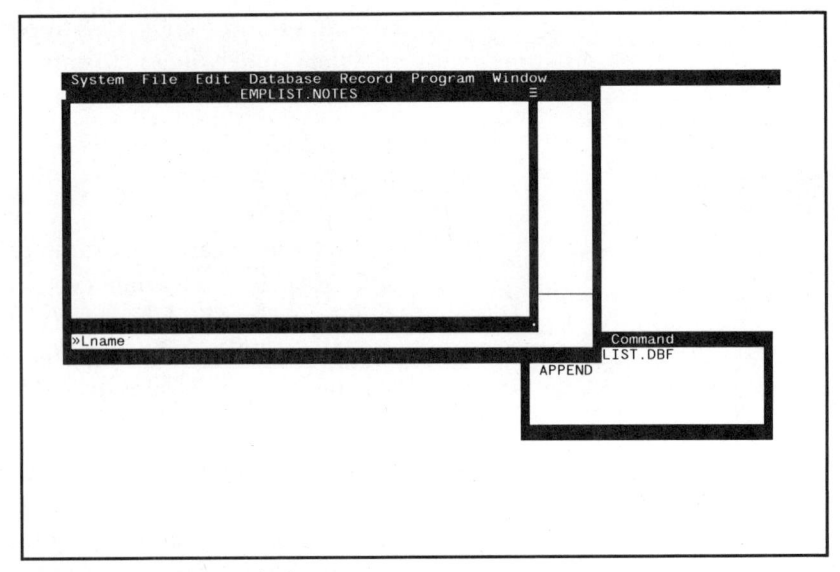

Figure 2.4: A memo window.

> ⦿ Because a memo field is not kept in the same file as the rest of the database, there is a danger of losing your memo data when you are copying a database file—for example, to transfer it to another computer. You must be sure to copy the memo file as well as the database file, and the easiest way to do this is by using the DOS wild-card character. For instance, to copy a database file named SAMPLE, use the DOS command **COPY SAMPLE.***, which will copy SAMPLE.DBF and also SAMPLE.FPT or SAMPLE.DBT.

Database files automatically get the extension .DBF (which stands for database file). For example, when you name your sample employee list file EMPLIST, it will be stored with the name EMPLIST.DBF. FoxPro memo files are given the extension .FPT (for FoxPro text). When you create your EMPLIST database later in this chapter, then, it will actually be stored in two files: EMPLIST.FPT as well as EMPLIST.DBF. In earlier dBASE compatible programs, memo files were given the extension .DBT (which stands for database text). These .DBT files could hold only character data.

Since FoxPro memo files can hold any data type—character or binary—FoxPro can use databases with these older forms of memo field without any difficulty.

When you are entering the definition of your sample database file, you will see that the cursor does not even move to the Width column for date, logical, and memo fields, since their widths are preset and cannot be changed.

No doubt, you have noticed that an actual piece of data can sometimes go into several different types of field. For example, numbers can go into character, numeric, or float fields, and dates can go into date or character fields. The real difference between field types lies in how the data can be used. You can perform numeric calculations, for example, only on numeric or float fields—not on numbers that are stored in character fields. In the earliest versions of dBASE, dates were stored as characters, and there was no date type. As a result, it was hard to arrange records in order of date. Now that there is a special date type, though, you can not only sort records in order of date, you can also perform calculations with dates—to find the number of days between two dates, for example.

When you are defining the structure of a database, it is best to use the numeric type only for fields that will actually have calculations performed on them. Beginners are often tempted to define the zip code field as numeric just because it has numbers in it. Actually, though, some zip codes—those from foreign countries—contain letters as well as numbers, and extended zip codes include a dash after the first five digits. Neither of these could be entered in a numeric field. Furthermore, because data in a character field can be sorted alphabetically and by number, it is possible to sort any zip code in order when Zip is a character field. There is no advantage, then, to using a numeric field except for the ability to perform calculations.

BREAKING DOWN THE DATA

The time to think about how much you need to break down the data for the uses that you are going to make of it is before you create the structure of your database. When even a very small business computerizes, entering names and addresses in its mailing list usually takes at least a week of full-time work for a data entry person (or for an overworked owner). There have been cases where, after the data entry was done, users decided to print out the names on their mailing list in alphabetical order—and only then realized that you cannot alphabetize by last name if the first and last name are in a single field. Sometimes these people have managed to get by without the alphabetical listings that they wanted; in other cases they have gone back, redefined the database, and spent an extra week redoing all their data entry.

Our sample application in this book will be a simple list of employees. As with most lists of names and addresses, it is best to break down the name into fields for first and last name, so you can alphabetize records, and also to have separate fields for city, state, and zip,

You usually do not need a separate field for a middle initial, which you can fit into the same field as the first name.

rather than a single field for all three. In this sort of application, you may well want to list just the people who live in a certain city or a certain state, and you usually want to print mailing labels in order of zip code; you can do these things if you have a separate field for each.

There are costs to creating fields for which you rarely have data—fields that, in many records, will be empty. For one thing, it takes data entry time to skip that field and leave it empty. In addition, a field takes up space on your disk whether there is any data in it or not. To save disk space, it is best not to create unnecessary fields and not to make fields wider than necessary.

Balance the advantages and disadvantages of breaking down your data. When in doubt, it is generally safest to break the data down more, rather than less.

ENTERING THE FIELD NAMES AND TYPES

Now you are ready to create a new database file by using the Structure dialog box that you called up earlier in this chapter, filling it out with the name, data type, and width of the fields you want. (If you have quit FoxPro and started it again since reading the beginning of this chapter, go back to the section entitled "How to Create a New File" and follow the numbered steps there to call up the Structure dialog box again before going on with the next set of numbered instructions.)

As you will see, as soon as you begin to fill out each field, FoxPro automatically defines the type to be Character and the width to be 10. Obviously, you will sometimes want to change these default assignments. You can move from column to column using Tab (or Shift-Tab, to move back a column). If you have a mouse, you can click the word you want to move to, but it is usually quicker to use Tab or Shift-Tab.

Once you have gotten to the column you want (the word or number in it will be highlighted), you can change its contents in one of two ways:

- Simply begin to type the contents you want. Any current contents will immediately disappear, and the new contents that you are typing will replace them.

> Other keys can sometimes be used to move from one column to the other, such as Enter to move right and the left arrow key to move left—but they do not work consistently in every column, so it is best to just get in the habit of using Tab and Shift-Tab to move among columns, and saving the left and right arrows for editing purposes. It is good to get used to these keys now, since you will find in the next chapter that FoxPro works in a similar way when you are editing the data in a database file.

- Use the right arrow key to move the cursor. The whole word will no longer be highlighted; instead, a cursor will appear on one letter of the word. This allows you to use the ordinary editing keys to make changes one character at a time.

When you use the first method above to change the data type, all you have to do is type the first letter of a data type, and FoxPro will automatically fill in its entire name. If you do not remember all the data types, you can press the space bar, and a popup will appear to let you choose among the different FoxPro data types.

The default width will change depending on the data types. If you choose the numeric or float data type, a default value of zero will appear for the number of decimal places, but you will be able to edit it. On the other hand, to accept a default value, just move the cursor to the next item. You will also see that, when you add a field in the structure dialog box, a shaded area appears to the left of the field name. This shaded area helps you to work with indexes, which will be covered in Chapter 4. You can ignore it for now.

1. Type **FNAME** in the Name column. As soon as you begin typing, "Character" appears in the Type column, and "10" appears in the Width column. These are the default assignments for these items. A small shaded area and a double-headed arrow also appear, to the left of the name, as shown in Figure 2.5.

2. You need to change the width from 10 to 15. When you have finished typing the field name, press Tab twice to move to the Width column. Press the right arrow key to change from a highlight to a cursor, which will be on the first digit. Press the right arrow key again to move to the second digit, press Del to delete the zero that is there, and type **5** to replace it. The number will now be 15.

3. Press Tab to move to the Name column of the next line. Type **LNAME**. Press Tab twice to move to the Width field. This time, instead of using the arrow and editing keys to change one character in the Width field, simply type **20** to replace the entire number. When you start typing, the 10 will disappear.

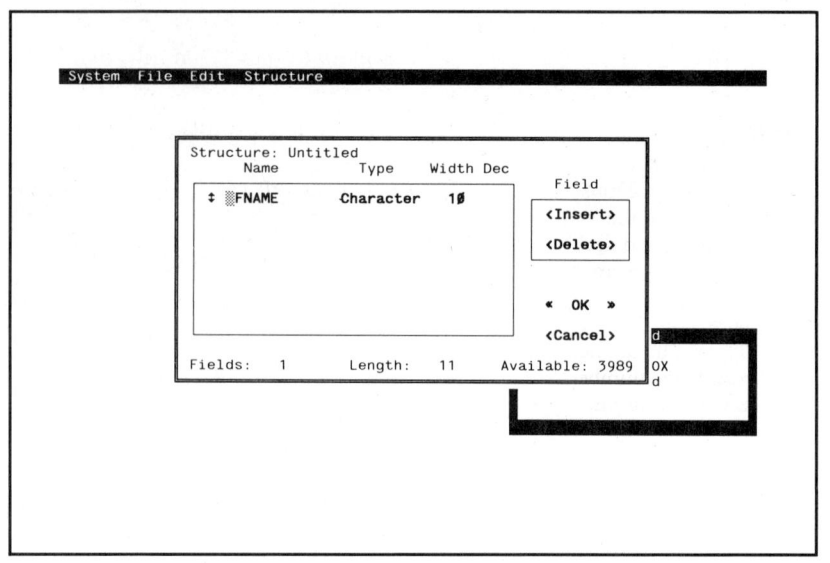

```
┌─────────────────────────────────────────────────────────┐
│ System  File  Edit  Structure                           │
│                                                         │
│           ┌─────────────────────────────────────┐       │
│           │ Structure: Untitled                 │       │
│           │   Name      Type      Width Dec     │       │
│           │                              Field  │       │
│           │ ‡ ▓FNAME    Character    1Ø         │       │
│           │                            <Insert> │       │
│           │                            <Delete> │       │
│           │                                     │       │
│           │                             « OK »  │       │
│           │                            <Cancel> │   d   │
│           │ Fields:  1   Length:  11  Available: 3989 OX│
│           └─────────────────────────────────────┘   d   │
│                                                         │
└─────────────────────────────────────────────────────────┘
```

Figure 2.5: The default data type and width appear as soon as you start typing.

> 4. Press Tab to move to the next line. Type **ADDRESS**. Press Tab twice. As the width, type **25**. Press Tab to move to the next line.
>
> 5. Type **APT_NO**. Press Tab twice. As the width, type **5**. Press Tab to move to the next line.
>
> 6. Type **CITY**. Press Tab twice. As the width, type **20**. Press Tab to move to the next line.
>
> 7. Type **STATE**. Press Tab twice. Type **2** as the width, and then press Tab to move to the next line.
>
> 8. Type **ZIP**. Press Tab twice. Type **5** as the width and press Tab to move to the next line.
>
> 9. Type **DATE_HIRED**. The first time through, you should try using the popup to change the data type, to get used to it and to give you an idea of another place to find the type names listed. Press Tab to move to the Type column, and then press the space bar to use the Type popup, illustrated in Figure 2.6. Press the down arrow three times, and then press the

If you have a mouse, you can use it to move to the Type column, use the popup, and make your selection from it—in the same way as you do when you are using a menu popup. Most people, though, once they learn the names of the data types, find it easier to use the keyboard when they are doing this sort of steady typing.

> In the Width column of a numeric field you must count spaces for the decimal point and decimal places if there are to be any. Thus, the decimal places you count for the Dec column are not *additional* to the number in the Width column.

space bar to select the Date type. Notice that the width automatically becomes 8: there is no choice of width for date fields.

10. As the next field name, type **WAGE**. Press Tab to move to the Type column. Type **N** for numeric type. (The whole word—Numeric—is automatically displayed.) Notice that the default width is 8. Since we will assume that everyone's hourly wage is under 100 dollars, we need a width of 5: two for the dollar figures, one for the decimal point, and two for the cents. Type **5** and press Tab to move to the Dec column. Type **2** and press Tab to move to the next line.

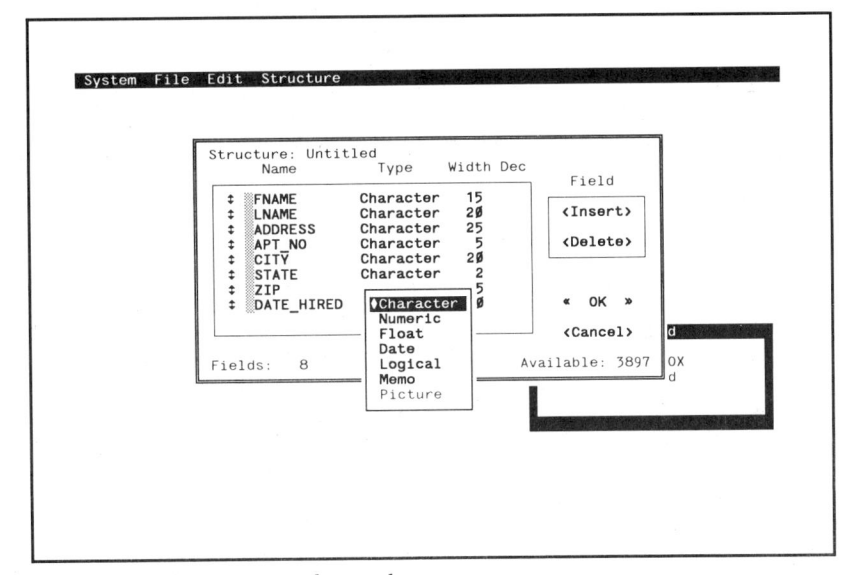

Figure 2.6: The popup to choose data type.

11. Type **PROBATION**. This is a logical field to see whether or not the employee is on probation. Press Tab to move to the Type column and type **L** make it a logical field. Notice that the width is automatically 1. Because you cannot change the width of a logical field, the cursor automatically moves to the next line.

12. Type **NOTES**. Press Tab to move to the Type column and type **M** to choose the Memo type. The width of a memo field is listed as 10, even when it is holding much more than that, as you will see. There is no need to change it.

13. When you choose the Memo type, the cursor moves to the next line and the list scrolls up to make room for the description of another field, but we have all the fields we need for this sample database. The Structure dialog box should look like Figure 2.7.

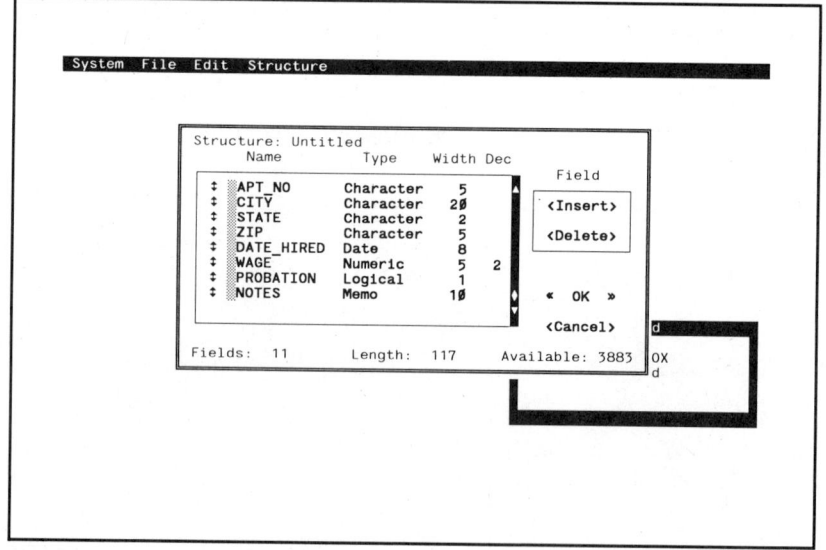

```
 System  File  Edit  Structure

          Structure: Untitled
              Name          Type      Width Dec
          ‡  APT_NO        Character    5            Field
          ‡  CITY          Character   20
          ‡  STATE         Character    2          <Insert>
          ‡  ZIP           Character    5
          ‡  DATE_HIRED    Date         8          <Delete>
          ‡  WAGE          Numeric      5    2
          ‡  PROBATION     Logical      1
          ‡  NOTES         Memo        10          «  OK  »

                                                   <Cancel>
          Fields:  11      Length:  117     Available: 3883
```

Figure 2.7: The structure dialog box with fields filled in. (Not all field names are visible.)

14. Scroll up to the top of the list of fields you entered in order to see if they are all correct. If you made any typographical errors, correct them in the same way that you changed the default values—either by typing the new value when the field is highlighted, or by pressing the right arrow key and then editing the existing value.

15. When you have confirmed that the definition is right, select the default text button, OK, either by clicking it with the mouse or by pressing Ctrl-Enter.

SAVING THE DATABASE FILE

When you select OK, the dialog box that lets you name the database appears—including a scrollable list with names of files and directories, as shown in Figure 2.8. (Of course, your list may look a bit different from this illustration, depending on what is in your directory.) The list on the left side of the dialog box lets you navigate through the DOS directory structure, so you can save your file in any subdirectory. The place where your cursor is located in this dialog box is a text box without the box around it, the place for you to type in the file name. For readers who are not familiar with DOS subdirectories, the next section contains a brief discussion of how they are organized; if you are familiar with DOS subdirectories, skip to the following section, "How to Save the File."

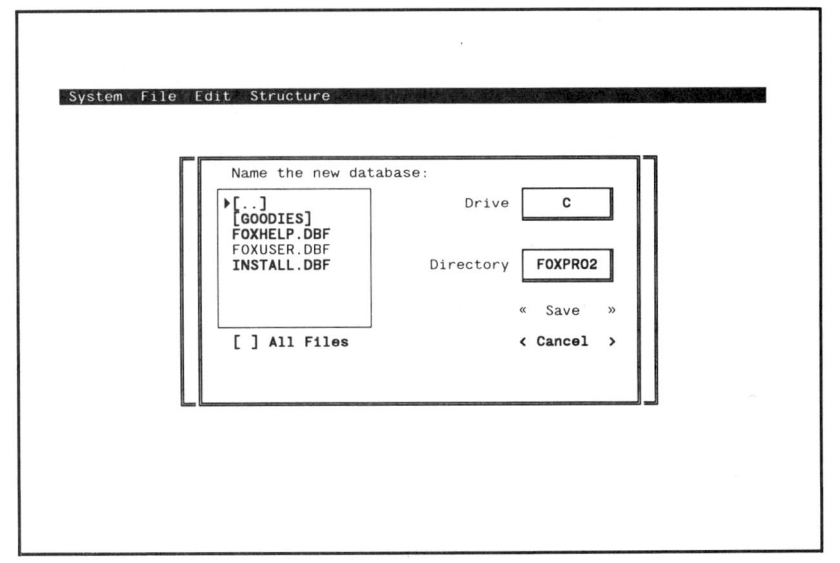

Figure 2.8: The dialog box for naming the new database file.

WORKING WITH THE DOS DIRECTORY STRUCTURE

DOS has a hierarchical subdirectory structure. This means that its subdirectories are arranged like the organization chart of a typical corporation, which has the president at the top, a number of vice-presidents directly under the president, a number of managers under

> To be even more complete, you can include the disk letter followed by a colon before the directory name. For example, C:\ is the root directory of the C disk and A:\MISC is the MISC subdirectory directly under the root directory of the A disk. If use several disks—for example, if you have more than one hard disk—it is good to get in the habit of including the disk letter in the directory name, as it will let you access the directory you want no matter what disk you are in. Here, we assume that you work in one disk and do not need to include the disk letter.

each vice-president, and so on. This sort of hierarchical structure lets each directory on your disk have a number of directories below it but only one directory directly above it; there is one directory at the top.

A directory is sometimes called a *child* of the directory above it and a *parent* of the directories below it. The directory at the top is called the *root directory*.

The root directory is represented by the backslash \ symbol. Other directories are referred to by listing all the directories above them, beginning with the root directory; each of these directories is separated by backslashes. For example, if you installed all of FoxPro's optional features, your root directory has a FOXPRO2 directory under it, which has a SAMPLE directory under *it*. The SAMPLE directory is referred to precisely as \FOXPRO2\SAMPLE. Likewise, SAMPLE has a directory under it named PRGS, and the full name of that directory is \FOXPRO2\SAMPLE\PRGS. Figure 2.9 illustrates a directory structure with these directories plus a few others.

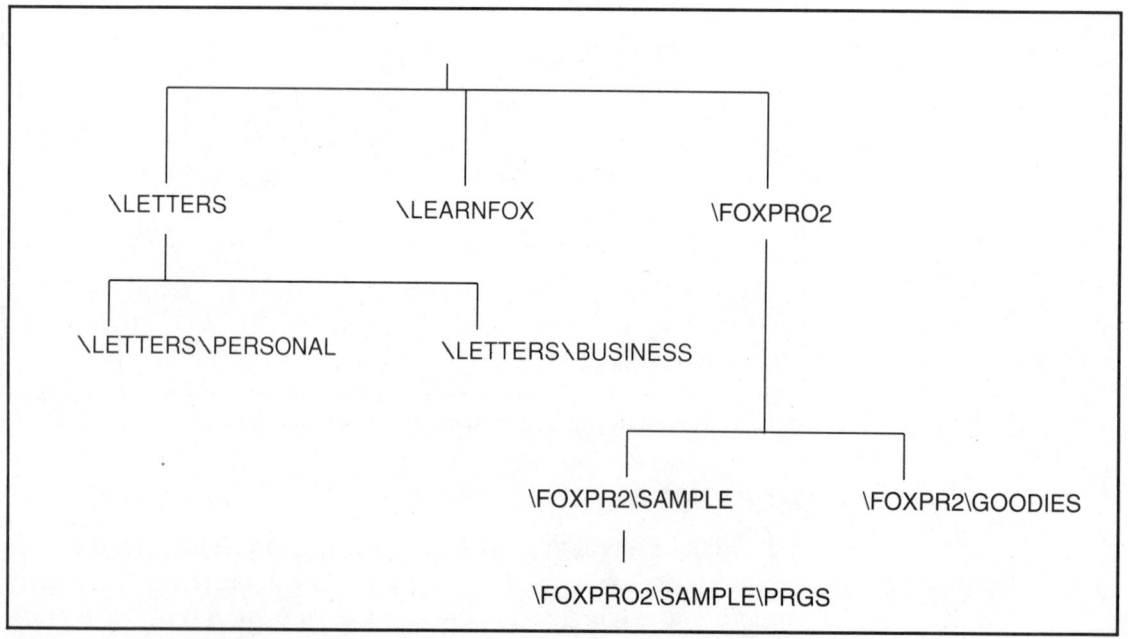

```
                          |
         ┌────────────────┼────────────────┐
      \LETTERS         \LEARNFOX         \FOXPRO2
         │                                   │
   ┌─────┴─────┐                        ┌────┴────┐
\LETTERS\   \LETTERS\                \FOXPR2\  \FOXPR2\
PERSONAL    BUSINESS                 SAMPLE    GOODIES
                                        │
                                  \FOXPRO2\SAMPLE\PRGS
```

Figure 2.9: A directory structure

By default, DOS commands apply only to the current directory. For example, the command

DEL FILE.TXT

would delete the file named FILE.TXT only if it were in the current directory. You can enter the full directory name, though, to use commands on files in any directory, using the same backslash delimiter to separate the file name from the directory name. For example,

DEL \FOXPRO\API\MISC\FILE.TXT

would work no matter what directory you are in when you enter it. Note that a space must follow any command word, but no spaces should occur within a file name or path.

A useful shortcut is to use two dots to refer to the parent of the current directory. The two dots (periods) stand for the entire name of the parent directory of the current directory.

Once you understand how to refer to directories, there are only three basic commands you need to work with them.

- **MD** stands for Make Directory. **MD** <*directory name*> creates a directory with a given name.
- **CD** stands for Current Directory or for Change Directory. **CD** <*directory name*> moves you into the directory you named.
- **RD** stands for Remove Directory. **RD** <*directory name*> removes the directory with that name, but it only works if that directory has no files in it or subdirectories under it.

These commands can use the full directory name or the same abbreviations of directory names as other commands. For example,

RD \FOXPRO\API\MISC

would remove that directory no matter which directory you were currently in. If you were already in the \FOXPRO\API directory, though, you could remove it by just entering **RD MISC**.

> If you prefer using a menu-driven method of working with files, you can use the Filer, discussed in Appendix B, instead of these three basic commands for working with subdirectories. In either case, though, you do have to understand the hierarchical organization of directories discussed above, in order to use FoxPro dialog boxes to navigate through the directory system.

That is really all you will ever need to know about DOS directories. You used **MD \LEARNFOX** earlier in this chapter to create a directory to use with this book. You can use **RD \LEARNFOX** to remove that directory when you are done with this book and have deleted your practice files. And you should understand the directory structure well enough that you will have no trouble moving through it.

HOW TO SAVE THE FILE

In the scrollable lists in FoxPro dialog boxes, the names of subdirectories that are under the current directory are in square brackets. A square bracket with two dots in it represents the parent directory of the current directory. You can move up and down the directory structure by selecting either the parent or one of the children directories of the current directory, and you can ultimately get to any directory on your disk in this way.

The popup control boxes to the right tell you the name of the current disk drive and current directory. The Drive popup control lets you select the disk you want to save to: for example, you can use it to select A if you want to save the file on a floppy disk in drive A. The Directory popup control will display all the parent directories up to the root, to let you move up quickly through a complex subdirectory structure. In the Directory control, FoxPro refers to the root directory simply by using the drive letter plus a colon, without the backslash used in DOS.

To move through most directory structures, you just need the scrollable list, and you can use it to save the new database file in the \LEARNFOX directory that you created at the beginning of this chapter.

1. The cursor should be at the lower left of the *Name the new database* dialog box, called up by selecting OK from the Structure dialog box. Type **EMPLIST** as the name of the database.

2. Move to the list of directories. Select the first item in the list, [..]. You have now moved from the FOXPRO directory up to the root directory.

3. This list is alphabetical. Select [LEARNFOX] from it, and a new scrollable list representing the contents of this directory appears. Of course, there are no files or subdirectories in this new directory, just [..] to let you move up to the parent directory, as in Figure 2.10.

4. Now that you have the proper file name (EMPLIST) and subdirectory (LEARNFOX), just select the default pushbutton, Save, to save the new database file.

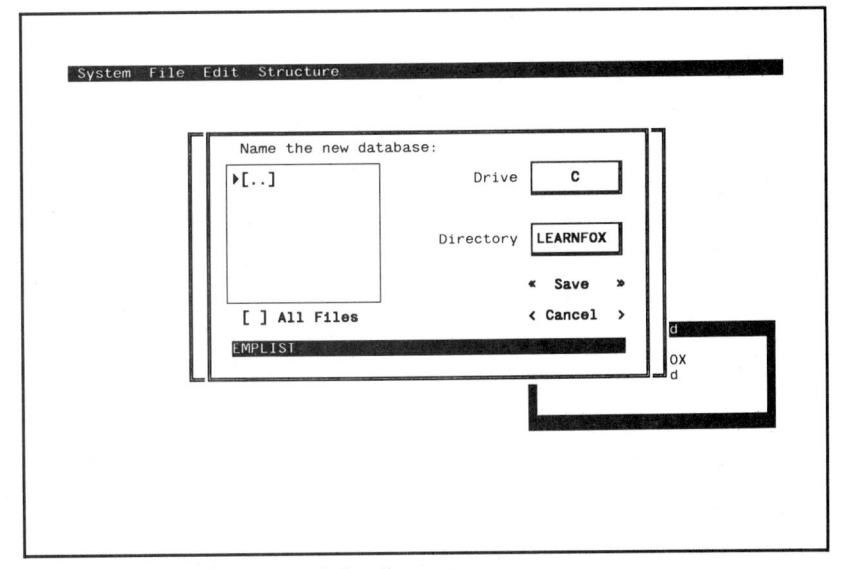

Figure 2.10: Moving around the directory system.

5. FoxPro will save the file and ask if you want to enter records now, as in Figure 2.11. Select the No pushbutton. (You can do this simply by pressing the letter **N**.)

In practice, you will find that you often create a database file under the pressure of necessity, and you will want to enter records as soon as you are done. For now, though, you should take a few moments to investigate how the program keeps track of what you are doing.

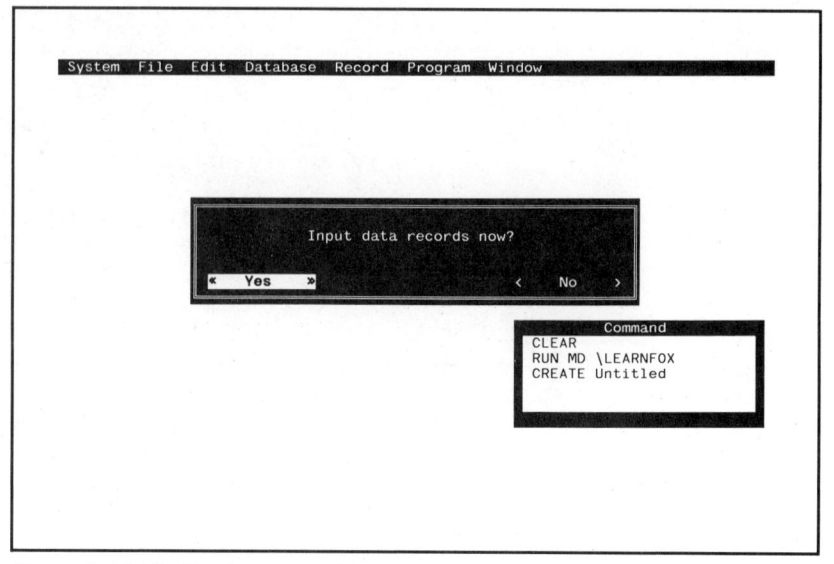

```
┌────────────────────────────────────────────────────────────┐
│ System  File  Edit  Database  Record  Program  Window      │
├────────────────────────────────────────────────────────────┤
│                                                            │
│                                                            │
│              ┌──────────────────────────────┐              │
│              │    Input data records now?   │              │
│              │  « Yes »            ‹ No ›   │              │
│              └──────────────────────────────┘              │
│                                   ┌──────────Command──────┐│
│                                   │ CLEAR                 ││
│                                   │ RUN MD \LEARNFOX      ││
│                                   │ CREATE Untitled       ││
│                                   └───────────────────────┘│
│                                                            │
└────────────────────────────────────────────────────────────┘
```

Figure 2.11: FoxPro lets you add records immediately.

THE DATABASE FILE IN THE BACKGROUND

You have learned all that you really need to know to create database files, but it is also useful to look a little deeper. In this section, you will work from the Command window and do a few things that you cannot do by using the menu system.

This section is not meant to teach you new techniques. It simply uses these new techniques to give you a deeper understanding of what happens more or less "behind the scenes" when you work with the menus. Therefore, you do not have to try to memorize the commands in this section. The menu system will be enough for almost all of your practical work.

You should take a moment to absorb the very important idea that when a given database file is in use it does not necessarily appear anywhere on your screen—that it can be hovering in the background and still be the database file that any operations which you choose from the menu will be performed on. For example, though it does not appear on the screen, the database file that you just created is in use. If you select Edit from the Database menu, for example, this is the database file that will appear in the Edit window.

OPENING AND CLOSING A DATABASE FILE

Normally, you use a database file by selecting Open from the File menu. The database file that you select from the dialog box does not appear on the screen, but it becomes available and can be manipulated with the Database or Record popup.

When you select Open, the command **USE** <*file name*> is generated in the Command window. This command is used to open a file from the command line or from within a program.

If a file is already in use, its name will be dimmed in the scrollable list of files when you select Open, and you will not be able to "reselect" the file. Another handy way of telling whether a file is in use is by entering the command **DISPLAY STRUCTURE** in the Command window. This will display the name of the current file and the names, types, and widths of its fields.

> You will see in Chapter 7 that you can use the View window to have multiple files in use at once, a feature that is used primarily with relational databases. To do this, though, you must create a separate work area for each file. There is always just one file in use in the current work area. You can also use the View window to close database files through the menu system.

Normally, only one database file can be in use at a time. If you open another database file, the current file will no longer be in use: it automatically closes and will be replaced by the one you opened. Thus, you rarely need to close a database file when you are working through the menu system—you simply use another file.

If it happens that you want to close a database file without opening another one, you cannot do so by selecting Close from the File menu. That menu option merely closes the current *window* and does not affect the database file in the background. If you did it now, it would close the Command window—but the EMPLIST database would still be open.

There is a simple command to close a database file, though. The command **USE** <*file name*>, which has the side effect of closing the current file as it opens the one you specify, will still have the side effect of closing the current file if you don't specify a file to be used. Thus, the command **USE** without a file name serves to close the current file.

A BIT OF EXPERIMENTING

Try some experimenting to see what kinds of things can occur in the background:

1. Select Open from the File menu and note that EMPLIST.DBF, the file you just created, is dimmed in the scrollable list in the Open dialog box. Try to select it, and you will see that it is impossible: the file is already open. Press Esc to close the dialog box.

2. Enter **DISP STRU** in the Command window, and FoxPro will display the structure of the EMPLIST file, as shown in Figure 2.12—another indication that this is the current file.

> Remember that you can use just the first four letters of each word in any FoxPro command. Here, you can abbreviate the command as **COPY STRU**. (You can abbreviate only FoxPro key words, not file names.)

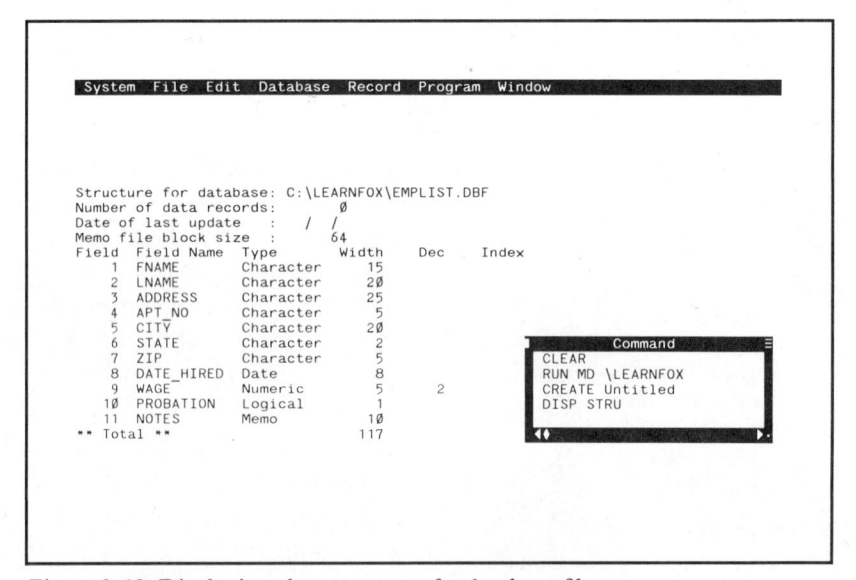

```
System  File  Edit  Database  Record  Program  Window


Structure for database: C:\LEARNFOX\EMPLIST.DBF
Number of data records:       0
Date of last update    :   /  /
Memo file block size   :      64
Field  Field Name  Type        Width   Dec   Index
    1  FNAME       Character      15
    2  LNAME       Character      20
    3  ADDRESS     Character      25
    4  APT_NO      Character       5
    5  CITY        Character      20
    6  STATE       Character       2
    7  ZIP         Character       5
    8  DATE_HIRED  Date            8
    9  WAGE        Numeric         5     2
   10  PROBATION   Logical         1
   11  NOTES       Memo           10
** Total **                      117
                                           ┌─── Command ───┐
                                           │ CLEAR         │
                                           │ RUN MD \LEARNFOX │
                                           │ CREATE Untitled │
                                           │ DISP STRU     │
                                           └───────────────┘
```

Figure 2.12: Displaying the structure of a database file.

3. Enter **USE** in the Command window to close the current file without opening a new one.

4. To see if the last command worked, enter **CLEAR** to clear the screen, and then enter **DISP STRU** again. Since no file is in use, FoxPro will display a dialog box to let you select a database whose structure you want displayed, as in Figure 2.13.

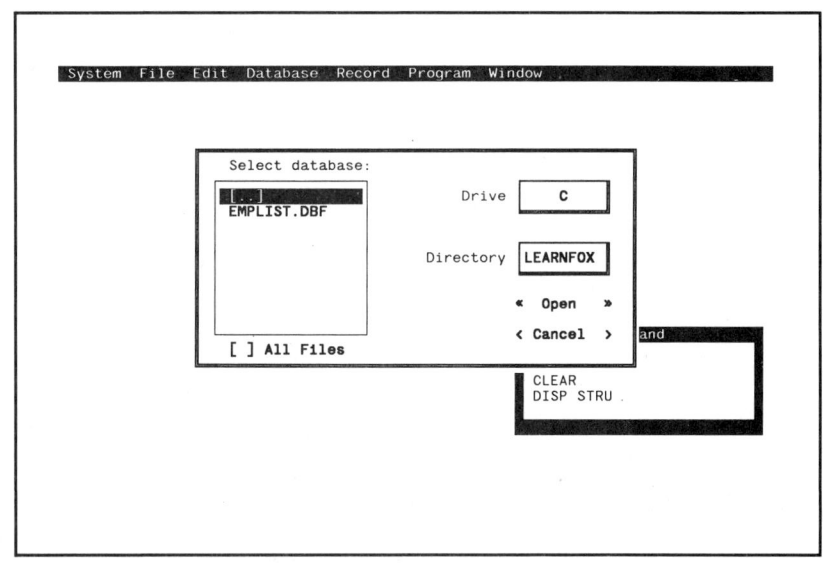

```
┌─────────────────────────────────────────────────────┐
│ System  File  Edit  Database  Record  Program  Window │
│                                                     │
│         ┌─────────────────────────────────────┐     │
│         │  Select database:                   │     │
│         │  ┌──────────┐         Drive  ┌───┐  │     │
│         │  │[..]      │                │ C │  │     │
│         │  │EMPLIST.DBF│                └───┘  │     │
│         │  │          │      Directory ┌────────┐│     │
│         │  │          │                │LEARNFOX││     │
│         │  │          │                └────────┘│     │
│         │  │          │           «  Open  »   │     │
│         │  │          │           <  Cancel >  │and  │
│         │  │[ ] All Files│                     │     │
│         └─────────────────────────────────────┘     │
│                              CLEAR                   │
│                              DISP STRU               │
│                                                     │
└─────────────────────────────────────────────────────┘
```

Figure 2.13: The Select Database dialog box.

5. Rather than selecting a database, press Esc to close this dialog box. FoxPro will display an error message telling you that it cannot execute the DISPLAY STRUCTURE command because no database is in use, as shown in Figure 2.14. This is an example of an alert: Press any key and it will disappear.

6. For one more look behind the scenes, enter

   RUN DIR \LEARNFOX

   You will see the files in the LEARNFOX directory, as shown in Figure 2.15. Notice that it includes EMPLIST.DBF, the database file, and EMPLIST.FPT, the memo file.

This bit of experimenting should help you realize that a database file is sometimes in use without there being any obvious indication of it on the screen.

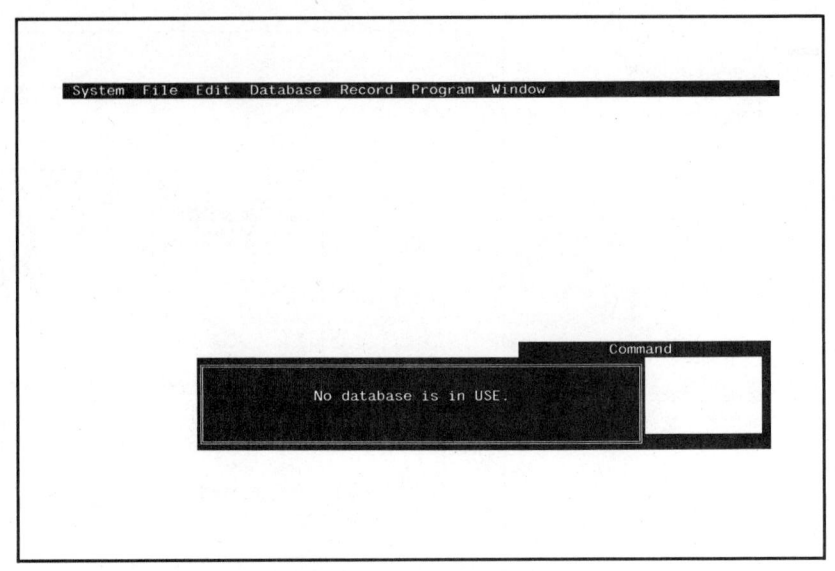

Figure 2.14: A FoxPro alert.

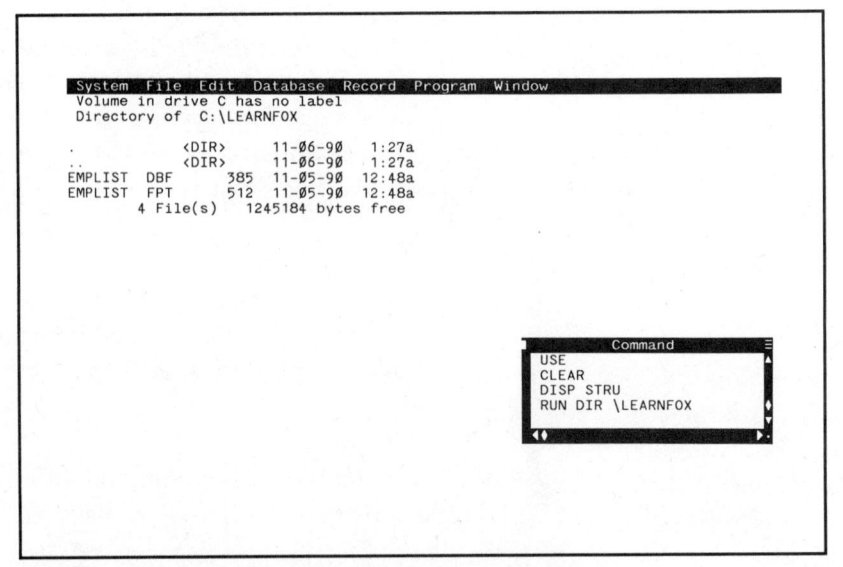

Figure 2.15: The EMPLIST database and memo files.

COPYING AND MODIFYING THE STRUCTURE OF A DATABASE FILE

Normally, you would use the menu system to define the structure of a new database file, but there are cases where it is easier to work from the command line. For instance, if you are creating a new database file that is similar to an existing one, you can work from the command line to copy the structure of an existing file to a new file. The FoxPro menu system does not offer an option to enable you to copy a file structure directly. As you will see in Chapter 5, it is possible to use the menu system to *trick* FoxPro into copying the structure, but it is simpler just to use the command **COPY STRUCTURE** from the Command window, as you will do in the following exercise. After you copy the structure of an existing file to a new file, you will use the menu system to modify the copy somewhat, a procedure that will address a common need in practice.

1. If you want, enter **CLEAR** in the Command window to clear the screen. Select Open from the File menu popup and select EMPLIST.DBF from the Open dialog box, shown in Figure 2.16. The dialog box used to open a file is very similar to the one that you used to name the file, so you should be comfortable with it. The command

    USE EMPLIST.DBF

    is generated in the Command window.

2. To copy its structure to a new file (which we will call TEMP since is it being used only temporarily, for illustration), enter

    COPY STRUCTURE TO \LEARNFOX\TEMP

    in the Command window.

3. To make TEMP the current file, select Open from the File menu again and the new file from the dialog box. Note that EMPLIST.DBF is dimmed: you cannot select it (open it) because it is already in use. Note also that the new file, TEMP.DBF, has automatically been given a .DBF extension.

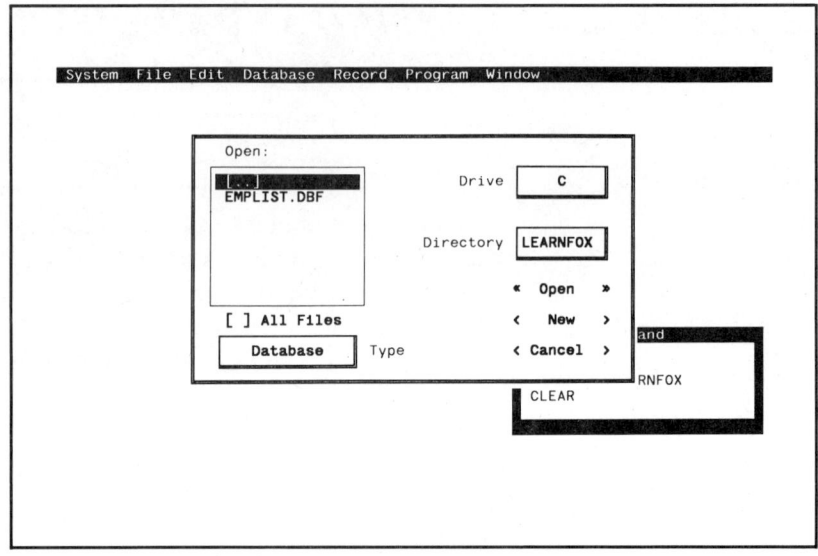

Figure 2.16: Opening a database file.

Now that you have copied the structure of an existing database file to a new one, you will practice modifying it slightly using the Setup dialog box (shown in Figure 2.17) from the Database menu popup.

This dialog box gives you control over the way in which a database file is displayed. It is very powerful and versatile. It will be further discussed in Chapter 4, which deals with indexes, as well as in later chapters. For now, you will just use it in a simple way to modify the structure of the new database.

> There are two Modify text buttons in the Setup dialog box discussed in Step 1. Do not select the one under the word Index in the upper right corner of the dialog box. If you do, press Esc to return to the Setup dialog box.

1. Select Setup from the Database menu. Then, from the Setup dialog box, select the Modify pushbutton that follows the word Structure in the upper left corner.

2. The Structure dialog box appears, the same dialog box you used when you were creating the structure of a new database from scratch, except that it is already filled out with a structure for the TEMP database, as shown in Figure 2.18. This structure is identical to the structure of EMPLIST.

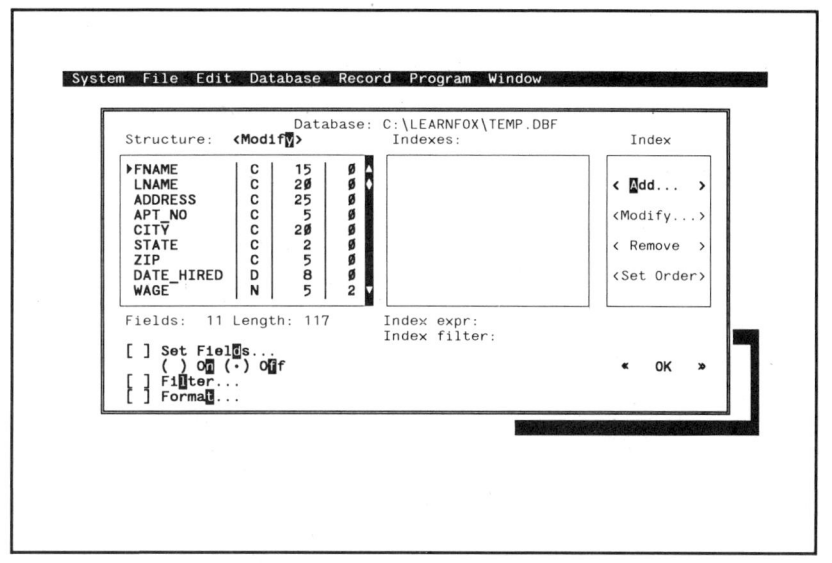

Figure 2.17: The Setup dialog box.

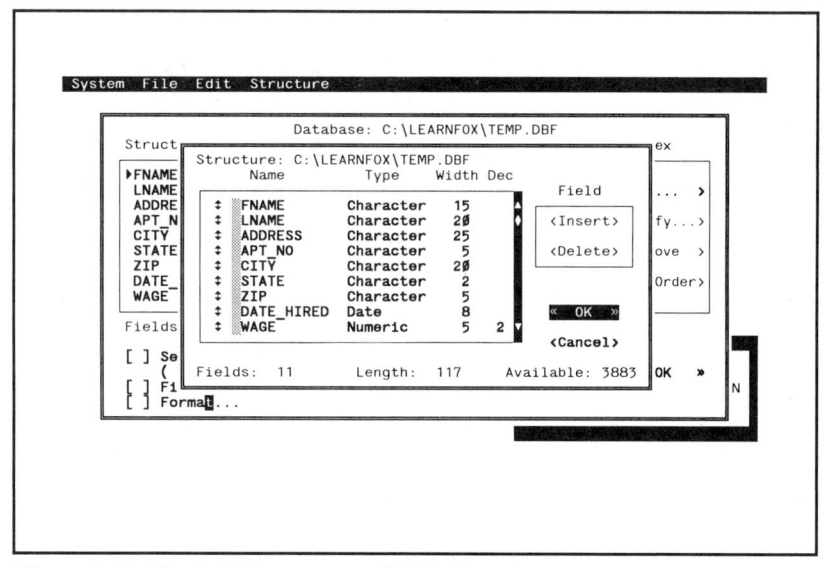

Figure 2.18: The initial structure of TEMP, copied from EMPLIST.

3. Try moving the FNAME field below the LNAME field so that the last name comes before the first name in this database. If you are using a mouse, simply move the pointer to the arrow to the left of FNAME, hold down the button, drag the field below the LNAME field, and release the button. If you are using the keyboard, press Tab twice to highlight the double arrow to the left of FNAME, press the space bar to highlight the field, press the down arrow key once to move it, then press Enter to complete the operation.

4. Try inserting a middle-initial field. Place the cursor in the ADDRESS field. Then, if you are using a mouse, it is easiest just to click the Insert pushbutton. Using the keyboard, use the Structure menu popup to select Insert Field. In either case, a field called NEWFIELD with character data type and the default width of 10 is inserted above the ADDRESS field, where the cursor was. Edit this field: Type **MI** (for Middle Initial) to change its name, and **1** to change its width.

> Notice the hot keys on the Structure menu: Ctrl-I to insert a field and Ctrl-D to delete a field. The hot keys are really the only convenient way to insert and delete fields using the keyboard.

5. Finally, delete the PROBATION field. Move the highlight to this field using the mouse or the down arrow key. Then select the Delete pushbutton, or select Delete Field from the Structure menu as you did when you were inserting a field. The PROBATION field disappears. The Structure dialog box should now look like Figure 2.19. (Note that the LNAME and FNAME fields in our screen have scrolled up beyond the top of the list box.)

6. Assuming that those are the changes you want, select the default pushbutton, OK. FoxPro will ask for confirmation that you want to make the structure changes permanent: select Yes. FoxPro will display the Setup window again: a system message in the upper right says "Database Structure Modified." Remember that there is no need to remove a system message; unlike an alert, it will just go away. Select OK to confirm what you have done and to remove the Setup dialog box.

Of course, you can also modify the structure of a file you have been using—for example, if you have been entering five-digit zip codes

CREATING A DATABASE STRUCTURE 69

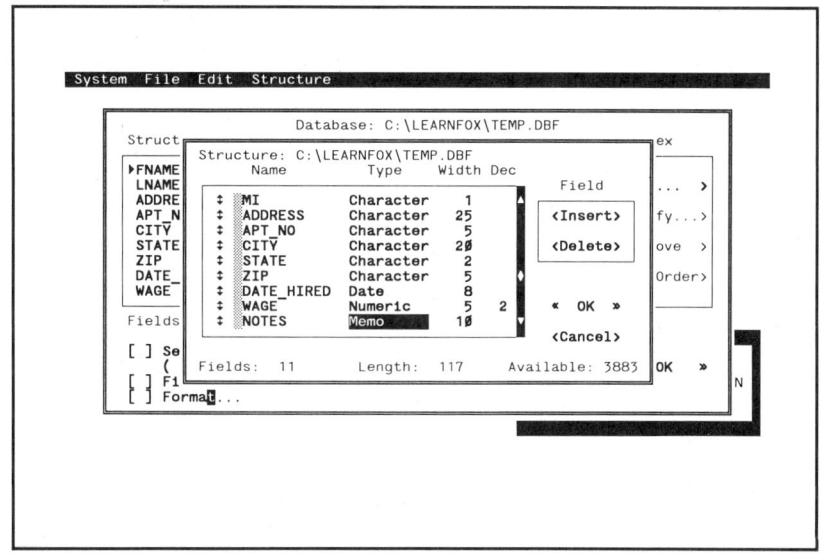

Figure 2.19: The new structure of TEMP.DBF.

and want to convert to extended zip codes. You should be aware, however, that you can lose data when you modify a file's structure—for example, if you mistakenly shorten a field so that it is no longer large enough to hold some of the data in it or if you mistakenly delete a field with data in it. For this reason, FoxPro automatically backs up a database file when you modify its structure, as you will see in a moment.

7. Remember that after you create a file it is in use. Enter **DISP STRU** and you will see that TEMP has the structure you defined.

8. To see exactly what you have created, enter

    RUN DIR \LEARNFOX

    Notice that the directory, shown in Figure 2.20, contains a .DBF and an .FPT file for both EMPLIST and TEMP; these are the database and memo files respectively. There are also backup files for TEMP, with the extensions .BAK and .TBK, since you modified its structure.

```
System  File  Edit  Database  Record  Program  Window
Volume in drive C has no label
Directory of   C:\LEARNFOX

     .           <DIR>        11-06-90    1:27a
     ..          <DIR>        11-06-90    1:27a
EMPLIST   DBF       385       11-05-90   12:48a
EMPLIST   FPT       512       11-05-90   12:48a
TEMP      BAK       385       11-05-90   12:57a
TEMP      TBK       512       11-05-90   12:57a
TEMP      DBF       385       11-05-90    1:02a
TEMP      FPT       512       11-05-90    1:02a
        8 File(s)     1187840 bytes free

                                        Command
                              USE C:\LEARNFOX\EMPLIST.
                              COPY STRU TO \LEARNFOX\T
                              USE C:\LEARNFOX\TEMP.DBF
                              RUN DIR \LEARNFOX
```

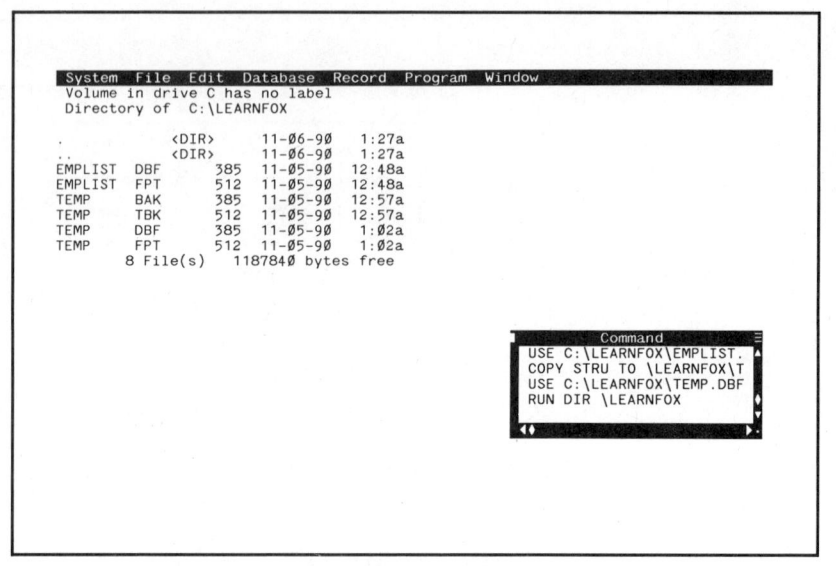

Figure 2.20: Database, memo, and backup files.

If you ever lose data and want to use the backup files as your database, you can do so in several ways. One easy one is by using the DOS command **COPY** <*file name*>**.BAK** <*file name*>**.DBF**, and **COPY** <*file name*>**.TBK** <*file name*>**.FPT** if there is a memo field as well.

Since this was just an exercise, you can simply delete the new file and backup files. FoxPro has its own commands to delete files, and the Filer utility covered in Appendix B lets you delete files using a menu-driven system; but it is usually easier to use the DOS **DEL** command. You can use the DOS wild-card character * (which stands for any word) to delete them all at once. Thus, to delete all the temporary files, enter

RUN DEL \LEARNFOX \TEMP.*

in the Command window.

If you want to take a break, select Quit from the File menu—or, if you are becoming accustomed to the Command window, just enter **QUIT**.

Chapter 3

Adding, Editing, and Viewing Data

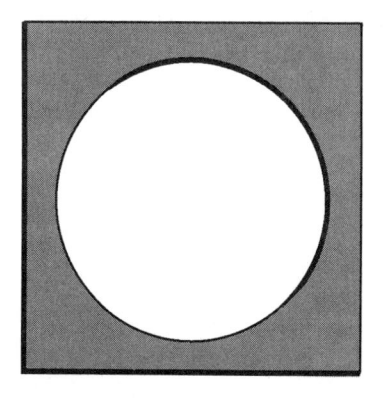

FOXPRO OFFERS TWO FUNDAMENTALLY DIFFERENT ways in which you can look at the database when you add, edit, or view data: the Change (or Edit) mode and the Browse mode.

The Change mode is designed to let you work on the database one record at a time. The fields of the record are thus arranged so that you can see the entire record, limited only by the size of the screen. Of course, some records have such wide fields or such a number of fields that you cannot see all the data in one record at one time using the Change window. Still, Change is essentially record-oriented, and its vertical field arrangement comes as close as possible to letting you see an entire record. Figure 3.1 shows a complete record and, because there is still room in the window, the beginning of the next record in the database.

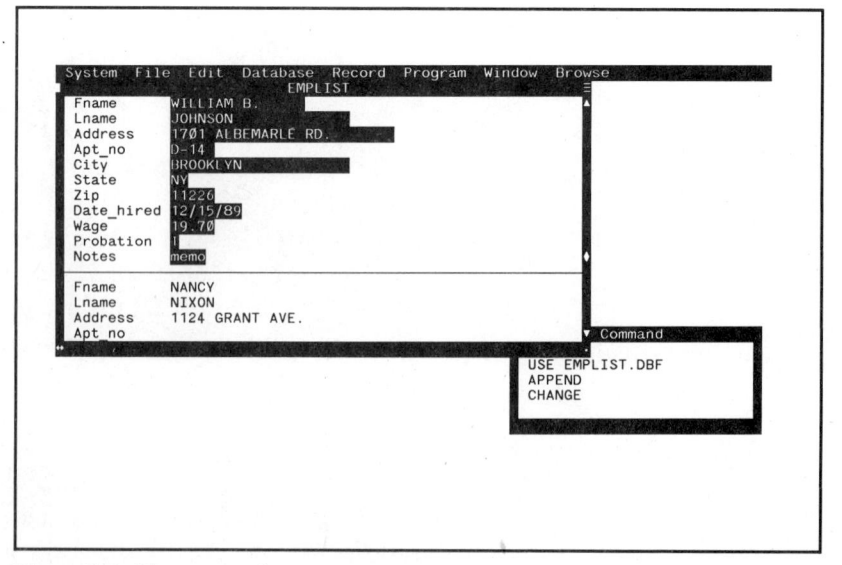

Figure 3.1: Change mode

The Browse mode is designed to let you look quickly through the entire database file, rather than looking at one record at a time. It displays the database in table form so that each record takes just one line, as shown in Figure 3.2. In the Browse mode, you can see many records at a time, but you usually cannot see all the fields of each record.

ADDING, EDITING, AND VIEWING DATA   75

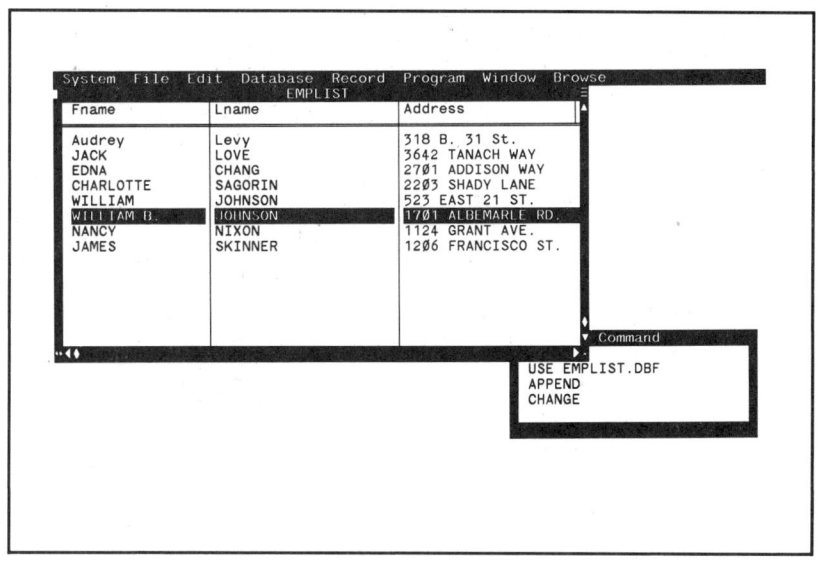

```
 System  File  Edit  Database  Record  Program  Window  Browse
                         EMPLIST
 Fname           Lname              Address

 Audrey          Levy               318 B. 31 St.
 JACK            LOVE               3642 TANACH WAY
 EDNA            CHANG              2701 ADDISON WAY
 CHARLOTTE       SAGORIN            2203 SHADY LANE
 WILLIAM         JOHNSON            523 EAST 21 ST.
 WILLIAM B.      JOHNSON            1701 ALBEMARLE RD.
 NANCY           NIXON              1124 GRANT AVE.
 JAMES           SKINNER            1206 FRANCISCO ST.

                                              Command
                                       USE EMPLIST.DBF
                                       APPEND
                                       CHANGE
```

Figure 3.2: Browse mode

> The command **EDIT** is more common than **CHANGE** in older dBASE compatible programs. **CHANGE** is more common in FoxPro.

Because Change is record-oriented, Change is on the Record menu popup; and because Browse is database-oriented, Browse is on the Database menu popup. Working from the Command window, you can simply enter **CHANGE** (or **EDIT**) to use the Change window or enter **BROWSE** to use the Browse window.

The Change and Browse windows are related. Whenever you choose either of these options, a Browse menu pad is added at the right of the menu bar. The first option on the new menu popup lets you switch from one mode to the other: if you are in Change mode, the first option is Browse, and if you are in Browse mode, the first option is Change. These options simply alter the way the database is displayed, without closing the window and interrupting your work. We will refer to the window created by either of them as the Browse/Change window, since you can toggle between the two modes.

Browse and Change are meant to let you work on existing records—to edit them or simply to look at them. If you want to create new records, there is an option on the Browse menu popup that lets you add a new record after you have selected Browse or Change, but you must choose it each time you want to add a new record, which is inconvenient when you are doing data entry.

To add several new records, you should select Append from the Record menu or enter the command **APPEND** in the Command window. This command continually maintains a blank record at the end of the database file as you fill in additional records. The screen in the Append mode starts out arranged as in the Change mode, with one field above another. When you are in the Append mode, you can scroll in the usual manner to reach other records in the file that you are appending to. Thus, in the Append mode you can edit previous records as well as add or change new ones; however, you would always have to scroll up from the bottom of a database file to edit previous records. For purposes of editing database records, Change is the better option.

Append also makes the Browse menu pad appear, which enables you to toggle the window from a Change-mode display to a Browse-mode display and vice-versa. You can add records with the window arranged in either way. No matter how the window is arranged, as long as Append is selected there will always be one blank record at the end of the file for you to fill in.

Of course, a database must be in use before you can utilize Browse, Change, or Append, which is to say that you must first select Open from the File menu or enter the command **USE** <*file name*> in the Command window. If no database is in use, Change and Append are not even available from the menu system, because you cannot access the Record popup that they belong to. You can select Browse—from the Database menu—when no database is in use, however, and FoxPro will display a dialog box to ask you which database you want, as shown in Figure 3.3. The same dialog box will appear if you enter the command **CHANGE**, **EDIT**, **BROWSE**, or **APPEND** in the Command window when no database is in use.

APPENDING DATA

If you try to change or browse a database before any records are in it—for example, the database from Chapter 2 which only has its fields defined—the Change/Browse window will simply be blank. You should append a few sample records first, so that you have something there to change and browse a bit later.

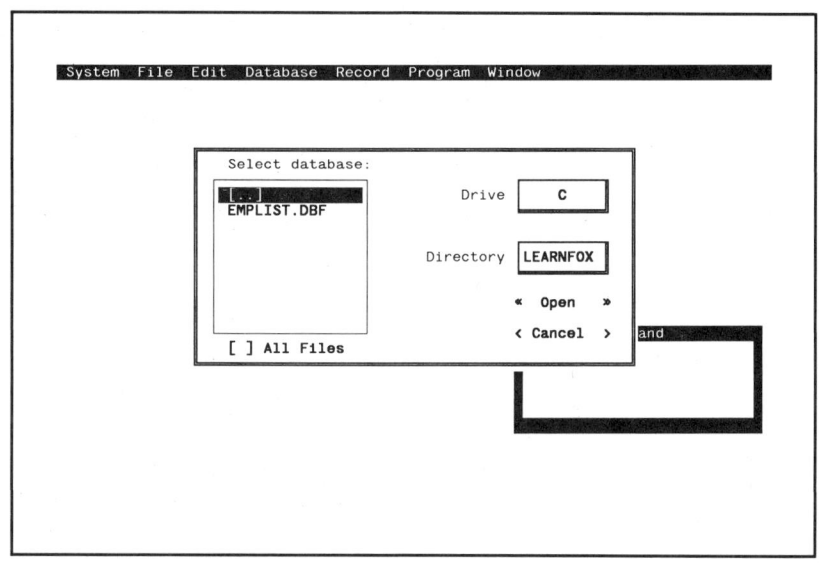

Figure 3.3: If no database is in use, FoxPro asks which database you want

Most of the sample entries in the exercises of this chapter will be made in Append mode. You will move around the file in the conventional ways, using the mouse or the right and left arrow keys to move within a field, the up and down arrow keys to move among fields, Tab or Enter to move to the next field, and so on.

When you are finished editing database records you may either save or discard the changes you made. Ctrl-End, Ctrl-W, clicking the close box, and selecting Close from the File menu are four ways to close the window and save the changes you made. Pressing Esc or Ctrl-Q closes the window and discards the changes you made to the current field.

Memo fields of the database will show the word *memo*. If there is any text in the memo, this word will begin with a capital M; if not, it will begin with a small m. To work with the contents of the memo field, press Ctrl-PgDn or double-click the memo field with the mouse, and a memo window will open. Enter or change the memo contents using the conventional editing keys. To close the memo window and save the changes you made, press Ctrl-W or select Close from the File menu. (Ctrl-End does not close a memo window—it moves the cursor to the end of the document.) Pressing Esc lets you discard the changes, but when you are in a memo field FoxPro gives you a warning before discarding.

All these features will be very obvious when you use them in the following exercises. First you will append some data in the ordinary way, with the fields one above another, as they are in the Change mode. Then you will append more data with the fields next to each other, as they are in the Browse mode. Throughout this book we will refer to the vertical arrangement of fields as the Change mode or display and the horizontal arrangement of fields as the Browse mode or display, in keeping with the "Browse/Change window" terminology. As you will see later, this window can be split to display information in both modes if you wish.

APPENDING DATA WITH THE CHANGE DISPLAY

In the last chapter, you used the FoxPro dialog boxes to move among subdirectories. Now that you have become familiar with these operations, you might as well make your work easier by getting into the LEARNFOX subdirectory to begin with, which will let you select the database file with less trouble.

1. Before starting FoxPro, use DOS to change directories. At the DOS prompt, enter **CD \LEARNFOX**. Then enter **FOXPRO** to start the program. (If you are already running FoxPro, just enter **RUN CD \LEARNFOX** in the Command window.) If you want, enter **CLEAR** in the Command window to clear the screen and make it easier to see.

2. To use your sample database, select Open from the File menu and select EMPLIST.DBF from the Open dialog box. (Notice that the command generated in the Command window is **USE EMPLIST.DBF**. The full name of the database file **\LEARNFOX\EMPLIST.DBF** is not needed, as the file is in the current directory.)

3. To add data to the file, select Append from the Record menu. The command **APPEND** is generated in the Command window, a Browse menu pad is added to the menu

Remember that, if you are working from the Command window, you do not need to include the .DBF extension. You can just enter **USE EMPLIST**, since the **USE** command applies only to database files anyway.

bar, and the Browse/Change window appears in the special form that it has when you are in the Append mode, shown in Figure 3.4.

Notice that the name of the database file is at the top of this window and that the record is arranged in what we are calling the Change display, with one field above another. The fields are highlighted in reverse video, so that you can see the maximum length of each field—the amount of space you have to fill in. The cursor also appears in the Fname field; it is the ordinary blinking cursor except that it is in reverse video.

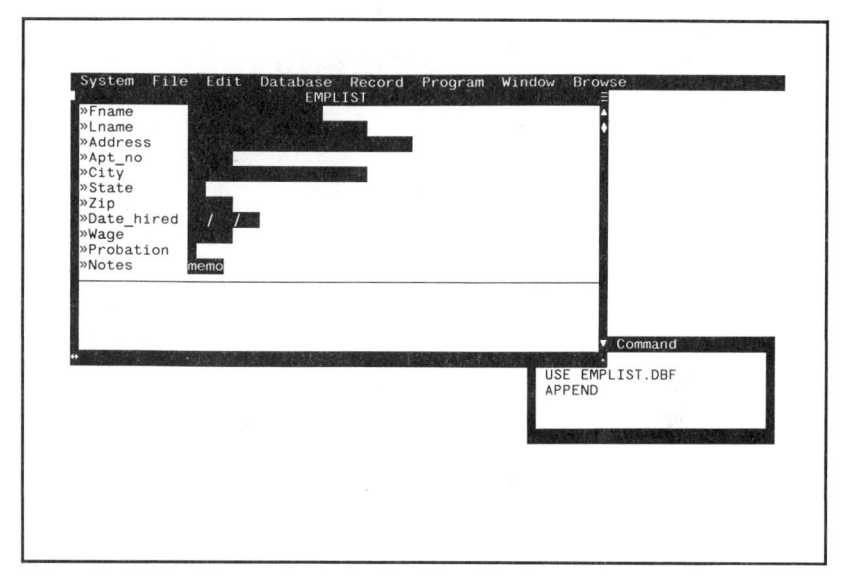

Figure 3.4: The "Append window" with a blank record

If you fill the entire length of a field, FoxPro beeps and goes on to the next field. As you will see, this saves a bit of time when you are entering fields of a fixed length, such as date fields. FoxPro will not accept invalid data in any field. If you try to enter a letter in the Wage field or Date_hired field, for example, it will beep and not accept it.

One important point to note—and one which is unique to the Append mode—is that, when you begin, all the fields of the record have the double right arrowhead >> to their left. This indicates that

It is common when using dBASE compatible database fields to enter blank records by mistake. If you create a blank record in FoxPro, the >> will disappear and the record will be saved. The >> sign thus makes it easy for you to tell whether you truly have a blank record or simply an unused one.

there is no data entered in the record: if you close the window at this point, that record will not be saved. On the other hand, as soon as you enter any data in the first field of the record, the >> will disappear from all the fields of the current record, and a new record with >> before each field will be added after the current record, as in Figure 3.5. This change indicates that the current record is no longer empty, and that it *will* be saved when you close the window. This is a major difference between selecting Append and selecting Change or Browse, which only let you add a new record by making an explicit choice from the Browse menu popup for each record to be added.

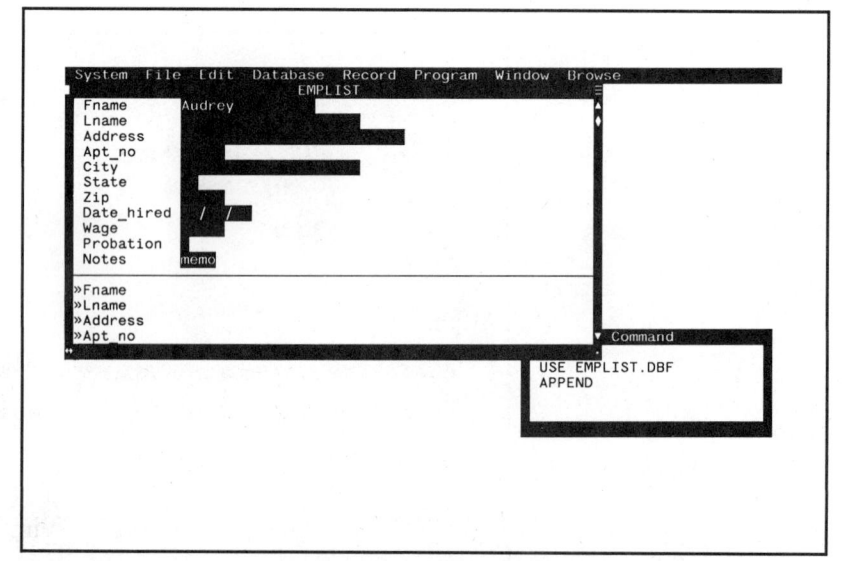

Figure 3.5: As soon as you enter data, a new blank record is appended

FoxPro (like other dBASE compatible programs) is sensitive to case differences in data. For example, if you tell it to search for SMITH (all uppercase) it will not find the record if the name was entered as Smith (upper and lowercase). For this reason, it is a common practice to enter names in all capital letters, to avoid difficulties in sorting and searching. However, when you have a long file, it is also common to have some names that were inadvertently entered in the ordinary format, with both capital and small letters. For the purposes of this exercise, you will enter the first record in the upper-and-lowercase format as begun in Figure 3.5, and the rest of the records in all capitals—so that you can see in later chapters what sort of difficulties this causes and how to get around them.

The samples in this exercise will also have other inconsistencies that often arise in data entry: for example, "Christmas" and "fund raising" will be spelled in more than one way. There will also be two people with the same name, as there often are in a large database. Though this is a small sample, it should give you an idea of some of the difficulties you usually come across in real life.

> The instructions tell you to press Tab to move to the next field, but you can actually press Tab, Enter, or the down arrow key. As usual, you should find the one that is most comfortable for you.

1. Type **Audrey** in the Fname field and press Tab. Notice that the >> signs to the left of all the fields in this record disappear, because this is no longer a blank record. At the same time, a new blank record with a >> sign before each field is added after it.

2. Type **Levy** in the Lname field and press Tab.

3. Type **318 B. 31 St.** in the Address field and press Tab.

4. Press Tab to skip the Apt_no field.

5. Type **Far Rockaway** in the City field and press Tab.

6. Type **NY** in the State field. Because the data fills the entire field, FoxPro beeps and the cursor automatically moves to the next field.

7. Type **11600** in the Zip field. Again, FoxPro beeps and moves to the next field.

8. Type **07/16/81** in the Date_hired field, and FoxPro beeps and moves to the next field.

9. You want to enter 8.00 in the Wage field. Simply type **8**, and then press Tab to move to the next field. FoxPro automatically justifies the number 8 and keeps the two zeroes.

10. Type **n** for no in the Probation field. The letter n appears for an instant and is then replaced by an F, as FoxPro translates

yes and no answers into **T**rue or **F**alse logic statements. FoxPro then beeps to tell you the field is full, and the cursor moves to the next field. (If you enter anything besides a capital or small T, F, Y, or N in a logical field, FoxPro beeps to show that you have made an invalid entry, and the cursor stays in the field.)

11. Since the Notes field is a memo field, press Ctrl-PgDn or double-click to use the memo window. You can see it is titled

    EMPLIST.NOTES

    to show that it is the Notes field of the EMPLIST database file. You can enter any text in the memo window, using the usual editing keys that you learned in Chapter 1. Try entering a note that is longer than one line: **Vacation time now totals more than three weeks per year. Works on annual Christmas fund-raising drive.** Notice the editor's word-wrap feature: when you get to the right edge of the window, the text automatically continues on the next line, as shown in Figure 3.6.

> If you did not want to enter anything in this memo field, you would just press Tab, Enter, or the down arrow key to move on to the next field.

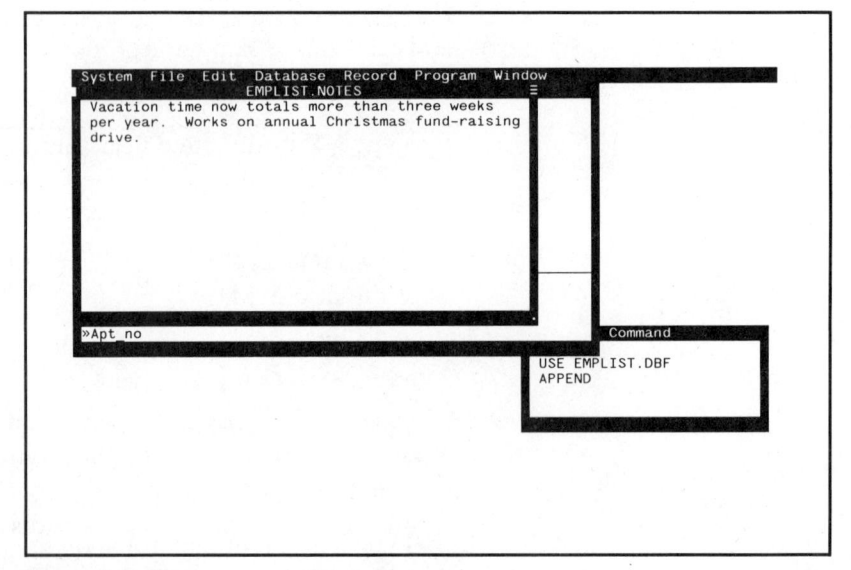

Figure 3.6: The memo window with text

ADDING, EDITING, AND VIEWING DATA 83

12. Try zooming the window, to get a better feel for word wrap. Click the zoom control, or select Zoom ↑ from the Window menu. The memo window now takes up the entire screen, and the text is automatically rewrapped to fit into the new size of the window, as shown in Figure 3.7. Zoom the window again to return it to its original size.

```
System  File  Edit  Database  Record  Program  Window
                       EMPLIST.NOTES
Vacation time now totals more than three weeks per year.  Works on annual
Christmas fund-raising drive.
```

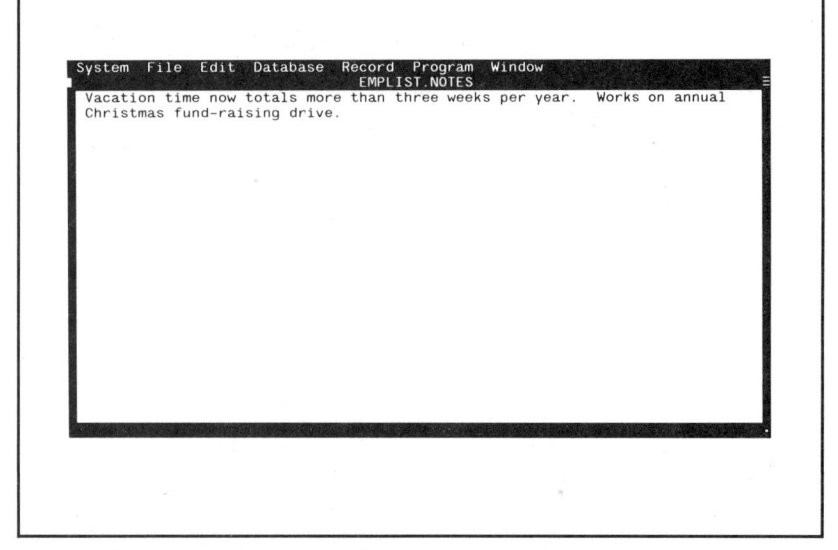

Figure 3.7: Text in the memo window is automatically rewrapped when the size of the window changes

13. When you have finished typing, press Ctrl-W or click the close box to close the memo window and return to the Browse/Change window. Then press Tab to move to the next field, the Fname field of the second record.

Try entering the following additional names to get used to the way the Append mode works and to give yourself some sample data to work with in the rest of the book. Be sure to press the Caps Lock key first so that you enter the following records as they are written, in all capital letters (except for the memo fields, some of which are entered with ordinary capitalization). Where the field indicates "(none)," leave that field blank.

- *Fname:* **JACK** *Lname:* **LOVE** *Address:* **3642 TANACH WAY** *Apt_no:* **18** *City:* **ELIZABETH** *State:* **NJ** *Zip:* **07200** *Date_hired:* **06/04/89** *Wage:* **16.20** *Probation:* **T** *Notes:* **Cannot work on Christmas fund raising drive.**

- *Fname:* **EDNA** *Lname:* **CHANG** *Address:* **2701 ADDISON WAY** *Apt_no:* **2B** *City:* **BERKELEY** *State:* **CA** *Zip:* **94706** *Date_hired:* **09/07/88** *Wage:* **9.75** *Probation:* **T** *Notes:* (none)

- *Fname:* **CHARLOTTE** *Lname:* **SAGORIN** *Address:* **2203 SHADY CIRCLE** *Apt_no:* (none) *City:* **EAST ORANGE** *State:* **NJ** *Zip:* **07000** *Date_hired:* **06/06/82** *Wage:* **22.75** *Probation:* **F** *Notes:* **ON XMAS FUNDRAISING COMMITTEE.**

- *Fname:* **WILLIAM** *Lname:* **JOHNSON** *Address:* **523 EAST 21 ST.** *Apt_no:* **F-23** *City:* **NEW YORK** *State:* **NY** *Zip:* **10022** *Date_hired:* **04/23/76** *Wage:* **6.25** *Probation:* **F** *Notes:* **LONG TERM AND LOYAL EMPLOYEE.**

- *Fname:* **WILLIAM B.** *Lname:* **JOHNSON** *Address:* **1701 ALBEMARLE RD.** *Apt_no:* **D-14** *City:* **BROOKLYN** *State:* **NY** *Zip:* **11226** *Date_hired:* **12/15/89** *Wage:* **19.70** *Probation:* **T** *Notes:* (none)

You should be accustomed, by now, to the way FoxPro works when you append data with the ordinary, Change-mode display.

APPENDING DATA WITH THE BROWSE DISPLAY

You will continue creating your sample database by appending another record with the Browse display. In this exercise, you will use the menu system to toggle the screen to this display, and then you will go on adding records in much the same way you did before.

1. If it isn't already there, move the cursor to the first field of the blank record. Then select the Browse menu pad. Since the Browse/Change window is now arranged in the Change display mode, the first option on the menu popup is Browse. Select that option to toggle the window to the Browse display.

2. The Browse/Change window is now large enough to show only a few fields of each record, and the cursor is right where it was before you toggled to the Browse display, as shown in Figure 3.8.

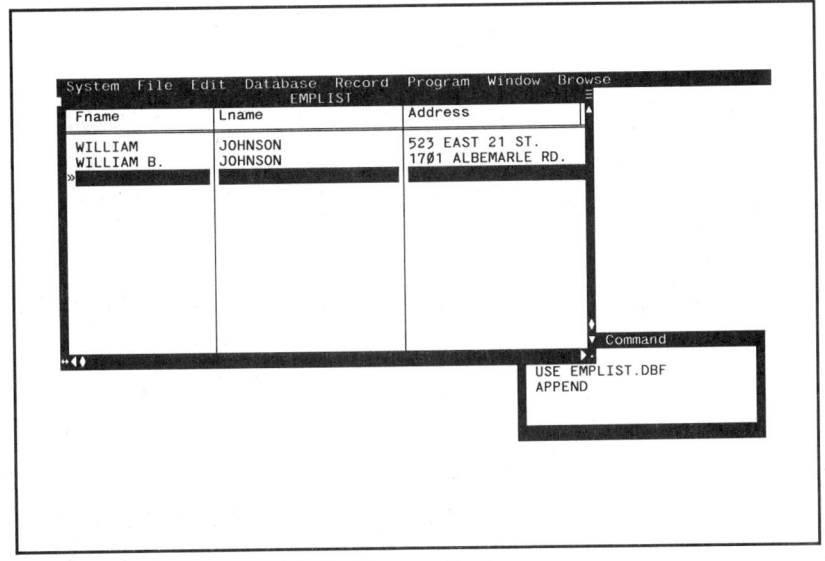

Figure 3.8: Appending with the Browse display

3. To enter the next record, type **NANCY** in the Fname field and press Tab. Notice that the >> symbol disappears from the left of the current record, and moves one line down, just as it moved one record down when you were working with the Change display.

4. Type **NIXON** in the Lname field and press Tab.

5. Type **1124 GRANT AVE** in the Address Field and press Tab. Then press Tab again to skip the Apt_no field.

6. Type **PALO ALTO** in the City field and press Tab.

7. Type **CA** in the State field. Notice that although the State field now looks wider than is needed to hold the two letters of a state's name, it still accepts no more than the two characters that are its defined width. It then beeps and goes on automatically to the next field.

8. Type **94300** in the Zip field.
9. Type **02/01/84** in the Date_hired field.
10. Type **18.25** in the Wage field.
11. Type **N** in the Probation field.
12. There is no entry in the Notes field. Leave the cursor in that field.

As you can see, it is equally easy to append records with either the Browse or the Change display. Now, in order to leave the file in the way you will next use it, you will toggle back to the Change display and then end your data-entry session.

1. Select the Browse menu pad. Notice that the first option on the menu popup now is Append, which toggles the screen back to the Change display that is standard in Append mode. Select the Append option.
2. Close the window to save your changes: press Ctrl-End, click the close box, or—if you insist on doing things the hard way—select Close from the File menu.

Remember that the EMPLIST database is still in use. Even if you selected Close from the File menu, you only closed the current window and not the database file itself.

CHANGING (OR EDITING) DATA

At this point, you should find it very easy to learn how to edit data. When you select Change from the Record menu, the database appears in a form very much like the Change display that you are familiar with from appending data. The only major difference, as you will see, is that since you are not in the Append mode, new records are not added at the end of the database automatically—you must use the menu system to add a blank record each time you want to add a record to the database.

> When you are editing, pressing Ctrl-Q closes the window and discards the changes that you have made in the current field without giving you any warning, as it does when you are appending. Although this is useful if you made changes by mistake, it must be handled with caution; otherwise you might discard changes you shouldn't.

To edit the data, you will use the conventional editing keys, and press Ctrl-End or Ctrl-W, or click the close box, to close the Browse/Change window and save the changes you made, just as you did with Append. You may edit memo fields, also, just as you did with Append. When you are editing, you are more likely than when you are appending to want to scroll among records, so you will be using the scroll bar or the PgUp and PgDn keys. You are also more likely to want to use the Undo feature of the editor, which you learned about in Chapter 1.

When you begin, you will see that not only is the EMPLIST file already open, as mentioned above, but that the record you worked on last is still the current record—the record with the cursor in it, displayed in the Browse/Change window as shown in Figure 3.9. FoxPro thus kept track of where the cursor was even after the window was closed. FoxPro has what is called a *pointer*, which remains on the current record until you either move it or close the database. The idea of the pointer is important, and you will look at it more thoroughly later in this chapter.

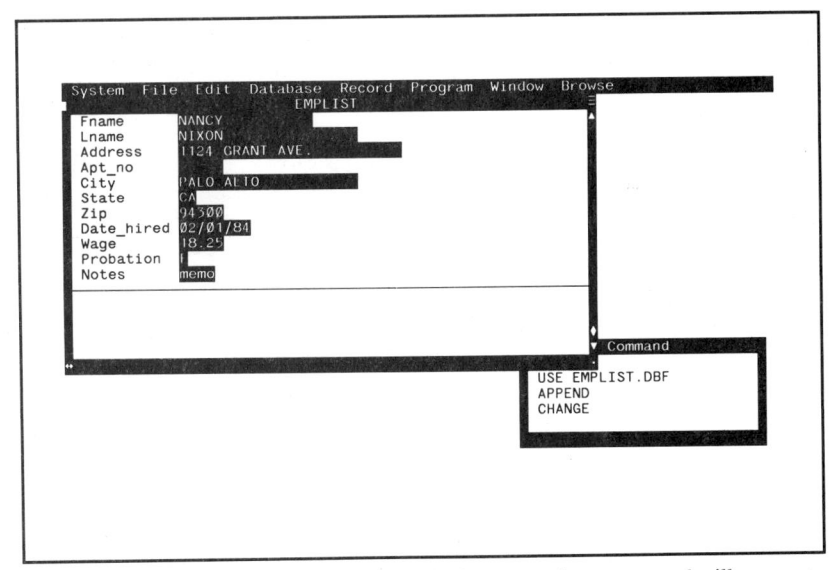

Figure 3.9: The Change window, with the last record you entered still current

> The command **CHANGE** is exactly equivalent to the command **EDIT**.

1. Select Change from the Record menu. This will display the Browse/Change window with the last record that you entered. Notice that the command **CHANGE** is generated in the Command window.

2. Try moving up and down through the file. After moving up, use the scroll bar or press PgDn repeatedly to try to move beyond the last record: you will see that you cannot. Try again, by using the down arrow key to move to the final field of the last record. When you try to go further, you will see that you cannot go beyond the last record and add a new record, as you could when you were in Append mode.

3. Let's say that you find that SHADY CIRCLE is supposed to be SHADY LANE. To correct it, use the keyboard or the mouse to move the cursor through the record to the first letter of CIRCLE. Press Ins to toggle into the typeover mode. Type **LANE**. Press Ins again to toggle out of the typeover mode. Press Del twice to delete the L and E of CIRCLE. You have corrected the error.

> If you delete the entire contents of a memo field, the word *memo* in the database will begin with a small m again, to show that the field is empty.

That's all there is to editing the content of fields; you can close the window and save the changes by pressing Ctrl-End or discard them by pressing Ctrl-Q. To edit a memo field, just move the cursor to the field, press Ctrl-PgDn to access the memo window, and edit the field just as you did when you were first entering it, using the conventional editing keys. Save the changes you made by closing the memo window, or discard the changes you made by pressing Esc.

A Browse menu pad was added to the menu bar when you selected Change, just as it was when you selected Append. Most of the options on this menu popup (shown in Figure 3.10) are far more useful when you are in Browse mode, and you will look at this popup in detail in the next section.

You will find that, in general, the only time you will want to use the menu when you are in Change mode is when you want to add a single extra record. Try it now:

1. Select Append Record from the Browse menu. Notice that a blank record has been added to the end of the file, and that your cursor immediately moves to this new record, ready to

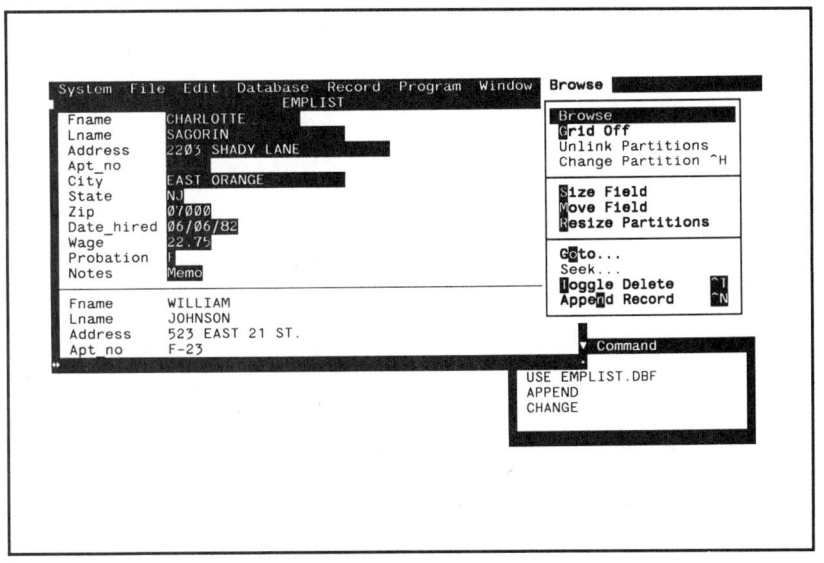

Figure 3.10: The Browse menu popup when you are in Change mode

enter data in it. Unlike the record that is added to the end of the database when you select Append from the Record menu, this new record does not exhibit the >> symbol, as shown in Figure 3.11. This means that a record created in this way *will* be saved as a *blank record* if you close the window immediately.

2. Make a sample entry in the record. For Fname, enter **JAMES**. For Lname, type **SKINNER**. For address, type **1206 FRANCISCO ST**. Skip the Apt_no field. For City, type **MENLO PARK**. For State, type **CA**. For Zip, type **94025**. For Date_hired, type **12/01/88**. For Wage, type **8.2**. For Probation, type **Y**. Type nothing in the memo field.

What happened when you selected Append Record is identical to what happens when you use the command **APPEND BLANK** from the Command window: the program adds a new blank record and makes it the current record. There actually is no advantage to using **APPEND BLANK** in the interactive mode, because to make an entry in the new record you would have to enter the command **CHANGE** (or **EDIT**). **APPEND BLANK** is very important in programming,

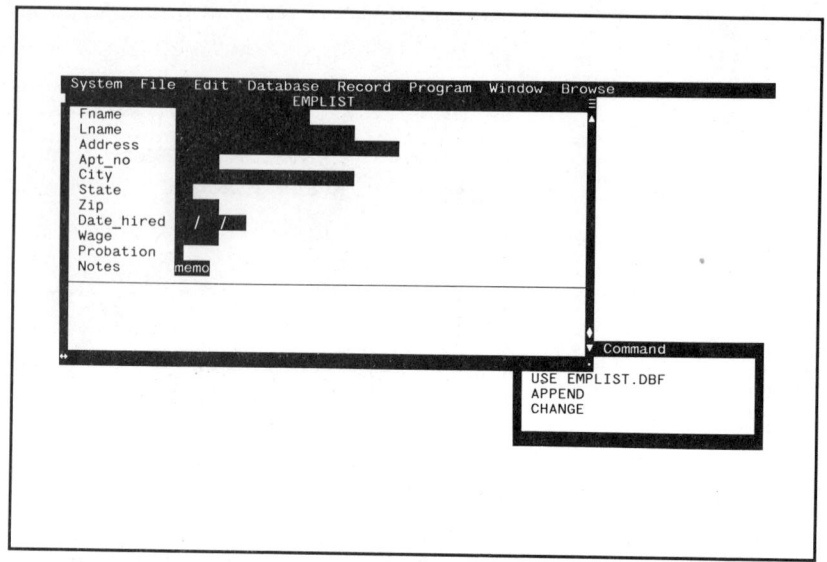

Figure 3.11: Adding a blank record to the file

though, since it lets you have complete control over users' access to the database—unlike **APPEND**, which lets users scroll through the entire database.

BROWSING THROUGH THE DATA

You probably noticed that when you are in the Change mode the first option on the Browse menu popup lets you toggle to Browse mode—just as you toggled from Change to Browse display when you were appending records. If you choose Browse from this popup, the Browse/Change window will be arranged like the Browse display you used in Append mode, except that now that you aren't in the Append mode you will not be able to append without explicitly making the menu choice to add a single blank record.

Since it is so similar to what you have already learned, you do not need extensive exercises with the Browse window. You can just play with it yourself to get the feel of it.

Because it lets you see many records at a time but does not let you see all the fields in each record, you often want to select which fields you can see in the Browse window. Imagine, for example, that you have a list of names, addresses, and telephone numbers, and you need to use this list in order to make telephone calls. The addresses would probably be of little help for this purpose, and the address fields would take up so much space that you would not normally be able to see the telephone number in the Browse window. As you will see, though, you can move the fields of the Browse window so that the telephone number is displayed immediately after the first and last name—making it much easier for you to do your telephoning.

There are a number of ways of altering the display of the Browse window, which are listed in this section. As you have seen, the options for altering the display of the window that are on the Browse menu popup are also available when you select Change, but they obviously are more useful when you are browsing through a file and cannot see the entire record. You should experiment with these options as you read their descriptions below. Experiment also to see how they work when you toggle back and forth between Change and Browse.

When you experiment, the first thing you should notice is that whenever you select Browse (from the Database menu), the command generated in the Command window is **BROWSE LAST**. This command can be used to open the Browse/Change window as it was when you last used it. This command is very useful in practice. For example, if you often telephone people, and you change the order of fields in the Browse window so that the telephone number is next to the name, FoxPro will save the setting even after you turn off your computer, and will display the fields in that order whenever you browse that file using **BROWSE LAST**.

RESIZING AND CHANGING THE ORDER OF FIELDS

The most common alteration you will want to make in the Browse window is to change the order and the size of the fields, so you can see the data you want. If you move the fields that you need to the left, and you make some of the fields smaller, you can generally see all of the data that you need within the Browse window. (Sometimes, of course, you will want to Zoom the window also).

Changing the size or order of fields in this way only affects how they are displayed in the Browse window, and does not affect the way that they are actually stored in the database, so there is no danger of loss of data.

USING A MOUSE

It is extremely easy to change field size or order using a mouse. You simply use the mouse to manipulate the list of field names above the records. First, though, check to see if you can see the grid lines to the right of each field name. If you cannot, select the Grid On option from the Browse menu.

- **size:** To change the size of a field, move the pointer to the grid line to the right of the field's name. Drag left or right to make the field smaller or larger.
- **order:** To change the order of a field, move the pointer to the field's name, then drag left or right to reposition the column where you want it.

USING THE KEYBOARD

If you are using the keyboard, you must use the Browse menu to change the size or order of fields.

- **size:** Select Size Field, then select the field whose size will be changed. The name of the current field is highlighted in reverse video. If it is not the field you want, use Tab or Shift-Tab to move to the field you want. Then press the left arrow key to shorten the field or the right arrow key to lengthen the field. When it is the size you want, press Enter.
- **order:** Select Move Field, then select a field to be moved. The name of the current field is underlined. If it is not the field you want, use Tab or Shift-Tab to move to the field you want. Then press the left arrow key or the right arrow key to move the field. When it is in the location you want, press Enter.

PARTITIONING THE WINDOW

You can divide the window into two partitions—which is a bit like having two separate windows that let you look at two parts of the database file at once.

Normally, the two partitions are linked: when you scroll through the records in one partition, records will automatically scroll through the other partition, so the same record is visible in both. However, you can use the menu to unlink partitions in order to view records independently. This menu option toggles from Unlink to Link; after you have unlinked partitions, you would choose Link to tie them together again. Figure 3.12 shows the difference between linked and unlinked partitions.

After you have partitioned the window, only one partition is active and available for editing. You can move around a partition in the same way that you move around any Browse/Change window, by using the scroll bar or by using the Tab, arrow, PgUp, and PgDn keys.

As you can see from the illustrations, the partitioned window is very versatile. Experiment with it when you read the following sections. The first section is for mouse users, the second is for keyboard users, and the third describes menu selections that are the same for both.

USING A MOUSE

Again, it is very simple to work with partitions using the mouse.

- **create, resize, or remove:** Move the pointer to the window splitter. This is an arrow with two heads pointing left and right that is in the lower left corner of the Browse window when no partitions have been created or on the bar separating the two partitions when partitions have been created. Dragging the splitter to the right divides the window into two partitions. As you drag the splitter, the partition on the left becomes larger and the one on the right becomes smaller. To resize the partitions, drag the partition splitter in the same way until the partitions are the size you want. To remove the partitions, drag the splitter until one is closed.

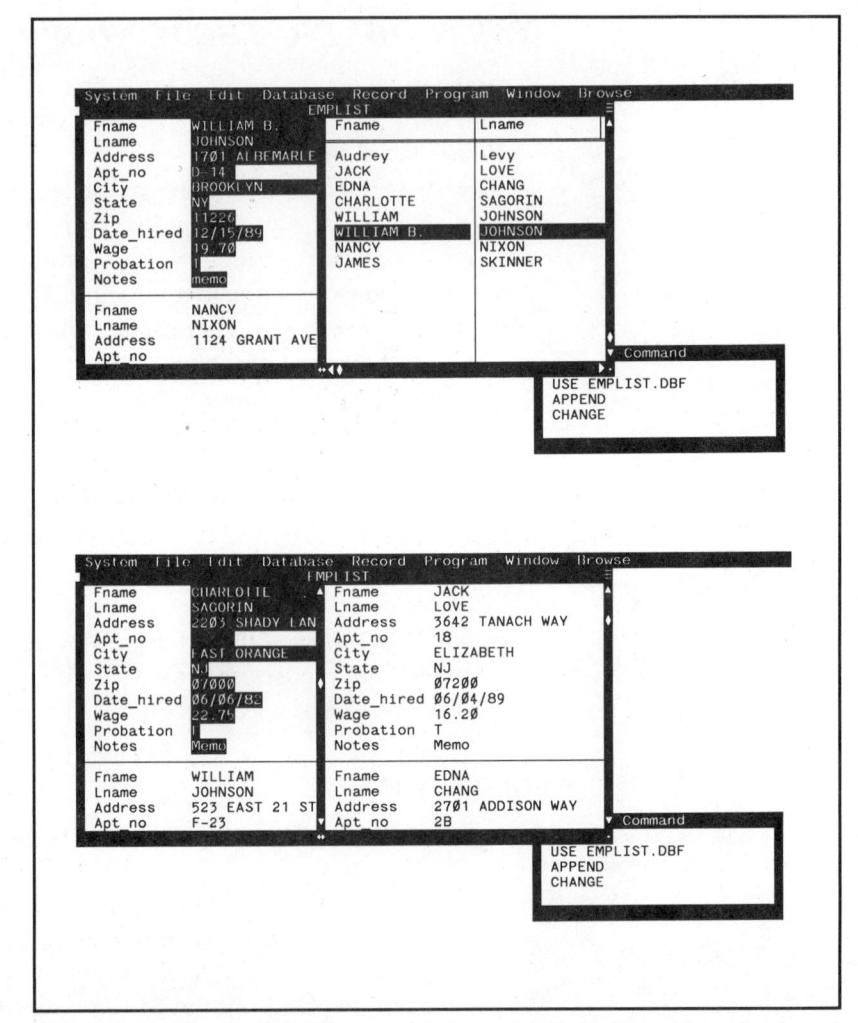

Figure 3.12: The Browse/Change window with linked partitions (top) and unlinked partitions (bottom)

- **to change:** To move the cursor from one partition to another, just click the partition that you want to be active.

USING THE KEYBOARD

Again, to work with partitions using the keyboard, you must make selections from the Browse menu.

- **create, resize, or remove:** Select Resize Partitions from the Browse menu. The window splitter (the arrow with two heads that is in the lower left corner of the Browse window when there are no partitions or at the bottom of the bar between the partitions when they have already been created) begins to blink, indicating that you can move the partition. Press the right arrow key, and the window splitter will move right, dividing the window into two partitions. As you press the right arrow key, the partition on the left becomes larger and the one on the right becomes smaller. Keep pressing the right and left arrow keys until the partitions are the size you want. Resize existing partitions in the same way. To Remove the partitions, press the arrow keys until one is closed.
- **to change:** Select Change Partition from the Browse menu, which will move you to the partition that you are not currently in.

LINKING AND UNLINKING PARTITIONS

Regardless of whether you are using a mouse or the keyboard, you must use the Browse menu to link and unlink partitions.

Normally, the two partitions are linked: if you scroll through one partition, you will automatically scroll through the other at the same time. Select Unlink Partitions from the Browse menu to separate the two, so that you can scroll through one without affecting the other.

When you have unlinked partitions, the Unlink Partitions option on the Browse menu popup is replaced by a Link Partitions option. Select this to tie the partitions together again.

DELETING A RECORD

There are a few additional features of the Browse menu popup.

Selecting Grid Off removes the vertical lines separating fields in the Browse window. If you select it while in the Change display, the lines will be removed when you toggle to the Browse display. After the lines are removed, this option changes to Grid On, which lets you replace the lines.

Goto and Seek from the Browse menu popup let you move through the database file by specifying the records you want and by using indexes. These options are identical to options available on the Record menu popup. Goto will be discussed later in this chapter; Seek will be discussed in Chapter 5.

The most important remaining option on the Browse menu is Toggle Delete, which lets you delete a record. To be more precise, selecting this option lets you mark a record for deletion—it does not actually remove the record from the database file. When a record is marked for deletion, a bullet appears to its left, as shown in Figure 3.13. The menu option is equivalent to the command **DELETE**.

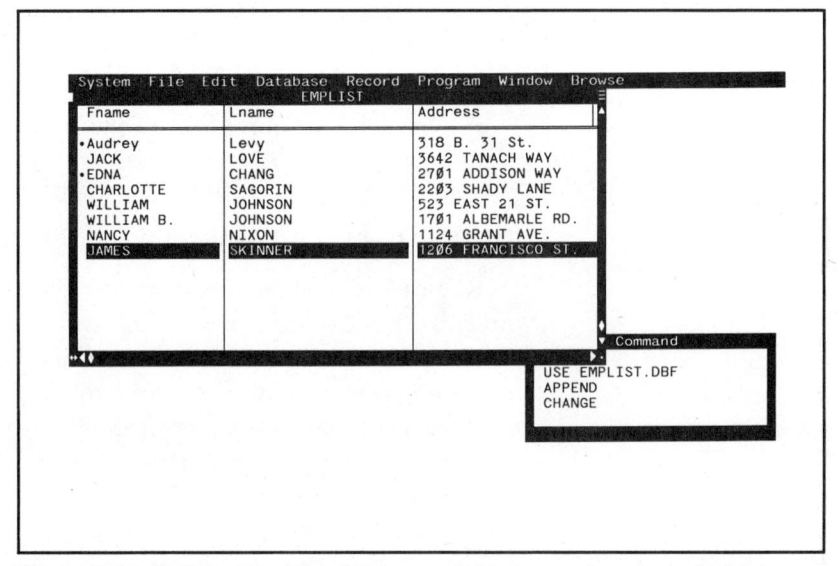

Figure 3.13: Bullets show that the first and third records are marked for deletion

If a record is already marked for deletion, selecting the same option will unmark it; that is why it is called Toggle Delete. In this situation, it is equivalent to the command **RECALL**.

Using this option from the Browse menu popup is very handy when you are editing or browsing a file, to delete or recall the record you are currently working on. In other situations, you may want the extra power that you get by selecting Delete from the Record menu and using the Delete dialog box, shown in Figure 3.14.

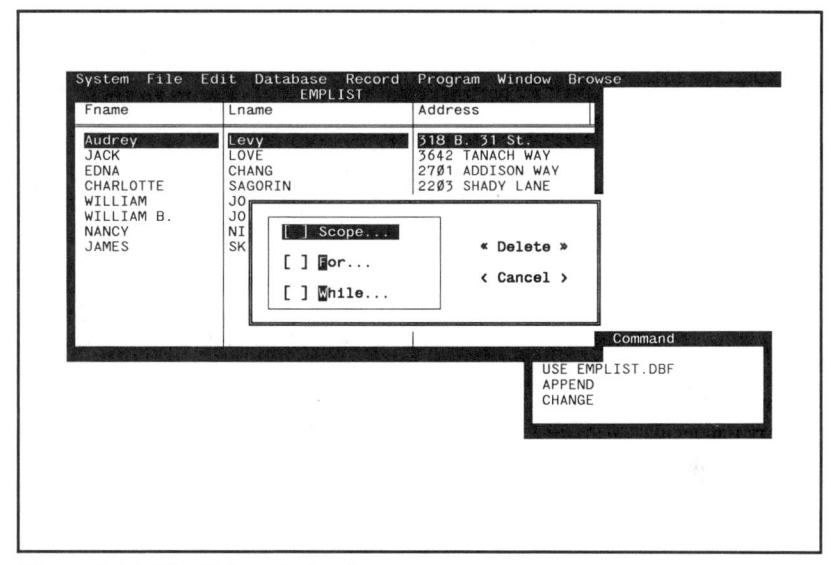

Figure 3.14: The Delete dialog box

> The For and While check boxes are the most useful, as they let you delete or undelete records that meet certain criteria. For example, you can delete all the records with less than a certain wage or recall the records that are not from California. This is essentially a matter of building a query into the **DELETE** command, and you should bear it in mind when you read the discussion of FOR and WHILE clauses in Chapter 5.

Selecting the default pushbutton Delete from this dialog box simply marks the current record for deletion, just as selecting Toggle Delete from the Browse popup does. As you can see, though, this dialog also includes Scope, For, and While check boxes, which let you mark more than one record at a time. These three check boxes are found in many different dialog boxes, and you will learn how to use them in Chapter 5. To give one example now, though, to give you an idea of what they can do, select Scope and then choose All from the Scope dialog box to mark all the records for deletion (or just enter the command **DELETE ALL** in the Command window).

Remember that these records are simply marked for deletion: you can select Recall from the Record menu to unmark them. The Recall dialog box, shown in Figure 3.15, has the same check boxes as the Delete dialog box. Selecting its default Recall pushbutton will unmark only the current record, however; for this example it is best to use the check boxes, which let you work with groups of records. Once again, use a scope of All to unmark all the records that you previously marked for deletion.

When you experiment with these features, you will see that Toggle Delete does not generate a command in the Command window; it resides entirely in the Browse window. On the other hand, Delete,

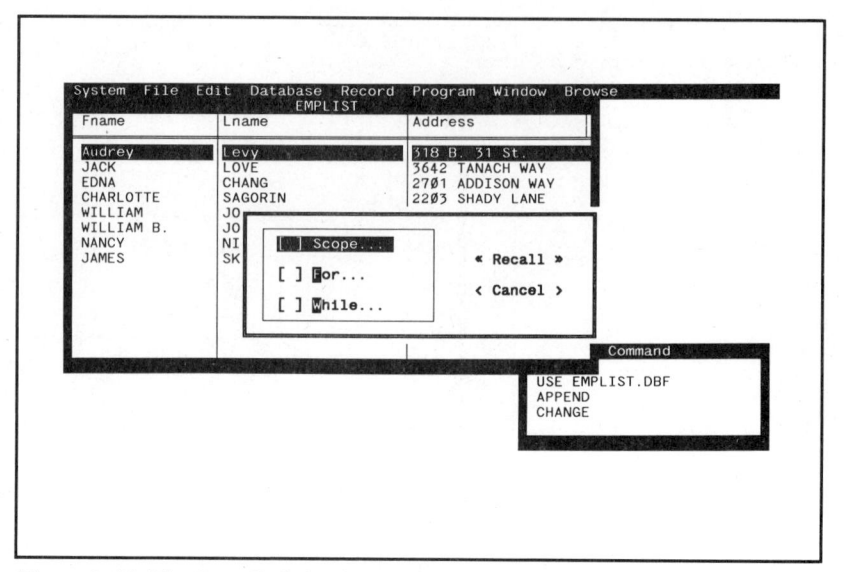

Figure 3.15: The Recall dialog box

from the Record menu, generates the command **DELETE NEXT 1** as well as FoxPro "talk" that says "1 records deleted." Similarly, Recall, from the Record menu, generates **RECALL NEXT 1** as well as talk that says "1 records recalled." The NEXT 1 at the end of each of these commands is not necessary: it specifies the scope of the commands (discussed at length in Chapter 5) to be 1, which means that they apply only to the current record. As it often does, FoxPro generates commands with more detail than is actually needed: this is the default scope for these commands, so you do not need to specify it if you are working from the Command window. Thus, to mark or unmark the current record from the Command window, simply enter the command **DELETE** or **RECALL**.

Records that are marked for deletion are not actually removed from the file until you select Pack from the Database menu or enter the command **PACK** in the Command window. When you "pack" the file, the program finalizes the deletion by copying all of the records that are not marked for deletion. These are copied to a new file, which replaces the old file. The process is called packing because it compresses the file into a smaller amount of space by removing the deleted records. Because it takes time to copy the records to a new file, it is done only when you select Pack; if you were working with a long file, there would be an annoying delay if the file were packed every time you deleted a record. When you pack a database, "talk" will appear on the screen behind the windows to tell you how many records were copied into the new version of the database file.

Most FoxPro commands that use records will use them regardless of whether they are marked for deletion, and this can sometimes cause problems. For example, if you search for records from the state of California, FoxPro will find those that are marked for deletion as well as those that belong in the file. The simplest way of dealing with this problem is to pack the database before using any command that you do not want deleted records to get in the way of. At the end of Chapter 5, after you have learned about logical expressions, you will be able to learn other methods of keeping records that are marked for deletion out of your way.

Finally, there is one very dangerous command that you should know about: **ZAP**, which eliminates all records from a file. It is equivalent to entering **DELETE ALL** and then **PACK**, except that it works much more quickly. After you enter **ZAP**, your records are gone forever: they cannot be recalled. This command is useful in programming, but it is so dangerous that it should probably not be usable from the command line; since it is used in dBASE compatible programs, though, you should be forewarned.

ZAP is most dangerous in combination with the environment command **SET SAFETY OFF**. Normally, FoxPro will ask you if you want to **ZAP** all your records before it executes this command. However, if you have entered the command **SET SAFETY OFF** (or turned Safety off using the View window) earlier in the session, **ZAP** will eliminate all your records without giving you any warning.

MOVING THE POINTER

There are times when you should know where the pointer is even if you can't see it. Furthermore, there are times when you want to move the pointer.

You have already seen that a pointer keeps track of the current record when you are changing or browsing a file. After you close the Browse window, the record that had the cursor on it last remains the current record as long as the file is still open; thus the cursor will still be on that record when you start to edit the file again. Likewise, you have seen that when you enter **DELETE** in the Command window, the record that the pointer is on will be marked for deletion. This occurs even if the Browse window is closed.

When you are working with the pointer, it is useful to remember that every record in your database file has a *record number*. Records are numbered sequentially as they are entered: the first record you entered in the database is record number 1, and so on.

It is possible to move the pointer even when the Browse window is closed and you cannot see the pointer. You do this by selecting Goto from either the Record or the Browse menu popups. Either of these will display the Goto dialog box, illustrated in Figure 3.16.

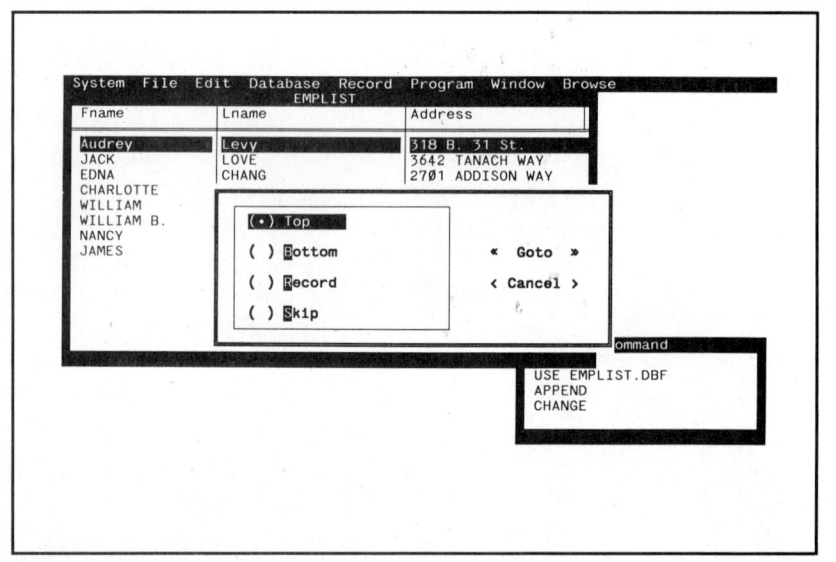

Figure 3.16: The Goto dialog box

As you can see, this dialog box gives you four choices of where to move the pointer:

- **Top:** moves the pointer to the first record of the database.
- **Bottom:** moves the pointer to the last record of the database.

- **Record:** displays a text box so you can enter the number of the record you want to move to. Though you usually will not know the exact number of the record you want, if you have an idea of its approximate number this option will generally be the fastest method for moving the pointer to the place you want in a long database. If you have a thousand records in the database, for example, and you know that the record you want was entered recently, say among the last hundred, you can use this command to "goto" record 900 and then scroll through the Browse window beginning at that point.

- **Skip:** displays a text box so you can enter the number of records by which you want to move the pointer from its current position. The number 1 is entered by default, but you can edit it to enter any number. If you keep the 1, for example, the pointer moves to the very next record; if you enter 1000, the pointer skips ahead 1000 records (assuming the file is that large). You can also use negative numbers: enter −1 to move to the previous record or −20 to move back twenty records.

Since the pointer is a very important concept, use this dialog box a bit to get a feel for it. Open the Browse window before moving the pointer, so you can see where it goes.

1. If necessary, enter **BROWSE** in the Command window, to open the Browse window with its default display, that lets you see all the records of EMPLIST.

2. Select Goto from the Record menu and select one of the radio buttons of the Goto dialog box. Remember you must select the default pushbutton, Goto, to execute the command. Do this several times to get a feel for moving the pointer.

3. When you are done, close the Browse window.

Notice that the commands that are generated as you make selections from this dialog box are almost identical to the selections you make.

GOTO commands have two forms: as a typing shortcut, you can simply enter the command **GO**, though **GOTO** is also valid.

- **GO TOP** (or **GOTO TOP**) moves the pointer to the first record.
- **GO BOTTOM** (or **GOTO BOTTOM**) moves the pointer to the last record.
- **GO [RECORD]** <*number*> (or **GOTO [RECORD]** <*number*>) moves the pointer to the record with the number indicated. (Do not type the square brackets—they simply serve to indicate that the word **RECORD** is optional.)
- **SKIP** <*number*> moves the pointer the indicated number of records from the current record. The number can be positive or negative.

You will see in the next section that there is an easy way of seeing the contents of the target record when you are working from the Command window, without opening the Browse window.

> In addition to a number, you can use any numerical expression with **SKIP** or **GO RECORD**. Expressions will be covered in Chapters 4 and 5.

SHORTCUTS USING THE COMMAND WINDOW

There are two commands for viewing the file that are very useful when you are working in the Command window or programming and that have no equivalent in the menu system.

- **DISPLAY** displays the contents of the current record on the screen.
- **LIST** displays the contents of all the records on the screen.

Both **DISPLAY** and **LIST** display records *behind* the windows. If any windows are opened, you might have to hide them to see the records. Both commands will display all the field names at the top of the display. In general, databases are too wide to fit all the fields across one screen, but FoxPro will wrap the display to the next line if it is too wide to fit otherwise. You can also use the **DISPLAY** and **LIST** commands with the names of the specific fields you want to see. For example, the command

```
LIST FNAME, LNAME, WAGE
```

would show you only those three fields of all the records in the database. Notice that the field names must be separated by commas. This form of the command lets you choose few enough fields that you can fit them into the width of one screen.

You will see in Chapter 5 that many commands can be used with this sort of field list. In some cases the word **FIELDS** must also be added before the list of fields; to avoid having to learn which commands require it, it is best to include it whenever it is relevant. Thus, it is easiest to use the command

LIST FIELDS FNAME, LNAME, WAGE

here, and this is the form these sorts of commands will take throughout the book.

It is easy to look at individual records in the database, then, by combining **GOTO** or **SKIP** commands with the

DISPLAY FIELDS <field names>

command. Once you get the **DISPLAY** command right, with the fields that you actually want, you can move the pointer to a different record by moving the cursor to the appropriate commands in the Command window and then reusing the **DISPLAY** command.

The limitation of the **LIST** command is that most database files are too long to fit on a single screen, and the records in the database will scroll by on the screen too quickly for you to read them if you use **LIST**. It can be genuinely useful, however, if you add **TO PRINT** at the very end of the command, which will send the listing to the printer as well as to the screen. This is usually the easiest way of getting a quick-and-dirty report on the data in your file.

LIST normally displays the record number of each record, but you can make the printed report look better by displaying the fields without the record number. Do this by adding **OFF** after the field list and before the words **TO PRINT** when entering the **LIST** command. For example, if you have a database of names, addresses, and telephone numbers, and you want to give someone a printed list of just the names and phone numbers, the absolutely easiest way to do it is by entering

LIST FIELDS FNAME, LNAME, PHONE OFF TO PRINT

☑ Like all commands, **DISPLAY** can be abbreviated to its first four letters: just type **DISP**.

☑ To clean up your printout while also making a more useful record of the listing, you can use **LIST TO FILE** <file name> instead of **LIST TO PRINT**. This version of the command will create the same listing in a plain DOS text file (also called an ASCII file). The advantage to this is that you can edit this file with any word processor that reads plain text files. The word processor will automatically handle the page breaks, and if you change the column headings a bit and add a header or footer for each page, you'll have a fairly respectable looking report.

(assuming, of course, that these are the names of the fields). This will give you a printed list of all the names and phone numbers in the file, in three columns, with the name of the field at the top of each column. Note that long lists will print continuously, without allowing for page breaks.

As a precaution, it is usually best to enter the command without **TO PRINT** first, to make sure that you have the fields that you want and that they actually fit into the width of the screen—which is the same as the width of the paper in a standard printer. If it is a long file, it will take time to list, but you can press Esc to stop the process. Once you have the fields right, use the up arrow key to edit the command, and add **TO PRINT**.

Try these steps to get a report on employee wages:

1. If necessary, close the Browse window and return to the Command window. Enter **CLEAR** to clear the screen.

2. Enter

    LIST FIELDS LNAME, FNAME, WAGE OFF

    The listing is shown in Figure 3.17.

```
System  File  Edit  Database  Record  Program  Window
LNAME              FNAME              WAGE
Levy               Audrey              8.00
LOVE               JACK               16.20
CHANG              EDNA                9.75
SAGORIN            CHARLOTTE          22.75
JOHNSON            WILLIAM             6.25
JOHNSON            WILLIAM B.         19.70
NIXON              NANCY              18.25
SKINNER            JAMES               8.20


                                            ┌─ Command ─┐
                                            │ CLEAR
                                            │ LIST LNAME, FNAME, WAGE
```

Figure 3.17: Using LIST to get a very quick report

3. If you want to try printing this listing, use the conventional editing keys to add **TO PRINT** to the end of the listing command, and press Enter.

Of course, one of the names is not properly capitalized, and the names are not in alphabetical order. But in Chapter 4 you will learn enough about expressions and indexes to deal with these problems. And in Chapter 5, when you have also learned about queries, you will use the **LIST** command again to produce a fairly respectable report.

You can also use **BROWSE** or **CHANGE** or **EDIT** in the Command window with this sort of field list. These options are particularly useful to fit all the information you want into the Browse window. You may also find it handy to use **BROWSE** with the option **NOEDIT**, so that you cannot make changes in the data inadvertently.

1. Enter

   BROWSE FIELDS LNAME, FNAME, WAGE NOEDIT

   to see just these fields in the Browse window, as shown in Figure 3.18.

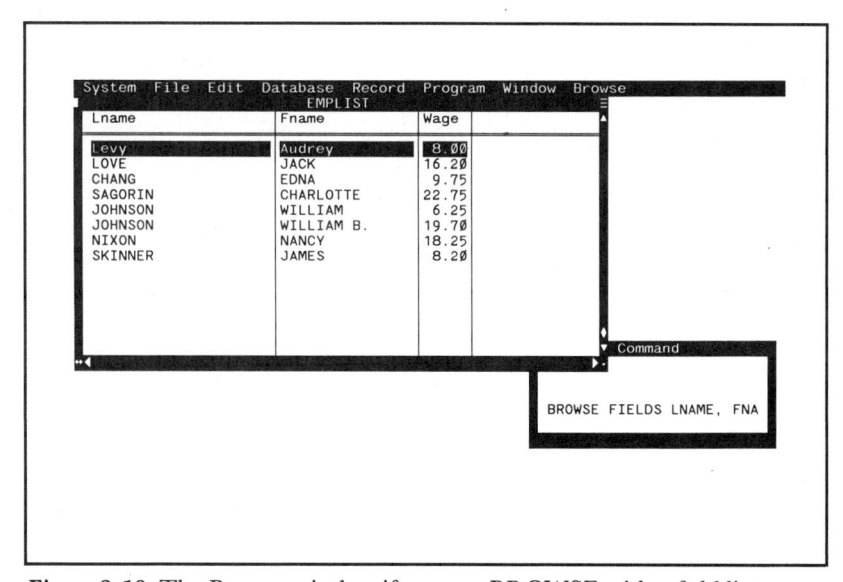

Figure 3.18: The Browse window if you use BROWSE with a field list

2. Try editing one of the fields and you will see that is it impossible. FoxPro just beeps and does not change the data. This is because you included **NOEDIT** in your command.

3. Close the Browse window. If you then enter **BROWSE LAST**, you will notice that the same options are still being used.

4. To return the Browse window to its default configuration so that you will be able to see all the fields in future exercizes, enter **BROWSE** in the Command window, then close the Browse window again.

There are many other options of this sort that you can use from the command line. If you are interested in them, see **BROWSE**, **EDIT** (or **CHANGE**), and **APPEND** in the Help window or in your reference manuals. Field lists can be used with many other commands besides these, and they will be covered in more detail in Chapter 5.

Chapter 4

Understanding Indexes and Expressions

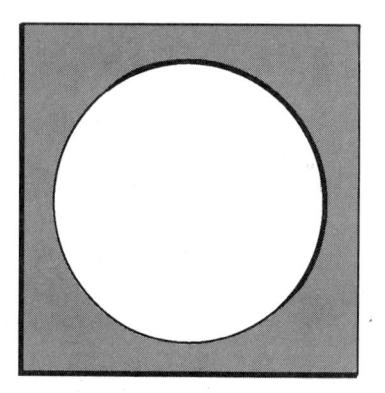

AN INDEX OF A DATABASE FILE IS A BIT LIKE AN INDEX of a book. A book's index lists subjects covered in the book in alphabetical order and refers you to the pages that they are on. Of course, it is much faster to look something up in the index and go to the right page in the book than it is to leaf through the entire book in order to find the topic that you are interested in.

If you are working with even a moderately large database file, any database program takes a long time to read through the entire file to look up a record you want. Even a very small business could easily have a mailing list with a few thousand names in it. If you had to look up names in a list this long, there could be agonizing delays if your program had to read through the entire list to find them.

On the other hand, the program could find the name very quickly if the file were indexed. The index would contain the names in alphabetical order and pointers showing where each name was in the actual database. There are methods of searching that let a database management program find a name very quickly in this sort of ordered list so that the program can retrieve records in large databases without any delay.

Of course, the computer can also use an indexed database much more powerfully than a person can use an indexed book. For example, the computer can list the entire database in index order so the user can look at the records in the database in alphabetical order by name, even though the actual order of the records in the database is different. Since you can have several different indexes for a single database, you can use the database in more than one order: you can look at the records in alphabetical order to find people's names, and then you can look at the records in zip code order to see which people live near each other.

TYPES OF INDEXES

Version 1 of FoxPro supported only one type of index. Each index was kept in a separate file, with the extension IDX. If you wanted the indexes to be kept up to date, you had to open each of these index files explicitly whenever you added data to or edited the database file.

Needless to say, opening the indexes was a bit of trouble. Often, people would forget to open all the indexes when they were doing a quick bit of data entry or editing. Then, when they used the file later with an order determined by an index that had not been updated, the records that they had added would not be visible.

Version 2 of FoxPro adds a second type of index to eliminate this problem. Unlike IDX files, each of which can hold only one index, *compound index* (*CDX*) files can hold multiple indexes in a single file. Each index in a compound index file is called an *index tag*.

One special type of compound index is called a *structural compound index*, which will open automatically whenever you open the database file it applies to. A structural compound index is automatically given the same name as the database file, with the extension CDX. (Compound indexes other than the structural compound index are called *independent* compound indexes, and they cannot be given the same name as the file.)

For most purposes, it is easiest to use a structural compound index file for all your indexes. All the indexes are updated automatically whenever you update the file, without your having to take the time to open them and without any danger of your forgetting to open them.

There are some cases, though, where it makes sense to use an independent compound index file or to use IDX files for your indexes. The one problem with having all of your indexes open at all times is that FoxPro takes some time to update each index when you are entering data. In general, this amount of time is so small that it is not noticeable, but if you have an extremely large number of indexes open, the time it takes to update them can slow data entry. In addition, FoxPro rebuilds all indexes whenever you pack a database to remove records that are marked for deletion, and it does take a noticeable amount of time to rebuild each index. If you have a very large number of tags in your structural index file, packing could become very slow.

For these reasons, then, if you have a large number of indexes, it is good to include as tags in the structural compound index file only those indexes that you need to keep updated. If you have a group of indexes that you use only once a year to produce reports, you should keep them in a separate, independent index file. Then, you can explicitly use that file and reindex once a year before producing the reports, rather than having the overhead of maintaining these indexes at all times.

In addition to compound index files, FoxPro has one other major improvement in indexing: *compact indexes,* which take up much less disk space than the IDX indexes used by version 1 or by other dBASE compatible programs. The fact that these indexes are smaller saves you disk space, and it also improves performance, because FoxPro spends less time reading the index from disk.

For the sake of compatibility, IDX index files can still be created in the older format as well as in the new compact format, though the compact format is preferable. CDX files all take advantage of the compact format.

USING SOME SIMPLE INDEXES

Some indexes are more complex than others. For example, if you want to use names in alphabetical order, you would not index only on the last name: in order to make sure that Aaron Smith comes before Xavier Smith, you need to use the first name as a "tie-breaker" to determine the order of records whose last names are the same. Furthermore, as you will see, a name entered using lowercase letters would come after a name that is entered in all capital letters. In the next section, you will learn to use *expressions,* which let you deal with this sort of problem.

CREATING SIMPLE INDEXES USING THE INDEX ON DIALOG BOX

To begin with, you can create a couple of simple indexes, each of which is based on a single field. Let's say that you need to use the records in zip code order when you produce your mailing labels, and that you also need to produce a special report that uses the records in order of the date the employee was hired. If you were working on an actual application, it would be easiest to include both of these indexes in a structural compound index file. As an exercise, however, in order to familiarize yourself with using various types of indexes, let's use an IDX file for one of them. Try creating these indexes:

1. Start FoxPro if necessary, making sure that you are in the \LEARNFOX subdirectory. If you want, enter **CLEAR** to clear the screen. Select Open from the File menu and select EMPLIST.DBF from the Open dialog box. A database file must be open before you can create an index for it.

2. To create the index file, select New from the File menu. Select the Index radio button in the New dialog box, and then select the default pushbutton, OK.

3. The Index On dialog box appears. The scrollable list in this box lets you index on a single field. Select ZIP from the scrollable list, and note that ZIP appears in the Index On box. The arrow to the left of the field name indicates that you are indexing in ascending order, beginning with the smallest zip code numbers. Select the IDX radio button: the Compact check box should be selected by default. The screen should look like Figure 4.1.

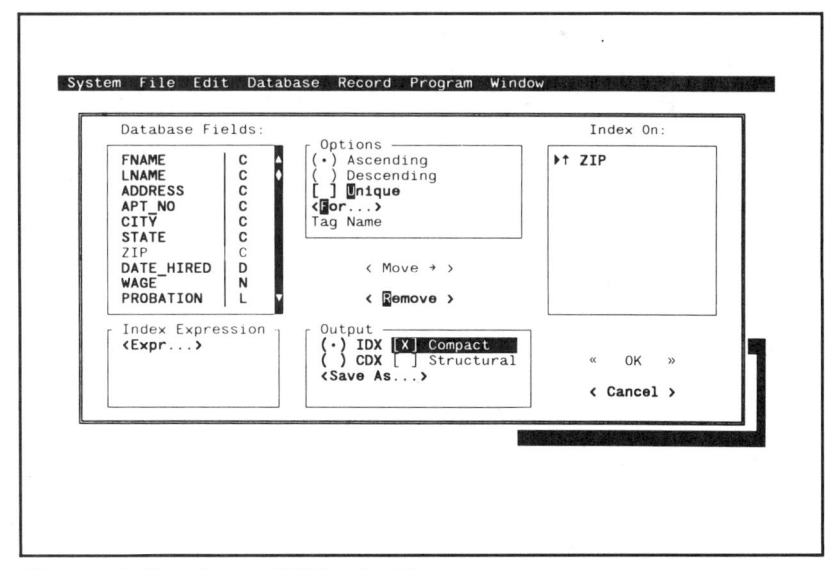

Figure 4.1: Creating an IDX index file

As you will see, managing the database can become a bit confusing after you have multiple indexes. To make your life simpler, always give index files descriptive names, such as ZIPS.

4. Finally, to name the index file, select the Save As pushbutton. FoxPro prompts you to enter the index file name. Notice the popup controls to let you change drive or to move quickly through the subdirectory structure, the scrollable list of file names and subdirectories, and the check box that lets you list All Files (rather than just index files); all of these work just as they do in the Open dialog box. You do not need to use any of these features now, so simply type **ZIPS** as the name of the index, as shown in Figure 4.2. Then select the default pushbutton OK to return to the Indexing dialog box. Notice that the full path name of the index is shown under the Save As pushbutton. Select the default pushbutton (OK) to create the index.

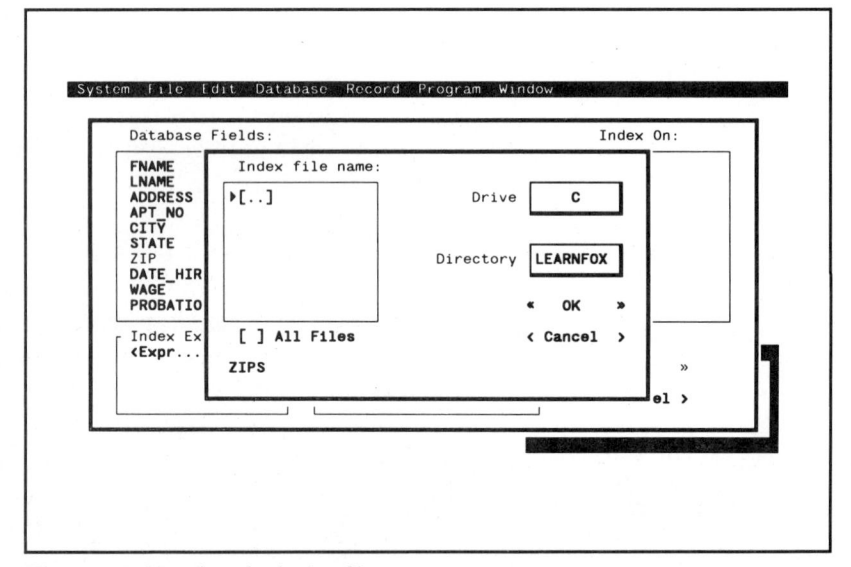

Figure 4.2: Naming the index file

5. Select Browse from the Database menu to look at the file: scroll right until you can see the Zip field, and note that the records are in zip code order. Or move the Zip field to the far left (as you learned to do in the last chapter) so you can see the zip code along with the names, as in Figure 4.3. Close the Browse window.

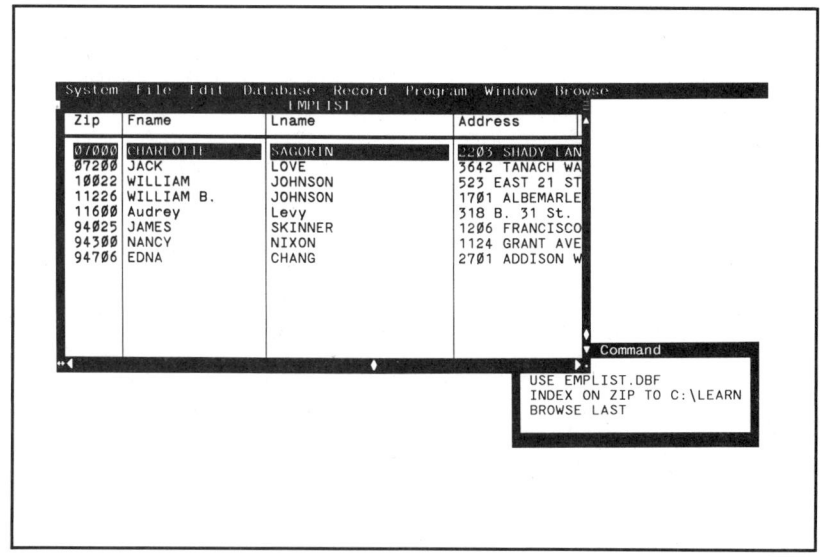

```
              System File Edit Database Record Program Window Browse
                                    EMPLIST
              Zip    Fname         Lname         Address
              07000  CHARLOTTE     SAGORIN       2203 SHADY LAN
              07200  JACK          LOVE          3642 TANACH WA
              10022  WILLIAM       JOHNSON       523 EAST 21 ST
              11226  WILLIAM B.    JOHNSON       1701 ALBEMARLE
              11600  Audrey        Levy          318 B. 31 St.
              94025  JAMES         SKINNER       1206 FRANCISCO
              94300  NANCY         NIXON         1124 GRANT AVE
              94706  EDNA          CHANG         2701 ADDISON W

                                                   Command
                                          USE EMPLIST.DBF
                                          INDEX ON ZIP TO C:\LEARN
                                          BROWSE LAST
```

Figure 4.3: The records displayed in zip code order

 .
6. Now, create an index on the DATE_HIRED field, but make it a tag of the structural compound index. Select New from the File menu. In the New dialog box, select the Index radio button, and then select OK. In the indexing dialog box, select DATE_HIRED from the scrollable list. The CDX radio button in the output box should be selected by default. Note that the Compact check box is automatically checked and is dimmed so that you cannot access it: a compound index must be compact. In addition, the Structural check box should be checked by default, and the name of the index is automatically displayed (C:\LEARNFOX\EMP-LIST.CDX, as the structural CDX file must have the same name as the database file). Notice also that the name of the field is automatically entered as the Tag Name. The screen should look like Figure 4.4. Select the default pushbutton, OK, to create this index tag. Again, FoxPro displays "talk" telling you the number of records indexed.

7. Now select Browse from the Database menu, and scroll right until you can see the Date_hired field, or move this field to the far left so you can see it along with the zip codes and names. Note that the records are now listed from the earliest

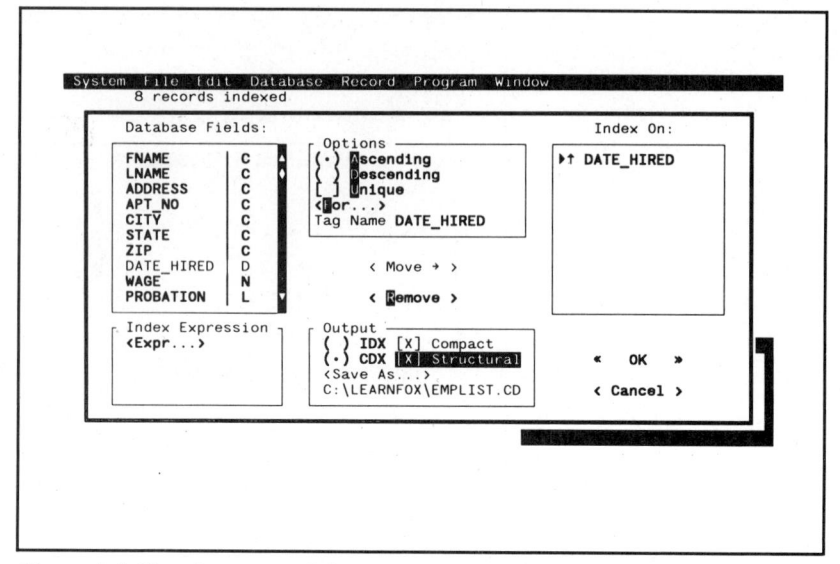

```
┌─────────────────────────────────────────────────────────────┐
│ System  File  Edit  Database  Record  Program  Window       │
│              8 records indexed                              │
│ ┌─Database Fields:─────┐ ┌─Options────────┐  Index On:      │
│ │ FNAME       C      ▲│ │(•) Ascending   │ ▶↑ DATE_HIRED    │
│ │ LNAME       C       │ │( ) Descending  │                  │
│ │ ADDRESS     C       │ │[ ] Unique      │                  │
│ │ APT_NO      C       │ │<For...>        │                  │
│ │ CITY        C       │ │Tag Name DATE_HIRED│               │
│ │ STATE       C       │ └────────────────┘                  │
│ │ ZIP         C       │                                     │
│ │ DATE_HIRED  D       │     < Move → >                      │
│ │ WAGE        N       │                                     │
│ │ PROBATION   L      ▼│     < Remove >                      │
│ └─────────────────────┘                                     │
│ ┌─Index Expression─┐ ┌─Output────────────┐                  │
│ │ <Expr...>        │ │( ) IDX [X] Compact│                  │
│ │                  │ │(•) CDX [X] Structural│  «   OK   »   │
│ │                  │ │<Save As...>       │                  │
│ │                  │ │C:\LEARNFOX\EMPLIST.CD│ < Cancel >    │
│ └──────────────────┘ └───────────────────┘                  │
└─────────────────────────────────────────────────────────────┘
```

Figure 4.4: Creating a tag of the structural compound index file

to the most recent date (and are no longer in zip code order). Close the Browse window.

8. If you changed the configuration of the Browse window to display the records as shown in the illustrations, enter **BROWSE** in the Command window to use the Browse window in its default configuration. Then close the Browse window, saving the default configuration.

Perhaps you were curious about why the Index On dialog box that lets you name the index includes a scrollable list of the names of existing indexes. You can choose one of these names if you want to overwrite an existing index, replacing it with an index of the same name based on the expression you have created—as you will do later in this chapter, when you index by name in two different ways.

OTHER FEATURES OF THE INDEX ON DIALOG BOX

You should familiarize yourself with the other features available through the Index On dialog box. First, the For pushbutton lets you index only records that meet certain logical criteria; this is essentially a matter of building a query into an index, which will be covered in Chapter 5.

The Unique check box excludes records with duplicate values in the field that you are indexing on; thus, only the first record that FoxPro finds with a given value in that field is indexed. This is an advanced feature, and it should be used with great caution to avoid overlooking data.

Finally, the Ascending and Descending pushbuttons let you choose whether the index arranges the records beginning with the smallest values or beginning with the largest values. The default is Ascending—from the smallest to the largest number for a numeric field; from the earliest to the most recent date for a date field; and in ASCII order from A to Z for a character field. (The difference between ASCII and alphabetical order will be discussed in a moment.) If you select the Descending text button, the records will be arranged in the opposite order.

INDEXING COMMANDS

When you created the indexes above, FoxPro generated these two commands:

```
INDEX ON ZIP TO C:\LEARNFOX\ZIPS.IDX COMPACT
INDEX ON DATE_HIRED TAG DATE_HIRED
```

These are typical variations of the following indexing command:

```
INDEX ON <expr>
TO <idx file name> | TAG <tag name> [OF <cdx file>]
```

(Actually, this entire command appears on one line in the command window.)

Before you can use this command, the database file must be in use. The basic command is **INDEX ON** followed by an expression. In the example, the expression was based on a single field; you will look at more complex expressions in a moment.

The expression can be followed by either **TO** <*idx file name*> or **TAG** <*tag name*>. The key word TO creates an IDX file with the name that is specified. The key word **TAG** creates a CDX index tag with the name that is specified; if it already exists, it adds that tag to the CDX file.

If the TAG clause is followed by the optional clause **OF** <*cdx file*>, the tag will be added to the CDX file whose name is specified—or this CDX file will be created to hold the tag. If this optional clause is left out, FoxPro uses the structural CDX file to hold the tag. Of course, its name does not have to be specified, since it is the same as the name of the database file.

An optional **COMPACT** clause creates the index in compact format. As you can see in the commands that were generated, it is not used with the tag of the CDX file, because that is automatically compact.

In addition, this command can have an optional **ASCENDING** or **DESCENDING** to specify the sorting order for the index. You can leave this off if you want the index to be sorted in ascending order, since ascending is the default order anyway.

Finally, the command can have an optional **FOR** <*expr*> clause and the optional **UNIQUE** key word, which are equivalent to the For pushbutton and the Unique check box in the indexing dialog box.

If you are creating indexes from the Command window, you do not have to include the full path name (if the index is in the current directory) or the extension. For example, you can just enter the command **INDEX ON ZIP TO ZIPS** or the command **INDEX ON DATE_HIRED TAG DATE_HIRED**. Once you get used to it, entering the commands in this way is easier than using the menu system.

CREATING SIMPLE INDEXES WITH THE STRUCTURE DIALOG BOX

You have learned to create indexes using the Index On dialog box, but there is also an easier way to create simple index tags for the structural compound index file.

When you were defining the structure of the database file, you learned that the shaded area to the left of each field name in the Structure dialog box could be used for creating indexes. Now you know enough about indexes to use this feature. You simply have to select this shaded area to toggle from No Index to Ascending Index to Descending Index. An index created in this way is automatically given the name of the field it is based on.

Whenever you create an index tag of the structural compound index file that is based just on a field name, an arrow is added next to that field name in the Structure dialog box. Existing Index tags can also be removed or changed from ascending to descending using this feature.

Indexes that are based on expressions and indexes in other files are not listed in the Structure dialog box, and you cannot work with them in this way, but the Structure dialog box does give you an easy way of creating simple indexes while you are defining the structure of a file.

Remember that you created the ZIPS index in a separate IDX file purely as an exercise to learn to use other types of indexes, and that it actually would be easier to have a ZIPS tag as part of the structural compound index file. Try creating that ZIPS tag now, using the Structure dialog box:

1. The EMPLIST database file should already be open. Select Setup... from the Database menu and then select the Modify pushbutton that is in the upper left of the dialog box, next to the word Structure, to use the Structure dialog box. (Do not select the other Modify pushbutton, in the box under the word Index. This second one, which you will learn to use later, is for modifying an index.)

2. Notice that the DATE_HIRED field has an upward pointing arrow to its left, instead of the shaded area that appears to the left of the other field names. This indicates that you have created an ascending index based on this field as a tag in the structural compound index file. The ZIP field does not have an arrow next to it, because the index you created for ZIP is in a separate IDX file. Select the shaded area to the left of the ZIP field name several times. Notice that it cycles from an up arrow to a down arrow to a shaded area.

3. Leave the item next to ZIP when it shows an up arrow, and select the default pushbutton (OK) to return to the Setup dialog box. Notice that the index tag EMPLIST:ZIP is now listed in addition to the index tag EMPLIST:DATE_HIRED.

In the same way, you could have selected the arrow to the left of DATE_HIRED in the Structure dialog box to make that index descending rather than ascending.

UNDERSTANDING EXPRESSIONS

Though simple indexes are useful for many purposes, there are times when they are not adequate—times when you want to index on an expression rather than just on a field. As you have seen, you cannot simply index on the Lname field to put the records in alphabetical order, since you also have to use the Fname field as a tie breaker.

In addition, you must make the index put capital and small letters in proper alphabetical order, since, by default, FoxPro indexes in ASCII order. You will be better at using FoxPro if you take a moment to understand what this means. ASCII stands for American Standard Code for Information Interchange. Just as Morse code represents each letter with a series of dots and dashes, ASCII represents each character with a number. The lowest numbers represent what are called control characters, such as carriage return. The first of the actual keyboard characters is ASCII character 32, which represents a blank space. After some punctuation marks and special characters come ASCII characters 48 through 57, which represent numbers. After some more special characters come the capital letters from A to Z, which are ASCII characters 65 to 90. And after a few more special characters come the small letters from a to z, ASCII characters 97 to 122. IBM-PC compatible computers also have what is called extended ASCII, with even higher numbered characters for foreign letters and for box-drawing characters.

If you index on a character field, FoxPro will order the information using ASCII numbers, and consider all small letters to come after all capital letters. Expressions let you overcome this problem and many others. They are useful not just in indexes but in almost everything you do in FoxPro, from producing simple mailing labels to writing advanced programs.

Later in this chapter, you will learn to create expressions using the "expression builder" dialog box, shown in Figure 4.5. Once you get accustomed to expressions, though, you will simply type them in.

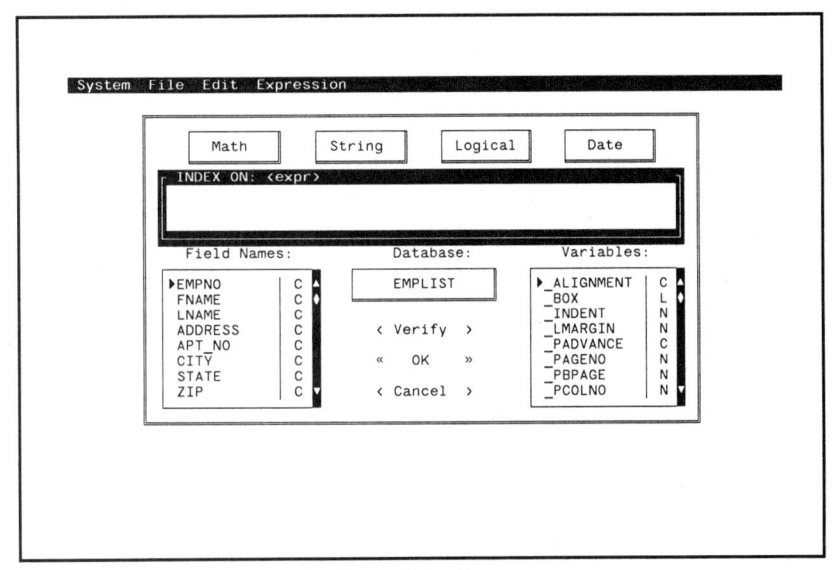

Figure 4.5: The expression builder dialog box

An expression can include several elements:

- field names
- memory variables
- constants (or literals)
- functions
- operators

FoxPro automatically creates certain memory variables when it runs, which are called system variables. Their names always begin with the underscore character: for example, one is named _ALIGNMENT. These are included in the Variables scrollable list; you will learn to use one of them in Chapter 6.

Field names, of course, are simply the names that you gave the fields of your database, such as FNAME and LNAME. As you will see, the names of all the fields in the database you are working with can be selected from a scrollable list in the expression builder dialog box.

Memory variables are used in more advanced expressions, and are useful primarily in programming. You will learn about them in Chapter 8. The names of all active memory variables can also be selected from the scrollable list of variables in the expression builder dialog box, but you will ignore them for now.

CONSTANTS

Constants (or *literals*) are letters, numbers, or dates that are used with their literal meaning. For example, if you wanted an expression to actually include the word "Name:" before each person's name, you would use the constant "Name:" as part of that expression. These are called constants because they are always the same, unlike the first name and last name, for example, which change for each record.

Constants that are used in expressions must include delimiters to indicate their data type.

- **Character constants**: must be enclosed in double quotation marks, single quotation marks, or brackets. For example, you could use "Name:" or 'Name:' or [Name:] in an expression to make it include **Name:**

- **Date constants**: must be enclosed in curly brackets. If you wanted to create an expression that calculated the number of days to the end of the year, for example, it would include a constant such as {12/31/92}.

- **Number constants**: are used without any delimiter. Simply use the number itself.

If you forget to use delimiters for a character field, FoxPro will think it is the name of a memory variable or of a field. If you get a puzzling error message saying that a variable cannot be found, it probably means that you mistakenly used a character constant without delimiters.

When you are working with constants, you have to remember that an entire expression must be of a single data type. Sometimes you must convert literals or fields from the date or number type to the character type in order to make them compatible with the rest of the expression. This is where functions come in handy.

FUNCTIONS AND OPERATORS

The four popup controls at the top of the expression builder dialog box divide all of FoxPro's functions and operators into four different types, depending on the type of data they work on. The Math popup lets you work with numeric data, the String popup with character data, the Logical popup with logical data, and the Date popup with date data.

Logical expressions are usually not needed in indexes, so they will not be discussed here. (They will be presented in the next chapter, which covers queries.) Figure 4.6 illustrates the three popups you will be working with in this chapter. As you can see, there are often too many operators and functions to fit in the popup, but you can scroll down to get more. Notice the word "text" at the top of the String popup; you can select this to put the quotation mark delimiters around text that you enter. Of course, you can also type in the quotation marks by hand.

> ? always prints the results of the expression, preceded by a new line. In Chapter 11, you will also learn to use ?? to print an expression without a new line. If you just use ? without an expression following it, it will just print a new line: this is an easy way to skip a line.

While you are learning about expressions, you will find it instructive to try them out by using the ? command, which prints an expression to the screen. For example, if you enter the command ? **"THIS IS A TEST"** in the Command window, the words THIS IS A TEST will appear on the screen, in the same place where the "talk" appears. Notice that ?, like all other commands, always evaluates an expression. For example, if you enter ? **FNAME**, FoxPro prints the content of the current Fname field. This example used ? with an expression made up of a single string constant. You will see how functions and operators work by using ? with more complex expressions.

FUNCTIONS

> A function does not actually transform or permanently change the data it is working on. It merely lets the expression use it in this new form.

A function returns a value. Usually this means that a function works on a piece of data in some way and that the "value" it returns is the data in a new form. For example, the index you create at the end of this chapter will use the function UPPER( ) to convert lowercase characters to uppercase. You will use this function in the form UPPER(LNAME) to return the data in the Lname field with all the letters capitalized so that a name originally written with lowercase letters will be arranged in correct alphabetical order rather than in ASCII order.

Some functions return a value that depends on the system. For example DATE( ) returns the current system date. Logical functions, which you will look at in the next chapter, return a value of True or False. Note that all functions end with parentheses, even functions such as DATE( ) that never have anything in the parentheses.

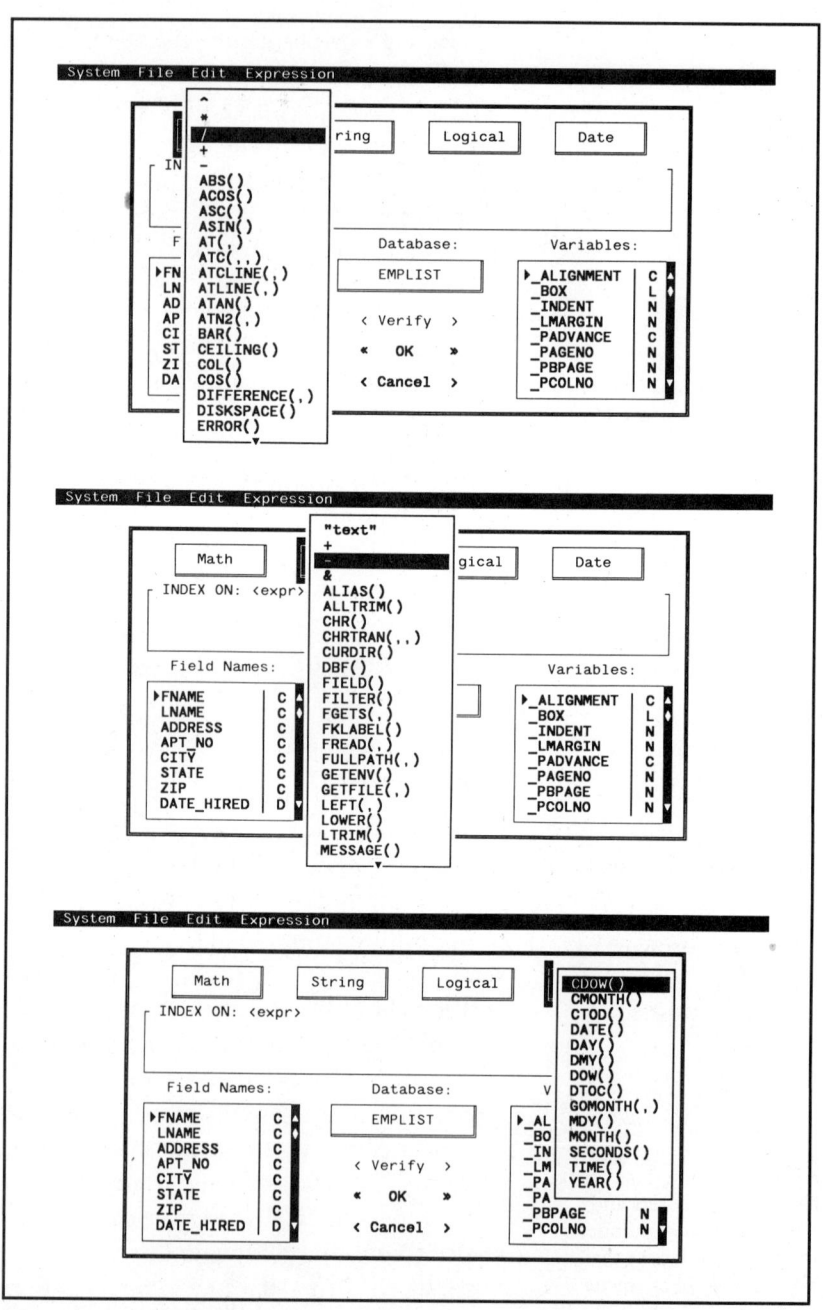

Figure 4.6: The Math, String, and Date popups in the expression builder dialog box

Try these two functions out:

1. Enter **?** to skip a line. (You must of course press Enter after the question mark.)

2. Enter **? UPPER("this is a test")**. FoxPro prints THIS IS A TEST on the screen.

3. Enter **? DATE( )**. FoxPro prints the system date, as shown in Figure 4.7. (Of course, the actual date on your screen will differ from the date in the illustration.)

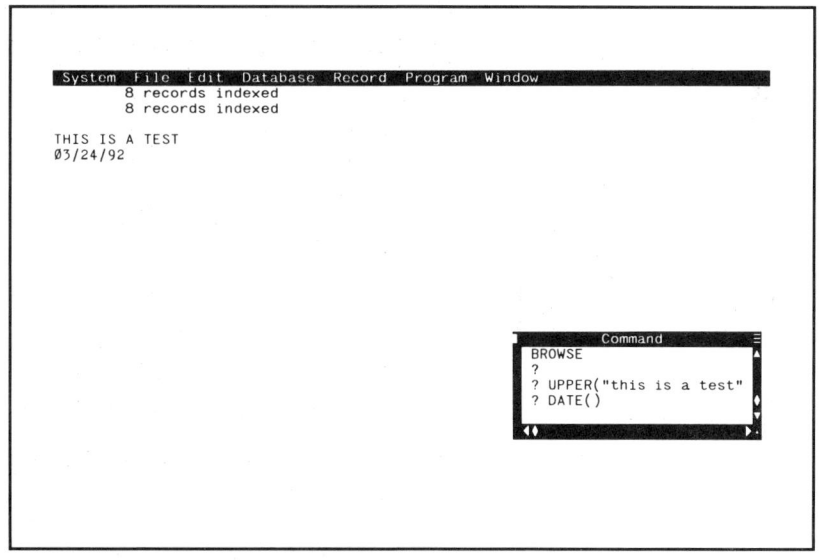

```
System  File  Edit  Database  Record  Program  Window
        8 records indexed
        8 records indexed
THIS IS A TEST
03/24/92






                                          ┌──────── Command ────────┐
                                          │ BROWSE                  │
                                          │ ?                       │
                                          │ ? UPPER("this is a test"│
                                          │ ? DATE()                │
                                          └─────────────────────────┘
```

Figure 4.7: Using ? to print expressions

FoxPro offers a tremendous number of functions, as you will see when you use the scrollable list to choose them. Until you begin programming, though, you can get by with a relatively small number of functions. The most important are listed here.

You will find the following functions useful for changing the case of character data. (The abbreviation *char exp* within the arrow brackets stands for character expression.)

> These functions act only on letters and do not affect any numbers or special characters that are included in character fields.

- **UPPER(<*char exp*>)** converts letters to uppercase. For example, UPPER(FNAME) returns the contents of the

Fname field in all uppercase letters, and UPPER("hEllO") returns the word HELLO.

- **LOWER(<*char exp*>)** converts to lowercase, as you might expect. For example, LOWER(FNAME) returns the contents of the Fname field in all lowercase letters, and LOWER("hEllO") returns hello.

- **PROPER(<*char exp*>)** converts to the capitalization used for a proper name, with the first letter of each word capitalized and rest lowercase. For example, PROPER(ADDRESS) returns the contents of the Address field, with the first letter of each word capitalized, as you would normally want on mailing labels. PROPER("hEllO") returns Hello.

Try testing these functions on the fields of your database. Your database file should still be open with the DATES index, since you indexed it earlier in this chapter. (If it is not, select Open from the File menu to open EMPLIST.DBF; then, if you want your results to match the illustrations, select Open again and open the DATES-.IDX index.)

1. Enter ? to skip a line.
2. Enter ? **LOWER(FNAME)** in the Command window. Fox-Pro will print the Fname field of the current record in all lowercase letters (even though you entered it in all uppercase).
3. Enter ? **PROPER(ADDRESS)** in the Command window. Fox-Pro will print the Address field of the current record with just the first letter of each word capitalized, as shown in Figure 4.8.

The next group of functions are useful for trimming blanks from character data. This is often necessary, because when you tell it to print the field Lname, for example, FoxPro not only prints the characters that are in the field, it also adds enough blanks at the end to fill the entire width of the field. These are called trailing blanks. Relatedly, if you convert a numeric field to the character type, FoxPro often adds blanks to the left of the number to pad it out. These are called leading blanks. Although there are times when blanks are indispensable (as you will see when you create your next index), there are also times when you want to get rid of them.

UNDERSTANDING INDEXES AND EXPRESSIONS *127*

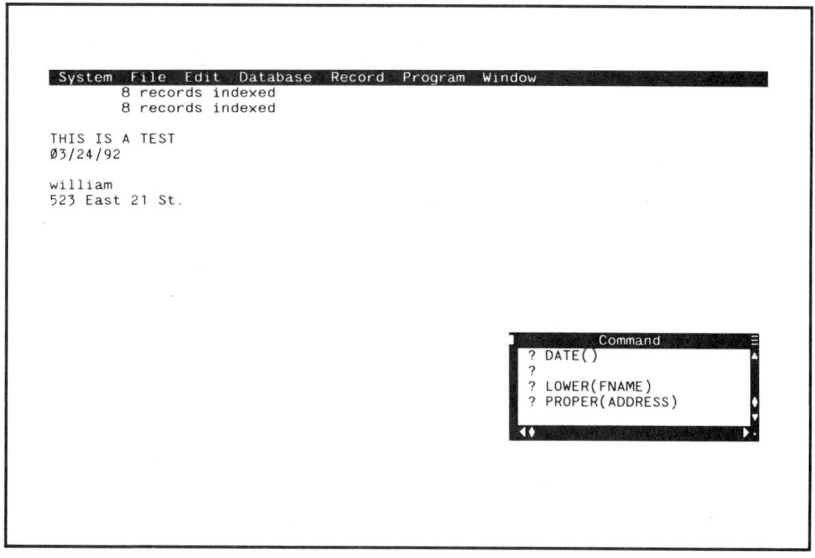

```
┌─System─File─Edit─Database─Record─Program─Window──────────────────┐
         8 records indexed
         8 records indexed
THIS IS A TEST
03/24/92

william
523 East 21 St.




                                              ┌──────Command──────┐
                                              │ ? DATE()          │
                                              │ ?                 │
                                              │ ?                 │
                                              │ ? LOWER(FNAME)    │
                                              │ ? PROPER(ADDRESS) │
                                              └───────────────────┘
```

Figure 4.8: Using functions to change the capitalization of character data

If you want, for example, to produce mailing labels or reports without unnecessary blank spaces in them, you would use these functions:

- **TRIM(**<*char exp*>**)** trims trailing blanks.
- **LTRIM(**<*char exp*>**)** trims leading blanks.
- **ALLTRIM(**<*char exp*>**)** trims both trailing and leading blanks.

Try these out:

1. Enter **?** to skip a line.
2. Enter **? TRIM("   THIS IS A TEST   ")**. FoxPro will indent the words THIS IS A TEST when it prints them, allowing for the leading blanks. (In this case, you cannot see that the trailing blanks have been trimmed.)
3. Enter **? LTRIM("   THIS IS A TEST   ")**. FoxPro will not indent the words THIS IS A TEST when it prints them, since it has trimmed off the leading blanks, as shown in Figure 4.9. The trailing blanks are still there, but you cannot see them.

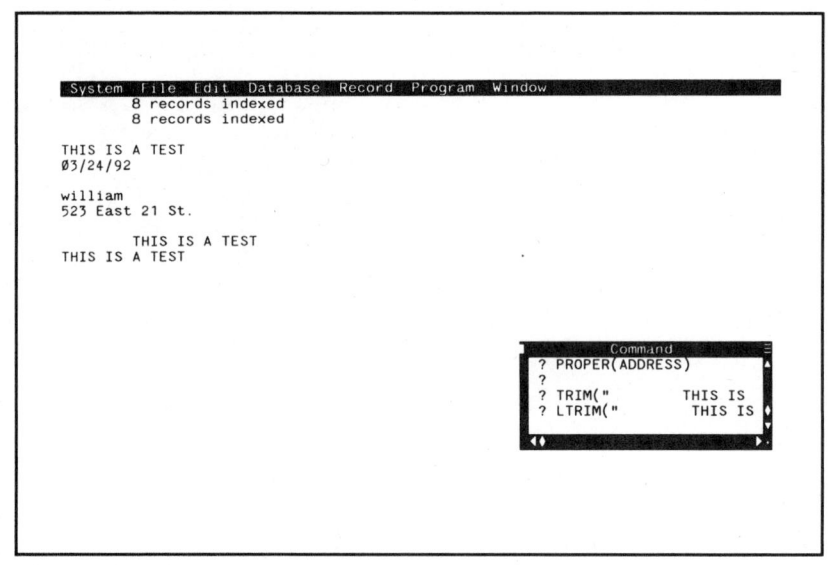

```
┌─────────────────────────────────────────────────────────────┐
│  System  File  Edit  Database  Record  Program  Window      │
│           8 records indexed                                 │
│           8 records indexed                                 │
│  THIS IS A TEST                                             │
│  03/24/92                                                   │
│  william                                                    │
│  523 East 21 St.                                            │
│              THIS IS A TEST                                 │
│  THIS IS A TEST                                             │
│                                                             │
│                                          ┌──── Command ───┐ │
│                                          │ ? PROPER(ADDRESS)│
│                                          │ ?              │ │
│                                          │ ? TRIM("   THIS IS│
│                                          │ ? LTRIM("  THIS IS│
│                                          └────────────────┘ │
└─────────────────────────────────────────────────────────────┘
```

Figure 4.9: Using functions to trim blanks from character data

The next group of functions is useful for converting data from one data type to another, which is necessary when you are creating an expression that combines data that is originally of two different types:

- **VAL(<*char exp*>)** converts character data to numeric data. For example, if you ever wanted, for some strange reason, to perform a calculation using a zip code, you could not perform it on Zip directly, since that field has been defined as the character type, but you could perform a calculation on VAL(ZIP).

- **DTOC(<*date exp*>)** converts date data to character data. For example, DTOC(DATE_HIRED) would return the contents of the Date_hired field as a character string in the same order that dates are displayed—ordinarily in the format **mm/dd/yy**, though the format can be changed using the View window, as explained in Chapter 7. This function should not be used for indexes, for the reasons explained below.

- **DTOS(<*date exp*>** converts date data to character data in ASCII format, **yyyymmdd**, for use in indexes. By way of comparison, note that DTOC( ) would ordinarily return character strings such as 12/31/91 and 01/31/92. Character strings are compared from left to right, so the second of these would come before the first in index order—because 0 comes before 1, FoxPro would never get to comparing the years. On the other hand, DTOS( ) would return the character strings 19911231 and 19920131, so that the first of these would come first: when the dates are in **yyyymmdd** format, sorting the character strings always puts them in order by date. Of course, you can use the date field by itself as the basis of a simple index; but if you are creating a more complex index that combines a date with some other form of character data, you should use DTOS( ) to convert the date to character data.

- **CTOD(<*char exp*>)** converts character data to date data. For example CTOD("10/12/90") uses the quotation mark delimiters to define 10/12/90 as a literal character string and uses the CTOD( ) function to convert the string to the date type. It is identical to {10/12/90}, which uses the curly bracket delimiters to define 10/12/90 as being the date type.

- **STR(<*number exp*>[,*length*][,*decimals*])** converts numeric data to character (sometimes called string) data. Notice the two optional clauses for length and decimals. If these are left out, the default length of the string is 10 spaces and the default number of decimal places is 0: any extra length is thus padded out with leading blanks and any decimal places are lost.

> Older dBASE compatible programs did not include the curly bracket delimiters for the date type, and the only way to use a date constant was in the form of CTOD("10/12/90"). You will see this form used frequently if you ever look at older books about dBASE or older programs written in dBASE compatible languages.

You will be trying out a few of these functions in the next section when you use operators to create more complex expressions. For now, you should try the STR( ) and VAL( ) functions, which are quite commonly used.

1. Enter **?** to skip a line.
2. Enter **? WAGE** and FoxPro prints 6.25, the contents of the current Wage field, indented one space to allow for the tens digit that is blank in this record.

3. Enter **? STR(WAGE)** and FoxPro prints 6, indented nine spaces. This shows the default width for STR( ), with no decimals and ten spaces wide.

4. Enter **? STR(WAGE,5,2)** and FoxPro prints 6.25, indented one space. The function returns a value that is five spaces wide (counting the blank tens place and the decimal point as taking one space each) including the two decimal places. This looks the same as it did when you entered ? WAGE, as you can see in Figure 4.10, but the difference is that now it is a character string that is being printed.

5. Compare these preceding STR( ) examples with VAL( ): Enter **? VAL("10")**, and FoxPro prints 10.00. By default, it prints two decimal places.

Next are a few functions that you will want to use on occasion to manipulate dates.

- **DATE( )** returns the current system date (determined from when you booted up your computer or, if you have one, the date in your computer's clock/calendar).

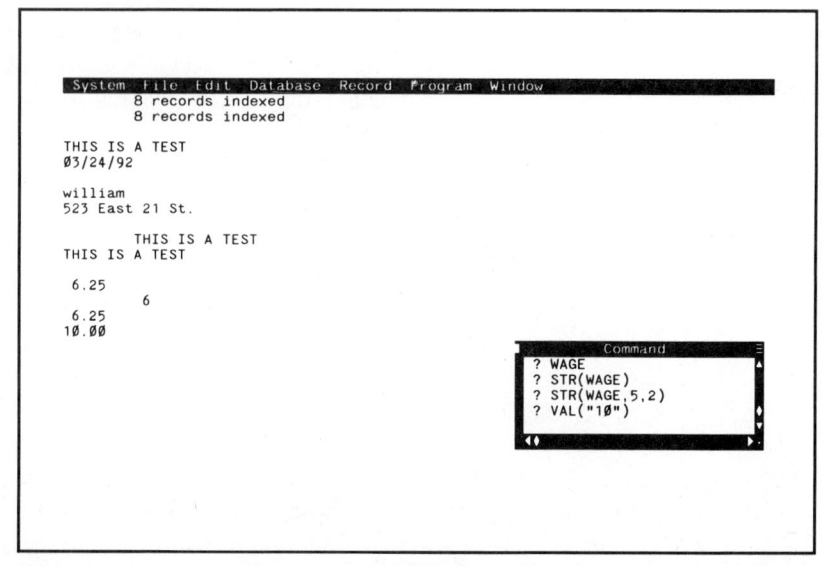

Figure 4.10: Using STR( ) to convert a number to characters and VAL( ) to convert characters to a number

- **DAY( ), MONTH( ), or YEAR( )** return the day, month, or year, respectively, of a date in number form. For example, since the date hired for the current record is 04/23/76, MONTH(DATE_HIRED) is 4.
- **DOW( )** returns the day of the week in number form. For example, since June 14, 1990 is a Thursday, and since Thursday is the fifth day of the week, DOW({06/14/90}) returns 5.
- **CDAY( ), CMONTH( ), or CDOW( )** return the day, month, or day of the week, respectively, of a date in character form. For example, CMONTH(DATE_HIRED) returns April for the current record.

You have already tried DATE( ). Take a minute now to try out a couple of other date functions:

1. Enter ? to skip a line.
2. Enter ? **CDOW({06/09/90})** to get the day of the week for that date. FoxPro prints Saturday.
3. Enter ? **CMONTH(DATE_HIRED)** to print the name of the month that the employee in the current record was hired, as shown in Figure 4.11.

Finally, two other functions that you might find instructive, even if they are not necessary, are ASC( ), which returns the ASCII number of any character, and the opposite function CHR( ), which returns the character for an ASCII number. For example, CHR(65) returns A, since the capital A is ASCII character 65. Likewise, ASC("A") returns the number 65. With these functions and ? you can use FoxPro as an ASCII chart. For example, ? **ASC("z")** lets you look up the ASCII number of that character: FoxPro prints 122 in response. These functions will be useful when you get to programming. You might also find that fooling around with them now will help you learn the ASCII system.

It often makes sense to read the parentheses of a function as if they were the word "of." For example, many people find that if they read TRIM(FNAME) as "the trim of Fname" or read VAL(ZIP) as "the

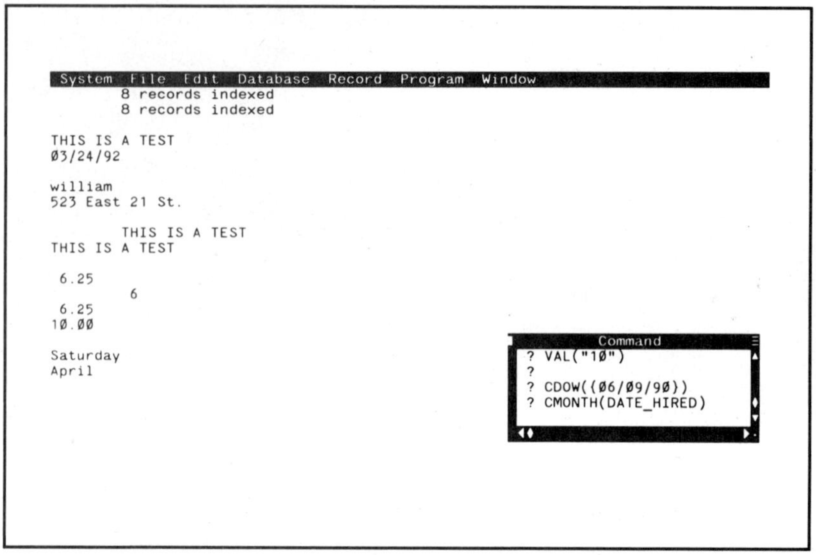

Figure 4.11: Using functions to work with dates

> Within an expression as a whole, the number of left parentheses must be equal to the number of right parentheses. In complex expressions, it is useful to count them to make sure you have not left anything out.

val of Zip,'' then it is easier for them to keep track of the meaning of the functions.

You can also use functions within functions. For example, if you use STR( ) to return the number in the Wage field as a character string, it will have leading blanks which you might not want. Since wages are different amounts and some strings may be longer than others, you cannot get rid of all the leading blanks with the STR( ) function itself: STR(WAGE,5,2) will have a leading blank if the amount is less than ten. You can use LTRIM(STR(WAGE,5,2)) to get rid of these leading blanks. The double parentheses at the end might seem a bit confusing at first, but if a complex expression confuses you, remember that it is evaluated from the inside out. First look at the innermost function, STR(WAGE,5,2) in this case. Once you understand that this is a number converted into string form, it is easy to see what LTRIM( ) is doing to it.

1. Enter ? to skip a line.
2. Enter ? **STR(WAGE,10,2)** to see the wage with a number of leading blanks, and then enter ? **LTRIM(STR(WAGE,10,2))** to see the same wage without any leading blanks.

UNDERSTANDING INDEXES AND EXPRESSIONS   **133**

3. Enter **? CDOW(DATE( ))** and FoxPro will print the day of the week that it is today, as shown in Figure 4.12 (though, of course, your current date will differ).

OPERATORS

The word "operators" sounds very technical and forbidding, but even if you have never used a computer before, you are already familiar with some operators, such as + and – , which are used to perform the operations of addition and subtraction in elementary arithmetic. FoxPro includes the usual arithmetic operators and similar operators that are used for strings and dates.

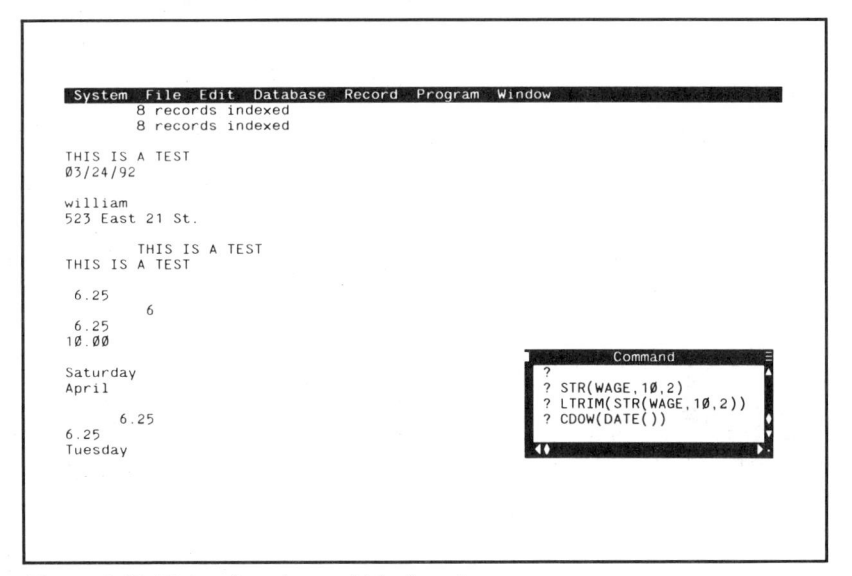

```
 System  File  Edit  Database  Record  Program  Window
        8 records indexed
        8 records indexed
THIS IS A TEST
03/24/92
william
523 East 21 St.
            THIS IS A TEST
THIS IS A TEST
    6.25
              6
    6.25
   10.00
Saturday
April                                   ┌──────Command──────┐
                                        │ ?                 │
                                        │ ? STR(WAGE,10,2)  │
         6.25                           │ ? LTRIM(STR(WAGE,10,2)) │
    6.25                                │ ? CDOW(DATE())    │
Tuesday                                 └───────────────────┘
```

Figure 4.12: Using functions within functions

The *arithmetic operators* are:

      +   addition

      –   subtraction

      *   multiplication

      /   division

^ or ** exponentiation (raising to a power)

( ) grouping—not a substitute for multiplication

Most of these signs should be familiar. Like virtually all computer applications and languages, FoxPro uses the asterisk for multiplication, instead of the × sign or even the parentheses commonly used in arithmetic or algebra. Since most computer monitors cannot use a superscript to represent an exponent, many programs use the caret: 5^2 indicates that the 2 should be above the line as a superscript, so that this stands for 5 squared (five to the second power). Some programs also use ** (to indicate that exponentiation is a step beyond multiplication); FoxPro lets you use either of these common symbols.

As in algebra, the parentheses are used for grouping, which indicates what is called the *precedence* of operations, that is, the order in which operations are performed. The difference that precedence makes is very obvious. For example, (2*3)+5 gives you a different result than 2*(3+5). In the first case, you multiply 2*3 first to get 6 and then add 5, so the final result is 11. In the second case, you add 3+5 first to get 8 and then multiply by 2, so the final result is 16.

If no parentheses are used, exponentiation takes precedence over multiplication and division; and multiplication and division take precedence over addition and subtraction. Though you probably never thought about it, this is the order of precedence that you are accustomed if you have gone through high school algebra. Think, for example, about the value of the algebraic expression

$2x^3 + 4$

If you're familiar with the math, you know not to multiply 2 times *x* first and then cube the result. Without any thought, you would cube the value of *x* first, then multiply the result by 2, and then add 4. This is the same order of precedence as in FoxPro: exponentiation, then multiplication or division, then addition or subtraction.

In general, though, it is good to use parentheses to indicate precedence even if the operations would occur in that order anyway, simply to make the expression easier to read. For example, (2*WAGE)+4 gives the same result as 2*WAGE+4, but it is easier to understand

> As you can see, you cannot leave out the multiplication sign in FoxPro as you do in algebra. You cannot use 2(3+5) to indicate that 3+5 is multiplied by 2. The asterisk must always be included to indicate multiplication.

immediately when you read it. Likewise, because spaces are optional before and after operators, you should use whatever spacing you need to make the expression easy to read.

Using the arithmetic operators with ? acts as a simple calculator, as shown in Figure 4.13:

1. Enter **?** to skip a line.

2. Enter **? 2*8** and FoxPro prints 16.

3. Enter **? 1/3** and FoxPro prints 0.33.

To perform a calculation, you simply print an arithmetic expression.

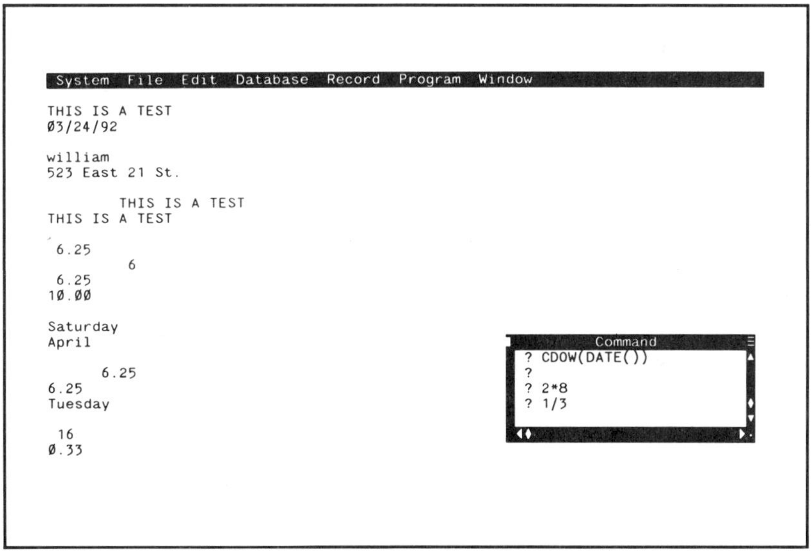

Figure 4.13: Using FoxPro expressions as a calculator

Notice that the FoxPro arithmetic operators print two decimal places by default. You can vary the number of decimal places, however, by using, for instance in the preceding example, STR(1/3,9,8) to print eight decimals.

In addition to the arithmetic operators, FoxPro includes a simple set of date and string operators.

Date operators simply let you add and subtract dates. They are the same as the arithmetic addition and subtraction operators. Thus, + adds dates. For example, {01/01/91} + 90 gives the date that is ninety days into calendar year 1991. Predictably, − subtracts dates. For example, DATE( ) − DATE_HIRED gives you the number of days between the current system date and the date hired for the current record—it tells you how long someone has been working for you.

Try these two simple date calculations:

1. Enter ? to skip a line.

2. Enter ? {06/06/90} − {05/06/90}. FoxPro prints 31, the number of days between the two dates.

3. Enter ? **DATE( ) + 7**. FoxPro prints the date a week after the current date, as shown in Figure 4.14.

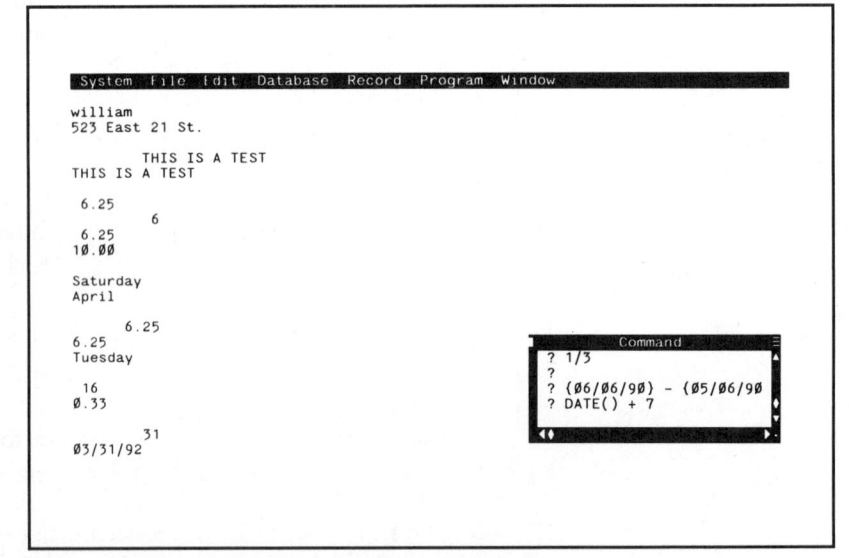

Figure 4.14: Using FoxPro calculations with dates

String operators are used to concatenate strings, that is, to put two strings together as one.

- \+ concatenates strings including blanks.
- − concatenates strings eliminating blanks.

The − to eliminate the blanks is simply a shortcut and is not actually necessary.

>   FNAME − LNAME

is the same as

>   TRIM(FNAME) + TRIM(LNAME)

since these fields only have trailing blanks to trim. When you actually work with FoxPro, you will find this shortcut very convenient. In this book, though, we will generally use the + operator to concatenate strings and will use functions to trim unnecessary blanks, in order to get you accustomed to the trimming functions and to give you more insight into what is happening when you concatenate strings.

Note that the string operators must be fiddled with a bit to print a full name, since a simple − concatenation would not leave a space between the strings. To print a name, you have to include a blank space as a constant. For example,

>   TRIM(FNAME) + " " + TRIM(LNAME)

would give you something like JOHN SMITH. The quotation marks may look strange at first, but you have to remember that they are enclosing the blank between them, which is a literal, and that this expression thus concatenates *three* character strings.

Even though the different types of operators look the same, you cannot use them to combine characters with dates or numbers. First, you must use functions to convert the data to the same data type. Since it is a very common error to forget to do this, let's make this error on purpose so you can recognize what it looks like.

1. Enter ? to skip a line.
2. Enter

   ? "Today is " + DATE( )

   and FoxPro will display the alert shown in Figure 4.15. Its error message is rather obscure, but you should remember to connect it with this error, which is one of the most common

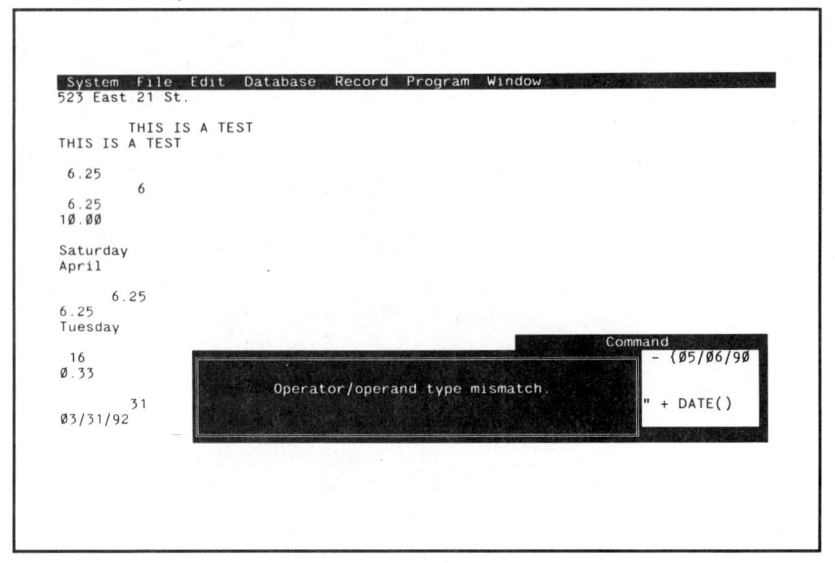

```
  System File Edit Database Record Program Window
523 East 21 St.
        THIS IS A TEST
THIS IS A TEST
    6.25
            6
    6.25
   10.00
Saturday
April
         6.25
  6.25
Tuesday
    16                                              Command
   0.33                                                    - {05/06/90
         31                 Operator/operand type mismatch.
  03/31/92                                          " + DATE( )
```

Figure 4.15: An alert appears if data types are mixed.

errors you will make when you work with expressions. Press any key to make the alert disappear.

What the alert means, of course, is that "Today is " is a different data type from DATE( ). Now let's fix the problem.

3. Enter

   ? "Today is " + DTOC(DATE( ))

   FoxPro will print a message that includes the current date.

4. Enter

   ? "The hourly wage of " + FNAME + LNAME + " is " + WAGE

   and FoxPro will display the same alert, because WAGE is a different data type from everything preceding it. Press any key to make the message disappear.

5. Use the up arrow key to edit the previous command. Enter

   ? "The hourly wage of " + FNAME + LNAME + " is " + STR(WAGE)

> Despite the fact that a lengthy command takes up more than one line on a printed page, you should of course type it as a single command without hitting Enter until you reach the end of the whole thing.

FoxPro will now print the expression, but it will be filled with unnecessary blanks and the wage will not have decimals. (You may have to hide the Command window to see it all.)

6. Edit the command again. Enter

   ? "The hourly wage of " + TRIM(FNAME) + " " + TRIM(LNAME) + " is " + LTRIM(STR(WAGE,5,2))

   The function TRIM( ) has eliminated the unnecessary blanks, but notice that you had to add a literal blank between FNAME and LNAME so it did not come out

   WILLIAMJOHNSON

   Likewise, do not forget to include the spaces after *of* and before and after *is*.

7. Edit the command once more to get the capitalization right and to add a dollar sign and a period at the end: Enter

   ? "The hourly wage of " + PROPER(TRIM(FNAME) + " " + TRIM(LNAME)) + " is $" + LTRIM(STR(WAGE5,2)) + "."

The results of this series of commands are shown in Figure 4.16.

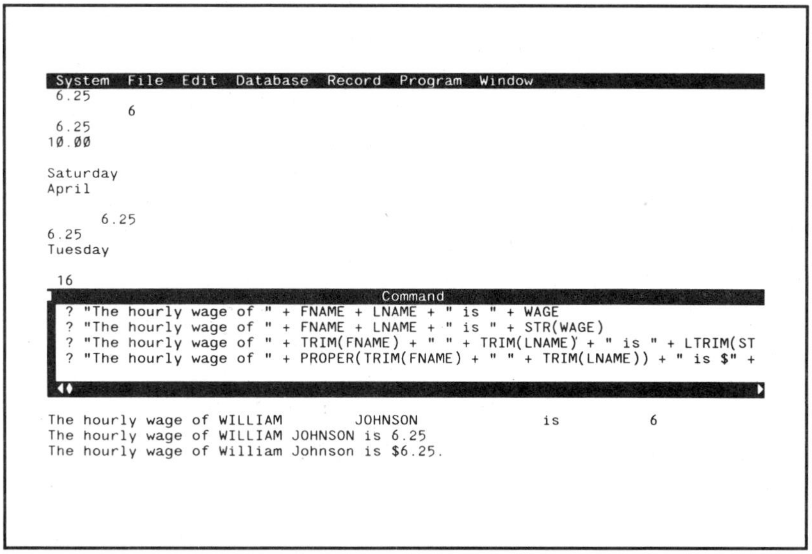

Figure 4.16: Getting a string expression right

The one other very common error, which you might have made while you were doing this exercise, is using unbalanced parentheses. Fortunately, the alert that tells you about this error is not difficult to understand.

USING EXPRESSIONS IN INDEXES

By now you should have a very solid understanding of expressions and know more than enough to start creating complex indexes using the expression builder. It is very common to use a complex index to alphabetize by name.

As you have seen, to put your records in alphabetical order, you need to index by last name using the first name as a "tie-breaker" when last names are the same. The way to do this is to index on the expression LNAME + FNAME.

FoxPro alphabetizes by comparing the ASCII numbers of characters in a word. The ASCII number for the blank character comes before any of the characters that represent letters, and this fact is vital for alphabetizing correctly. Thus, because fields in FoxPro are padded with trailing blanks to fill their entire width; SMITH comes before SMITHERS. FoxPro compares these names letter by letter to alphabetize them, and when it gets up to the E in SMITHERS and the first trailing blank following SMITH, it compares those two characters and decides that the blank, hence SMITH, comes first. For this reason, you cannot trim blank spaces using the TRIM( ) function or the − operator when you are indexing alphabetically by name.

In ASCII order, small letters all come after capital letters. To make sure that your list is alphabetized in dictionary order, rather than ASCII order, you should use the function UPPER( ) to capitalize the letters of the expression that you are indexing on. In the next example, you will start off by indexing on LNAME + FNAME, to see what ASCII order looks like, then you will index on the expression UPPER(LNAME + FNAME), to get proper dictionary order.

Though these are simple expressions, you will create them the long way in order to get experience with the expression builder dialog box,

> You could also index on the expression UPPER(LNAME) + UPPER(FNAME), which is identical to UPPER(LNAME + FNAME).

illustrated in Figure 4.17. As you have seen, the expression builder includes four popup controls across the top, which let you access the Math, String, Logical, and Date functions and operators. It also includes a scrollable list of field names on the lower left, with all except the memo fields of the current database. The scrollable list on the lower right includes all memory variables: since you have not created any, it contains only system variables, beginning with an underscore. The popup control in the center lets you select database files, which will be useful when you are working with relational databases (to be covered in Chapter 7). The Verify pushbutton right under it lets you make sure that an expression is valid; you are quite familiar with the OK and Cancel pushbuttons right under that. The expression that you will create will appear in the large text box that stretches all the way across this dialog box and has the words "INDEX ON: <expr>" on its upper edge. Alternately, you may type expressions directly in this text box. After you have built or entered an expression, you must select the Move pushbutton to place it into the Index On box.

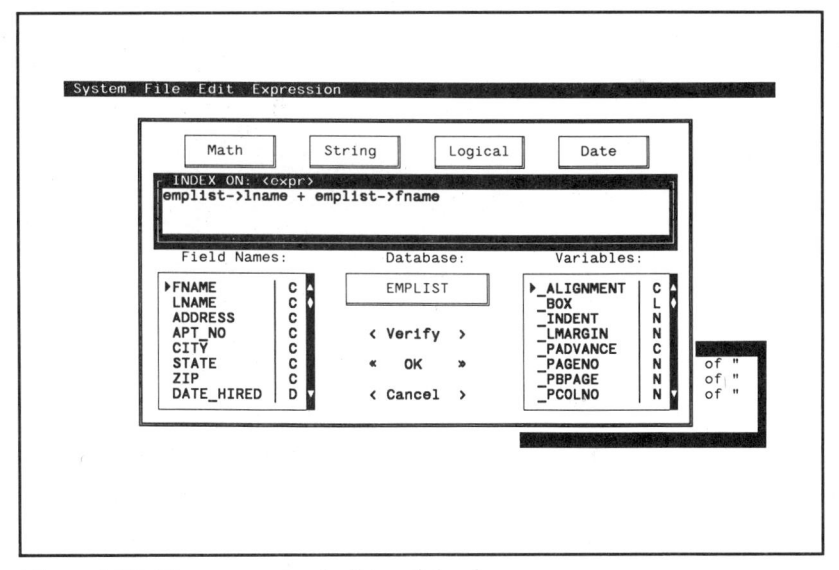

Figure 4.17: The expression builder dialog box

Though it would be easier to type the simple expressions you are using now, you will use the expression builder to create them as an exercise:

1. If you want, enter **CLEAR** to clear the screen. Then, as you did earlier, create the index by selecting New from the File menu, then the Index radio button, then OK.

2. When the Index On dialog box (which you used before) appears, select the Expr pushbutton to call up the expression builder.

3. Select LNAME from the scrollable list of field names. This causes lname to appear in the text box.

4. Since you will be combining two character fields, select the String popup control, then select +. This causes the + to appear after the field name in the text box.

5. To complete the expression, select FNAME from the scrollable list of field names. It is added to the text box after the +, so that it now says lname + fname.

6. To make sure the expression is valid, select the Verify pushbutton. An "Expression is valid" message should appear in the upper right of your screen.

7. Since this is the expression you want to index on, select the default OK pushbutton. The expression builder dialog box disappears, and the expression that you generated is filled in under the Expr pushbutton of the Indexing dialog box. (Remember that you could have just typed the expression in here, rather than using the expression builder.) Finally, select the Move pushbutton to move this expression to the Index On box.

8. Now, select the CDX radio button and the Structural check box, in order to add this new index as a tag to the structural compound index file. As the Tag Name, enter **NAMES**. (FoxPro does not automatically give this tag a name, as it does when a tag is based on a single field.)

9. Select OK to create the index.

10. The Index File Name dialog box appears. You do not need to change the drive or directory: just type **NAMES** as the name of the new index. Then select OK. The command

    INDEX ON LNAME + FNAME TAG NAMES

    is generated in the Command window. The "talk" tells you that records have been indexed.

11. To check the effect of the index, select Browse from the Database menu. Notice that all the names are now in alphabetical order except Audrey Levy's. JACK LOVE comes before Audrey Levy, as shown in Figure 4.18, because capital *LO* comes before *Le* in ASCII order. Close the Browse window.

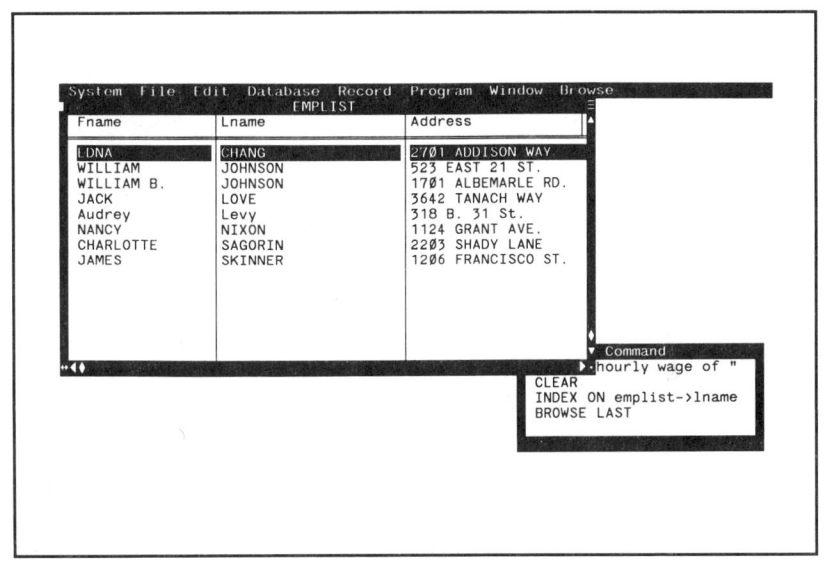

Figure 4.18: Indexing in ASCII order does not alphabetize properly.

To correct this error, you will create the new index UPPER (LNAME + FNAME)), which will compare the two strings using capital leters. Then you will again give the index the name NAMES, so that it overwrites the old, incorrect NAMES index. You could also modify the index by selecting the Modify pushbutton, but the method you use here will give you experience in opening and overwriting indexes. The one problem you will run into is that FoxPro will not let you overwrite an index when it is open, since that could corrupt your data. In this exercise, then, you will open the ZIPS index to close the NAMES index.

1. Select Open from the File menu, then the popup control (which now says Database), and then Index. (Notice, incidentally, the pushbutton New: you can also create new indexes with this dialog box, as you will in the next step.) Select ZIPS.IDX from the scrollable list of indexes in the Open dialog box (shown in Figure 4.19) to open the ZIPS index. Notice the command generated: **SET INDEX TO ZIPS.IDX**. (If you want, select Browse from the Database menu to see that the file has changed to zip code order, then close the Browse window to continue the exercise.)

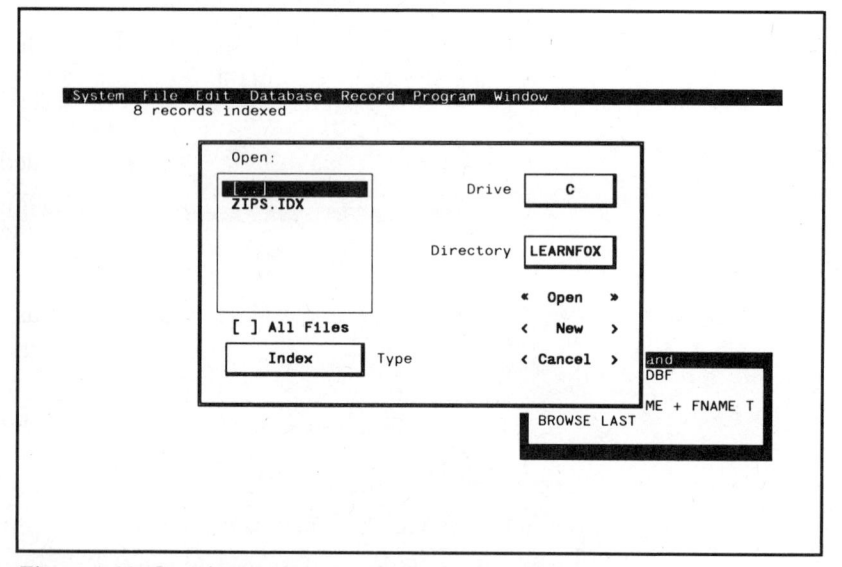

Figure 4.19: Opening an index with the Open dialog box

2. To create a new index in a different way, again select Open from the File menu. The dialog box already has Index as its type, since you selected that earlier. Select the pushbutton New, which calls up the same Index On dialog box you have been using to create indexes all through this chapter. Select the Expr pushbutton to get the expression builder again.

3. Select the String popup control. Scroll down and select the UPPER( ) function from the popup. Notice that the cursor is now in the UPPER( ) function's parentheses in the expression box.

4. Select LNAME from the scrollable list of fields. LNAME now appears in the parentheses, and the cursor moves outside.

5. Press the left arrow key once to move the cursor back one space into the parentheses. Select the String popup control and select + from the popup. The + goes into the parentheses, and the cursor moves out of the parentheses again.

6. Press the left arrow once again to move the cursor back into the parentheses. Select FNAME from the scrollable list of fields to complete the expression you want. Select Verify to make sure it is right.

7. Select OK. The expression is filled in under the Expr pushbutton in the Index On dialog box. Select the Move pushbutton to move the expression into the Indexing On dialog box.

8. Since you want to overwrite the earlier NAMES index you already created, enter **NAMES** as the tag name. Then select OK and FoxPro displays an alert asking if you want to overwrite an existing index (not the same as overwriting a currently *open* index). This alert is shown in Figure 4.20. Select Yes (you can just press Y).

9. Select Browse from the Database menu and you will see that the records are now in proper alphabetical order, not ASCII order. Audrey Levy is now before JACK LOVE, as in Figure 4.21. Close the Browse window.

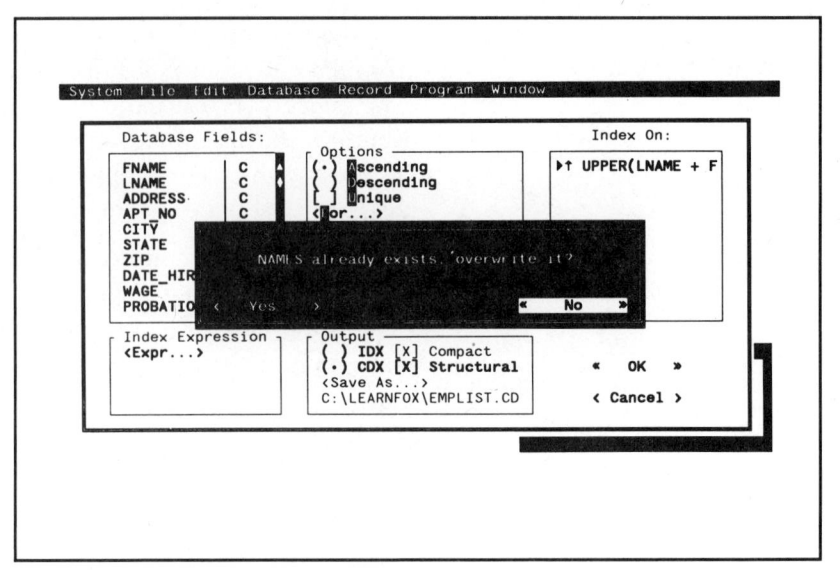

Figure 4.20: FoxPro displays an alert before overwriting an existing index.

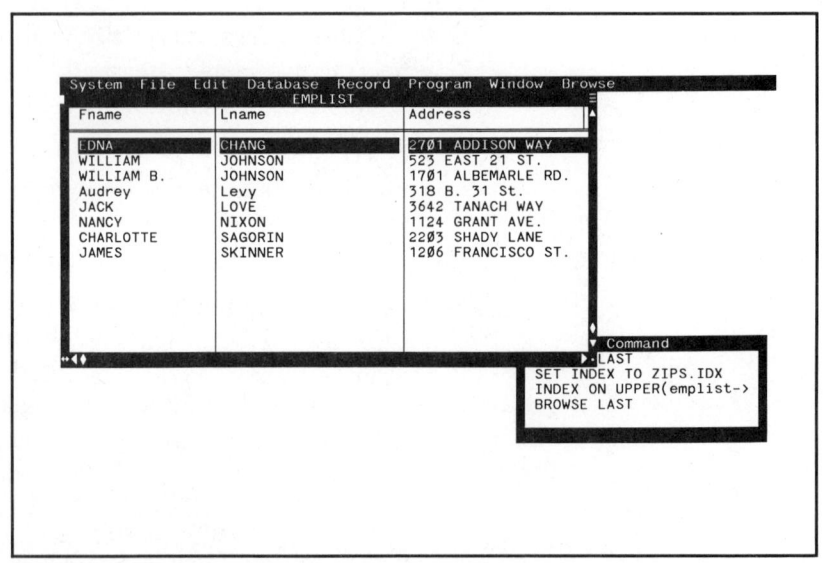

Figure 4.21: Records indexed in proper alphabetical order by name

Going through the steps of recreating the index was a useful lesson in using the expression builder, but it also shows that it is sometimes easier to use the Command window. You could have created the new index by closing the first index, pressing the up arrow key to move the cursor to the command

> INDEX ON LNAME + FNAME TAG NAMES

then just editing that command so it reads

> INDEX ON UPPER(LNAME + FNAME) TAG NAMES

and pressing Enter.

As you can see, using the expression builder is a bit unwieldy, because there are so many functions and operators to choose among. However, the expression builder lets beginners create expressions, and it is useful as a learning tool, to get you familiar with FoxPro's functions and operators. After you have used it for a while, you will find that you have learned the FoxPro functions that you use frequently and that it is usually easier just to type expressions into the Index On dialog box than to use the expression builder—though the expression builder will still be useful for expressions that use more obscure functions.

FoxPro functions are all listed in the Help window. If any function in the scrollable lists of the expression builder puzzles you, you can always open the Help window to find out what it does. Playing with the Help window and expression builder together, in this way, is an easy way to learn FoxPro functions.

USING INDEXES

You have learned all you need to create indexes—both indexes based on a single field and more complex indexes based on an expression. Now, you will see how to use the indexes that you have created. Indexes are managed with the Setup dialog box, which you use by selecting Setup... from the Database menu.

What you will do most often using this dialog box is select the index tag or the index file that determines the order in which the records are displayed. This index is called the *controlling index*.

When you first open a file using the menu system, the records are displayed in natural order—that is, in the order you entered them.

You have seen that, when you first create an index tag or file, it automatically becomes the controlling index, and the records are displayed in *that* order. In most cases, of course, you want to work with indexes that you already created, and you will want to make one of them the controlling index by using the Setup dialog box.

Another important thing you may do using the Setup dialog box is to open IDX index files or independent compound index files. (You may also open them using the Open dialog box, which you display by selecting Open from the File menu and selecting the Index radio button.)

As you know, the structural compound index file is automatically opened whenever the file is opened, so that its tags are always updated when you edit or add data to the database. Other indexes, though, must be added explicitly if you want them updated. Though it is easiest to use the structural compound index for most purposes, there are cases where you will want to use other types of index files, and so you should learn how to work with them.

SELECTING THE CONTROLLING INDEX

The index that is currently the controlling index has a small bullet to its left in the scrollable list of indexes in the Setup dialog box. When you first open a database file, though, there is no controlling index: the records are used in the order in which they were entered.

The four pushbuttons to the right of the scrollable list are used to manage indexes, and the last of them is used to determine which is the controlling index. If the index that is selected in the scrollable list is not currently the controlling index, this last pushbutton says *Set order*. Selecting it makes that index the controlling index. If the index that is selected in the scrollable list is the controlling index, then this pushbutton says *No order*. Selecting it returns the records to the natural order in which they were entered, with no controlling index.

Try changing index order. The database file should already be open with NAMES as the controlling index:

1. Select Setup... from the Database menu to use the Setup dialog box. Note the bullet next to EMPLIST:NAMES in the scrollable list of indexes.

2. Select EMPLIST:DATE_HIRED in this scrollable list. (If you are using the keyboard, just move the highlight to it.) Then select the Set Order pushbutton. Note that a bullet appears to the left of this index name and, now that the selected index is the controlling index, the pushbutton changes to No Order.

3. Select the default pushbutton (OK). Note that FoxPro generates the command **SET ORDER TO TAG DATE_HIRED**.

4. Select Browse from the Database menu. Scroll right so you can see the DATE_HIRED field, and notice that the records are in order of date hired. Then close the Browse window.

5. Select Setup... from the Database menu. The DATE_HIRED index tag should still be selected in the scrollable list, so the No Order pushbutton should be accessible. If it is not, select it. Then select the No Order pushbutton and select the OK pushbutton. Note that FoxPro generates the command **SET ORDER TO**. Next, select Browse from the Database menu and note that the records are no longer in any index order. Then close the Browse window.

The command **SET ORDER TO [** <*index name*> | <*tag name*>**]** specifies the index or tag to be the controlling index. If no index or tag name is specified, however, it removes the controlling index so that records are in natural order. You can also use **SET ORDER TO** with a number or numeric expression that refers to the order in which the indexes were opened. See the Help window or documentation for more information on this use of the command. Many FoxPro commands that begin with **SET** work similarly if the clause following **TO** is omitted; these commands will be discussed in more detail in Chapter 7.

USING OTHER TYPES OF INDEXES

As mentioned previously, the structural compound index is easy to use because it is opened automatically when you open the file, but it is not always the fastest approach to working with your data. For this reason, you must learn to work with other types of indexes, which you may open and close explicitly.

ADDING INDEXES

You also use the pushbuttons of the Setup dialog box to open and close simple indexes and independent compound indexes—adding them to or removing them from the scrollable list of indexes. Try opening the ZIPS.IDX index file that you created earlier in this chapter:

1. If you want, enter CLEAR to clear FoxPro "talk" from the screen. Then select Setup... from the Database menu to use the Setup dialog box.

2. Select the Add... pushbutton. FoxPro displays the Open Index File dialog box, shown in Figure 4.22, which lists all index files in the current directory. (If you have indexes in other directories, you may move among directories in the usual ways: either by selecting ... or a subdirectory name from the scrollable list of file names or by using the directory popup control.) Notice that EMPLIST.CDX is dimmed in the scrollable list, because it is already open. Select ZIPS.IDX from this scrollable list, and, if necessary, select the default pushbutton (Open). Note that ZIPS is added to the scrollable list of indexes in the Setup dialog box.

> A FOXUSER.DBF file and the FOXUSER.CDX file displayed in this list are automatically created and maintained by FoxPro to hold information about the way you have set up the program. For example, if you have moved the command window, these files hold its new location. You can simply ignore them.

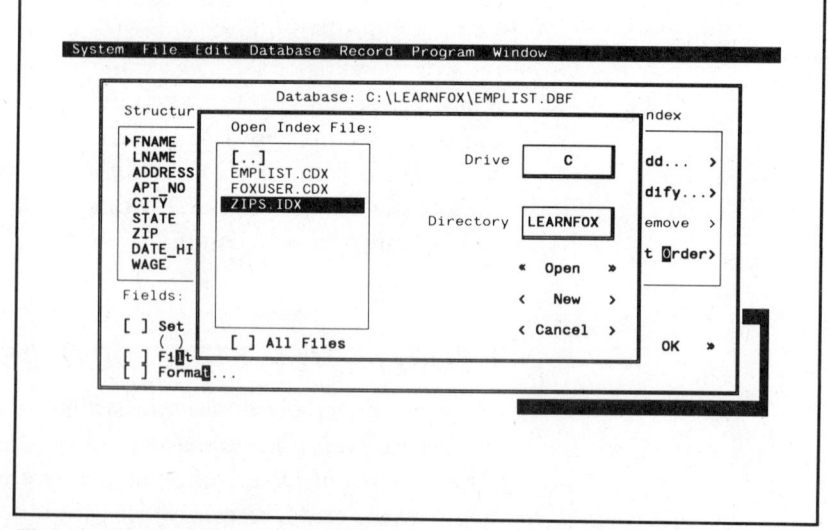

Figure 4.22: Opening an index file

You can open an independent compound index file in the same way. All of the tags will be added to the list of indexes. Notice that, in this list, the names of tags of compound index files are preceded by the file name, like the tags in the EMPLIST file. On the other hand, the name of an IDX file stands alone, like the ZIPS file you just added. Notice also that, as you scroll among these index and tag names, the expression that each is based on is displayed under the scrollable list; if the index had a FOR clause, that would be displayed under the scrollable list as its Filter.

You close an index file in much the same way: select the Remove pushbutton. You will try this in the next section.

REINDEXING

As you know, you do not have to worry about maintaining the structural compound index file. It is open whenever the database file is open, so it is updated whenever you add or edit data, without your thinking about it.

If you use indexes apart from the tags of the structural compound index file, however, you probably do not want to keep them open at all times: you put them in separate files in the first place so that FoxPro will not have the overhead of maintaining them whenever you modify your data. Instead, you want to reindex in order to update them only when you need to.

To learn how to do this, let's add a record without the ZIPS.IDX index open, and then reindex to update the ZIPS index:

1. In the Setup dialog box, select the ZIPS index in the scrollable list of indexes. Then select the Remove pushbutton to remove it from the list and select the OK pushbutton.

2. Select Append from the Record menu. As the new record, enter *Fname:* **MICHELLE** *Lname:* **PERLOW** *Address:* **224-1423 RESEARCH BLVD.** *Apt_no:* **22-41** *City:* **SANTA CLARA** *State:* **CA** *Zip:* **94304** *Date_hired:* **05/18/88** *Wage:* **9.75** *Probation:* **N** *Notes:* (none). Now, select Browse from the Browse menu, to see this record among the others. Once you have seen that it is in proper order in the Browse window, press Ctrl-End or click the close box to save the change.

3. Now select Open from the File menu, and select ZIPS.IDX from the Open dialog box. When you open an index in this way, FoxPro automatically makes it the controlling index.

4. Select Browse from the Database menu. The new record is not in the Browse window, as shown in Figure 4.23, because ZIPS was not open when you appended it.

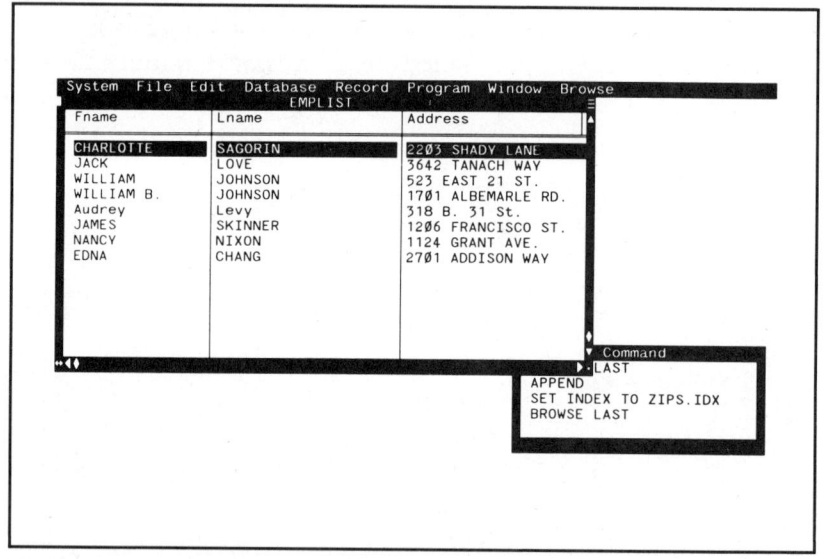

```
System  File  Edit  Database  Record  Program  Window  Browse
                     EMPLIST
Fname            Lname             Address
CHARLOTTE        SAGORIN           2203 SHADY LANE
JACK             LOVE              3642 TANACH WAY
WILLIAM          JOHNSON           523 EAST 21 ST.
WILLIAM B.       JOHNSON           1701 ALBEMARLE RD.
Audrey           Levy              318 B. 31 St.
JAMES            SKINNER           1206 FRANCISCO ST.
NANCY            NIXON             1124 GRANT AVE.
EDNA             CHANG             2701 ADDISON WAY

                                              Command
                                        LAST
                                        APPEND
                                        SET INDEX TO ZIPS.IDX
                                        BROWSE LAST
```

Figure 4.23: The new record is nowhere to be seen using ZIPS as the controlling index.

5. Select Reindex from the Database menu. Talk appears to inform you that FoxPro is reindexing the file. Close the Browse window, then select Browse from the Database menu to open it again. The Browse window reappears with the new record included, as shown in Figure 4.24. Close the Browse window.

6. Now, you have learned how to work with IDX files—and the same principles apply to independent CDX files—and you can see how much easier it is to include indexes as tags of the structural compound index file. Since you created a ZIP tag earlier, you can simply delete the ZIPS.IDX file, now that it

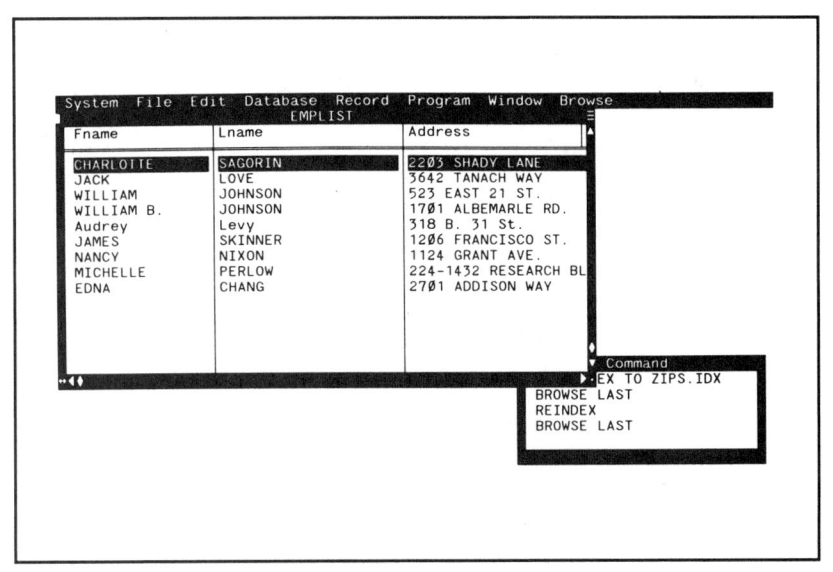

Figure 4.24: After reindexing, the new record reappears.

is no longer needed for instructional purposes. As you know, the FoxPro **RUN** command lets you do this by using the DOS **DEL** command: in the command window, enter **RUN DEL ZIPS.IDX**.

Reindexing applies to all the indexes that are open when you select Reindex, not just to the controlling index. If you have multiple IDX and independent CDX files that you want to update, you should open them all by selecting the Add pushbutton in the Setup dialog box to add each to the list of open index files; then select Reindex to reindex them all.

A REVIEW OF THE SETUP DIALOG BOX

You have already looked at virtually all of the features of the Setup Dialog box, shown in Figure 4.25, but you should take a moment to review it systematically.

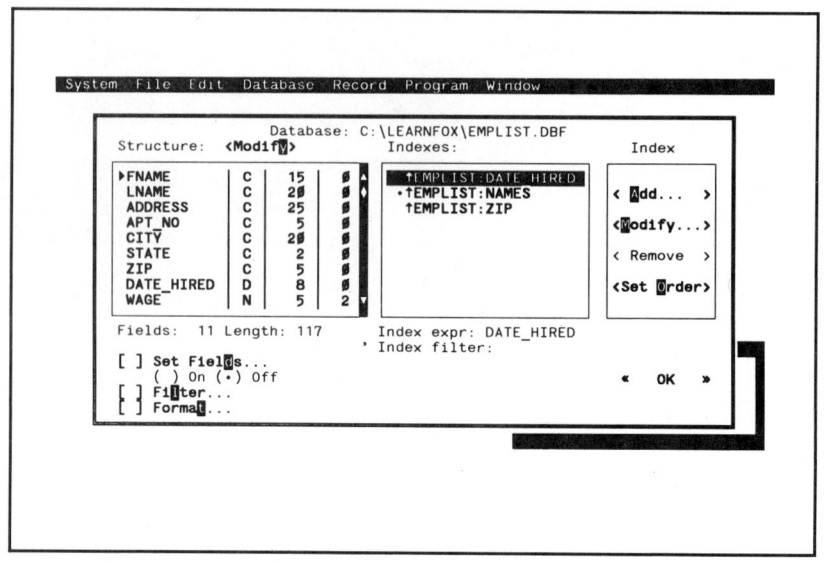

Figure 4.25: The Setup dialog box

The Indexes box (which includes a list of all indexes that are currently open) and the four pushbuttons to its right are central to using this dialog box to manage indexes.

The list automatically includes all the index tags of the structural compound index file, which are always open. You may open other index files and add them to the list by selecting the Add pushbutton. You may remove indexes (apart from tags of the structural compound index file) by selecting them in the list of indexes and then selecting the Remove pushbutton.

The Set Order pushbutton makes the selected index the controlling index, the one that determines the order of the records. If the index selected in the list is already the controlling index, this button changes to No Order, to give you the option of returning the database file to the natural order in which they were entered.

Selecting the Modify pushbutton calls up the Index On dialog box, which displays the specifications of the selected index. You may change these specifications to modify that index. Don't confuse this pushbutton with the Modify button above the field list, which lets you modify the structure of the database file, as you learned in Chapter 2.

The Set Fields and Filter check boxes are used in queries, which are covered in Chapter 5. The Format check box is used to choose an FMT file, an obsolescent type of data-entry form.

When you work from the menu system, you must always follow two steps to open a file and make an index into the controlling index. The first generates the command **USE**, and the second generates the command **SET ORDER TO** <*tag name*>. Once you gain more experience, you might prefer working from the command line, where you can combine these two steps in one command, such as

USE EMPLIST ORDER NAMES

This command would let you use the EMPLIST file with the NAMES index as the controlling index. See the entry under USE in the Help window or any FoxPro reference for other command options that let you use other types of index files.

SORTING

As you know, indexing a file changes only the apparent order of the records, while the actual way that they are arranged in the database file remains the same. It is possible, however, to change the actual order of the records by choosing Sort from the Database menu.

When you sort, you create a new database file to place the sorted records in. Sorting is rarely used in FoxPro, since it is slower and clumsier than indexing, but you should take a moment to look at the features of the Sort dialog box, illustrated in Figure 4.26.

Of course, it is impossible to sort or index on memo fields, so the scrollable list in the field picker leaves out memo fields.

The upper portion of this dialog box contains a field picker. Select the field that you want from the scrollable list labeled Database Fields, on the upper left, and then select the Move → pushbutton to move it into the box labeled Sort Order, on the upper right.

You can sort on more than one field. Add fields to the Sort Order list in order of their importance: a field lower on this list is only used as a tie-breaker if all the fields higher than it are identical. For example, to sort on the full name, you would put LNAME first and FNAME second in the Sort Order box. The order you end up with would be the same as if you indexed on the expression LNAME + FNAME. If you change your mind about adding a field to the Sort Order list, you can remove it by using the Remove pushbutton.

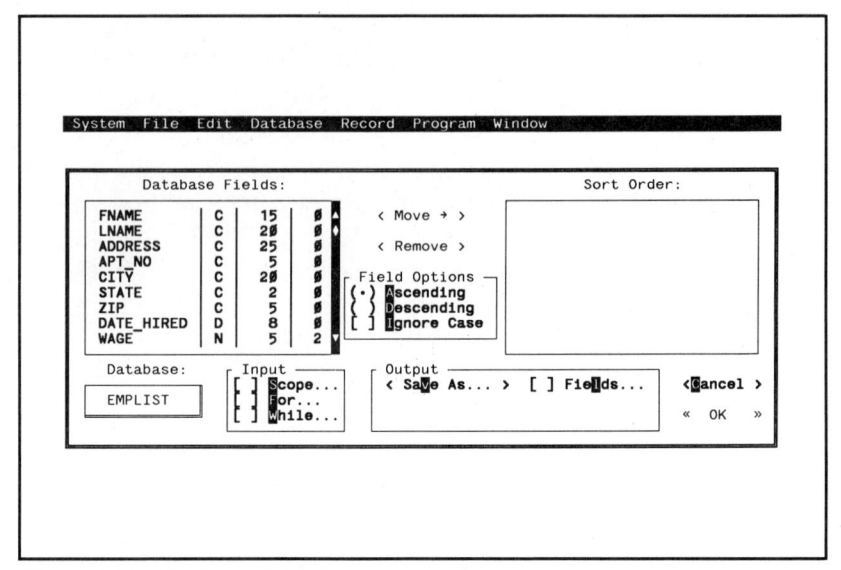

Figure 4.26: The Sort dialog box

The box labeled Field Options, in the center of the dialog box, includes two radio buttons to let you sort in Ascending or Descending order (with Ascending as the default) and a check box to let you choose to ignore case (upper and lowercase). To sort in alphabetical order by name, you should check this box in addition to moving LNAME and FNAME to the Sort Order box.

The Database popup control on the bottom left lets you access other databases that are open and create a sorted file that includes fields from more than one existing file. To do this, you must be working with a relational database and must open multiple files simultaneously and relate them to each other, a relatively advanced feature of FoxPro that you will learn about in Part II of this book. The Input box in the bottom center includes Scope, For, and While check boxes that let you choose which records go into the new file; similar check boxes are used in many FoxPro dialog boxes, and you will learn about them in the next chapter.

The Output box next to the Input box includes a Fields check box: selecting it displays a new dialog box that lets you choose which fields will be included in the new sorted file.

After you have chosen all of the sort options you want, you may choose the Save As pushbutton. The Sort Destination File dialog box appears. Within this dialog box, enter a new name for the output file, and then select the Save pushbutton; or you could simply have typed the name for the new file in the text box under the Save As pushbutton. When you are finished, select the OK pushbutton of the Sort dialog box.

Rather than using the Sort dialog box, you can enter the command **SORT TO** <*file name*> **ON** <*field list*>. See the entry in the Help window for a discussion of all the options for this complex command.

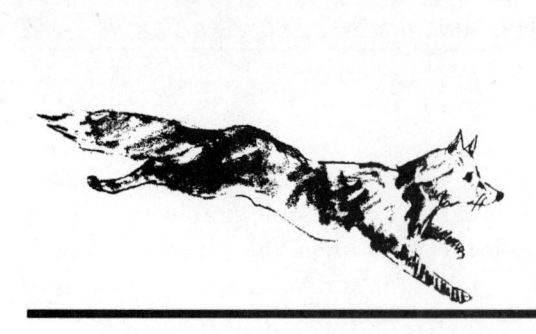

Chapter 5

Using Queries
and Logical Expressions

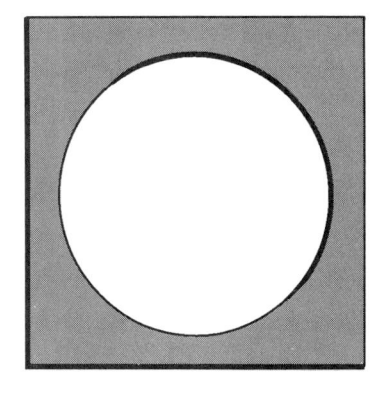

A QUERY TELLS A DATABASE PROGRAM TO FIND records that meet some criterion—for example, to find the record of a person with a certain name, or to find all of the records with addresses in the state of California. Obviously, you want different types of results from these two queries. For the first you want one record and for the second you want a whole list of records. FoxPro gives you several methods of making queries, which are useful for different purposes:

- You can find a single record that meets the criterion. Then, if you want, you can repeat the query to see if there is a second record that meets the criterion. This method is useful for tasks such as looking up someone by name. Repeating the query is useful if you get someone else with the same name the first time you try.

- You can find all the records that meet the criterion by combining queries with commands that work with the entire database. For example, you can build a query into the Copy command, so that records that meet the criterion are copied into a new file when you use that command. This method has many uses. For example, it can be used to produce mailing labels for everyone who meets the criterion—for example, for every employee who lives in California.

- In addition to these two basic ways of querying, FoxPro gives you special query techniques. You can create what is called a *filter*, which lets you use the entire database just as you normally would as it filters out the records that do not meet the criterion. You can also build a query into an index in such a way that the index is automatically updated as the file is maintained; after you do this, only records that meet the criterion are accessible when the database is used with that index as the controlling index.

This chapter will mainly deal with the first two of these methods. You will find later in the chapter that it is easy to use the same principles with other commands and special techniques.

WORKING WITH LOGICAL EXPRESSIONS

> In an actual application, of course, if you think there is any possibility of the state's not being capitalized, you should use the expression UPPER(STATE) = "CA". The examples leave out the UPPER( ) function to save you the trouble of entering it and because state names are less often miscapitalized than people's names.

Any query must contain an expression that is either true or false—that is, a logical expression. For example, if you wanted to make a query to find the employees who live in California, you would have to use the expression STATE = "CA". Later, you will examine this sort of expression in more detail. For now, just note that it makes FoxPro look at each record to see if the contents of the State field are equal to the letters CA. If they are, the expression STATE = "CA" is evaluated as true. If not, the expression is evaluated as false.

It is important to understand that the criterion you use in a query must be a logical expression that FoxPro evaluates as true or false. By printing a couple of sample expressions using **?**, you can get a firm grasp of the fact that FoxPro *evaluates* expressions:

1. If necessary, start FoxPro and enter **CLEAR** to clear the screen.
2. In the Command window, enter **? 1 + 1**. FoxPro prints **2**.
3. Enter **? 1 + 1 = 2**. FoxPro prints **.T.**, as shown in Figure 5.1.

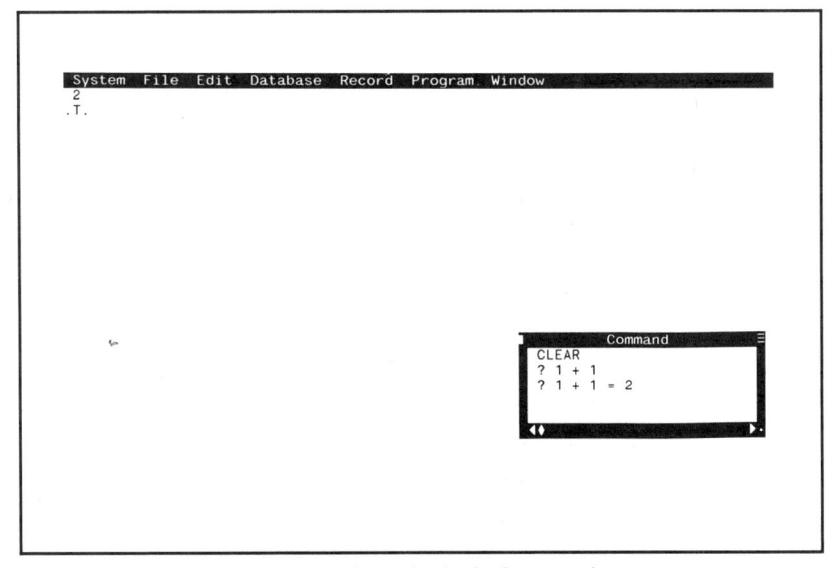

Figure 5.1: Evaluating a numeric and a logical expression

In the first example, FoxPro evaluates the expression 1 + 1 and comes up with the result 2. The operation it performs to get this result is addition, indicated by the + operator.

In the second example, FoxPro evaluates the expression 1 + 1 = 2 and comes up with the result .T., which stands for True. (As you will see, FoxPro often uses dots in this way as delimiters in logical expressions.) The operation it performs to get this result is comparison, indicated by the = operator.

LOGICAL FUNCTIONS

Operators are not the only expression elements that give a result of true or false. Some functions, called logical functions, will also return .T. or .F. Though they generally are used in programming, logical functions are sometimes handy during ordinary use of FoxPro.

One common example is the function EOF( ), which stands for End Of File. As long as the pointer is on one of the records of the file, EOF( ) is false. If you are at the last record, though, and you use the command **SKIP** to move the pointer to the next record, EOF( ) will become true, to indicate that you are beyond the point where records exist.

EOF( ) also becomes true if you make a query and FoxPro does not find what you are looking for. The pointer goes through all of the records looking for the criterion you gave it, and passes by the last record without finding it. To indicate this, it makes EOF( ) true. You will use this function in Chapter 9 when you start programming.

RELATIONAL OPERATORS

Logical functions and operators are included in the Logical popup control of the expression builder dialog box, shown in Figure 5.2. Although all the operators on this popup are referred to loosely as logical operators, it is more precise to divide them into *relational* and *logical* operators.

Relational operators are used to make comparisons. They can be used to compare numbers, strings, or dates.

The = operator, which you glanced at earlier, is an example. You can use expressions such as DATE_HIRED = {10/10/85} or

USING QUERIES AND LOGICAL EXPRESSIONS   *163*

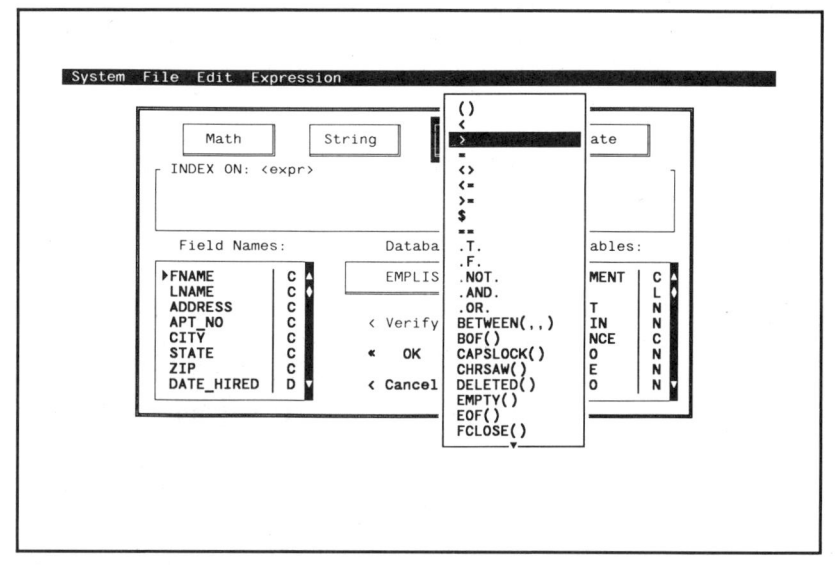

Figure 5.2: The Logical popup control of the expression builder

WAGE = 10 or UPPER(LNAME) = "SMITH" to find records where those fields have those values.

Though relational operators can be used with data of various types, the data being compared must be of the same type. For example, you could not use UPPER(LNAME) = {10/10/85}. Since there is a character expression to the left of the = and a date expression to the right, FoxPro would display an alert with an error message saying there is a type mismatch, as shown in Figure 5.3. On the other hand, FoxPro would let you use the expression UPPER(LNAME)- = DTOC({10/10/85}) without displaying an error message; though you obviously will not find someone with this name, the logical expression is valid, because it compares two character expressions.

The relational operators are listed in Table 5.1. Most will probably be familiar to you, since they are used in mathematics. There are three operators meaning "not equal." You may use whichever one you find convenient when you are typing from the keyboard. Only one is actually included on the popup.

Except for $ and = =, all of these operators can be used with character, numeric, or date data. $ and = = can be used only for character data.

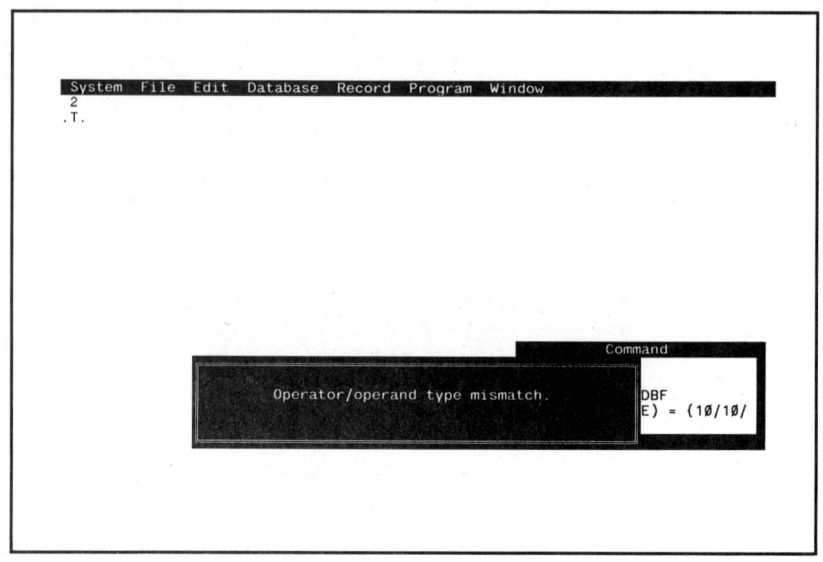

Figure 5.3: Alert indicating there is a data type mismatch

Table 5.1: The Relational Operators

OPERATOR	MEANING
=	is equal to
>	is greater than
<	is less than
> =	is greater than or equal to
< =	is less than or equal to
< > or # or ! =	is not equal to
$	is contained in (used only for character data)
= =	is identical to (used only for character data)

< >, which is commonly used in mathematics, is the only symbol for "not equal to" included on the Logical popup. # was common in earlier dBASE compatible languages, but it is sometimes confusing to beginners, who tend to read an expression like WAGE # 10 as "wage number 10" rather than as "wage not equal to 10." In dBASE compatible languages, this # sign is supposed to represent an equals sign with two vertical lines through it to show that is not true. ! was added to FoxPro as another way of representing "not," which it represents in other computer languages; it is used in combination with = to mean "not equal to."

$ is used to search for a substring. For example, you can use the expression ''BROADWAY'' $ UPPER(ADDRESS) to find the records of people who live on a street named Broadway. You can read this expression as ''BROADWAY is contained in upper of

USING QUERIES AND LOGICAL EXPRESSIONS   165

> If you enter the command **SET EXACT ON**, only strings that are identical will match, even if you use =. To go back to the default method, enter the command **SET EXACT OFF**. You can also use these commands through the View window, which will be discussed in Chapter 7.

ADDRESS." This operator applies only to character data; it can be used to search memo as well as character fields.

Though the difference may not be obvious, = =, which means "is identical to," is not the same as =, which means "is equal to." For example, if you search for UPPER(LNAME) = "SMITH", FoxPro will find people named SMITHSON and SMITHERS as well as SMITH. This feature of = is generally useful, as you will see. However, where you want only an exact match, you could use = =. Since these operators are tricky, you should try them out.

1. Enter **? "SMITHSON" = "SMITH"**. FoxPro evaluates the expression as true and prints .T.

2. Enter **? "SMITHSON" = = "SMITH"**. (You can do this most easily, of course, by editing the previous command.) FoxPro evaluates the expression as false and prints .F., as shown in Figure 5.4.

One other point you should consider, while you are at it, is that in these comparisons, FoxPro uses the second string as the criterion and compares the first string with it. In Step 1, for example, it uses

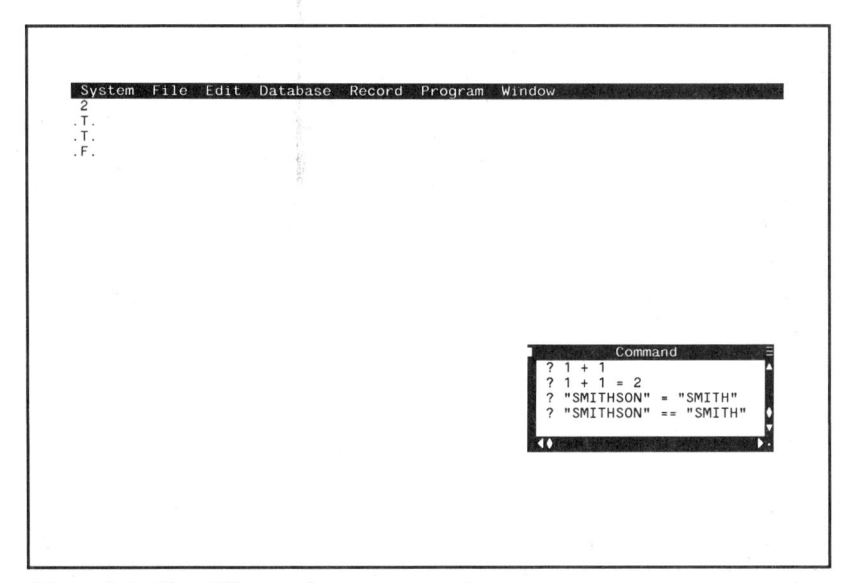

```
System  File  Edit  Database  Record  Program  Window
2
.T.
.T.
.F.




                                                    Command
                                              ? 1 + 1
                                              ? 1 + 1 = 2
                                              ? "SMITHSON" = "SMITH"
                                              ? "SMITHSON" == "SMITH"
```

Figure 5.4: The difference between = and = =

"SMITH" as the criterion, and it looks through "SMITHSON" to see that all the letters in "SMITH" are matched. Thus, it would not find that the reverse, "SMITH" = "SMITHSON", is true: when it looks at "SMITH", it would not find that all the letters in "SMITHSON" are matched. Try this out by entering ? **"SMITH" = "SMITHSON"**. FoxPro evaluates the expression and prints .F.

This example shows why actual queries have the form LNAME = "SMITH" rather than "SMITH" = LNAME. For the same reason, you can find all the names that begin with the letter A by using the criterion UPPER(LNAME) = "A".

LOGICAL OPERATORS

Though the relational operators that were listed in Table 5.1 are loosely referred to as logical operators, this section will look at the logical operators in the stricter sense of the term. These operators, used to create more complex expressions, are shown in Table 5.2.

Table 5.2: The Logical Operators

OPERATOR	MEANING
.AND.	both halves of the expression must be true for the entire expression to be evaluated as true
.OR.	either half of the expression must be true for the entire expression to be evaluated as true
.NOT. or !	the expression that follows must be untrue for the entire expression to be evaluated as true
( )	used for grouping

This book uses .NOT. for the sake of clarity, but you can use ! instead to save time.

In earlier dBASE-compatible languages, the AND, OR, and NOT logical operators had to be used with dot delimiters—the period on each side of the word. FoxPro version 2, however, lets you use AND, OR, and NOT with or without delimiters—partly to save you typing but primarily to make the language compatible with SQL (covered in Chapter 7), which is added to version 2 of FoxPro. This book will keep the dot delimiters, since they make it clearer that logical expressions are being used, which is useful when you are learning the language. If you want, you can omit the delimiters to save typing and to become accustomed to both ways of writing logical expressions.

USING .AND., .OR., AND .NOT.

The logical operators are used to build complex expressions, and you should look at a few examples to see how they work.

.AND. and .OR. are both used to build a complex expressions out of two *logical* expressions. For example, if you wanted to find records of employees who live in California, you would use the expression STATE = "CA". If you wanted to find employees who live in New York, you would use the expression STATE = "NY". And if you wanted to find employees who live in either state, you would combine the two with .OR. to make the complex expression

```
STATE = "CA" .OR. STATE = "NY"
```

It is important to remember that ordinary language does not use the words "and" and "or" in exactly this way. People might say colloquially "I want a list of the employees from California or New York." But they might also say "I want a list of the employees from California and New York," intending no difference in meaning. When you are working with computers, though, you have to use .AND. and .OR. in their precise logical sense. The complex expression

```
STATE = "CA" .AND. STATE = "NY"
```

would only be true if both halves of it were true—that is, if FoxPro found a record where the contents of the State field were, at the same time, both CA *and* NY, which, of course, is impossible.

The effect of the .AND. and .OR. operators is that .AND. is *ex*clusive—the expression is true only if both halves are true at once, which can exclude a lot of records—and .OR. is *in*clusive: the expression is true if either half is true, so that more records are included.

.OR. is thus used for broadening your queries: for example, for finding people from more than one state. .AND. is useful for narrowing your queries by adding more criteria. For example, the expression

STATE = "CA" .AND. WAGE < 10

would be used to narrow the query so that it finds only some of the employees from California: those with wages less than $10.

The use of .NOT. is more obvious. You use it before an expression to reverse the meaning of the expression. For example, .NOT. STATE = "CA" could be used to find the records for all the states except California; that is, it would find every record that is left out by the expression STATE = "CA". You simply have to remember to use .NOT. before the entire logical expression it refers to.

USING PARENTHESES FOR COMPLEX EXPRESSIONS

You can combine complex logical expressions with .AND. and .OR. indefinitely, creating more and more complex expressions. When expressions contain more than one of these operators, it is best to group them using parentheses to indicate precedence.

For example, let's say that you want to find employees from California and from New York who earn less than average wages for the area. You know that the average wage in California is $10 and that the average wage in New York is $11.

To find the records from California, you would use the expression

STATE = "CA" .AND. WAGE < 10

To find the records from New York, you would use the expression

STATE = "NY" .AND. WAGE < 11

Then, to find all the records you want, you would combine these two with .OR. to get

(STATE = "CA" .AND. WAGE < 10) .OR. (STATE = "NY" .AND. WAGE < 11)

> If you find these operators confusing, you should add the words "it is true that" when you read the expressions to yourself. Read STATE = "CA" .OR. STATE = "NY" as "it is true that the STATE equals CA or it is true that the STATE equals NY," and you will not confuse the .AND. with the .OR. operator. Likewise, .NOT. is sometimes clearer if you read it as "it is not true that." Thus, it is probably best to read .NOT. STATE = "CA" as "it is not true that the STATE equals CA."

ORDER OF PRECEDENCE

In Chapter 4, you saw that if you leave out parentheses, numeric expressions are evaluated in default algebraic order. In fact, all FoxPro expressions are evaluated in the following order of precedence if you leave out parentheses:

1. exponentiation
2. multiplication and division
3. addition and subtraction
4. character string concatenation
5. relational operators
6. .NOT.
7. .AND.
8. .OR.

The reason for some of this order of evaluation is obvious. Clearly, FoxPro has to evaluate numeric expressions before it can compare them: for example, if it is evaluating the expression 1 + 1 = 2, it must use the addition operator + to evaluate 1 + 1 before it can use the relational operator = to see if the entire expression is true.

Likewise, FoxPro must give relational operators precedence over logical operators. For example, if it is evaluating STATE = "CA" .OR. STATE = "NY", it must evaluate STATE = "CA" to see if it is true and must evaluate STATE = "NY" to see if it is true before it can determine if the entire complex expression is true. There is no need to use parentheses to make the order of precedence clearer.

On the other hand, when you get down to the logical operators themselves, things become less obvious. It is possible to leave out the parentheses and to rely on the default order of precedence when you are working with expressions that have more than one logical operator, but it makes expressions that are this complex hard to read, which makes errors more likely. Moreover, these errors are often hard to detect, since they will only result in your query not finding every record you want. For these reasons, it is best always to use parentheses in expressions whenever they may be useful for clarity, even if they are not needed.

TO INDEX OR NOT TO INDEX

One basic choice that you must make before making queries is whether or not to use an index.

There are many cases where using an index is essential. For example, if you are looking up employees by name in a large database, the delays would be intolerable if you did not use an index and the program had to read through every record in sequence to find each name that you wanted.

There are also cases where an index is not useful. If all of your employees lived in two states, for example, it would be foolish to use an index to search for state names. The program would have to read through about half the file anyway just to read all the records with the state you wanted, so using an index would not save much time. In this case, maintaining an index is more trouble than it is worth.

Likewise, there is no need to use an index to produce a report if you plan to go do something else while the report is being printed. If time is not a concern, there is no reason to go to the trouble of maintaining an index.

In version 1 of FoxPro and in other dBASE compatible programs, you had to use the index explicitly in order to do an indexed search: as you will see, this is a tedious process.

One of the most impressive innovations in version 2 of FoxPro is *Rushmore* technology, which automatically makes use of existing indexes to optimize queries, and which is blindingly fast—up to a thousand times faster than other dBASE compatible programs can process similar queries. Rushmore substitutes for older forms of indexed query, and it is so much easier to use that it makes them virtually obsolete.

Rushmore will be discussed in a moment, but first you should compare the two older types of queries. The older type of indexed query is still included in the FoxPro menu system, so you must learn about it to fully understand the FoxPro interface. It also is invariably used in older programs, because it was so much faster than an unindexed query, so you need to learn about it if you ever want to maintain existing programs. Finally, though they are rare, there are some occasions where you can invent ways to do explicitly indexed queries even though Rushmore will not kick in automatically; you will look at an example later in this chapter.

FOR AND WHILE CLAUSES

There are two different clauses that you can add to FoxPro commands depending on whether you want to query with or without explicitly using an index.

- **FOR clauses:** If you precede a logical expression with the word FOR, FoxPro will do the search whether or not there is an index. If there is no index, it will read through the entire file in sequence, starting with the first record, to find records where that expression is true.

- **WHILE clauses:** If you precede a logical expression with the word WHILE, FoxPro will assume that the pointer is already on the first record that you want and that all of the records that you want follow immediately after that record. It is called a WHILE clause because the search continues only while the criterion remains true.

If you are working in the Command window, there are many different commands that you could use with, for example, the clauses FOR STATE = "CA" or WHILE STATE = "CA" in order to build a query into the command. If you are working from the menu system, likewise, you will find that many dialog boxes have For and While check boxes—like the Copy To dialog box shown in Figure 5.5.—which let you build queries into these menu choices and thus generate commands that include FOR and WHILE clauses.

The Scope and Fields check boxes that are grouped with the For and While check boxes in this dialog box are useful for refining queries, but they involve side issues that are not essential. They will be covered later in this chapter.

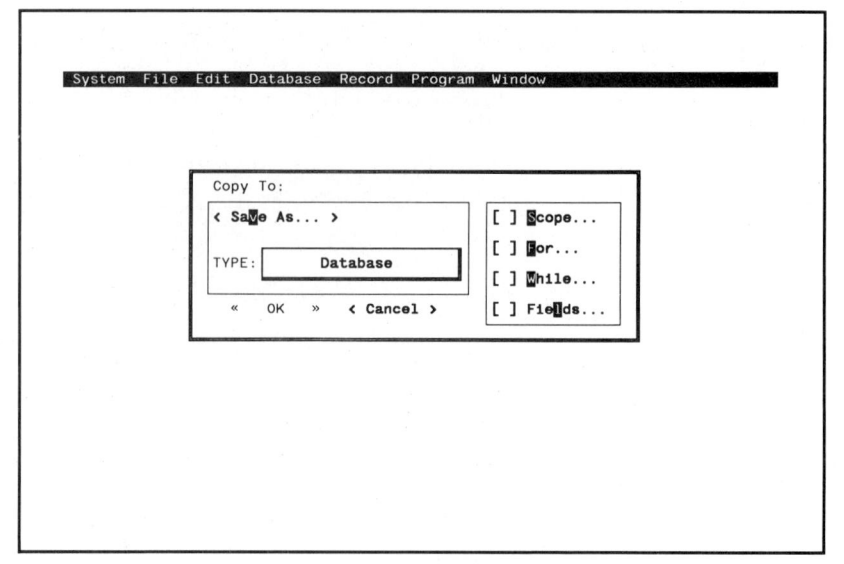

Figure 5.5: A dialog box with For, While, Scope, and Fields check boxes

PREPARING TO USE WHILE

Using a FOR clause with a command is very simple. Using a WHILE clause is a bit more difficult. It will be easier to understand by looking at an example.

Let's say that you have a very large database and that you want to use just the records of the employees whose names begin with the letters L through O. You could do this by using a command that includes the clause WHILE UPPER(LNAME) > = "L" .AND. UPPER(LNAME) < "P".

Before you can use this command, though, you must first be using the EMPLIST database with the NAMES index tag as the controlling index, so the names are already in alphabetical order (or the file must be sorted in that order). Then you must put the pointer on the first record that begins with L. Only then can you use a command containing this WHILE clause. When you use a WHILE clause, FoxPro begins by looking at the current record (where the pointer is) to see if it meets the criterion. If it does, then FoxPro looks at the next record and sees if it meets the criterion. It continues to look at records in this manner until it finds a record that does not meet the criterion, at which point it stops the search.

Think about the pitfalls this process involves—since they sometimes come up and it will be helpful if you can recognize the disease when you see the symptom:

- If you used a WHILE clause on a file that was not indexed or sorted, it would not find all the records that matched. They would be scattered through the file, and FoxPro would certainly find a record that did not match before it found every record that did match.

- If you used a WHILE clause without moving the pointer to the first record that matched, it would look at the current record, and if it didn't meet the criterion, would stop searching without having found *any* records.

- If you had an indexed file and the pointer was on a record that matched, but was not on the *first* record that matched, then the query would find only the records that came *after* that location of the pointer, not those that came before.

None of these problems can occur when you use a FOR clause.

RUSHMORE TECHNOLOGY

Though they require extra work and can create extra problems, it used to be common to use WHILE clauses, because the extra speed that you gained by doing an indexed search made all the trouble worthwhile. If you were working with even a moderately large database file, commands with FOR clauses would seem to take forever.

The Rushmore technology added in version 2 of FoxPro changes this entirely. If an index exists which can be used to speed the search, Rushmore automatically uses it when you use a FOR clause. You do not have to do the extra work that a WHILE clause requires.

If you want to do fast searches based on the contents of a certain field, it is easiest to create an index tag based on that field as part of the structural compound index file. As you know, FoxPro will automatically maintain the index for you when you modify the database.

And, whenever you do a query based on this field, FoxPro will automatically use Rushmore technology to optimize the search.

For Rushmore to work, there must be a *basic optimizable expression* as either part or all of the expression that the query is based on.

A basic optimizable expression takes one of these two forms:

<index expression> <relational operator> <constant>

or

<constant> <relational operator> <index expression>

For example, since you have a NAMES index tag based on the expression **UPPER(LNAME + FNAME)**, either **UPPER(LNAME + FNAME) = "SMITH"** or **"SMITH" = UPPER(LNAME + FNAME)** is a basic optimizable expression.

Notice, though, that the index expression must exactly match the expression on which the index is based: **UPPER(LNAME) = "SMITH"** is not an optimizable expression, given the indexes that you have for your database. You do have to do the extra work of typing **FOR UPPER(LNAME + FNAME) = "SMITH"** in order to save all the preparation that you would have to do before using the clause **WHILE UPPER(LNAME) = "SMITH"**.

The relational operators for basic optimizable expressions are

=, <, >, <=, >=, <>, #, !=

Basic optimizable expressions cannot include **$** or **==**.

If only part of the query expression is optimizable, Rushmore optimizes the query to the extent possible. For example, you have an index tag based on DATE_HIRED but none based on STATE. Thus, if you used a command with the clause **FOR DATE_HIRED > {01/01/90} .AND. STATE = "CA"**, FoxPro could only partially optimize the search.

In the standard version of FoxPro 2.0, Rushmore is disabled whenever there are more than 500,000 records in total in all open databases. To use Rushmore with more records than this, you must use the extended version of FoxPro, which is distributed with the standard version of FoxPro but which requires a computer with extended memory and at least a 386 processor. Rushmore is also disabled if a WHILE clause is actually included in a command, even if the command also contains a FOR clause that could use Rushmore.

You might want to disable Rushmore if a command with an optimizable FOR clause modifies the index key that the FOR clause is based on. In this case, the group of records that Rushmore selects become outdated as the command is executed, so you could get an inaccurate result using Rushmore. You can disable Rushmore by adding the clause **NOOPTIMIZE** at the end of a command that could use it or by entering the command **SET OPTIMIZE OFF**, which disables it until you enter **SET OPTIMIZE ON**.

The circumstances where Rushmore could be used but is not, however, are very rare. A FOR clause optimized by Rushmore can be used in virtually every case where a WHILE clause was used in the past. If the index exists that lets you use the WHILE clause, then you can almost always use a FOR clause with an optimizable expression instead—though you might have to use a slightly different expression, as you saw in the examples using the NAMES index.

The most important exceptions involve sorted databases, which can use WHILE clauses even though there is no index that can be used to optimize a FOR search, and cases (one of which you will look at below) where you can use another index to arrange records in the order you need for a WHILE clause, even though there is no index that Rushmore could use to optimize a FOR clause.

MAKING QUERIES FOR SINGLE AND MULTIPLE RECORDS

As you have seen, you can use queries to find either a single record or all records that match a certain criterion. In either case, you can decide to do a search that is explicitly indexed or one that is not.

UNINDEXED QUERIES FOR A SINGLE RECORD

The most common way of querying for a single record is to use the command **LOCATE FOR**. You could also select Locate from the Record menu and use the For check box in the Locate dialog box that appears (shown in Figure 5.6).

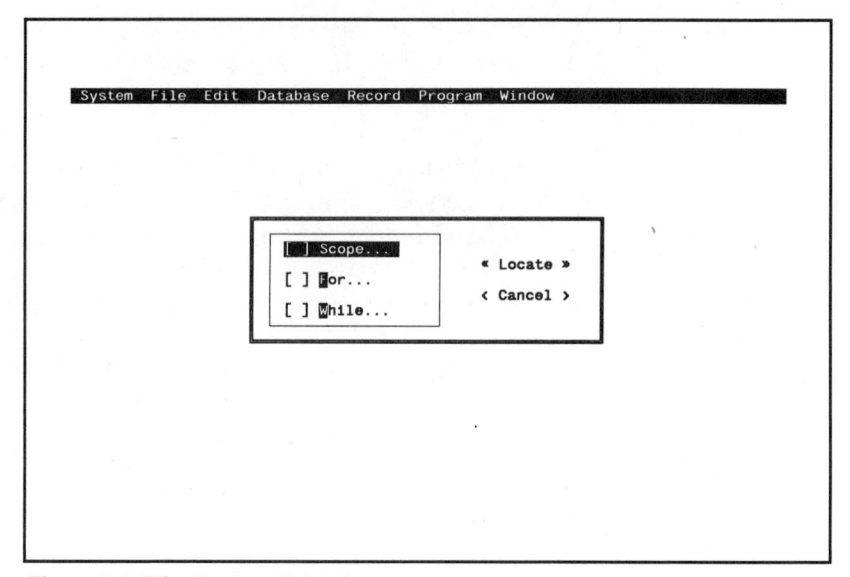

```
┌─────────────────────────────────────────────────────────┐
│   System  File  Edit  Database  Record  Program  Window │
│                                                         │
│                                                         │
│              ┌─────────────────────────────┐            │
│              │ [■] Scope...    « Locate »  │            │
│              │ [ ] For...      < Cancel >  │            │
│              │ [ ] While...                │            │
│              └─────────────────────────────┘            │
│                                                         │
└─────────────────────────────────────────────────────────┘
```

Figure 5.6: The Locate dialog box

> Though it is possible to use both a FOR and a WHILE clause in a command in this way, it is confusing and should be avoided. If you do use both, the WHILE clause takes precedence.

As you can see, the Locate dialog box has a For, a While, and a Scope check box. Many dialog boxes have these three check boxes together, but in this case, arranging them this way is a bit misleading, since they are not parallel options here, as they usually are. **LOCATE** *must* have a FOR clause; the WHILE and SCOPE clauses are optional and merely limit the number of records that FoxPro searches through. (When you look at Scope at the end of this chapter, you will see that it merely lets you specify that some command be carried out on the next 10, 20, or whatever number of records you choose. The While option can also be used in combination with FOR to carry out the **LOCATE FOR** command only for as long as the WHILE condition is true.

The basic way of using the Locate dialog box, then, is by checking the For check box. When you do so, the expression builder will appear, so you can enter the logical expression that you will be using as the criterion for your search. For example, to find the record for somebody named Johnson, you would enter the expression UPPER(LNAME) = "JOHNSON".

If there is no index based on the LNAME field, **LOCATE FOR** will begin with the first record in the database file and read through it sequentially until it finds a match, regardless of where the pointer is when you begin. If there *is* an index based on this field, Rushmore will take over and will optimize the search. If it does not find any record that matches, FoxPro "talk" will display a message saying "End of Locate Scope." In addition, the pointer will be set at the end of the file position, so that the function EOF( ) is true. Given the indexes that you have for your database, if you have a large database file and want Rushmore to optimize the search, you must use the expression **UPPER(LNAME + FNAME) = "JOHNSON"**, as you learned earlier.

If **LOCATE FOR** finds the record you want, but you also want to see the next record that meets the criterion, select Continue from the Record menu (or use the command **CONTINUE**).

Try these two commands, which you are bound to use frequently for the everyday work of looking up records:

1. Select Open from the File menu, and when the Open dialog box appears, select EMPLIST.DBF. In order to see the pointer being moved by the commands, open the Browse window by selecting Browse (from the Database menu popup).

2. Select Locate from the Record menu to display the Locate dialog box.

3. Select the For check box to display the expression builder. Note that above the text box it says FOR Clause: <expL> to remind you that a logical expression is needed in the FOR clause. To create this expression, first select the String popup control, and select UPPER( ) from the list that pops up. Select LNAME from the Field Names list. Then select the Logical popup control, and select = from the list that pops up. Select the String popup control again, and select "text" from the list that pops up. Type **JOHNSON** in the quotation marks that have appeared. This gives you the complete expression you want, as shown in Figure 5.7. (Alternately, you simply could have typed the expression UPPER (LNAME) = "JOHNSON".)

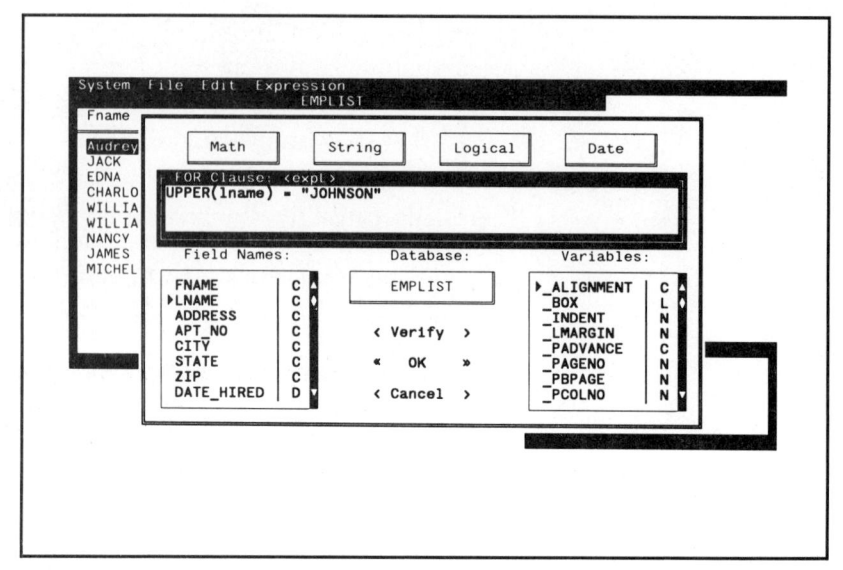

Figure 5.7: Building the expression to be located

4. Select the default pushbutton, OK, to return to the Locate dialog box. Select the default pushbutton, Locate, to find the first record that matches the criterion. The pointer moves to the first record with the last name of Johnson, as shown in Figure 5.8.

5. Select Continue from the Record menu popup. The pointer moves to the next record with the last name of Johnson, as shown in Figure 5.9.

The command generated in the Command window is

LOCATE ALL FOR UPPER(lname) = "JOHNSON"

As usual, generated commands contain more than is really needed. The word ALL is the scope of the command, and (as you will see later in this chapter) merely means that the entire database file is searched. Since this is the default scope, it is not necessary to include it if you are typing in the Command window. From the Command window, you could simply enter **LOCATE FOR LNAME = "JOHNSON"**.

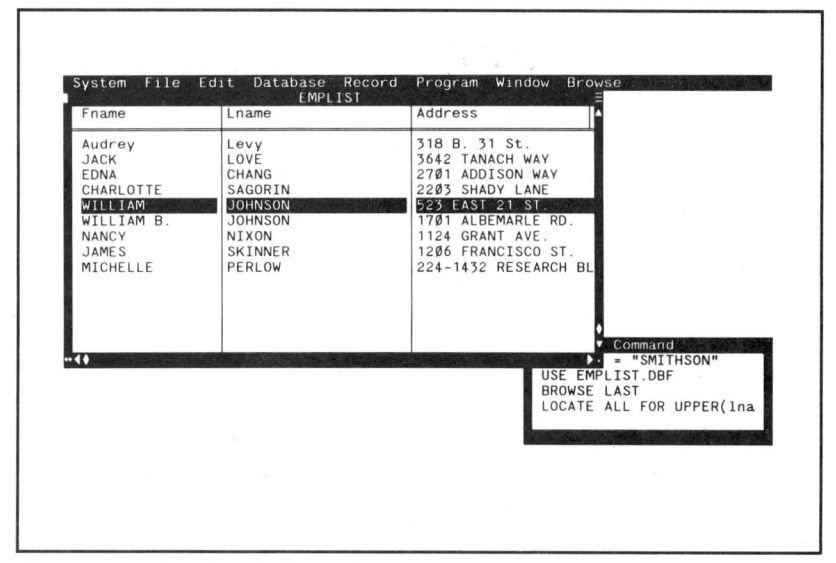

Figure 5.8: Using LOCATE to find a record

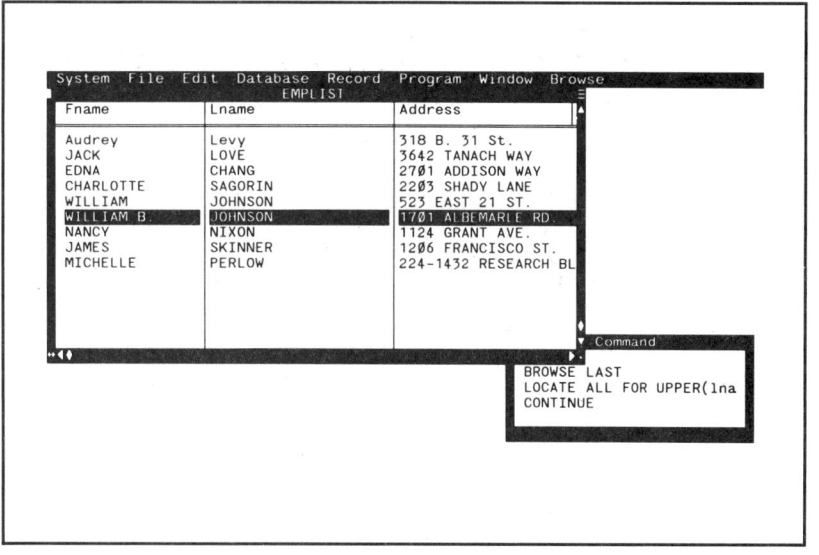

Figure 5.9: Using CONTINUE to find the next record with the same value

> You can also use **LOCATE** and **CONTINUE** without opening the Browse window, to move the pointer without its being visible to the user. This is often essential in programming, where you want the user to be able to search for a given record in order to view or edit it but you don't want to give the user access to the entire file.

> Normally, the pointer will move to the end of a file if the search is unsuccessful. But if you use the command **SET NEAR ON** before using **SEEK**, the pointer will be placed at the record that comes nearest to matching; then you can browse nearby records. This is very useful if, for example, you misspelled a name. **SET** commands will be discussed in Chapter 7, as part of the discussion of the View window.

Of course, this exercise in using LOCATE and CONTINUE does not seem very useful when you are working with this small a file, where you can see the two Johnsons as soon as you open the Browse window. These commands are essential, however, when you are working with a larger file that has people named Johnson scattered all through it.

INDEXED QUERIES FOR A SINGLE RECORD

SEEK lets you find the first record in an indexed file that matches the criterion, and it is generally used before you use a command with a WHILE clause based on the same criterion.

Before you use **SEEK**, the database must be indexed on the field that your query is based on, and that index must be active as the controlling index. If it does not find a match, the pointer is put at the end of the file and EOF( ) becomes true.

Since SEEK works only on the indexed field, it can let you enter the criterion in an easy way: you simply have to enter the *value* that the indexed field must match, and not an entire logical expression. To find the first person named JOHNSON in a file indexed on UPPER(LNAME) + UPPER(FNAME), you simply need to use the command **SEEK "JOHNSON"**. FoxPro assumes that you want to find that value of the expression that is currently the main index, so it will search for the first record where UPPER(LNAME) + UPPER(FNAME) = "JOHNSON". (Remember that there is a match as long as the beginning of the string you are searching matches; thus, this criterion will be true as long as the last name is Johnson.)

To do a seek using the menu system, select Seek from the Record menu, and FoxPro will display the expression builder so you can enter the expression that matches the main index. As you will see, the expression builder reminds you that you do not have to enter the entire logical expression that is your criterion. You just enter the second half of the expression, which FoxPro assumes you want to match with the fields in the main index. Try it:

1. Select Setup from the Database menu, and then EMP-LIST:NAMES from the list of indexes, and the Set Order

pushbutton to make it the controlling index. Then select the default pushbutton (OK). The names in the Browse window are now listed alphabetically.

2. Select Seek from the Record menu. The expression builder appears with the words Value to SEEK <expC> above the text box where you enter the expression, to remind you that you just need a character expression here, and not a logical expression as you do with most queries.

3. Type **"LOVE"** in the text box, as shown in Figure 5.10. (If you want, you can select "text" from the String popup control to put the quotation marks in the text box.) Then select the default pushbutton, OK. FoxPro moves the pointer to the proper record.

4. Select Seek again from the Record menu. Then type **"LEVY"** in the expression builder's text box, and select the default pushbutton, OK. FoxPro finds the appropriate record, even though it comes before the current location of the pointer, and even though the case does not match.

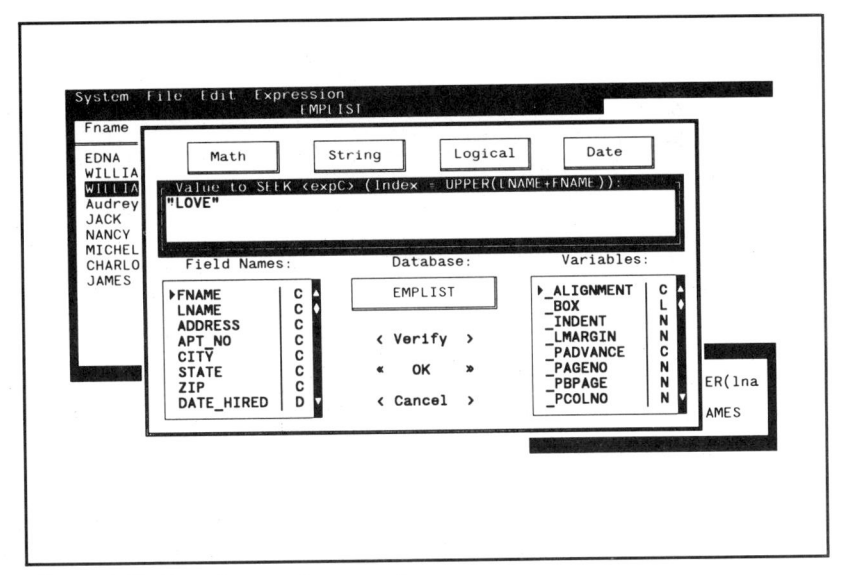

Figure 5.10: Entering a value to seek

The example above shows that **SEEK** does an indexed search of the entire database: it does not just begin where the pointer is.

When you are entering the criterion for the **SEEK** command, think carefully about the exact expression that the index uses. At first, it might seem puzzling that **SEEK** seemed to ignore capitalization when it found "LEVY". Remember, though, that **SEEK** was searching using the main index, thus, the expression based on UPPER(LNAME) + UPPER(FNAME). The index expression capitalized the LNAME field; thus, it *did* match the criterion "LEVY".

After you have done a **SEEK** in this way, the index is still open as the controlling index, and the pointer is on the first record with the value you want. This leaves you all ready to use a command with a WHILE clause.

> If you want to find the next single record that meets the criterion after you have used a **SEEK**, all you need to do is look at the next record in the Browse window. Since this is a search on the key field of the index, the next record that matches the criterion (if there is one) is simply the next record in the file.

QUERIES FOR MULTIPLE RECORDS

When you query for all the records in a file that match the criterion, many database management programs automatically put the results of a query in a new database file, which they call the Answer file or something similar. Then, if you want a report or mailing labels that contain only the records that match the query, you must produce the report or labels using the Answer file.

FoxPro and other dBASE compatible programs do not require you to go through this unwieldy process. You can add a FOR or a WHILE clause to many commands—including the commands that you use to produce reports or labels—and, in essence, build the query into the command.

As an exercise to learn how to use the FOR and WHILE clauses, you will make a query that works like a conventional query that puts all the matching records into a new file. There are times when you need to make this sort of simple query. It is very easy to do this using FoxPro by selecting Copy To from the Database menu and checking For or While in its dialog box—or by using the **COPY** command with a FOR or WHILE clause—to copy the records that match the criterion into a new file. You can even name the new file ANSWER.DBF if you want.

You have already learned how to make queries using **LOCATE** and **SEEK** for a single matching record. By using **COPY** with FOR and WHILE clauses, you will get a general idea of how to make queries for all the matching records in a file—so that you will also be able to use FOR and WHILE with other menu choices or commands.

AN UNINDEXED MULTI-RECORD QUERY

Since FOR is easier, you should try it first:

1. If you want, close the Browse window and enter **CLEAR** to clear the screen. Select Copy To from the Database menu popup, and when the Copy To dialog box appears, select the For check box.

2. Select STATE from the list of field names. Select the Logical popup control and select = from the popup that appears. Then select the String popup control and select ''text'' from the popup that appears. Type **CA** in the quotation marks. Select the default pushbutton OK to confirm the expression and return to the Copy To dialog box.

3. Type **ANSWER1** in the text box under the Save As pushbutton. This will be the file containing all the records that match your STATE = ''CA'' criterion. The dialog box should now look like Figure 5.11. Select OK to copy.

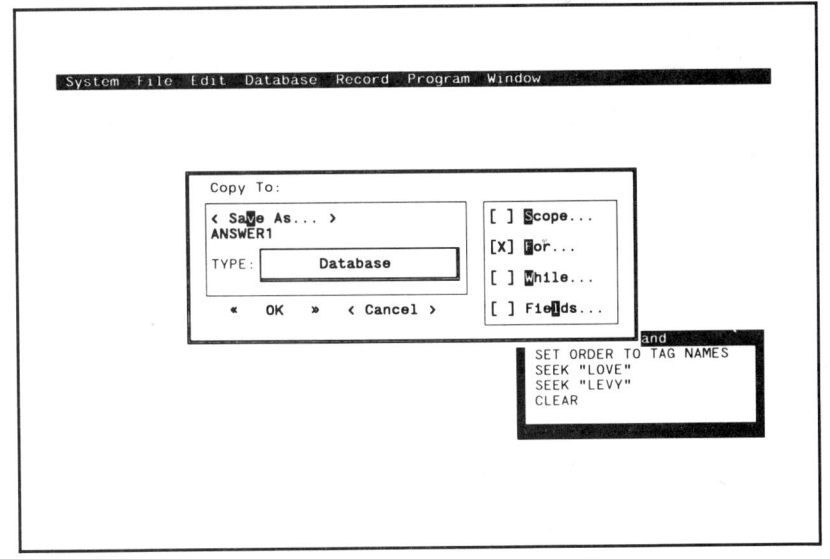

Figure 5.11: Using COPY FOR to create an Answer file

4. Select Open from the File menu. When the Open dialog box appears, use the Type popup control to select Database. Then select ANSWER1.DBF from the scrollable list of files. Select Browse from the Database menu to view it. Scroll until you can see the State field, and you will see that all the records are from California. Then close the Browse window.

The command generated in the Command window is

COPY TO ANSWER1 FOR state = "CA"

AN INDEXED MULTI-RECORD QUERY

You can also do the same thing using WHILE, but you must perform the preliminaries first: use the file with an index and place the pointer on the first matching field.

Even though this database file is not indexed on the State field, you can use a WHILE clause with it if you remember that California residents have zip codes beginning with a 9. After making the ZIP index tag the controlling index, you can use the command **SEEK "9"** to find the first record from California. Then you can use the clause **WHILE STATE = "CA"** to find all of the records from California.

This example shows that sometimes you can use a WHILE clause even though there is no index that would let Rushmore optimize a FOR clause. In this case, you could actually use FOR ZIP = "9" instead of WHILE STATE = "CA", because it happens to be the case that all "9" zip codes are in one state, but in other cases, it would be harder to use a FOR clause than a WHILE clause.

1. Select Open from the File menu. When the Open dialog box appears, select EMPLIST.DBF from the list of files. Select Browse from the Database menu (though it is not necessary) so you can see what you are doing.

2. Select Setup from the Database menu. Select EMPLIST:ZIP from the list of Indexes, and then select the Set Order push button to make it the controlling index. Select the default OK push button to generate the command SET ORDER TO TAG ZIP. Scroll right in the Browse window until you can see the State and Zip fields.

3. Select Seek from the Record menu. Type "**9**" in the expression builder's text box as the character expression to seek. (Do not forget to include the quotation marks.) Then select OK. The pointer moves to the first California record, as shown in Figure 5.12.

4. Select Copy To from the Database menu popup. When the Copy To dialog box appears, select the While check box. The heading of the expression builder text box asks for a WHILE Clause: <expL>. Type **STATE = "CA"** as the logical expression (or create the same expression using the expression builder). Then select OK.

5. In the Copy To dialog box, type **ANSWER2** in the text box under the Save As pushbutton, as the name of the file to copy to. Then select OK to copy the file.

6. To see the result, select Open from the File menu. When the Open dialog box appears, use the Type popup control to select Database. Then use the list of files to select ANSWER2.DBF. Select Browse from the Database menu and scroll right until you can see the State and Zip fields.

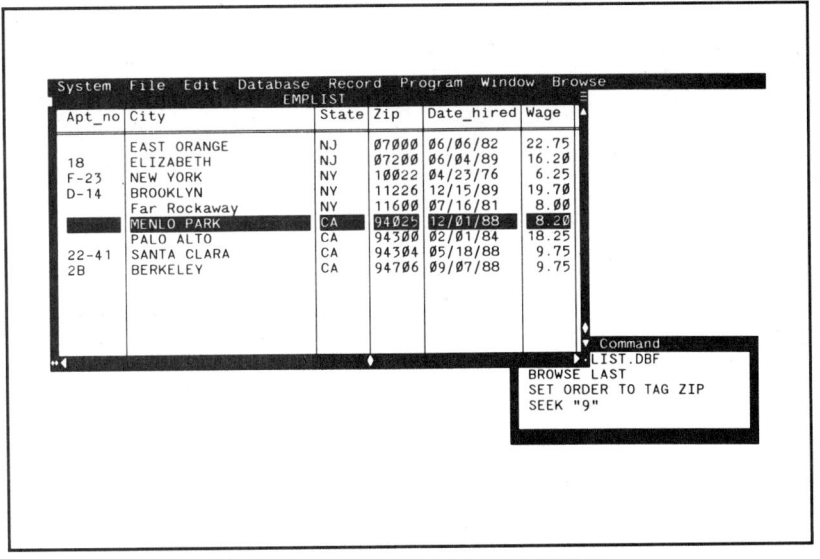

Figure 5.12: Moving the pointer to prepare to use WHILE

Notice that the file has the same records as the ANSWER1 file but that they are in zip code order. Even though this file is not indexed, that is the order in which you copied the records.

If you were working from the command line, you would have entered

    USE EMPLIST ORDER ZIP

then

    SEEK "9"

and then

    COPY TO ANSWER2 WHILE STATE = "CA"

TRICKING FOXPRO INTO COPYING THE STRUCTURE

You will find it instructive at this point to try making an error. Use **COPY WHILE** without using **SEEK** first, so that the pointer is not on a matching record to begin with.

1. Repeat Steps 1 and 2 from the previous exercise to open and browse the EMPLIST file, make the ZIP tag the controlling index, and view the State and Zip fields.

2. Skip Step 3 from the previous exercise, which uses Seek to move the pointer. Then repeat Step 4 to enter a WHILE clause in the Copy To dialog box. Repeat Step 5, but enter ANSWER3 as the name of this file, and then copy the file. To view the result, open ANSWER3.DBF and select Browse, as you did in Step 6.

As you can see, the ANSWER3 file has no records in it. The current record did not meet the criterion of the WHILE clause, so FoxPro did not go any further. You may now close the Browse windows.

In Chapter 2, you learned the **COPY STRUCTURE** command, which you used from the Command window to create a new database with the same structure as an existing one. What you just did is equivalent to copying the structure.

To trick FoxPro into copying the structure using the menu system, just use **COPY TO** with some untrue criterion. Using an impossible criterion, such as WHILE 1 = 2, ensures that FoxPro will not copy any records.

But there is an even easier way of doing it. Remember that when FoxPro uses a WHILE clause, it performs whatever you have instructed it to do until it reaches a record for which it evaluates the logical expression as .F.. You can save it the trouble of doing the evaluation by simply entering .F. as the logical expression of the WHILE clause to begin with.

There is no need to index when you do this. The index is used with WHILE just to make sure that all the matching records are found, a consideration which does not apply in this case.

To save time, try doing this from the Command window:

1. Enter **USE EMPLIST**.
2. Enter **COPY TO ANSWER4 WHILE .F.**
3. When FoxPro is done copying, enter **USE ANSWER4** and then enter **DISP STRU**. You will see that the file has the same structure as EMPLIST but no records, as shown in Figure 5.13.

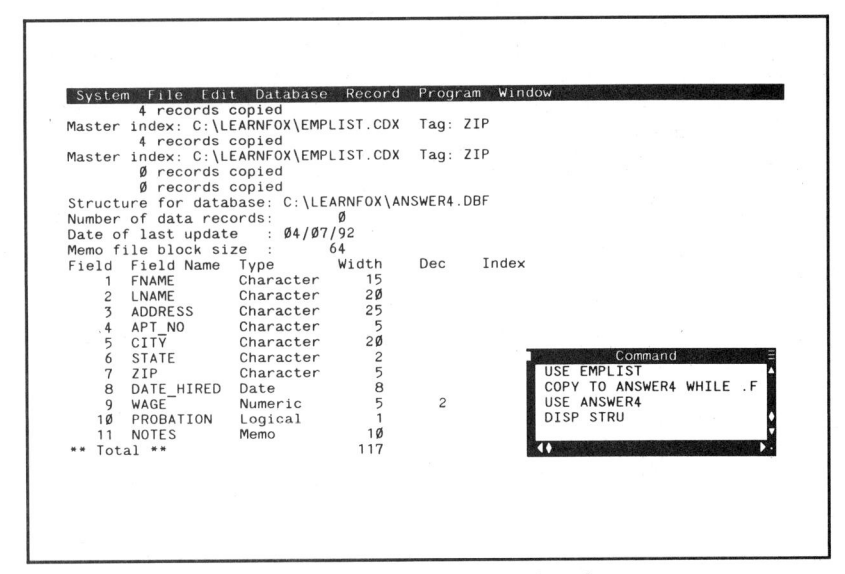

Figure 5.13: FoxPro has been tricked into copying just the structure.

Of course, you can do the same thing from the menu system by repeating all the steps you used in the previous examples but entering .F. in the expression builder text box: you can type it in or select it from the Logical popup.

QUERYING WITH OTHER DATA TYPES

It is very simple to search character or numeric fields. You generally use the equals, greater than, and less than operators with both these data types. The = operator is used most commonly when you are searching character fields, and the >, <, > =, and < = operators are most common when you are searching numeric fields. It will take an extra moment, though, to look at how to search memo and logical fields.

The "included-in" operator, $, can be used for character fields, but is most commonly used to find a substring in a memo. In the next exercise, for example, you will look for employees who are connected with the Christmas fund-raising drive. The only trick to this query is figuring out all the different ways you might have entered the data in the memo field. You need to search for both XMAS and CHRISTMAS in both upper and lower case. Even then, you should read each memo individually, since one says that the employee *cannot* help with the fund raising.

When you are basing a query on a logical field, you do not need to use a logical expression. You may recall that logical expressions are evaluated as true or false. The content of a logical *field,* however, is already one of these values (.T. or .F.). Thus, to find all the people in the EMPLIST database who are on probation, you can use a query with FOR followed by the logical field PROBATION. FoxPro will evaluate this logical field just as it would evaluate any logical expression: as true or false. Likewise, you could use the criterion FOR .NOT. PROBATION to find the records of employees who have .F. in the field.

The following exercise will perform queries using **COPY** with a **FOR** clause, though you could just as well use **LOCATE FOR** and **CONTINUE**.

1. If you want, enter CLEAR to clear the screen. Enter USE EMPLIST to open the EMPLIST database file. Then select Copy To from the Database menu. Type **ANSWER5** in the

text box as the name of the file to copy to, and select the For check box. In the expression builder, type

"XMAS" $ UPPER(NOTES) .OR. "CHRISTMAS" $ UPPER (NOTES)

and select OK. Then select OK from the Copy To dialog box to execute the command.

2. Select Open from the File menu and select ANSWER5.DBF from the scrollable list of file names. Select Browse from the Database menu to view the file. Look at the Notes fields of each record to see that all match the criterion of the query, as shown (for example) in Figure 5.14. When you are done, close the Browse window.

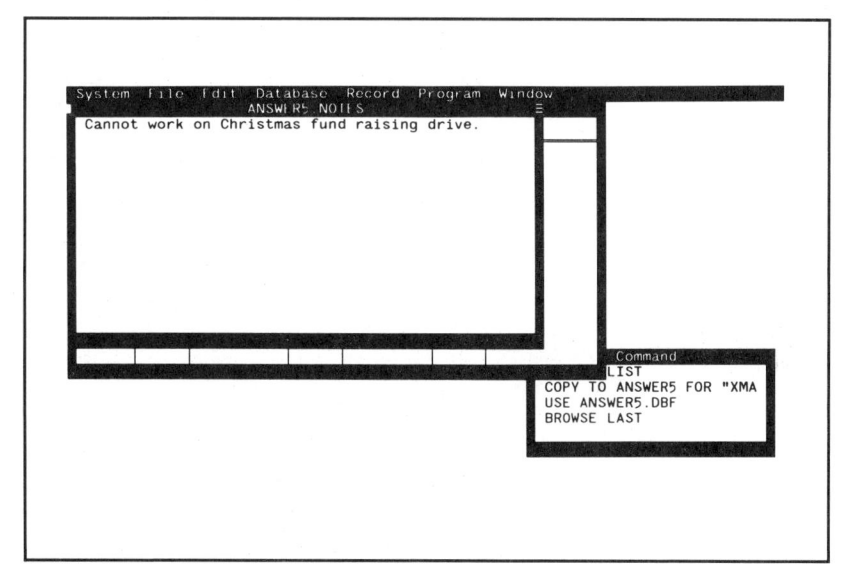

Figure 5.14: Looking at the results of a query for a memo field

3. Again select Open from the File menu popup and select EMPLIST.DBF from the scrollable list of file names. Select Copy To from the Database menu. Type **ANSWER6** in the text box near Save As. Then select the For check box. When

the expression builder appears, select the field PROBATION from the scrollable list of field names: this field name will complete the FOR clause in the expression builder. Select OK to use this expression, and select OK to execute the command.

4. Select Open from the File menu once more and select ANSWER6.DBF from the scrollable list of file names. Select Browse from the Database menu popup to view the file. Scroll to see the Probation field and confirm that all of them are .T., as shown in Figure 5.15. Close the Browse window.

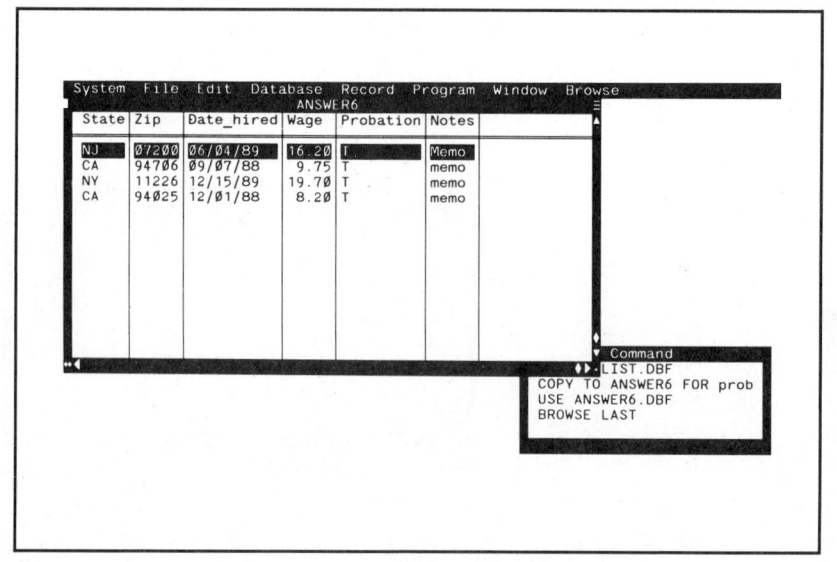

Figure 5.15: Looking at the results of a query for a logical field

When you were looking at the memo fields, you might have noticed that fund raising was spelled in three ways: fund raising, fund-raising, and FUNDRAISING. This gives you an idea of what you are up against when you are searching memo fields.

DEALING WITH DELETED RECORDS

One problem that you will have to deal with when you are using any of these query techniques is how to handle records that are marked for deletion.

In many cases, you do not want these records: you may have removed them from your file, and you do not consider them part of your data, but you may not have gotten around to using the **PACK** command to finalize the deletion.

Yet FoxPro, by default, includes records that are marked for deletion in the output of commands, and this can sometimes create problems. For example, if you use a FOR clause to find the records of certain people you want to telephone, FoxPro will include records that you have marked for deletion—and you might end up telephoning people you thought you had scratched off your list.

You now know enough to be able to deal with these problems in several ways.

The most obvious technique is to use **PACK** before you use any command where deleted records might cause a problem. This method does not take any thought, but it can waste time if you are working with a large database. If you delete records frequently and use these commands frequently, you might have to pack your database dozens of times, which might take hours.

Another way to handle the problem is to use the **SET DELETED** command. You can access this command through the menu system by using the View window, which is discussed in Chapter 7, but it is also easy to use it through the Command window. If you enter the command **SET DELETED ON**, commands that select records will not include any records that are marked for deletion. If you enter the command **SET DELETED OFF**, the commands will include records marked for deletion again.

> Many people find the **SET DELETED** command confusing, since **SET DELETED ON** is the command that turns *off* the deleted records. It is easy to remember if you realize that it means: set the feature that eliminates deleted records on.

You can also use the function DELETED( ) in combination with a single command. If a record is marked for deletion, DELETED( ) returns .T.; if it is not, DELETED( ) returns .F.. By adding .AND. .NOT. DELETED( ) to a logical expression, then, you can do a query that leaves out records marked for deletion. For example, you can use the command

    COPY TO ANSWER1 FOR STATE = "CA" .AND. .NOT. DELETED( )

(all on one line) in order to make a query that is similar to the first one you made in this section but that leaves out deleted records.

You can access DELETED( ) through the logical popup of the expression builder, so you can also generate this function by working with the menu system.

As you can see, there are many ways of accomplishing the same task when you are using FoxPro. The dBASE compatible language gradually grew, with more commands and functions to let you do things more conveniently. There is no need to learn all of the commands and functions—since many of them just do the same things in different ways that different users prefer. You should just be aware of them and learn the ones that let you do what you want in a way that is easiest for you.

SPECIAL TECHNIQUES

You have learned the basic techniques for making queries to find either one record or all the records that match a criterion:

- to do a search for a single record without explicitly using the index, use **LOCATE FOR** and **CONTINUE**
- to do a search for a single record based on the controlling index, use **SEEK**
- to do a search for all matching records without explicitly using the index, use a FOR clause
- to do a search for all matching records based on the controlling index, use a WHILE clause

These techniques are the workhorses that you will constantly use when you are working with FoxPro.

FoxPro also provides two special techniques that you might find make your job much easier on occasion. Both of these are similar to what you have already learned, and it should be easy for you to pick them up at this point.

SETTING A FILTER

There are often times when you want to perform a long series of commands, all of which apply only to records that meet some criterion. Obviously, it would be unwieldy to use the For check box or a

FOR clause with each of these commands separately. For this reason, FoxPro also gives you the option of setting a filter.

After you set a filter, you do not need to worry about adding the criterion to each command. Records that do not meet your criterion are filtered out indefinitely, until you remove the filter.

Using the menu system, you can set a filter by selecting Setup from the Database menu popup. Then use the Filter check box of the Setup dialog box, which lets you enter a criterion in the expression builder. After you do this, only those records that match the criterion will be used with commands you select. The filter will continue to be active until you remove the check from the check box.

1. If you want to clear the screen, enter **CLEAR**. Select Open from the File menu. Then select EMPLIST.DBF from the Open dialog box.

2. Select Setup from the Database menu. When the Setup dialog box appears, select the Filter check box. The expression builder appears, with SET FILTER Expression: <expL> over the text box. Type **STATE = "CA"** in the text box (or use the expression builder to create the same expression). Then select OK.

3. The expression you created appears next to the Filter check box of the Setup dialog box, as shown in Figure 5.16. Select OK, and note that the command generated is

   SET FILTER TO STATE = "CA"

4. Select Browse from the Database menu. Since the filter has been set, only the California records are visible. Only they will be used with any command.

5. Select Setup from the Database menu and select the Filter check box again. The expression builder appears, with STATE = "CA" entered as the expression in its text box. Press Del to delete the expression. Then select OK to return to the Setup dialog box. The check in the Filter check box disappears, and the command **SET FILTER TO** is generated in the Command window. Select OK, and you can see all the records in the Browse window again. Close the Browse window.

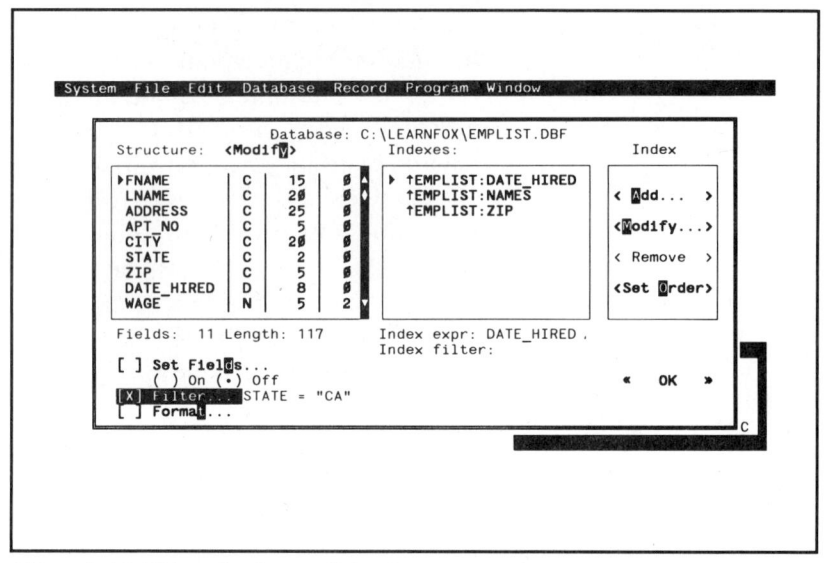

Figure 5.16: Using the Setup dialog box to set a filter

> In some cases, filters are useful for simplifying commands. Even if you only want to use the criterion once, it is sometimes easier to understand what you are doing if you use a filter to set up the criterion, then use the command, and then remove the filter. This is particularly true if the command has many other clauses besides the FOR clause. When you have multiple criteria that would have to be combined, creating a complex and difficult to understand logical expression, it also may be easier to use a filter for one criterion and a FOR clause for the other.

You can create a filter from the Command window by entering **SET FILTER TO** <*logical exp*>. You can remove the filter by entering the command **SET FILTER TO** without any logical expression included; you might want to read this as "set filter to nothing."

Keep in mind that a filter works like a FOR clause: Rushmore is used to increase speed if the filter is based on an index expression; otherwise, FoxPro reads all the records in the file to find the matching ones. In the latter case, the filter is slow if you are working with a large file.

BUILDING A QUERY INTO AN INDEX

You saw in the last chapter that the Index dialog box contains both a For and a While check box. Now you know how to use these check boxes: you use them to create indexes that include only the records which meet a certain logical expression. For example, you can create an index that includes only records of employees who live in California. Whenever you update the database with that index active, records will continue to be included in that index as long as they are from California. Any time you want to query for records in California, all you have to do is use the file with this index as its main index, and FoxPro will return even the most recent California additions to the database; records not from California will be disregarded.

It is most common to create the index using the For check box, rather than going through the extra trouble of using While. In the following example, then, you will use the For check box to see how powerful a query built into an index is.

1. Select New from the File menu. From the New dialog box, select the Index radio button. Then select OK.

2. When the Index On dialog box appears, move the cursor under the Expr pushbutton and type

   UPPER(LNAME) + UPPER(FNAME)

   (Or you could select the Expr pushbutton and use the expression builder to create this same expression.) As the tag name, enter **CALNAMES**. Then select the Move pushbutton to move the expression to the Index On box.

3. Select the For pushbutton. The expression builder appears. Type **STATE = "CA"** in the push box, or use the expression builder to create this same logical expression. Then select OK.

4. The Index On dialog box now includes both the expression to index on and the logical expression of the FOR clause, as in Figure 5.17. Select OK to create the index. Note that the command generated is like the usual **INDEX** command plus the usual FOR clause:

   INDEX ON UPPER(LNAME) + UPPER(FNAME) FOR STATE = "CA" TAG CALNAMES

5. Select Setup from the Database menu. Select the NAMES index tag from the Indexes list, and select the Set Order pushbutton to make this the controlling index. The Setup dialog box should now look like Figure 5.18. Select OK.

6. Select Browse from the Database menu. You now can see all the records in the Browse window in alphabetical order. Select Append Record twice (from the Browse popup) in order to enter these two new employees:

   Fname: **JOSEPH** *Lname:* **CRUZ** *Address:* **1450 VALENCIA ST.** *Apt_no:* **4** *City:* **SAN FRANCISCO** *State:* **CA** *Zip:* **94101**

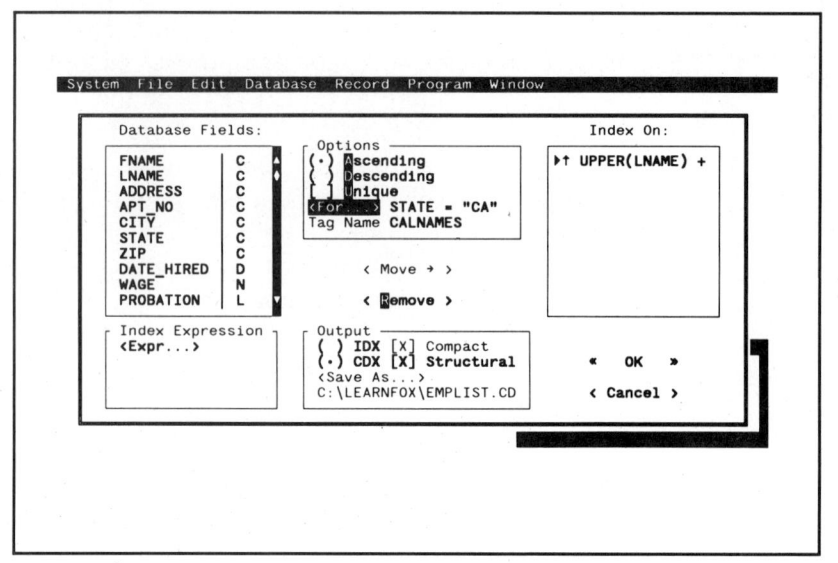

Figure 5.17: Indexing with a FOR clause

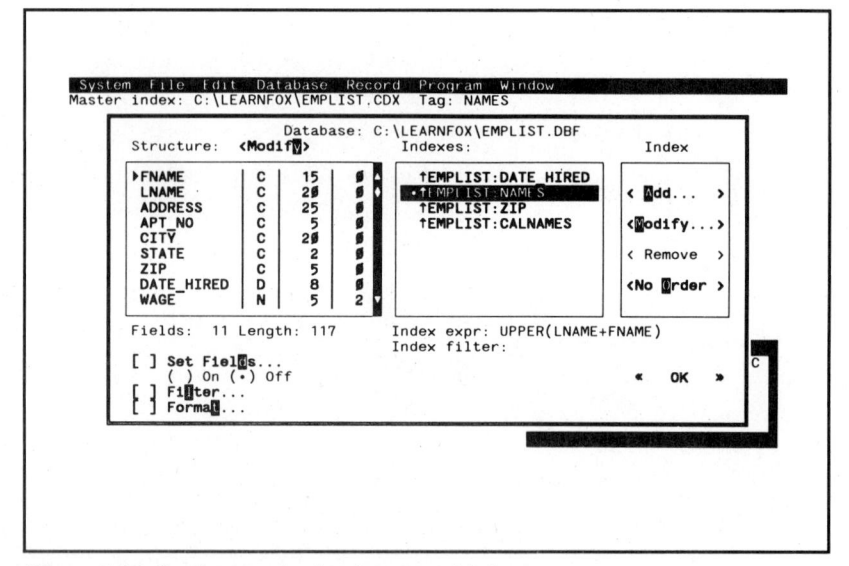

Figure 5.18: Setting up the database to add data

Date_hired: **03/04/90** *Wage:* **19.00** *Probation:* **T** *Notes:* (none)

Fname: **HENRIETTA** *Lname:* **JOHNSON** *Address:* **2204 GRAND CONCOURSE** *Apt_no:* **18-F** *City:* **BRONX** *State:* **NY** *Zip:* **10405** *Date_hired:* **03/12/90** *Wage:* **6.05** *Probation:* **T** *Notes:* (none)

Then press Ctrl-End to save the changes.

7. Select Setup again from the Database menu. Select CAL-NAMES from the list of indexes. Then select Set Order to make it the controlling index, and select OK. Then select Browse from the Database menu. Notice that the Browse window includes the one new record from California that you just added.

8. Select Setup once again from the Database menu. Select DATE_HIRED from the list of indexes. Then select Set Order to make it the controlling index, and select OK. Notice that both of the new records that you just added are at the end of the database, since they are the two with the most recent Date_hired. Close the Browse window.

Despite its power, the query built into an index obviously is not useful for every purpose. You have to weigh the time saved by building the query into an index against the time lost by having to maintain the index.

RESTRICTING THE QUERY

In general, the dialog boxes that you use to make queries include a check box for Scope as well as ones for For and While. Some of these dialog boxes also include a check box for Fields.

Unlike For and While, the Scope and Fields check boxes are not essential to making queries. They are simply conveniences that let you restrict what will appear in the result. If you think of how the database appears in the Browse window—in the form of a table—

then Scope cuts the query off vertically by determining how many *records* will be considered, and Fields cuts the query off horizontally, by determining which *fields* will appear in the result.

SCOPE

Scope merely refers to the number of records that FoxPro searches in the course of performing a command. Many commands can be used with Scope clauses: they do not necessarily have any inherent relation to FOR and WHILE clauses.

The Help window can tell you which commands can be used with Scope clauses and where they must be placed if other clauses are also used. Descriptions of these commands include the word [*scope*] to indicate where a Scope clause goes, with the square brackets indicating that it is optional. The word *scope,* though, is not actually used in the clause. Instead, Scope clauses consist of any of the following words:

- **ALL** The command acts on all of the records of the database (unless some other clause, such as a FOR or a WHILE clause, restricts it)
- **NEXT** <*number*> The command acts on whatever number of records is specified, counting the *current* record (where the pointer is) as the NEXT 1.
- **RECORD** <*number*> The command acts on the record whose number is specified. This option is not often useful, as you do not usually know the numbers of particular records in your database.
- **REST** The command acts on the records beginning with the current record and continuing until the last record in the file.

Commands have a default scope—the scope that is usually most convenient to use them with. For example, **DELETE** has a default scope of NEXT 1, since you usually want to delete just the current record. You have already used **DELETE** without specifying a scope, and you have seen that it just deletes the record where the pointer is.

> Record numbers always refer to the order in which the records appear in the actual database—not to the order in which they seem to appear because an index is being used. Record 1 is the first record that you entered in the database, not the first record in alphabetical order or any other index order.

> One other minor difference between the two is that **DISPLAY ALL** will display records one screen at a time, pausing and asking you to press any key to see the next screen. This difference makes **DISPLAY ALL** the easiest way of scrolling through data to view it on the screen if you are working from the Command window.

But you can also use commands such as **DELETE ALL** or **DELETE NEXT 10** to override the default scope.

In Chapter 3, you learned two commands which both let you view data, the main difference being that one—**DISPLAY**—lets you view one record and the other—**LIST**—lets you view the entire database. Now you can see that the main difference between these commands is their default scope. **DISPLAY ALL** is virtually identical to **LIST**, and **LIST NEXT 1** is virtually identical to **DISPLAY** (though there are a couple of other, very minor, differences apart from their scope).

To see how to use these options through the menu system, by using a Scope check box, you will try deleting all of your records. Don't worry—remember that this command just *marks* records for deletion, and you can use Recall with a Scope check box to get them all back.

1. If you want to clear the screen, enter **CLEAR**. Select Delete from the Record menu. When the Delete dialog box appears, select the Scope check box. When the Scope dialog box appears, as shown in Figure 5.19, select the All radio button. Then select OK to return to the Delete dialog box, and select Delete. Notice that the command **DELETE ALL** has been generated. Select Browse from the Database menu, and note that all the records have bullets to their left to indicate that they are marked for deletion.

2. Select Recall from the Record menu. When the Recall dialog box appears, select the Scope check box. When the Scope dialog box appears, select the All radio button. Then select OK to return to the Recall dialog box and select Recall. Notice that the command **RECALL ALL** is generated and that all the bullets have disappeared from the Browse window to indicate that the records are no longer marked for deletion. Close the Browse window.

When you first used the Scope check box with either Delete or Recall, the Next radio button was chosen and the default scope 1 was written to its right. Because this is the default scope of the command, just the current record is deleted or recalled if you do not use the Scope check box at all.

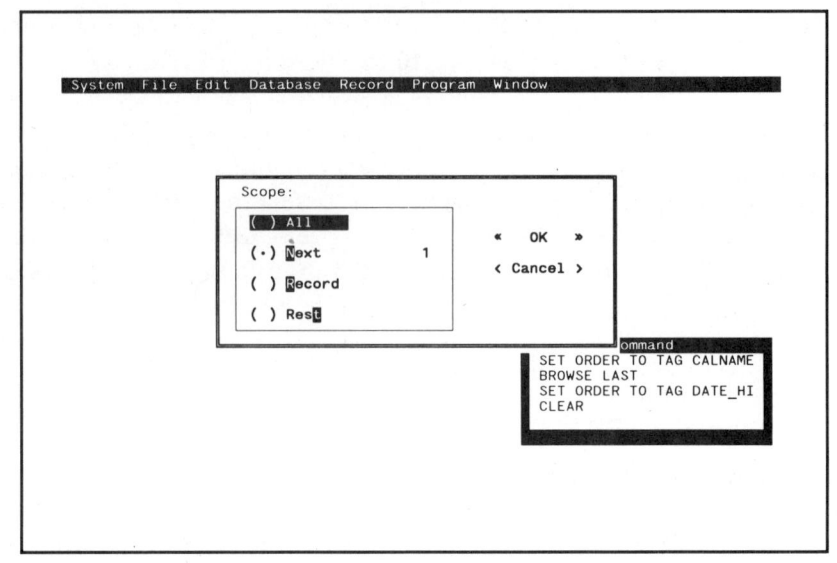

```
┌─────────────────────────────────────────────────────────────┐
│  System  File  Edit  Database  Record  Program  Window       │
│                                                              │
│                                                              │
│              ┌──────────────────────────────┐                │
│              │ Scope:                       │                │
│              │   ( ) All          « OK  »   │                │
│              │   (•) Next    1              │                │
│              │   ( ) Record    < Cancel >   │                │
│              │   ( ) Rest                   │                │
│              └──────────────────────────────┘                │
│                                    ┌─────────ommand──────┐   │
│                                    │ SET ORDER TO TAG CALNAME │
│                                    │ BROWSE LAST          │   │
│                                    │ SET ORDER TO TAG DATE_HI │
│                                    │ CLEAR                │   │
│                                    └──────────────────────┘   │
│                                                              │
└─────────────────────────────────────────────────────────────┘
```

Figure 5.19: The Scope dialog box

FIELDS

Just as you can use a command with a Scope clause to restrict the records that the command applies to, you can also use a command with a FIELDS clause to restrict the fields that it applies to. You should check the Help window to see where the fields list fits into the syntax of any given command.

Unlike a Scope clause, which cannot contain the word *scope,* a FIELDS clause can either contain the word FIELDS followed by a list of fields (or expressions) or it can simply contain the list of fields (or expressions). In either case, commas must be included between each of the fields or expressions in the list. Some commands *require* the word FIELDS. To avoid confusion, it is best to always use the word FIELDS if you are working from the Command window.

Like a scope, a fields list can be combined with many commands and can also be used in conjunction with FOR or WHILE clauses. For example, try using Copy to create a new file that has only the names and addresses of the employees who live in California.

1. If you want to clear the screen, enter **CLEAR**. Select Copy To from the Database menu.

> You can use a FIELDS clause with expressions instead of just with field names in order to make the output look better. For example, in the next exercise, you will use PROPER(TRIM (FNAME) + " " +LNAME) to get a better-looking listing than you would get with just FNAME, LNAME.

2. When the Copy dialog box appears, select the For check box. In the text box of the expression builder, enter **STATE = "CA"** (or use the expression builder to create this expression). Then select OK to return to the Copy dialog box.

3. Select the Fields check box. FoxPro displays the field picker dialog box shown in Figure 5.20. Select the FNAME, LNAME, ADDRESS, APT_NO, CITY, STATE, and ZIP fields from the scrollable list of fields to move them to the Selected Fields list. Then select OK to return to the Copy dialog box. Enter **ANSWER7** in the text box near Save As and select OK to copy the file.

4. Select Open from the File menu, and select ANSWER7 from the list of files in the Open dialog box. Select Browse from the Database menu to look at the new file. Scroll right to see that it includes only the fields you listed and only the records from California. Close the Browse window.

5. Since all these ANSWER files were just created as exercises, you can delete them now. Enter **USE** to close the current file. Then enter **RUN DEL ANSWER?.*** to use DOS to delete all these files.

The DOS command uses two wild-card characters. ? stands for any single character; it makes the command include all the files with numbers following the word ANSWER. * stands for any word; it makes the command include the memo files with .FPT extensions as well as the database files with .DBF extensions.

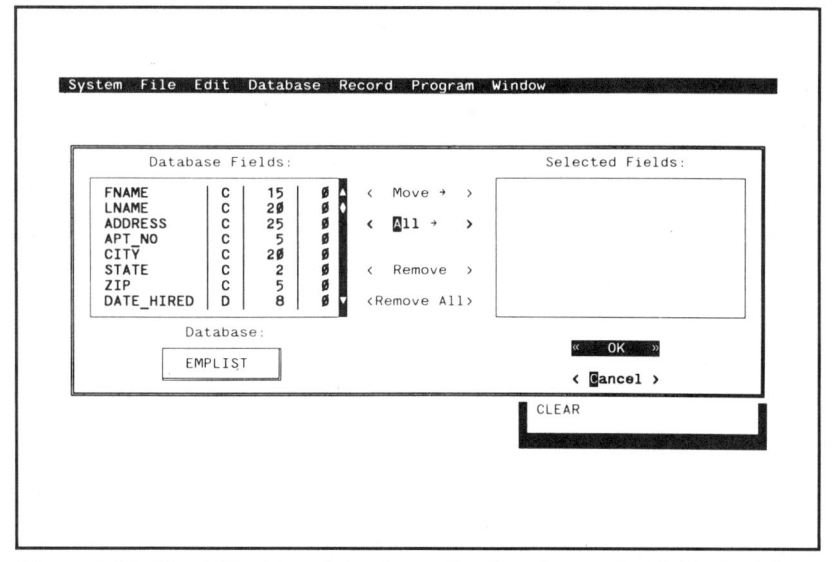

Figure 5.20: The field picker dialog box called by selecting the Fields check box

Many menu selections include only For, While, and Scope check boxes in their dialog boxes, and leave out the Fields check box. If you are working with these menu choices, you can still restrict the fields they apply to by using the Setup dialog box first.

You can set fields in much the same way that you set a filter. You use the Filter check box of the Setup dialog box to set a filter that works just like having a FOR clause in a command. Likewise, you can use the Set Fields check box of the Setup dialog box in the same way. It works just like having a FIELDS clause in a command—with one difference: the Set Fields check box has On and Off radio buttons under it. This allows you to turn off the fields setting temporarily and then turn it on again without going through the bother of choosing the fields again.

You can do the same thing working from the Command window by using the command **SET FIELDS TO** <*field names*>. This command is used together with the commands SET FIELDS OFF and SET FIELDS ON, which temporarily suspend and reactivate the field setting you have chosen. The command **SET FIELDS TO ALL** will make all of the fields in the current database active.

THE EASIEST POSSIBLE REPORT ON A QUERY: LIST WITH OPTIONS

Remember in Chapter 3 you used the command **LIST** to create the simplest possible report—easier than anything you can do with the menu. You can also use **LIST** in combination with a FOR clause and a field list to create rather precise custom reports without using the special report generator (which you will learn about in the next chapter). Of course, the appearance of the report will not be as good as it would be if you had used the report generator to design it, but **LIST** is the easiest way to get a quick printout of your data for your own use—for example, if you simply want to print out names and phone numbers of people who live in California, so you can telephone them today.

Since you can use expressions as part of the field list, you can even include calculated fields in the report. Try, for example, getting an alphabetical listing of the names and wages of your employees who live in California, and add a calculated field, using the expression

40 * WAGE to calculate basic weekly wages (assuming that all employees work a base 40-hour week).

1. Enter **USE EMPLIST ORDER NAMES**

2. Enter **CLEAR**, then

   LIST FIELDS LNAME, FNAME, WAGE, 40*WAGE FOR STATE = "CA" OFF

3. To make the listing look nicer, you can combine the first and last names, so the listing has a single name column. Enter

   LIST FIELDS PROPER(TRIM(FNAME)+ " " +LNAME), WAGE, 40*WAGE FOR STATE = "CA" OFF

If the listing on the screen, shown in Figure 5.21, looks good to you, you can add TO PRINT at the very end of the command in order to get a quick printout of the data you need.

If you want a report that includes page breaks, page headers and footers, and the like, you can add TO FILE <*file name*> after OFF to save the output of the report in a plain ASCII text file. Most word processors can import ASCII files (some call them DOS text files)

> Remember that the OFF used with the **LIST** command simply makes the command leave out the record numbers, which you do not want in an alphabetical listing. OFF usually comes at the end of a **LIST** command—only TO PRINT and TO FILE can come after it—so, to avoid confusion, you must remember that it has nothing to do with the preceding clauses.

> Do not use proportional fonts when you print the data of a text file generated by FoxPro. Remember that FoxPro pads out the space between columns by using the blank character. Proportional fonts use less space for blanks than for other characters, so that they will not align the columns properly. Of course, you can use proportional fonts to add a report title.

```
 System  File  Edit  Database  Record  Program  Window
 LNAME                  FNAME               WAGE    40*WAGE
 CHANG                  EDNA                 9.75    390.00
 CRUZ                   JOSEPH              19.00    760.00
 NIXON                  NANCY               18.25    730.00
 PERLOW                 MICHELLE             9.75    390.00
 SKINNER                JAMES                8.20    328.00

 PROPER(TRIM(FNAME)+" "+LNAME)  WAGE    40*WAGE
 Edna Chang                      9.75    390.00
 Joseph Cruz                    19.00    760.00
 Nancy Nixon                    18.25    730.00
 Michelle Perlow                 9.75    390.00
 James Skinner                   8.20    328.00

                                        Command
                               USE EMPLIST ORDER NAMES
                               CLEAR
                               LIST FIELDS LNAME,FNAME,
                               LIST FIELDS PROPER(TRIM(
```

Figure 5.21: Using LIST with options to create a report

and they can add any formatting you want to the data. You can change the headings above the columns and even use a variety of fonts if your word processor supports them.

You can see now how worthwhile it is to know about FoxPro commands—and about the different types of expressions and clauses that can be used with many of them. Though they have taken you a bit of extra time to learn, the extra power that they give you will more than repay you for the trouble. As you have just seen, a one-line command can produce an entire report for you.

Of course, there are also times when you want reports with more sophisticated features—for example, reports that group your data to make it easier for you to analyze. For these, you can use the FoxPro report generator, which you will learn about in the next chapter.

Chapter 6

Generating
Reports and Mailing Labels

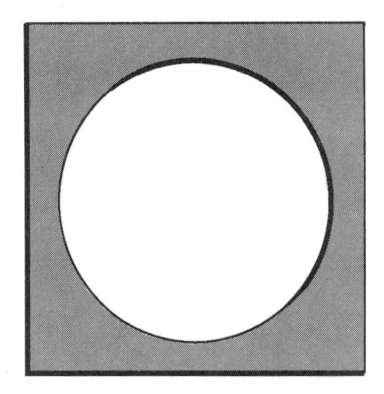

REPORTS AND MAILING LABELS ARE AMONG THE most important applications of any database program. Now that you have a thorough background in FoxPro basics, it will be easy for you to learn to use the program's report and label generators. These features of FoxPro let you lay out the report or labels on the screen—an easy, visual approach to designing the final product.

To make the best use of these features, you must be able to use FoxPro expressions to specify what will be in the report or label, to use indexes to print out the data in the order you want, and to use FOR or WHILE clauses to determine what data is printed out. For example, you can use expressions such as PROPER(ADDRESS) to capitalize reports and labels properly. You can use indexes to print out reports in alphabetical order or mailing labels in zip code order. And you can use a FOR clause to print out labels only for a state you specify.

By now, you have a strong enough background in these fundamentals that it should be easy for you to use them with the report and label generators.

CREATING REPORTS

There are two steps to creating FoxPro reports. First, you must design the *report form*. Then you can actually produce the report.

The report form determines how field data, text, and graphics are laid out, and also lets you group and summarize data.

You create a new report form in the same way you create a new database file or a new index: simply select New from the File menu and then select the Report radio button. This command lets you use the report layout window, shown in Figure 6.1. As usual, FoxPro names the report form Untitled until you select Save As from the File menu to save it and give it a name. (If you are working from the Command window, you can enter the command **CREATE REPORT** to use the report layout window in this way. Alternately, you can enter **CREATE REPORT** <*file name*> to name the report from the beginning.)

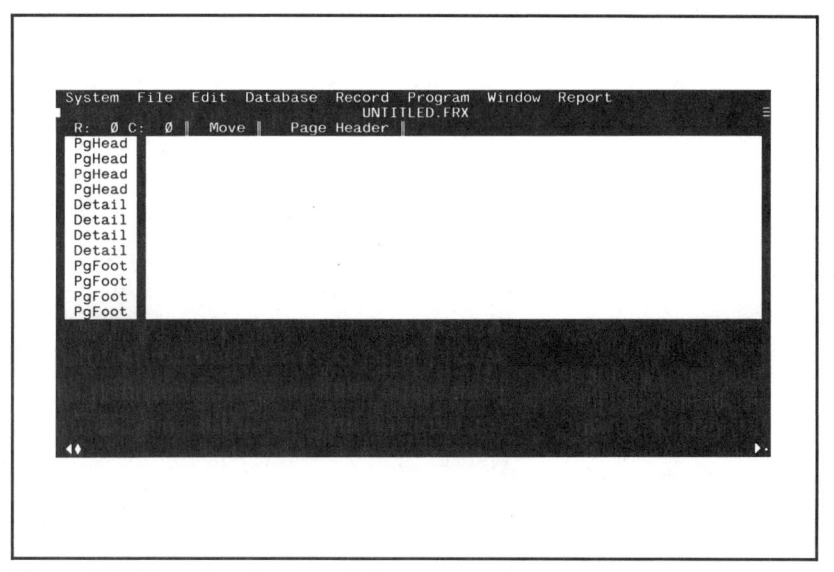

Figure 6.1: The report layout window

Before you can create a report, it is best to open the database file and the index you want to use for the report. (As you will see later, you can save the report's "environment" so that the index is opened automatically when you want to produce the report.)

As you can see from the illustration, a Report menu pad is added to the menu bar when you are using the report layout window. You can see that the report is divided into bands: you can use the menu to add expressions or graphic characters in any of these bands, and you can simply type text into them.

Also notice the status line at the top of the window. The numbers at the left, next to R and C, tell you the Row and Column of the cursor location. The word to the right of that tells you what action is currently being performed, such as moving the cursor, drawing a box, or defining a field. The final item of the status line tells you the band where the cursor is located.

The report layout window will be discussed in detail in the next section.

> DBASE, FoxBase, and other earlier dBASE compatible programs saved report forms with the extension .FRM. If you are running older applications on FoxPro, it will be able to use these .FRM reports without any trouble, and will include them in the list of report forms for you to choose from. The one possible confusion arises if you are working from the command line, where you can enter the report's name without the extension: If there are two reports with the same name, FoxPro will use the one with the .FRX extension and ignore the one with the .FRM extension.

When you have finished designing the report and save it, FoxPro adds the extension .FRX to the name you give the report. The .FRX file is actually a database file that holds information about the report; it has an associated memo file with the extension .FRT.

You can modify an existing report form, also, in the obvious way. You selected New from the File menu popup to *create* a report form; now you select Open to *modify* one. After selecting Open, you would select the Report radio button, and select from the scrollable list the name of the report form you want to modify. (From the Command window, simply enter **MODIFY REPORT** <*file name*>.)

Once you have designed and saved the report form that you want, you can use it at any time to produce actual reports. To do this, you select Report from the Database menu, and FoxPro displays the Report dialog box shown in Figure 6.2.

To determine which report form is used, you can either type the name of any existing report form for the current database into the text box, or select the Form pushbutton to choose from a list of all the reports for the current database. As you can see from the figure, this dialog box includes an Environment check box. If you saved the environment when you created the report form, checking this option will

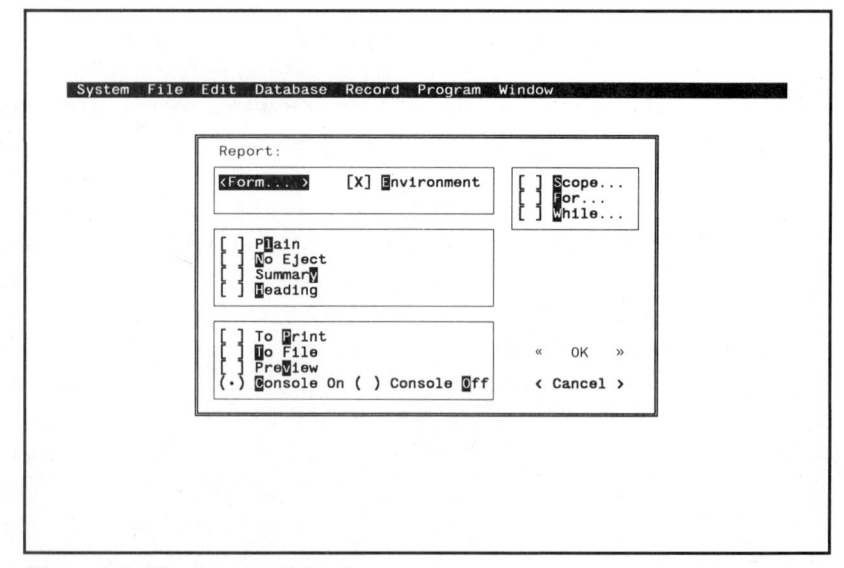

Figure 6.2: The Report dialog box

automatically open the index you need and set the other environmental variables that you saved.

This dialog box also includes Scope, For, and While check boxes, so that you can select which records to include in the report. If you have designed a report form that lists employee names and addresses, for example, you can use the For check box to print out the report with only the employees from California, only the employees who earn more than a certain wage, or whatever.

The dialog box also includes a set of check boxes that let you choose these printing options:

- **Plain:** prints the report with a page header only on the first page, and suppresses headers on following pages.
- **No Eject:** stops the printer from automatically ejecting a page before printing it.
- **Summary:** prints only the data in the summary band of the report. (You will learn below how to add this summary band.)
- **Heading:** lets you add an extra heading line to each page of the report—just type the extra heading in the text box.

Finally, this dialog box also has check boxes that let you decide whether to send the report to the printer, to a text file on disk, or simply to preview it on the screen. The Console On and Console Off radio buttons next to these check boxes determine whether the report is displayed on the screen while it is produced.

Working from the Command window, enter **REPORT FORM** <*file name*> to produce a report. The most important options with this command are a FOR or WHILE clause to determine which records are printed, which can be followed by TO PRINT or TO FILE <*file name*> to send the output to the printer or a text file respectively. (See the Help window for all the options that can be used with this command.)

This discussion has given you a general idea of the two-step process of creating reports: designing the report form and then producing the report. Now we will look in detail at how to design a report form.

> Reports will be printed or sent to a text file more quickly if you select the Console Off radio button. Remember also that the command to produce a report, like most commands, is interrupted if you press Esc—a feature that is often useful when you are producing a report on large databases.

THE REPORT LAYOUT WINDOW

The layout window that you use to design report forms is divided into three bands, each with several lines. There are bands for page header, detail, and page footer. The header and footer, of course, appear at the top and bottom of each page. You use the detail band to enter an example of what you want included in the report. The data that you want in the report is entered in the detail band just once; the final, printed report repeats it for each record to be included.

In addition to the three bands that are in the report layout window to begin with, you can use the Report menu popup to add bands for the following:

- **title:** The report title appears only once at the beginning of the report, unlike the header, which is repeated at the top of each page.

- **summary:** The report summary appears at the end of the report, unlike the footer, which is repeated at the bottom of each page. It is common for the summary to include some calculation—for example, the total number of workers and the total payroll.

- **groupings with headers and footers:** Groupings let you divide your data. For example, you can group all the employees by state.

You can choose to have your titles and summaries on pages separate from the rest of the report. Groupings also can begin at whatever point they naturally occur or, if you choose, on a new page. You can also use the menu to add or remove lines for each band. Bands may be any number of lines, but the entire report form may have no more than a total of 255 lines for all the bands combined.

Any of the bands can include

- **fields or field expressions,** which you place by using the Report menu

- **text** that you simply type anywhere on the form and which you can edit by using the Report menu

- **lines or boxes,** which you add using the Report menu. These simple graphics are created using the line characters that are part of the extended DOS character set. They can be used to make the report look more attractive and to highlight important data.

The Report menu also lets you preview the page, that is, to see on the screen what the printed report will look like. If you are not satisfied with the layout you created, it is very easy to change it.

Anything that you enter in the report layout window is an *object*. A block of text becomes an object when you press Enter or reach the end of a line. Before you press Enter, you can edit the text in the ordinary way. After you press Enter, it can be selected and manipulated, but can be edited only by selecting the Text option from the Report menu popup. Fields and expressions, lines and boxes, and even words or lines of text are all treated as objects, which you can select and then move or delete using either a mouse or the keyboard, in the ways described below.

MANIPULATING OBJECTS USING A MOUSE

To place the pointer or the cursor on a box, you must place it on one of the lines that makes up the border of the box.

To select an object in the layout window using the mouse, put the pointer on it and click. To select more than one object at once, hold Shift the whole time you are clicking on the objects.

Once the objects are selected, drag them to move them. When they are located where you want them, click anywhere outside the object (or press Enter) to deselect them. Pressing Del or Backspace will delete any objects that are selected.

To resize an object, place the pointer on it and press Ctrl and the mouse button. The box blinks to show that it is selected. Drag the mouse to make the box larger or smaller, and release the mouse button to deselect it when it is the right size.

MANIPULATING OBJECTS USING THE KEYBOARD

You can move the cursor anywhere in the layout window by using the arrow keys. Or you can press Tab or Shift-Tab to move the cursor from object to object.

To select an object in the layout window using the keyboard, place the cursor on it and press the space bar. To select more than one object at once, hold the Shift key while using the arrow key to move the cursor; when the cursor is in the new object, press Shift and the space bar to select it.

Once the object is highlighted to show it is selected, use the arrow keys to move it. When it is located where you want it, press Enter to deselect it. You can delete an object that is selected by pressing the Del or Backspace key.

To resize an object, place the cursor on it and press Ctrl and the space bar. The box blinks to show that it is selected. Use the right or down arrow keys to resize the box. Press Enter to deselect it when it is the right size.

> Since you can only move the bottom and right lines of a box to resize it using the keyboard, it is best to move it before resizing it, if you need to do both. First move the upper left corner of the box to where you want it to be. Then adjust the right and bottom lines.

MANIPULATING MULTIPLE OBJECTS

You can also select multiple objects by creating what is called a *selection marquee*.

Using a mouse, begin with the pointer outside of the objects you want to select, then hold down the mouse button and drag to create a box (the marquee) around the objects. Select the objects within the marquee by releasing the mouse button.

Using the keyboard, start by placing the cursor outside of the objects you want to select, then press the space bar while using the arrow keys to draw the marquee around the objects. Press Enter to select the objects within the marquee.

COPYING OBJECTS AND USING MULTIPLE REPORT WINDOWS

You can use the Edit menu in the ordinary way to cut or copy and paste objects. After the object or objects are selected, just select Cut or Copy from the Edit menu. Then, at a later time, you can select Paste from the Edit menu to paste whatever was cut or copied to the new location of the cursor.

You can even cut or copy and paste among windows. You can open multiple report windows to work on several report forms. Use them in the same way you use any windows: cycle among them or resize

> You can open any number of reports simultaneously. The only limitations are the amount of memory your computer has and the number of file handles in your CONFIG.SYS file.

and move them so you can see more than one report form on the screen at a time.

For example, imagine that you need to create a report with features similar to some you have already laid out on an earlier report. After selecting New from the File menu to create the new report form, select Open from the File menu and open the report that you can borrow features from. Select the objects you need, and select Copy from the Edit menu. Then close that report window, and paste them in the location where you want them in the new report.

ADDING STYLES AND COMMENTS TO OBJECTS

If you select a text object by placing the cursor on it and pressing Enter or by double clicking it with the mouse, FoxPro displays a dialog box that lets you select a style (bold, italic, underline, superscript, or subscript) or add a comment to the object.

If you select the Comment check box, FoxPro lets you enter information for the object (or edit a comment you entered earlier). The information is not displayed in the report and is purely for your own use. It can be a description of the object or any other text you want to enter as a reminder for yourself.

THE REPORT MENU

Most of the options of the Report menu popup, shown in Figure 6.3, are simple and easy to use. If you select Field, however, you call up the Report Expression dialog box, which contains a number of special features. These special features are not often needed. We will cover them here briefly, but keep in mind that the best way to learn to create reports is to look through the entire Report menu relatively quickly to see what it can do.

PAGE LAYOUT

If you select Page Layout from the Report menu, you can use the Page Layout dialog box shown in Figure 6.4 to set margins, page length, and the like.

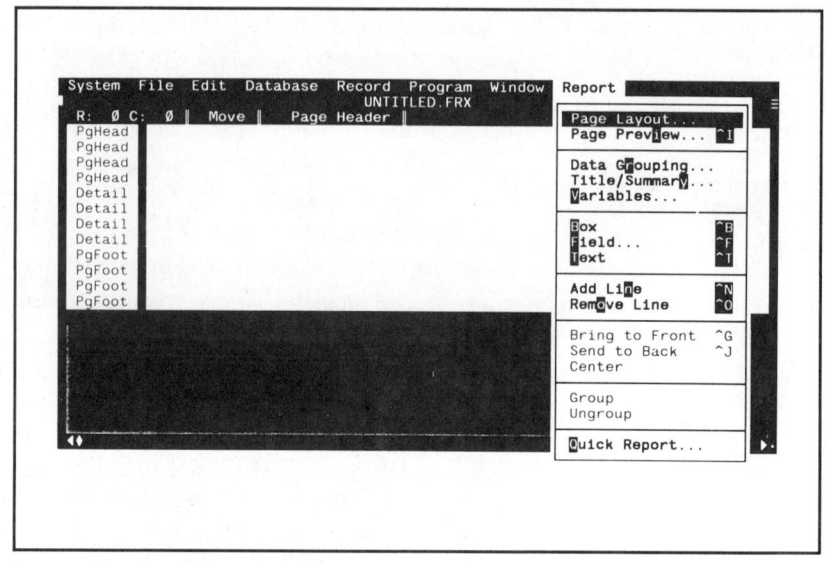

Figure 6.3: The Report menu popup

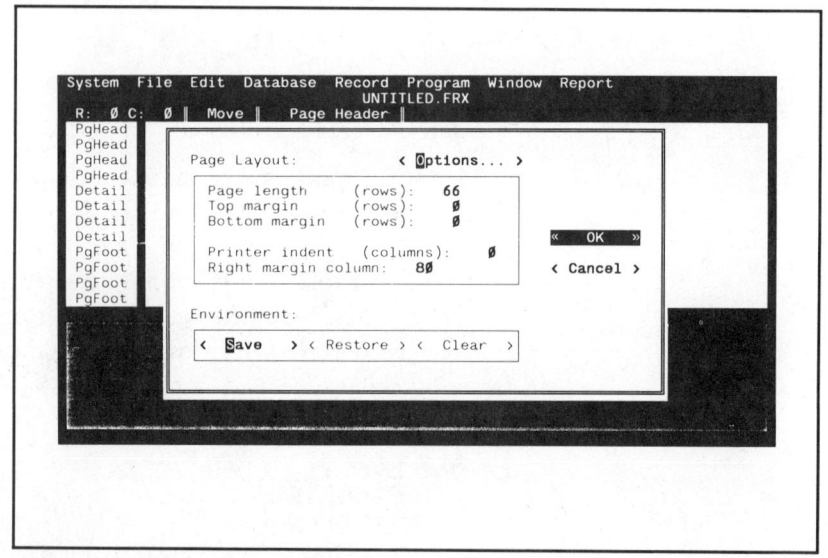

Figure 6.4: The Page Layout dialog box

Page Length determines how many lines will be printed on a single page. FoxPro subtracts the number of lines for the top and bottom margins from the total number of lines on the page to determine how many lines to print. The default Page Length setting of 66 lines is what most printers print on ordinary 8½-by-11-inch paper. Change this setting only if you are using some unusual paper (such as legal-size paper) or have a printer (such as an HP LaserJet) that does not print the standard 66 lines per page.

Top Margin and Bottom Margin determine the number of blank lines that appear at the top and bottom of each page. On most printers, six lines are equal to one inch, and this is often a good setting for each margin.

Printer Indent (Columns) determines the size of the left margin. Most fonts on most printers print ten characters to the inch; so 10 is often chosen for the left margin.

> It is best to set the left and right margins when you first begin designing the report, so that you can take the ultimate printing width into account as you lay out the data.

The Right Margin Column (in combination with the printer indent) determines the size of the right margin. Your computer screen displays 80 characters across, and most printers print only 80 characters of an unproportioned font. (At 10 characters per inch, most printers will not print more than 80 characters even though 8½-inch paper has enough space for 85.) If you choose 10 for the printer indent so that there is a 1-inch left margin, choosing 65 for the right margin column will create a 1-inch right margin: the 10 columns of the left margin plus the 65 columns of text add up to 75 columns, which is 10 columns, or 1 inch, away from the right edge of the page. These are standard margins; of course, the actual right and left margins you choose depend on how much data you have to fit into your report and how wide your printer is. A report can be a maximum of 255 columns wide.

If you select the Options pushbutton of this dialog box, FoxPro displays the Options dialog box, with the following check boxes:

- **Page eject before printing:** FoxPro sends a form-feed to the printer before printing the report, so it begins on a new page.

- **Page eject after printing:** FoxPro sends a form-feed to the printer after printing the report, so that the final page of the report is ejected even if it is not completely filled with text.

- **Plain Page:** The report is printed with the page header on the first page only, not on the following pages.
- **Summary Report:** The detail band is not printed, only the summary bands.
- **Add Alias:** An alias is added to all fields in the report. This is an advanced option needed only by programmers who open the database file with another name.

The three Environment buttons at the bottom of this dialog box have the following functions:

- **Save:** lets you save the environment settings, such as the index that is open, so they are used automatically when the report is produced. If you do not select this option, FoxPro displays an alert that lets you save the environment when you save the report form.
- **Restore:** lets you restore the environment settings for the report. Ordinarily, the Environment check box of the Open dialog box is checked by default when you open a report file, so the environment is restored automatically. If you open the report file without the restoring the environment, however, you can use this pushbutton to restore it at any time.
- **Clear:** clears the environment settings for the report. Though the settings are cleared from memory, they are still saved on disk. To change them permanently, save the new environment when you save the report form.

To save the report, you can select Save from the File menu or press Ctrl-W if you are using the keyboard. FoxPro then gives you the option of saving the environment if you have not already. To discard changes, select Close from the File menu, click the close box, or press Esc. FoxPro then gives you the option of saving or discarding changes.

PAGE PREVIEW

If you select Page Preview from the Record menu you can see on the screen how the report will look when it is printed out. Page

Preview does not display type styles, such as bold, underline, or italic, but it does include text, field expressions, lines, and boxes, just as they will appear in the printed report.

If your report is wider than your screen, you can scroll right and left to see the entire width of the report. At the bottom of the Page Preview window is a status line which tells you the column where the cursor is and also includes two pushbuttons—Done and More.

You can go through the report a screen at a time by selecting More, or select Done at any time to stop previewing the report.

DATA GROUPING

Selecting Data Grouping from the Report menu popup lets you group data. A grouped report might, for example, print the data for each state separately, and it could include a header and footer for each state. Often the group footer includes a calculated field that summarizes the data in the group.

When you add a grouping, new bands appear in the report layout window to hold the group header and group footer. You can work with these bands in the same way you work with any other bands.

Selecting Data Grouping calls up the Group dialog box, shown in Figure 6.5. As you can see, this dialog box lets you add, change, or delete a grouping. The scrollable list on the left represents groups that have already been added; you can select a group from the list to change or delete. This list can include up to 20 levels of groupings. For example, you can group by state, by city within each state, and so on. In the illustration, records have been grouped by state; within each state, they are grouped by city; and within each city, they are grouped by zip code. Notice how the bands for these groupings are placed in the report layout window (still visible on the left behind the dialog box).

When you add a new grouping or change an existing one, the Group Info dialog box shown in Figure 6.6 appears to let you specify how the data is grouped.

By far the most important feature of the Group Info dialog box is the Group pushbutton. You can type the expression that you want the group to be based on to the right of this pushbutton, or you can select it to call up the expression builder to create the expression.

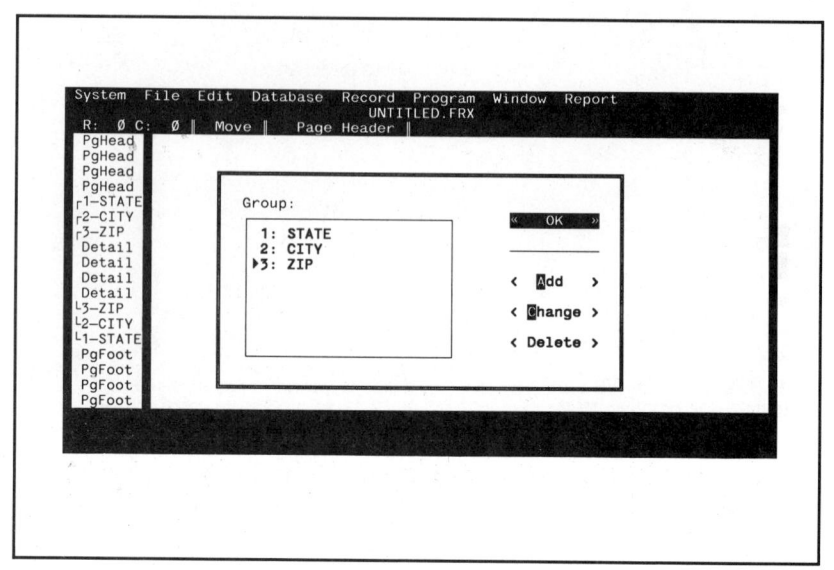

Figure 6.5: The Group dialog box

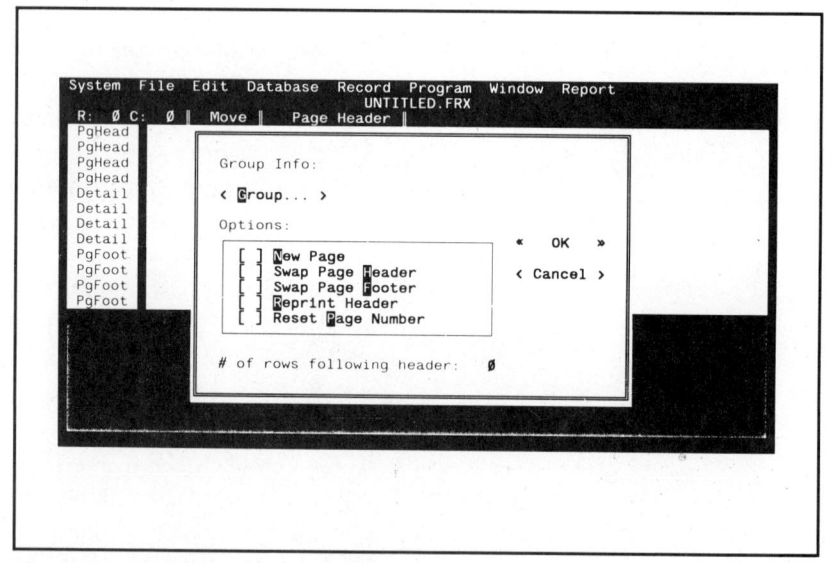

Figure 6.6: The Group Info dialog box

Usually, the grouping expression is something simple—a field name such as STATE. You might also want to use a simple expression such as UPPER(STATE), if there is a chance that the state names are not all capitalized.

Apart from this basic feature, the Group Info dialog gives you a few optional check boxes:

- **New Page:** makes each new group start on a new page.
- **Swap Page Header:** makes the group header appear on the first page of each group instead of the ordinary page header.
- **Swap Page Footer:** makes the group footer appear on the last page of each group instead of the ordinary page footer.
- **Reprint Header:** If the group occupies more than one page, the group header is printed at the top of each page.
- **Reset Page:** Resets the page number so that the numbering for each group begins with page 1.

> To use the Swap Page Header or Swap Page Footer features, the group header or footer must be the same size as the ordinary page header or footer.

In addition, this dialog box lets you specify the number of lines that should be skipped after each header.

The New Page check box is automatically selected when Swap Page Header or Swap Page Footer is selected, since these can only be used if each new group begins on a new page.

There is one important precaution that you must remember if you use data groupings: you must index your data properly to make sure that the data is grouped correctly. If you group on State without indexing, for example, FoxPro will print a new group footer and header each time it comes to a record where the state is not the same as it was in the previous record. The options on the menu system just make the report print the previous group's footer and the new group's header whenever there is a change in the data in the expression that you are grouping on.

What if you want to group by state but you also want the names of the employees within each state to be alphabetized? You have to index on UPPER(STATE+LNAME+FNAME) or on some equivalent expression. The index itself must put the records in the order needed by the grouping.

TITLE/SUMMARY

Selecting Title/Summary from the Report menu displays the Title/Summary dialog box shown in Figure 6.7, which lets you add a title or summary to the report.

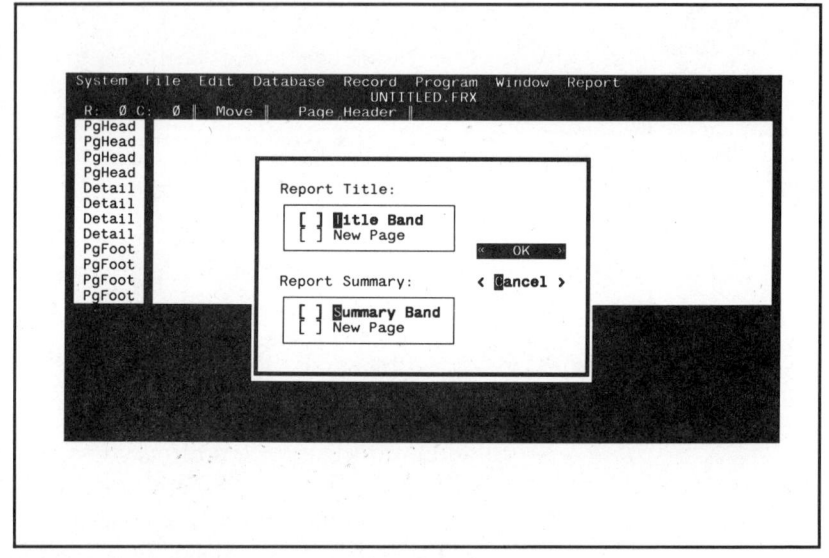

Figure 6.7: The Title/Summary dialog box

As you can see from the illustration, there are two check boxes under both Report Title and Report Summary. Checking the first adds a title band or summary band to the report layout window. You can work in these bands in the same way that you work in other bands. Checking the second check box in each pair makes FoxPro print out the report title or report summary on a separate page.

You might want to use the title band not just for a one- or two-line title but for an abstract of the report. Similarly, you could use it for a cover letter to each person who gets the report. These are cases where you would want it to appear on a separate page.

Of course, the title actually appears below the header of the first page, even though the title *band* is above the page header band. Similarly, Summary actually appears above the footer of the last page, even though its band is below the page footer band.

VARIABLES

Selecting Variables from the Report menu lets you add memory variables to the report form. This is an advanced report feature that is used primarily in programming. Memory variables are discussed in Chapters 8 and 9.

BOX

When you select Box from the Report menu, FoxPro places a small box at the location of the cursor. The box is blinking to show that it can be resized immediately. If you are working with the keyboard, use the down arrow and right arrow keys to make the box larger or the up arrow and left arrow keys to make it smaller; press Enter when the box is the size you want. If you are working with the mouse, click on the box and drag it to move its right and bottom edges, making it larger or smaller.

You create lines in exactly the same way you create boxes: just reduce the box's width to zero to make a vertical line, or reduce its height to zero to make a horizontal line. (You cannot draw diagonal lines—only vertical or horizontal.)

If you select an existing box by double clicking it with the mouse or by putting the cursor on it and pressing Enter, you will call up the Box dialog box, shown in Figure 6.8. As you can see from the illustration, this dialog box includes radio buttons that let you choose the characters that will make up the box or line. The basic choices are single line, double line, and panel (a wider line), but you can also select Character to display the dialog box shown in Figure 6.9 that lets you choose any DOS character. For example, you might want to create a box made of asterisks to highlight some very important data.

You can add a comment to a box just as you would for a text object, by selecting the Comment check box.

If the box you are drawing occurs entirely in the detail band of the report, the Float As Band Stretches check box appears in this dialog box. If it is selected, the box will expand vertically if you make the band larger to display more field data. If it is not selected, the box will remain the same size when you expand the band, so that the additional data will end up outside the box. If you put a box around a

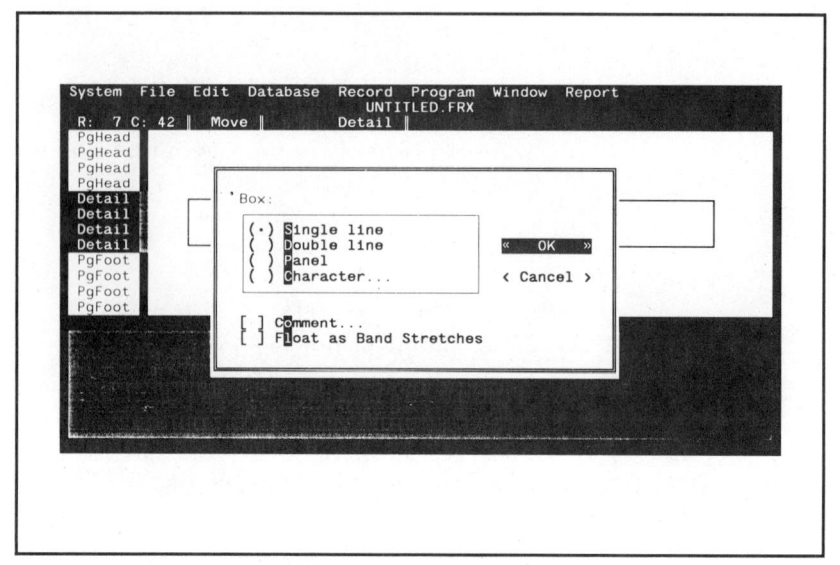

Figure 6.8: The Box dialog box

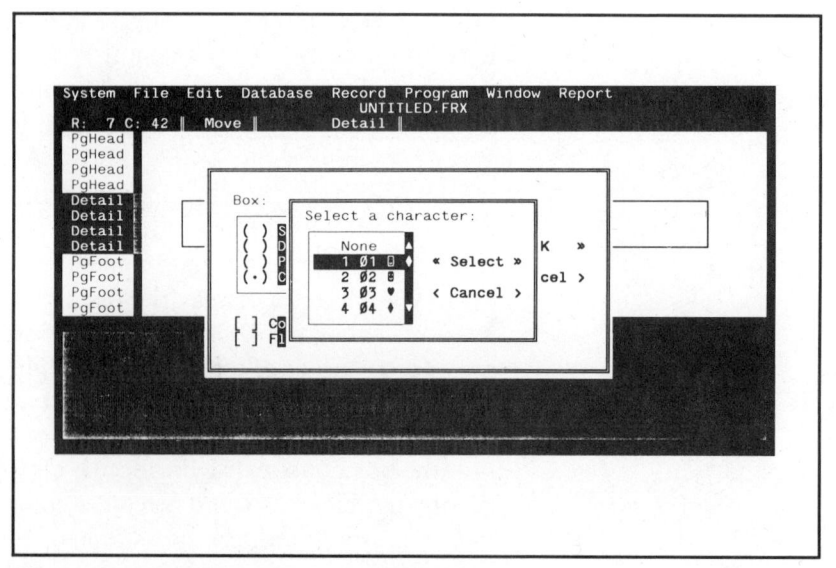

Figure 6.9: The Select a Character dialog box

memo field, you should select this check box so that longer memos do not overflow the size of the box.

Remember that a box or line is an object, and you can move, resize, or delete it as you do other objects. See the previous sections on Manipulating Objects Using a Mouse and Using the Keyboard.

FIELD

Selecting Field from the Report menu popup calls up the Report Expression dialog box shown in Figure 6.10, which lets you place field expressions in the report layout window as follows: First place the cursor where you want the field to be located. Then select Field from the Report menu. Then type the expression to the right of the Expr pushbutton (or select the Expr pushbutton to call up the expression builder, which you can use to create the expression just as you did in earlier chapters). When you move the cursor after entering the expression (by pressing Tab or using the mouse), the expression's width is automatically entered. Choosing OK places the expression.

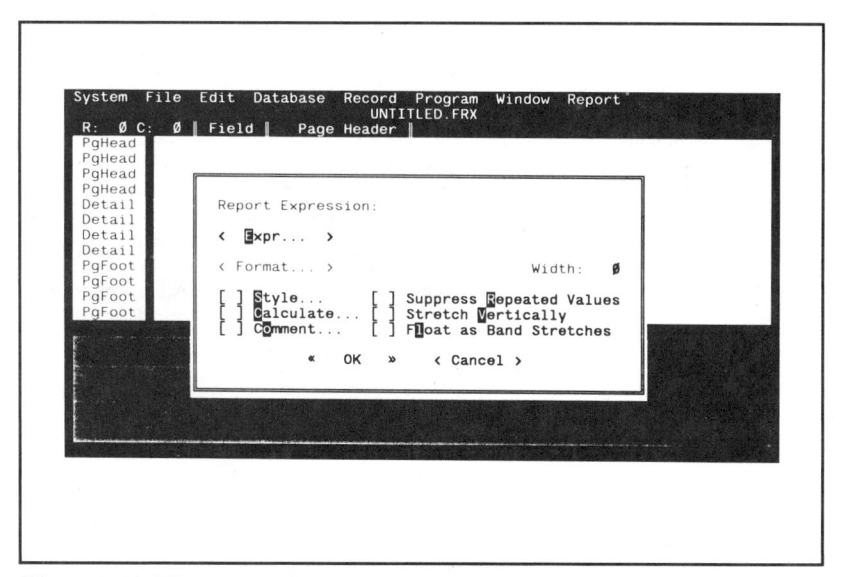

Figure 6.10: The Report Expression dialog box

You can include a page number in an expression by selecting _PAGENO from the list of memory variables. This should be used in the header or footer for long reports.

Formatting Fields The Format pushbutton of the Report Expression dialog box calls up the Format dialog box shown in Figure 6.11, which lets you format the field you are placing in a variety of ways. As you can see from the illustration, this includes four radio buttons to indicate the data type of the field that is being formatted—Character, Numeric, Date, or Logical. The Editing Options check boxes change according to the data type of the field being formatted. The options for all the data types are summarized in Table 6.1.

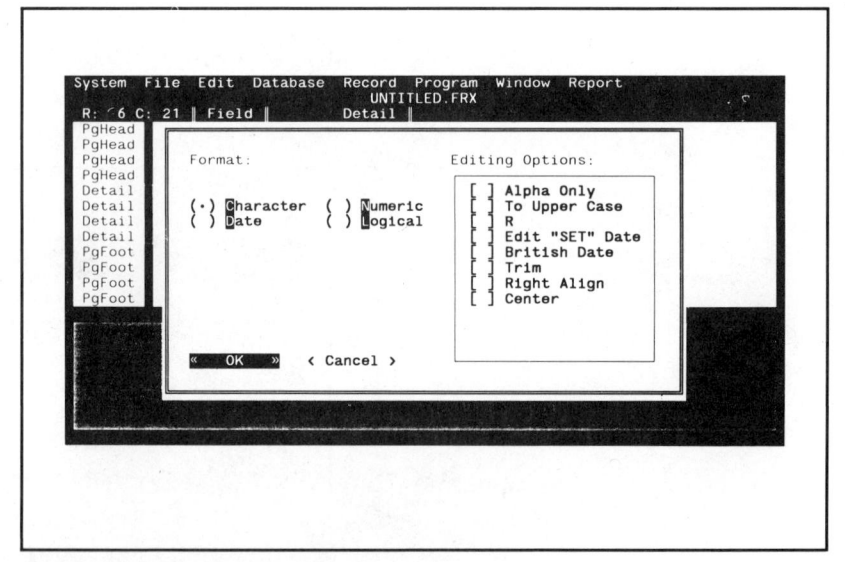

Figure 6.11: The Format dialog box

In addition to the options that are available through check boxes, you can enter *templates* to the right of the word Format in the upper left of the dialog box, to format an expression on a character-by-character basis. A template is a series of symbols that control the format of the entry. The special formatting characters are summarized

Table 6.1: Editing Options Check Boxes Available for Formatting Data

Radio Button Selected	Check Boxes Available	Effect
Character	Alpha Only	only letters are allowed
	To Upper Case	letters are capitalized
	R	non-format characters used literally are inserted into the data rather than overwriting it
	Edit "SET" Date	the date is displayed using whatever format is determined by the current SET DATE command (an environment command covered in Chapter 7)
	British Date	the date is displayed in the European format
	Trim	both leading and trailing blanks are trimmed
	Right Align	data is right-justified
	Center	data is centered on the line
Numeric	Left Justify	data is left-justified, like character data
	Blank If Zero	if the expression's value is zero, nothing is printed
	(Negative)	negative numbers are printed in parentheses, as they usually are in accounting
	Edit "SET" Date	the date is displayed using whatever format is determined by the current SET DATE command
	British Date	the date is displayed in the European format

Table 6.1: Editing Options Check Boxes Available for Formatting Data (continued)

Radio Button Selected	Check Boxes Available	Effect
Numeric	CR If Positive	CR (which stands for Credit) appears after all positive numbers
	DB If Negative	DB (for Debit) appears after all negative numbers
	Leading Zero	pads out the length of the field with leading zeros
	Currency	displays the expression in currency format
	Scientific	displays the expression in scientific (exponential) notation
Date	Edit "SET" Date	the date is displayed using whatever format is determined by the current SET DATE command
	British Date	the date is displayed in the European format
Logical	none	none

in Table 6.2. Any character apart from these special characters can also be used in a template as a literal, which means the character itself will appear in the formatted expression. For example, you can format Social Security numbers using the template **999-99-9999**. In this case, the 9s are symbols that display numbers, and the hyphens are literals.

> Text is always displayed on the screen in Normal style—even when you preview the page using Page Layout from the Record menu. The attributes you choose are visible only when you print out the report.

Selecting Type Style Selecting the Style check box in the Report Expression dialog box calls up the Style dialog box shown in Figure 6.12, which lets you determine the type style in which the fields will be printed. You can also enter a printer code in the text box to

Table 6.2: Special Characters for Format Templates

Character	Effect
A	displays only letters
L	displays only logical data
N	displays only letters or numbers
X	displays any character
9	displays only numbers when used with character data, or displays numbers and signs when used with numeric data
#	displays numbers, blanks, and signs
$	displays a dollar sign in a fixed location before a numeric value (if the value includes leading blanks, there will be a space between the dollar sign and the number)
$$	displays a floating dollar sign before a numeric value (if the value includes leading blanks, the dollar sign will move right so there is no space between it and the number)
*	uses asterisks to fill the leading blanks of a numeric value (this is often used on printed checks)
.	shows the location of a decimal point
,	adds commas to separate values to the left of the decimal point

determine the style: these codes can usually be found in the user's manual that comes with the printer. This is an advanced option, however, and is not recommended unless you have technical knowledge about printer codes.

Creating Computed Fields Selecting the Calculate check box calls up the Calculate dialog box shown in Figure 6.13, which lets you

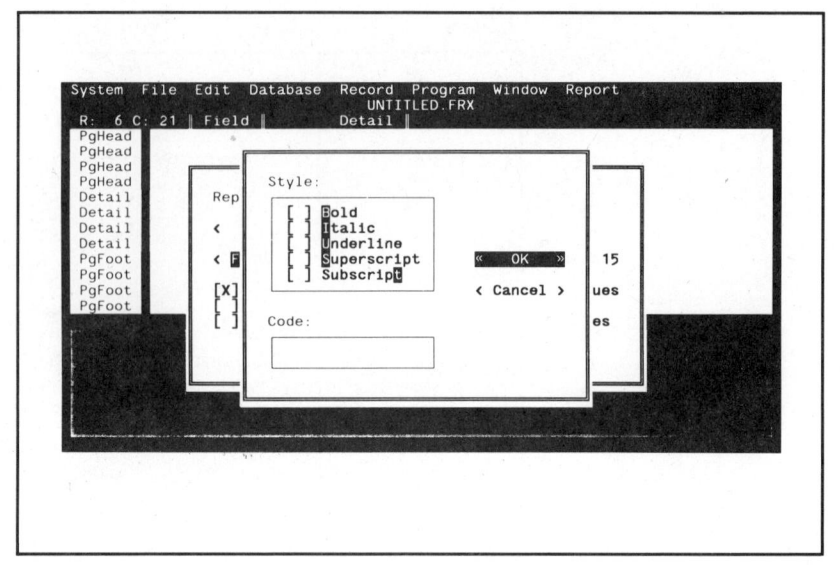

Figure 6.12: The Style dialog box

create computed fields. As you can see, this dialog box contains eight radio buttons, to select the calculation to be performed on the field:

- **Nothing:** no calculation is performed
- **Count:** counts the number of fields
- **Sum:** totals all the values of the field
- **Average:** finds the average value in the field
- **Lowest:** finds the lowest value in the field
- **Highest:** finds the highest value in the field
- **Std Deviation** and **Variance**: perform these statistical calculations

> The default calculation in the Calculate dialog box is Nothing. If you do not select the Calculating check box and use this dialog box, then no calculation is performed.

For example, if you had WAGE as the field expression in the Report Expression dialog box and you checked the Calculate check box, and then selected the Average radio button in the Calculate dialog box, you would create a calculated field that finds the average wage. Notice that the Calculate dialog box includes the Reset popup control, which determines when the calculation will be done. The default

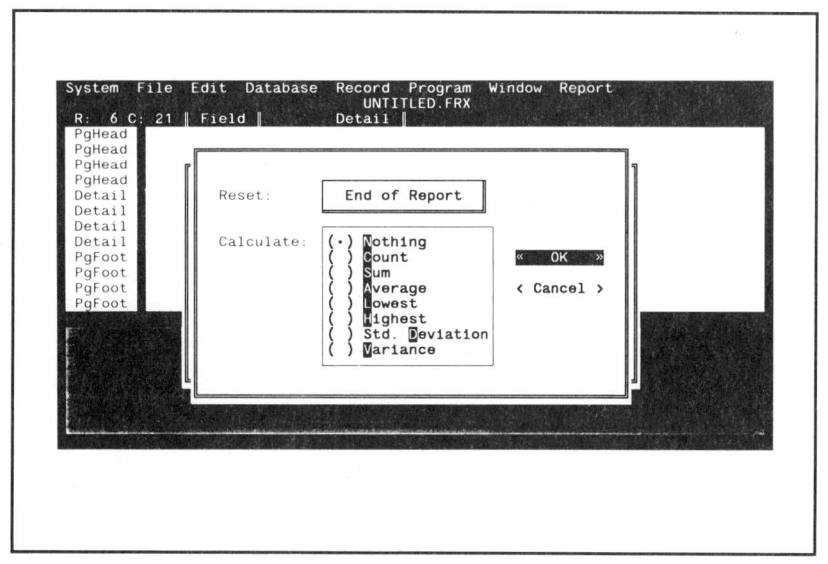

Figure 6.13: The Calculate dialog box

is End of Report, which does the calculation only once, at the end, obviously. If you have grouped data, you can also select the name of any of your groups from the popup, and perform the calculation for each group; or you can select End of Page from the popup, for example, if you want to put the total in a footer. The Calculate field itself must always be numeric.

Other Features of the Report Expression Dialog Box If you select the Suppress Repeated Values check box, then if the value of the field is the same for more than one record, only the first occurrence of the value will be printed. For example, if you have a report that is indexed by state, you might want to put the State field at the far left of the report and select this option so that each state's name appears only once.

Select the Stretch Vertically check box to have the contents of the field wrap onto the lines that follow when there is not enough space to hold it on a single line. If you select Float As Band Stretches, the field will be printed on the line following the last line of a vertically stretched field. Fields that use this option must themselves be on a line below the first line of a vertically stretched field.

Selecting the Comments check box lets you add a comment, as it does with other types of objects.

Finally, you should remember that after a field expression is placed it is an object, and you can select it and manipulate it as you do any object. See the previous sections on Manipulating Objects Using a Mouse and Using the Keyboard.

TEXT

Unlike the case with boxes and field expressions, you do not have to use the Report menu to position text in the report layout window. If you wish, you can select Text from the Report menu popup at any time to enter the Text mode, but the main reason for doing so would be to edit text that has already been added.

To add text, you can just put the cursor where you want it to begin and start typing. Until you either press Enter or reach the end of a line, you can edit the text; after that, the line of text you added is treated as an object and must be selected and manipulated like a box or graphic object. The whole block of text is then treated as a single object.

To edit text after it becomes an object, you can select the object and then select Text from the Report menu. Alternatively, you can edit text by moving the mouse pointer to it and pressing Ctrl while you click the mouse, or by moving the cursor to it and pressing Ctrl and the space bar.

If you select a text object that is in the detail band by using the mouse or by placing the cursor in the text and pressing Enter, the Text dialog box, shown in Figure 6.14, appears.

- **Style:** This check box calls up the same Style dialog box discussed in the previous section on field objects. The Style dialog box lets you determine the type style in which the text is printed.
- **Comment:** This lets you add comments, as with other objects.
- **Float As Band Stretches:** If you check this box, the text will be printed on the line following the last line of a vertically stretched field.

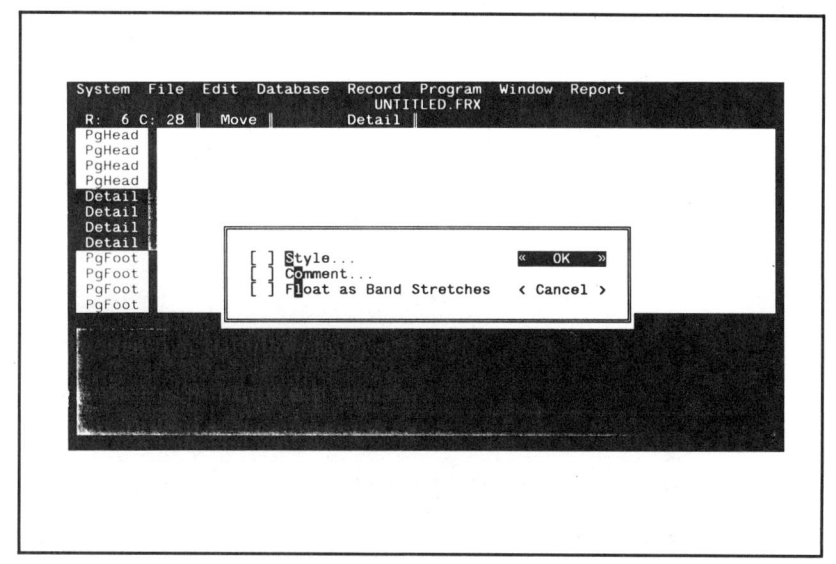

Figure 6.14: The Text dialog box

ADD LINE

Selecting Add Line from the Report menu popup lets you make bands larger by adding a line to them. The new line is added above the current position of the cursor.

> If you press Shift when you open the Report menu—by pressing Shift-Alt-R if you are using the keyboard or by holding down the Shift key while you pop up the menu using the mouse—the popup will include an Add Line After option instead of the ordinary Add Line option. This option inserts the line after the current position of the cursor.

REMOVE LINE

Selecting Remove Line from the Report menu lets you make bands smaller by deleting the line that the cursor is on. If you have already entered anything on this line when you select this option, FoxPro will ask if you want to delete the objects on the line. If you choose Yes, it will delete both the line and the objects on it.

BRING TO FRONT AND SEND TO BACK

These two options change the way in which overlapping expressions appear. For example, if you draw a line that partly covers a text object but you actually want the text object to appear in front of the line, you can use either one of these options to rearrange them: select the text object and then select Bring to Front, or alternatively, select the line object and then select Send to Back.

CENTER

Select an object and then select Center from the Report menu in order to center the object on its line. Note that the location of the "center" of the line depends on the margins that you choose by selecting Page Layout. Furthermore, if you are centering a field object, you must choose the Center check box from the Format dialog in addition to choosing this option.

GROUP AND UNGROUP

Selecting Group combines all the objects that are currently selected, so that they can be manipulated as a single object. This is simply a convenience to let you work with them more easily during design. Selecting Ungroup breaks them up into individual objects again.

QUICK REPORT

Selecting Quick Report from the Report menu calls up the Quick Report dialog box shown in Figure 6.15. You can use this dialog box to place field data in the report automatically, so you do not have to place each field expression individually.

You can see that this dialog box contains two radio buttons and two check boxes:

- **Column Layout:** places the fields in the detail band one next to another, from left to right.

- **Form Layout:** places the fields in the detail band one above another, from top to bottom. The detail band will automatically stretch to hold all the fields.

- **Title:** determines whether the field name will be included. It is placed above each field (if they are arranged in column layout) or to the left of each field (if they are arranged in form layout).

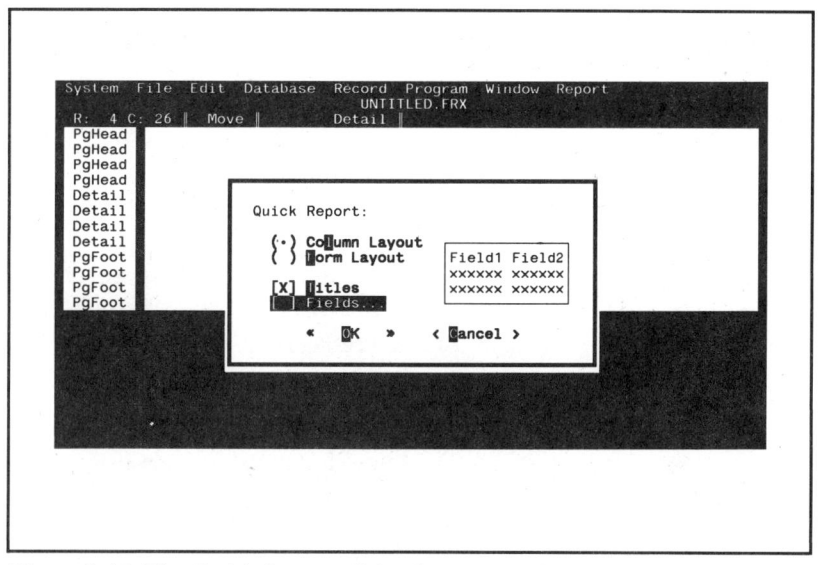

Figure 6.15: The Quick Report dialog box

- **Field:** displays the field picker dialog box (which you looked at in the last chapter) to let you choose which fields are initially displayed in the quick report.

Since it only includes fields and not field expressions, the Quick Report option is of limited use.

A SAMPLE REPORT

With this background, you should have no trouble creating a sophisticated sample report. In this exercise, you will create a report that groups employees by state, listing their names (alphabetically) and their wages. Among other features, the report will include group footers with the number of employees and the average wage for each state and a report footer with the same information for all the employees.

1. If necessary, start the program by entering **CD\LEARNFOX** and then **FOXPRO**. Then enter **CLEAR** if you want to clear the screen. You will begin work on the report by opening the

database file and creating the index needed to create a report grouped on state and arranged alphabetically by name within each state. Thus, select Open from the File menu and select EMPLIST.DBF. Then select New from the File menu, select the Index radio button, and select OK. When the Index On dialog box appears, type

UPPER(STATE + LNAME + FNAME)

under the Expr pushbutton (or use the expression builder to create this expression). As the Tag Name, enter **ST_NAME** (for State Name). Select the Move pushbutton to move the expression to the Index On box. Then select OK to create the index.

2. The EMPLIST file is now open with this new index tag active as the controlling index, so you are ready to design the report. Select File New from the File menu popup, select the Report radio button, and then select OK to call up the report layout window.

3. Set the report margins using Page Layout from the Report menu. Make the top margin 6 rows, the bottom margin 6 rows, the printer indent 10 columns, and the right margin column 65. Then select OK.

4. Add a title and summary band to the report: Select Title/Summary from the Report menu. Select both the Title Band and the Summary Band check boxes. Select OK.

5. Add a few extra lines to the title band: The cursor should already be in the title band. Select Add Line from the Report menu to add an extra line. Repeat this step two more times, so the title band has four lines in all.

6. Add the title: Press the down arrow to move the cursor to the second line of the title band, and type

   Employee Wages by State

   Press Enter to finish creating this text object. Now select the text object you just created. (Since the cursor is in it, you can just press the space bar.) Then select Center from the Report menu to center it on the line. Press Enter to deselect it.

7. Put a box around the title: Move the cursor to row 0, column 19 (one row up from and two columns to the left of where the title begins). Then select Box from the Report menu. Use the keyboard or the mouse to stretch the box so it is centered around the title, as shown in Figure 6.16.

8. Create the page header: First remove one line from the PgHead band. Move the cursor to that band and select Remove Line from the Report menu. Move the cursor to the top line of the page header band and to the left edge of the screen. Select Field from the Report menu. To the right of the Expr pushbutton, type

"data accurate as of " + DTOC(DATE( ))

Press Tab and note that the width of the expression you entered, 28, automatically appears. (If it does not, the expression contains an error.) Select OK. Note also that the expression as it now appears on the report seems incomplete. This is because it can take up only 28 spaces, the actual width the expression's *result* will occupy on the report.

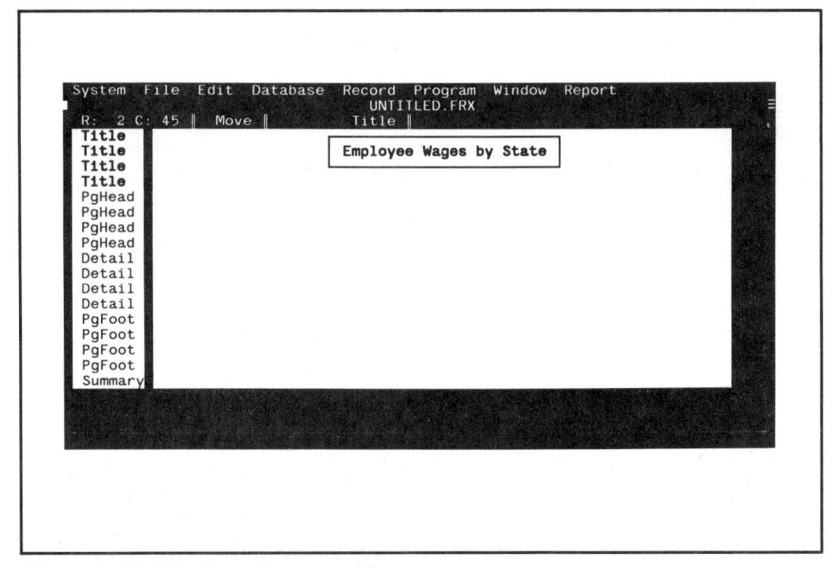

Figure 6.16: The boxed report title

9. Add group bands: Select Data Grouping from the Report menu. When the Group dialog box appears, select Add. Then, when the Group Info dialog box appears, type **STATE** to the right of Group, and select OK. This returns you to the Group dialog box where STATE is added as group 1. Select OK. Notice that the group header and footer named 1-STATE have been added to the report layout window.

10. Add the group header: Move the cursor to that band. Select Add Line twice from the Report menu so that there are three lines in the band. Move the cursor to its second line, at the left edge of the screen. Select Field from the Report menu. In the Report Expression dialog box, to the right of the Expr pushbutton, type (in all capital letters)

    "EMPLOYEES IN THE STATE OF " + UPPER(STATE)

    and press Tab. The width—28—is entered automatically. Select OK.

11. Enter the detail line: Move to the detail band. Select Remove Line twice from the Report menu to make it just two lines. Move the cursor to the second line of the band, flush with the left margin. Select Field from the Report menu. Since the WAGE of the detail line is not used in a calculation, you can enter the entire detail line as a single string expression. In the Report Expression dialog box, to the right of the Expr pushbutton, type

    PROPER(LNAME + " " + FNAME) + " $" + LTRIM(STR(WAGE,5,2))

    This expression capitalizes the last and first name properly and puts a blank between them to make sure there is a space between columns. It also uses STR( ) to convert the wage from a number to a string five characters long, with two decimal places. It adds this to the expression with a space and a dollar sign before it, using LTRIM to make sure that there is no space between the number and the dollar sign. Press Tab, and the width—42—is automatically entered. Select OK.

GENERATING REPORTS AND MAILING LABELS   *239*

12. Add the group footer, which will summarize how many workers there are in the given state and their average wage: Move the cursor to the group footer line. Select Add Line three times from the Report menu so that there are four lines in the band. Move the cursor to the second line in the band, at the left margin. Select Field from the Report menu to call up the Report Expression dialog box. You can count any field to get the number of workers; we'll use LNAME. Enter this to the right of the Expr pushbutton. If it is not already selected by default, select the Calculate check box to call up the Calculate dialog box. Select the Reset popup control and select STATE from the popup that appears; then select the Count radio button; and select OK to return to the Report Expression dialog box. Since a computed field must be numeric, select Format, then select the Numeric radio button and select OK. Since you know that there will be no more than 99 employees in any of the states, enter **2** as the width of the computed field. Then select OK. Only the first two letters of the field name, in this case LN, are displayed to show where the number goes.

> Do not press the space bar to add spaces between columns. It will only select the object, since the cursor is on the object that you just finished creating.

13. You can continue with text to the right of this number: Press the right arrow key to leave one blank space after the field. Then select Field from the Report menu. In the Report Expression dialog box, type

    "EMPLOYEES FROM " + STATE + ": AVERAGE WAGE"

    to the right of the Expr pushbutton. Press Tab to automatically add the width—31—and select OK.

14. Press the right arrow key to leave a space before the amount of the wage. You want to left-justify this amount so that there are no extra spaces between it and the preceding text if the number is small. Select Field from the Report menu. In the Report Expression dialog box, type **WAGE** to the right of the Expr pushbutton. Select the Calculating check box. In the Calculate dialog box, select the Reset popup control and select STATE

from the popup. Select the Average radio button, then select OK. In the Report Expression dialog box, select the Format pushbutton to call up the Format dialog box, and select the Numeric radio button. Among the editing options, select the Left Justify and Currency check boxes; then select OK. Back in the Report Expression dialog box, increase the Width to 6 to allow for the dollar sign you just added, and then select OK.

15. Add a page footer: Move the cursor to the last line of the footer band. Type

    Report on wages by state

    and press Enter. Then press the space bar to select the new text object, select Center from the Report menu to center it, and press Enter to deselect it.

16. Finally, add the report summary: Move to the summary band. Select Add Line three times from the Report menu to make it a total of four lines. (The extra lines are not visible as you add them, because they appear beyond the bottom of the screen.) Move the cursor to the fourth line, at the left margin. Adding the summary line at this point is almost exactly like totaling the wages for each state as we did in Step 14. First, though, repeat Step 12, which you used to add the group footer—but select the popup control, End of Report, so that it gives the count of employees in the entire database.

17. Press the right arrow to leave a space after the field, then type

    EMPLOYEES IN TOTAL: AVERAGE WAGE

    Then repeat Step 14, which you used to add the average to the group footer, but, once again, set the popup control to End of Report, to get an overall average. The layout window is shown in Figure 6.17 (though some of the layout has scrolled beyond the top of the window).

18. Select Page Preview from the Report menu to preview the report. The first screen displayed should look like Figure 6.18. Select More if you want to page through the report. Select Done when you have seen enough.

Figure 6.17: The final layout of the report

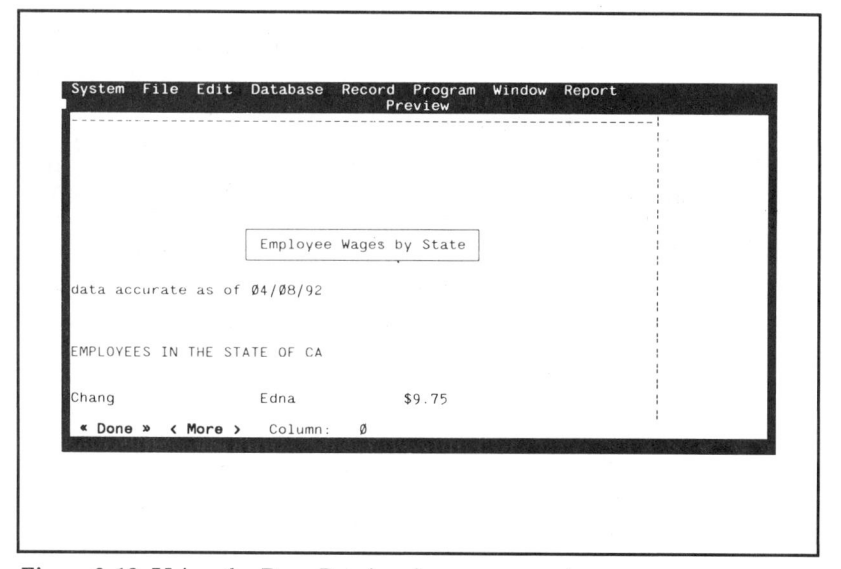

Figure 6.18: Using the Page Preview feature to test the report

19. Select Save As from the File menu to use the Save Report As dialog box. Type the name **ST_WAGE** (for the State Wage report), as in the report name, and select Save. Now that you are finished designing the report, close the report layout window as you would any window.

20. Now select Report from the Database menu. Note that in the Report dialog box, shown in Figure 6.19, the Environment check box is already checked by default, which means that the index will be opened automatically. Select the Form pushbutton at the upper left to call up the Report file dialog box, and select ST_WAGE.FRX.

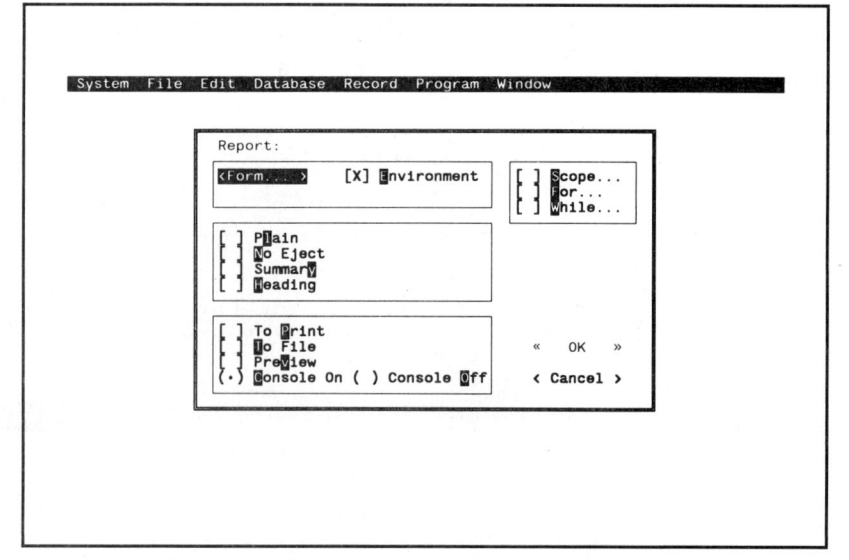

Figure 6.19: The Report dialog box

21. In the Report dialog box, neither To Print nor To File have been checked, but the Console On radio button is selected. This means that when you produce the report, it will be displayed on the screen but will not go to the printer or to a text file. (You can change these settings if you want.) Select OK to produce the report. Be patient: it can take a while before it scrolls by. If you are just producing it on the screen, all the information is displayed just as it would be on paper.

You might want to modify this report and try other features of the report generator on your own. For example, you could try different type styles or try making each group start on a new page, or try using the _PAGENO memory variable in the expression builder to add a page number.

CREATING MAILING LABELS

FoxPro's mailing label generator works a bit like its report generator. Of course, creating labels is much simpler, since labels do not need to include graphics, summary fields, titles, footers, or many of the other features of reports.

As with reports, there are two steps to creating FoxPro labels. First, you design the *label form,* which determines how field data (and other text, if you want it) is laid out. Once you have the label form you want, you can actually produce the labels.

You create a new label form in a familiar way: select New from the File menu and then select the Label radio button. This calls forth the label layout window, shown in Figure 6.20. When you are using the label layout window, a Label menu pad is added to the menu bar.

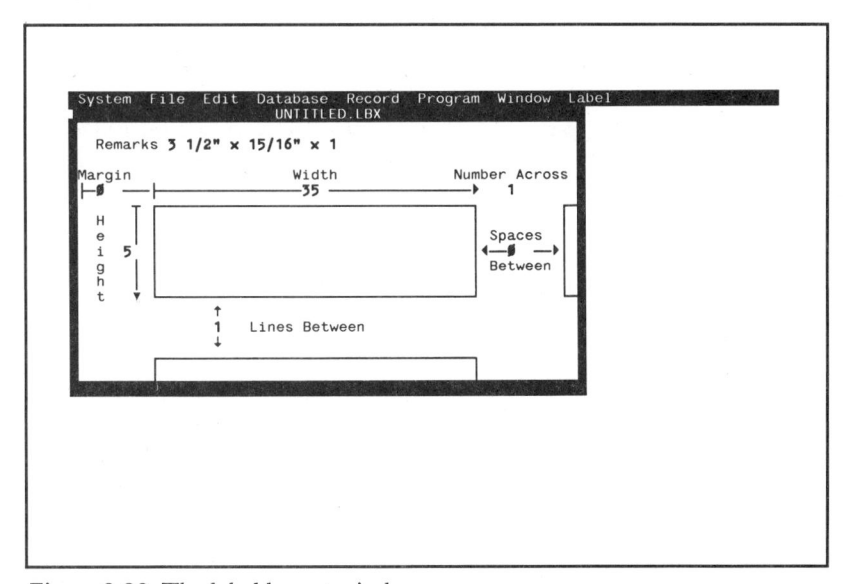

Figure 6.20: The label layout window

A database should be open before you create labels, since the label form (like the report form) uses fields from the current database; you should also open the appropriate index if you want your labels to be printed out in a special order. As usual, FoxPro names the label form Untitled.

If you are working from the Command window, you can enter the command **CREATE LABEL** <*file name*> to name the label form from the beginning; of course, you should first enter

USE <*database file name*> ORDER <*index tag name*>

As with reports, you can modify an existing label form by selecting Open from the File menu or by using the command **MODIFY LABEL** <*file name*>.

The next section explains in detail how you use the layout window to design the label form. You can use the menu to select from a number of standard layouts, and you can also customize any of the standard layouts. You fill in the layout with FoxPro expressions to show where the field information should be.

Once you have the layout you want, you will save it in the usual way by selecting Save As from the File menu. As with reports, you can save the index and other environment settings.

After you have designed and saved the label form, you can print the labels at any time by selecting Label from the Database menu to call up the Label dialog box, shown in Figure 6.21.

This dialog box is very similar to the dialog box you use when you select Report from the Database menu to print a report. As you can guess, the Form pushbutton lets you choose which of the existing label forms to print, and the Environment check box next to it lets you use the environment setting that you saved when you created the labels. The Scope, For, and While check boxes let you print labels for records that meet certain criteria. The To Print and To File check boxes let you send the labels to the printer or to an ASCII file, and the Console On and Console Off radio buttons determine whether the labels are displayed on the screen, just as with reports.

The one difference is the Sample check box. This feature lets you print a single sample label in order to check the alignment of the label

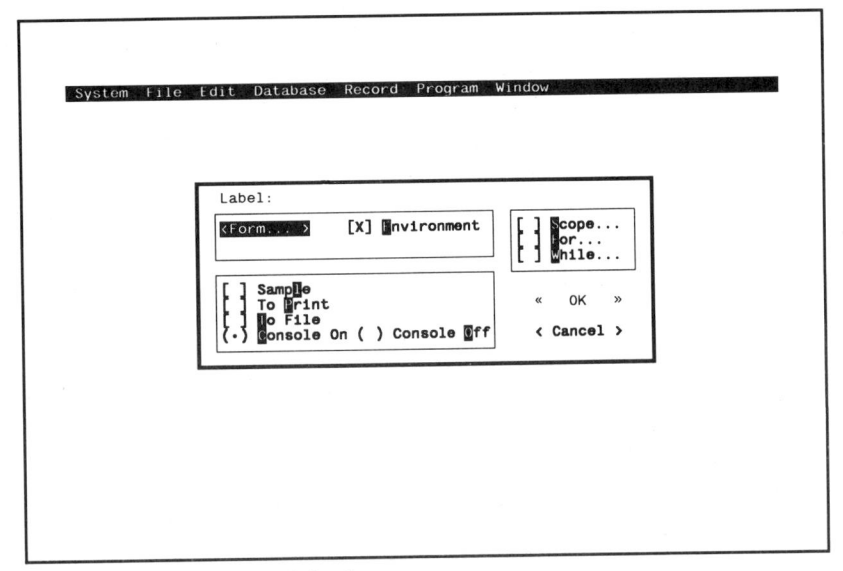

```
┌─────────────────────────────────────────────────────┐
│                                                     │
│     System File Edit Database Record Program Window │
│                                                     │
│                                                     │
│         ┌─────────────────────────────────────┐     │
│         │ Label:                              │     │
│         │ <Form...>   [X] Environment  [ ] Scope... │
│         │                              [ ] For...   │
│         │                              [ ] While... │
│         │ [ ] Sample                          │     │
│         │ [ ] To Print              «   OK   »│     │
│         │ [ ] To File                         │     │
│         │ (·) Console On ( ) Console Off  < Cancel >│
│         └─────────────────────────────────────┘     │
│                                                     │
│                                                     │
└─────────────────────────────────────────────────────┘
```

Figure 6.21: The Label dialog box

paper in your printer. The sample label will contain asterisks to show you where data goes on the label. After the sample is printed, a dialog box appears asking if you want another sample. If the printer is out of alignment, you can move the label paper and then select Yes from this dialog box to see if the new alignment is correct. If the paper is correct, select Do Labels to print all the labels.

From the Command window, you would enter **LABEL FORM** <*file name*>. The most important option for this command is a FOR or a WHILE clause, which can be followed by either TO PRINT or TO FILE <*file name*>. See the Help window for all the options used with this command.

LAYING OUT LABELS

As you have seen, the label layout window starts you off with the default layout of 3 1/2″ × 15/16″ × 1. If you look back at Figure 6.20 again, you will see that these standard labels allow 5 lines of text per label and have one blank line between labels.

You can select Layout from the Label menu popup to choose among these standard layouts:

- $3\ 1/2'' \times 15/16'' \times 1$
- $3\ 1/2'' \times 15/16'' \times 2$
- $3\ 1/2'' \times 15/16'' \times 3$
- $4'' \times 1\ 7/16'' \times 1$
- $3\ 2/10'' \times 11/12'' \times 3$ (Cheshire)
- $6\ 1/2'' \times 3\ 5/8''$ envelope
- $9\ 7/8'' \times 7\ 1/8''$ envelope
- $3'' \times 5''$ Rolodex
- $4'' \times 2\ 1/4''$ Rolodex

As you can see, not all of these layouts are restricted to labels. If your printer is capable of it, they also let you print directly on the two standard sizes of envelope, on 3-by-5-inch index cards (or that size Rolodex cards), and on the other standard size of Rolodex cards.

If none of these standard layouts is adequate, you can start with the one that is closest to what you need and customize it by simply changing the settings in the layout window. For example, you can see that the left margin back in Figure 6.20 is 0; if you want to add a 1-inch left margin, just change that number to 10 (assuming that you are using a standard printer with ten characters per inch). Likewise, you can edit the width, height, lines between, spaces between, and number across to create any label layout you choose, and edit the remarks to change the size description.

When you have the right layout size, just enter expressions in the sample label on the window. You can use the expression builder to do this by selecting Expression from the Label menu popup, or you can just type in the expressions.

Remember that any text enclosed in quotation marks (or in the other delimiters that FoxPro allows for character literals) is a valid FoxPro expression. If, for example, you run a membership organization and you are using a FOR clause to print labels for people who have not paid their dues, you can include the expression "PLEASE PAY YOUR DUES" somewhere on the label.

> Notice this other difference from the report layout window. When you are designing reports, you must use the menu to add expressions, since anything you just type is treated as text. On the other hand, there are only expressions on label forms. Thus, you can just type expressions in as well as using the menu to add them.

Often, a line of a label must include the contents of two fields with just a blank space between—for example, the first name field and the last name field. You can use the expression

TRIM(FNAME) + " " + TRIM(LNAME)

to print this, but since it is so common, FoxPro also gives you a shortcut. If you simply separate each field expression with a comma, FoxPro trims the contents and puts one space between.

If there is a possibility that an expression will evaluate to a blank space, you should add a semicolon after it so there will not be a blank line left in the labels. You will do this for the apartment number when you are creating sample labels, since that field is blank in many records.

That's about all there is to creating label forms. The Label menu popup, shown in Figure 6.22, is very easy to understand. It has just seven features, many similar to features of the Report menu:

- **Page Preview:** lets you see on the screen how the labels will appear in print. It works just like the feature with the same name on the Report menu.

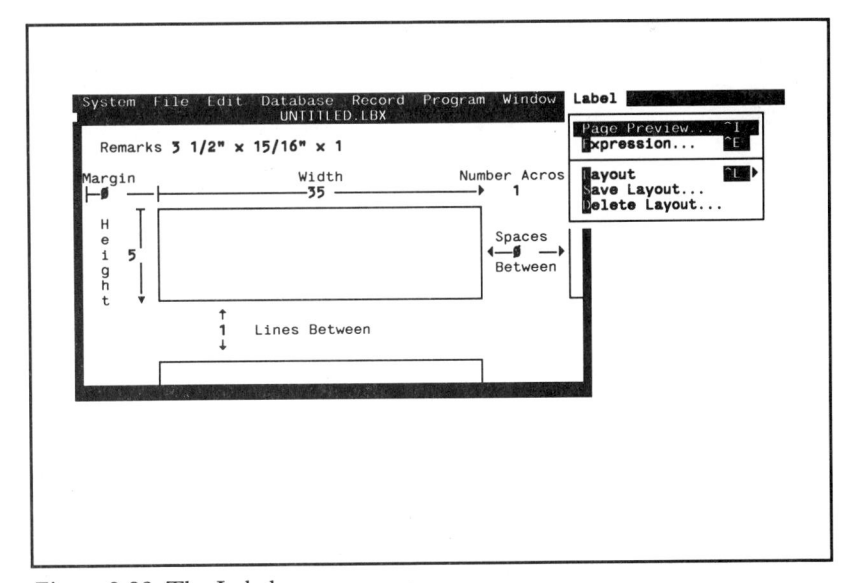

Figure 6.22: The Label menu popup

- **Expression:** lets you use the expression builder to enter expressions in the label layout window. Remember, though, that you can also just type expressions into the layout window.
- **Environment:** lets you save, restore, or clear the working environment.
- **Style:** lets you make the current line bold, italic, underline, superscript, or subscript, or lets you specify a printer code.
- **Layout:** lets you choose among the standard label layouts.
- **Save Layout:** lets you save a customized layout you have designed, adding it to the list of available layouts you can choose from when you select Layout. Then, whenever you are designing labels for the paper or cards that you created this layout for, you can just select this layout as if it were a default layout and fill in the fields.
- **Delete Layout:** lets you delete a label form that you designed and saved.

Now, you should have no trouble laying out some sample labels:

1. If necessary, enter **CLEAR** to clear the screen. If you do not already have EMPLIST.DBF open, select Open from the File menu and open it. Assuming that you want the labels in zip code order, select Setup from the Database menu, and use the Setup dialog box to make ZIP the controlling index.

2. To start designing the labels, select New from the File menu popup, select the Label radio button in the New dialog box, and select OK.

3. The label layout window appears, with the cursor on the first line of the label form. Type

    PROPER(FNAME),PROPER(LNAME)

    and press Enter. On the second line, type

    PROPER(ADDRESS)

and press Enter. The third line contains the apartment number with ten spaces before it, so it is indented, and a semicolon after it, so there is no blank line for addresses without an apartment number: type

"<10 spaces>" + APT_NO;

and press Enter. Finally, the fourth line should have the city name followed by a comma and a blank space, followed by the capitalized state name, a blank space, and the zip code: type

PROPER(TRIM(CITY)) + ", " + UPPER(STATE) + " " + ZIP

and press Enter. The final form is shown in Figure 6.23.

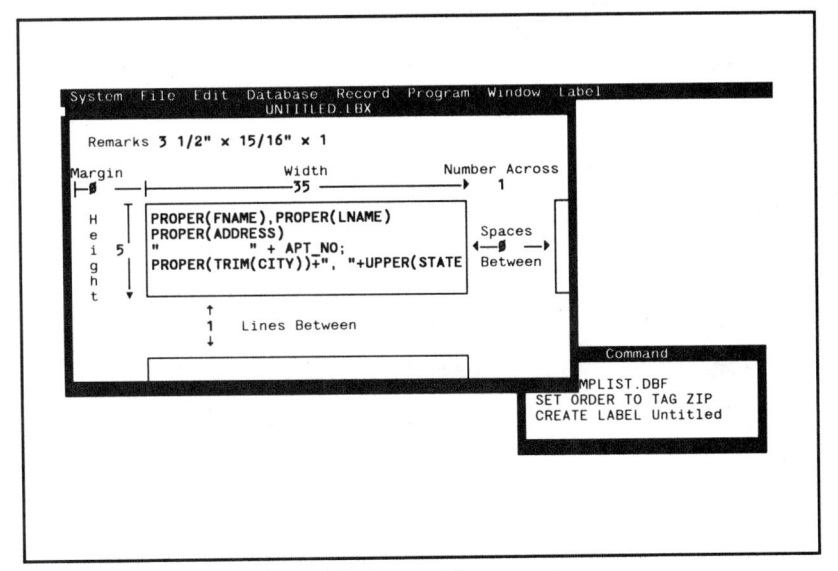

Figure 6.23: The label form, filled out with expressions

> Some early releases of FoxPro did not implement the feature that suppresses blank lines. Check your page preview window to see if blank lines are suppressed.

4. To check the form you created, select Page Preview from the Label menu. When you are finished, select Done.

5. You should also try some other layouts. Select Layout from the Label menu, select other default layouts, and select Page Preview to see how they look.

6. Now, try customizing the default settings. Select Layout from the Label menu and select the second standard layout to get two-across labels. Then change the width from 35 to 42 and change the number of spaces between from 2 to 1. Change the Remarks line to 4″ × 15/16″ × 2. This setting lets you print on a fairly common type of two-column label paper. This layout is shown in Figure 6.24.

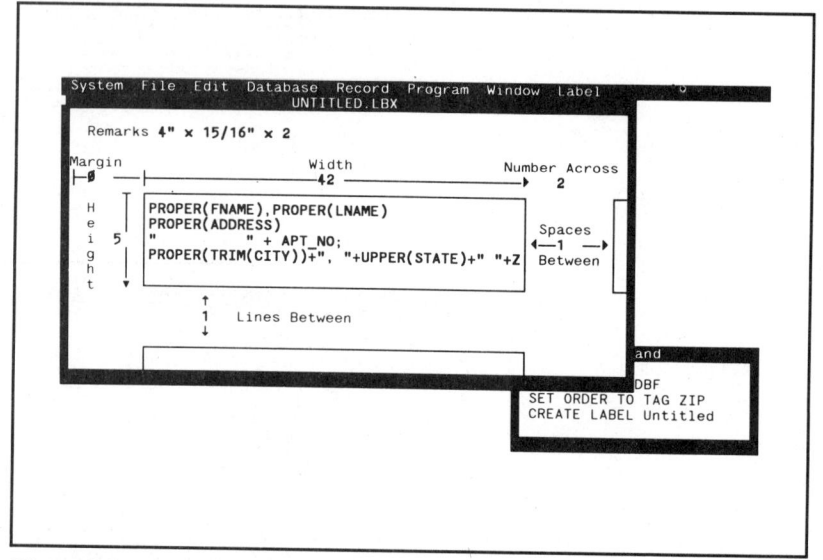

Figure 6.24: A custom label form

7. Save this custom layout. Select Save Layout from the Label menu. When the Save As dialog box appears, select OK to save it under the suggested name. Select Layout again from the Label menu to confirm that your custom layout has been added at the end of the list of layouts, as shown in Figure 6.25.

8. Save the label form. Select Save As from the File menu. Enter the name **TWO_COL**, since this form prints two column labels, select Save and select Yes to save the environment. Then close the label layout window as you would any window.

9. Select Label from the Database menu. The Label dialog box is the same as the dialog box you used to produce reports. Select Form, and then, from the Label File dialog box, select

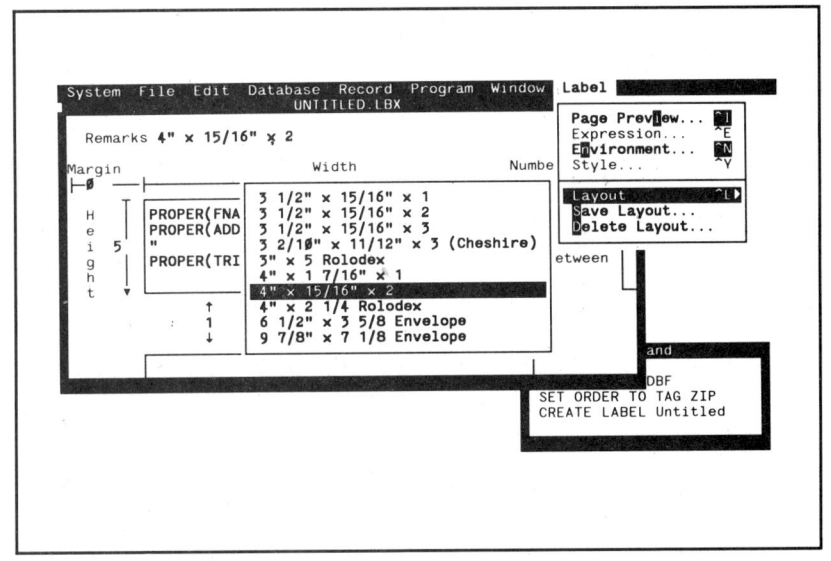

Figure 6.25: The label menu popup with the custom form added

TWO_COL.LBX. Select OK from the label dialog box to send the labels to the screen.

WHAT NEXT?

Now you have learned all the basic features of FoxPro that are needed for most ordinary purposes. You can define the structure of a database; add, edit and view data; create indexes; query to find data you want; and create reports and mailing labels. This is all you need to know for most basic database applications.

At this point, you must choose how to continue your work with FoxPro.

If you have an application that you can manage with the techniques that you have learned so far—such as running a mailing list— you might want to go ahead and get practical experience with that application without learning any more about FoxPro. Before you do this, though, you should look at the brief discussion of relational databases in the next chapter to see if you might need these techniques to manage your data.

If you want to go right ahead with this book, you can either go ahead to Part II or skip right to Part III, depending on your interests.

Part II covers more advanced FoxPro techniques. It takes you through the menu options that have not been covered yet. It also teaches you to create keyboard macros and to work with relational databases. If you want to become a power user, go on to Part II.

Part III includes an introduction to computer programming with FoxPro, teaches you to use the screen builder and menu builder, and leads you through creating a menu-driven mailing list application that includes popup menus and dialog-box controls such as check boxes and pushbuttons. If you are eager to learn about programming, you can skip Part II for now and go right to Part III. You should go back to Part II later, however, when you want to learn advanced techniques to add more power to your programming.

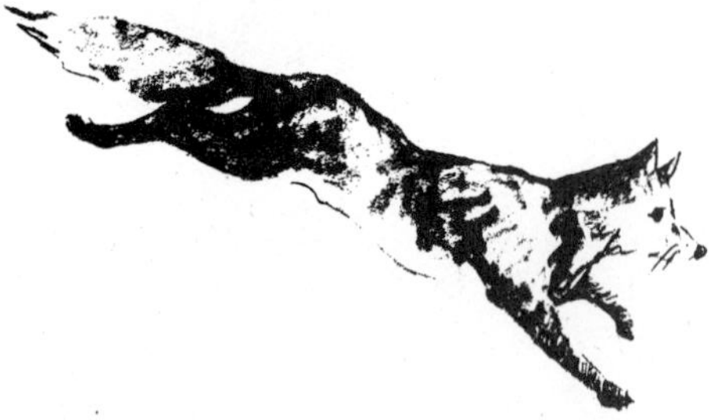

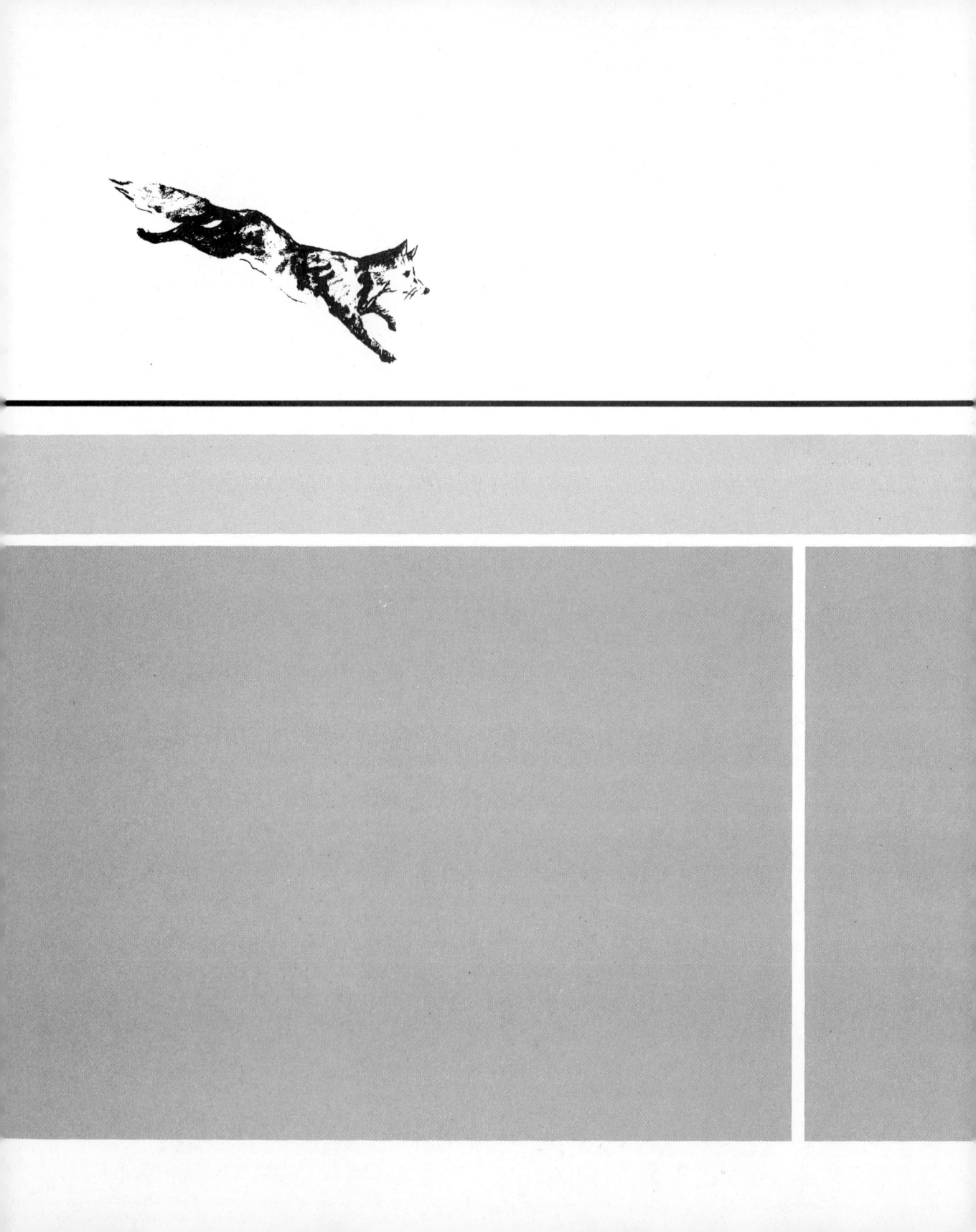

Part II

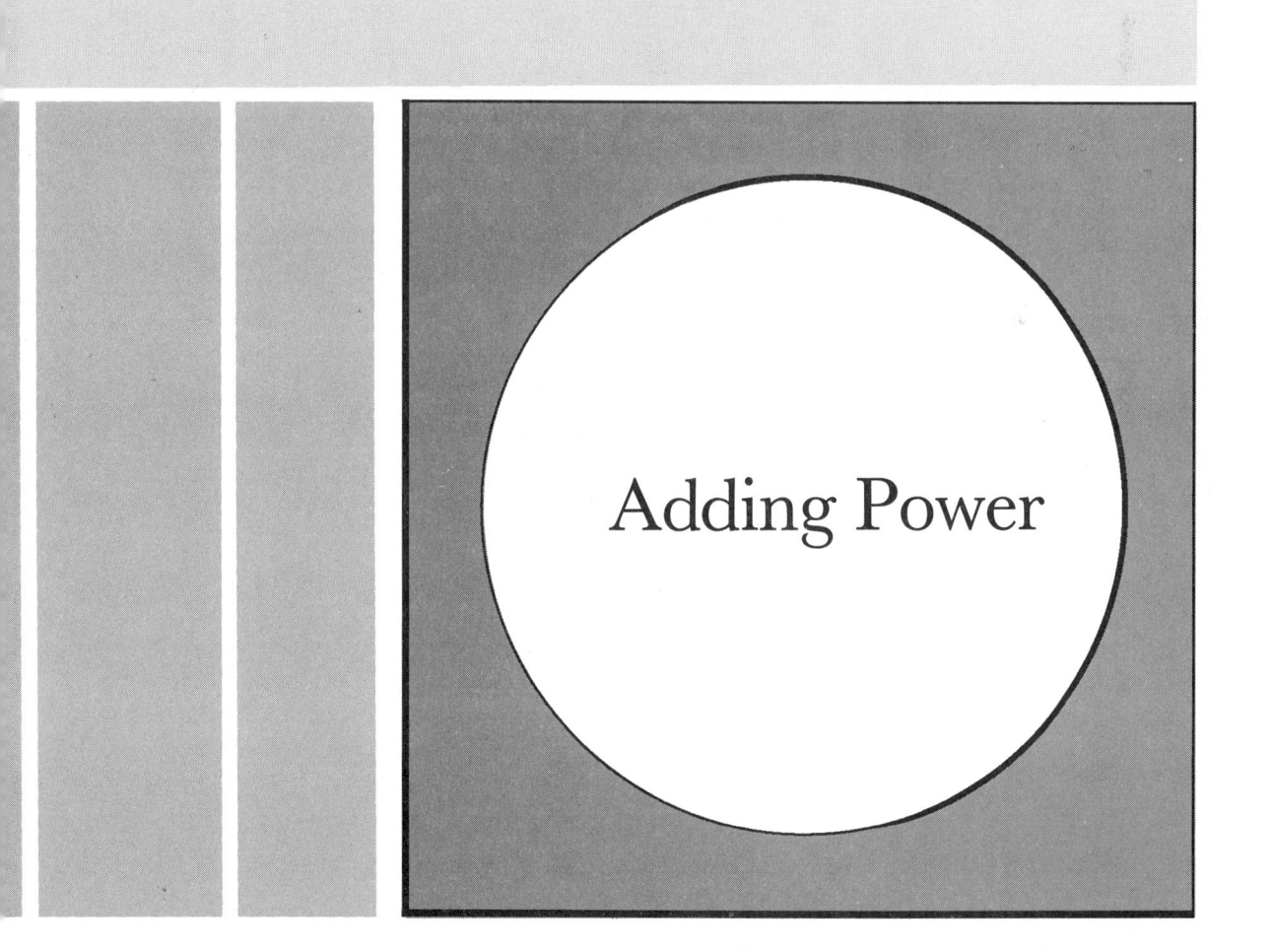

Adding Power

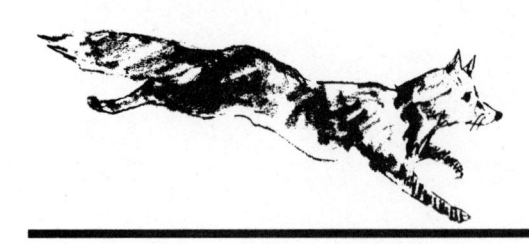

Chapter 7

Using Relational Databases,
the View Window, and RQBE

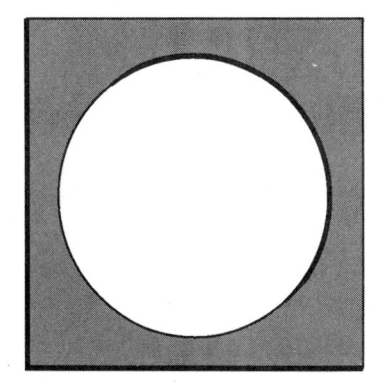

THE VIEW WINDOW, ACCESSED FROM THE WINDOW menu popup, is one of the most powerful and advanced features of FoxPro. This window lets you set up a special view of your data—an entire working environment. You can then save this environment in a file so that you can use it whenever you want.

Actually, you created views earlier when you were working with reports and labels, but these were relatively simple views, saved and recalled automatically only because the Environment check box was selected by default. The View window lets you control many features of the FoxPro environment.

Most obviously, the View window lets you control environment settings, some of which you have looked at earlier. For example, you have seen that you can use **SET DELETED ON** or **SET DELETED OFF** to determine whether FoxPro commands act on records that are marked for deletion. This is one of a large number of environment settings that you can control using the View window.

In addition, the View window lets you use the same Setup dialog box that you can access by selecting Setup from the Database menu. As you remember from earlier chapters, you can use the Setup dialog box to determine which indexes are open, to set a filter that determines which records the user can access (in the same way that a FOR clause does), or to set fields so that the user can access only certain fields in the database file.

You can begin to see why this is called a view of the data. If you let the user see only certain records and certain fields of those records, and if you also control settings such as whether deleted records are processed, then you are determining how the user *sees* the data. You might take your EMPLIST database and set it up for one user to see only names and addresses from California, and for another user to see the names and wages for all employees. The two users' views of the data are so different that they would hardly know that they are using the same database file.

The final feature of the View window is its most powerful: it lets you set up relational databases. As you will see in a moment, there are times when you should break up your data so it is stored in several database files and relate these files to each other. The View window lets you open more than one database file at a time and to set a relation of this sort between two separate files. Then, when you scroll through one file, the pointer automatically moves to the corresponding record in the other file. If you wish, you can even set up the view so the user can open a Browse window to scroll through the records of one file and automatically see the corresponding records of the other file in the same Browse window—without ever knowing that more than one database file is in use.

As of version 2, FoxPro includes a second method of working with relational databases. The FoxPro language now incorporates features of SQL, the **S**tructured **Q**uery **L**anguage, which is the industry standard for working with relational databases in mainframe environments, and is gradually becoming the standard on microcomputers also. By using SQL, you can query relational databases without doing all the preliminary housekeeping work of setting a relation: it is all done within a single SQL query. Even more remarkable is the fact that FoxPro includes a Relational Query By Example (RQBE) facility, which generates SQL commands.

After learning the theory of setting up relational databases and learning about the View window, you will see how to work with relational databases using RQBE.

UNDERSTANDING RELATIONAL DATABASES

When businesses first computerized, as you learned in the introduction to this book, they discovered an unexpected benefit of abandoning their paper files: they could avoid unnecessary repetition of data.

When records were kept on paper, the payroll department kept records on a form with each employee's name, address, and wages; the benefits department kept records on a form with each employee's name, address, and eligibility for benefits; the human resources development department kept records on a form with each employee's name, address, and training; and so on. In a large business, basic information such as the name, address, and Social Security number of each employee might be repeated dozens of times. If the employee moved, a dozen different forms had to be updated.

Computer scientists developed a number of methods of avoiding this repetition, and the relational database eventually emerged as the method of choice.

Before you can set up a relational database, you must *normalize* the data—break it down in a way that minimizes repetition. In the example above, you obviously would want to keep the employee's name, address, and other basic data in one file, the records of wages in a second file, the records of eligibility for benefits in a third file, the records of courses taken in a fourth file, and so on.

In order to relate these files to each other, you must use some key field in all of them, such as an employee number or Social Security number. Imagine that one file has the employee number and basic data such as name and address. And imagine that, whenever employees are paid, the employee number, the date, and the wage is entered in a second file. These two files can be related to each other using the employee number. A view can be set up that lets the payroll department scroll through the records and look at the name, address, date, and wage just as if they were in a single database file. This is an example of a *one-to-many relationship*: each employee has one name and address, but many weeks of wages.

> Though it is meaningful, the Social Security number is acceptable as a key field, since it is unique for each person and never changes.

Notice that the key field must be unique: it cannot be duplicated in more than one record in the file on the "one" side of the relation. If two employees had the same employee number, for example, there would be no way of knowing which one of them corresponded to a wage record with that employee number. The key field must also be unchanging: if you ever change its value in a record on the "one" side of the relation, than you will have no way of relating the records on the "many" side to it. For these reasons, you should use some arbitrary value, such as an employee number, as the key field, and you should never use some meaningful value, such as the person's name. A meaningful value might be duplicated; and it might change. For example, two people may have the same name; furthermore, people sometimes change their names.

Needless to say, the job of normalizing the data, breaking it down to avoid repetition, can be very complex if you are computerizing a large corporation. There is an entire theory of database normalization that you should study if you become interested in advanced database programming. For most applications on microcomputers, though, normalization is just a matter of common sense: you simply have to look for one-to-many relationships.

In the example you looked at above, one employee gets many paychecks. In some applications, there are also *many-to-many relationships*.

One common example is enrollments of students in classes: each student can take many classes, and each class can have many students enrolled in it. This sort of relationship will not really be covered in this book, because many-to-many relationships are not common in applications on microcomputers. It is good for you to know that they exist, however, just in case you run across one—so that you will not try to handle it as a one-to-many relationship. The theory of databases with many-to-many relationships is covered in more advanced books. Since they are broken down into pairs of one-to-many relationships, they can be handled using techniques similar to the ones you will learn for one-to-many relationships.

It is also possible to create *one-to-one relationships.* For example, you could conceivably keep a person's name and address in one file and other data in another file, adding an employee number to both files to relate them. Of course, this is not something you would normally do: whenever there is a one-to-one relationship, it is easier to keep all the data in one file. There might be cases, though, where you would want to create a one-to-one relation between two files that you had not anticipated using together, assuming that they have some field, such as Social Security number, that you can use as the key.

WORKING WITH THE VIEW WINDOW

In this chapter, you will use the example of wages for employees and keep the data in two related files. You will add an employee number to a file which already has the basic data on the employee (the EMPLIST file), and you will create a WAGES file with the employee number, date, and wage.

SETTING UP A RELATIONAL DATABASE

To relate two files using the FoxPro View window, you must open them both at once. In the past, you have always found that the current file is automatically closed when you open a new file, but the View window, shown in Figure 7.1, lets you use several database files in different work areas. The pushbuttons on the upper left of the

View window let you use its four different panels. The View panel, shown in the illustration, is the most powerful and is discussed first. The other three pushbuttons let you access the On/Off, Files, and Misc panels, which are used to make simple environment settings that will be covered later in this chapter.

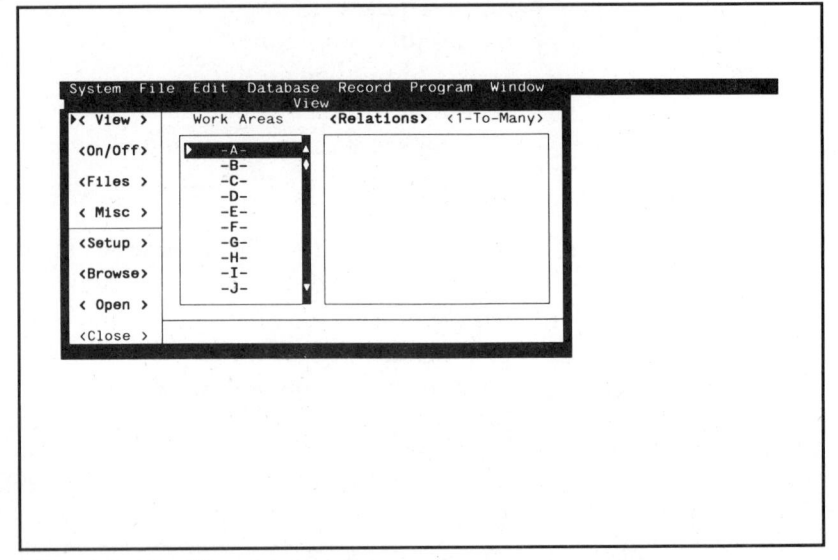

```
System File Edit Database Record Program Window
                        View
>< View >      Work Areas    <Relations>  <1-To-Many>
<On/Off>          -A-
                  -B-
<Files  >         -C-
                  -D-
< Misc  >         -E-
                  -F-
<Setup  >         -G-
                  -H-
<Browse>          -I-
                  -J-
< Open  >
<Close  >
```

Figure 7.1: The View window

As you can see from the illustration, the View window lets you use ten work areas, each designated with a letter from A to J. You can move among these work areas and open a different database file in each of them.

You can always use the database in the current work area in the same ways that you have used databases in the past. For example, you can refer to its fields simply by using the field name, as usual.

No matter which work area you are in, though, you can use the fields of any file that is open in any other work area, by referring to them in one of the following ways, all of which use the period or arrow operator that you have seen before in commands generated by FoxPro:

- the appropriate letter (from A to J), followed by the period or arrow operator and the field name

- the appropriate number (from 1 to 10), followed by the period or arrow operator and the field name
- the file name (or alias), followed by the period or arrow operator and the field name

The arrow operator is made up of two characters, a hyphen followed by a greater-than sign.

You can also move among work areas by using the command **SELECT** with any of the preceding methods to refer to the work area. For example, if you have the EMPLIST file open in Work Area A, you can move to that work area and use that file in the ordinary way by entering **SELECT A** or **SELECT 1** or **SELECT EMPLIST**. Notice that the period or arrow operator is not used to move among work areas. It is used only to refer to fields that are not in the current work area.

If you wanted, you could open different databases in different work areas in order to make it easy to look at different lists when you are working on several. You can then move back and forth among the work areas and use the database in each one without having to open it every time. You could still use the period or arrow operator to access a database in another work area, even though it is unrelated to the database in the current work area: you would get the data from the record where you left the pointer the last time you were working on that database.

You get the most power from the multiple work areas, however, when you use the View window to set a relation between two database files, so the pointer in one moves automatically whenever you move the pointer in the other.

In order to better understand how to set a relation, you should consider the nature of the many-to-one relationship of the data. Your EMPLIST.DBF file contains one record for each employee, and your WAGES.DBF file will contain many records for each employee. When you scroll through the records in the WAGES file, you can find the corresponding data from the EMPLIST file; as you look at each week's wages, you can also look at the name of the person who has that employee number.

For this reason, you must be in a work area of the file that is on the "many" side of the many-to-one relationship when you set the relation and when you use the relational database. The file on the "one"

> Programmers sometimes open files with an alias, to make it easier to follow the code. You can do this by using the command **USE** <*file name*> **ALIAS** <*alias name*>, after which you can refer to the file by its alias rather than its name.

> The **SET RELATION** command actually lets you relate files by record number as well as by key field, but this feature is not really useful. To create a genuine relational database, you must set the relation into an indexed key field.

side of the many-to-one relationship must be indexed on the key field (in this case, on the employee number field)—FoxPro needs this index to look up the name of the person with the same employee number as the current record in the WAGE file.

The file on the many side of a many-to-one relationship is sometimes called the *parent* or *controlling file*. The file on the one side of the relationship merely fills in the details; it is sometimes called the *child file*. Notice that you cannot logically make an entry in the WAGES file unless there is already an entry with the same employee number in the EMPLIST file. If you did, you would be entering wages for someone who is not an employee. This is always true of a database with a many-to-one relationship: you cannot logically enter a record in the file on the "many" side of the relation unless there is already a record with the same key field in the file on the "one" side.

This should become clear in the exercise. First you will simply set the relation and see how the pointers move in both files. Bear in mind that although the key fields in the example will have the same name in the two files when you set the relation, they do not need to. You can specify any field in the "many" file and the relation is set into the field that the "one" file is indexed on.

> In this example, just the total wage is recorded. In a real application, of course, you would probably want to keep more data in the wages file—for example, the number of hours worked. This example is simplified to save you time in data entry and to let you concentrate on the main issue: relating the two files.

1. First you must create the WAGES file. Select New from the File menu and select the Database radio button; then select OK. When the Structure dialog box appears, create a database with the fields shown in Figure 7.2. Select OK. In the Name the New Database dialog box, type WAGES and select Save.

2. FoxPro asks if you want to enter records now. Select Yes and enter the following sample records, whose use will become clear to you in a moment: When the Wages window appears, enter as the first Empno **A01**, as the Date, **08/06/90**, and as the Wage, **720.00**. As the second record, enter Empno **A01**, Date, **08/13/90**, Wage, **740.00**. As the third record, enter Empno **A02**, Date **08/06/90**, Wage **530**. As the fourth record, enter Empno **A02**, Date **08/13/90**, Wage **590.00**. That's two weeks of wages for two employees, as shown in Figure 7.3. Close the Wages Edit window, saving the data.

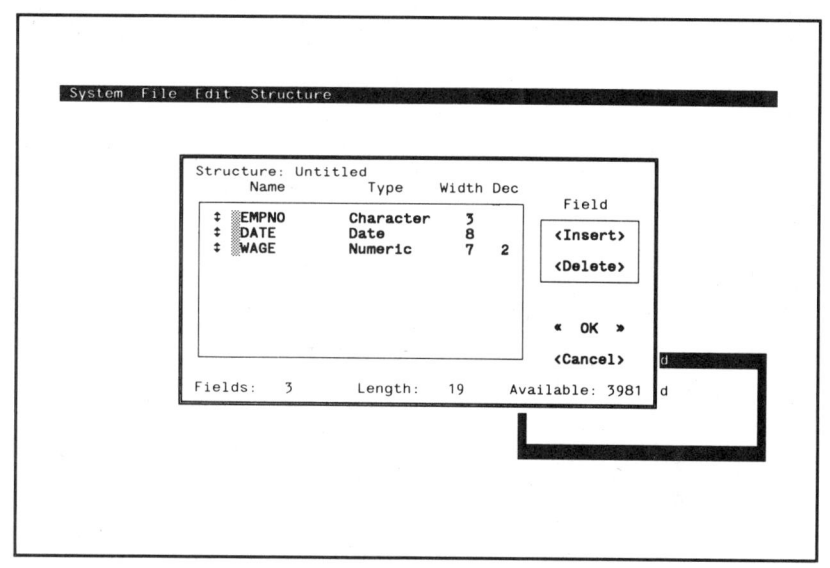

Figure 7.2: The structure of the WAGES file

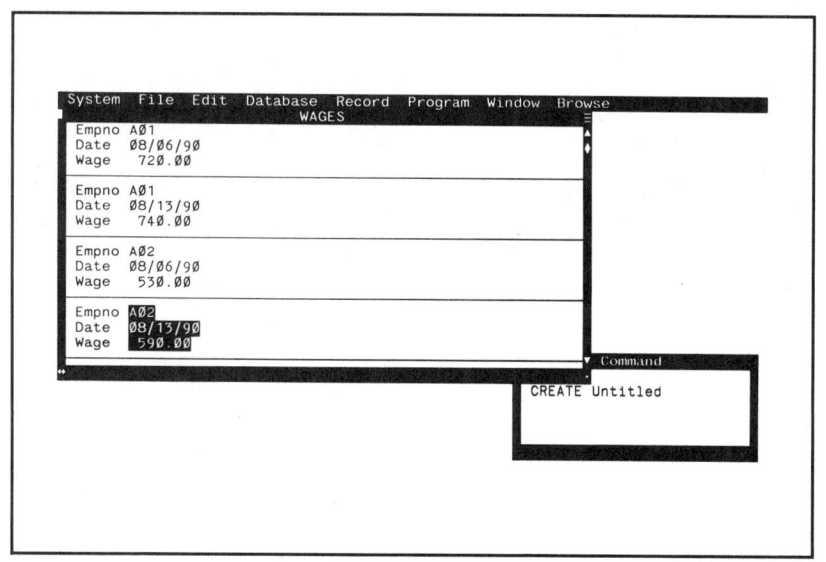

Figure 7.3: Data entered in the WAGES file

> Remember that there are two Modify pushbuttons in the Setup dialog box. You need to use the one next to the word Structure, not the one under the word Index.

3. Now, since the View window includes the entire Setup dialog box, you can use it to modify the structure of the EMPLIST database to add an employee number. Select View from the Window menu to call up the View window. Note that the WAGES file that you have created is already active in Work Area A, and the other work areas are free. Move the highlight to Work Area B and press Enter to select it. The command **SELECT B** is generated in the Command window and the Select dialog box automatically appears. Select EMPLIST.DBF to open it in Work Area B, generating the command

   USE C:\LEARNFOX\EMPLIST.DBF

4. To modify the structure of EMPLIST, select the Setup pushbutton from the View window. From the Setup dialog box, select the Modify pushbutton. When the Structure dialog box appears, move the highlight to the FNAME field; then select the Insert pushbutton or select Insert Field from the Structure menu to add a new field. Change the name of the field that is added from NEWFIELD to **EMPNO**, keep its type as Character, and change its width from 10 to **3**. Select the shaded area to its left to create an index tag. The structure should look like Figure 7.4. Then Select OK and, to make the structure change permanent, select Yes. When you return to the Setup dialog box, the new field is added at the beginning of the scrollable list of field names. Select OK.

5. Now, you need to add employee numbers to EMPLIST; since this is the file on the "one" end of the one-to-many relationship, the employee numbers must be unique, and the file must be indexed on employee number. Select the Browse pushbutton of the View window (or select Browse from the Database menu), and simply add the numbers from A01 to A11, as shown in Figure 7.5. Then close the Browse window, saving the changes, to return to the View window.

6. To make the EMPNO tag the controlling index, select Setup, then EMPLIST and EMPNO in the list of indexes,

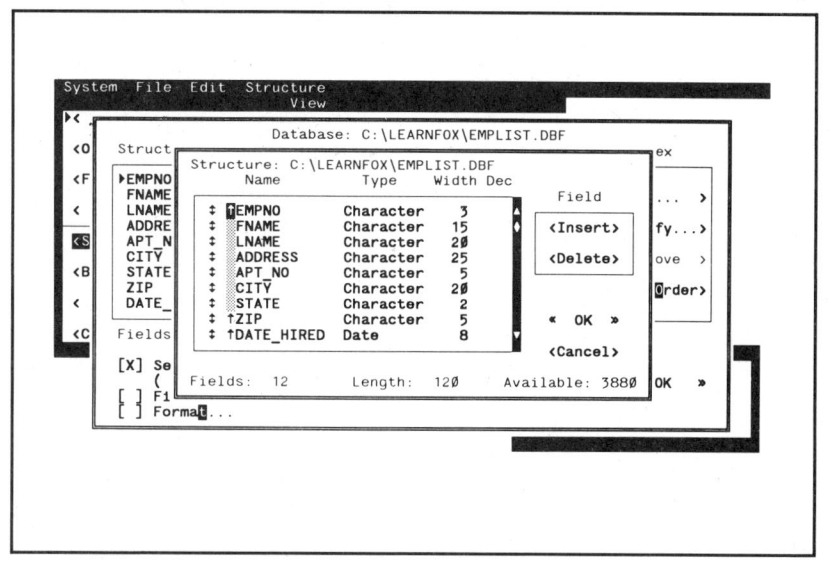

Figure 7.4: The modified structure of EMPLIST

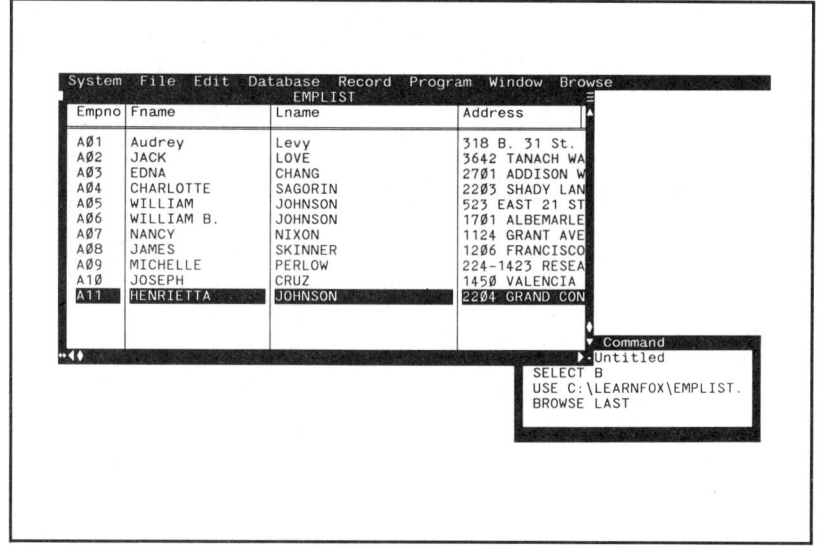

Figure 7.5: EMPLIST with employee numbers added

and the Set Order pushbutton. Then select OK to return to the View window.

7. Now you are ready to set the relation. Remember that you must be in the work area of the file on the "many" side of the relationship and set the relation into the file on the "one" side of the relationship, since FoxPro needs to look into the EMPLIST file to find one record that matches each record in the WAGES file. Move the View window's highlight to WAGES and press Enter to generate the command **SELECT A**. If FoxPro also opens a Browse window and generates the command **BROWSE LAST**, close the Browse window to return to the View window. Then select the Relations pushbutton. Notice that WAGES, the name of the current file, appears in the Relations window, with an arrow pointing to the space under it for the file that the relation is set into.

8. Move the highlight to EMPLIST and press Enter to select it as the file that the relation is set into. The expression builder appears to let you choose the expression in WAGES that corresponds to the indexed expression in EMPLIST. Notice that you can use any expression from the file on the "many" side of the relationship, but that you must relate it to the indexed expression in the file on the "one" side of the relationship. If it is not already there by default, type **EMPNO** in the text box. Then select OK. Now that the relation is set, EMPLIST appears under WAGES, with the arrow pointing into it, as in Figure 7.6. The command **SET RELATION TO EMPNO INTO EMPLIST** is generated.

Now that the relation is set, you can browse both files and see that when you move the pointer in the WAGES file, FoxPro automatically moves the pointer to the corresponding record in the EMPLIST file. This exercise will help you understand how the relation affects the pointers in the two files. (In a later exercise, you will set up the relational database in more practical ways, for example by including fields from the two files in the same Browse window.)

1. Select the Browse pushbutton to browse the WAGES file (which is in the current work area). Move up to the first

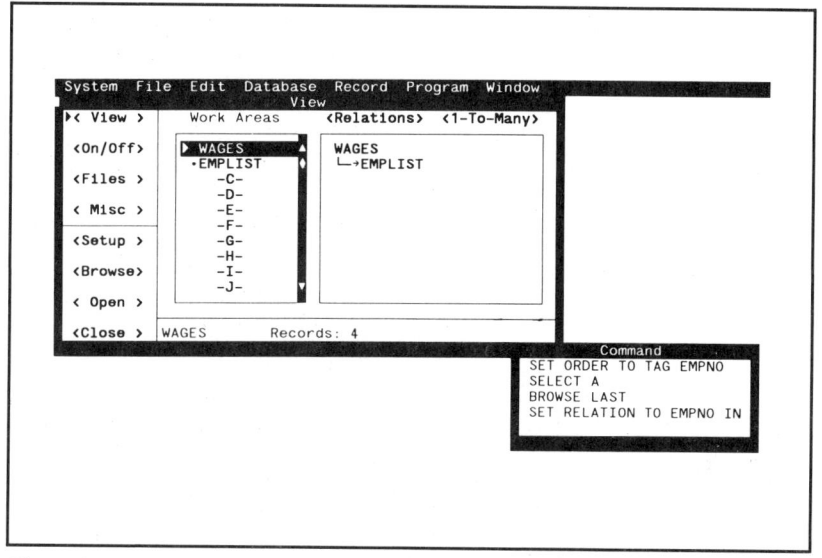

```
System  File  Edit  Database  Record  Program  Window
                          View
 < View  >   Work Areas    <Relations>  <1-To-Many>
 <On/Off>   ▶ WAGES        WAGES
             ·EMPLIST       └→EMPLIST
 <Files  >   -C-
             -D-
 < Misc  >   -E-
             -F-
 <Setup  >   -G-
             -H-
 <Browse>    -I-
             -J-
 < Open  >
 <Close  >  WAGES      Records: 4
                                              Command
                                   SET ORDER TO TAG EMPNO
                                   SELECT A
                                   BROWSE LAST
                                   SET RELATION TO EMPNO IN
```

Figure 7.6: The relation of WAGES set into EMPLIST, shown in the View window

record, which has an EMPNO of A01. Now, select View from the Window menu to bring the View window to the front. Move the cursor to EMPLIST and press Enter to generate the command **SELECT B**. If FoxPro does not automatically open a Browse window, select the Browse pushbutton. Note that the pointer is also in the record in this file that has the Empno of A01.

2. Remember that any open window is added at the end of the Window menu popup, with a number before it to let you use that window quickly. Select 1 WAGES from the Window menu to bring the WAGES Browse window to the front again. Move the cursor down to the fourth record, which has the employee number A02. Then select 0 EMPLIST from the Window menu to bring the EMPLIST Browse window to the front again. Note that the pointer has automatically moved to the second record, which has the EMPNO of A02, corresponding to the EMPNO of the record where the cursor was moved in the WAGES file.

3. Now test the fact that the relation works only one way. Move the pointer back up to the first record of the EMPLIST Browse window, which has the Empno of A01. Then select 1 WAGES from the Window menu to move back to the WAGES Browse window. The pointer is still where you left it, on the fourth record, which has the Empno of A02. Select 0 EMPLIST from the Window menu to return to the EMPLIST Browse window. The pointer is not where you left it: it moves back to the second record, so that its Empno corresponds with the current Empno in the WAGES file. Now close both Browse windows to return to the View window.

Of course, it would take too much time to set the relation each time you wanted to use this relational database. In the next section, you will save and reuse the view, after you see how to make use of the related files.

USING A RELATIONAL DATABASE

Now that you have set the many-to-one relation and seen how moving the pointer in the WAGES file (the controlling or parent file) automatically moves the pointer to the corresponding record in the EMPLIST file, you can begin to make use of this relational database. First, you will create a Browse window of the sort that you could use for entering and viewing data. Then you will use a command with a Fields check box to include fields from both files. Finally, you will take a look at reports and labels for relational databases.

BROWSING RELATED FILES

As you remember, many FoxPro commands can be used with field lists. Once a relation is set up, you can use these commands with a list that includes fields from both files. You just need to use the period or the arrow operator to refer to fields in the file not in the current work area. Remember what you learned in the last section, when you were browsing through the two files: you should always arrange to have the controlling file in the current work area, so that FoxPro can automatically move the pointer in the file that the relation is set into.

One particularly interesting command to use with relational databases is **BROWSE FIELDS** <*field list*>, since the Browse window you set up is saved and reused automatically each time you select Browse from the Database menu, generating the command BROWSE LAST. If you use **BROWSE FIELDS** <*field list*> once to create the Browse window, the Browse window will be displayed in the same way whenever you select Browse from the Database menu.

As an exercise, try creating a Browse window that includes all the fields of the WAGES file, and the Empno and name fields of the EMPLIST file, to see how easy this makes data entry. Having the Empno fields from both files will let you see clearly that the fields added to the Browse window from the EMPLIST file correspond to the current record in the WAGES file. It will also show you an important pitfall that you must avoid when you are working with relational databases.

Before you begin, make sure that you closed both Browse windows at the end of the last exercise, and that the work area of the WAGES file is the current work area.

○ The key field from the file on the "one" side of any many-to-one relation must be protected from being changed accidentally, otherwise it can cause irrecoverable loss of data. The Empno field from the EMPLIST file is included in the Browse window in this exercise only for instructional purposes.

1. Select Command from the Window menu to bring the Command window to the front. Enter

   BROWSE FIELDS EMPNO, DATE, WAGE, EMPLIST – >
   EMPNO, EMPLIST – >LNAME, EMPLIST – >FNAME

   all on one line to get the Browse window shown in Figure 7.7. Notice that each record you entered in the WAGE file has the corresponding employee number, last name, and first name from the EMPLIST file displayed next to it.

2. Add a new record: Select Append Record from the Browse menu. In the first Empno field (which you may remember is the Empno of the HOURS file), type **A03**. The corresponding EMPLIST fields Empno, Lname, and Fname are instantly filled in, as shown in Figure 7.8. To finish filling in the record, type **08/06/90** and type **498.00**.

3. For comparison, see what happens if there is no corresponding record in the EMPLIST. Select Append Record from the Browse menu. Type **A23** in the Empno field. The fact that no corresponding empno, lname, and fname appear lets you

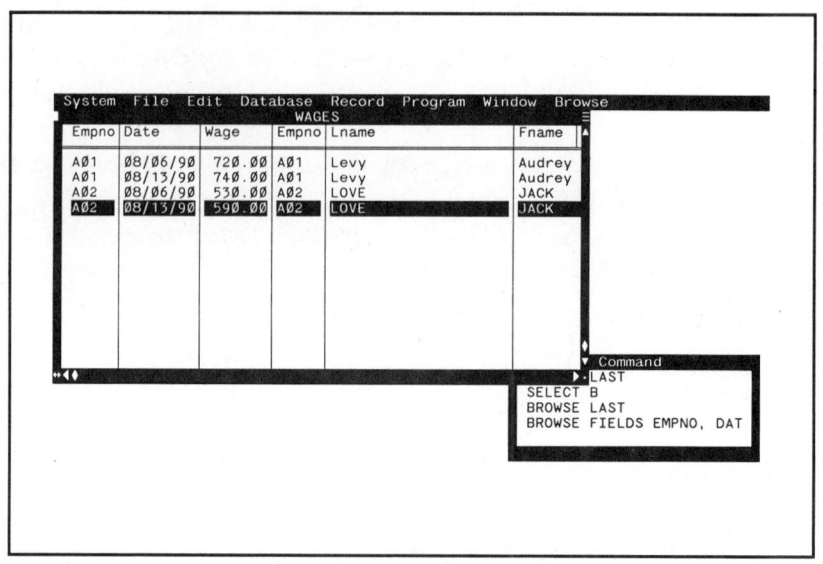

Figure 7.7: Browsing fields from two related database files

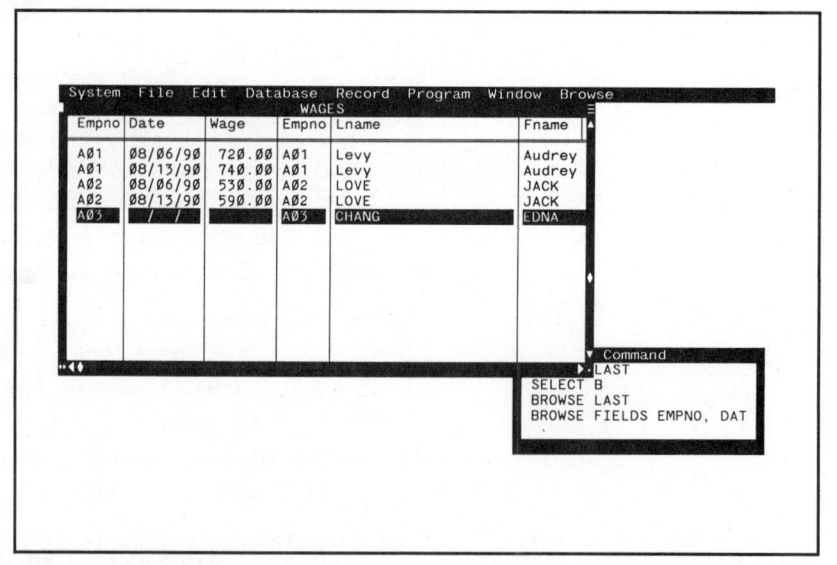

Figure 7.8: Fields that correspond to the Empno you enter are automatically filled in.

know that you have made an error in data entry: you have begun to enter wages for a worker who does not exist in your list of employees. Correct the error by editing A23 so it is **A03** instead. The empno and name appear. As the date, enter **08/13/90**, and as the wage, enter **480.00**.

4. Now, imagine that you make a very dangerous error. Move the cursor to the next field in the same record, the Empno field that comes from the EMPLIST file. Change this number from A03 to **A04**. Instantly, this empno and the lname and fname disappear from this record, as shown in Figure 7.9. You have just edited the EMPLIST file by mistake, so that there is no longer a record there with the empno of A03: fields disappeared because there is no longer a record in the EMPLIST file that corresponds to these records of the WAGES file.

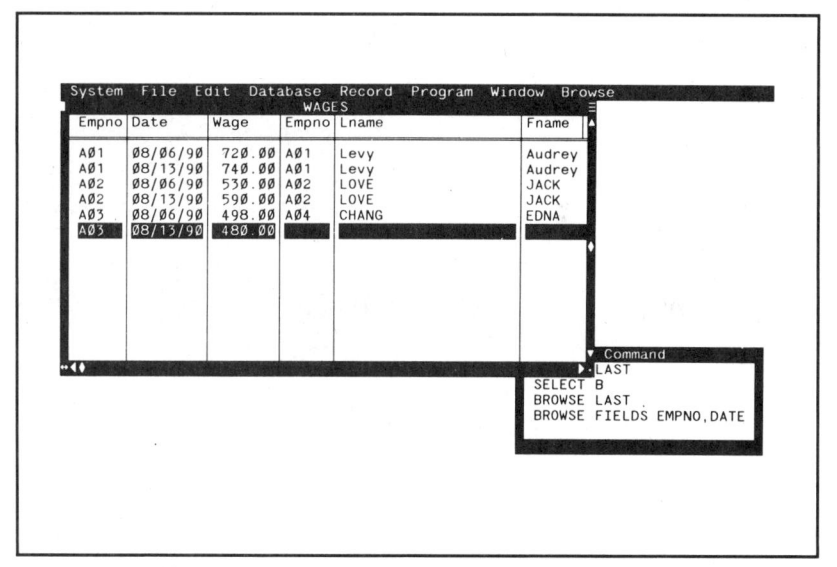

```
System  File  Edit  Database  Record  Program  Window  Browse
                        WAGES
 Empno  Date      Wage     Empno  Lname           Fname
 A01    08/06/90  720.00   A01    Levy            Audrey
 A01    08/13/90  740.00   A01    Levy            Audrey
 A02    08/06/90  530.00   A02    LOVE            JACK
 A02    08/13/90  590.00   A02    LOVE            JACK
 A03    08/06/90  498.00   A04    CHANG           EDNA
 A03    08/13/90  480.00
                                                        Command
                                                     LAST
                                                     SELECT B
                                                     BROWSE LAST
                                                     BROWSE FIELDS EMPNO,DATE
```

Figure 7.9: The data vanishes.

5. To fix this mistake, select View from the Window menu. In the View window, move the cursor to the work area with EMPLIST in it and press Enter, to generate the command **SELECT B**. If FoxPro does not automatically open a Browse

window, select the Browse pushbutton. In the new Browse window, you can see that two records have the empno of A04. Hopefully, you remember that Edna Chang is the one that used to be A03. Edit the file so Edna Chang again has number **A03** and close this EMPLIST Browse window, saving the change. Close the View window to see your WAGES Browse window again. The empno, lname, and fname reappear in the record where they were missing.

6. Now that you have seen what can go wrong, you will save this view and then reuse it as an exercise. First, make sure the WAGES work area is selected. Then save the view: Select View from the Window menu to open the View window again. Then select Save As from the File menu, and FoxPro displays the Save View As dialog box, shown in Figure 7.10. Type the name **WAGEENTR** and select Save, generating the command

   CREATE VIEW C:\LEARNFOX\WAGEENTR.VUE

7. Now, watch how easy it is to use this view at any time in the future, even after you have quit FoxPro. Select Quit from the File menu to end this session; then, at the DOS prompt,

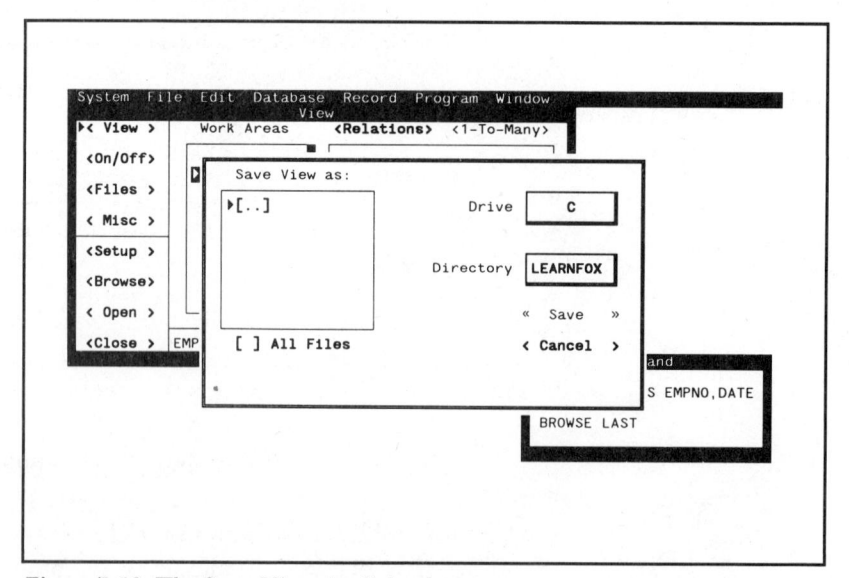

Figure 7.10: The Save View As dialog box

enter **FOXPRO** to start FoxPro again. (If you want, enter **CLEAR** to clear the screen, or start the program using **FOXPRO −T**).

8. Select Open from the File menu. From the Open dialog box, select the Type popup control as in Figure 7.11. Select View as the type. Select WAGEENTR.VUE from the scrollable list and note that FoxPro generates the command **SET VIEW TO WAGEENTR.VUE**. Now, select Browse from the Database menu, and the Browse window that you set up to display fields from the two files reappears. Close the Browse window.

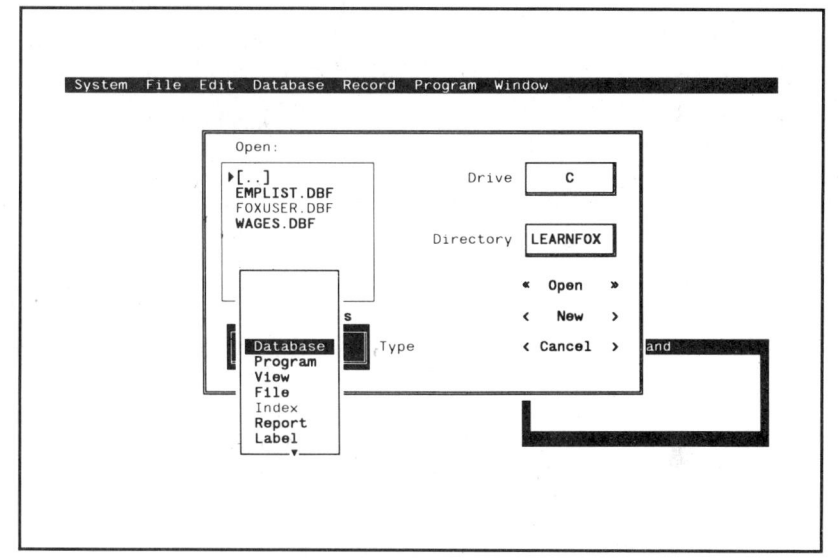

Figure 7.11: Using the Type popup to open a View file

You can see that it is almost as easy to open a view—with up to ten files, the relations among them, and other environment settings—as it is to open a single database file. You can imagine how much of a convenience this is if you have to switch between ten different views of your data in the course of the day, or if you are writing a program that constantly switches from one view to another.

USING THE FIELDS CHECK BOX

If a dialog box has a Fields check box you can use it to choose the fields from the file that the relation is set into, in the same way that

> The Set Fields box of the Setup window cannot be used in this way. It can only be used to exclude fields from the file in the current work area, and not to include fields from related files. To set fields permanently in this way, you should use RQBE (covered later in this chapter) rather than the View window.

you used a fields list when you were working from the Command window. Let's try using the Fields check box of the Copy To dialog box:

1. Select Copy To from the Database menu popup. When the Copy To dialog box appears, select the Fields check box. When the field picker appears, use the Database popup control to select EMPLIST, as in Figure 7.12; then select LNAME and FNAME from the Database Fields scrollable list and move them into the Selected Fields box on the right (using the Move pushbutton for each field). Then use the Database popup control to select WAGES, and select DATE and WAGE from the Database Fields scrollable list. The field picker should now look like Figure 7.13. Select OK.

2. You have returned to the Copy To dialog box, and you are ready to copy the selected fields to a new file. In the Save As text box, type **TESTCOPY**, and then select OK.

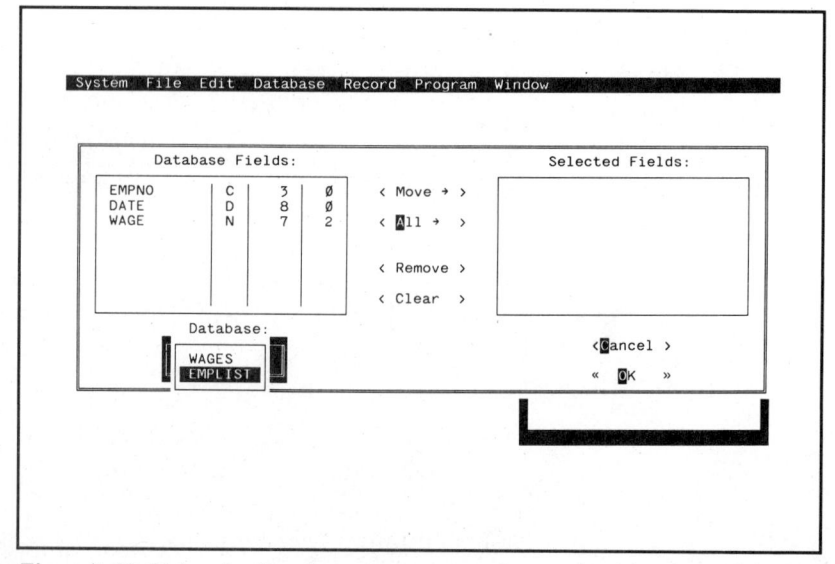

Figure 7.12: Using the Database popup control to work with related database files

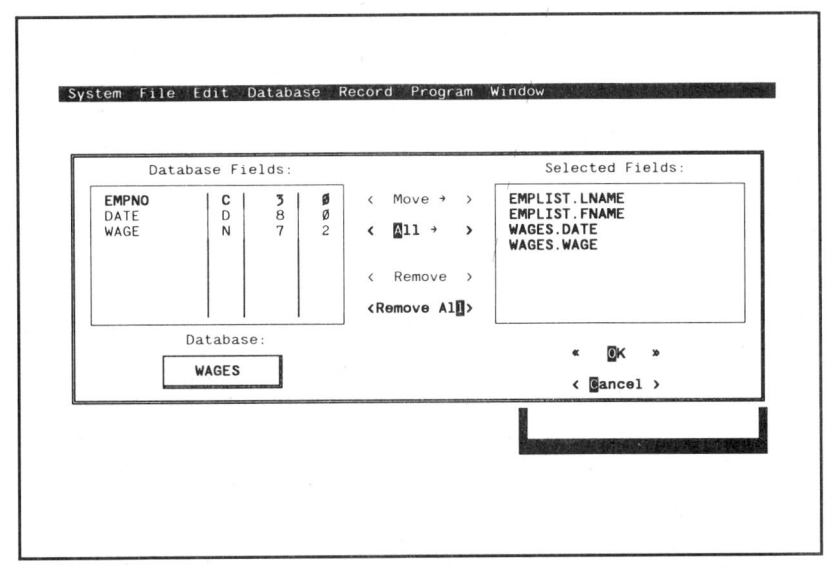

```
┌─────────────────────────────────────────────────────────────┐
│ System  File  Edit  Database  Record  Program  Window       │
│                                                             │
│     Database Fields:                    Selected Fields:    │
│   ┌──────────────────┐              ┌────────────────────┐  │
│   │ EMPNO  C  3  0   │   < Move  >  │ EMPLIST.LNAME      │  │
│   │ DATE   D  8  0   │              │ EMPLIST.FNAME      │  │
│   │ WAGE   N  7  2   │   < All   >  │ WAGES.DATE         │  │
│   │                  │              │ WAGES.WAGE         │  │
│   │                  │   < Remove >                         │
│   │                  │   <Remove All>                       │
│   │                  │                                      │
│        Database:                          «  OK  »          │
│        ┌────────┐                                           │
│        │ WAGES  │                         < Cancel >        │
│        └────────┘                                           │
└─────────────────────────────────────────────────────────────┘
```

Figure 7.13: The field picker with fields from two related database files

3. To see the result, select View from the Window menu to re-open the View window. Move the highlight to Work Area C and press Enter to generate the command **SELECT C**. If the Select Database dialog box does not appear automatically, select the Open pushbutton of the View window. Select TESTCOPY.DBF from the scrollable list of file names and then select the Open pushbutton. If necessary, select the Browse pushbutton of the View window to browse this file to see the TESTCOPY file. You will find that it has the fields from both the EMPLIST and WAGES files, as shown in Figure 7.14. Close the Browse window.

REPORTS USING RELATIONAL DATABASES

You can use data from related files just as easily when you are creating reports. You can use the Database popup of the expression builder to access fields from different database files, much as you did in the previous section.

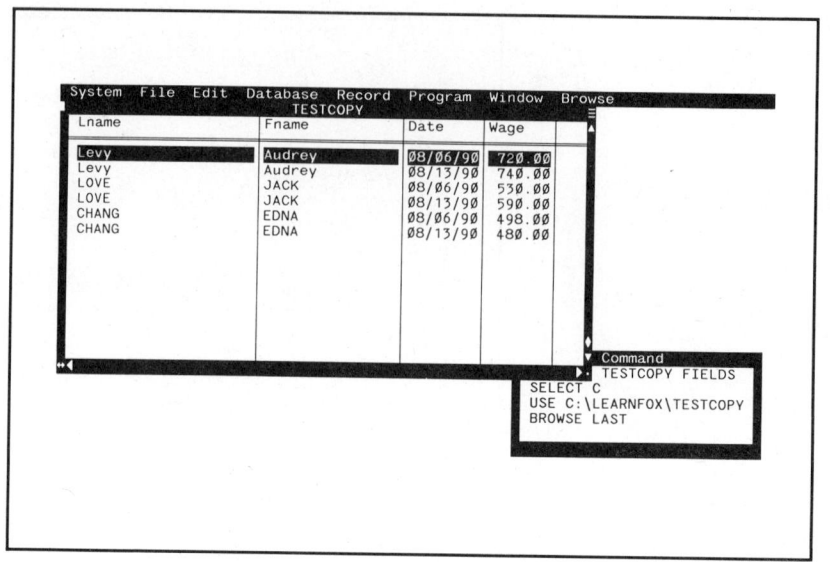

```
┌─────────────────────────────────────────────────────────────────┐
│ System  File  Edit  Database  Record  Program  Window  Browse   │
│                      TESTCOPY                                    │
│  Lname          Fname           Date        Wage                 │
│  Levy           Audrey          08/06/90    720.00               │
│  Levy           Audrey          08/13/90    740.00               │
│  LOVE           JACK            08/06/90    530.00               │
│  LOVE           JACK            08/13/90    590.00               │
│  CHANG          EDNA            08/06/90    498.00               │
│  CHANG          EDNA            08/13/90    480.00               │
│                                                                  │
│                                          Command                 │
│                                          TESTCOPY FIELDS         │
│                                          SELECT C                │
│                                          USE C:\LEARNFOX\TESTCOPY│
│                                          BROWSE LAST             │
└─────────────────────────────────────────────────────────────────┘
```

Figure 7.14: Fields from related files copied into a single file

1. Select Work Area A, the work area in the View window with the WAGES file. Remember, you are creating a report on the *controlling file,* the file which is on the "many" side of the relationship. This file must be in the current work area when you use the report, as when you use any command with this relational database.

2. Select New from the File menu. Select the Report radio button and then select OK to call up the report layout window. Press the down arrow key four times to move the cursor to the detail band.

3. Select Field from the Report menu to call up the Report Expression dialog box. Select the Expr pushbutton to call up the expression builder. Select the Database popup, which lets you select fields from any database, just as you did when you were using the Copy To dialog box above.

4. Select EMPLIST from this popup, as in Figure 7.15. Select LNAME from the scrollable list of field names. Select OK to return to the Report Expression dialog box, where this field name, complete with the file name and arrow operator, now

appears in the text box to the right of the Expr pushbutton. Of course, you could have typed it here if you wanted. If you do type it in, use the period or the arrow operator before the field name.

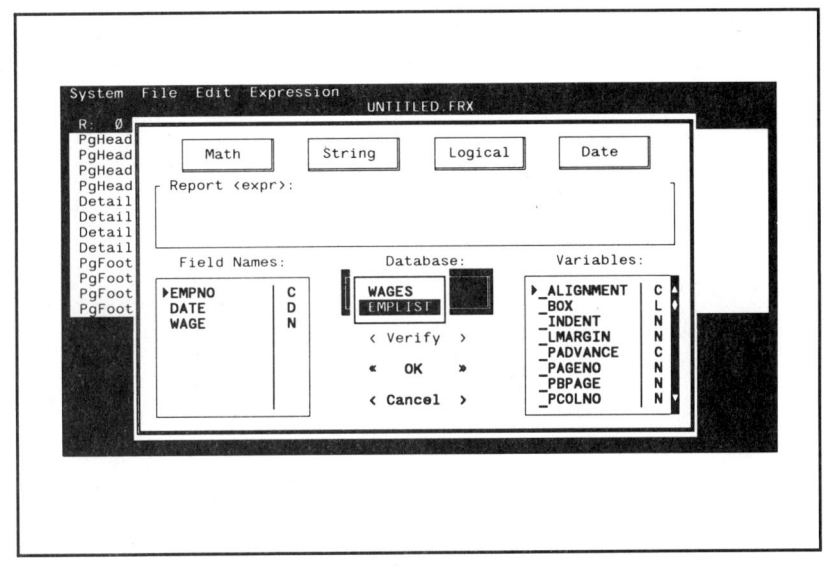

Figure 7.15: Adding fields from related files to a report

5. Select OK to place this field in the report. In an actual application, of course, you would place other fields from both related files in the layout window. Since you have learned what you need from this exercise, though, you should just close the report layout window. When FoxPro asks, type **Y** to discard the changes. You should also close any Browse windows that are open and return to the View window.

You can create labels using related files by selecting Expression from the Label menu popup and using the expression builder or by simply typing field names that include the period or arrow operator into the label form. It is unlikely, however, that you will have the name and address data that is needed for most labels in more than one file.

It is easy to create reports or labels that use related files, but this exercise does point out one possible pitfall. When you used the Database popup, TESTCOPY.DBF was on it, because it was open in Work Area C, even though it is not related to the other two files and has nothing to do with this report. Sometimes this popup makes things look a bit too easy; the fact that a database file is on it does not mean that this file is properly related to the other files. You must have a firm grasp of which files you are using and must set the relation between them before you create a report or work with any command that uses fields from multiple files.

CLOSING A VIEW

When you were working with just a single file open, you learned that you could close a database file by entering the command **USE** without any file name following it.

When you are using multiple work areas, though, this command only closes the database file in the current work area—just as the command **USE** <*file name*> only opens the file in the current work area.

The easiest way to do the housekeeping work of closing files when you are done using a view is to enter the command **CLOSE ALL**, which closes all files of all types in all work areas and selects Work Area 1, starting you off again with a clean slate.

Leaving files open can cause unexpected results later on. To make sure you avoid this error in the future, try closing files the wrong way first and then closing files the right way:

1. Enter **USE** in the command window. To see if a file is in use, enter **LIST**. Since no file is open, FoxPro displays the Open dialog box to let you choose a database file. Press Esc and FoxPro displays an alert saying no file is in use. Press any key to get rid of the alert.

2. Enter **SELECT B** and then enter **LIST**. FoxPro lists the EMPLIST database.

3. Enter **CLOSE ALL**. Select View from the Window menu to confirm that all database files are closed and Work Area A is selected. Close the View window.

ONE-TO-MANY RELATIONS

Unlike some other database programs, FoxPro lets you set one-to-many relations as well as the many-to-one relations that you have already learned about. Setting a one-to-many relation is easy to do.

First, you must set a relation just as you did earlier, using the View window or the **SET RELATION** command, but with the file on the "one" side of the relationship as the parent (controlling) file. Whenever you are in the work area of a file that is a parent file, the 1-To-Many pushbutton of the View window is activated, and you can select it to use the Establish 1-To-Many Relationship dialog box, shown in Figure 7.16.

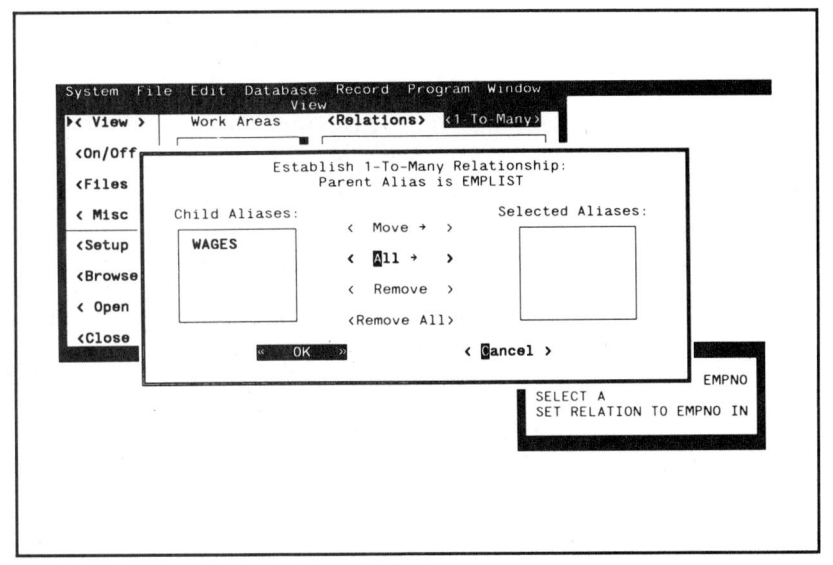

Figure 7.16: The Establish 1-To-Many Relationship dialog box

> These files are called aliases rather than files because it is permissible to refer to a file by another name when you open it. As long as you open the file in the ordinary way, though, the file alias is identical to the file name.

As you can see, the name of the parent file, the file whose work area was selected when you called up this dialog box, is listed at the top of the dialog box. All of its child files are listed in the Child Aliases box, and you can move any of them to to the list of Selected Aliases in order to specify that it is part of a one-to-many relationship.

As an example of a one-to-many relationship, try creating a view with the EMPLIST file as the parent file and the WAGES file as the child file, since there can be many entries in the WAGES file for each employee in EMPLIST:

1. You should be at the command window. If you have not already done so, enter **CLOSE ALL** to close the previous view. Then enter **USE EMPLIST**. Enter **SELECT B** and **USE WAGES**. The WAGES file must be indexed to set a

relation into it, so enter **INDEX ON EMPNO TAG EMPNO**. Now, to set the relation, enter **SELECT A** and then **SET RELATION TO EMPNO INTO WAGES**.

2. Now, to see what you have done, select View from the Window menu. Select the 1-To-Many pushbutton to use the Establish 1-To-Many Relationship dialog box, and select the All→ pushbutton to move the name of the WAGES file to the list of Selected Aliases.

3. That is all it takes to establish a one-to-many relationship. Save this view in case you want to use it again. Select Save As from the File menu, enter the name **EMPWAGES**, and select the Save pushbutton. Then close the View window to return to the command window.

4. Now, you will use the **BROWSE FIELDS** command as an exercise in using this relational database. Remember that EMPLIST is the file in the current work area, so you can refer to its fields by name; to refer to the fields in the WAGES file, though, you must use the arrow or period operator. In the command window, enter **BROWSE FIELDS LNAME, FNAME, WAGES – >DATE, WAGES – >WAGE**. You can play with the Browse window if you want. When you are done, close the Browse window and enter **CLOSE ALL** to close the view: remember that, since you saved it, you can open this view again at any time.

The Browse window is shown in Figure 7.17. As you can see, fields from the parent file appear only once. There is a shaded area under them to fill in the blank spaces if there are multiple records in the child file.

Notice that the command **SET SKIP TO WAGES** was generated in the command window. The command **SET SKIP TO** <*list of file aliases*> specifies that the parent file in the current work area is in a one-to-many relationship with all of the files whose aliases (or names) are listed. The file names in the list must be separated by commas if there are more than one, and all must already have been made children files of the file in the current work area.

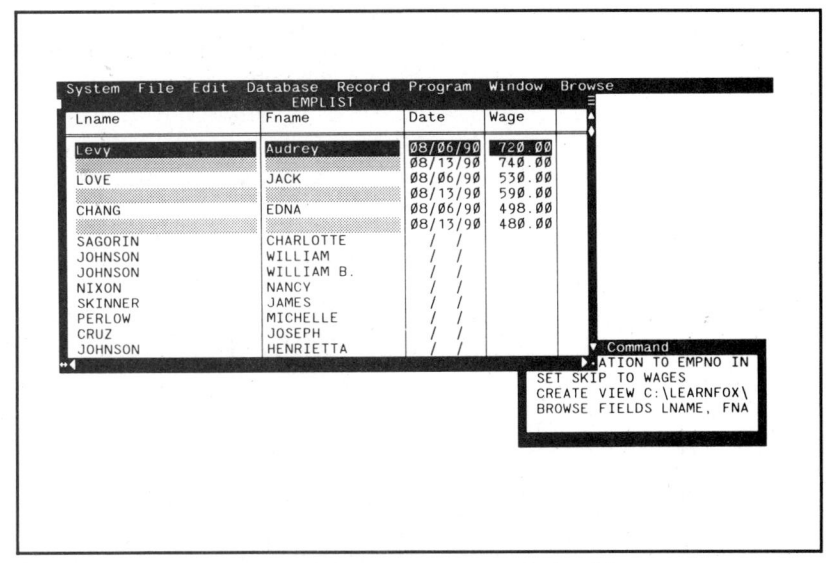

```
System  File  Edit  Database  Record  Program  Window  Browse
                         EMPLIST
 Lname              Fname           Date       Wage
 Levy               Audrey          08/06/90   720.00
                                    08/13/90   740.00
 LOVE               JACK            08/06/90   530.00
                                    08/13/90   590.00
 CHANG              EDNA            08/06/90   498.00
                                    08/13/90   480.00
 SAGORIN            CHARLOTTE         /  /
 JOHNSON            WILLIAM           /  /
 JOHNSON            WILLIAM B.        /  /
 NIXON              NANCY             /  /
 SKINNER            JAMES             /  /
 PERLOW             MICHELLE          /  /
 CRUZ               JOSEPH            /  /
 JOHNSON            HENRIETTA         /  /
                                                     Command
                                              ATION TO EMPNO IN
                                              SET SKIP TO WAGES
                                              CREATE VIEW C:\LEARNFOX\
                                              BROWSE FIELDS LNAME, FNA
```

Figure 7.17: Browsing fields of a one-to-many relationship

WARNING

The most important thing you should have learned from all these exercises is how much damage you can do by modifying the indexed key field of the database that the relation is set into. If you do this by mistake, you could end up with a list of wages and employee numbers without having any way of finding out which employee has a given employee number. Or you could end up with lists of customer numbers, sale dates, and amounts of money owed to you without having any way of finding out the names, addresses, or phone numbers of the customers you have to bill.

Never include a key field of this sort in the Browse window in the way that we did in the exercise. That example was meant to teach you graphically about a danger you need to avoid. Do not even include this sort of key field in the Browse window that you use to update the file itself; instead, use a Browse window with all the *other* fields. This way, you can change the name and address but you cannot change the employee number or customer number even by mistake. Moreover, do not delete records in this file unless you are archiving all of your old data and beginning a new cycle of data entry. If you do delete a record in this file, you will not be able to use the corresponding records in the related file. Finally, always keep your database files backed up, in case the mistake does occur despite your precautions.

In fact, because of this danger, the best way to use a relational database is by writing a program that adds the key field automatically and never lets the user change them. It is better yet if the user never even sees them.

USING ENVIRONMENT SETTINGS

The View panel that you just used to set relations is the most complex and powerful panel of the View window, since setting relations requires using multiple databases at once, creating or opening the proper index, and so on.

The View window also has three other panels that let you make simpler environment settings: the On/Off, Files, and Misc panels. The pushbuttons in the upper left of the View window let you access its four panels. When you use the View panel, there are also four pushbuttons in the lower left, which let you do things you might need to do while working with relational databases: Setup, Browse, Open, and Close. When you work with any of the other three panels, the lower left is empty: because they are simpler, there is no need for these extra features.

THE ON/OFF PANEL

Selecting the On/Off pushbutton lets you use the On/Off panel of the View window, shown in Figure 7.18 with its default settings. You can see from the help line at the bottom of the panel that it gives you access to features equivalent to commands which use **SET** with ON or OFF.

For example, you learned in Chapter 5 that you can deal with deleted records by using the commands **SET DELETED ON** and **SET DELETED OFF**. Selecting the Deleted check box in this panel is equivalent to using these commands. As you see, the check box is blank by default. You should remember that the default setting of the Deleted feature is *off*: the feature does *not* ordinarily screen out records marked for deletion. By selecting the check box, you set it *on*: the feature *does* screen out records marked for deletion.

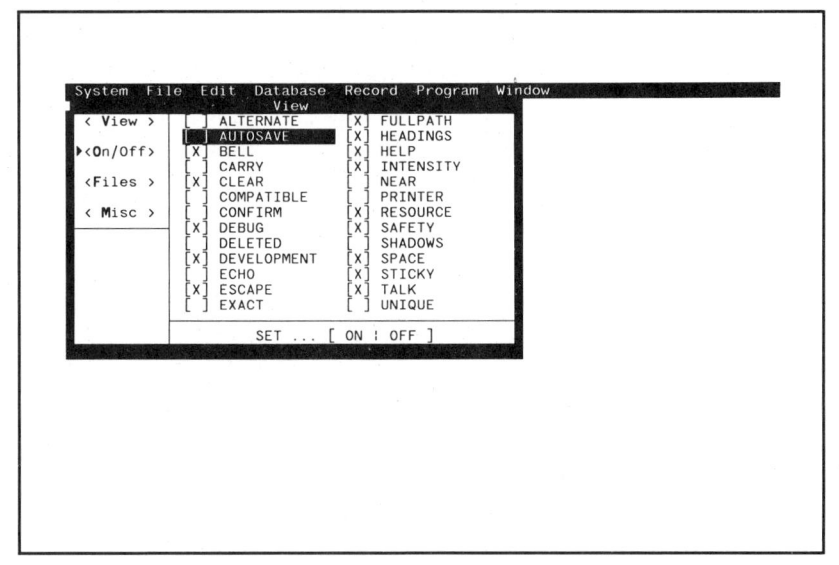

```
System  File  Edit  Database  Record  Program  Window
                        View
    < View >     [ ] ALTERNATE    [X] FULLPATH
                 [ ] AUTOSAVE     [X] HEADINGS
  ►<On/Off>      [X] BELL         [X] HELP
                 [ ] CARRY        [X] INTENSITY
    <Files >     [X] CLEAR        [ ] NEAR
                 [ ] COMPATIBLE   [ ] PRINTER
                 [ ] CONFIRM      [X] RESOURCE
    < Misc >     [X] DEBUG        [X] SAFETY
                 [ ] DELETED      [ ] SHADOWS
                 [X] DEVELOPMENT  [X] SPACE
                 [ ] ECHO         [X] STICKY
                 [X] ESCAPE       [X] TALK
                 [ ] EXACT        [ ] UNIQUE
                        SET ... [ ON : OFF ]
```

Figure 7.18: The On/Off panel of the View window with default settings

Deleted is one of the very few default environment settings that you would want to change as a user. You have already looked at a couple of others in earlier chapters.

Remember that if you set Near on, a **SEEK** command that cannot find a match positions the pointer at the record nearest to the value you were searching for, so that you can browse around and look for the record you want. You can see from the illustration that Near is off by default. You might want to select this check box when you are doing searches where you might not be sure of an exact spelling or number.

Likewise, you can see from the illustration that Exact is off. With earlier dBASE compatible programs, it was common at times to set Exact on to find only exact matches of character strings that you were searching for, leaving out words or names that began with the string you were searching for but which had more letters after it. You will still run across this command, though it is not as useful now that the = = operator has been added in FoxPro.

You might also want to set Printer on sometimes, in order to print whatever scrolls by on the screen. Set Alternate, which saves to a text file everything that scrolls by on the screen, is also useful, but it must be used in combination with **SET ALTERNATE TO** (covered in the next section), which specifies the name of the text file; Alternate is therefore dimmed until you have used **SET ALTERNATE TO**.

Other settings in this panel are useful mainly in programming. Setting Bell off stops FoxPro from sounding a beep when you reach the end of a field and automatically move to the next one. You may be tempted to set Bell off primarily because the beep can be annoying, but you will find if you do that the data you are entering in one field sometimes runs into the next field without your realizing it. Setting Bell off is really useful, however, in programs where you have built in some other way of controlling this problem. Likewise, setting Talk off can be useful when you are programming applications wherein you don't want to confuse the user with the FoxPro talk; but there is no reason to set the talk off when you are using FoxPro itself.

Some commands are dangerous. Setting Safety off, in particular, lets FoxPro destroy data without warning you.

These are some of the most important and interesting On/Off commands. A comprehensive listing is provided under SET in the Help window or in your *Commands and Functions* reference.

THE FILES PANEL

Selecting the Files pushbutton lets you use the Files panel of the View window, as shown in Figure 7.19. This panel controls environment settings that have to do with files. All of its features are equivalent to **SET ... TO** commands.

- **Default Drive:** lets you use a popup to choose the default drive used for all file input and output. For example, to use data that is on a floppy disk in your A: drive, just select A as the default drive. This feature is equivalent to the command

   SET DEFAULT TO <*letter of drive*>

> In the actual command, the letter designating the drive must be followed by a colon—for example, **A:**—despite the fact that the colon is not included in the popup control.

- **Path:** lets you specify a path for FoxPro to search when the file is not found in the directory. Selecting this check box calls up a dialog box that lets you enter the drive and directory for FoxPro to search in. You can eliminate this search path by selecting the Clear Path pushbutton. This feature is equivalent to the command

   SET PATH TO <*list of paths*>

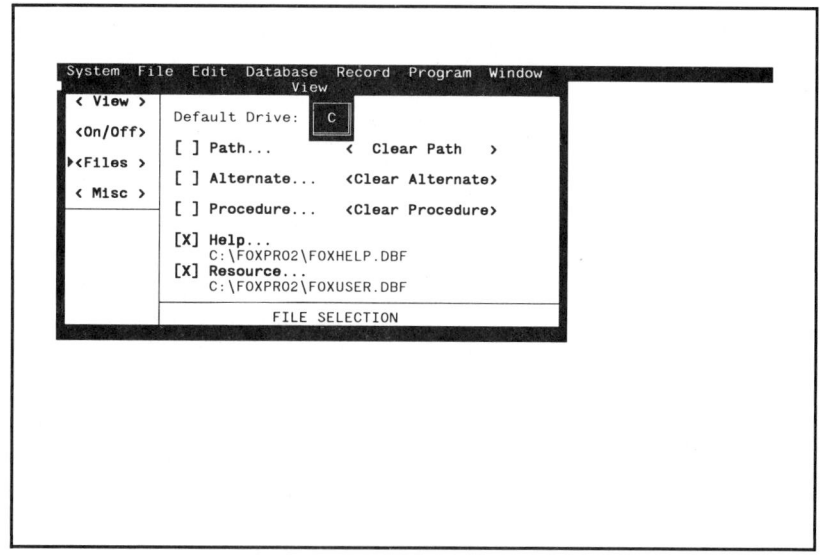

USING RELATIONAL DATABASES, THE VIEW WINDOW, AND RQBE 287

```
System  File  Edit  Database  Record  Program  Window
                    View
  < View >    Default Drive:  [C]
  <On/Off>
                [ ] Path...        <  Clear Path  >
 ><Files >
                [ ] Alternate...   <Clear Alternate>
  < Misc >
                [ ] Procedure...   <Clear Procedure>

                [X] Help...
                    C:\FOXPRO2\FOXHELP.DBF
                [X] Resource...
                    C:\FOXPRO2\FOXUSER.DBF
                         FILE SELECTION
```

Figure 7.19: The Files panel of the View window

- **Alternate:** lets you specify the name of a text file where screen output will be saved. Selecting this check box displays the Open dialog box, where you can select an existing file or enter the name of a new file. This feature is equivalent to

  SET ALTERNATE TO <file name>

  Remember that it has to be used in combination with the command **SET ALTERNATE ON**, or its equivalent, which you can access from the On/Off panel; using **SET ALTERNATE ON** or **OFF** allows you to use or disable the storage of screen output temporarily. Select the Clear Alternate pushbutton to eliminate it entirely.

- **Procedure:** is used in programming to specify a procedure file for FoxPro to use while executing a program. It is equivalent to the command **SET PROCEDURE TO** <*file name*>, which will be covered in Chapter 9. The use of the procedure file can be ended by selecting Clear Procedure.

- **Help:** lets you specify which file is to be used when the user selects Help from the System menu (or presses F1). You can create your own help files if you are creating an application where the user does not need and would only be confused by all the information in FOXHELP.DBF, the help file that comes with FoxPro—which, as you can see, is the default help file. This feature is equivalent to the command

SET HELP TO <*file name*>

You can also set Help on or off using the On/Off panel; the default setting for Help is *on*.

- **Set Resource To:** lets you specify the resource file that FoxPro uses. The resource file stores information about the location and size of your Browse windows, color selections, and other preferences. By default, FoxPro automatically creates a resource file named FOXUSER.DBF if, for example, you change your Browse window; then it uses this file to set up the Browse window when you use the command **BROWSE LAST** in a later session. You can create a variety of resource files with different names and use them for different purposes. You can also set Resource on or off using the On/Off panel; the default, of course, is *on*.

THE MISC PANEL

Selecting the Misc pushbutton lets you use the Misc panel of the View window, as shown in Figure 7.20. This panel controls a number of miscellaneous environment settings. Its features are listed below:

- **Date:** lets you choose among date formats. The default is AMERICAN (mm/dd/yy). Other date format options are ANSI (yy.mm.dd), BRITISH or FRENCH (dd/mm/yy), GERMAN (dd.mm.yy), ITALIAN (dd-mm-yy), and JAPAN (yy/mm/dd); also USA (mm-dd-yy), MDY (mm/dd/yy), DMY (dd/mm/yy); and YMD (yy/mm/dd). Any of these can be used with the command **SET DATE TO** plus one of the capitalized format names listed above. Other features of the date format are controlled by the check boxes to the right of this popup.

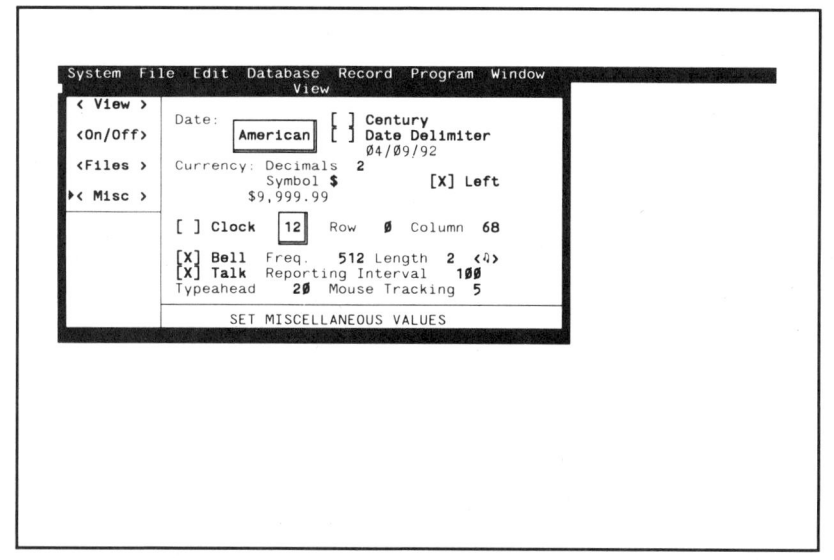

USING RELATIONAL DATABASES, THE VIEW WINDOW, AND RQBE **289**

```
System  File  Edit  Database  Record  Program  Window
                              View
< View >     Date:         [ ] Century
<On/Off>              American  [ ] Date Delimiter
                                    04/09/92
<Files >    Currency: Decimals  2
                      Symbol  $           [X] Left
>< Misc >            $9,999.99

            [ ] Clock   12    Row  0   Column  68

            [X] Bell  Freq.      512 Length  2  <4>
            [X] Talk  Reporting Interval    100
            Typeahead    20  Mouse Tracking  5
                 SET MISCELLANEOUS VALUES
```

Figure 7.20: The Misc panel of the View window

- **Century:** lets you display the entire four-digit year, not just the last two digits. The equivalent command is **SET CENTURY ON** or **OFF**.

- **Date Delimiter:** lets you change the delimiter used between the numbers for the year, month, and day. Check the check box and type the delimiter you want in the sample date displayed below it.

- **Currency:** lets you specify the way that currency is displayed. The default is with two decimal places, a dollar sign, a comma to mark thousands (and millions and so on), a decimal point to mark cents, and left-alignment *on*. Edit any of these specifications and use the Left check box to set left-alignment on or off.

- **Clock:** lets you use and adjust the system clock. When the check box is checked, the system time is displayed on the screen. The command equivalent is **SET CLOCK ON**. The popup lets you display the time in 12- or 24-hour format.

Edit the Row and Column items to determine where on the screen the time is to be displayed—or use the command

SET CLOCK TO <*row, col*>

- **Bell:** lets you adjust FoxPro's beep. Enter a frequency from 19 to 10000 to change its pitch and a length from 1 to 19 to determine how long it lasts. The equivalent command is

  SET BELL TO <*frequency, duration*>

  Remember that there is also a command **SET BELL ON** or **OFF**, which you can access through the On/Off panel.

- **Talk:** is used to determine how frequently certain commands display information about their status—for example, the **INDEX** command, which displays talk telling you how many records have been indexed as it executes. As you can see (in Figure 7.20), the default is 100, but you can enter a number from 1 to 32,767. This feature is equivalent to the unfortunate command

  SET ODOMETER TO <*number*>

  inherited from earlier versions of dBASE. It is used in combination with the Talk check box. Setting Talk off eliminates these status messages entirely.

- **Typeahead:** lets you determine how many characters FoxPro holds in its keyboard buffer. The buffer is a small area of memory reserved to hold keystrokes until FoxPro is able to display them; it can hold up to 128 keystrokes. You can use the buffer, for example, when you first start FoxPro, since it takes a while for the program to display the screen: If your buffer is large enough, you can type **USE EMPLIST**, press Enter, type **BROWSE LAST**, and press Enter, all while you are waiting; when the screen finally appears, these commands will be in the Command window and will be executed.

- **Mouse Tracking:** lets you determine how sensitive your pointer is to the movement of your mouse. The sensitivity ranges from 1 to 10, with 1 being the least sensitive.

If you are a fast typist and have a slow computer (such as an XT compatible), **SET TYPEAHEAD** is one of the most useful of these environment commands. The default setting does not store enough keystrokes in the buffer, but increasing it will let you type more while you are waiting for FoxPro to do other things.

Remember that all the environment settings from all these panels are saved when you save the view in a .VUE file. They will all be in effect again whenever you open that .VUE file. You can see how powerful a tool the .VUE file can be.

RELATIONAL QUERY BY EXAMPLE AND SQL

As of version 2, FoxPro includes a second method of setting up relational databases: the **SELECT** command that is used in SQL.

SQL (the Structured Query Language) is the standard query language for working with relational databases on mainframe computers, and it is now being added to the more powerful microcomputer database management systems.

The SELECT command of SQL, now a part of the FoxPro language, can be used like any other FoxPro command. It lets programmers set up relational databases with a single command, without doing all the preliminary housekeeping of opening multiple files and setting a relation. Because it only takes a single line of code, it optimizes the performance of the program.

FoxPro not only gives you all the power of the SQL SELECT statement, it also gives you a simple method of generating SELECT statements by making selections from a dialog box. This method is called *Relational Query By Example* (RQBE).

THE RQBE WINDOW

You can also modify an existing query in the usual way. Either select Open from the file menu and select the query's name in the Open dialog box; or enter **MODIFY QUERY** <*query name*> in the command window.

You create an SQL query using Relational Query By Example in the same way you create any other object. Select New from the File menu, select the Query radio button, and select OK to generate the command **CREATE QUERY Untitled** in the command window; you name the query later by selecting Save As from the File menu. Or simply enter the command **CREATE QUERY** <*query name*> in the command window.

When you create or modify a query, FoxPro displays the RQBE Window, shown in Figure 7.21.

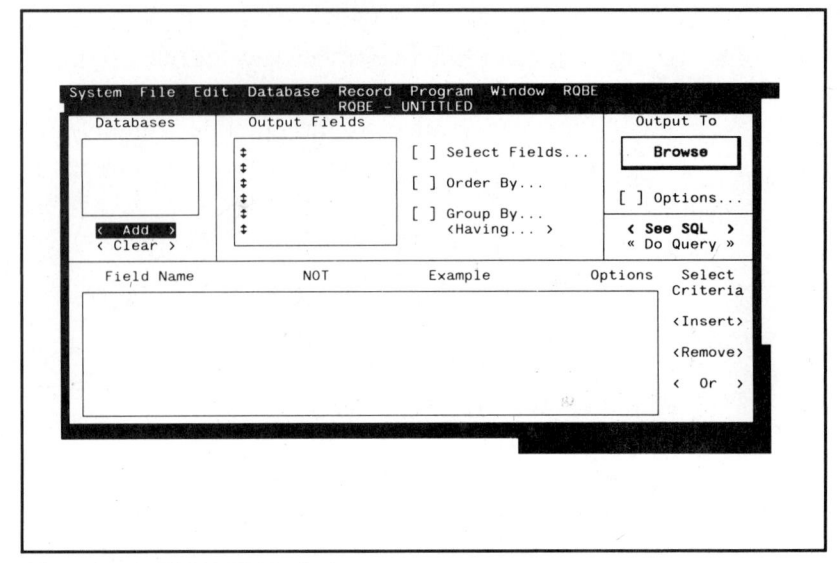

```
                System File Edit Database Record Program Window RQBE
                                     RQBE - UNTITLED
      Databases            Output Fields                                    Output To
   ┌──────────────┐    ┌──────────────────────┐                          ┌──────────┐
   │              │    │  ‡                   │   [ ] Select Fields...   │  Browse  │
   │              │    │  ‡                   │   [ ] Order By...        └──────────┘
   │              │    │  ‡                   │                          [ ] Options...
   │              │    │  ‡                   │   [ ] Group By...
   │              │    │  ‡                   │        <Having...>       < See SQL >
   │   < Add >    │    │  ‡                   │                          « Do Query »
   │   < Clear >  │    │                      │
   └──────────────┘    └──────────────────────┘
        Field Name             NOT            Example          Options   Select
                                                                         Criteria
   ┌──────────────────────────────────────────────────────────────────┐  <Insert>
   │                                                                  │
   │                                                                  │  <Remove>
   │                                                                  │
   │                                                                  │  < Or >
   └──────────────────────────────────────────────────────────────────┘
```

Figure 7.21: The RQBE window

In the illustration, no database file names are listed in the Databases box and no field names are listed in the Output Fields box. If a database file is open in the current work area when you create the query, FoxPro automatically includes its name in the Databases box and all its fields in the Output Fields box. If you are using only a few fields from each file, though, it is easier to not have any database files open when you create the query.

You can add databases to the Databases box by selecting the Add pushbutton under that box. You can remove the selected database from that box by selecting the Clear pushbutton.

Whenever you add more than one database file to this box, FoxPro displays the Join Condition dialog box, and you must specify the way in which the new file is related to the other database files in the list. This dialog box includes three popup controls:

1. Use the left popup control to select a field from the database that you just added.

2. Use the center popup control to select the relation between the fields: LIKE, EXACTLY LIKE, MORE THAN, or LESS THAN. You can also use the NOT check box to invert any of these relations.

3. Use the right popup control to select a field from an existing database.

> LIKE is equivalent to the = operator, and EXACTLY LIKE is equivalent to the = = operator.

You should always set up relational databases so that you can use LIKE in the center popup control. For example, using the database from in the earlier exercises in this chapter, you might want the records in the two database files to be joined whenever EMPNO in the EMPLIST file is *LIKE* EMPNO in the WAGES file, as shown in Figure 7.22.

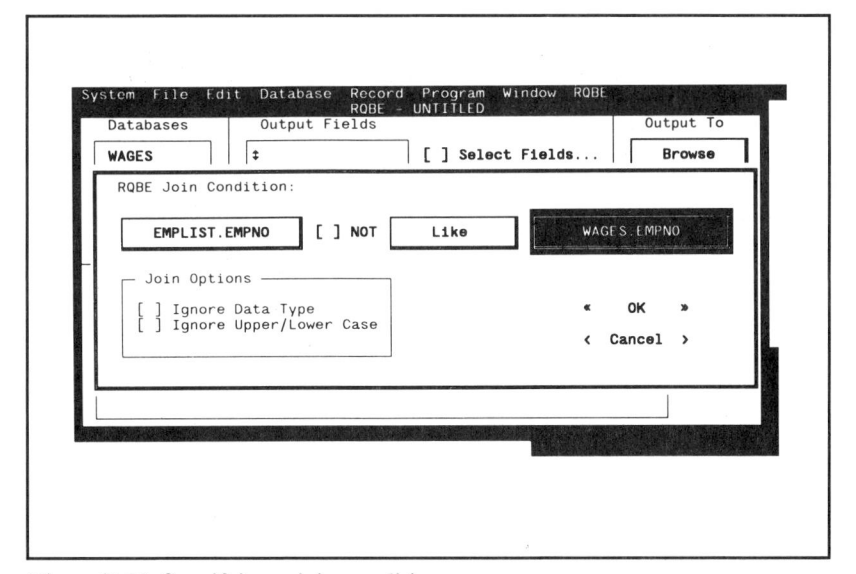

Figure 7.22: Specifying a join condition

You might want to use EXACTLY LIKE, MORE THAN, LESS THAN or the NOT check box to join files for other purposes, but you should not need them when you are joining files of a relational database on the basis of a common key field. Note that using these criteria can sometimes produce a result with a very large number of fields, so you should not use them lightly.

All the join conditions you create in this way are listed in the Select Criteria box that takes up the entire bottom half of the RQBE window. You can use the Remove or Insert pushbuttons to the right of this box to remove an existing join condition or to insert a blank line where you can add a new one.

> You can change the order of fields in the Output Fields box by dragging the arrows to the left of the field name with the mouse. Using the keyboard, press Tab until the field you want to move is selected, then press Ctrl-up arrow or Ctrl-down arrow.

You can specify the fields to be included in the result of the query by using the Select Fields check box to its right. This displays a field picker dialog box, shown in Figure 7.23, which lets you select fields from the currently selected database file. (All the selected fields are listed in the Output Fields box.) You should have no trouble using this dialog box, because it works like other field pickers that you have used in earlier chapters.

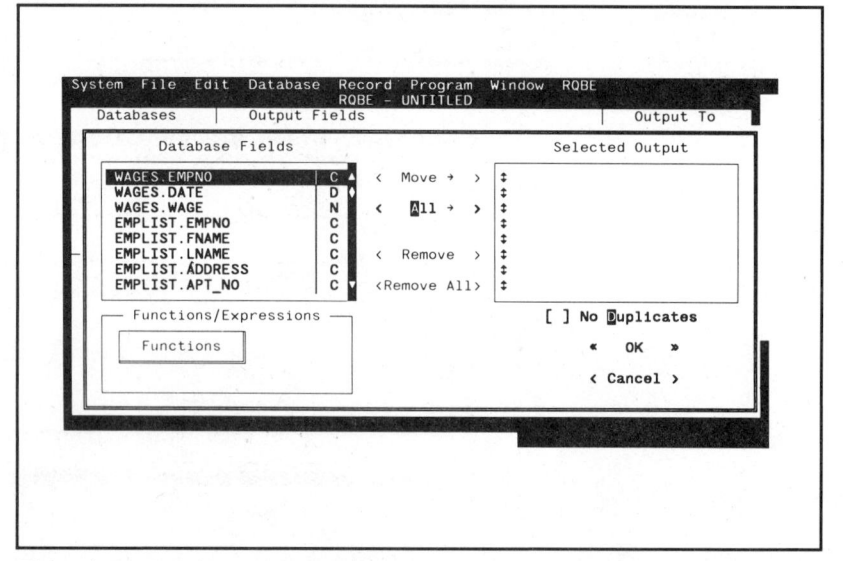

Figure 7.23: Selecting output fields

You can specify the order in which records should be listed as a result of the query by selecting the Order By check box, which displays the dialog box shown in Figure 7.24. Again, it should be easy for you to use this dialog box, because it works like the dialog boxes you used for indexing and sorting in Chapter 4.

Selecting the Group By check box calls up a dialog box that lets you specify how the result of the query should be grouped. Finally, the Output To popup control lets you specify where the result of the query will appear. There are four options:

- **Browse:** The result is displayed temporarily in a Browse window.

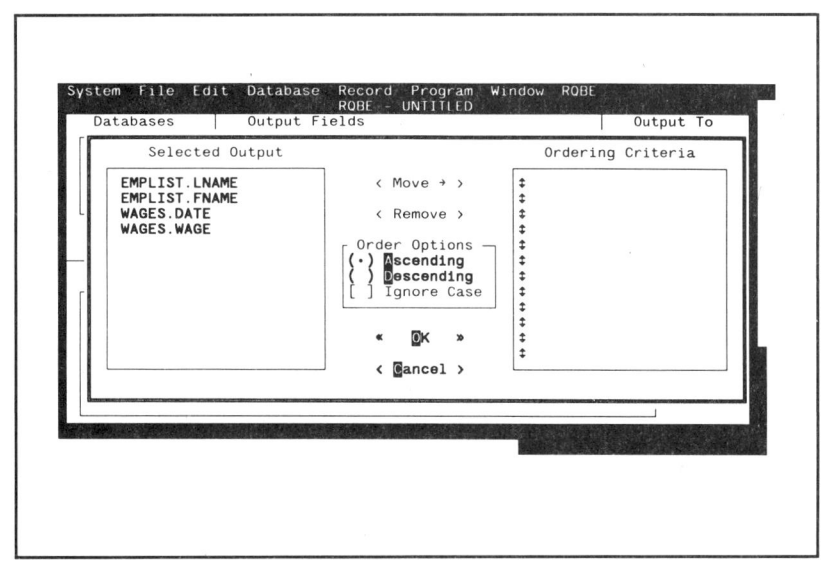

Figure 7.24: Determining the order of the records in the output

- **Report/Label:** The result is displayed in a new or existing Report or Label form.

- **Table/DBF:** The result is stored permanently in a database file. The Open File dialog box appears so you can specify the file name.

- **Cursor:** The result is stored temporarily in a database file. As long as it remains open, you can use this database file like any other—for example, you can Browse it or create a report on it—but once you close it, it is discarded.

    If you select Report/Label, the Options check box under this popup control is enabled. If you check it, FoxPro displays the RQBE Display Options dialog box, shown in Figure 7.25. The options in this dialog box are also easy to understand: the radio buttons on the upper left let you select whether you want a screen display, a report, or a label. If you select Report or Label, the check boxes underneath are activated.

The Report/Label Form Name check box displays the Open File dialog box, so you can choose an existing report or label form—or

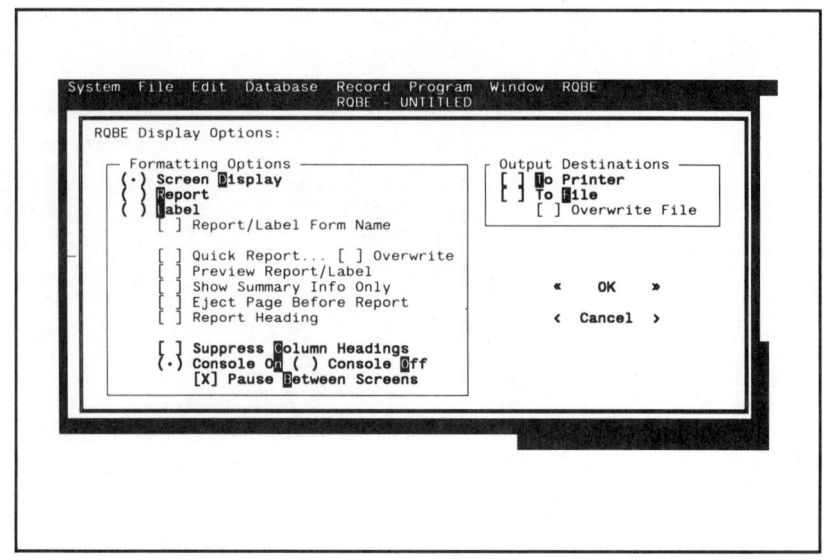

```
┌─────────────────────────────────────────────────────────────────┐
│  System  File  Edit  Database  Record  Program  Window  RQBE   │
│                          RQBE - UNTITLED                        │
│ ┌─RQBE Display Options:─────────────────────────────────────┐  │
│ │ ┌─Formatting Options──────────────┐ ┌─Output Destinations─┐│  │
│ │ │ (·) Screen Display              │ │ [ ] To Printer      ││  │
│ │ │ ( ) Report                      │ │ [ ] To File         ││  │
│ │ │ ( ) Label                       │ │   [ ] Overwrite File││  │
│ │ │     [ ] Report/Label Form Name  │ └─────────────────────┘│  │
│ │ │                                 │                        │  │
│ │ │     [ ] Quick Report... [ ] Overwrite                    │  │
│ │ │     [ ] Preview Report/Label                             │  │
│ │ │     [ ] Show Summary Info Only        «    OK    »       │  │
│ │ │     [ ] Eject Page Before Report                         │  │
│ │ │     [ ] Report Heading                <  Cancel  >       │  │
│ │ │                                                          │  │
│ │ │     [ ] Suppress Column Headings                         │  │
│ │ │     (·) Console On  ( ) Console Off                      │  │
│ │ │     [X] Pause Between Screens                            │  │
│ │ └──────────────────────────────────────────────────────────┘  │
│ └───────────────────────────────────────────────────────────┘  │
└─────────────────────────────────────────────────────────────────┘
```

Figure 7.25: The RQBE Display Options dialog box

you can type the name in the text box below. The other check boxes are like options for reports and labels that you learned about in Chapter 6 and are self-explanatory.

Finally, you can select the See SQL pushbutton in the RQBE window to see the SQL programming code that the query will generate, and you can select the Do Query pushbutton to execute the query. You will look at this SQL code in a moment. First let's try a sample query.

A SAMPLE QUERY

As an exercise in using the RQBE window, you will set up the same many-to-one relationship between the WAGES file and the EMPLIST file that you created using the View window earlier in this chapter. You can use RQBE to browse fields of this relational database, as you did earlier using the BROWSE FIELDS command.

1. Select New from the File menu. Select the Query radio button, and select OK to use the RQBE window. FoxPro asks you to select a database: press Esc or select the Cancel pushbutton, so no database file is in use when you begin.

2. Select the Add pushbutton. Then select WAGES.DBF from the list of files in the Select Database dialog box and select the Open pushbutton.

3. Select the Add pushbutton again, select EMPLIST.DBF from the list of files, and select Open. The RQBE Join Condition dialog box appears. Select the left popup control and select EMPLIST.EMPNO. Leave the center popup as Like. Select the right popup and select WAGES.EMPNO. Select the OK pushbutton to return to the RQBE window, and note that the criterion you just created is displayed in the Select Criteria box.

4. Select the Select Fields check box. Use the field picker to Move EMPLIST.LNAME, EMPLIST.FNAME, WAGES.DATE, and WAGES.WAGE to the Selected Output box. Then select OK.

5. Select the Do Query pushbutton to display a Browse window with the two files joined, as in Figure 7.26.

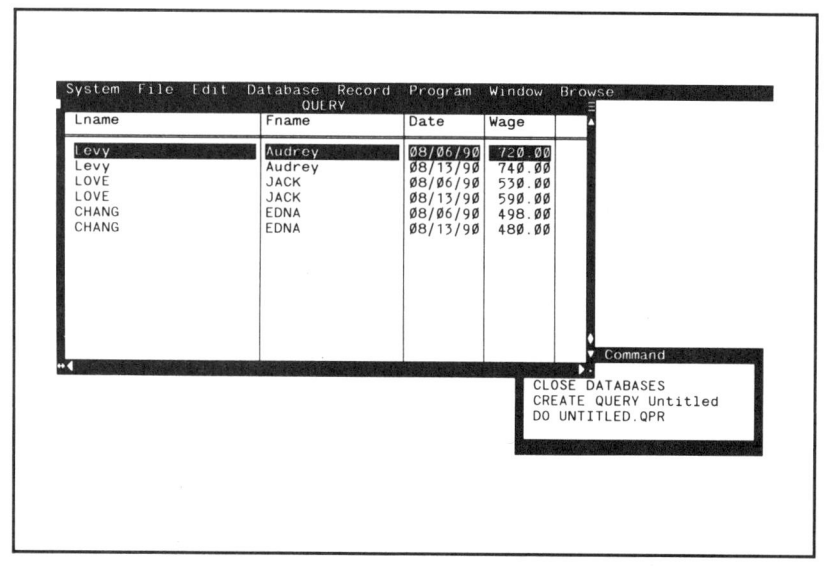

Figure 7.26: The result of this query

6. Close the Browse window to return to the RQBE window. Select Save As from the File menu. Enter EMPWAGES as the name of the file, and select the Save pushbutton.

If you want, you can experiment with other features of the RQBE window. For example, you can try alphabetizing the records by name: select the Order By check box, select LNAME and FNAME as the ordering criteria, and select the Ignore Case check box so the file is in alphabetical (rather than ASCII) order. Or you can try selecting Cursor from the Output To popup control and work with the temporary database file that is created.

THE SELECT COMMAND

If you select the See SQL pushbutton, you will see that the query saved as EMPWAGES generated the code shown in Figure 7.27. This is an example of the simplest sort of SELECT command that you can use to work with a relational database.

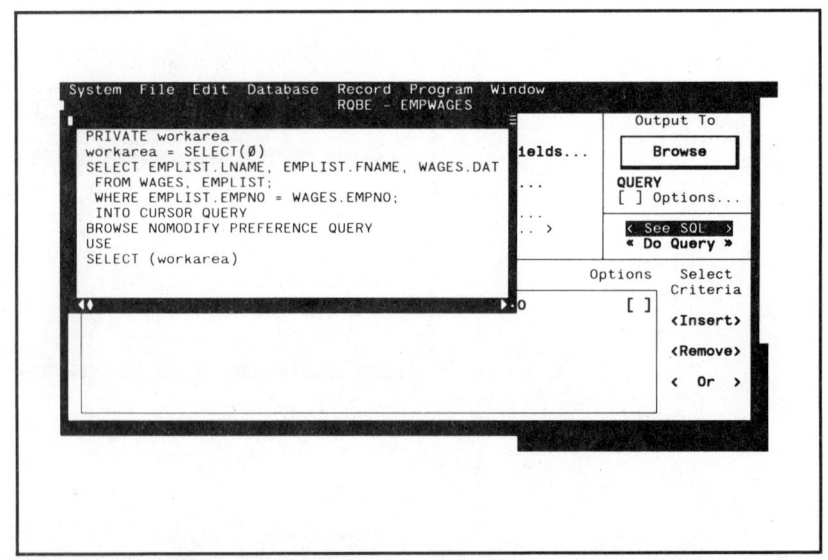

Figure 7.27: The SQL SELECT command that was generated by the EMPWAGES query

The first and last two lines of this code are not part of the query itself. The first two lines, **PRIVATE workarea** and **workarea = SELECT(0)**, just create a memory variable named **workarea** and assign the value of the currently selected work area to it. The last two lines **USE** and **SELECT (workarea)** simply close the database file created by the SQL query and select the initial work area (whose value is stored in the variable **workarea**). These are just routine housekeeping chores.

The query itself is contained in the **SELECT** command:

```
SELECT EMPLIST.LNAME, EMPLIST.FNAME, WAGES.DATE;
   WAGES.WAGE;
FROM EMPLIST, WAGES;
WHERE WAGES.EMPNO = EMPLIST.EMPNO;
INTO CURSOR QUERY
```

Though this query is written on several lines to make it easier to understand, it is actually a single line of code: as you will see when you learn programming in Part III of this book, you can type a line of code on several lines if you a put a semicolon at the end of each to indicate that the end of the line is not actually the end of the command.

The first clause of the command is the word SELECT followed by a list of select items, which could be constants or calculated fields as well as the database fields listed here. The FROM clause lists the database files that contain the data, and the WHERE clause lists the join conditions that relate the files to each other. Finally, the INTO clause determines where the results of the query go: the options for this clause are:

- **CURSOR:** Store them in a temporary database file
- **DBF** *<file name>* or **TABLE** *<file name>*: Store them in permanent database file
- **ARRAY:** Store them in an array of memory variables (a programming feature discussed briefly in Chapter 9)

You can see from Figure 7.27 that, because you selected BROWSE as the destination of the query's results, FoxPro uses TO CURSOR to store them in a temporary file, then uses a BROWSE command to browse that file, and, when you are finished browsing, uses the command USE to close (and eliminate) that file.

The SELECT command has many options, which you can find in the Help window or in any reference to FoxPro commands. Now that this discussion has introduced you to its basics, you should have no trouble adding additional clauses to use its other features.

Chapter 8

Getting the Most
from the Menu System

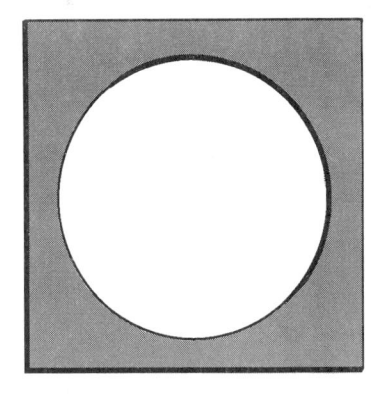

IN THE FIRST PART OF THIS BOOK, YOU LEARNED ALL the features of the menu system that are essential to using FoxPro to manage simple databases. You learned to create and modify the structure of a database, to add, view, and edit data, to make queries, and to produce reports and mailing labels—the basic things you need to know to manage any simple application. In Chapter 7, you learned to use the View window and RQBE. In combination with the commands you learned in the first section, these give you all the essential skills you need to manage more complex applications that require relational databases.

This chapter takes you beyond the essentials and introduces you to the features of the menu system that give you extra power. It includes three main sections.

In the first, you learn to use keyboard macros, which you access through the System menu popup, to save keystrokes. Macros can make your work with FoxPro easier, by saving you repetitive data entry. As you become more advanced, you can also use them to automate commands and give yourself extra power. (The other features of the System menu are covered in Appendix B; they are not directly related to using FoxPro to manage data.)

In the second section, you learn to use more advanced editing and word-processing techniques. You learn the remaining features of the File menu, which let you create text and program files and print them—essentially, using FoxPro as a word processor or programmers' text editor. And you learn the features of the Edit menu popup which were not covered in Chapter 1. All these things will be handy if you write programs or use long memo fields, though they are not needed for routine data entry and editing.

In the third section, you learn techniques that let you manipulate data more powerfully. This includes the remaining features of the Database and Record popups.

Finally, there is a brief fourth section that describes how to change the colors of your screen—something that is not often needed by users but is included in case you have one of the odd color displays that does not work well with the default colors of FoxPro.

KEYBOARD MACROS

Many programs let you create keyboard macros. A macro simply records a series of keystrokes and assigns them to some special key or key combination, so that you can press one key or key combination each time you need to use the series of keystrokes you have recorded.

Macros are a convenience to save you time in entering keystrokes that you use frequently. Though you can save any sequence of keystrokes in a macro, generally you will use them to save data-entry time. For example, if you have to enter a large number of records with addresses in San Francisco, you can create a macro that stores the keystrokes needed to type SAN FRANCISCO, to move to the State field, and to type CA. Macros are also useful for customizing the editor, for example, to make it work like an editor that you are more familiar with.

FoxPro lets you assign a macro to any of the function keys—the keys on the left or top of your keyboard, labeled with F and a number—and to a large number of key combinations that use Ctrl, Alt, or Shift with function keys or letter keys: remember that only letter keys and function keys can be used in macros, not numbers, special characters, or editing keys. The permissible combinations of keys are

- any function key except F1 and F10
- Shift plus any function key except F10
- Ctrl plus any letter or function key
- Shift-Ctrl plus any letter or function key
- Alt plus any single letter or function key except F10
- Shift-Alt plus any single letter or function key except F10
- Ctrl-Alt plus any single letter or function key except F10
- Ctrl-Shift-Alt plus any single letter or function key except F10

FoxPro does let you use Alt-F10 (and Shift-Alt-F10, Ctrl-Alt-F10, and Ctrl-Shift-Alt-F10), but only when followed by a letter. This gives you even more combinations of keystrokes that can be assigned macro values.

This gives you a possible total of 255 different keyboard macros, probably more than you will ever need—and probably more than you could ever remember. The maximum number of keystrokes that you can store in any macro is 1,024—again, probably more than you will ever need.

The function keys by themselves are assigned default macro values if you have never created macros for them. F1 is help, and because this is very useful, it cannot be assigned another value. The other function keys' default values are left over from the days when dBASE did not have a menu interface; they let you enter the most common commands at the command line. These default macros are no longer useful now that it is easier to use the menus. As you will see, you can save new default values for these function keys so that they will be set automatically whenever you start FoxPro.

Selecting Macros from the System menu calls up the Keyboard Macros dialog box, shown in Figure 8.1. When this dialog box is displayed, a Macros menu pad is added to the menu bar; the Macros popup is shown in Figure 8.2. As you can see, the menu popup simply duplicates the choices that you can make by using the pushbuttons of the dialog box—the menu is added so that you can use the Control-key combinations as an alternate way of making these choices, if you find it more convenient.

> Default macros that you create are saved in a file named DEFAULT.FKY in either your FoxPro home directory or in the current directory. Until you create new defaults, this file does not exist, and FoxPro simply generates the standard defaults when the program is started. If default macros that you have saved are not available when you start FoxPro, search for the DEFAULT.FKY file.

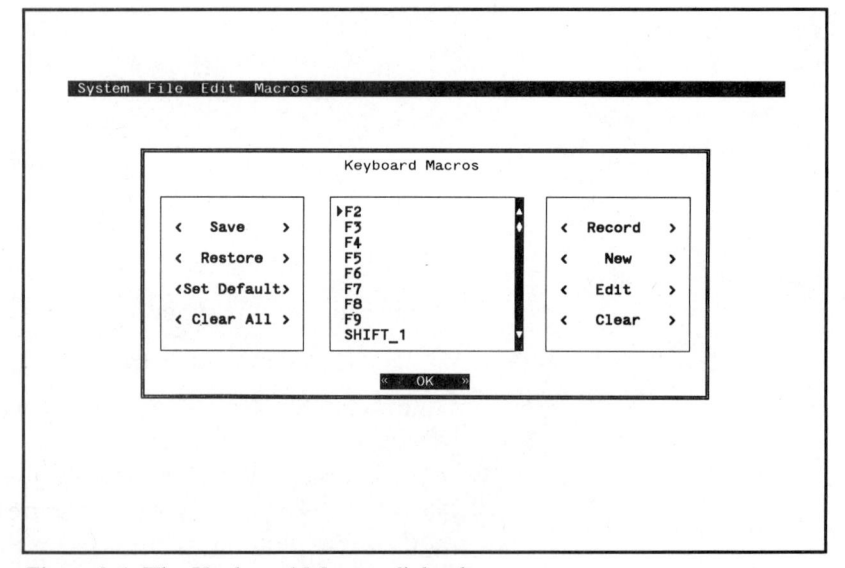

Figure 8.1: The Keyboard Macros dialog box

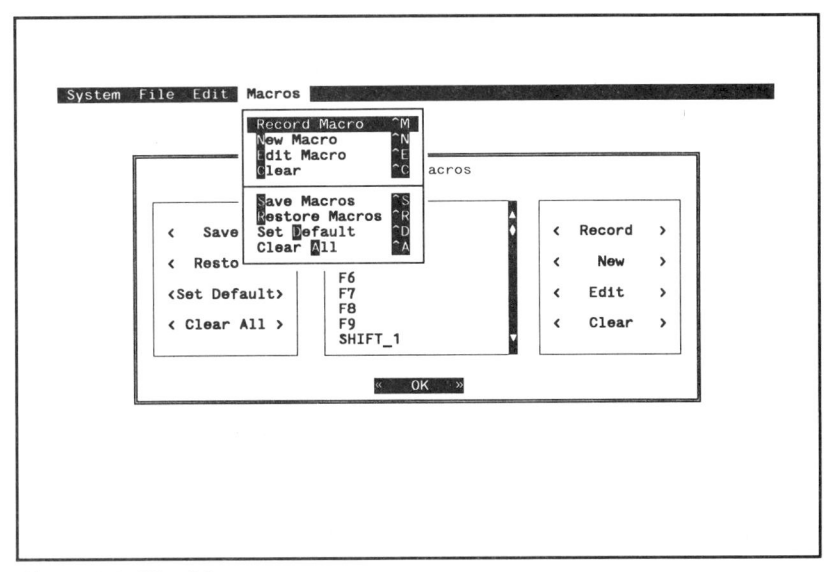

Figure 8.2: The Macros menu popup

RECORDING AND USING A NEW MACRO

You can create a new macro either by selecting the Record pushbutton of the Keyboard Macros dialog box or by selecting Record Macro from the Macros menu popup. In addition, you can create a new macro at any time by pressing Shift-F10 (which is why Shift-F10 is one of the combinations that you cannot assign your own macro to).

Though it is not necessary, it generally makes it easier to understand what you are doing if you create the macro at the same point in FoxPro where you will use it. For example, to create a macro that fills in a city and state name, first open the Browse window and move the cursor to the City field. Then select New Macro from the Macro menu or press Shift-F10 to create the macro. Of course, you will often realize that it is handy to create a macro when you are already in the situation where it is used.

When you make any of these choices, FoxPro displays the Macro Key Definition dialog box, shown in Figure 8.3. Enter the key combination that you want to use to activate the macro—for example, press F2 or press Ctrl-Alt-A. FoxPro will not let you enter illegal

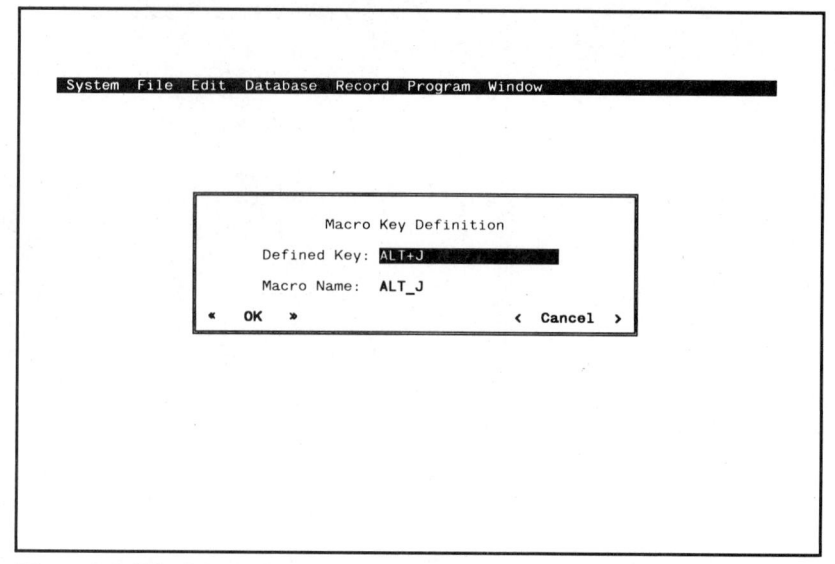

```
┌─────────────────────────────────────────────────────┐
│  System File Edit Database Record Program Window    │
│                                                     │
│                                                     │
│            ┌─────────────────────────────┐          │
│            │     Macro Key Definition    │          │
│            │  Defined Key: ALT+J         │          │
│            │  Macro Name:  ALT_J         │          │
│            │ «  OK  »          < Cancel >│          │
│            └─────────────────────────────┘          │
│                                                     │
│                                                     │
└─────────────────────────────────────────────────────┘
```

Figure 8.3: The Macro Key Definition dialog box

combinations. If you enter a keystroke combination that you have already defined as a macro, it will display the Overwrite dialog box, shown in Figure 8.4, which gives you the following choices:

- **Overwrite:** Replace the existing macro with the new macro that you are defining.

- **Append Keystrokes:** Add the new keystrokes at the end of the existing macro.

- **Cancel:** Do not replace the existing macro.

Once you come up with an acceptable key combination, it appears in the Macro Key definition dialog box, along with a suggested name for the macro (based on the key combination), as you can see in Figure 8.3. You can change this name if you wish and enter any name up to 20 characters long. When the keystrokes and name are right, choose OK to begin creating the macro.

Then enter any combination of keystrokes that you want saved in the macro. These might be just text—for example, type **SAN FRAN-CISCO**, press Tab, and type **CA** to save yourself time entering that city and state in each record in a database file.

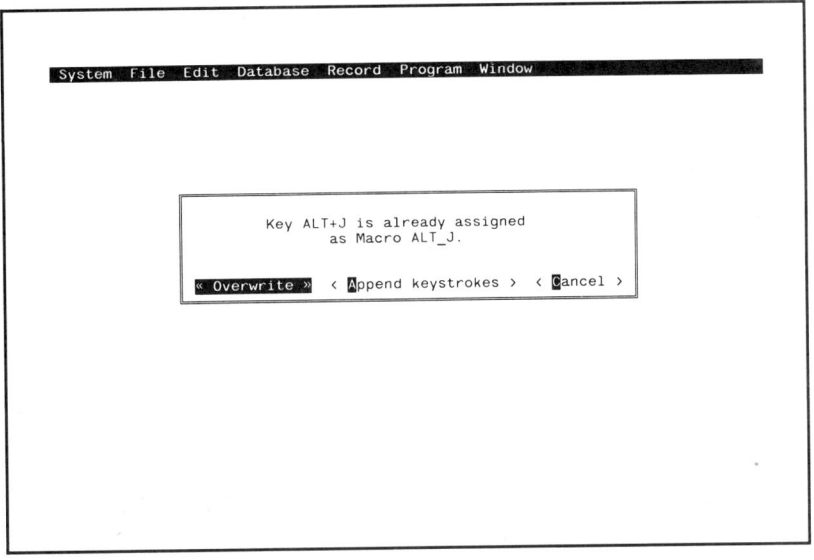

```
┌─────────────────────────────────────────────────┐
│ System File Edit Database Record Program Window │
│                                                 │
│                                                 │
│          ┌─────────────────────────────────┐    │
│          │   Key ALT+J is already assigned │    │
│          │        as Macro ALT_J.          │    │
│          │ « Overwrite »  < Append keystrokes >  < Cancel > │
│          └─────────────────────────────────┘    │
│                                                 │
│                                                 │
└─────────────────────────────────────────────────┘
```

Figure 8.4: The Overwrite dialog box

The keystrokes might involve commands—including editor commands or even the keystroke versions of menu choices. If you are accustomed to an editor that lets you delete a line by pressing Ctrl-Y, for example, you can create a Ctrl-Y macro that does just that.

When you are finished entering the keystrokes you want recorded, press Shift-F10 to stop recording. The Stop Recording dialog box appears, as shown in Figure 8.5. The choices that this dialog box gives you are easy to understand:

- **Insert Literal:** Record the literal value of the next keystroke instead of the value assigned to it by an existing macro.

- **Insert Pause:** Stop execution of the macro temporarily and let the user type in text.

- **OK:** Save the macro as it has been entered.

- **Discard:** Do not save the macro.

- **Continue:** Return to the point where you were when you left off and continue to create and record the macro.

Insert Pause is the most interesting of these. It lets the user interrupt the macro in order to type text of any length; then, when the user presses

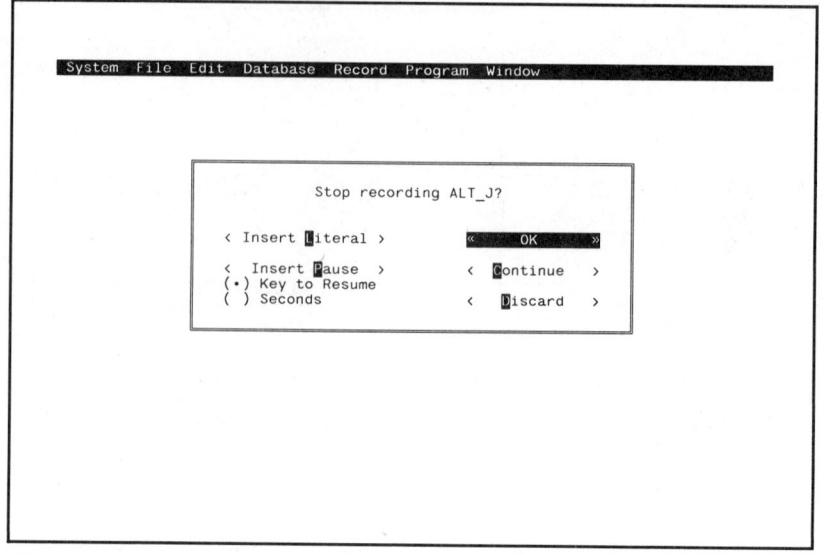

```
┌─────────────────────────────────────────────────────────────┐
│ System  File  Edit  Database  Record  Program  Window       │
│                                                             │
│                                                             │
│              ┌─────────────────────────────────────┐        │
│              │        Stop recording ALT_J?        │        │
│              │                                     │        │
│              │   < Insert Literal >    «   OK   »  │        │
│              │                                     │        │
│              │    < Insert Pause >   < Continue >  │        │
│              │   (•) Key to Resume                 │        │
│              │   ( ) Seconds         <  Discard  > │        │
│              │                                     │        │
│              └─────────────────────────────────────┘        │
│                                                             │
│                                                             │
└─────────────────────────────────────────────────────────────┘
```

Figure 8.5: The Stop recording dialog box

Shift-F10, the macro continues. For example, you can create a macro that enters your return address at the top of a letter, pauses, and then enters the salutation. To use the macro, you let it enter the return address, then you take advantage of the pause to enter the address of the person you are writing to, and then you press Shift-F10 to let the macro continue, which it does by skipping a line, typing the word *Dear,* and leaving the cursor where you need it to type the rest of the name.

The Insert Pause pushbutton has two radio buttons associated with it, which let you control how the pause is ended:

- **Key to Resume:** When the macro pauses, FoxPro prompts you to press the same key that you used to start the macro in order to resume execution of the macro.

- **Seconds:** The pause lasts a certain time before the execution of the macro resumes. The default value is one second, but you can enter a different number.

In general, Key To Resume is the better choice, since it lets you take as much time as you need to make the entry. Seconds is useful primarily if you want the macro to continue executing after a pause even if no value is entered.

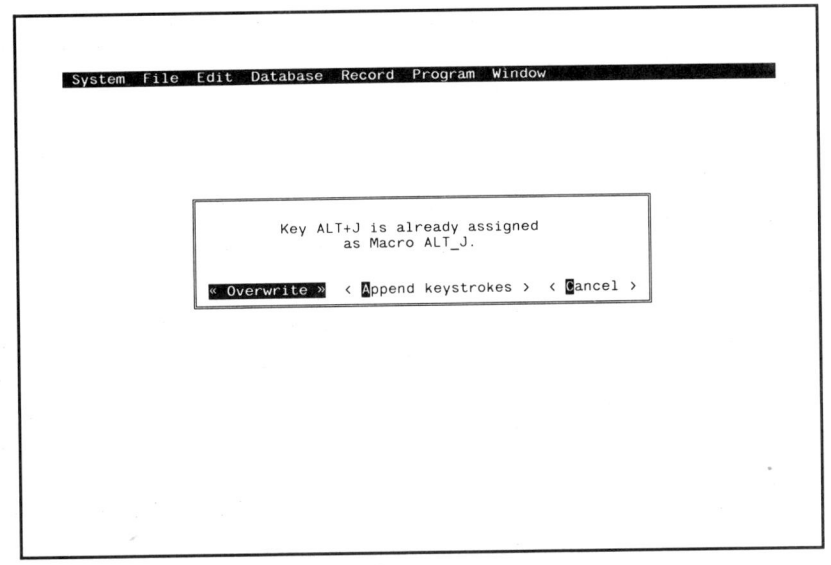

```
┌─────────────────────────────────────────────────────────┐
│  System File Edit Database Record Program Window        │
│                                                         │
│                                                         │
│              ┌───────────────────────────────┐          │
│              │  Key ALT+J is already assigned│          │
│              │         as Macro ALT_J.       │          │
│              │« Overwrite » < Append keystrokes >  < Cancel > │
│              └───────────────────────────────┘          │
│                                                         │
└─────────────────────────────────────────────────────────┘
```

Figure 8.4: The Overwrite dialog box

The keystrokes might involve commands—including editor commands or even the keystroke versions of menu choices. If you are accustomed to an editor that lets you delete a line by pressing Ctrl-Y, for example, you can create a Ctrl-Y macro that does just that.

When you are finished entering the keystrokes you want recorded, press Shift-F10 to stop recording. The Stop Recording dialog box appears, as shown in Figure 8.5. The choices that this dialog box gives you are easy to understand:

- **Insert Literal:** Record the literal value of the next keystroke instead of the value assigned to it by an existing macro.
- **Insert Pause:** Stop execution of the macro temporarily and let the user type in text.
- **OK:** Save the macro as it has been entered.
- **Discard:** Do not save the macro.
- **Continue:** Return to the point where you were when you left off and continue to create and record the macro.

Insert Pause is the most interesting of these. It lets the user interrupt the macro in order to type text of any length; then, when the user presses

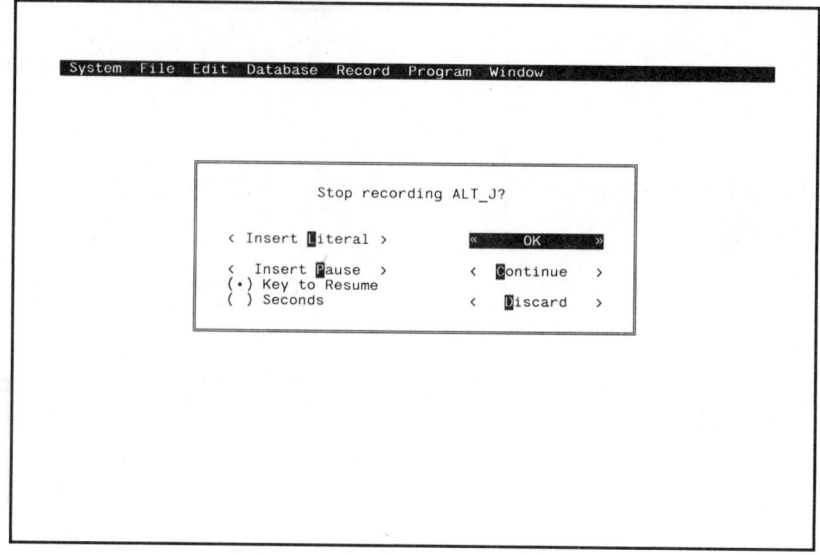

Figure 8.5: The Stop recording dialog box

Shift-F10, the macro continues. For example, you can create a macro that enters your return address at the top of a letter, pauses, and then enters the salutation. To use the macro, you let it enter the return address, then you take advantage of the pause to enter the address of the person you are writing to, and then you press Shift-F10 to let the macro continue, which it does by skipping a line, typing the word *Dear,* and leaving the cursor where you need it to type the rest of the name.

The Insert Pause pushbutton has two radio buttons associated with it, which let you control how the pause is ended:

- **Key to Resume:** When the macro pauses, FoxPro prompts you to press the same key that you used to start the macro in order to resume execution of the macro.

- **Seconds:** The pause lasts a certain time before the execution of the macro resumes. The default value is one second, but you can enter a different number.

In general, Key To Resume is the better choice, since it lets you take as much time as you need to make the entry. Seconds is useful primarily if you want the macro to continue executing after a pause even if no value is entered.

That's all there is to recording a macro. To summarize the basic steps:

1. To start recording, select Macro from the System menu and either select the Record pushbutton of the Keyboard Macros dialog box or select Record Macro from the Macros menu popup. Or you can just press Shift-F10.

2. When the Macro Key Definition dialog box appears, press the key combination you want to assign to the macro, and select OK.

3. Enter the keystrokes that you want to record in the macro.

4. Press Shift-F10 to stop recording, and select OK from the Stop Recording dialog box.

Once the macro has been recorded, use it by pressing the key combination that you entered in the Macro Key Definition dialog box.

If a macro does not work properly, the problem probably results from your being in the wrong place when you used it. To give an obvious example, if you saved the keystrokes needed to type San Francisco, you must be in the City field of your database when you use the macro.

EDITING A MACRO

When you create a macro, FoxPro stores it in text form so that you can edit it if necessary. Special keys are represented by self-explanatory names such as {TAB} for the Tab key, {RIGHT ARROW} for the right arrow key, and {LEFTMOUSE} for the left mouse button. Note that these names are in curly brackets.

To edit a macro, select it in the Keyboard Macros dialog box, then select the Edit pushbutton or select Edit Macro from the Macros menu. FoxPro displays the Macro Edit dialog box shown in Figure 8.6. You can edit the name of the macro and the defined key that plays it as well as the macro's contents.

The illustration shows a macro meant to speed data entry by typing **SAN FRANCISCO**, tabbing to the next field, and typing **CA** when you press Alt-S.

> If you assign Alt-key combinations such as this one to macros they can interfere with your using the keyboard to work with the menu system. When this macro is active, you can no longer use Alt-S to pull down the system menu. Likewise, Ctrl-key combinations can interfere with Ctrl-key shortcuts for using the menu system. If you do not have a mouse, you should be very careful to choose combinations for macros that do not interfere with your work.

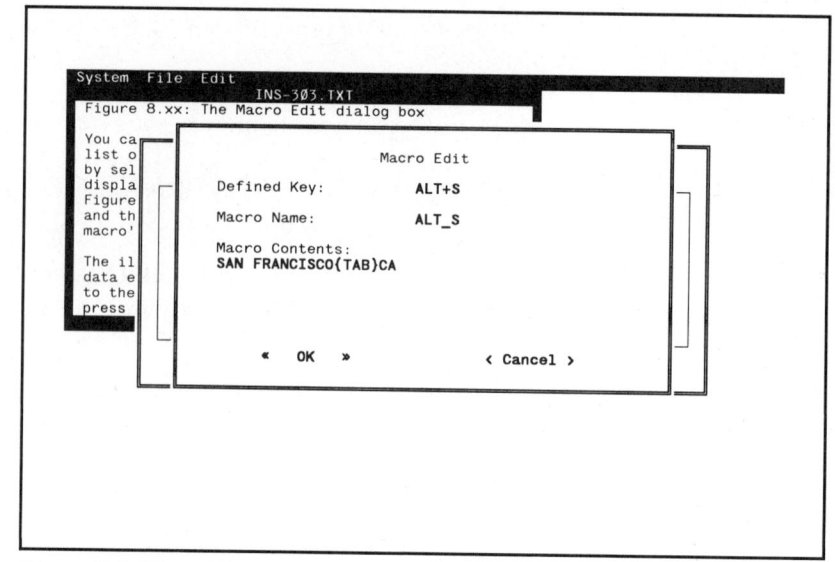

Figure 8.6: The Macro Edit dialog box

It is useful to edit macros in this way to correct minor errors: for example, if you spelled San Francisco incorrectly when you were recording the macro, it would be easier to edit the macro than to rerecord it.

For most errors, though, it is easiest to start from scratch and record the macro again. Give it the same name as the one with the error, and select the Overwrite pushbutton from the alert that Fox-Pro displays.

FoxPro also lets you use the macro editor to create new macros, by selecting the New pushbutton of the Keyboard Macros dialog box or selecting New Macro from the macros menu. Writing anything but the simplest macros in this way, however, is a very difficult and often frustrating exercise in computer programming. It is generally best to record macros rather than writing them.

WORKING WITH CURRENT AND SAVED MACROS

Once you have created a macro using the methods outlined above, it is a *current macro,* which appears in the scrollable list in the Keyboard

Macros dialog box. Current macros exist only temporarily, unless they are saved.

Macros that you have saved in past sessions are kept in disk files with the extension .FKY. They do not appear in the scrollable list in the Keyboard Macros dialog box, and thus are not usable until you restore them and add them to the list of active macros.

Dividing macros into sets lets you group macros for different applications. For example, there might be one group that you use when you are editing programs, and others that you use when are you doing data entry in different files. All of the macros that are being used at a given time appear in the scrollable list, and you can save them all as a set with a single name. Then you can recall and use that set whenever you need it.

To save the current set of macros, select the Save pushbutton from the Keyboard Macros dialog box or choose Save Macros from the Macros menu popup. The familiar Save As dialog box appears, with all of the sets of macros in the current directory in its scrollable list. Select one of these names to overwrite an existing macro set, or enter a new name to create a new macro set.

To use a set of macros that has been saved, select the Restore pushbutton from the Keyboard Macros dialog box or Restore Macros from the Macros menu. The familiar Open dialog box appears, with the heading Restore Macros From File above a scrollable list of macro set names. Select any one and select Open to use those macros.

Remember that the macros you restore are added to the macros that are already open, which are in the scrollable list of the dialog box. At some point you might want to get rid of some or all of the current macros before adding new ones. To get rid of a macro, select it from the scrollable list, and then select the Clear pushbutton or select Clear from the Macros menu. To get rid of all the current macros, select the Clear All pushbutton or select Clear All from the Macros menu. These options only clear the macros from current memory—they do not erase the file where they are saved on disk.

Finally, to make the current set of macros the *default* set, the set that is automatically used whenever you start FoxPro, just select the Set Default pushbutton or select Set Default from the Macros menu popup. FoxPro asks you to confirm this selection, then it stores the current macros in a file named DEFAULT.FKY, which it automatically uses to set the default whenever it is started. You can begin by saving one or two macros that you always find useful as the default, and add more default macros as you invent more.

ADVANCED EDITOR TECHNIQUES

Most of the features of the File menu that you have not yet learned are connected with creating and printing text files. When you use these features, you are moving in the direction of using the FoxPro editor as a word processor or programmer's text editor—something more than just using it for the routine tasks of entering data or entering commands in the Command window. Since these features are useful in combination with the Edit menu, learning the remaining features of these two menu popups together will make you into an advanced user of the FoxPro editor.

CREATING A TEXT OR PROGRAM FILE

You have used New from the File menu to create database, index, report, and label files just by selecting the respective options from the radio buttons in the New dialog box. You can also use this dialog box (shown in Figure 8.7) to create ordinary text files and to create program files by selecting the File and Program radio buttons. Simply type the text or the program into the window that is opened; select Save As from the File menu when you are done.

You can also create text or program files from the Command window by entering **MODIFY FILE** <*file name*> or **MODIFY COMMAND** <*file name*>.

Both text and program files are ordinary ASCII files. Unlike the files created by many word processors, they do not have special control characters of their own; both have just the standard ASCII characters.

The difference between them is in the default editor settings that they use. The major difference is that the default editor setting for text files includes the word-wrap feature, which automatically moves the cursor to the next line when you get to the right margin. Since

> Unlike most files that you create selecting New from the File menu, text and program files are not created using a command that begins with **CREATE.** Instead, the command beginning with **MODIFY** both creates and modifies these files.

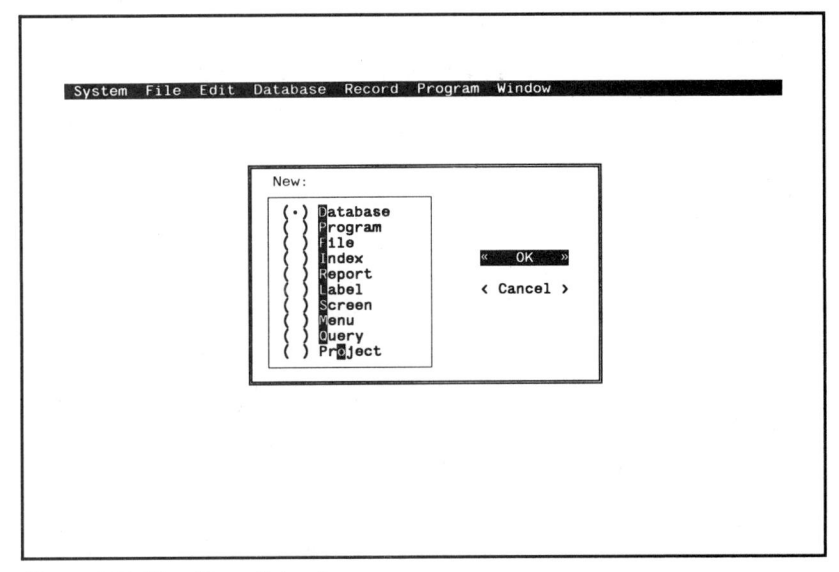

Figure 8.7: The New dialog box

program files must keep each command on a line of its own, the program editor sets word-wrap off by default.

SETTING UP THE PRINTER AND PRINTING A FILE

Select Printer Setup from the File menu to display the Printer Setup dialog box, shown in Figure 8.8.

The popup control here lets you choose the device to print to. The default is PRN, which represents your default printer. You can also use this control for printers at other ports by selecting LPT1, LPT2, or LPT3, or COM1, COM2, or COM3. To print to a file, select File from the same popup; you must also specify the name of the file that the output goes to, either by selecting the File pushbutton and entering the file name in the Print To dialog box or simply by typing the file name next to the File pushbutton. The Print On and Print Off radio buttons determine whether or not output goes to the printer. Adjust the margins by typing values next to the Left Margin and Right Margin items. When you have filled in the values you want, select the OK pushbutton to use these settings, and then go on to

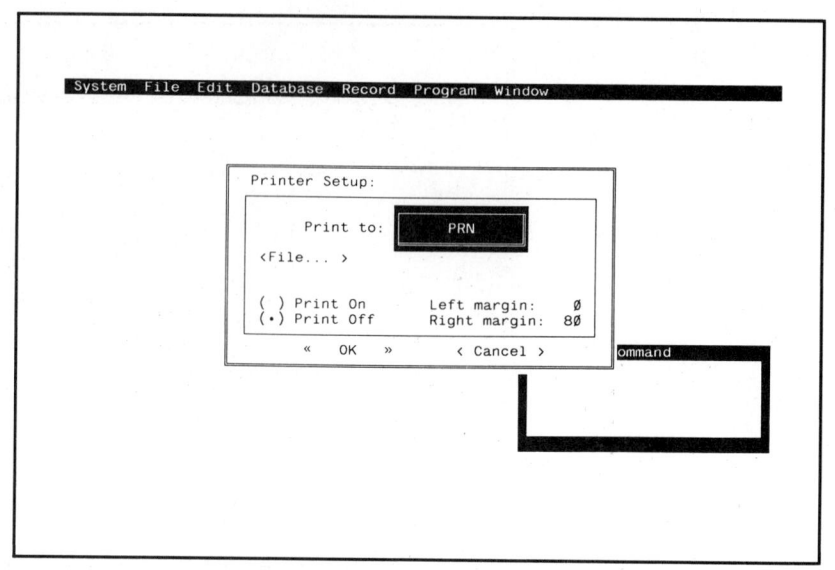

```
┌─────────────────────────────────────────────────────┐
│  System  File  Edit  Database  Record  Program  Window │
│                                                     │
│         ┌─────────────────────────────────┐         │
│         │ Printer Setup:                  │         │
│         │                                 │         │
│         │      Print to:    ███PRN███     │         │
│         │    <File... >                   │         │
│         │                                 │         │
│         │    ( ) Print On   Left margin:  0 │       │
│         │    (•) Print Off  Right margin: 80│       │
│         │         «  OK  »    < Cancel >  │ ommand  │
│         └─────────────────────────────────┘         │
│                                                     │
└─────────────────────────────────────────────────────┘
```

Figure 8.8: The Printer Setup dialog box

print the file using the Print dialog box; or choose Cancel at any time to remove the Printer Setup dialog box without activating the settings you entered.

The Print dialog box, shown in Figure 8.9, is displayed by selecting Print from the File menu.

Use the Windows popup control of this dialog box to choose the source of the text that will be printed. You can choose to print any of the following:

- the text in the clipboard (that is, text that you have used the Edit menu to cut or copy)
- the text in the Command window
- the text in any open editing window (that is, the text of a program or text file)
- the text in any file that is not open

You can select the first three of these from the Window popup control. For the fourth, printing the text in a file that is not open, select the File pushbutton to choose the file you want from a scrollable list

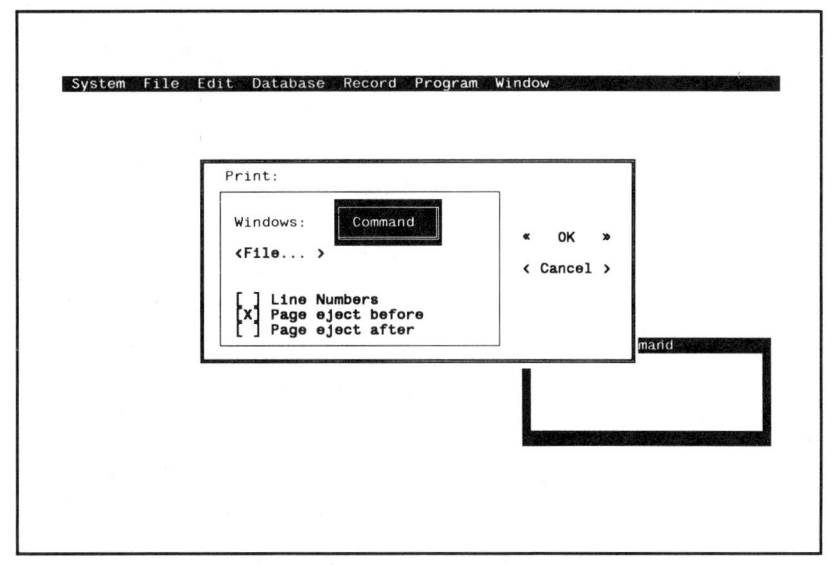

```
┌─────────────────────────────────────────────────────────┐
│ System  File  Edit  Database  Record  Program  Window   │
└─────────────────────────────────────────────────────────┘

        ┌─────────────────────────────────────────┐
        │ Print:                                  │
        │                                         │
        │ Windows:  ┌─────────┐                   │
        │           │ Command │    «  OK  »       │
        │ <File... >└─────────┘                   │
        │                         < Cancel >      │
        │ [ ] Line Numbers                        │
        │ [X] Page eject before                   │
        │ [ ] Page eject after                    │
        │                                         │
        └─────────────────────────────────────────┘
```

Figure 8.9: The Print dialog box

in the Print File dialog box, or just enter the name of the file you want to print next to the File pushbutton.

If you select the Line Numbers check box, FoxPro numbers the lines of the file that it prints. This feature is meant primarily for programmers. The other two check boxes let you eject a page before and after printing.

THE EDIT MENU

In Chapter 1, you learned the basics of using the editor, such as moving the cursor and marking text. You also learned a few features of the Edit menu popup: Undo, Redo, Cut, Copy, and Paste.

The two next features on this popup are very simple:

- **Clear:** deletes (or clears) text that is marked. Since you can also delete marked text simply by pressing Del or Backspace, there is little need to use Clear.

- **Select All:** marks (or selects) all the text in the document. This is sometimes a handy shortcut.

After these two simple features, there is a group of very useful features that let you move around the document, search for specific words, and even do search-and-replace. There is also a feature that lets you change the default settings of the editor. With the addition of these features, the FoxPro editor is as powerful as many commercial word processors. They are covered in detail here.

GOTO LINE

Selecting Goto Line from the Edit menu calls up the Goto dialog box, shown in Figure 8.10, which lets you move the cursor to any line in the document, if you know its line number. (If the word-wrap feature is on, this feature is disabled, because the line numbers will change whenever the text is rejustified.) Just enter the number of the line you want to move to and then select Goto to execute the command.

FIND

Selecting Find from the Edit menu calls up the Find dialog box, shown in Figure 8.11. The items in this dialog box let you search

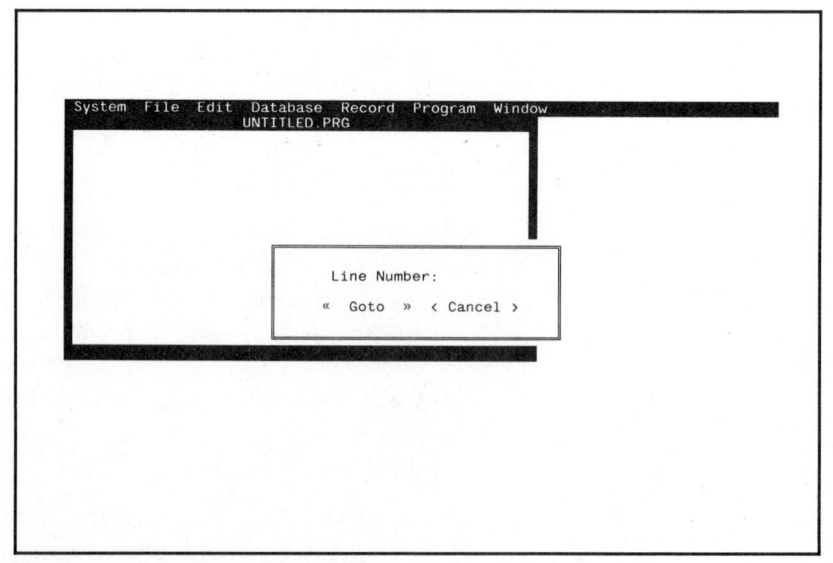

Figure 8.10: The Goto dialog box

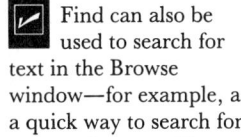

> Find can also be used to search for text in the Browse window—for example, as a quick way to search for a person's name. Note that when you are in the Browse window, the Find dialog box does not include the Replace With text box.

for text—a word, several words, or just a few letters—in the current document.

Just type the text you are searching for in the Look For text box. You can search for control characters by using **\r** to stand for carriage return, **\t** to stand for tab, **\n** to search for the new line character, and **** to search for the backslash. Just type these codes in the Look For text box, along with any other text. For example, type **\tThe** to find the word The at the beginning of a paragraph.

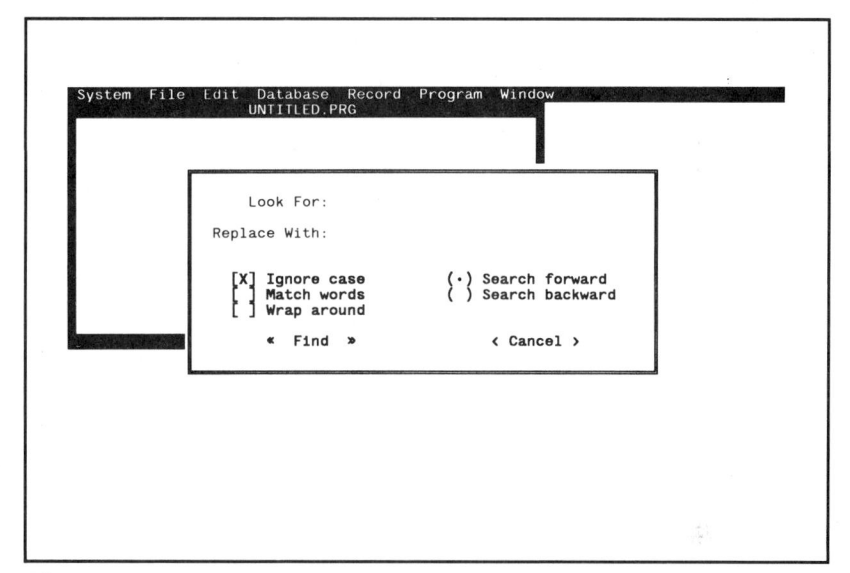

```
 System  File  Edit  Database  Record  Program  Window
                       UNTITLED.PRG


        Look For:

        Replace With:

         [X] Ignore case        (·) Search forward
         [ ] Match words        ( ) Search backward
         [ ] Wrap around

              «  Find  »              < Cancel >
```

Figure 8.11: The Find dialog box

As you can see, this dialog box includes three check boxes:

- **Ignore Case:** This feature tells the search to disregard differences in capitalization. For example, if you search for HELLO, it will find not only HELLO but also Hello, hello, and so on.

- **Match Words:** If you check this, the search looks for an exact match only, and will not find a word that has the word you are looking for embedded in it. For example, if you search for top, it will not find stop or estoppel.

- **Wrap Around:** If you check this, the search will look from the location of the cursor to the end of the file, and then will "wrap around" and continue the search at the beginning of the file. This option lets you search through the entire file without first moving to the beginning of the file.

There are also two radio buttons in this dialog box. By default, the Search Forward radio button is selected, and so the editor begins at the location of the cursor and looks for the next occurrence of a match. By selecting the Search Backward radio button, you can make it look for the preceding occurrence of a match.

If you want to replace the text you are searching for with some other text, type the new text in the Replace With text box. This replacement is not made automatically, however; you must also select one of the following options from the Edit menu in order to make the replacement.

FIND AGAIN

Selecting Find Again from the Edit menu repeats a search you just made without your having to fill out the dialog box again. This comes in quite handy since files usually have the word you are looking for more than once, and the first one you find is not necessarily the one you want.

REPLACE AND FIND AGAIN

Selecting Replace And Find Again from the Edit menu replaces the text you just located (which matches the text in the Look For text box of the Find dialog box) with the text you entered in the Replace With text box, and then continues the search for the next occurrence of the text in the Look For box.

REPLACE ALL

Selecting Replace All from the Edit menu replaces every occurrence of the text in the Look For text box with the text in the Replace With text box.

PREFERENCES

> If you select Preferences from the Edit menu when you are using the expression builder, you can use another Preferences dialog box to select additional features, such as the options that appear on the operator/function popups.

Selecting Preferences from the Edit menu calls up the Preferences dialog box, which lets you change the default settings of the editor. As you can see from Figure 8.12, the default settings are different for text, program, and memo windows. When you read the descriptions of this dialog box's features, look at these illustrations and note that some of them are not available for all types of windows.

The default settings are usually the settings you need for the type of file you have chosen. For example, if you are creating a text file, you ordinarily want to have a word-wrap feature, so that the right margin automatically determines where to break a line without you having to keep track of where the margin is. If you are creating a program file, though, you need to keep each command on its own line and press Enter at the end of each command, so that FoxPro knows when the command is complete, even if that means going beyond the visible right margin for some commands.

FoxPro's word-wrap defaults are set accordingly. If you create a new text file, the Wrap Words check box of the Preferences dialog box is automatically checked. If you create a new program file, it is automatically not checked. You do not even have to look at the dialog box; just type and you will find that these defaults are in effect.

If you do want to change default editor settings, for some reason, you can use the following check boxes of the Preferences dialog box to do so:

- **Wrap Words:** determines whether the word-wrap feature is used, as you have just seen.
- **Auto Indent:** automatically indents each line the same amount as the previous line. This is usual in programming, where you want to line up commands one below the other to make the program easier to read.
- **Make Backup:** automatically makes backup files. When you save a new version of a file, the previous version is saved in a file with the extension .BAK.
- **Add Line Feeds:** saves files with a carriage return and line feed at the end of each line. If this is not checked, files are saved with a carriage return and line feed only where you

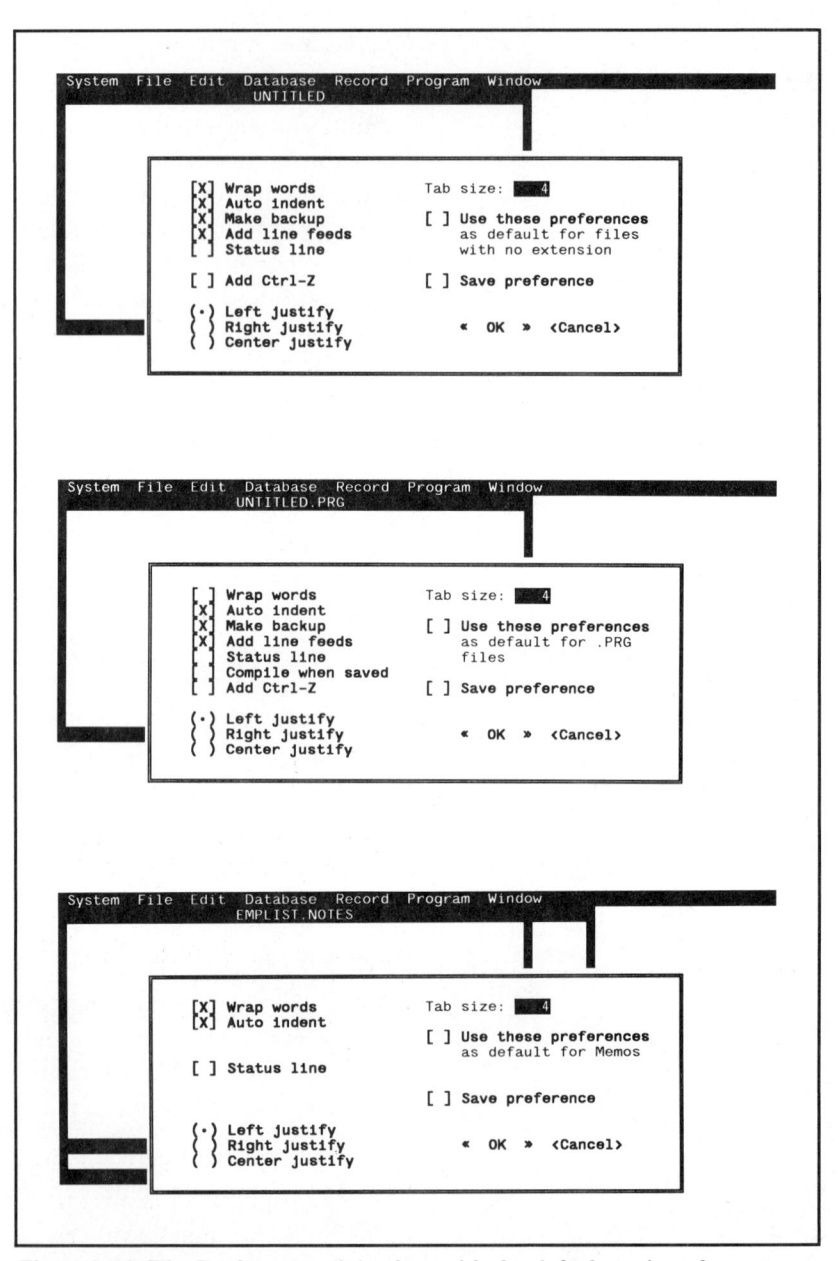

Figure 8.12: The Preferences dialog box with the default settings for text, program, and memo files

pressed Enter, making it possible to rejustify the text the next time you edit it.

- **Status line:** adds a status line at the top of the editing window. This line includes a *bullet* if the text has been modified since it was saved, the *column* the cursor is in, the *line* the cursor is in (if Word Wrap is off), **Ins** if the editor is in Insert mode, **Over** if it is in Overwrite mode, **Num** if NumLock is on, and **Caps** if CapsLock is on.

- **Add Ctrl-Z:** uses the control character Ctrl-Z (ASCII character 26) to mark the end of a file.

In addition, if you are editing a program file, this dialog box has one other check box, Compile When Saved. If you select this, the program will automatically be compiled each time you save the file.

The radio buttons under this list of check boxes control how the text is justified. Most text, of course, is left-justified, but these radio buttons also let you right-justify or center every line of a file.

The Tab Size box lets you choose how many spaces are skipped each time you press the Tab key.

The check box marked Use These Preferences As Default lets you use the conditions specified in this dialog box as the default settings for all text or program files with the same extension or for all memos.

The check box marked Save Preference can be used more freely. If you check it, these preferences will be used every time you edit this file.

ADVANCED TECHNIQUES FOR MANIPULATING DATA

Continuing to move across the menu bar, we come to the Database and Record menu pads.

There are a number of very useful features of the Database menu popup that you have not learned about yet. These fall into two categories on the popup: those involving two database files, and the arithmetic commands. You have already learned half of the commands that involve two database files (Copy To, which copies records from one file to another, and Sort, which sorts the records of one file into another); there are two other commands in this group that you have not yet learned about. Append From appends records to the current file from another file, and Total adds numeric values from one file and puts the results in another file. The other category on this popup includes a number of arithmetic commands, none of which you have yet learned: Average, Count, Sum, and Calculate.

There is also one command on the Record menu popup that you have not yet learned: Replace lets you change the contents of a single record or a whole group of records.

Though these commands are not essential to the basic work of maintaining your database, there are times when they are very handy.

APPEND FROM

Selecting Append From from the Database menu calls up the Append From dialog box, shown in Figure 8.13. This dialog box lets you add records to the currently open database from another file.

To choose the file to append records from, type its name to the right of the From pushbutton or select the From pushbutton to select it from a list of files.

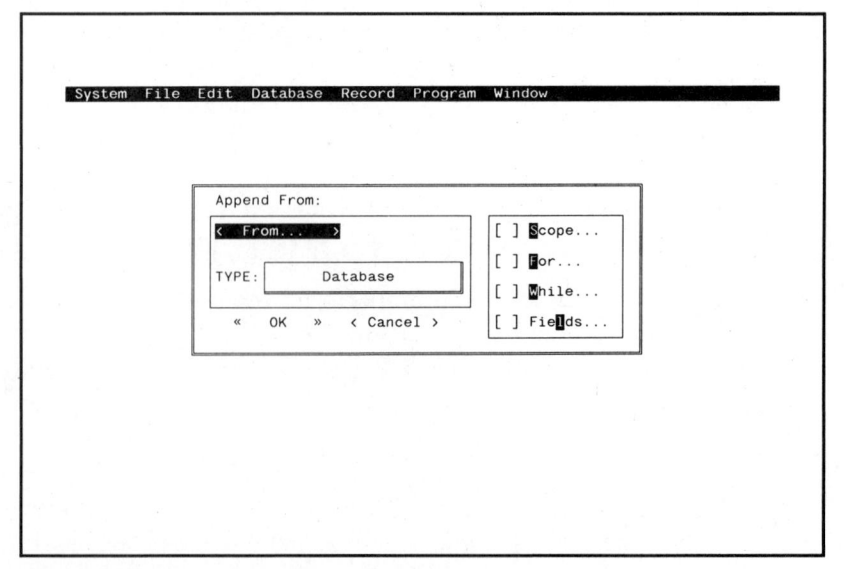

Figure 8.13: The Append From dialog box

As you can see, this dialog box has Scope, For, While, and Fields check boxes, which you are very familiar with from Chapter 5 of this book. You can use these check boxes in the ways you have learned, to determine which records to append from the selected file to the currently open file. For example, to append only those with addresses in California, you would check For and enter the logical expression STATE = "CA".

The Type popup of this dialog box is particularly useful, since it lets you append records from other types of files besides DBF database files. Select this popup control and you will be given the choice of appending from the following types of files:

- **Database:** a standard FoxPro database file (or any other dBASE compatible database file with a .DBF extension)

- **Delimited With Tabs:** a text file with tabs between the data in each field

- **Delimited With Commas:** a text file with commas between the data in each field

- **Delimited With Spaces:** a text file with a single space separating each field

- **System Data Format (SDF):** a text file where the records all have the same length and all end with a carriage return and line feed

- **Symbolic Link Format (SYLK):** an interchange format with no extension; columns become fields and rows become records

- **Data Interchange Format:** an interchange format with the extension DIF; columns become fields and rows become records

- **Microsoft Excel 2.0:** an Excel spreadsheet with the extension XLS

- **Microsoft Multiplan 4.01:** a Multiplan Binary File Format document with the extension MOD

- **Symphony 1.0:** a Symphony spreadsheet with the extension WRK

- **Symphony 1.1/1.2:** a Symphony spreadsheet with the extension WR1
- **Lotus 1-2-3 1A:** a Lotus 1-2-3 spreadsheet with the extension WKS
- **Lotus 1-2-3 2.x:** a Lotus 1-2-3 spreadsheet with the extension WK1
- **Lotus 1-2-3 3.0:** a Lotus 1-2-3 spreadsheet with the extension WK3
- **Paradox 3.5:** A Paradox 3.5 database file
- **RapidFile 1.2:** A RapidFile database file
- **Framework II:** A Framework II spreadsheet

When you append data from any of these spreadsheet formats, cells become fields and rows become records.

Delimited With Commas is important because many database programs allow you to export data from their own file type to comma-delimited files. These files normally have character fields in quotation marks as well as having commas between fields. If you have this type of text file, exported from some other database, you can simply use Append From from the Database menu with the Delimited With Commas type to import it into FoxPro.

The Copy To dialog box also has a Type popup control, which lets you copy FoxPro data to these formats so that they in turn can be used by other, noncompatible programs.

Working from the Command window, you can use the command **APPEND FROM** <*file name*> to add records from another file to the current database file.

For more information, see the commands **APPEND FROM** and **COPY TO** in the Help window.

TOTAL

Selecting Total from the Database menu calls up the Total On dialog box, shown in Figure 8.14. This dialog box lets you compute totals for the numeric fields in the current database and create a new database file with corresponding fields to store the answers.

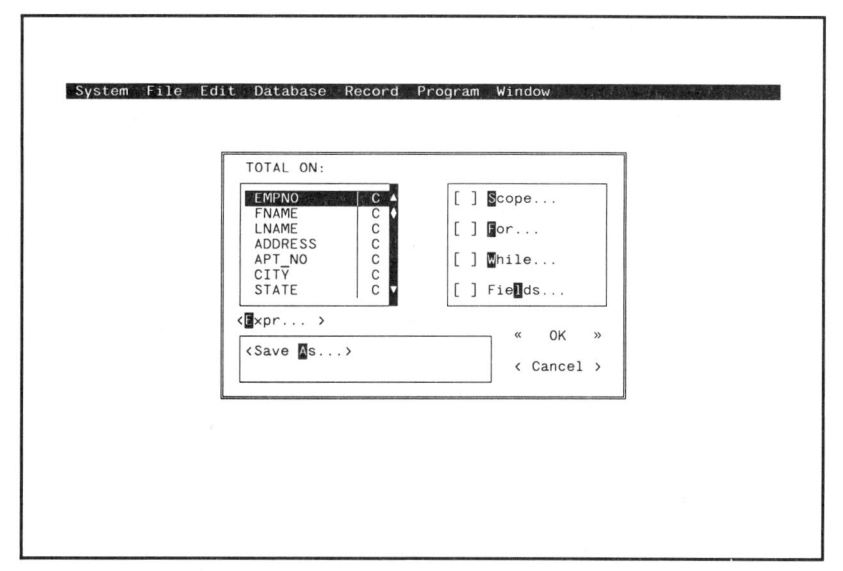

```
  System  File  Edit  Database  Record  Program  Window
```

```
                TOTAL ON:
                EMPNO      C      [ ] Scope...
                FNAME      C
                LNAME      C      [ ] For...
                ADDRESS    C
                APT_NO     C      [ ] While...
                CITY       C
                STATE      C      [ ] Fields...

                <Expr...>
                                       «  OK  »
                <Save As...>
                                       < Cancel >
```

Figure 8.14: The Total On dialog box

The key to understanding how Total works depends on the fact that you must enter a field name or expression to the right of the Expr pushbutton. You can do this by selecting a field name from the scrollable list, by selecting the Expr pushbutton to call up the expression builder, or simply by typing the field name or expression to the right of this pushbutton. The command then finds numeric totals based on this expression. For example, if you select STATE, the new database that is created will include totals for each state.

For Total to work, the database must be sorted on this same key field or expression, or it must be in use with an index based on this same key field or expression as the controlling index that determines the order of its records.

The check boxes in the Total On dialog box are optional. The Scope, For, and While check boxes let you limit the records that are included in the total, in the ways that you learned in Chapter 5; and the Fields check box lets you limit which fields are totaled. If you do not use the Fields check box, all the numeric fields in the database will be totaled.

The Save As pushbutton displays the familiar Save As dialog box, so you can type in a name for the new file. Of course, you can also simply enter the name next to this pushbutton.

> As before, these commands are written using the usual conventions: the parts of the command that are in square brackets are optional.

Because of the preparation it requires, it is often more convenient to perform this operation from the Command window. Use the following command:

TOTAL ON <*field expression*> TO <*file name*> [FIELDS <*field list*>] [FOR <*logical expr*>] [WHILE <*logical expr*>]

(all on one line, of course). You can prepare to use the command by indexing first, for example:

USE EMPLIST
INDEX ON STATE TO STATES
TOTAL ON STATE TO EMPTOTAL

It is probably easier to create the index and then total from the command line than it is to use the menu system for the same task.

Notice that, in this case, we create an IDX index file, since we do not always need this index to be updated.

CALCULATIONS USING MEMORY VARIABLES

As you can imagine, it is often inconvenient to create an entire new database file just to hold the totals from your current file. Though the **TOTAL ON** command creates the new file automatically, you have to go through the trouble of opening and browsing it to see the totals, and then you probably will have to delete it when you are done with the totals.

The next four commands that you will look at let you perform calculations without creating a new file to hold the results. Instead, the results go into *memory variables*. Memory variables are very important to computer programming, and you will learn more about using them in Chapter 9, but it is very easy to learn enough to use them now to hold the results of these commands.

The names of the fields in a database are variables, because their value can change as you move from record to record. If you enter the command **? STATE**, for example, the letters that FoxPro prints can change depending on which record the pointer is on.

The values of the fields in your databases are stored permanently when you quit FoxPro. But FoxPro also lets you create temporary variables which are lost when you quit the program. These variables are not stored on disk like database files. They are just kept in your computer's memory, and so they are called memory variables. It is conventional to give memory variables names beginning with the letter M.

You can create a memory variable from the Command line and assign it a value by using the command **STORE** <*value*> **TO** <*variable name*> or the command <*variable name*> = <*value*>. The equals sign in the second version of the command should not be confused with the = operator that is used for comparison in logical expressions: in this case it actually creates the variable and assigns the value to it, and it should be read as "let <*variable name*> equal <*value*>." You can use either of these commands to change the value of an existing memory variable as well as to create a new one.

In the following short exercise you will create and print a couple of different variables. You will notice that, when you assign a value to a variable, the value is displayed as FoxPro talk (unless you have set Talk off). When you print the variable, the number includes leading blanks. As you learned in Chapter 4, you can control its width and number of decimal places by using the STR( ) function.

1. In the Command window, enter **STORE 20 TO MVAR1**.

2. Enter **? MVAR1** and FoxPro prints 20.

3. Enter **MVAR2 = 10**. Then enter **? MVAR2** and FoxPro prints 10.

4. Try changing the value of an existing variable. Enter **MVAR1 = 25**. Then enter **? MVAR1** and FoxPro prints 25.

5. You can also perform calculations using memory variables. Enter **? MVAR1 − MVAR2** and FoxPro prints 15. Enter

    ? (MVAR1 * 2) − (MVAR2/2)

    and FoxPro prints 45.00, as shown in Figure 8.15.

It is possible to create memory variables of any FoxPro data type—except, of course, Memo. (At this point, you only need to use numeric memory variables.) The data type depends on the delimiters you use when you create the variable. For example, the command MVAR3 = "HELLO" would create a memory variable of the character type with the word HELLO stored in it. Just remember

```
┌─────────────────────────────────────────────────────────────────┐
│ System  File  Edit  Database  Record  Program  Window           │
│ 20                                                              │
│        20                                                       │
│ 10                                                              │
│        10                                                       │
│ 25                                                              │
│        25                                                       │
│         15                                                      │
│         45.00                                                   │
│                                                                 │
│                                             ┌──── Command ────┐ │
│                                             │ MVAR1 = 25      │ │
│                                             │ ? MVAR1         │ │
│                                             │ ? MVAR1 - MVAR2 │ │
│                                             │ ? (MVAR1 * 2) - (MVAR2 / │
│                                             └─────────────────┘ │
└─────────────────────────────────────────────────────────────────┘
```

Figure 8.15: Using memory variables

that any value that you store in a memory variable is temporary and will be lost when you quit FoxPro or turn off your computer.

With this background, you should have no trouble using the following options on the Database menu popup that involve memory variables.

AVERAGE

Selecting Average from the Database menu calls up the Average dialog box, shown in Figure 8.16. This dialog box lets you find the average value for numeric fields or expressions in your database and store the answer in memory variables.

If you select the Expr check box in this dialog box, you can enter a field name or field expression for the command to average: for example, enter WAGE to find the average wage. You can use only a numeric expression with this command. If you do not enter an expression, the command will average every numeric field in the current database.

The averages are displayed on the screen, as part of the FoxPro talk (unless, of course, you have set Talk off).

> Both this Average command and the AVG() function give you the *arithmetic mean,* which is calculated by adding a list of numbers and dividing the sum by the number of numbers in the list. This is the most common use of the word average, which is sometimes used in other senses.

```
┌────────────────────────────────────────────────────────────┐
│  System  File  Edit  Database  Record  Program  Window     │
│                                                            │
│                                                            │
│              ┌─────────────────────────────────┐           │
│              │ Average:       Memory Variables:│           │
│              │ [■] Expr...   ┌──────┬──────┐   │           │
│              │ [ ] Scope...  │      │      │ « OK »        │
│              │ [ ] For...    │      │      │ < Cancel >    │
│              │ [ ] While...  │      │      │   │           │
│              │   To Variable:└──────┴──────┘   │           │
│              └─────────────────────────────────┘           │
│                                                            │
└────────────────────────────────────────────────────────────┘
```

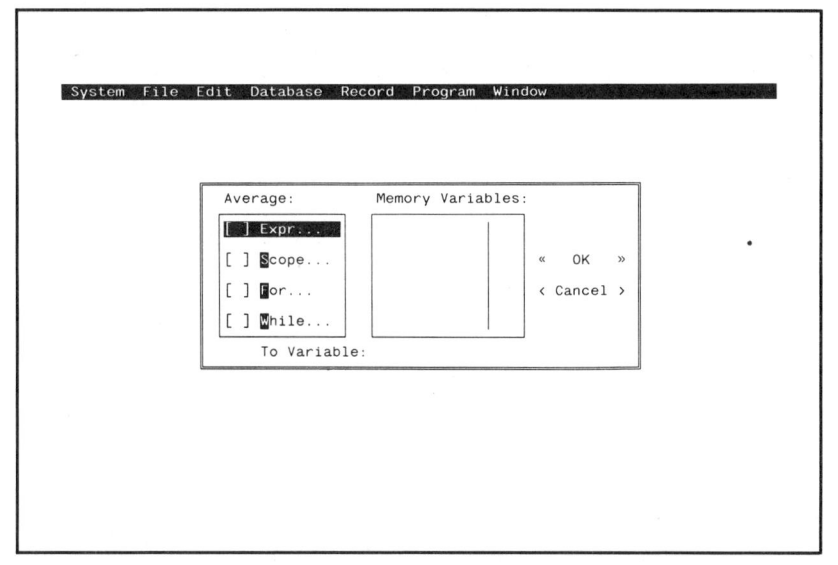

Figure 8.16: The Average dialog box

If you enter an expression to average on, then you can also enter the name of a memory variable to hold the result. You can create a new memory variable by entering its name in the To Variable text box. Or you can store the result in an existing memory variable, replacing its current value, by selecting its name from the Memory Variables list.

Ordinarily, you will get the average of all the records in the current database file. You can restrict the records that are averaged, though, by selecting the Scope, For, or While check box—for example, if you want the average wage for one state.

You can use similar options from the Command window using the **AVERAGE** command. The basic syntax is **AVERAGE** <*num expr*> **[TO** <*memvar*>**]**. The <*memvar*> in the optional TO clause of course indicates the name of the memory variable. You can also add a Scope or a FOR or WHILE clause before TO <*memvar*>. For more details, see the Help Window.

COUNT

Selecting Count from the Database menu calls up the Count dialog box, shown in Figure 8.17. This dialog box lets you count how many records there are in the current database.

🎯 Remember that, as you learned before, all of these commands include records that are marked for deletion unless you use the command **SET DELETED OFF** before you execute them, or use one of the other methods of dealing with deleted records that you learned in Chapter 5. This is not only important when you are counting records but also when you are summing, averaging, and performing other calculations.

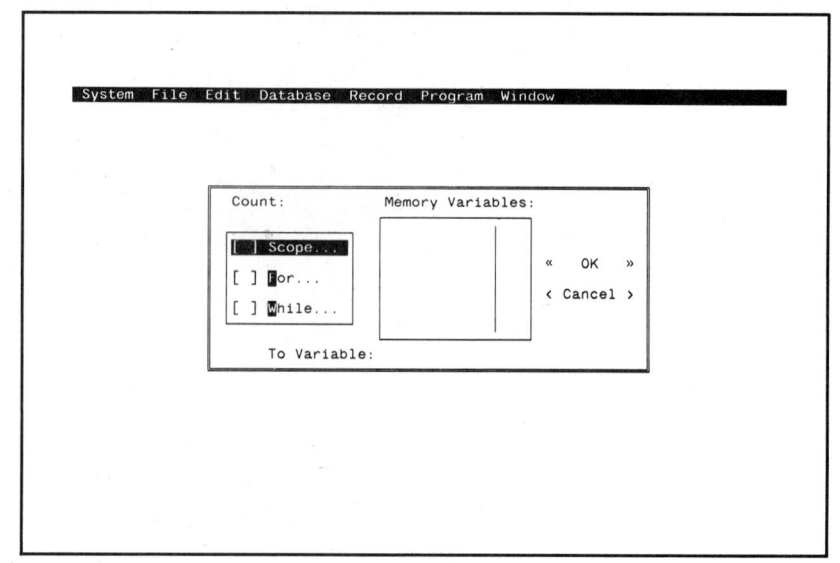

Figure 8.17: The Count dialog box

As you can see by comparing the illustrations, Count is very similar to Average, except that it does not have an Expr check box. This is because you do not need an expression to count on: FoxPro simply counts each record once.

Like the Average, the Count of records is displayed as part of the FoxPro talk. You can store it to either a new or an existing memory variable in the same way, and you can restrict the number of records in the same way by using the Scope, For, or While check box. (The usual check boxes are included even though you obviously would never want to use Count with a Scope.)

You can use similar options from the Command window using the COUNT command. The basic syntax is **COUNT [TO** <*memvar*>**]**. You can also add a Scope or a FOR or WHILE clause before TO <*memvar*>. For more details, see the Help window.

SUM

Selecting Sum from the Database menu calls up the Sum dialog box, shown in Figure 8.18. This lets you find the sum of numeric fields or expressions in your database and store the answer in memory variables.

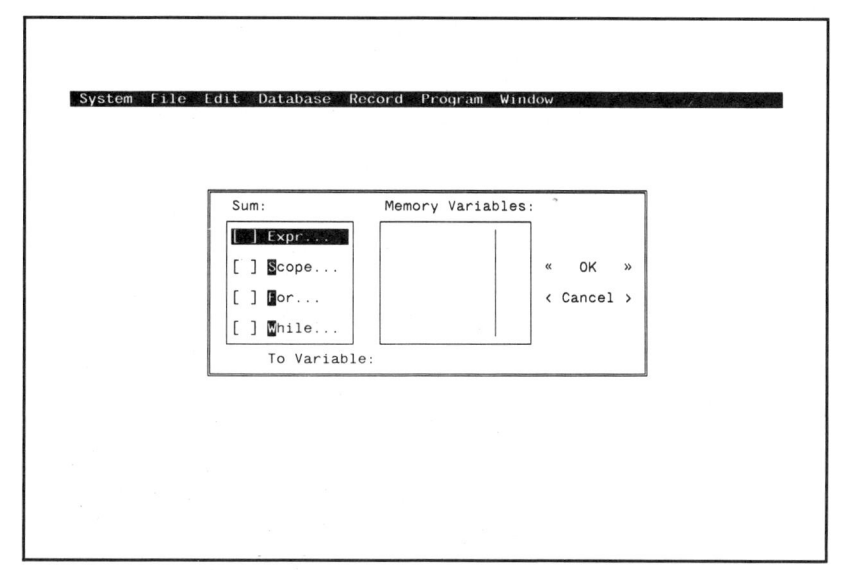

```
┌─────────────────────────────────────────────────────────────┐
│                                                             │
│       System  File  Edit  Database  Record  Program  Window │
│                                                             │
│                                                             │
│              Sum:              Memory Variables:            │
│              [ ] Expr...       ┌──────────┐                 │
│              [ ] Scope...      │          │    «   OK   »   │
│              [ ] For...        │          │    < Cancel >   │
│              [ ] While...      │          │                 │
│                 To Variable:   └──────────┘                 │
│                                                             │
└─────────────────────────────────────────────────────────────┘
```

Figure 8.18: The Sum dialog box

As you can see by comparing the illustrations, Sum works in a way that is identical to Average. By default, it sums all numeric expressions and displays the result as talk. You can check the Expr check box to enter a numeric expression to be summed (such as WAGE), and you can store the result in a new or existing memory variable. Select the Scope, For, or While check box to restrict the records that are summed. From the Command window the basic syntax is **SUM** <*num expr*> **[TO** <*memvar*>**]** with a Scope or a FOR or WHILE clause.

CALCULATE

Selecting Calculate from the Database menu calls up the Calculate dialog box, shown in Figure 8.19. This dialog box lets you perform a number of different calculations.

This dialog box works just like the others you have looked at, with one exception: to use it, you *must* select the Expr pushbutton. This calls up a special version of the expression builder dialog box, which has only the Math popup control and only a limited number of options available, as shown in Figure 8.20.

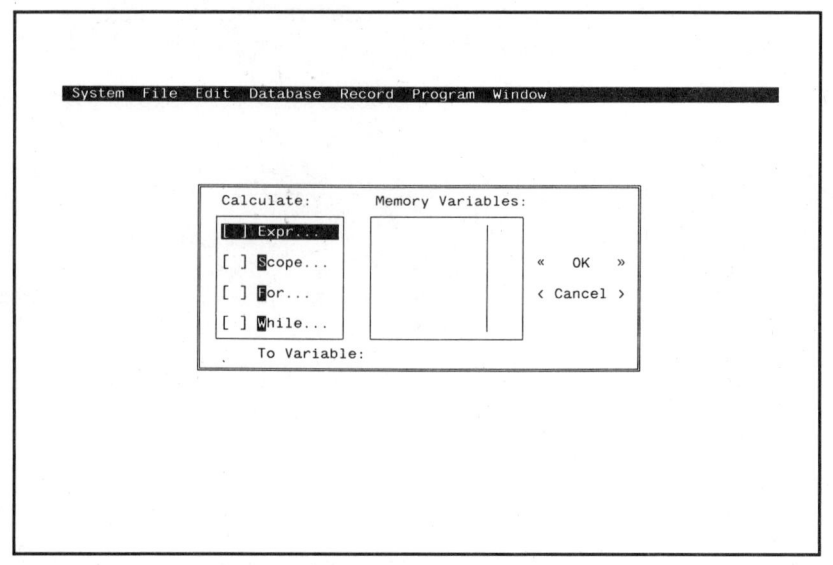

Figure 8.19: The Calculate dialog box

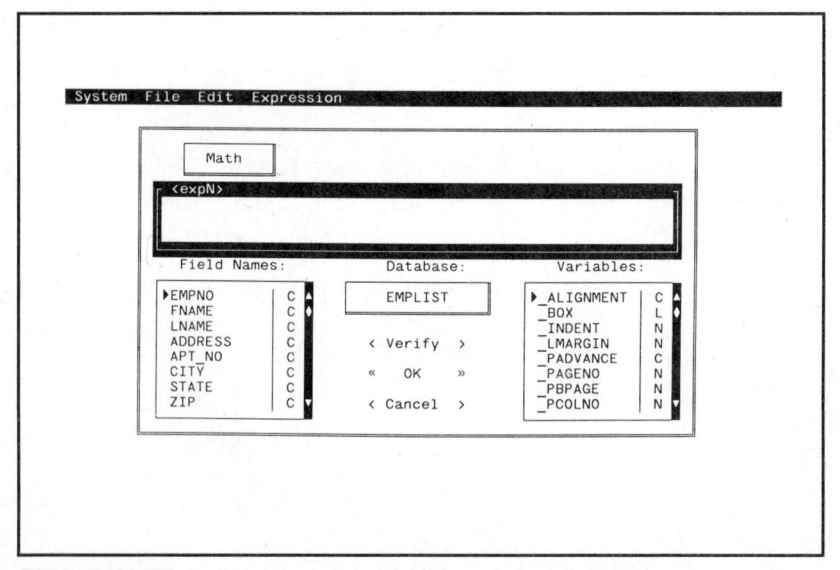

Figure 8.20: The special expression builder used with Calculate

Note that some of these calculation functions are used with no expressions, some require numeric expressions, and some (indicated by just <*exp*>) can be used with numeric, character, or date expressions.

- **AVG(<*num exp*>)** finds the average (arithmetic mean) for the expression
- **CNT( )** counts the number of records in the database
- **MAX(<*exp*>)** finds the largest value of the expression
- **MIN(<*exp*>)** finds the smallest value of the expression
- **NPV(<*num exp*>,<*exp*>,<*num exp*>)** finds net present value of periodic future cash payments, discounted at some interest rate
- **STD(<*num exp*>)** finds standard deviation, the degree to which the field values vary from the average
- **SUM(<*num exp*>)** finds the sum
- **VAR(<*num exp*>)** finds the variance from the average, which is the square root of the standard deviation.

The use of most of these functions is obvious. For more information look under **CALCULATE** in the Help window.

You can see that some of these functions—SUM( ), CNT( ) and AVG( )—duplicate other menu choices. One advantage of Calculate, though, is that you can perform several calculations at once. If you use the expression builder to create a list of functions, separated by commas, all the calculations will be performed and displayed as talk. If you want to store them to memory variables, simply create a list of an equal number of memory variables, also separated by commas.

From the Command window, the basic form of this command is **CALCULATE** <*exp list*> [**TO** <*memvar list*>].

REPLACE

There is one very useful option on the Record menu popup that you have not yet learned. Selecting Replace from the Record menu lets you replace the value in a field of the current database with some new value.

This option is very useful when it is used with the scope of ALL: it lets you change or fill in a given field in every record in the database. For example, say that you modify the structure of your database to add a new logical field, and that the field should start off by being true for every record: instead of using the keyboard to type the entry in each record, you can use Replace with the All check box.

The default scope for Replace is NEXT 1; so if you do not specify a scope it only replaces the value of the current record.

The Replace dialog box, shown in Figure 8.21, is easy to use. Just select the field whose value you want to change (from the scrollable list of field names), and type the new value to the right of the With pushbutton.

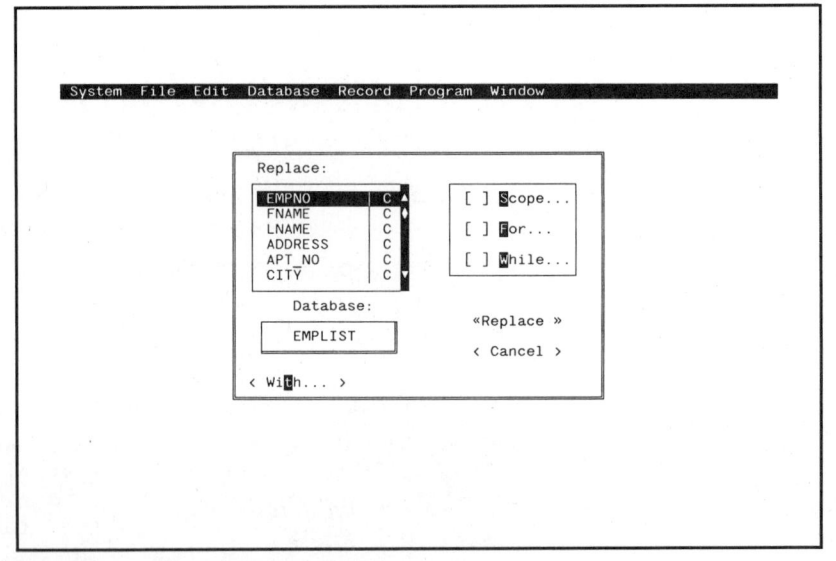

Figure 8.21: The Replace dialog box

To create an expression that you want to replace the current value with, you can select the With pushbutton to call up the expression builder. For example, if every employee got a cost-of-living raise of 10 percent, the new wage would be 1.10 times as great as the current wage, so you would select WAGE as the field whose value should be changed, and use the expression WAGE * 1.1 as its new value, and use ALL as the scope.

Use the For or While check boxes in the usual way to restrict the records that the command affects—for example, if only employees from California get a cost-of-living raise. Remember, though, that the default scope is NEXT 1. If you want FoxPro to look through the entire database for employees from California (rather than just checking the next record to see if it is from California), then you must use the Scope check box and enter the scope of ALL in addition to using a FOR or WHILE clause.

Working from the Command window, the basic form of this command is **REPLACE** [<*scope*>] <*field name*> **WITH** <*expr*>. Remember, again, that if the optional <*scope*> is omitted, the default is NEXT 1. For example,

    REPLACE PROBATION WITH .T.

only acts on the current record;

    REPLACE ALL PROBATION WITH .T.

acts on the entire database. A FOR or WHILE clause can be added at the end of the command, for example,

    REPLACE ALL PROBATION WITH .T. FOR STATE = "NJ"

SETTING COLORS

There is one remaining command that you should look at briefly. Selecting Color from the Window menu calls up the color picker dialog box, shown in Figure 8.22. This dialog box lets you control the colors of your FoxPro display—or, if you are using a monochrome monitor, the intensity of your display. This feature is not often needed except by programmers; it is useful mainly if you have an unusual color monitor that is hard to read when FoxPro's default colors are used.

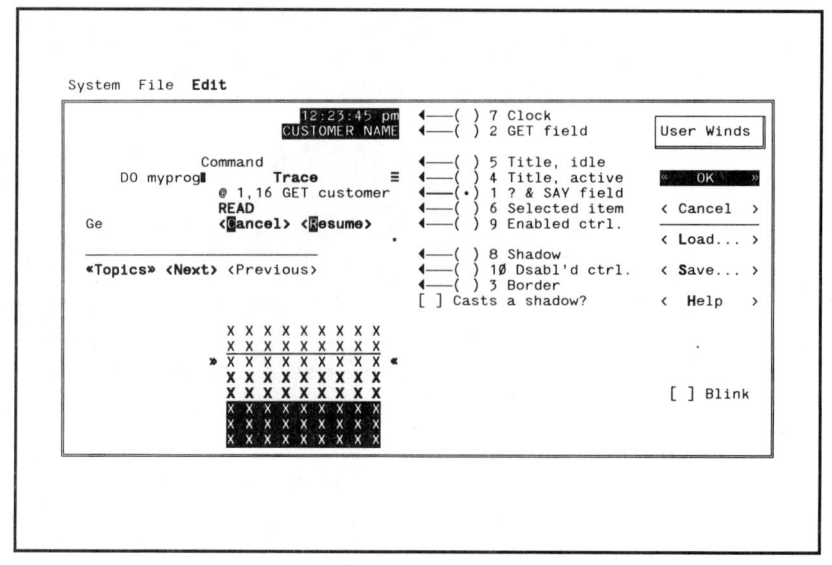

Figure 8.22: The color picker dialog box

You can change the colors of many different features of your display. The popup control in the upper right of this dialog box gives you these choices:

- **Usr Winds:** user windows
- **Usr Menus:** user menus
- **Menu Bar:** the main menu bar and menu pads
- **Menu Pops:** menu popups
- **Dialogs:** dialog boxes and system messages
- **Dlog Pops:** popup controls and scrollable lists within dialog boxes
- **Alerts:** alerts (error messages)
- **Windows:** system windows
- **Wind Pops:** popup controls and scrollable lists within windows
- **Browse:** the Browse/Edit window
- **Report:** the report layout window

The list also includes numbered Schemes. Schemes 12 through 16 are reserved for use in later versions of FoxPro and Schemes 17 through 24 may be used by programmers.

Once you have selected the feature whose color you want to change, choose Load to select from a scrollable list of available color sets, and select one that is suited to your computer. The Cast a Shadow ? check box is used to add a shadow behind the selected feature, and the Bright check box is used to intensify the background color of the feature associated with the current radio button; use the Blink check box to make this feature blink.

Once you have the color combinations you want, select Save. FoxPro prompts you to enter a name for this new color set. To use the color set during the current session, select OK.

It is very unusual for a user to need to change the default colors of FoxPro, but this summary of the basics of using the color picker gives you an idea of what you can do. If you do need to use the color picker, see your *User's Guide* for more details.

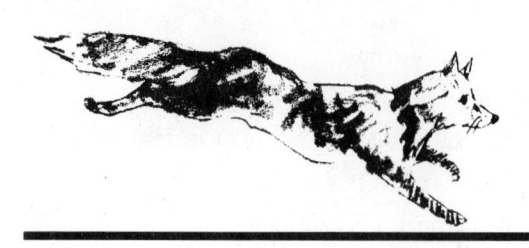

Chapter 9

Expanding Your Capabilities through Programming

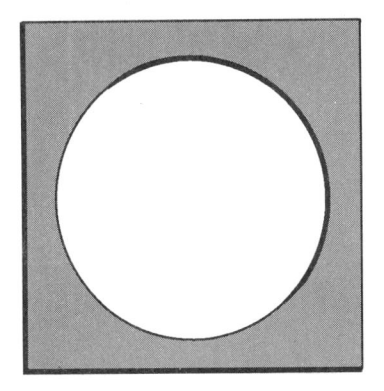

THIS CHAPTER IS A GENERAL INTRODUCTION TO computer programming using FoxPro as an example. It will teach you the basic commands that FoxPro programmers use to interact with the user and to organize the flow of their programs. At the same time, it will use these commands to teach you the basic principles that apply to any programming language.

Many people believe that the FoxPro/dBASE language is the best introduction to computer programming. It has the usual features of most programming languages, but it also has special features that will let you set up genuinely useful database-management systems not long after you begin learning.

When you learn most programming languages, you have to work on trivial exercises until you have mastered the language. You generally must read an entire book or take an entire course on the language without creating any real programs; you don't begin to write programs that anyone would actually want to use until you get to an advanced level.

Early versions of dBASE, which could be used only by entering interactive commands at the dot prompt, were difficult enough to learn that programmers were in great demand. They were asked to create menu-driven systems that would let users do what they needed for their own applications without having to know anything about dBASE itself. The programmer would define the structure of database files, create reports and labels, and write a program to tie them together.

It is possible for a relative beginner at FoxPro programming to create this sort of system without much trouble, and with the programming tools included in version 2 of FoxPro—the screen and menu generators—it is not difficult to give this program a very impressive interface, including windows, popup menus, and such features as pushbuttons.

After spending this chapter learning the basics, you will go on to learn about the screen generator in Chapter 10. Then, in Chapters 11 and 12, you will design and program a general purpose, menu-driven mailing list application for users who want to keep track of names and addresses and produce mailing labels.

STRUCTURED PROGRAMMING

Apart from the ease with which it can be used to create useful applications, FoxPro is a good introduction to computer programming because it is a *structured* programming language.

In this respect, FoxPro is greatly superior to most versions of BASIC. The usual practice of teaching students BASIC as their first programming language has probably made many students abandon programming as too difficult. BASIC is one of the older programming languages, which means for one thing that many BASIC programs are extremely difficult to understand, since it was invented before computer scientists knew how to create languages that could make it easy for programmers to follow the logic of their programs.

The central processing unit of every computer has a built-in *instruction set*. For example, there are circuits designed to add numbers and to move data from one location in the computer's memory to another. Each of these circuits is activated by a binary code made up of ones and zeros, and the earliest programmers actually had to learn all these codes and what they did in the computer they were working with in order to write programs. Programs written in this binary code are said to be written in *machine language*.

Before long, computer scientists devised the idea of using an English-like word to symbolize each of these codes. You could write programs made up of these words and use a special program to translate them into machine code. This sort of translation is something that a computer can do very easily: when it sees the word ADD or MOV, for example, it replaces the word with the binary code that tells the central processing unit to add two numbers or to move data. Assembly language, which is still commonly used, is this sort of language. The program used to translate each word into binary code is called an assembler.

Assembly language represented such an advance over machine languages that it came to be known as the second generation of computer languages. However, although assembly language is a tremendous advance over lists of binary numbers, it is still very difficult to use. It is a language that is based on how the hardware works—not on how people think—and using it requires rigorous technical training.

During the 1950s and 1960s, as businesses began to computerize, it became apparent that it would be impossible to get enough programmers with the technical knowledge needed to write programs in assembly language. Computer scientists began to develop what were known as *high-level languages,* which were designed to be easy to learn and understand. The best known of the early ones were COBOL and BASIC. There were claims that such third-generation languages would make programming so easy that computer programmers would not be needed anymore: the managers of businesses would just write programs for themselves. Of course, these claims were much too optimistic, but it was possible for businesses to hire people who had never used computers, train them for a few months, and then start them working as programmers.

The earliest of these third-generation languages had a major flaw, though, which made programs much more difficult to understand and maintain. This flaw had to do with the way that they redirected *the flow of program control.*

The simplest program is just a list of instructions, which are executed one after another. Most programs, though, redirect the sequence of execution, in order to use some instructions more than once. For example, a program to write a report might have a series of instructions that write a page's footer, skip a number of lines, and then write the header of the next page. Of course, these instructions have to be executed many times when a report is produced, but the programmer only needs to write them once: the program can contain instructions that direct the flow of control to those lines every time the footer and header are needed.

The earliest third-generation languages, imitating control flow in assembly language, used the command **GOTO** in this sort of situation. BASIC, for example, gives each line of programming code a number. If the code for producing a footer and header is at line 10200, the program uses the command **GOTO 10200** or perhaps the command **GOSUB 10200** each time that it uses that code.

Needless to say, a program written this way is very difficult to follow. You need to flip through pages of code to find line 10200 in order to understand what that command actually does. And it is likely that the code you find there will contain another **GOTO** that sends you flipping though the pages again. Programs written in this way get so twisted up that programmers began referring to them as

> Even today, the most popular versions of BASIC—GW-BASIC and BASICA, which are distributed with IBM-PC compatible computers—use **GOTO** and **GOSUB**, and so are not structured. Some more recent versions of BASIC, such as QuickBASIC and Turbo BASIC, do allow you to do structured programming, but they also contain the commands used by older, unstructured programs; learning them as your first language tends to teach bad programming habits.

"spaghetti code." It is possible (though just barely) to keep the logic in your mind when you are writing the program, but it is much more difficult to follow the logic when you are debugging the program or when you go back to the program a year later to modify it; it is almost impossible to unravel the code if you have to modify a program that someone else wrote.

Structured programming was developed to make it easier to understand and maintain programs. Computer scientists proved that the command **GOTO** was not necessary. Any program could be written using only three types of control flow:

- **sequence:** the most basic type of control flow. Sequence simply means that commands are executed one after another, as they appear in the code.
- **selection:** the use of IF and ELSE to select one of a pair of alternatives. If a condition is true, the program does one thing; otherwise (ELSE), it does something else.
- **iteration (or looping):** the use of repetition. The same commands are repeated again and again as long as some condition is true.

Structured programming also involved breaking down a program into modules or procedures. Rather than a single long listing, with **GOTO** twisted all through it, structured programs are broken down into parts that are easier to understand. In the example above, there might be one procedure to print the footer and header, which might be named PAGEBRAK, since it occurs between pages; then, whenever you needed it, you would use a command like **DO PAGEBRAK** or **PERFORM PROCEDURE PAGEBRAK** (depending on the language you are using).

You can imagine how much easier it is to understand a program with commands like **DO PAGEBRAK** than one with commands like **GOTO 10200**. Breaking down the program into separate procedures also makes it easier to maintain, since a procedure can be changed without there being unexpected changes elsewhere in the program. As you will see when you write a program in the next chapter, it is much easier to test and debug programs one procedure at a time than it is to test an entire program.

In summary, then, structured programming is marked by two features: first, control flow is based on sequence, selection, and iteration, and does not use **GOTO**; and, second, long programs are broken down into smaller modules. Though they are not referred to as a separate generation, structured programming languages make programs so much easier to understand, test, and maintain that they are as important an advance in programming technique as a new generation. Later in this chapter, you will learn the basic techniques of structured programming, all of which have been adopted by Fox-Pro and other dBASE compatible languages.

The next major advance over structured programming was the development of fourth-generation languages, which make it easy to perform special tasks. The way that FoxPro lets you create files is typical of fourth-generation languages. Many third-generation languages make you save data on disk one line or one character at a time. FoxPro's low-level file handling functions do much the same thing. If you wanted to find a record in a database file, you might have to write a program that figures out how many characters after the beginning of the file that record begins. If you wanted to index the database, you would have to create an index file with pointers that let your program find the address of each record in the database file. Of course, FoxPro does all that for you automatically: you just need to know the command **GOTO** or **INDEX ON**.

Many FoxPro commands, such as **LOCATE**, **SEEK**, and **SET RELATION TO** do things that would take extra programming time and work if you were using a general purpose third-generation language. But they are easy to do using a fourth-generation language that is designed for the special purpose of managing a database.

> Languages designed for artificial intelligence are generally known as fifth-generation languages, but they have not yet become as popular as people predicted when they were first introduced.

SOME PRELIMINARY DETAILS

There are a few preliminary details that you should know before you write your first sample programs in the next section.

Programs are plain ASCII text files, which can be created with most text editors or with word processors that create plain ASCII files (which some word processors call DOS files).

FoxPro and other dBASE compatible languages require you to start a new line for each line of programming code: the new line is the delimiter that lets FoxPro know where a single command begins and ends. For this reason, you cannot use an editor with a word-wrap feature that breaks up a line simply because it reaches the right margin. Without word-wrap, you can simply keep typing the code beyond the right margin. (If you select New from the File menu and then select the Program radio button, or if you enter the command **MODIFY COMMAND** <*file name*>, the FoxPro editor will have its word-wrap feature turned off.)

> A semicolon within a character string will not break the string. If you need to break a line at a point where you are in a character string, you can break the string into two strings at that point and use the semicolon followed by the plus (+) sign. Don't forget that each string must be enclosed in quotation marks.

If you want to be able to read your code more easily, you can keep it from going beyond the right margin; you can break a long line in two by adding a semicolon (;) at the place you want it to break. This will make FoxPro ignore the indication that the next line is a new line, and read the two lines as a single command. Of course, the listings in this book will use ; to fit the command in the width of the page. When you see this character, you can either type the code as it is in the printed listing, or you can leave out the ; and continue typing the code on a single line.

FoxPro ignores extra blank spaces. You can skip lines, and add extra blank spaces or tabs whenever you think that will make the program easier to read. When you break a line in two using the ; character, for example, it is good to indent the second line to make it clear that it is a continuation of the same command. Likewise, as you will see, indentation is very important in making it easier to understand a program's control flow.

Programs should also contain comments, which are used solely to make it easier for people to understand the program. The program itself does not use the comments.

FoxPro includes three commands that let you add comments. An asterisk * or the word **NOTE** at the beginning of a line signals FoxPro to ignore everything on that line. Using an asterisk at the beginning of the line is the most common way of adding comments. It is also a good idea to add a few hyphens after the asterisk: though they are not required, they make the comments stand out so they are easier to follow.

The symbol && is used to add comments to the right of your programming code (rather than on a separate line). This double ampersand may be used anywhere in the line. FoxPro executes the command to its left, and ignores only the text to its right.

Programs are often difficult to follow when you come back to them after not working with them for a year. The logic that seemed so obvious

The command **SET ESCAPE OFF** disables the Esc key so that you cannot use it to stop a program. You can add this command to the beginning of a program you have created, to keep the user under your control at all times, but you should not add it until after you have finished your programming and debugging work, so you can use the Esc key yourself.

to you when you were writing the program suddenly seems mysterious: it is hard to figure out what you were doing. For this reason, it is good to write a comment before each major activity that the program performs, identifying what the program is about to do.

You can run a program by entering **DO** <*program name*> or by selecting Do from the Program menu and selecting the name from the scrollable list. You can stop a program from running by pressing Esc. When you do this, FoxPro displays an alert that gives you three choices:

- **Cancel:** stops execution of the program permanently. This is the default choice.
- **Suspend:** stops execution of the program temporarily and returns you to the Command window. You can start the program again from the point where you left off by selecting Resume from the Program menu or by entering the command **RESUME**.
- **Ignore:** ignores the fact that you pressed Esc, and continues execution of the program.

If there is an error in your program, FoxPro displays an alert with the same choices plus an error message: it also displays the line in the code that contains the error and lets you edit it, as you will see when you test the first program.

TALKING TO THE USER: INPUT/OUTPUT

One basic element of any programming language is input/output: the commands that the program uses to communicate with the user. The FoxPro/dBASE standard includes two different sets of input/output commands.

Unformatted input/output prints a message for the user or gets information from the user at the location on the screen where the cursor happens to be. You have seen one of these commands, **?**, which simply moves the cursor to the new line and prints a line of text there.

If there is no room for a new line, this command makes everything on the screen scroll up to make room for it.

Formatted input/output, on the other hand, lets you control where on the screen messages appear. Every message to the user and every space for the user to fill in text is in a specific place on the screen and does not move; the screen does not scroll up as it does when you use the ? command.

In this section, you will learn both of these types of input/output. Both of these are commonly used in connection with variables. As you learned in Chapter 8, FoxPro lets you create two types of variables:

- **fields:** Each field in a database file is a variable and can be used in input/output. For example, if you enter the command **USE EMPLIST** followed by the command **? FNAME**, FoxPro will print the first name of the first record in the EMPLIST file. If you then enter the command **SKIP** followed by the command **? FNAME**, FoxPro will print the first name of the second record in the file. FNAME is a variable because its value changes. The values in fields are stored permanently on your disk.

- **memory variables:** It is also possible to create temporary variables that exist only in the memory (RAM) of your computer and that are lost when you quit FoxPro. In Chapter 8, you learned two equivalent commands to create memory variables: **STORE** <*value*> **TO** <*memvar*> and <*memvar*> = <*value*>. In this section, you will also learn how to create a memory variable that the user assigns a value to. It is conventional to give memory variables names that begin with the letter M.

The index numbers of arrays can be enclosed either in square brackets or in parentheses. FoxPro supports both one- and two-dimensional arrays.

In addition, FoxPro lets you create a special type of memory variable called an *array*, which lets you have a number of variables that have the same name and that are distinguished by an index number. For example, you might use variables with the names **m_var[1]**, **m_var[2]**, **m-var[3]**, and so on. These are often convenient to use because you can refer to them all in just a few lines of code by using a variable as the index number. For example, if you created a numeric variable named **m_cntr**, you could refer to all the variables above as

m_var[m_cntr] by assigning m_cntr the values 1, 2, 3, and so on. Arrays will not be used in the exercises in this book, but they are introduced here both because they are a common feature of programming languages and because they are used by some dialog boxes in the screen generator, so they will be mentioned in Chapter 10. For information on FoxPro arrays, see either **DECLARE** or **DIMENSION** in the Help window: either of these commands can be used to create an array.

The programs that you write to test input/output will use both field and memory variables. You will begin by learning unformatted input/output and then go on to learn formatted input/output.

UNFORMATTED INPUT/OUTPUT

You have already used the most important of the unformatted output commands: **CLEAR** to clear the screen and **?** to print a line of text to the screen. In programming, **?** is sometimes used without any character expression following it, to print a blank line in order to skip a line. There are a couple of other variations on this command. **??** prints a line of text without printing a carriage return first, and **???** prints a line of text to the printer. Like **?**, these commands are used with FoxPro expressions, and can include literals, functions, and variables.

You can also send text to the printer, as you know, by adding **TO PRINT** at the end of certain commands. For example, you can use **LIST TO PRINT**. If you want to send text to the printer and the command you are using does not work with the clause TO PRINT, use the command **SET PRINT ON** before entering the desired command to print unformatted output that is displayed onscreen; then enter **SET PRINT OFF** to stop printing.

One other use of **?** that is very important in programming is to make the computer beep in case the user makes an invalid entry or some other error. The command **?** can be used to print any ASCII character, and the beep happens to be ASCII character number 7. Thus, the command **? CHR(7)** will make the computer beep.

Another output command that is used only in programs is **TEXT ...ENDTEXT**. You can add a block of text of any length as a substitute for the three dots in this command. (The words TEXT and ENDTEXT must each be on separate lines.) All of the text will be displayed on the screen and, if you use **SET PRINT ON** first, it will also be sent to the printer.

Finally, there are times in programs when you do not want output displayed on the screen. To suppress the screen display, you can use the command **SET CONSOLE OFF**. For example, you can use this in combination with **SET PRINT ON** if you want something sent to the printer but not displayed on the screen. Then, when you are done, use the commands **SET CONSOLE ON** and **SET PRINT OFF** to return to normal.

Notice that, as a fourth-generation language, FoxPro often gives you many ways to do the same thing, so that you can choose the one that is most convenient for you. For example, the program

```
? "Hello, "
?? FNAME
```

does the same thing as the program

```
? "Hello, " + FNAME
```

Likewise, the program

```
SET PRINT ON
? "This line is going to the printer."
SET PRINT OFF
```

produces the same result as

```
??? "This line is going to the printer."
```

These output commands do things that are similar to things you have done earlier in this book working from the command line. You are doing something completely new, though, when you use the Fox-Pro commands that get input from the user.

The most basic unformatted input command is

```
INPUT [<char exp>] TO <memvar>
```

This command gets input from the user and creates a memory variable to store it in. If the optional character expression is included, that character expression is used as a prompt. **INPUT** will keep repeating the prompt until the user makes a valid entry.

You will have no trouble understanding how this command works if you write a very simple program to test it. Before running this program, you should enter the command **SET TALK OFF** in the Command window, so that FoxPro does not display talk to the screen and disrupt the display that your program has set up. In an actual application, you would include the command **SET TALK OFF** in the program itself.

After running the sample program, you should change the listing to add an error to it, so you can see how FoxPro helps you with debugging.

The program listings in this book follow the common programming convention of writing words of the FoxPro language in capital letters and writing variables and comments in small letters. This is merely meant to make the program easier to read: capitalization does not matter to the program, except in the case of literals, such as "How old are you?", which are printed to the screen with the capitalization they have in the program. You can type the program in all capitals if you find it easier.

1. Enter **CD\LEARNFOX** and then **FOXPRO** if necessary. If you want, enter **CLEAR** to clear the screen.

2. To create the program, select New from the File menu. Select the Program radio button and select OK. Enter the program shown in Figure 9.1. Then select Save As from the File menu. Enter **TEST1** as the name of the new file, then select the default text button, Save. FoxPro automatically adds the .PRG extension. Close the Program window after writing and saving the program.

3. Enter **SET TALK OFF** (or select View from the Window menu and use the View window to set the talk off).

4. Select Do from the Program menu. When the Do Program File dialog box appears, select TEST1.PRG from the scrollable list.

```
************************************
*TEST1.PRG
*sample program to illustrate the use of INPUT
************************************

CLEAR
?
?
INPUT "How old are you? " TO m_age
?
? "Next year you will be " + LTRIM(STR(m_age + 1))
?
?
INPUT "Enter any number to continue " TO dummy
```

Figure 9.1: A sample program to test INPUT

Select the default text button, Do, to run the program. FoxPro automatically compiles it and runs it, creating the screen shown in Figure 9.2.

5. If you did not have any errors in the program, try adding one to get a demonstration of FoxPro's debugging capabilities. Edit TEST1.PRG again and eliminate the final parenthesis following the function that prints the age, so it now reads as **LTRIM(STR(m_age + 1)**, with unbalanced parentheses. Save it in this new form and then run it. When you get to the line with the error, FoxPro displays an error message plus the program code with a highlight on the line that has the error, as shown in Figure 9.3.

6. Select the default text button, Cancel. FoxPro automatically opens an edit window to let you edit the program, with the cursor in the line where the error is. Add the closing parenthesis at the end of the line. Save the file, then close the editing window and run the program again to make sure it is correct.

```
How old are you? 39
Next year you will be 40

Enter any number to continue
```

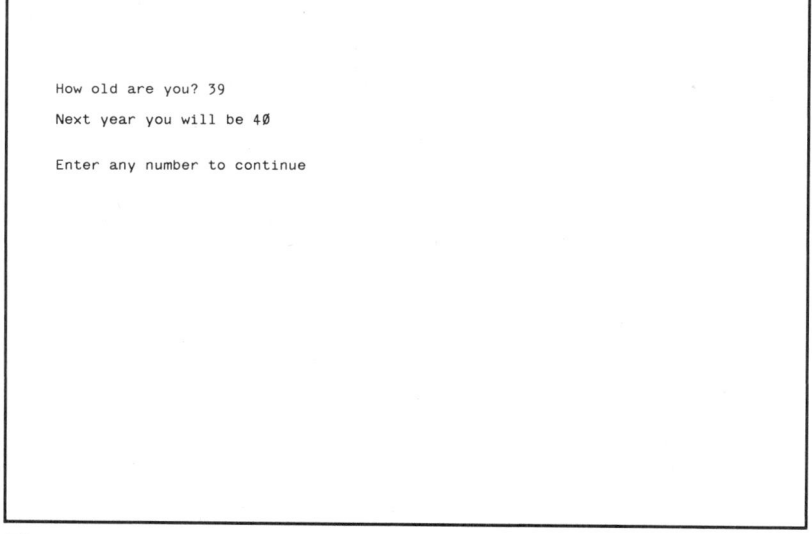

Figure 9.2: The output of the sample INPUT program

```
                     TEST1.PRG
CLEAR
?
?
INPUT "How old are you? " TO m_age
?
? "Next year you will be " + LTRIM(STR(m_age + 1)
?
?
INPUT "Enter any number to continue " TO dummy
```

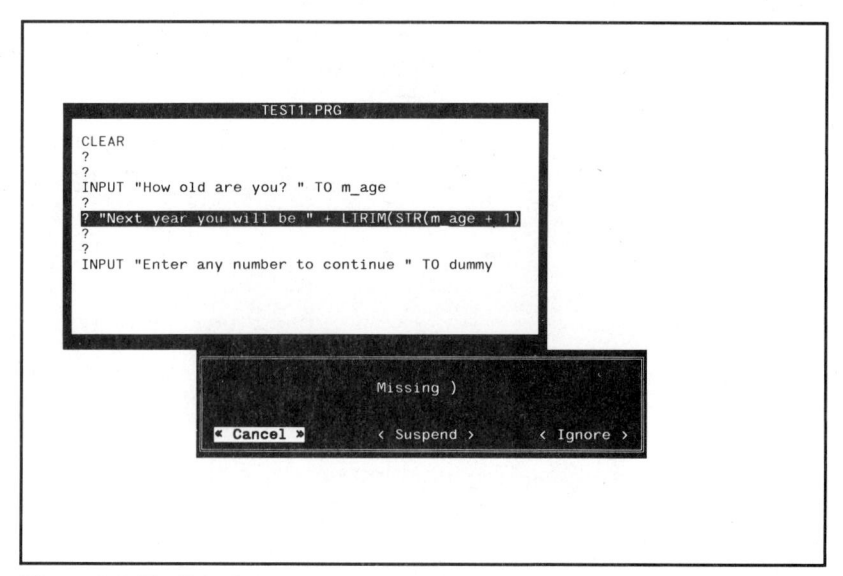

```
                    Missing )
    « Cancel »        < Suspend >        < Ignore >
```

Figure 9.3: FoxPro shows you your error

As you can see when you run the program, the character expression "How old are you? " appears as a prompt for the user; when the user makes an entry, it is stored as a variable and then used by the program as part of the next message to the user. A second **INPUT** command is used to make the program pause so that the user has time to read this message; because **INPUT** must save the user's response in a variable, this second occurrence of the command saves the user's choice in a memory variable named dummy because it is never actually used. Notice that this program used **?** to skip lines so that this prompt would not be right at the top edge of the screen.

The major limitation of the **INPUT** command is that the data type of the memory variable it creates is determined by the data type of the user's input. What this means is that, in order to use this command to get a date or a character string, you would have to tell the user to enter the data with the proper delimiters. To get the user's name, for example, you would have to use a command like:

INPUT "Enter your name surrounded by quotation marks" TO mname

Likewise, in TEST1, you had to have the user enter another number to continue at the end of the program. **INPUT** does not cause any trouble when you actually want to get a number, but it is not at all user-friendly when you are working with other data types.

Because it is common to use an unformatted input/output command to get text, there is another command that is like **INPUT** but that reads any input as a character expression. The command

ACCEPT [<*char exp*>] TO <*memvar*>

works very much like **INPUT** except that it reads whatever the user enters as a character string. Unlike **INPUT**, which creates a memory variable whose data type depends on what the user enters, **ACCEPT** always creates a memory variable of the character type. If necessary, you can then use the functions that you learned in Chapter 4 to use this input as if it were another data type—VAL( ) for the numeric type and CTOD( ) for the date type.

As with **INPUT**, the optional character expression that you use with **ACCEPT** appears as a prompt for the user. Try a sample program to test **ACCEPT**. The easiest way to create this program is by editing the program you created earlier, then saving it under a new name:

1. In the Command window, enter **MODI COMM TEST1**.
2. When the edit window appears, edit the program so it looks like Figure 9.4.
3. Select Save As from the File menu. Save this program under the name of TEST2. FoxPro adds the .PRG extension.

```
************************************
*TEST2.PRG
*sample program to illustrate the use of ACCEPT
************************************

CLEAR
?
?
ACCEPT "What is your name? " TO mname
?
INPUT "How old are you? " TO m_age
?
?
?
? "Sorry, " + PROPER(mname)
? "Next year you will be " + LTRIM(STR(m_age + 1))
?
ACCEPT "Press Enter to continue " TO dummy
^Z
```

Figure 9.4: A sample program to test ACCEPT

4. To run the program, enter **DO TEST2** in the Command window (or edit the command line that FoxPro generated when you ran TEST1).

The output of the program is shown in Figure 9.5.

```
What is your name? CHARLES
How old are you? 39

Sorry, Charles
Next year you will be 40

Press Enter to continue
```

Figure 9.5: The output of the sample ACCEPT program

There is one other input command that you will often find useful. Both **INPUT** and **ACCEPT** require the user to type something and then press Enter before the program continues. Often, there are times when you want to let the user press just one key, without having to press Enter afterwards. To do this, use the command

WAIT [<*char exp*>] [TO <*memvar*>]

Notice that the clause TO <*memvar*> is optional in this command: often it is just used to stop the program until the user is ready to continue, and you do not have to create a dummy variable to do this with **WAIT**, as you did with **INPUT** and **ACCEPT**.

In addition, if you do not include any character expression as the prompt, **WAIT** will display the default prompt,

Press any key to continue...

For example, if your program has reached a point where it is ready to print something, you can use the code

```
? "Make sure your printer is ready and"
WAIT
```

This will display the message

```
Make sure your printer is ready and
Press any key to continue...
```

Just the word **WAIT**, then, could substitute for the entire last line in both of the previous programs. It would not only display the correct prompt automatically but would also have the advantage of letting the user press any key rather than having to press Enter.

The **WAIT** command is also useful to get a yes or no from the user. For example, programs often include code like:

```
WAIT "Do you want to print the report (y/n) " TO yesorno
```

> In cases such as this one, where the memory variable is created, used immediately, and discarded, programmers often do without the initial m in the name of the variable, as it is not really required when the function of the variable is so obvious.

This displays the prompt and creates a memory variable named yesorno to hold the user's response; the program can decide whether or not to set the printer on depending on the contents of that variable. The advantage of using **WAIT** in this sort of situation is that it lets the user make the choice with just one keystroke, without pressing Enter; though this feature might not seem too important when you read about it, it can change the feel of a program entirely.

FORMATTED INPUT/OUTPUT

The FoxPro/dBASE language also provides a command for formatted input/output which is very versatile. In its place, it can perform the functions of virtually all of the unformatted input/output commands, and more.

> Though it is most common to use numbers, you can also use numeric expressions

The basic form of this command is:

```
@ <row>,<column> [SAY <exp>] [GET <variable>]
READ
```

with this command. For example, you can use variables as the row and column numbers so the location of the cursor changes in the course of the program. You will look at a program that does this later in this chapter.

The first clause, @ <*row*>,<*column*>, places the cursor; that is, it determines where on the screen the input/output will appear. The screen has 25 rows, numbered from 0 to 24, and 80 columns, numbered from 0 to 79. If you want a message on the next-to-the-last line of the screen indented 20 spaces from the left, for example, you can use a command beginning @ 23, 20.

The second clause, **SAY** <*exp*>, determines what the prompt will be.

The third clause, **GET** <*variable*>, creates a field for the user's input. Depending on your system, this field is displayed in reverse video or some other enhanced display.

The important thing to remember about this command is that the variable used after **GET** must be defined in advance: unlike the unformatted input commands, this command does not create a variable. Though this makes you go through an extra step as a programmer, it also gives you more control. The data type of the variable that you create determines the data type of the variable that is entered.

In addition, the value you give the variable appears as a default value. It is common to define the variable as a series of blank spaces, so that the user has a blank data-entry field of the proper length. Programmers often use the function SPACE(<*num exp*>) to do so: this function returns a number of blank spaces equal to the expression. Though you can simply use a series of blank spaces in quotation marks to define the variable, it is often easier to use this function.

You can also give the variable a useful default value: for example, if California is the input you expect most often, you can give the variable the value "CA". The user can then confirm that default by pressing Enter or they can change it by typing over it.

Finally, after you use the @...**SAY**...**GET** command, you must use a separate command, **READ**, to make the program pause to get the user's input. The advantage of this is that you can write a long series of @...**SAY**...**GET** commands and then use **READ** just once at the end to get the user's input for all of them. Thus, rather than just getting input one line at a time, as you did with unformatted input/output commands, you can present the user with an entire data-entry screen before getting any input.

Notice that the SAY and GET clauses in this command are both in brackets, indicating that they are optional. It is most common to use both clauses in a command. The variable that you GET will appear just to the right of the prompt that you SAY. It is also common, though, to leave one of them out and use the command just to print a prompt or just to get input without a prompt.

In general, the user must press Enter after each input. If the input fills up the entire width of the field, though, FoxPro will beep (assuming that you have not set Bell off) and go on to the next field, just as it does in ordinary data entry.

Try an example to get a feel for the basics of this command. Enter the program listed in Figure 9.6 in a file named TEST3.PRG, then compile and run it. Its output is shown in Figure 9.7. Notice the three steps in this program: define the variables, use the command **@...SAY...GET**, use the command **READ**. Notice in particular how much control the **READ** statements give you. You can determine exactly how much is displayed on the screen when the user inputs data. When you run this sample program, for example, the final line does not appear on the screen until after the user has entered the data in the earlier lines, and gotten up to the first **READ**. Until then, users can move back and forth among the first two data-entry fields, using the up and down arrows, Tab and Shift-Tab, or the mouse if they have one. All of the GET commands that have not yet been read are called *pending GETs*, and they are all activated when you reach a **READ** command.

Rather than using **READ**, you can use the command **CLEAR GETS** to deal with pending GETs. For example, if you want to display the fields of a record in reverse video but not let the user edit them, you can use **@...SAY...GET** commands to display them all

```
************************************
*TEST3.PRG
*sample program to illustrate formatted input/output
************************************

mcity = SPACE(15)
mstate = "CA"
mkey = " "

CLEAR
@ 12,0 SAY "Enter the city: " GET mcity
@ 14,0 SAY "Enter the state: " GET mstate
READ
@ 20,0 SAY "Press any key to continue... " GET mkey
READ
```

Figure 9.6: A program to illustrate formatted input/output

```
                    Enter the city: BERKELEY
                    Enter the state: CA



                    Press any key to continue... ▊
```

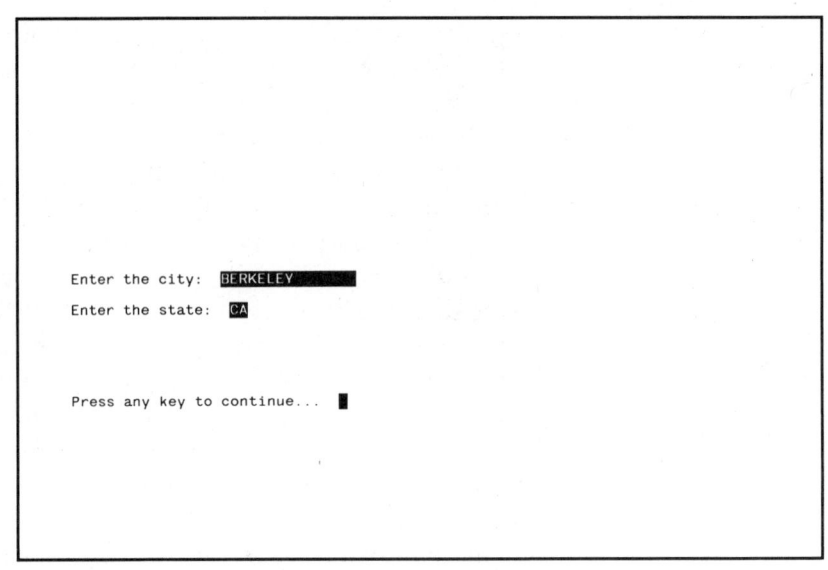

Figure 9.7: The output of the formatted input/output program

and then use the command **CLEAR GETS** to make them inaccessible to the user. All the GETs executed before the **CLEAR GETS** are no longer pending. Thus, you can use another **@...SAY...GET** command to get input from the user without the user being able to move back to the fields of the record and edit them.

No doubt you have noticed that the screen this program creates looks like part of a data-entry screen for a typical database. In fact, the most important use of the **@...SAY...GET** command is to design data-entry screens. Rather than defining memory variables, you can use the field names as the variables after GET, and the user will be able to edit the fields of the current record of an open database file.

There are many optional clauses that you can use with **@...SAY ...GET** commands: to control the input that they will accept, to display help messages telling the user what to enter, to display error messages if the user enters invalid output, and so on. Variations on the **@...SAY** command are used to draw boxes and variations on the **@...GET** command are used to create interface features such as pushbuttons. All these features are designed to make the **@...SAY- ...GET** command an extremely powerful tool for creating data input/output screens.

▪ In many cases, programmers prefer not to give users this sort of direct access to the database file. Instead, they create memory variables with the same values as the fields of the current record and let the user edit these memory variables. Then, they use the **REPLACE** command to put the new values of these memory variables in the database file.

The FoxPro screen generator creates programs made up largely of this command in its various forms, so the options for this command and other commands related to it will be covered in detail in Chapter 10. What you have learned so far is enough to let you use this command as you experiment with sample programs in the rest of this chapter.

CONTROL FLOW

The simplest program is just a list of commands, executed from beginning to end. The thing that really makes computer programs powerful, though, is the ability to direct the flow of program control. As you learned earlier in this chapter, the three types of control flow used in structured programs are sequence, selection, and iteration (or looping).

Sequence simply means that one command is executed after another. This is the only form of control flow used in the sample programs that you have tried so far. Now that you have learned about input/output, you are ready to work with more sophisticated forms of control flow.

LOOPING

The most important command used for iteration in FoxPro/dBASE compatible languages is the **DO WHILE** loop, which has the following form:

```
DO WHILE <logical exp>
   ...
ENDDO
```

The ellipsis between the first and last line stands for any number of lines of programming code.

Each time the program reaches this **DO WHILE** command, it checks to see if the logical expression evaluates as true. If it is, the program executes the commands that follow. When it gets to **ENDDO**, it loops back up to the **DO WHILE** and checks again to see if the logical expression evaluates as true; if it is, it executes the same commands.

It will continue repeating this loop until the program discovers that the logical expression does not evaluate as true, at which point it will skip all these commands and instead execute the command that follows **ENDDO**.

Of course, the lines of code within the loop must do something that ultimately makes the condition untrue, otherwise the program will continue executing this series of commands forever. This is a common error in programming, called an *infinite loop*. If your program seems to die—to stop doing anything at all—what has probably happened is that it has come to some infinite loop that does not display anything on the screen: it is actually performing some group of instructions over and over again and never getting up to a command that makes it do something that you would notice. Alternatively, a program may display the same thing over and over again as the result of an infinite loop. If either of these things happens, press Esc to interrupt the program and look through the code to see where and why a loop is executing indefinitely.

> On the rare occasions where Esc does not work, remember that you can always get out of an infinite loop by turning off the computer.

> FoxPro runs so quickly that you might not be able to see every location of the > symbol in TEST4.PRG and TEST6.PRG: it seems to jump across the screen. You can see it in every column in TEST5.PRG, where you add a delaying loop to slow its movement.

Consider a simple example of looping, which makes your screen look a bit like a primitive video game. Enter the listing in Figure 9.8 in a file named TEST4.PRG and run it: a bit of the output is shown in Figure 9.9.

```
***********************************
*TEST4.PRG
*a sample program to demonstrate looping
***********************************
col_cntr = 0
DO WHILE col_cntr < 80
    CLEAR
    @ 10,col_cntr SAY ">"
    col_cntr = col_cntr + 1
ENDDO
WAIT
```

Figure 9.8: A sample program to demonstrate looping

Notice the way this program is indented. Whenever you have a **DO WHILE** loop, you should indent the code that is within the loop. This does not affect the way that FoxPro runs the program, but it does make it much easier for you to understand.

```
                                                                      >
          Press any key to continue ...
```

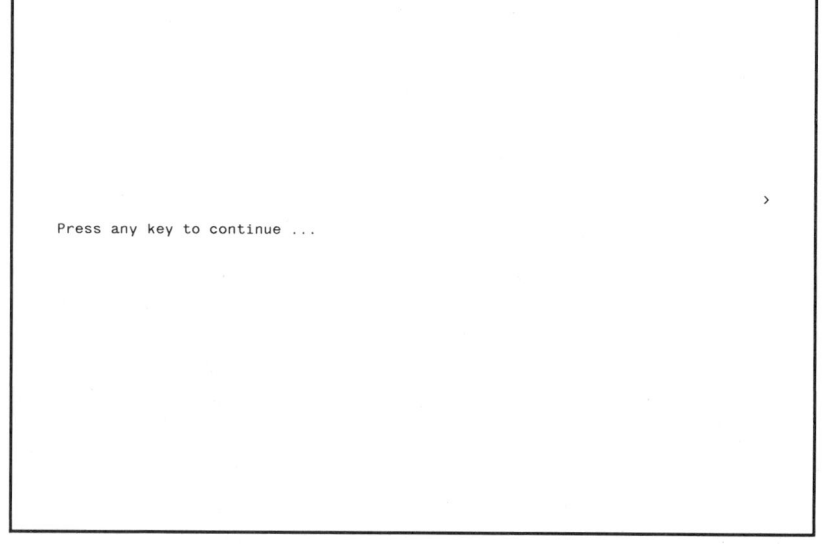

Figure 9.9: Output of the sample looping program, showing the > character after it has moved to column 79

How exactly does this program work?

First, you create a variable named col_cntr, a counter which will hold all the column numbers that you use in the program. You must define this variable before the program comes to the **DO WHILE** command: because you gave it a value of zero, the logical expression that follows **DO WHILE** is true, and so the code within the **DO WHILE** loop is executed. This code clears the screen and then uses the **@...SAY** command to display the character > at row 10, column 0 (since the value of *10,col_cntr* is 10,0 this time through the loop).

Then the program increments the value of col_cntr by one. The line of code that does this, **col_cntr = col_cntr + 1**, looks strange to many beginning programmers. People are used to the meaning of the = sign in arithmetic, where it signifies equality: in arithmetic, of course, the equation **col_cntr = col_cntr + 1** would be absurd, since a number cannot equal one more than itself. In FoxPro, though, as in most computer languages, the = sign represents *assignment*. This line of code should be read as "make col_cntr equal to col_cntr plus one," or as "let col_cntr equal col_cntr plus one." Since the value of col_cntr was 0 when the program got to this line, it makes its value equal to 1.

When the program gets to **ENDDO**, it sends it back up to the top of the loop, where it checks the condition following **DO WHILE** once again. Since col_cntr is now equal to 1, the condition is still true, so the program again executes the code in the loop. It clears the screen and then prints the > sign at row 10, column 1, so that it looks as if the sign has moved one column to the right. Then it makes the value of col_cntr equal to 2, adding 1 to its current value of 1.

Thus, it continues going through the loop and printing the > sign at column 2, column 3, and so on. When col_cntr is equal to 79, though, it prints the > sign at row 10, column 79. Then it adds 1 to col_cntr and makes its value 80. At this point, when it checks the condition of the **DO WHILE** loop, it finds that it is no longer true that col_cntr < 80 and so it does not execute the code in the loop again. Instead, it continues with the next line of code after **ENDDO**.

This program illustrates the basic principle of a **DO WHILE** loop: some code within the loop ultimately makes the condition following **DO WHILE** untrue.

NESTED DO WHILE LOOPS: A SIMPLE EXAMPLE

It is not uncommon to use one **DO WHILE** loop within another. This is known as *nesting*.

Consider a simple example, where you just use the inner loop as a delay mechanism. Let's say you decide that the > sign moved across the screen too quickly in the previous program, so you slow it down by adding a loop that simply wastes time by counting to 100 (since it actually takes the program time to do the counting). If you have a very fast computer, you might want to use a number larger than 100.

You can edit the previous example to add this loop, as shown in Figure 9.10, and save it in the file TEST5.PRG. Then compile and run it by entering **DO TEST5**.

Each time it goes through the main loop, the program makes tim_cntr equal to zero; then it must add 1 to it 100 times before it can continue. Notice how much more slowly it runs than it did before you added this extra loop.

```
*************************************
*TEST5.PRG
*a sample program to demonstrate a delaying loop
*************************************
col_cntr = 0
DO WHILE col_cntr < 80
    CLEAR
    @ 10,col_cntr SAY ">"
    col_cntr = col_cntr + 1
    tim_cntr = 0
    DO WHILE tim_cntr < 100
        tim_cntr = tim_cntr + 1
    ENDDO
ENDDO
WAIT
```

Figure 9.10: Adding a delaying loop within the main loop

MORE ADVANCED NESTED LOOPS

Nested loops are more complex if both change the value of meaningful variables. For example, let's say that you want the > sign not just to go across the columns of row ten, but to go across the columns of all the rows, one after another. You can add a loop to count rows outside of the loop that counts columns. Edit TEST4.PRG to add this extra outer loop, as shown in Figure 9.11, and then save it under the name of TEST6.PRG and run it by entering **DO TEST6**.

The indented lines inside the main loop (the six lines beginning with **col_cntr = 0**) are essentially the same as the earlier program, TEST4.PRG. These lines display the > sign on each column across the screen. The difference is that they do not just go across row 10, as the earlier program did: instead, they are nested in a larger loop

```
*************************************
*TEST6.PRG
*a sample program to demonstrate nested loops
*************************************
row_cntr = 0
DO WHILE row_cntr < 25
    col_cntr = 0
    DO WHILE col_cntr < 80
        CLEAR
        @ row_cntr,col_cntr SAY ">"
        col_cntr = col_cntr + 1
    ENDDO
    row_cntr = row_cntr + 1
ENDDO
```

Figure 9.11: A more complex example of nested loops

that executes them on all the rows, one row after another. To begin with, the row_cntr is 0. The program displays > at 0,0, at 0,1, at 0,2, and so on until it has gone through all the columns and displayed it at 0,79. Then, it finds that the condition col_cntr < 80 is no longer true, so it stops executing the inner **DO WHILE** loop and goes to the next line of code following the inner **ENDDO**, which adds 1 to row_cntr. Then it reaches the final, outer **ENDDO**, which sends it back up to the first **DO WHILE** to see if the condition is true. Because row_cntr is still less than 25, it executes this outer loop again. First, it makes col_cntr equal 0. Then it executes the inner loop, displaying > at 1,0, at 1,1, at 1,2, and so on until it has gotten up to 1,79. Then it makes row_cntr equal to 2, so that the next time through, the inner loop displays > in all the columns of the next row. It keeps doing this until it has displayed > across all the columns of all 25 rows. Then, finally, when row_cntr equals 25, the condition of the outer loop is no longer true.

This program shows how important it is to indent code properly. When one loop is nested in another, it is very difficult to follow unless it is indented in a way that makes the logic clear.

LOOPING THROUGH A DATABASE FILE

Finally, try one example that uses a **DO WHILE** loop with a database file. It is common in programs to go through an entire file by using the function EOF( ) in the condition of a **DO WHILE** loop. You should remember from Chapter 5 that FoxPro makes this function true after you move the pointer beyond the last record. Thus, you can use it to display all the records in a file by using the code shown in Figure 9.12. Try creating and running this program; the screen output is shown in Figure 9.13.

This little program is essentially equivalent to the command **LIST PROPER(TRIM(fname) + " " + lname)**. It simply reads through the entire file and prints the first and last name from each record. When it gets past the last record, the condition of the **DO WHILE** loop is no longer true, so the program stops. You can begin to appreciate how good it is to be using a fourth-generation language, because it has commands such as **LIST**, which relieves you of the task of having to write programs like this.

> Most programmers prefer to use the command **SCAN WHILE** rather than **DO WHILE** to loop through a file in this way, since it runs slightly faster. For more details, see **SCAN WHILE** in the Help window.

```
************************************
*TEST7.PRG
*a sample program that loops through the records of a file
************************************

USE emplist
CLEAR
?
?
DO WHILE .NOT. EOF()
        ? PROPER(TRIM(fname)+" "+lname)
        SKIP
ENDDO
?
USE
WAIT
```

Figure 9.12: A program to loop through a database file

```
Audrey Levy
Jack Love
Edna Chang
Charlotte Sagorin
William Johnson
William B. Johnson
Nancy Nixon
James Skinner
Michelle Perlow
Joseph Cruz
Henrietta Johnson

Press any key to continue ...
```

Figure 9.13: The output of the program TEST7.PRG

SELECTION

Selection is the third method of control flow used in structured programming.

FoxPro includes two basic methods of selection. When there are just one or two choices, it is most convenient to use the **IF...ELSE ...ENDIF** command. When you have a larger number of choices, it is most convenient to use the **DO CASE...ENDCASE** command.

IF...ELSE...ENDIF

The **IF...ELSE...ENDIF** command is fairly straightforward and easy to understand. It takes the form

    IF <*logical exp*>
    ...
    ELSE
    ...
    ENDIF

The ellipses represent any number of lines of code. If the logical expression is true, the code following the IF clause is executed. If the expression is not true, the code following the ELSE clause is executed.

This command can also be used without any else clause, in the form

    IF <*logical exp*>
    ...
    ENDIF

The code is executed if the expression is true.

For example, let's revise the previous program to give the user the choice of whether or not to get the listing. Edit TEST7.PRG, the program you just wrote, and nest the loop that prints the names within an IF statement, as shown in Figure 9.14; save it under the name of TEST8.PRG and run it. The output (if you enter **y** to get the listing) is shown in Figure 9.15.

```
************************************
*TEST8.PRG
*a sample of a DO loop nested in an IF statement
************************************

USE emplist
CLEAR
?
WAIT "Do you want a listing (y/n)? " TO yesno
IF UPPER(yesno) = "Y"
        ?
        DO WHILE .NOT. EOF()
                ? PROPER(TRIM(fname)+" "+lname)
                SKIP
        ENDDO
ENDIF
?
USE
WAIT
```

Figure 9.14: A DO loop nested in an IF statement

```
Do you want a listing (y/n)? Y

Audrey Levy
Jack Love
Edna Chang
Charlotte Sagorin
William Johnson
William B. Johnson
Nancy Nixon
James Skinner
Michelle Perlow
Joseph Cruz
Henrietta Johnson

Press any key to continue ...
```

Figure 9.15: The output of TEST8.PRG

If the user does not press **y**, the program will not execute the **DO WHILE** loop at all and would go to the **WAIT** command.

As an example of a program with both an IF and an ELSE clause, try giving the user the choice of whether or not to capitalize the names. Edit TEST8.PRG, the program you just wrote, so that it matches the program in Figure 9.16. Save it under the name of TEST9.PRG and run it: its two possible outputs are shown in Figure 9.17.

```
***********************************
*TEST9.PRG
*a sample of a DO loop combined with IF/ELSE
***********************************
USE emplist
CLEAR
?
WAIT "Do you want the names capitalized (y/n) " TO yesno
?
DO WHILE .NOT. EOF()
        IF UPPER(yesno) = "Y"
                ? UPPER(TRIM(fname)+" "+lname)
        ELSE
                ? PROPER(TRIM(fname)+" "+lname)
        ENDIF
        SKIP
ENDDO
?
USE
WAIT
```

Figure 9.16: Combining a DO loop and an IF/ELSE statement

```
Do you want the names capitalized (y/n) y
AUDREY LEVY
JACK LOVE
EDNA CHANG
CHARLOTTE SAGORIN
WILLIAM JOHNSON
WILLIAM B. JOHNSON
NANCY NIXON
JAMES SKINNER
MICHELLE PERLOW
JOSEPH CRUZ
HENRIETTA JOHNSON

Press any key to continue ...
```

```
Do you want the names capitalized (y/n) n
Audrey Levy
Jack Love
Edna Chang
Charlotte Sagorin
William Johnson
William B. Johnson
Nancy Nixon
James Skinner
Michelle Perlow
Joseph Cruz
Henrietta Johnson

Press any key to continue ...
```

Figure 9.17: Two possible outputs of TEST9.PRG

Notice that this program could also be written with two separate **DO WHILE** loops—one to print all the names capitalized and the other to print them with normal capitalization, as shown in Figure 9.18. The only difference is that the code is more compact in the original form.

```
Do you want a listing (y/n)? Y

Audrey Levy
Jack Love
Edna Chang
Charlotte Sagorin
William Johnson
William B. Johnson
Nancy Nixon
James Skinner
Michelle Perlow
Joseph Cruz
Henrietta Johnson

Press any key to continue ...
```

Figure 9.15: The output of TEST8.PRG

If the user does not press **y**, the program will not execute the **DO WHILE** loop at all and would go to the **WAIT** command.

As an example of a program with both an IF and an ELSE clause, try giving the user the choice of whether or not to capitalize the names. Edit TEST8.PRG, the program you just wrote, so that it matches the program in Figure 9.16. Save it under the name of TEST9.PRG and run it: its two possible outputs are shown in Figure 9.17.

```
************************************
*TEST9.PRG
*a sample of a DO loop combined with IF/ELSE
************************************
USE emplist
CLEAR
?
WAIT "Do you want the names capitalized (y/n) " TO yesno
?
DO WHILE .NOT. EOF()
        IF UPPER(yesno) = "Y"
                ? UPPER(TRIM(fname)+" "+lname)
        ELSE
                ? PROPER(TRIM(fname)+" "+lname)
        ENDIF
        SKIP
ENDDO
?
USE
WAIT
```

Figure 9.16: Combining a DO loop and an IF/ELSE statement

```
Do you want the names capitalized (y/n) y

AUDREY LEVY
JACK LOVE
EDNA CHANG
CHARLOTTE SAGORIN
WILLIAM JOHNSON
WILLIAM B. JOHNSON
NANCY NIXON
JAMES SKINNER
MICHELLE PERLOW
JOSEPH CRUZ
HENRIETTA JOHNSON

Press any key to continue ...
```

```
Do you want the names capitalized (y/n) n

Audrey Levy
Jack Love
Edna Chang
Charlotte Sagorin
William Johnson
William B. Johnson
Nancy Nixon
James Skinner
Michelle Perlow
Joseph Cruz
Henrietta Johnson

Press any key to continue ...
```

Figure 9.17: Two possible outputs of TEST9.PRG

Notice that this program could also be written with two separate **DO WHILE** loops—one to print all the names capitalized and the other to print them with normal capitalization, as shown in Figure 9.18. The only difference is that the code is more compact in the original form.

```
*************************************
*TEST10.PRG
*a less elegant method of combining a DO loop with IF/ELSE
*************************************
USE emplist
CLEAR
?
WAIT "Do you want the names capitalized (y/n) " TO yesno
?
IF UPPER(yesno) = "Y"
        DO WHILE .NOT. EOF()
                ? UPPER(TRIM(fname)+" "+lname)
                SKIP
        ENDDO
ELSE
        DO WHILE .NOT. EOF()
                ? PROPER(TRIM(fname)+" "+lname)
                SKIP
        ENDDO
ENDIF
?
USE
WAIT
```

Figure 9.18: A less compact way of combining a DO loop and an IF/ELSE statement

DO CASE...ENDCASE

The **DO CASE...ENDCASE** command is useful when there are a larger number of choices.

It is possible to use the **IF...ELSE...ENDIF** command to select among multiple choices, by nesting one **IF...ELSE...ENDIF** within another. Consider the program shown in Figure 9.19, which simply tells the user what number was entered. Figure 9.20 shows two possible outputs of this program.

Look carefully at how this program works. All of the other **IF...ELSE** commands are nested within the first ELSE. Thus, if the user enters 1, the program executes the command under the first IF, then it skips all the lines between the first ELSE and the last ENDIF. If the user does not enter 1, though, the program executes the line under the first ELSE, and it checks to see if the user entered 2. If the user entered 2, it skips all the lines nested in the second ELSE, but if the user did not enter 2, it executes the line under the second ELSE and checks whether the user entered 3. Likewise, if the user did not enter 3, it checks to see if the user entered 4. Finally, if the user did not enter 4, it prints an error message.

This program is an example of what is called an IF ELSE ladder, and you do see it in programs on occasion. Needless to say, though, it

```
*************************************
*TEST11.PRG
*a sample IF/ELSE ladder
*************************************
CLEAR
?
?
WAIT "Type a number between 1 and 4 >  " TO usr_nmbr
?
IF usr_nmbr = "1"
     ? "You typed one."
ELSE
     IF usr_nmbr = "2"
          ? "You typed two."
     ELSE
          IF usr_nmbr = "3"
               ? "You typed three."
          ELSE
               IF usr_nmbr = "4"
                    ? "You typed four."
               ELSE
                    ? "Error: entry not between 1 and 4."
               ENDIF
          ENDIF
     ENDIF
ENDIF
?
WAIT
```

Figure 9.19: An IF/ELSE ladder

is difficult for the programmer to read. Thus, FoxPro gives you another command, **DO CASE**, which does the same thing. The program in Figure 9.21 works just like the previous one and produces identical output.

DO CASE works just like an IF-ELSE ladder. The program looks through the CASE statements to find if one is correct. If it is, the program executes the code following that CASE statement and, after it is done with that block of code, goes on to the code following END-CASE. OTHERWISE works like the final ELSE of the IF-ELSE ladder: the statements following it are executed if the conditions in all of the CASE statements are untrue. **DO CASE** may also be used without OTHERWISE: if none of the conditions are true, no code is executed.

EXIT AND LOOP

If you use one of these methods of selection within a **DO WHILE** loop, you can create an infinite loop deliberately and use the command **EXIT** to break out of it.

```
************************************
*TEST10.PRG
*a less elegant method of combining a DO loop with IF/ELSE
************************************
USE emplist
CLEAR
?
WAIT "Do you want the names capitalized (y/n) " TO yesno
?
IF UPPER(yesno) = "Y"
        DO WHILE .NOT. EOF()
                ? UPPER(TRIM(fname)+" "+lname)
                SKIP
        ENDDO
ELSE
        DO WHILE .NOT. EOF()
                ? PROPER(TRIM(fname)+" "+lname)
                SKIP
        ENDDO
ENDIF
?
USE
WAIT
```

Figure 9.18: A less compact way of combining a DO loop and an IF/ELSE statement

DO CASE...ENDCASE

The **DO CASE...ENDCASE** command is useful when there are a larger number of choices.

It is possible to use the **IF...ELSE...ENDIF** command to select among multiple choices, by nesting one **IF...ELSE...ENDIF** within another. Consider the program shown in Figure 9.19, which simply tells the user what number was entered. Figure 9.20 shows two possible outputs of this program.

Look carefully at how this program works. All of the other **IF...ELSE** commands are nested within the first ELSE. Thus, if the user enters 1, the program executes the command under the first IF, then it skips all the lines between the first ELSE and the last ENDIF. If the user does not enter 1, though, the program executes the line under the first ELSE, and it checks to see if the user entered 2. If the user entered 2, it skips all the lines nested in the second ELSE, but if the user did not enter 2, it executes the line under the second ELSE and checks whether the user entered 3. Likewise, if the user did not enter 3, it checks to see if the user entered 4. Finally, if the user did not enter 4, it prints an error message.

This program is an example of what is called an IF ELSE ladder, and you do see it in programs on occasion. Needless to say, though, it

```
************************************
*TEST11.PRG
*a sample IF/ELSE ladder
************************************
CLEAR
?
?
WAIT "Type a number between 1 and 4 >  " TO usr_nmbr
?
IF usr_nmbr = "1"
     ? "You typed one."
ELSE
     IF usr_nmbr = "2"
          ? "You typed two."
     ELSE
          IF usr_nmbr = "3"
               ? "You typed three."
          ELSE
               IF usr_nmbr = "4"
                    ? "You typed four."
               ELSE
                    ? "Error: entry not between 1 and 4."
               ENDIF
          ENDIF
     ENDIF
ENDIF
?
WAIT
```

Figure 9.19: An IF/ELSE ladder

is difficult for the programmer to read. Thus, FoxPro gives you another command, **DO CASE**, which does the same thing. The program in Figure 9.21 works just like the previous one and produces identical output.

DO CASE works just like an IF-ELSE ladder. The program looks through the CASE statements to find if one is correct. If it is, the program executes the code following that CASE statement and, after it is done with that block of code, goes on to the code following END-CASE. OTHERWISE works like the final ELSE of the IF-ELSE ladder: the statements following it are executed if the conditions in all of the CASE statements are untrue. **DO CASE** may also be used without OTHERWISE: if none of the conditions are true, no code is executed.

EXIT AND LOOP

If you use one of these methods of selection within a **DO WHILE** loop, you can create an infinite loop deliberately and use the command **EXIT** to break out of it.

```
Type a number between 1 and 4 >  3
You typed three.
Press any key to continue ...
```

```
Type a number between 1 and 4 >  m
Error: entry not between 1 and 4.
Press any key to continue ...
```

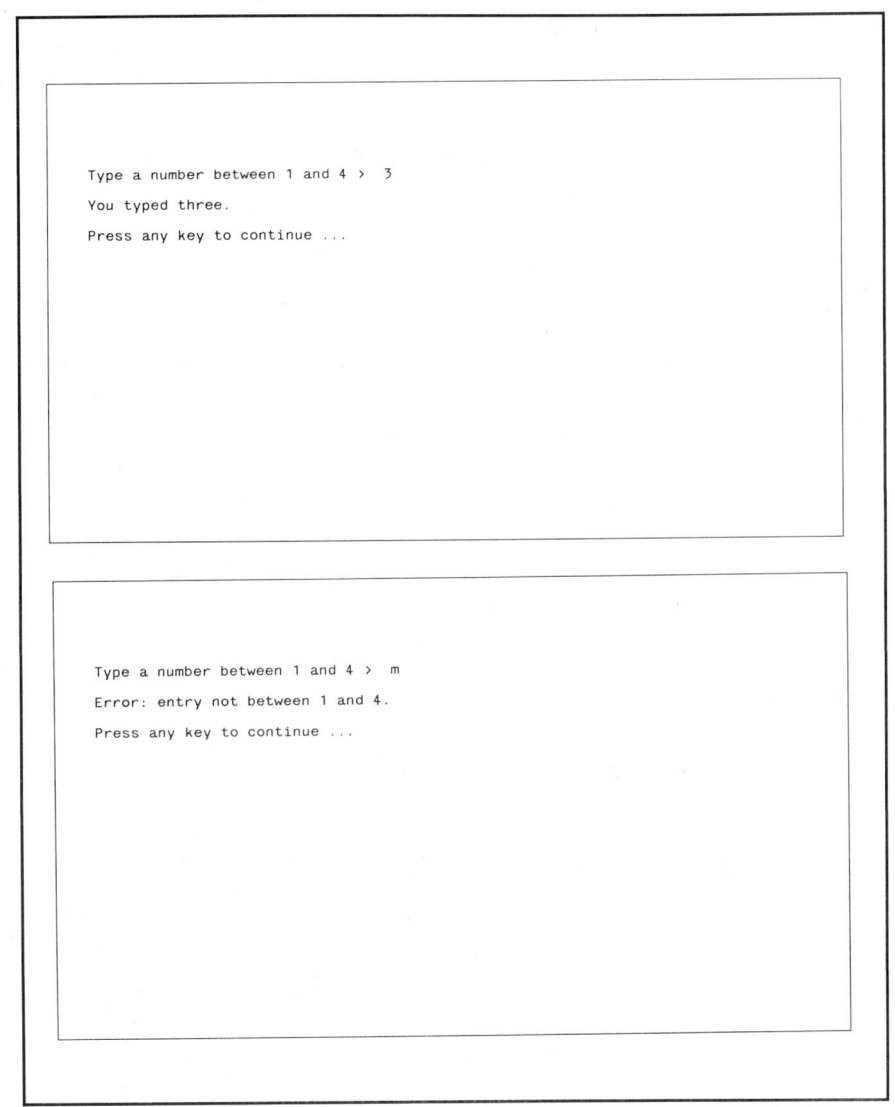

Figure 9.20: Two possible outputs of the preceding IF/ELSE ladder

EXIT and **LOOP** are two commands that programmers use when they want to make loop control explicit. **EXIT** breaks out of the loop and directs control to the statement following **ENDDO**. **LOOP** returns control to the **DO WHILE** statement. This makes it possible

```
************************************
*TEST12.PRG
*a sample of DO CASE
************************************
CLEAR
?
?
WAIT "Type a number between 1 and 4 >  " TO usr_nmbr
?
DO CASE
     CASE usr_nmbr = "1"
          ? "You typed one."
     CASE usr_nmbr = "2"
          ? "You typed two."
     CASE usr_nmbr = "3"
          ? "You typed three."
     CASE usr_nmbr = "4"
          ? "You typed four."
     OTHERWISE
          ? "Error: entry not between 1 and 4."
ENDCASE
?
WAIT
```

Figure 9.21: A DO CASE statement

to return to the beginning of the loop without executing some of the commands that are in it.

It is often clearer to put an **EXIT** command within an infinite loop rather than putting the condition after **DO WHILE**. You can create an infinite loop by using a condition that is always true, for example, **DO WHILE 1 = 1**. You can use a more elegant command, though, if you remember that FoxPro evaluates any condition of this sort and executes the loop if it evaluates as .T. To save it the trouble, you can just use the condition **DO WHILE .T.**

Try rewriting the TEST12.PRG to add an infinite loop using the **EXIT** and **LOOP** commands, as in Figure 9.22. Save this program in a file named TEST13.PRG and run it. Its output is shown in Figure 9.23.

Notice that the command **LOOP** is not actually needed in this case: the program would loop up when it reached the final **ENDDO** anyway. The condition at the end of the program could be rewritten as:

```
WAIT "Do you want to try again? (y/n)" TO yesno
IF UPPER(yesno) <> "Y"
    EXIT
ENDIF
```

```
**********************************
*TEST13.PRG
*a sample of EXIT and LOOP
**********************************
DO WHILE .T.
     CLEAR
     ?
     ?
     WAIT "Type a number between 1 and 4 >  " TO usr_nmbr
     ?
     DO CASE
           CASE usr_nmbr = "1"
                ? "You typed one."
           CASE usr_nmbr = "2"
                ? "You typed two."
           CASE usr_nmbr = "3"
                ? "You typed three."
           CASE usr_nmbr = "4"
                ? "You typed four."
           OTHERWISE
                ? "Error: entry not between 1 and 4."
     ENDCASE
     ?
     WAIT "Do you want to try again? (y/n) " TO yesno
     IF UPPER(yesno) = "Y"
           LOOP
     ELSE
           EXIT
     ENDIF
ENDDO
```

Figure 9.22: Using EXIT and LOOP to control a loop

```
Type a number between 1 and 4 >  3

You typed three.

Do you want to try again? (y/n)
```

Figure 9.23: The output of TEST13.PRG

and the program would run in exactly the same way. In this case adding **LOOP** is merely a stylistic convenience, to make the program easier to understand. In other cases, **LOOP** is used to bypass some of the commands within a **DO WHILE** loop.

PROCEDURES AND PARAMETERS

As you learned at the beginning of this chapter, an essential part of structured programming is dividing the program up into smaller procedures or modules, so that each one can be written, tested, and debugged individually.

In early versions of the dBASE language, each module had to be kept in a separate .PRG file, and it is still possible to write programs in this way.

To call a program in another file, you simply use the command **DO** <*file name*> within a program, just as you have been doing from the command line. Control of the program passes to the program that you have called. When that program is done, control returns to the following line in the calling program.

Control returns to the calling program automatically when it reaches the end of the called program. You can also use the command **RETURN** anywhere in the called program to return control to the calling program (or, if you used the program directly from the command window, to return to FoxPro).

One principle of structured programming, though, is that it is best for control to flow to the bottom of each procedure, so it is not good style to use **RETURN** in the middle of a module. Many programmers put **RETURN** at the end of each module, even though it is not needed, to make the flow of the program explicit.

RETURN TO MASTER is a variation on the command **RETURN**, which returns control to the first .PRG file executed, rather than to the file that called the current one.

THE SCOPE OF VARIABLES AND PASSING PARAMETERS

As you will see in Chapter 11, dividing a program into separate modules makes the program much easier to develop, debug, and maintain. The modules are truly separated from one another, though, only if the variables in one module can be independent of the variables used in other modules.

For example, if you create a general-purpose procedure to be reused many times, you should be able to use it without having to worry that a statement assigning a value to a variable in that procedure might change the value of a variable somewhere else in the program. When you create a variable named **m_counter** in the main program, you should not have to worry about whether the program calls another procedure that also happens to contain a variable named **m_counter**.

To develop modules of a program independently, then, you should be able to control whether or not a memory variable is accessible to all the modules of the program. This is called the *scope* of the variable.

By default, a memory variable initialized in any module remains active until program control returns to the code that called that module—either because it reaches a **RETURN** command or because it reaches the end of that module. In other words, the variable is accessible to any module called by that module directly or indirectly.

You can change the default scope of variables by using two simple commands at the beginning of any PRG file or procedure:

- **PRIVATE** <*memvar list*> limits the availability of the specified memory variables to the active PRG file or procedure and to modules called by it directly or indirectly. If a module that calls the PRG or procedure happens to have a variable with the same name, FoxPro considers it a different variable from the one that is declared private.

- **PUBLIC** <*memvar list*> makes the specified memory variables available to all programs and procedures. (Though this command can be used at the beginning of any module, it is best to use it in the highest-level module where the variables are used.)

PRIVATE, of course, is useful if you are writing a minor module that is called by many other modules, and you do not want to worry about whether the other modules use variables of the same name. PUBLIC is useful if you *want* the value assigned to the variable in one module to be available to all the other modules of the program.

> As you will see in a moment, you can also pass parameters from the Command window.

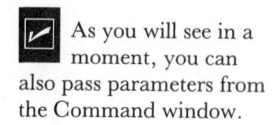

Apart from these two alternatives, though, there are also many cases where you want the values of variables to be available to only two modules. To let the calling module pass the value of a variable to the module that it calls, you use the command **PARAMETER** <*memvar list*> as the first command in the module that is called. Then, the simplest way of passing a parameter to that module when you call it is to use the command **DO...WITH** <*expr list*>. The expressions in the list following **DO...WITH** are assigned in order to the memory variables in the list following **PARAMETER**, and thus are passed to the module that is called.

The principles that are discussed in this section cannot be illustrated in small sample programs as easily as the principles discussed in earlier sections of this chapter. You can really see the use of breaking a program into procedures, controlling the scope of variables, and passing parameters only when you are working with a long program, and these principles will be illustrated at greater length in the program you develop in Chapters 11 and 12. However, it will make it easier to understand **PARAMETER** if we use some very small examples here.

Try writing a procedure to capitalize the initial letter of a string. As you know, FoxPro has the function PROPER( ) to capitalize the first letter of each word of a string—as well as the functions UPPER( ) and LOWER( ) to make all the letters of a string upper or lowercase—but it does not have a function to capitalize just the first letter of a *string*. The procedure shown in Figure 9.24 will print the string in this form. Try it out:

> If there is a typographical error in your program code that you must correct, the procedure file will automatically be closed when you edit it. You must use the command **SET PROCEDURE TO MYPROCS** again before retesting it.

1. Enter the listing in Figure 9.24 in a file with the name **MYPROCS.PRG**.

```
******************************
*PROCEDURE INITCAP
*a procedure to capitalize the first letter of a
*character string and make all the other letters lower case
******************************

PROCEDURE initcap
PARAMETER mstring

? UPPER(SUBSTR(mstring,1,1)) + LOWER(SUBSTR(mstring,2))
```

Figure 9.24: A procedure to capitalize the first letter of a string

2. After saving the file, and returning to the Command window, enter the command **SET PROCEDURE TO MYPROCS**.

3. Enter **?** to skip a line. Then enter the command **DO INITCAP WITH "KNOW THYSELF!"**

As you can see from Figure 9.25, the program prints the string you entered with only the first letter capitalized.

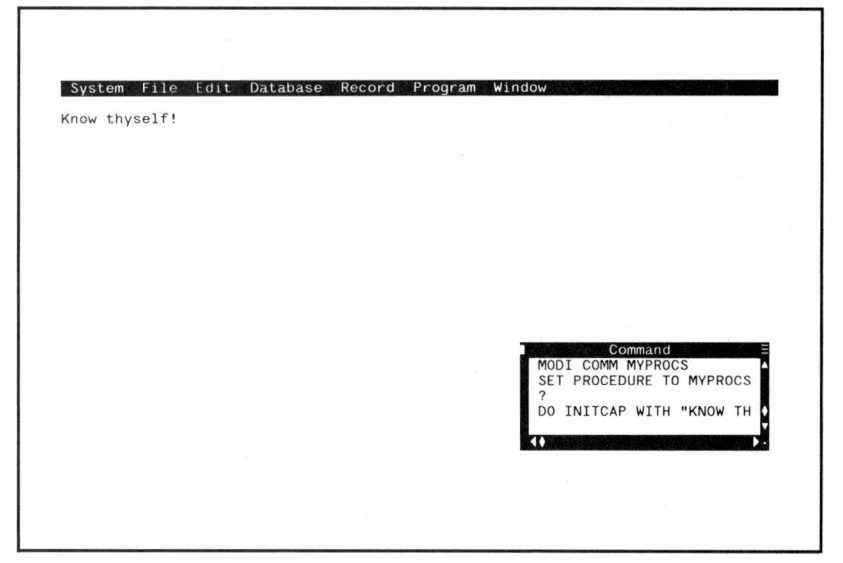

Figure 9.25: Using the capitalization procedure

It is easy to see how this program works. The expression following WITH in the **DO** command is passed to the INITCAP procedure as a parameter, so it is assigned to the variable **mstring**, used in the **PARAMETER** command of that procedure.

Things become a bit more tricky when you want to pass a parameter to the called procedure and then pass a new value back to the calling procedure. As you can see in the program in Figure 9.26, you assign the variable a value in the calling module. That variable is assigned to the parameter, and is altered in the called module. As a result, the value is changed in the calling module as well. In this way, you can pass the values of variables back and forth between two modules without worrying about whether the variables have the same name in both modules. This makes the modules much more independent of each other and makes the program more structured. Try entering and running this program in the usual way.

```
******************************
*TEST14.PRG
*a program to test passing parameters
******************************

SET TALK OFF
mproverb = "KNOW THYSELF!"
DO initcap WITH mproverb
? mproverb


******************************
*PROCEDURE INITCAP
*a procedure to capitalize the first letter of a
*character string and make all the other letters lower case
******************************

PROCEDURE initcap
PARAMETER mstring

mstring = UPPER(SUBSTR(mstring,1,1)) + LOWER(SUBSTR(mstring,2))
```

Figure 9.26: A program to test passing parameters

USER-DEFINED FUNCTIONS

You are no longer limited to the functions that are provided as part of the FoxPro language. If they are inadequate for your purposes, you can create functions of your own, which you can use just like the program's built-in functions.

FoxPro lets you use the command **FUNCTION** just as you use the command **PROCEDURE**. In fact, the way that these two commands work is identical, but as a matter of programming style it makes sense to use **FUNCTION** at the beginning of a user-defined function and **PROCEDURE** at the beginning of a procedure, in order to make the program easier to understand when you are modifying or debugging it.

The real difference between procedures and user-defined functions is the way you pass parameters and return a value. So far, you have used the word **RETURN** by itself to return control to the calling function. Remember, though, that by definition a function returns a value. If you end a user-defined function with the command **RETURN** <*expr*>, the expression is returned to the calling program as the value of that function.

User-defined functions are used just like ordinary functions. Rather than passing a value to the user-defined function by using the command **DO...WITH**, you simply put the value (or values) being passed to the function in the parentheses following it. The function itself begins with **FUNCTION...** followed by the **PARAMETER** <*parameter list*> command, and the value or values passed to it are assigned to the variables in the parameter list in order, just as they are with ordinary procedures. When the function reaches the command **RETURN** <*expr*>, the expression returned is used as the value of the function, just as it is with one of the built-in functions of FoxPro.

This sounds complicated when it is described, but it will be very easy to understand when you create a user-defined INITCAP( ) function, to do the same thing as the procedure you just wrote.

1. If you want, enter **CLEAR** in the Command window to clear the screen. Then enter **MODI COMM MYFUNCTS** to edit a new program file that holds the user-defined functions you create, and enter the code shown in Figure 9.27.

2. After you have saved the file and returned to the Command window, enter the command **SET PROCEDURE TO MYFUNCTS** to make this new file the active procedure file. Then enter ? to skip a line and enter ? **INITCAP(KNOW THYSELF!)**.

FoxPro displays **Know thyself!**.

```
*******************************
*INITCAP()
*a user defined function to capitalize the first letter of a
*character string and make all the other letters lower case
*******************************

FUNCTION initcap
PARAMETER mstring

RETURN UPPER(SUBSTR(mstring,1,1)) + LOWER(SUBSTR(mstring,2))
```

Figure 9.27: The code for the user-defined function

As you see, the new value is returned as the value of the INITCAP( ) function itself: you use this function that you created yourself in the same way that you use built-in functions such as UPPER( ) and PROPER( ). Just place the parameter that you pass to the function in the parentheses of the function, and the expression that is returned is the value of that function. User-defined functions, like any functions, can be used in programs in the same way that they are used in the Command window.

User-defined functions, though, can be much more powerful than FoxPro's built-in functions, because they can do much more than return a value. They can contain virtually any command that a program or procedure can, and they execute all these commands—as any procedure does—before they get to the **RETURN** command and return a value. The other commands they execute do not necessarily have to have anything to do with the value that is returned. As you will see in the next chapter, you can make user-defined functions do all sorts of useful things.

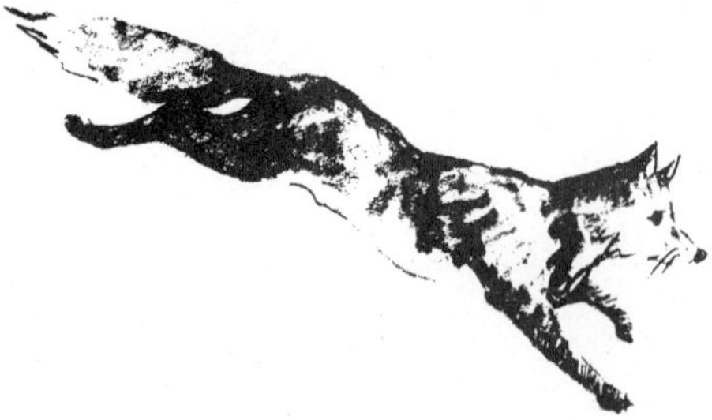

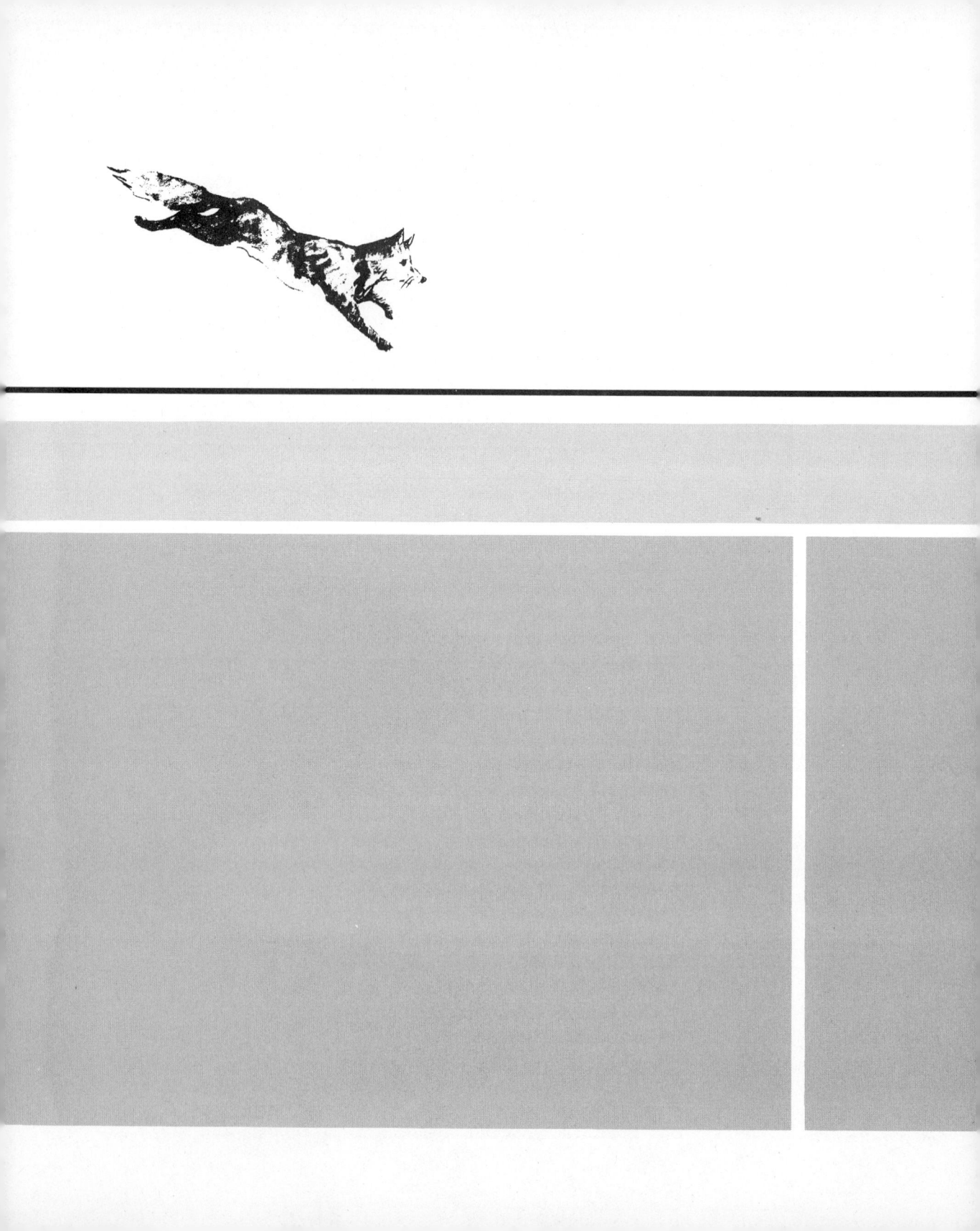

PART III

Programming with FoxPro

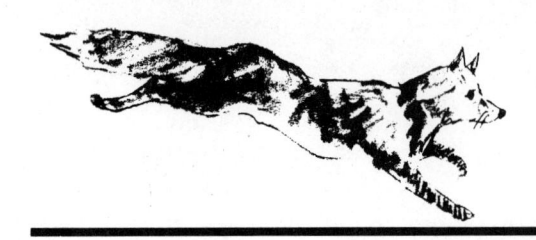

Chapter 10

Understanding the Screen Builder

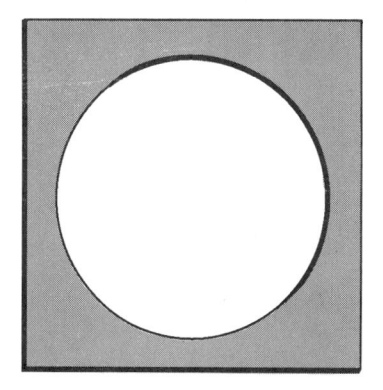

THE SCREEN BUILDER IS ONE OF THE MOST POWERFUL new programming tools added to version 2 of FoxPro. It lets you design a screen that includes fields, text, and boxes—as previous screen builders for dBASE-compatible programs have all done—but what makes it truly impressive is that it also lets you add all the other features of the FoxPro interface. With relatively little effort, you can now create screens with pushbuttons, radio buttons, check boxes, popup controls, and scrollable lists that look and work like the equivalent features of FoxPro itself.

You can even go beyond FoxPro's standard interface and simulate icons. You can add "invisible buttons," defining a certain area of the screen as a button without displaying a pushbutton symbol. Then you can design an icon of your own to display at that location. The user will activate the invisible button by clicking the icon.

Much of the code created by the screen builder is made up of @...GET commands and related commands. You looked at the simplest form of this command in Chapter 9. Now, as you learn the features of the screen builder, you will also learn the optional clauses that you can use with @...GET, READ, and related commands. It only takes a slight variation on the simple @...GET command to create interface features such as pushbuttons and radio buttons.

You can also use two other features of the FoxPro interface in your own programs: windows and popup menus. The screen builder can create windows, and FoxPro includes a separate menu generator to produce popup menus, which work like FoxPro's own menu bar.

This chapter will describe the screen builder. Chapter 11 will include exercises in using the screen builder to create screens for the sample program that you write in that chapter. You will learn about the menu generator in Chapter 12.

CREATING SCREENS AND GENERATING CODE

You create screens in the familiar way: Select New from the File menu, select the Screen radio button, and select the OK pushbutton to generate the command **CREATE SCREEN Untitled**; then name the

> Likewise, you can modify an existing screen in the usual way. Select Open from the File menu. Select Screen from the popup control, select the name of the screen you want to modify from the scrollable list and select the Open pushbutton to generate the command **MODIFY SCREEN** (<*screen name*>.)

screen by selecting Save As from the File menu. As usual, if you are working from the Command window, you can name the screen when you first create it, by entering the command **CREATE SCREEN** <*screen name*>.

When you use this command, FoxPro displays the screen builder window and adds a Screen pad to the menu bar. The screen builder window and menu are shown in Figure 10.1.

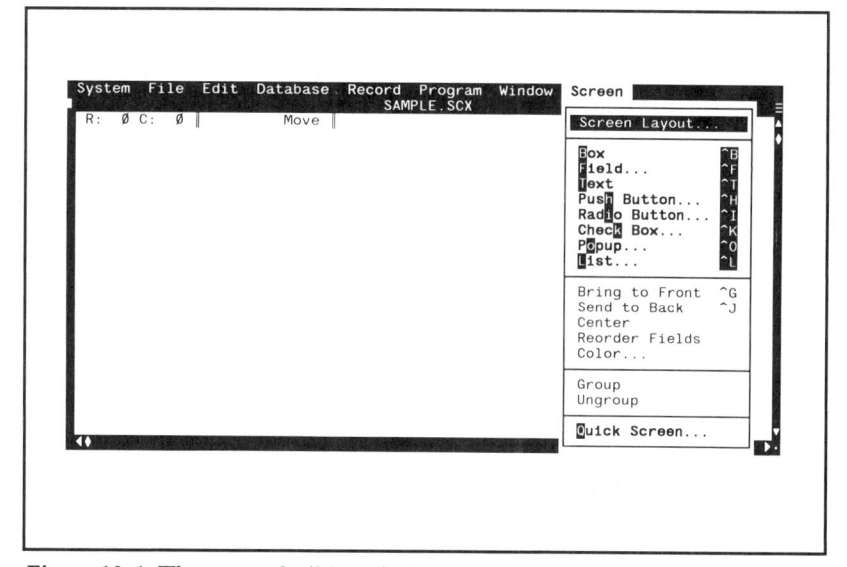

Figure 10.1: The screen builder window and menu

You will look at the features of the menu in detail in the rest of this chapter, but you should get a quick overview of it now. The first selection, Screen Layout, lets you choose general layout features that apply to the entire screen. The next group of selections lets you add objects to the screen. As you can see, you can add boxes, database fields, or text as well as interface features such as pushbuttons and radio buttons. The next two groups of selections let you manipulate objects in special ways. The final selection lets you create a Quick Screen—to lay out all the fields and field names of the database file on the screen, rather than having to place them one at a time.

When you are using the screen builder, you can select *Generate* from the Program menu to display the dialog box shown in Figure 10.2.

Notice that it lets you include more than one screen. The features of all the screens listed are compiled into a single program. This is one of the most powerful features of the screen builder: you can create screens, which you can use as parts of many different screen sets. Several screen elements of this sort are distributed with FoxPro, including CONTROL.SCX, a general-purpose control panel of radio buttons designed for the ordinary tasks of file editing. In Chapter 11, when you write a sample program, you will combine this control panel with a screen that you create to display the fields of a database file, to let the user edit a sample database file. The Generate dialog box will be discussed in more detail at the end of this chapter.

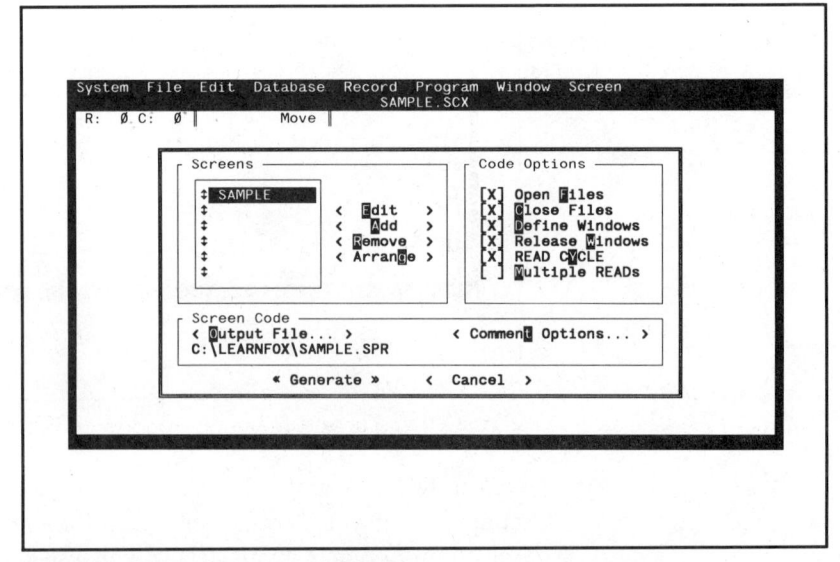

Figure 10.2: The Generate dialog box

Screen specifications are stored in an ordinary database file with the extension SCX. When you select Generate from the Program menu, FoxPro generates the programming code needed to display that screen, which is kept in a file with the extension SPR. This file is an ordinary FoxPro program, like the ones you wrote in PRG files, and you use it with the usual command **DO** <*file name*>. Because it does not have the default PRG extension, you must enter the complete file name to run it—for example, **DO SCREEN1.SPR**.

MANIPULATING OBJECTS

When you looked at the Screen menu, you might have noticed that the Quick Screen feature and some of the menu features that let you place objects are similar to features of the report generator, which you learned about in Chapter 6. In fact, some operations, such as placing a box, are exactly the same in the screen builder as in the report generator. Once you have placed an object, you can also select it and manipulate it as you do when you are using the report generator.

You can display a dialog box for any object by placing the cursor on it and pressing Enter or by double-clicking it with the mouse. Every dialog box includes a Comment check box, with which you add a comment to any object or edit a comment you added earlier. These comments are purely for your own use and do not affect the code that is generated.

Most dialog boxes also control other features of objects, and they will be covered when each object is discussed below. As you will see, you must use the dialog box when you first place most objects, though some objects (such as boxes) can be placed without using a dialog box. After an object is placed, you can access its dialog box in the ways described above if you want to change its features.

THE LAYOUT DIALOG BOX

Selecting *Screen Layout* from the Screen menu calls up the dialog box shown in Figure 10.3, which lets you control general features of the entire screen.

The radio buttons at the top of this dialog box determine whether the screen is placed on the desktop or in a window.

THE DESKTOP

If the DeskTop radio button is selected, the screen covers your entire computer screen. You can edit the Row and Column settings to control the size of the area where you can place objects, but the size of the desktop remains the same. The desktop cannot be brought forward over windows and cannot be assigned other attributes that can

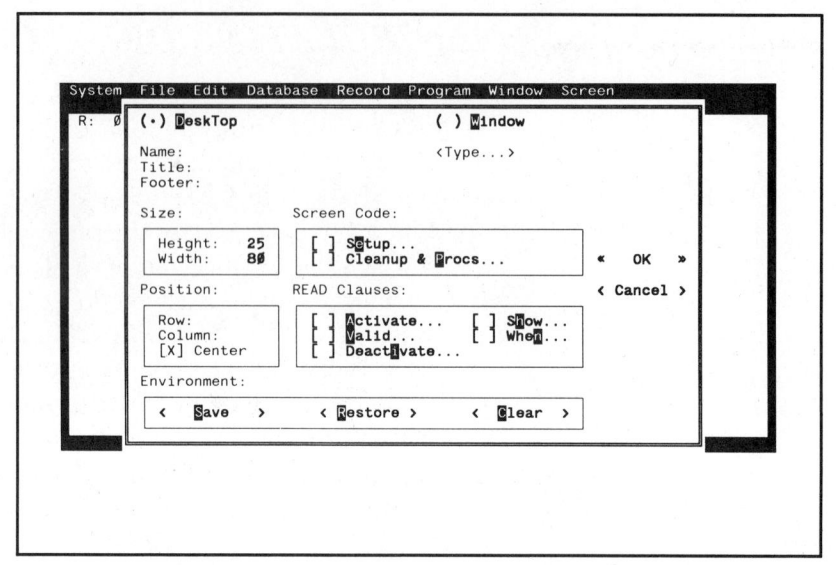

Figure 10.3: The Screen Layout dialog box

be assigned to windows: features that are specific to windows, discussed below, are dimmed if DeskTop is selected. The desktop, then, is just a sort of base that you can place windows on top of, it is not as versatile as windows, which can be used either under or above other windows.

WINDOWS

If the Window radio button is selected, you can enter a name, title, and footer, height and width, and position for the window in the locations provided in this dialog box. These features are used as follows:

- **Name:** Used to refer to this window within programs. If you do not enter a name for the window, FoxPro generates one. It makes it easier to maintain the program, though, if you enter a meaningful name, rather than letting FoxPro generate one made of random characters.

- **Title:** Appears centered in the top bar of the window. If you do not enter a title, none is used.

- **Footer:** Appears centered in the bottom bar of the window. Again, if you do not enter one, none is used.

- **Size:** Lets you enter the height and width of the window.

- **Position:** Lets you specify the row and column where the window is located. Alternatively, if you check the Center check box, the window is centered in the display.

WINDOW TYPES

> This position can be altered when you generate the code, if you select the Arrange pushbutton in the Generate dialog box, covered later in this chapter.

If you select Window, the Type pushbutton is also activated. Select it to use the dialog box shown in Figure 10.4, to add the following attributes to the window:

- **Close:** If this check box is selected, the user can close the window

- **Float:** If this check box is selected, the user can move the window

- **Shadow:** If this check box is selected, the window has a "shadow" behind it to highlight it.

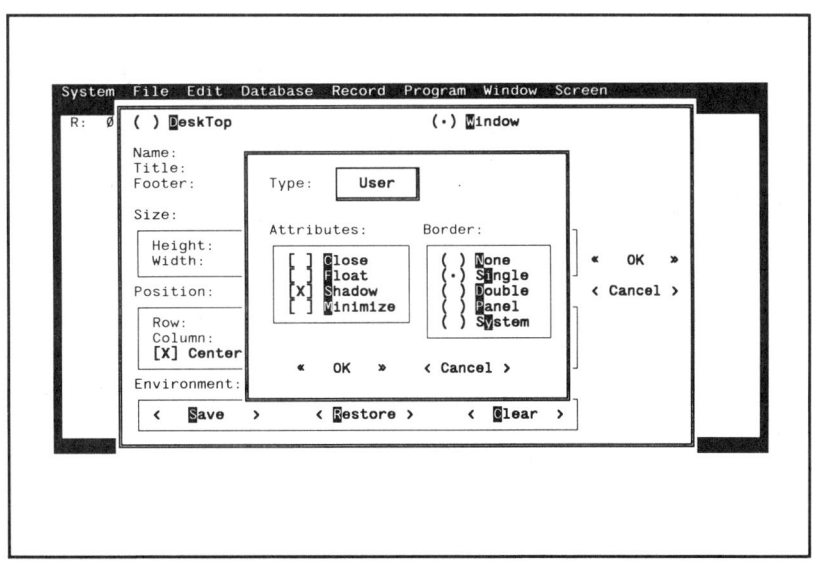

Figure 10.4: The Type dialog box

- **Minimize:** If this check box is selected, the window can be shrunk to a text "icon," as FoxPro windows are when you select Zoom ↓.

- **Border:** Select the None radio button for no border, the Single radio button for a single-line border, the Double radio button for a double-line border, the Panel radio button for a wide border like the border of FoxPro windows, or the System radio button for a wide border with controls visible.

In addition, you can use the Type popup to select among different predefined window attributes. As you can see in the illustration, the User type has a single-line border and Shadow checked by default, but you can change these attributes to design window types of your own. The other types have the following attributes:

- **System:** System border; Close, Float, Minimize, and System are checked.

- **Dialog and Alert:** Double-line border; Float and Shadow are checked.

By using these predefined types, you can develop a consistent interface for your programs without having to keep track of the different types of windows you use for different purposes.

> If you select System as the border and select the Close option, the Close box will be visible on the window border. If you select some other border and select the Close option, you may still click the upper-left corner of the window to close it though no Close box is visible.

WINDOW COMMANDS

The basic commands used for creating windows involve a two-step process. First you must DEFINE the window. Then you can control the display of the window on the screen.

The basic command for defining a window is

```
DEFINE WINDOW <window name> FROM <row>,<col>
    TO <row>, <col>
[FOOTER <char exp>]
[TITLE <char exp>]
[DOUBLE | PANEL | NONE | SYSTEM |  <border definition>]
[close | NOCLOSE]
[float | NOFLOAT]
[grow | NOGROW]
```

> For optional clauses used to determine colors and to define a window within another window, see listing under DEFINE WINDOW in the Help window.

```
[zoom | NOZOOM]
[MINIMIZE]
[SHADOW]
[FILL <char exp>]
```

The two pairs of row and column numbers define the upper left and lower right corner of the window. The other options generally correspond in obvious ways to the options in the dialog boxes you looked at earlier in this section.

After a window has been defined using this command, you can activate it for use with the command **ACTIVATE WINDOWS** <*window name list*>, or you can display it without letting it be used by means of the command **SHOW WINDOWS** <*window name list*>. You can stop displaying the window without deactivating it by using the command **HIDE WINDOWS** <*window name list*>: this does the same thing that you do to a FoxPro system window when you select Hide from the Window menu. You can deactivate it with **DEACTIVATE WINDOWS** <*window name list*>. Finally, you can remove the window definition from memory entirely by using the command **RELEASE WINDOWS** <*window name list*>.

When a window is active, @...SAY...GET commands automatically display output within that window, as opposed to a position relative to the overall screen. For example, **@ 0,0 SAY**... will display the output in the upper left corner of the current window, not in the upper left corner of the screen.

That summarizes just the basics of creating and using windows. For more details, see these commands in the Help window. The cross references under these basic commands in the Help window will refer you to related useful commands and functions.

SCREEN CODE

Because FoxPro cannot open windows in front of dialog boxes, these text-editing windows are opened behind the Layout dialog box. You can use them after selecting the OK pushbutton.

The other features of the Layout dialog box are available whether DeskTop or Window is selected.

The Screen Code box lets you add extra code to the code generated automatically by the screen builder. If you check either the Setup or the Cleanup & Procs check box, FoxPro opens a text-editing window where you can enter the code. The code entered for Setup is performed before the screen is displayed, of course.

You can also use the Cleanup & Procs editing window to enter Cleanup code that is performed after the screen has been used or to enter procedures that are used repeatedly by features of the screen. For example, you will see later that you can add VALID clauses to individual objects, but if you are using the same VALID clause for more than one object in the screen, you can include it in a procedure here rather than retype it.

READ CLAUSES

The Activate, Valid, Deactivate, Show, and When check boxes of the Layout dialog box generate optional clauses for the READ command in the final code. If you select any of these, FoxPro displays a dialog box similar to the one shown in Figure 10.5: the figure shows the Activate dialog box, but the others are identical except for the name in the upper left corner.

By selecting the proper radio button, you can use these dialog boxes to enter or edit a procedure or expression in the text-editing area of this dialog box. (As a convenience, the Edit pushbutton opens an edit window behind the dialog box, so you can have a separate window in which to edit these instead. This is very handy for longer procedures.)

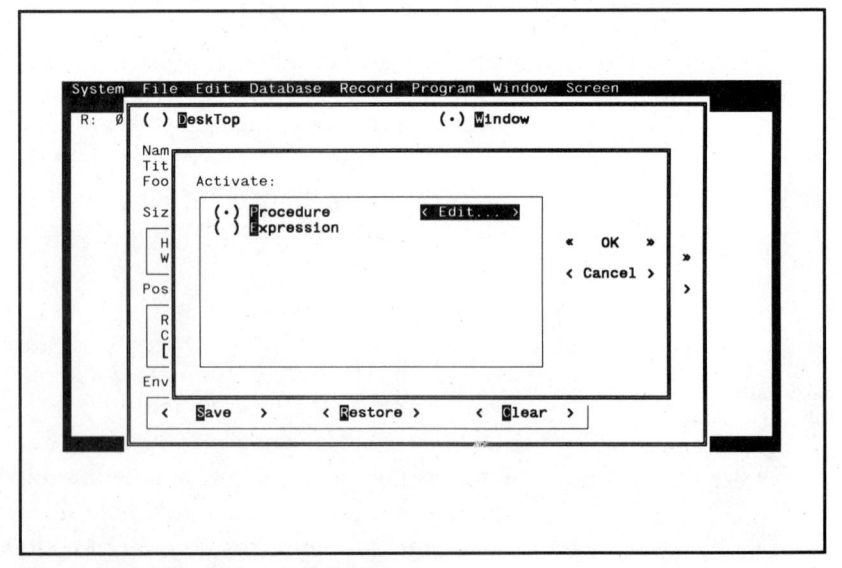

Figure 10.5: The Activate dialog box

> When you create code snippets, an additional menu option, Open All Snippets, is added to the Screen menu. Selecting it opens editing windows for all the snippets.

The code you enter here is called a *code snippet*. When the code for the entire screen is generated, these snippets will be included in options for the **READ** command. For explanations of the effect of these advanced programmiong options, see the options ACTIVATE, VALID, DEACTIVATE, SHOW, and WHEN under the **READ** command in the Help Window.

As you will see later, in addition to adding these clauses to the READ clause through the layout window, you can add similar clauses with code snippets to individual objects by using these objects' dialog boxes. These clauses are referred to as *Read level* and *Object level* clauses respectively.

ADDING CODE SNIPPETS

The optional Read level and Object level clauses of both the @...GET and READ commands usually contain logical expressions. For example, the VALID clause often contains a logical expression that determines whether the entry is valid or not. A VALID clause can also contain a numeric expression to move the cursor the number of fields specified or to leave the cursor on a current field if the number is zero.

If you select the Expression radio button of the dialog box you use to define these optional clauses, FoxPro simply uses the expression you enter in the optional clause of the @...GET or the READ command in the generated code. If you select the Procedure radio button, FoxPro generates a user-defined function containing the procedure you entered and uses this function in the optional clause.

Remember that user-defined functions can execute almost any command that procedures can execute, but they must return a value at the end. You can take advantage of this fact by selecting the VALID check box and entering procedures that do whatever you want. Then, at the end of the procedure, simply add a final line of code, such as **RETURN 0**, which lets FoxPro use the procedure as a user-defined function. In this way, you can use the VALID clause to execute whatever commands you want. You "trick" the program into executing the code under the guise of checking whether the input is valid or not.

In fact, using the VALID clause in this way is so important that, if you do not add the RETURN command at the end, FoxPro generates the command **RETURN .T.** and adds it at the end of the procedure you entered. It is most common to add the command **RETURN 0** at the end, however, so that the cursor simply remains on the current field after all the code in the procedure is executed.

You can see how powerful code snippets are. If you add procedures to VALID clauses, FoxPro executes them whenever it READs the input. It is supposedly checking whether the data entered is valid or not, but the VALID clauses can actually include any programming features that you want to add to the screens you design, and they become built-in parts of the objects. Examples of this powerful use of the screen generator are included in Chapter 11.

ENVIRONMENT

You can use the Save pushbutton at the bottom of the Layout dialog box to save the environment, i.e., the database files and indexes that are open.

If you have used this Save pushbutton, the environment is saved permanently when you later select Save from the File menu to save the screen file on disk. Use *both* this pushbutton and the Save menu selection to save the environment permanently on disk.

> If you do not save the screen in this way, a dialog box appears when you save the file, giving you the option of saving the environment.

Ordinarily, when you open a screen file, the environment check box is checked, so that the environment is restored. If it is not checked, though, you can select the Restore pushbutton to restore the environment.

Finally, the Clear pushbutton clears the environment from memory. (It does not remove environment settings that have been stored to disk.)

BOXES

Selecting *Box* from the Screen menu lets you add boxes or lines in the same way you do when you are using the Report Design window. FoxPro begins by placing a small box at the location of the cursor. Using the keyboard, you can press the down arrow and right arrow to make the box larger (by moving its bottom edge down or its right edge further right), or you can press the up arrow and left arrow to make the box smaller (by moving its bottom edge up or its right edge further left). Using the mouse, you can simply drag its lower right corner to make it larger or smaller. In either case, its upper left corner remains at the location of the cursor while you are resizing. If you want, you can select and move the box after it is the proper size, in the same way you move any object.

You can make horizontal or vertical lines by making boxes with a height or width of zero.

You do not use a dialog box to place a box, but after you have created one, you can use the Box dialog box, shown in Figure 10.6, in the same way you would use the dialog box for any object: double-click on the border of the box with the mouse, or move the cursor to the border of the box with the keyboard and press Enter.

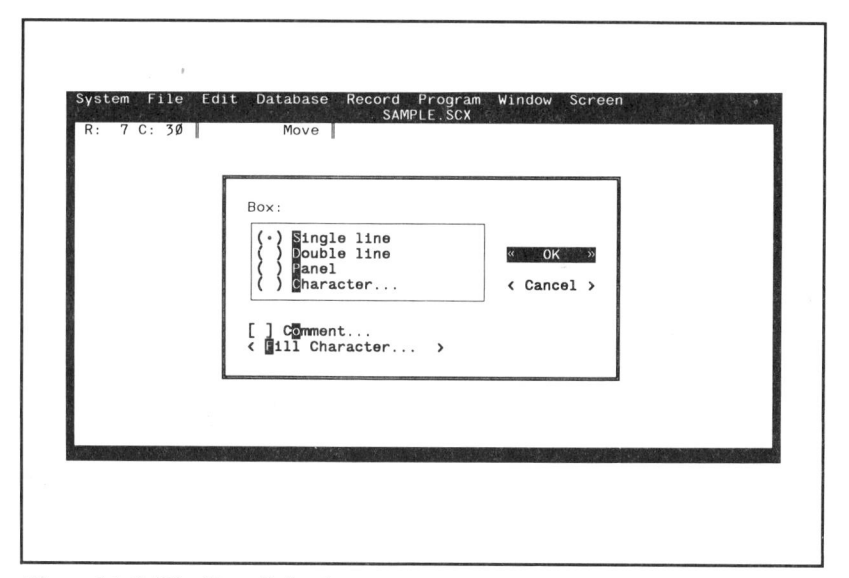

Figure 10.6: The Box dialog box

The radio buttons let you select the border of the box: single line, double line, panel (a wide line), or any character. The Fill Character pushbutton lets you fill the entire box with any character. If you select either the Character radio button or the Fill Character pushbutton, FoxPro displays a list of ASCII characters for you to choose from.

As always, the Comments check box lets you enter a comment for your own purposes.

This selection generates the command @ <*row*>,<*column*> TO <*row*>,<*column*>, which draws a box with the first row and column specified as the upper left corner and the second row and column as the lower right corner. Optional clauses of this command determine the border and fill character.

FIELDS

Selecting *Field* from the Screen menu calls up the Field dialog box, shown in Figure 10.7, which lets you place fields or memory variables on the screen and control their features.

When the Say radio button is selected, most options in the dialog box are disabled. You can use the Get pushbutton to select the variable to be displayed, and you can use the Comment and Refresh check boxes. The other options are dimmed, as they do not apply when a variable is just being displayed and cannot be edited.

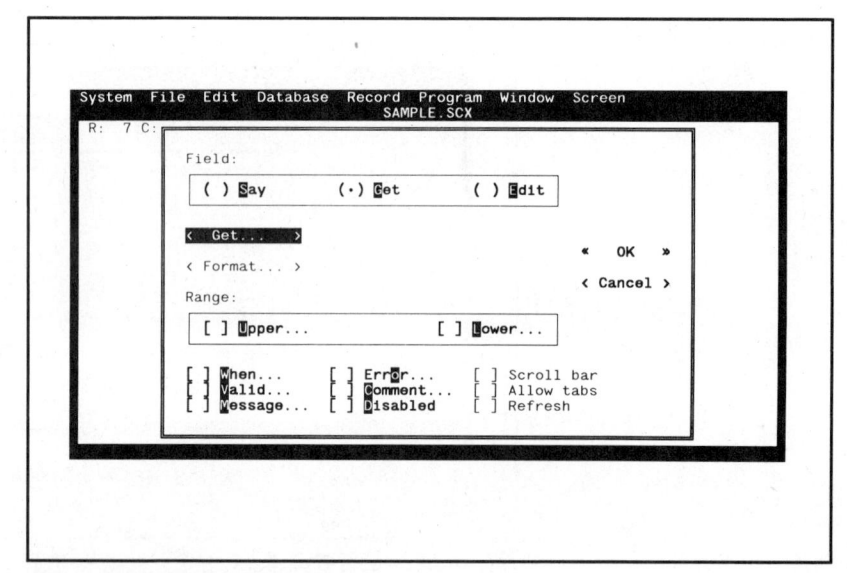

Figure 10.7: The Field dialog box

Typically, the Get radio button is selected, and this dialog box generates the ordinary @...GET <*var*> command that you learned about in Chapter 9, with a field name as the variable that is displayed and that can be edited when READ is executed.

If the Say radio button is selected, however, it generates the command @...SAY <var>, which simply displays the contents of the variable and does not let the user edit it.

If the Edit radio button is selected, it generates the command @...EDIT <var>, which lets the user scroll through the data-entry area to edit data that is larger than the area itself. This is particularly useful for editing memo fields.

SPECIFYING THE FIELD OR VARIABLE TO DISPLAY

Selecting the Get pushbutton displays the dialog box shown in Figure 10.8, which lets you use scrollable lists to select the database field or memory variable to place.

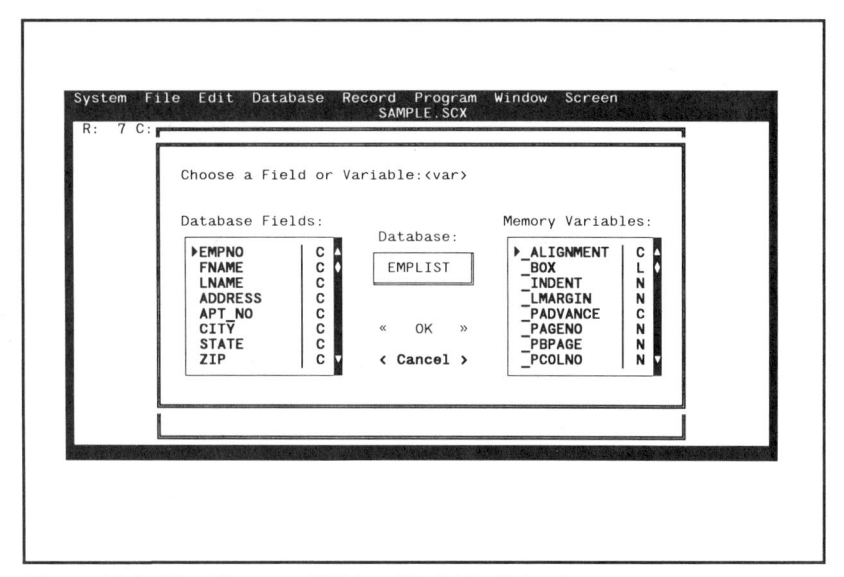

Figure 10.8: The Choose a Field or Variable dialog box

PICTURE TEMPLATES AND FUNCTIONS

You can type *picture templates* or *picture functions* in the text box to the right of the Format pushbutton of the Field dialog box, and these will be used to generate a PICTURE clause that formats the data.

Picture templates are used to format a variable on a character-by-character basis. For example, the template symbol ! converts any character that is entered to upper case, and the template symbol 9 lets the user enter only a number. Thus, if you wanted to validate the EMPNO field in the sample database that you have been using in this book, you could use the commands:

```
APPEND BLANK
@ 5,3 SAY "Enter the employee number" GET empno
    PICTURE "!99"
...
READ
```

FoxPro displays the value in the EMPNO field in the current record, which is made up of three blank spaces. When the user edits it, FoxPro automatically converts any letter entered as the first character to upper case and allows only numbers to be entered as the second and third letters.

Picture functions are used to format the entire variable. Function symbols can be used in a PICTURE clause if they are preceded by @ (to specify that they are function rather than template symbols), or they can be used in a FUNCTION clause without the @. For example, the function symbol ! capitalizes all the letters in an entry: if you wanted to make sure the first name was entered in all capital letters, you could use the command

```
@ 7,3 SAY "Enter the first name" GET fname PICTURE "@!"
```

or you could use the command

```
@ 7,3 SAY "Enter the first name" GET fname FUNCTION "!"
```

You can also use multiple picture templates and functions in a single PICTURE Clause.

Table 10.1 lists the effects of all the picture template symbols, and Table 10.2 lists the effects of all the picture function symbols. If you use any character that is not listed in Table 10.1 in a picture template, it is displayed literally. For example, you might get a Social Security number by using the command:

@ 10,3 SAY "Social Security Number:" GET ssn PICTURE "999-99-9999"

This picture function would display three spaces, where only digits could be entered or edited, a hyphen, two spaces for digits, another hyphen, and four spaces for digits. You could not move the cursor onto the hyphens or alter them: the cursor would skip right over them, as it skips over the / characters in a date field.

Table 10.1: Picture Template Symbols

Symbol	Effect
A	allows only alphabetic characters to be entered
L	allows only logical data to be entered
N	allows only alphabetic characters or numerals to be entered
X	allows any character to be entered
Y	allows only a capital or small Y or N to be entered, and converts the entry to uppercase
9	allows only numerals to be entered in a character field, or numerals and signs to be entered in a numeric field
#	allows numerals, signs, and blanks to be entered
!	capitalizes lowercase characters that are entered
$	displays the currency symbol defined by SET CURRENCY
*	fills leading blanks of a numeric value, using asterisks

By default, literal characters that are inserted in this way are saved in the database file.

You would have to create a character field that is eleven spaces wide to hold the Social Security numbers that are entered. If you also

Table 10.2: Picture Function Symbols

Symbol	Effect
A	allows only alphabetic characters to be entered
B	left-aligns numeric output
C	displays CR after a positive number (used only with numeric data in the SAY clause)
D	displays dates in the current SET DATE format (used with date, character, and numeric data)
E	displays dates in the European (or British) format (used with date, character, and numeric data)
I	centers text within a field (used only with the SAY clause)
J	right-aligns text within a field (used only with the SAY clause)
L	displays leading zeros instead of blanks to fill numeric fields (used only with numeric data in the SAY clause)
M <list>	specifies preset choices, which are listed with commas separating them (if the GET variable is not one of the choices in the list when READ is executed, it is replaced by the first choice on the list)
R	literal characters of the picture template are not saved in the database file
S <number>	limits the width of the field displayed to the number specified (used only with character data)
T	trims leading and trailing blanks
X	displays DB after a positive number (used only with numeric data in the SAY clause)
Z	displays a field as blank if its value is zero (used only with numeric data)
(	displays negative numbers enclosed in parentheses (used only with numeric data in the SAY clause)

Table 10.2: Picture Function Symbols (continued)

SYMBOL	EFFECT
!	converts letters to uppercase, but does not prevent the entry of other characters (used only with character data)
^	displays numeric data using scientific (exponential) notation (used only with numeric data)
$	displays data in currency format, as defined by the SET CURRENCY command

use the picture function **@R**, however, the literal characters are not saved in the database file: you would only have to use a field nine spaces wide to hold Social Security numbers. This picture function used to be very useful when disk space was scarce, but now it is not generally needed.

You must type picture templates in by hand: there is no way to "build" or generate them. On the other hand, you may either type in picture functions or generate them by selecting the Format pushbutton to call up the Format dialog box. The check boxes in this dialog box change depending on whether it is formatting character, numeric, logical, or date data. Figure 10.9 shows the selections corresponding to character and numeric data.

OPTIONAL CLAUSES

Many of the check boxes in the Field dialog box let you enter expressions or code snippets, which are used to generate optional clauses for the command. As you can see by looking at the dialog box in Figure 10.10, these object-level clauses are added in the same way as the Read-level clauses that can be added in the Screen Layout dialog box discussed previously (in the section on READ clauses and illustrated in Figure 10.5). The clauses entered in the Screen Layout dialog box were added to the READ command; the clauses entered here are added to the GET command for the particular object.

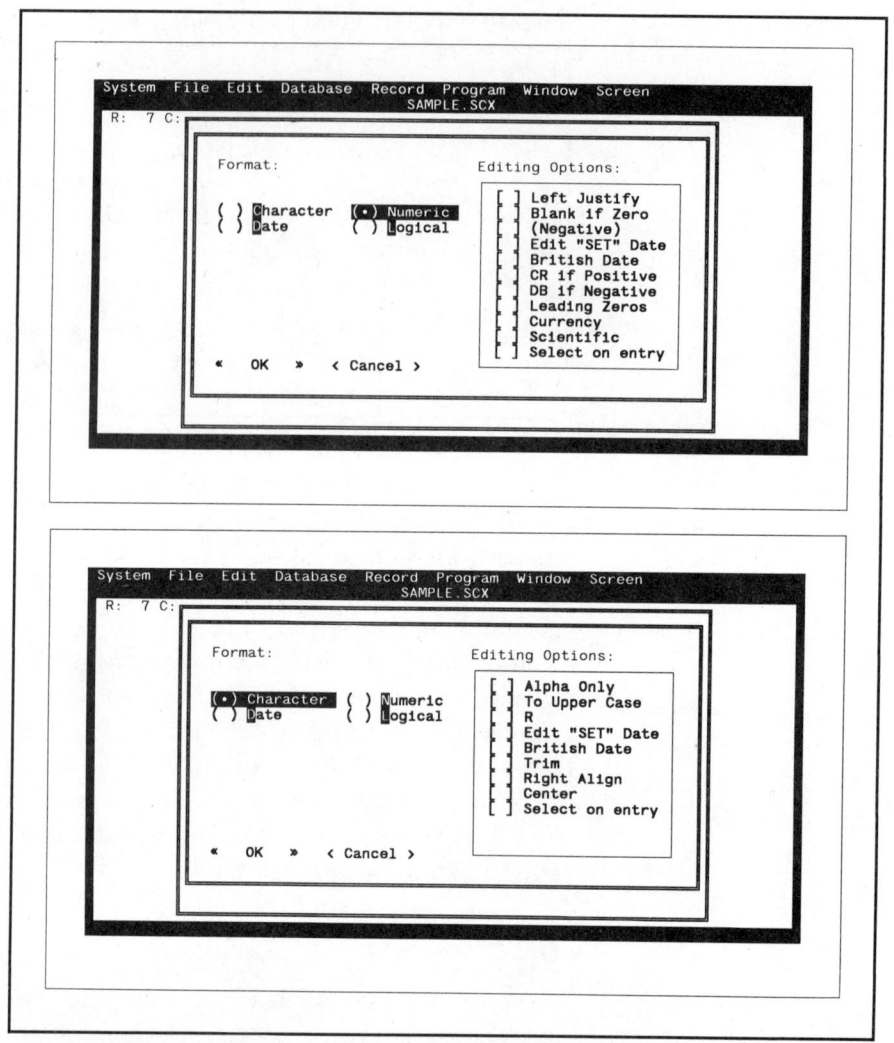

Figure 10.9: The Format dialog box for different data types

> The comma is included before the second expression even if the first expression is omitted.

An @...GET <*var*> command can contain the optional clause **RANGE [**<*expr1*>**][,**<*expr2*>**]** if the variable is character, numeric, or date data. The first expression is the lower limit and the second expression is the upper limit of the data that will be accepted as valid. If the clause is used, either the first or second expression may be omitted, but not both.

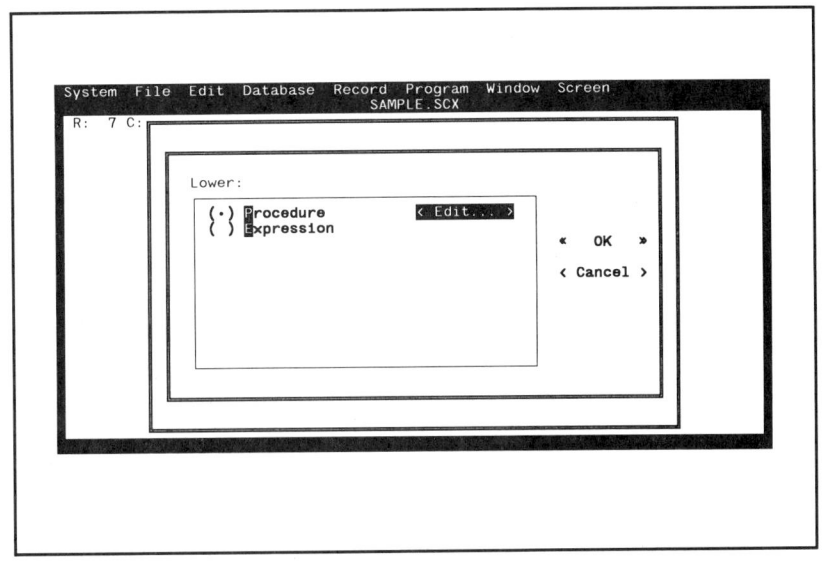

```
      System File Edit Database Record Program Window Screen
                               SAMPLE.SCX
       R:  7 C:

           Lower:
             (·) Procedure            < Edit... >
             ( ) Expression                              «   OK   »

                                                        < Cancel >
```

Figure 10.10: Entering the lower limit of a range

You select the Upper and/or Lower check boxes of the Range box to generate this clause. In most cases, you enter a simple expression in the dialog box that is displayed. For example, the lower limit for a date might be {01/01/92}, and its upper limit might be {12/31/92}.

The optional clause **WHEN** <*log exp*> lets the user edit the field only when the logical expression is true. The When check box lets you add this clause.

The optional clause **VALID** <*exp*> lets you check the validity of a data entry. It was originally meant to check whether an entry is valid or not. As mentioned earlier, though, the Valid check box is often used to add a procedure that contains a wide variety of commands, with a final command—for example, RETURN 0—to "trick" Fox-Pro into thinking the procedure is being used to validate the data.

The optional clause **MESSAGE** <*char exp*> lets you add a help message: the character expression is displayed at the bottom of the screen whenever the cursor moves to the field. The Message check box lets you add this clause.

The optional clause **ERROR** <*char exp*> lets you display an error message. If the VALID clause evaluates to false, the message

"Invalid Input" is displayed by default. Adding an ERROR clause lets you display the specified character expression instead.

OTHER FEATURES OF THE FIELD DIALOG BOX

The Comment check box lets you add a comment for your own use, as you can with all types of objects.

The Disabled check box prevents the user from editing the field. The field is displayed, but the cursor skips over it.

The Refresh check box can be used only if the Say radio button is selected. This box must be checked to make the value of the field displayed by the SAY clause change automatically when the pointer moves to a new record, in the same way that fields displayed by GET clauses change when the pointer moves. Checking the Refresh check box generates the optional clause **SHOW** <*log exp*> as part of the READ command. For more information on how this clause works, see READ in the Help window.

The Scroll Bar and Allow Tabs check boxes can be used only if the Edit radio button is selected. The Scroll Bar check box places a scroll bar at the side of editing regions that are at least two lines deep, to make it easier for the user to scroll through the contents of the field. The Allow Tabs check box lets the user enter the Tab character within the edit field. If this is not checked, pressing Tab moves the user to the next field; if it is checked, the user must press Ctrl-Tab to move to the next field.

TEXT

Selecting *Text* from the Screen menu toggles you to the text mode so you can edit text: the word "text" appears on the status line in the upper left of the window.

You can begin typing text without using this menu selection, because the screen toggles to text mode automatically. As long as you continue to type text, you can use the editing keys to edit it on a character-by-character basis. Once you press Enter, though, all of the characters that you typed become a single object, which can be manipulated like other objects. To edit a text object on a character-by-character basis again, you must select Text from the screen menu.

CONTROLS

The next five features of the Screen menu let you produce the special controls that the FoxPro language makes available: pushbuttons, radio buttons, check boxes, popups, and scrollable lists.

As you will see, the commands used to create these features are like @...GET commands that use special picture functions and cannot include a SAY clause. As always, you can specify these picture functions using either the clause **PICTURE** '@ <*char exp*>' or the clause **FUNCTION** ' <*char exp*>'. As you will see, the picture function for each control begins with a specification code made up of a special character, such as * or ^ or &, or made up of an asterisk plus a letter. The specification code is followed by a space and then by the option displayed by the control, or by a list of options separated by semicolons if the command can be used to display multiple options.

Like ordinary @...GET commands, these commands are activated by a READ command. You can put any combination of @...GET commands on the screen and they will all be activated at once when the program executes the READ command. These commands also offer optional clauses similar to those offered by ordinary @...GET commands. Selecting the menu options lets you generate these commands and their optional clauses. The discussions below introduce you to all the basic features for these commands, but for a thorough discussion, see @..GET in the Help window: each is treated as a separate @...GET command.

PUSHBUTTONS

An asterisk is the specification code for a pushbutton: its picture function must begin with a asterisk followed by a list of the prompts used in the pushbuttons being created. For example, to create two pushbuttons with the prompts OK and Cancel, you can use the clause **PICTURE** '@* **OK;Cancel**' or the clause **FUNCTION** '* **OK;Cancel**'. FoxPro adds the angle brackets around the prompts that are listed.

If you want the pushbuttons to have hot keys, put a backslash and less than sign \< before the character to be used as a hot key. For example, if you use the clause **PICTURE** '@* \<**Yes;**\<**No**', the user will be able to press Y or N to select Yes or No. If you want a pushbutton disabled, put two backslashes \\ before it in the list. If you want a default pushbutton, accessible by pressing Ctrl-Enter, put a backslash plus an exclamation point \! before it in the list, and if you want to let the user select one of the pushbuttons by pressing the Esc key, put a backslash plus a question mark before it. For example, use the clause **PICTURE '@* \!OK;\?Cancel'** to make OK the default pushbutton and to let the user select Cancel by pressing Esc. You can also combine these features.

In the basic form of the command—

@ *<row,col>* GET *<var>* FUNCTION
<char exp> | PICTURE *<char exp>*

—the row and col numbers specify the location of the first prompt in the list. The name of the variable that is specified holds the user's choice. If you define the variable as numeric, the number of the button that the user selects is stored in that variable: in the example, if the user selects OK, the variable is assigned the value 1, and if the user selects Cancel, it is assigned the value 2. You must write the code that tells the program what to do based on the value of that variable.

Selecting Push Button from the Screen menu lets you use the dialog box shown in Figure 10.11 to generate this basic command and its optional clauses.

The prompts are entered in the Push Button Prompts text-editing box, one prompt to a line. These can include \ codes used to define hot key, default text buttons, and so on. A double-headed arrow to the left of each one you enter lets you change the order of the list in the usual way.

The Horizontal and Vertical radio buttons determine whether the pushbuttons are arranged one next to another or one above another.

The Terminating check box determines whether choosing any of these pushbuttons terminates the READ. By default, this box is not checked, and the user can continue to select other controls or to enter and edit text after selecting a pushbutton. If this box is checked, the program continues with the line of code following the READ after the pushbutton is chosen. You would want to select this box, for example, for the OK and Cancel pushbuttons.

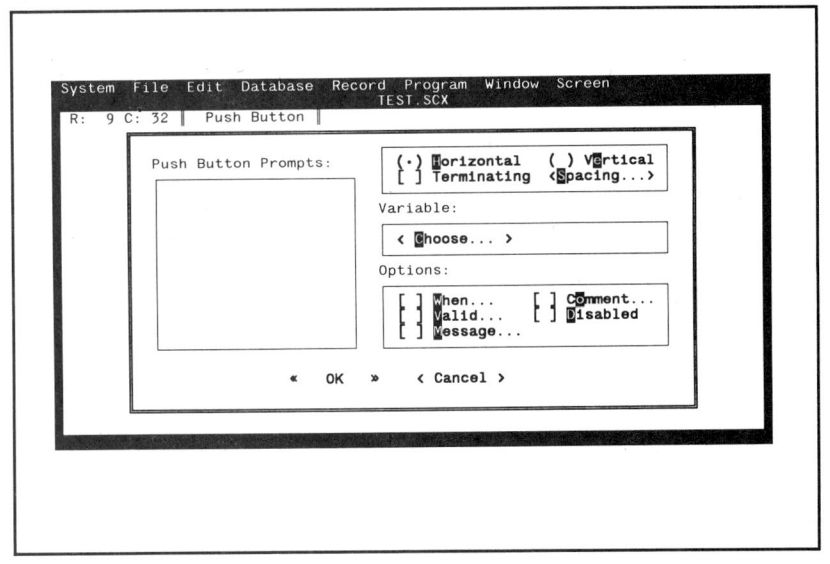

Figure 10.11: The Push Button dialog box

Selecting the Spacing pushbutton lets you alter the spacing between pushbuttons: by default, there is one space between pushbuttons that are arranged horizontally, and one line between those that are arranged vertically.

In the Variable text box, you can enter the name of the variable that the user's choice will be stored in. If no such variable already exists, FoxPro creates it and gives it a default value of 0. Select the Choose pushbutton to choose a database field or an existing public memory variable as the variable.

The When check box lets you generate the optional clause **WHEN** <*log var*>. The pushbuttons can be selected only if the logical variable evaluates to true.

The Valid check box lets you generate the optional clause **VALID** <*log var*>. As mentioned earlier, a user-defined function is often used in the VALID clause.

The Message check box lets you generate the optional clause **MESSAGE** <*char exp*>, which displays the character expression as a Help message when the pushbutton is selected.

The Comment check box lets you add a comment for your own use, as always.

The Disabled check box generates the optional clause **DISABLE**, which prevents the user from accessing the pushbuttons. Though they are visible on the screen, they cannot be selected.

The Initial popup can be used to select an initial value for the variable.

Note that the When, Valid, Message, and Disabled check boxes generate optional clauses in the command. On the other hand, the Horizontal, Vertical, and Terminating check boxes generate the optional additions **H**, **V**, and **T** to the Picture clause: for example, **PICTURE '@*VT OK;Cancel'** arranges these pushbuttons vertically and makes them terminating.

RADIO BUTTONS

*R is the specification code for a radio button: its picture function must begin with ***R** followed by a list of the prompts used in the radio buttons being created. For example, to create three radio buttons with the prompts Upper, Proper, and Lower (which you can use to determine caplitalization) you can use the clause **PICTURE '@*R Upper;Proper;Lower'** or the equivalent clause beginning with **FUNCTION**. You can define hot keys for radio buttons as you do for pushbuttons, by putting \< before a letter of the prompt.

The basic form of the command—

@ <row,col> GET <var> FUNCTION
<char exp> | PICTURE <char exp>

> As always, you must write the code to determine what the program will do based on the value of the variable.

—works very much like the command for pushbuttons. The row and col numbers specify the location of the first radio button in the list. If you define the variable as numeric, the number of the radio button that the user chooses is assigned to that variable. If you want one of the radio buttons to be selected initially, assign the variable the value of that button. In the example above, if you want Proper capitalization to be selected by default, use the command <var> = 2 to initialize that variable before you use the @...GET command.

Selecting Radio Button from the Screen menu lets you use the dialog box shown in Figure 10.12 to generate this basic command and its optional clauses.

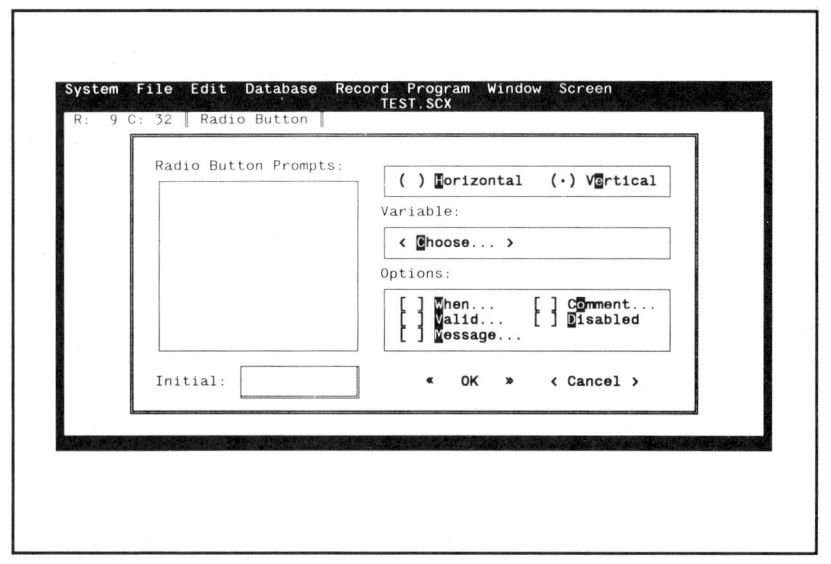

Figure 10.12: The Radio Button dialog box

The features of this dialog box are very similar to those of the Push Button dialog box. You list the prompts in the Radio Button Prompts box. You determine the arrangement of the radio buttons by selecting the Horizontal or Vertical radio buttons. You enter the variable that the choice is assigned to in the Variable text box, or use the Choose pushbutton to select it. You use the check boxes to add an optional WHEN, VALID, MESSAGE, or DISABLE clause, which work like the equivalent clauses for pushbuttons, and you use the Initial popup to determine which radio button is selected initially.

CHECK BOXES

An asterisk followed by C is the specification code for a check box: its picture function consists of *C followed by the prompt that the check box uses. For example, to create a check box that capitalizes text, you can use the clause **PICTURE '@*C Capitalize'** or the equivalent clause using **FUNCTION**. This command can have only a single prompt. You can give it a hot key in the usual way, by putting \< before one of the letters of the prompt.

> The box is checked if you assign the variable any non-zero numeric value.

In the basic form of the command—

@ <row,col> GET <var> FUNCTION
  <char exp> | PICTURE <char exp>

—the row and col numbers specify the location of the check box. The variable may be numeric or logical: if the box is checked, it is assigned the value of **1** or **.T.**, and if the box is not checked, it is assigned the value of **0** or **.F.**. Whether or not the box is checked by default depends on the initial value you assign the variable.

Selecting Check Box from the Screen menu lets you use the dialog box shown in Figure 10.13 to generate this basic command and its optional clauses.

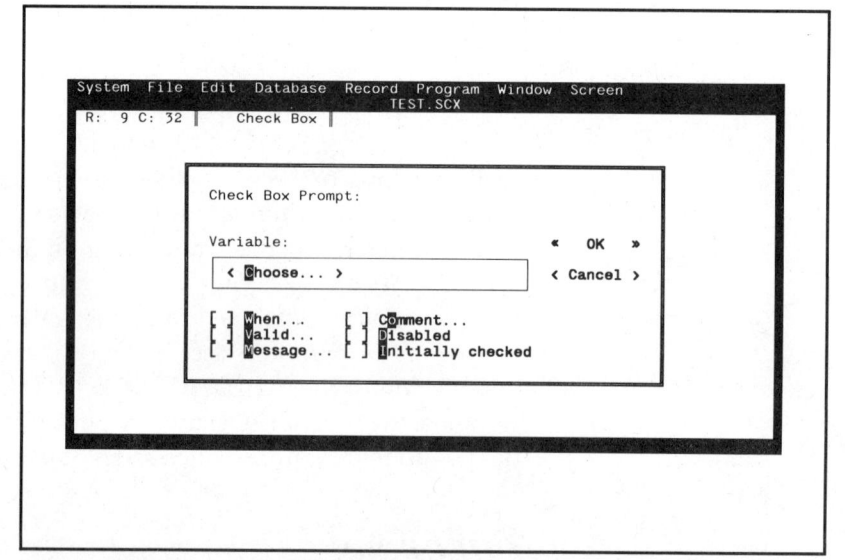

Figure 10.13: The Check Box dialog box

This command cannot include a list of prompts, so you can only enter a single prompt in the dialog box. As usual, you enter the variable the choice is assigned to or select the Choose pushbutton to choose it. Check boxes generate the usual optional WHEN, VALID, MESSAGE, and DISABLE clauses and let you add a comment for your own purposes. The final check box lets you determine if the box is checked by default.

POPUP CONTROLS

A caret ^ is the specification code for a popup control, and it is followed by a list of the options that the popup displays. For example, to create a popup control to let the user choose among four data types, you can use the clause **PICTURE '@^ Character;Number;Date;Logical'** or the equivalent FUNCTION clause. Since there are often more options to a popup than you want to list, you can use the optional clause **FROM** <*array name*> to read them from an array instead.

In the basic form of the command—

@ <*row,col*> GET <*var*> FUNCTION
  <*char exp*> | PICTURE <*char exp*>

—the row and col numbers specify the location of the upper left corner of the popup control. If the variable defined is the character type, the prompt that is chosen is assigned to that variable; if it is numeric type, the number of that prompt in the list is assigned to the variable.

Selecting Popup from the Screen menu lets you use the dialog box shown in Figure 10.14 to generate this basic command and its optional clauses.

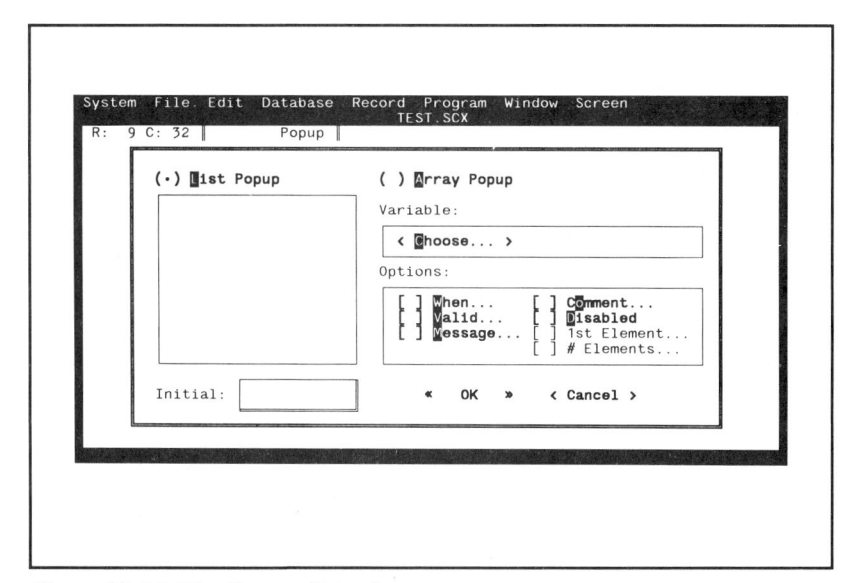

Figure 10.14: The Popup dialog box

If the List Popup radio button is selected, you can list the options on the popup in the box as usual; if the Array Popup radio button is selected, you can enter the name of the array to read them from.

In either case, you can enter or choose the name of the variable as usual and use the check boxes to generate the usual WHEN, VALID, MESSAGE, or DISABLE clause or to add a commment for your own use. You can use the Initial popup to select the initial value of the variable, which is displayed in the popup control box before it is selected and the entire list is displayed.

The 1st Element and # Elements check boxes can be used only if the Array Popup radio button is selected. By default, all of the elements of the array are used in the popup. If you use these check boxes, though, you can determine which element of the array will be the first element used and how many elements will be used in total.

SCROLLABLE LISTS

An ampersand (&) is the specification code for a scrollable list, used in its picture function. However, you cannot list the options available as part of the picture function for scrollable lists, as you can for other controls. There are several ways of specifying the option; the most common is to store them in an array.

In the basic form of the command—

@ *<row,col>* GET *<var>* | *<field>* FUNCTION *<char exp>* | PICTURE *<char exp>* FROM *<array>*

—the row and col numbers specify the location of the upper left corner of the list. When the user chooses from the list, the variable is assigned a number equal to the number of the user's choice in the list; alternatively, you can store the choice in the specified field of a database file. The clause **FROM** <array> specifies the array that the options in the list come from. For other details about this very complex command, see the Help window.

Selecting *List* from the Screen menu lets you use the dialog box shown in Figure 10.15 to generate this command. Note that, since the picture function cannot contain a list of options, this dialog box does not contain a text-editing area to enter prompts, as the other control dialog boxes do. Instead, the List Type box lets you select where the elements of the list come from, as mentioned, From Array is most common. Enter the variable that holds the user's choice in the text box, or select the Choose pushbutton to select the memory or field variable.

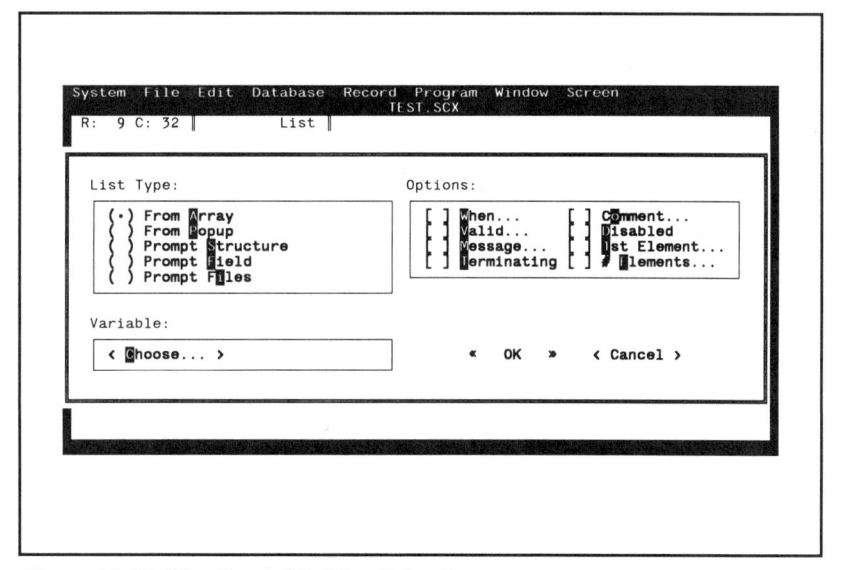

Figure 10.15: The Scrollable List dialog box

The check boxes in the options box generate the usual optional clauses, and the two new check boxes. If you are reading list elements from an array, the list includes all the elements of the array by default. You can use only part of the array, however, by selecting the 1st Element and # Elements check boxes to specify which element of the array the list should begin with and how many elements of the array it should include in total.

INVISIBLE PUSHBUTTONS

*I is the specification code for an invisible pushbutton: its picture function must begin with *I, but this is not followed by a list of the prompts separated by semicolons, as there are no prompts displayed; instead it can be followed by a series of semicolons, which indicates how many invisible buttons there will be. If no semicolons are included, only one invisible button is created; each semicolon added creates an additional button.

Additional picture function options are similar to those available for pushbuttons:

N:	do not terminate the READ when an invisible button is chosen
T:	terminate the READ when an invisible button is chosen
H:	arrange the buttons horizontally
V:	arrange the buttons vertically

If these are omitted, the buttons are non-terminating and vertical by default.

The picture function should followed by the clause **SIZE** <*num exp*>,<*num exp*>[,<*num exp*>] to control the size of the invisible buttons. The first and second numeric expressions specify the buttons' height and width. The optional third expression specifies the number of rows (for vertical buttons) or columns (for horizontal buttons) between buttons. If the third expression is left out, no rows are placed between vertical buttons, and one column is placed between horizontal buttons.

As usual, the row and col numbers following @ specify the location of the first invisible button, and the variable following **GET** holds the user's selection.

After using an @...**GET** command to define invisible buttons in this way, you can use @...**SAY** commands to display characters in the same locations as the buttons. You can use ASCII line-drawing characters or other special characters to simulate icons in these locations. Then, when the user clicks an icon, that invisible button will be selected.

> You can use all the ASCII characters by using the function **CHR**(<*num exp*>, which returns the ASCII character equivalent to the specified number.

CONTROLLING THE SCREEN DESIGN

You have seen how to place objects on the screen builder window. The next few options in the Screen menu let you manipulate these objects to control the design of the screen.

Bring to Front and *Send to Back* let you change the "stacking order" of objects. As you add objects, new ones are put in front of existing ones. These options let you change this order by moving the selected object to the front or the back of the stack. For example, if you draw a line that partly covers a field, you could use one of these options to place the field on top of the line instead.

Center places the selected object in the center of the line within the screen or window.

Reorder Fields determines the order in which the user accesses the fields on the screen. By default, pressing Tab moves the user through the objects in the order in which they were placed on the screen. The fields are numbered in this order. Selecting *Bring to Front* or *Send to Back* changes this order: Bring to Front makes the object behave as if it were the last one placed, and Send to Back makes it behave as if it were the first one placed; in both cases, the numbering changes correspondingly.

> If an object is selected when you select Reorder Fields, that object becomes last in order.

Selecting *Reorder Fields* automatically makes the user access the fields from top to bottom and from left to right: this does not always apply to grouped fields, described below.

Selecting *Color* calls up the Screen Color Picker dialog box, shown in Figure 10.16, which lets you control the color of the object that is currently selected. Selecting the Default radio button gives that object the color that type of object normally has in FoxPro. Selecting the Custom radio button enables the Scheme popup, which lets you select among custom color schemes that you have defined.

> Grouping objects can change the order in which they are accessed. If their order is changed unexpectedly, it can be altered again after they are ungrouped.

Selecting *Group* combines all the objects that are currently selected, so that they can be manipulated as a single object. This is simply a convenience to let you work with them more easily during design. Selecting Ungroup breaks them up into individual objects again.

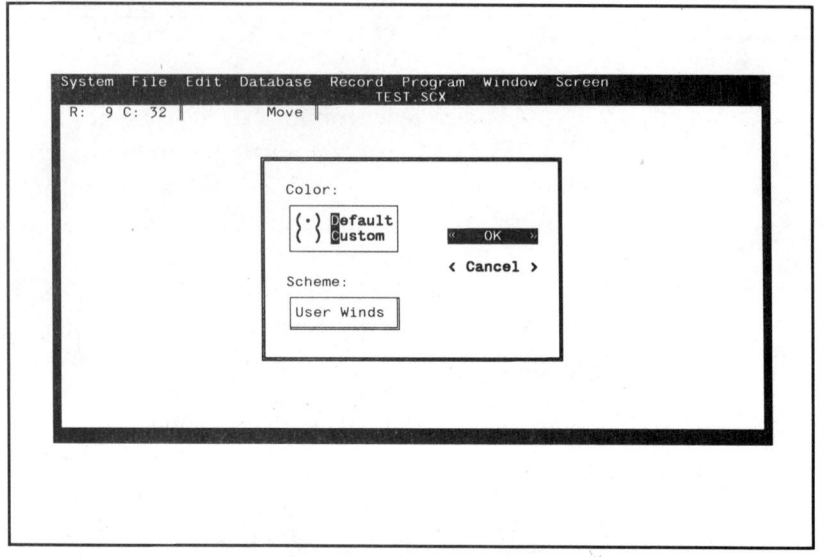

Figure 10.16: The Screen Color Picker dialog box

QUICK SCREEN

Selecting *Quick Screen* calls up the Quick Screen dialog box, shown in Figure 10.17, which lets you lay out all or some of the fields in the database on the screen.

Quick Screen is accessible only if there are no objects on the screen builder window, and it is generally the easiest way to begin designing a screen—much easier than placing the fields individually. Once you have created a quick screen, you can move the fields and edit field titles to be exactly what you want.

The radio buttons at the top let you choose between two basic layouts of the fields. The box on the right illustrates the layout that is chosen. Row Layout places the fields one above the other. Column Layout places the fields one next to the other; if the fields cannot fit across the width of the screen, they wrap to the following lines. Column layout should be used in conjunction with the Maximum field width setting, described below.

If the Titles check box is checked, the name of each field is displayed as its title, to its left.

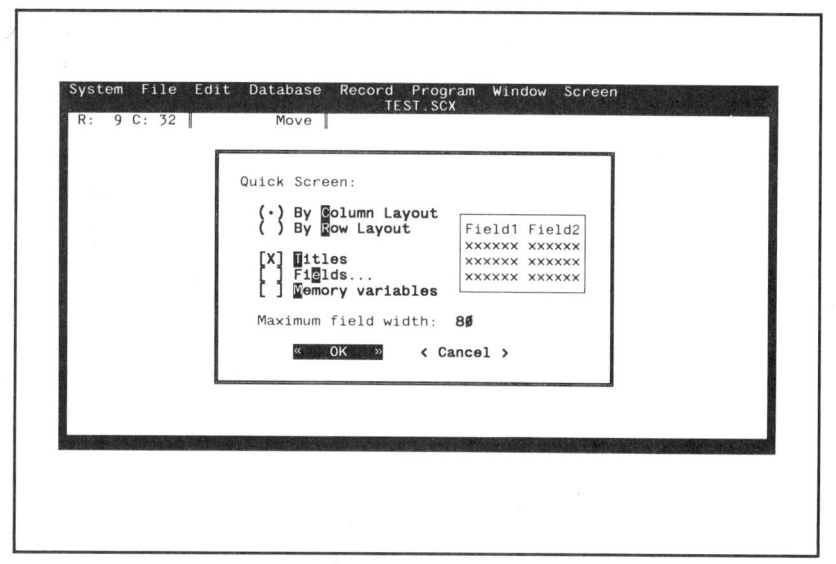

Figure 10.17: The Quick Screen dialog box

If you select the Fields check box, you can use the familiar Field Picker dialog box to select which fields are included in the layout. If this box is not checked, all the fields are included.

Selecting the Memory Variables check box automatically creates memory variables for all the fields. Programmers often prefer to read user input into memory variables, rather than letting the users access the database fields themselves.

By default the Maximum field width setting is equal to the width of the screen or the defined width of the window minus two. You may set it at any length less than the width of the window. Any data in fields that does not fit in this display width is truncated.

If you select the Column Layout pushbutton but maximum field width is 80, FoxPro will not be able to create columns: it will allow the full 80 characters for each field, so only one field can fit on each line.

GENERATING CODE

Once you have finished designing the screen, you must generate the programming code that displays that screen. When the screen builder window is open, you can select *Generate* from the Program menu to use the Generate dialog box, shown in Figure 10.18.

As mentioned at the beginning of this chapter, you can generate programs based on multiple screens. The scrollable list in the upper left of this dialog box lists all the screen designs that will be used to generate the code, and the four pushbuttons next to it lets you control these screens' designs.

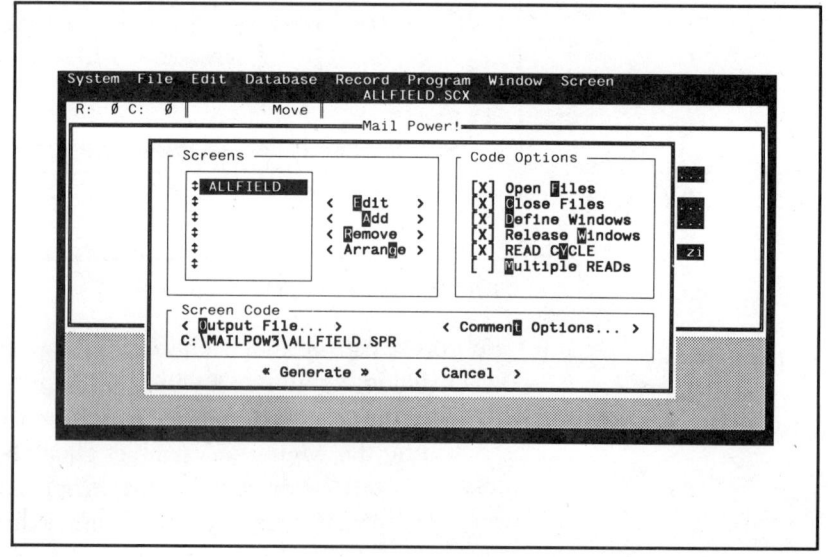

Figure 10.18: The Generate dialog box

- The Edit pushbutton calls up the screen design window to let you change the design of whichever screen is selected in the list.
- The Add pushbutton displays a dialog box with a scrollable list that lets you select screen design files to add to the list.
- The Remove pushbutton lets you remove files from the list.
- The Arrange pushbutton displays the screen shown in Figure 10.19, which lets you arrange the screen designs, specifying the location of each.

```
┌─────────────────────────────────────────────────────────┐
│ System  File  Edit  Arrange                             │
│  ┌──────────────────────Controls──────────────────────┐ │
│  │                     Mail Power!                    │ │
│  │                                                    │ │
│  │                                                    │ │
│  │                                                    │ │
│  │                                                    │ │
│  │                                                    │ │
│  └────────────────────────────────────────────────────┘ │
│                                                         │
│                                                         │
│                                                         │
└─────────────────────────────────────────────────────────┘
```

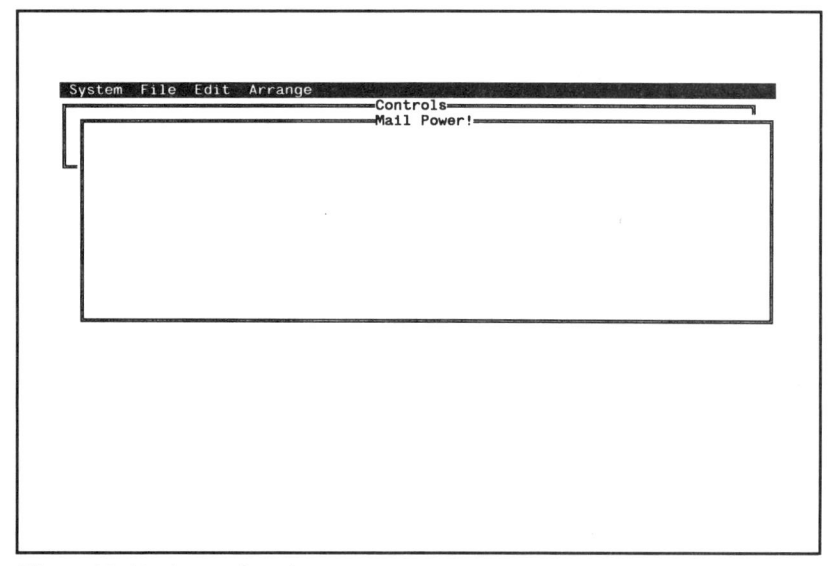

Figure 10.19: Arranging the screens

In the illustration, based on the sample program you will write in the next chapter, two screens, both of which are windows, were in the scrollable list of the Generate dialog box when the Arrange pushbutton was selected. One screen is named ALLFIELD, and has the heading **Mail Power!**, which is displayed at the top of its window. The other is called ED_CNTRL and has the heading **Controls**.

When you use this screen, an Arrange menu is added to the menu bar, which is shown in Figure 10.20. Notice that the names of the two screens are added at the bottom of this menu, and that there is a bullet next to ALLFIELD to indicate that it is currently selected; note also that this window (with the name Mail Power!) is on top of the other on the screen.

The options on the Arrange menu are self-explanatory. You can specify the name of the output file where the code will be stored by selecting the Output File pushbutton to select among existing screen program files, or you can type a file name under this pushbutton. By default, the name under the pushbutton is the same as the name of the screen design, but with the extension SPR.

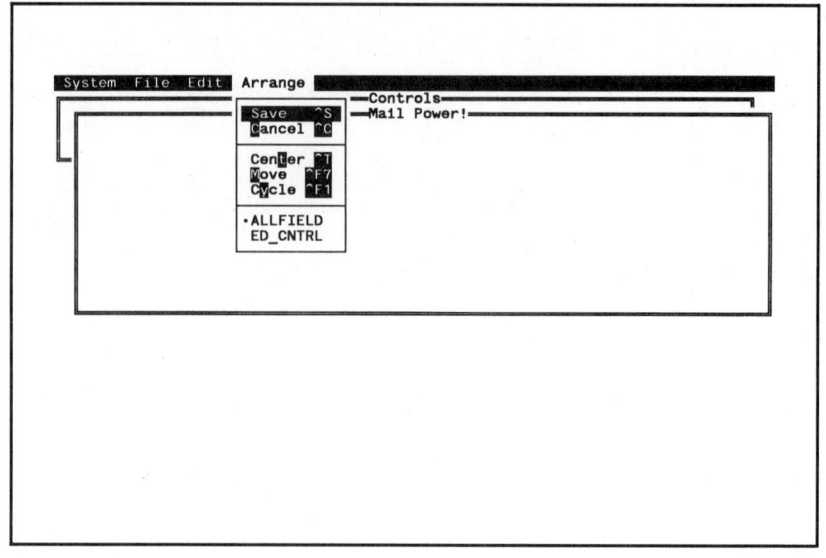

Figure 10.20: The Arrange menu

You can select the check boxes on the right of the Generate dialog box to control certain features of the code that will be generated:

- **Open files:** Code is generated to open the database files and indexes and to set relations at the beginning of the screen program.

- **Close files:** Code is generated to close the files at the end of the screen program.

- **Define windows:** DEFINE WINDOW commands are generated to define the windows in the screen.

- **Release windows:** RELEASE WINDOWS commands are generated to remove the definition of the windows from memory at the end of the screen program.

- **READ CYCLE:** The command READ CYCLE is generated, rather than the ordinary READ command, so the READ does not terminate when the cursor moves beyond the last GET field (or before the first one), but continues to cycle through the fields.

- **Multiple READs:** A READ statement is generated between the format commands for each screen panel, instead of a single READ CYCLE for all the screen panels.

These options are meant for advanced programmers, and you can generally just leave them checked by default.

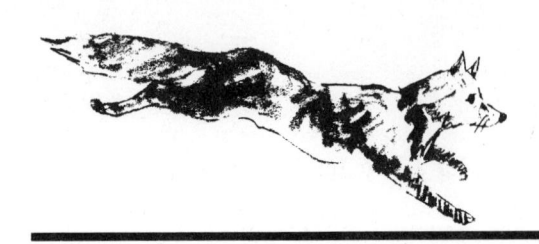

Chapter 11

Write Your Own
Professional Menu Application

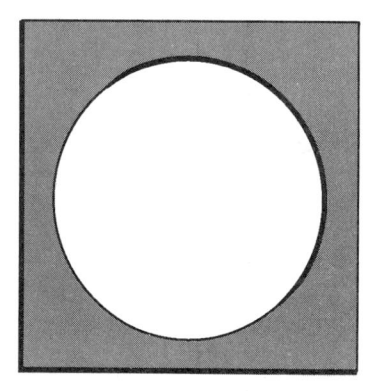

IN THIS CHAPTER, YOU WILL WRITE A COMPLETE mailing list application using the FoxPro commands and programming techniques that you learned in previous chapters. This application could act as a stand-alone program to let a user

- keep track of a list of names and addresses
- print mailing labels and reports
- export names and addresses to a text file so that they can be used by many word processing programs to perform mail-merge (inserting the names and addresses in form letters)

You will write the entire program in this chapter, but you will write it in a fairly simple form. In the next chapter, you will modify the program using some more advanced programming tools.

ANALYSIS

Before you begin programming, you must analyze the problem you are dealing with. Professional programmers who are computerizing a business must go through a long process of analysis. Usually, they begin by analyzing all the paper forms the business uses, and organizing the data kept on all these forms into a single *data dictionary*. Once they have the data listed in one place, they can see how it should be normalized: generally, a problem this complex requires a relational database. Before programming, they often use data flow diagrams to show what department or what report uses each element of data. The data flow suggests how their programs should be organized. In short, programmers generally gather and analyze a tremendous amount of information before they write even a line of code.

Of course, this mailing list application is simple enough that the analysis can be relatively brief. Even with a simple application, though, you should outline the program in writing before doing any programming. An excellent way of doing this, which you will use in this chapter, is the *structure diagram*. As you will see, this diagram sketches out the basic functions that the program must perform and thus gives you an idea of how the program should be broken down into procedures.

First, though, you should consider the database file and indexes that the program must use. We can call the file MAILLIST.DBF. The fields that it needs are fairly obvious: in addition to name and address, the program should also keep track of telephone numbers, to make it a complete address book program. Thus, the fields that are needed are

- Mr., Mrs., Ms., or an honorific
- first name
- last name
- company name
- address
- city
- state
- zip
- telephone number

Even when the data is this simple, you should list it in writing as part of your analysis. If you just start programming without analysis, it is very easy to forget, for example, that you need an honorific in this program. When you create the structure diagram and think about exporting the data for mail-merge, however, you will be reminded that your user may want to begin a letter with the salutation Dear Mr. So-and-So, Dear Ms. So-and-So, or Dear Prof. So-and-So, and that it is impossible to do this unless you have a separate field for title or honorific.

As you can see, analysis is a dynamic process. Things that you do in the later stages of analysis make you think about and maybe change the things you have already done in earlier stages of analysis. As I mentioned, it is best to put everything in writing in advance: it is much easier to change written notes before you begin programming than to change the code you have already written. It is very disturbing to suddenly realize, when you are in the middle of a project, that you left a field out of your database, and that you have to redesign your data-entry screens and reports and perhaps also rewrite many procedures in your program.

Make key decisions during analysis. Should this program have a field for notes? Should it have two lines for the address?—or should you assume that the user can use the company name line for the first line of a two-line address? The time to think about these things is before you begin programming: make a decision that you can stick with, because it becomes more and more difficult to change as the project progresses.

One important question is how to handle deleted records. An extreme solution would be to let the user recall deleted records until they are packed, as you can with FoxPro itself. This is a bit confusing for a simple program such as this one, though. At the other extreme, you could **SET DELETED ON** so deleted records cannot be used, and you could automatically **PACK** the records at some time (for example, whenever the user exits from the program), then the user would not even know about packing and would have the impression that records were permanently deleted as soon as they made that selection from the menu. This option has the disadvantage of wasting time by packing unnecessarily, though: if you had a large database, it could take a long time to quit the program.

Though there are arguments for both of the preceding options, this program will take a middle course: it will **SET DELETED ON**, so that the user will not be able to access deleted records, and will also provide for a menu option to finalize deletions, so that there will not be any time wasted. This feature would have to be explained to the user; if this were an actual commercial program, it would be explained in the documentation.

It should be fairly obvious to you what indexes you will need for this program. Users will want to produce reports in alphabetical order and to produce mailing labels in zip code order (if the program is to be used for bulk mailing). Which of these indexes the program should generally use as the main index will become more clear when you create the structure diagram.

MAKING A STRUCTURE DIAGRAM

The structure diagram simply shows all the programs or procedures that make up the entire mailing program, diagrammed in a way that makes it obvious how they are related to each other. The *main menu* is at the top of the structure diagram for this program: when the program starts, it presents the user with a menu of the basic functions that the program performs. Each choice from the main menu calls another module of the program, which displays a submenu with choices.

To organize the menu system, we can divide the program's functions into four parts:

- **Data:** lets the user add, edit, look up, or delete records
- **Reports:** creates printed reports, Rolodex cards, and the like
- **Labels:** creates a variety of different mailing labels
- **Export:** creates text files to be used for mail merge

Since each of these presents the user with a menu, we can call them DATAMENU, REPTMENU, LABLMENU and EXPTMENU.

These options give us the first cut at a structure chart, shown in Figure 11.1. Note that the structure chart shows graphically how these modules are related to each other—that the main menu calls the other menu programs. Of course, the main menu would also need an option that lets the user quit the program, but this need not be included in the structure chart, because it does not require using a separate program or procedure.

Now, what else needs to be added to this structure chart? In this first version of the program, you will use a simple type of menu

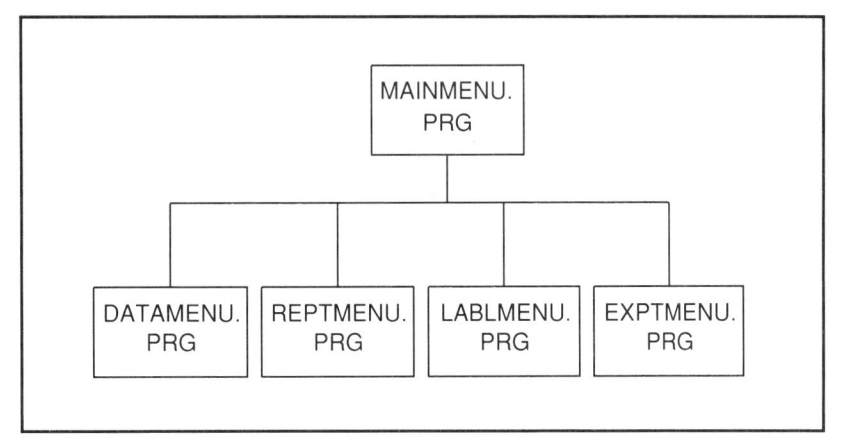

Figure 11.1: The first step in creating the structure chart

screen that was commonly used in dBASE III programming. As you will see, all five menu screens will have similar headers, and it is best to put the header in a separate module called by each of them. We can call this the SCRNHEAD procedure. Using these old-fashioned menus will give you valuable experience with the basics of control flow, with procedures and parameters, and with actually writing @...SAY...GET commands, rather than using the screen builder to generate them. In the next chapter, you will replace them with pop-up menus, like the ones used in FoxPro itself.

The program must let the user edit existing records and append new records to the database file. To do this, you will use the screen builder to generate two custom screens: EDITSCRN.SPR and APNDSCRN.SPR.

In addition, the program must let the user look up a name and provide for editing or deleting the record for a given name. In any case, the program must ask the user for the name, must search for that name in the file, and must display an error message if the name cannot be found.

When the same series of steps must be used more than once in the program, that is the clue to put those steps in a separate module. Putting repetitive steps in a separate program or procedure saves some time when you are writing the program, and it saves a tremendous amount of work if you need to modify this feature of the program and to keep it consistent wherever it is used. Thus, in light of the previous discussion on looking up names, you should add a procedure (that you can call LOOKUP), which will be used by DATAMENU for looking up, editing, and deleting records. You will also create several custom screens to display messages and get input from the user when you are looking up records, but there is no need to worry about these details at this stage of the analysis.

The Report menu should let the user produce an alphabetical listing of the names, addresses, and telephone numbers in the mailing list; you can create this report using the report generator. In addition, you should create a report that includes only names and telephone numbers, since this is something that users commonly need. FoxPro's mailing label generator lets you print out data on 4″ ×

2¼″ or on 3″ × 5″ Rolodex or index cards, and you can also give these choices to the user as options on the Report menu.

The Label menu should simply give the user the choice of creating as many different size labels as possible, since this is meant as a general-purpose program to be used by many users. We will let the user choose among all the label forms that are currently listed as standard forms by the FoxPro label generator. In an actual application, you might want to add even more label forms, since the user will not be provided with the tools to create custom forms.

Finally, the Export submenu will simply use the **COPY** command to copy the database to a text file. In an actual application, you would also add special procedures to export the data in the forms needed by popular word processors. In this sample program, though, the EXPORT menu does not need to call any procedures: it will simply include a number of **COPY** commands.

Our analysis, then, finally gives us the structure diagram shown in Figure 11.2. When you study this diagram it will become clear which index is most important. Virtually all of the modules do better with the names in alphabetical order: for example, it is best to have the records in alphabetical order to modify them (so the user can find a name by paging through them), to export names (in mail-merge files—in alphabetical order), and to produce alphabetical reports. The only exception is the Label menu, which should use records in zip code order. Thus, it is best to open the file with the NAMES index tag as the controlling index when the program begins. You should make the ZIPS index the controlling index only when the user produces labels—and, to avoid confusion, you should make the NAMES index the controlling index again as soon as the user is done producing labels.

You can also see by looking at the structure diagram that this program is moderately complex. It would be difficult to start writing a single program file that does all these things, as they used to do in the days before structured programming. The structure diagram, though, breaks it up into small pieces, each of which is easy to understand and relatively easy to write the program for.

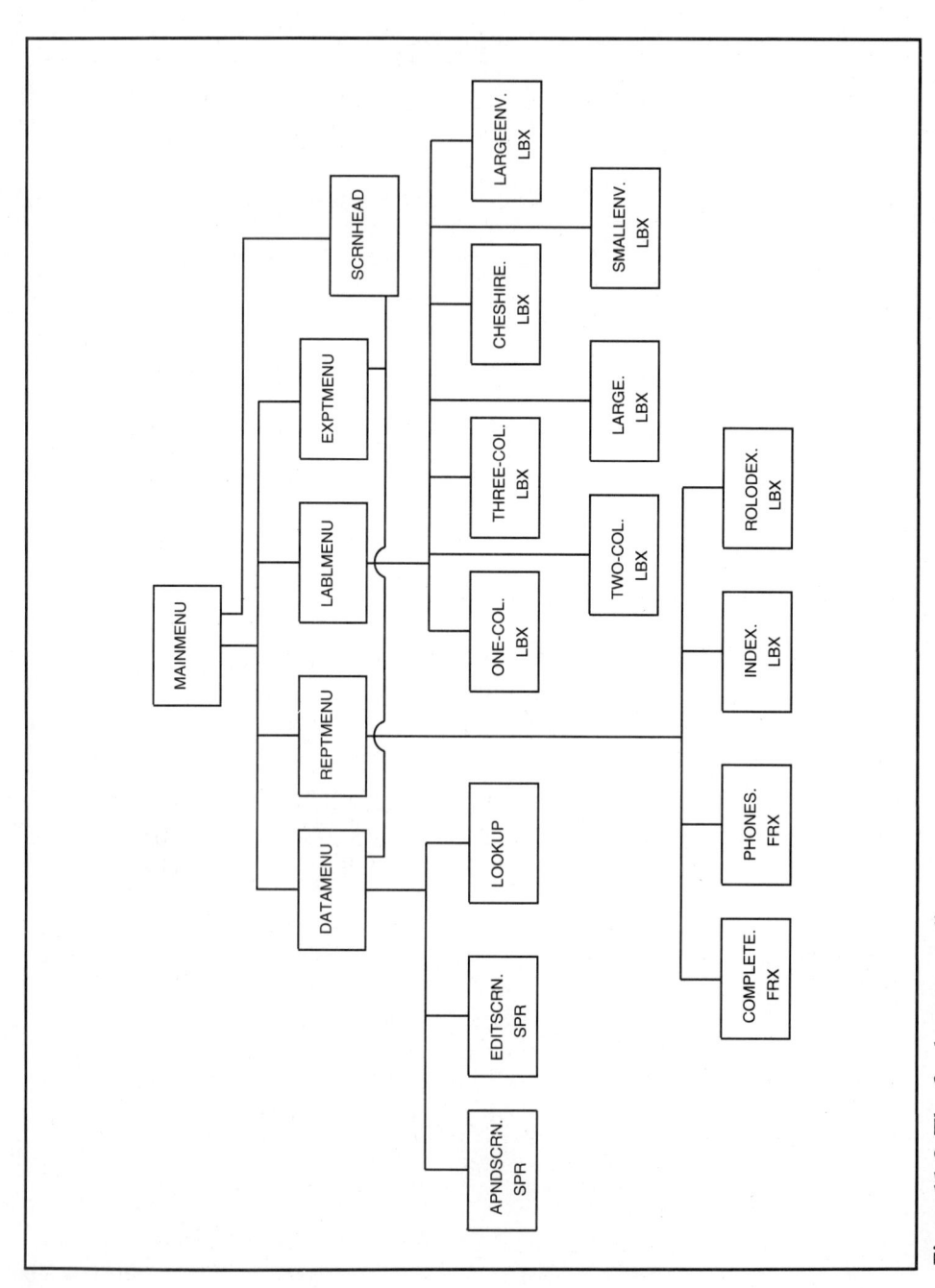

Figure 11.2: The final structure diagram

THE MAIN MENU

In a more complex program, there would be further formal analysis for each procedure. Often, this analysis would involve writing *pseudocode,* an outline of the exact step-by-step method that the final program will use, but written in plain English, with some of the details left out so that it is easy to follow. Pseudocode can often be translated into the final programming code rather easily.

In a program this simple, written in a programming language that is very much like plain English, more formal analysis is not necessary, but you do need to think about exactly what the main menu module will do before you write it.

To begin with, it should display a title screen, with the program name and copyright. If you were writing a commercial program, you might use an editor that lets you use line-drawing characters to create the title screen: making the letters out of the line characters can give you an attractive title. Here, though, you can simply display the program's name and copyright using regular characters in the center of the screen.

While the user is looking at the title screen, the program should **USE** the database file and index files, creating a slight delay before the main menu appears; you can also use a delaying loop to give the user enough time to read the title screen. The program code that is listed makes the loop count up to 1000, but if you have a fast or a slow computer, you may want to use a higher or lower number. At the same time, the program should **SET** environmental variables: for example, you should **SET TALK OFF**, so that FoxPro talk does not confuse the user. Another important environment command to use in programs is **SET SYSMENU OFF**, which prevents the user from accessing the FoxPro menu bar. If this command is omitted, the user will be able to access the menu bar in the usual ways—for example, pressing Alt-S to pull down the System menu popup—even if the menu bar is not visible.

Then, you can display the main menu with a heading at the top; the four choices on the structure diagram, plus Quit; and a line near the bottom asking the user to enter a choice. You will use a conventional menu program—a series of **@...SAY** statements to display the options and get the user's choice, followed by a **DO CASE**

> An easy way to create an attractive title screen is to draw it with an editor that lets you use line characters. Then, when you have the title screen that you want, just add an **@...SAY** statement at the beginning of each line—beginning with **@ 0,0**—to display the screen row by row. Of course, you must use quotation marks to enclose what you have drawn on each line, including any blank spaces that are needed.

statement that makes the program perform some action that depends on the choice that was entered. This menu program must be in a **DO WHILE** loop, so that the menu screen is displayed repeatedly as long as the user does not select Quit.

Under ordinary circumstances, you would probably use the screen generator to create the menu screen, so that you can center the choices easily and use graphic characters to add boxes. As an exercise, though, you will write this menu by hand, using a series of **@...SAY** commands: you should get experience with writing these programs before you get in the habit of generating them, just as you should learn to do arithmetic problems by hand before you start using a calculator.

To make it easy for the user to enter choices, you use the first letter of each choice as the entry. With **SET CONFIRM OFF**, if you use an **@...SAY...GET** statement to get the choice, and if you define the variable that the statement "GETs" as just one character long, then the user can just press a single key to make the choice, without pressing Enter afterwards. Because this keystroke fills up the field, FoxPro beeps and goes on without waiting for the user to press Enter, just as it does when you are doing data entry in a Browse window.

This makes it very convenient to move up and down a menu tree, but the beeps are a distraction when you are using the menu. When you are setting the environmental variables, then, you should also **SET BELL OFF**. Then you can make the menu system beep only if the user makes an error, by using the command **? CHR(7)**. Of course, the beep is useful when you are doing data entry, so that you know if you have filled a field; thus, you should **SET BELL ON** when the user is modifying the data (but **SET BELL OFF** again after that is done).

Finally, just before the user quits the program, you should return all the environment variables to their default setting, using the commands **SET TALK ON**, **SET SYSMENU ON**, **SET BELL ON**, and **SET DELETED OFF**. If someone is using this program as an application within FoxPro, rather than as a stand-alone application, they probably want the environment to be back at its default settings when they are through with it: you do not want to leave them with the

Deleted setting *on*, for example, because they might inadvertently overlook records that are marked for deletion at a later time, when they are working with another database. Remember when you are testing this program that if you have to interrupt it by pressing Esc, the environment settings that the program has created will still apply. Enter these commands in the Command window to return to the default environment.

With this background discussion, you should have no trouble understanding the listing in Figure 11.3, which is a very typical example of an older FoxPro/dBASE menu program. (Do not type this in yet: you will create a new directory for it in the next section.)

> This program uses a conventional form of capitalization meant to make it easier to read. The capitalization of commands, functions, and the names of fields and variables does not actually affect the way the program runs. Only the capitalization of string literals is significant.

```
*****************************************************
* MAILPOW.PRG
* a menu-driven, general purpose mailing-list program
*****************************************************

*------display the title screen
CLEAR
@ 11,34 SAY "MAILPOWER!"
@ 14,14 SAY "copyright: Advanced Technology Development Systems"

*------use database and set environment
SET TALK OFF
SET BELL OFF
SET SYSMENU OFF
SET DELETED ON

USE MAILLIST ORDER NAMES

*------delay to let user read screen
counter = 0
DO WHILE counter < 1000
    counter = counter + 1
ENDDO

*------create the main loop, to repeat the menu indefinitely
DO WHILE .T.

    *------create a variable to hold the user's choice
    choice = " "

    *------display main menu and get user's choice
    DO scrnhead WITH "Main Menu"
    @ 8,25 SAY "D - Data"
    @ 10,25 SAY "R - Reports"
    @ 12,25 SAY "L - Labels"
    @ 14,25 SAY "E - Export for mail merge"
    @ 16,25 SAY "Q - Quit MAILPOWER!"
    @ 22,26 SAY "What is your choice > " GET choice PICT "!"
    READ
```

Figure 11.3: The Mail Power! main menu program

```
*------perform option that user chose
*------or beep if choice was invalid
DO CASE
    CASE choice = "D"
        DO datamenu
    CASE choice = "R"
        DO reptmenu
    CASE choice = "L"
        DO lablmenu
    CASE choice = "E"
        DO exptmenu
    CASE choice = "Q"
        EXIT
    OTHERWISE
        ? CHR(7)
ENDCASE
ENDDO

*------close the database and return environment to
*------default settings before exiting.

CLOSE DATABASES
SET TALK ON
SET BELL ON
SET SYSMENU ON
SET DELETED OFF

*QUIT




*******************************************
*PROCEDURE SCRNHEAD
*a general purpose screen header
*called by the MAIN program and by
*procedures DATAMENU, REPTMENU, LABLMENU, EXPTMENU, LOOKUP
*******************************************

PROCEDURE scrnhead
PARAMETER menuname

CLEAR
@ 0,0   SAY "MAILPOWER! " + menuname
@ 0,70  SAY DATE()
@ 1,0   SAY "_____";
            +"_____"
```

Figure 11.3: The Mail Power! main menu program (continued)

Look carefully at how the main loop of this program works, since it is an excellent example of the basic forms of control flow, looping, and iteration. It is an infinite loop, with the condition **DO WHILE .T.** at the top. The only way to get out of it is by pressing Q to execute the command **EXIT**, which directs program control to the line following the **ENDDO**.

If you press another key instead of Q, either one of the **CASE** statements will execute a related program or the **OTHERWISE** statement will beep, depending on whether your choice was valid or invalid. Then, program control will be move to the next line after the **ENDCASE** of this **DO CASE** statement. That line is **ENDDO**, the end of the main loop, which directs control back to the beginning of this **DO WHILE** loop and displays the menu once again.

You will avoid a couple of common errors when you write this sort of program if you remember that the commands **CLEAR** and **choice** = " " must be inside the main loop. The variable *choice* must be made equal to a blank each time around, otherwise the value that it was given the last time through the loop would be displayed by the command **GET choice**, and the field where you enter your choice would not be blank. Of course, the screen also must be cleared each time the menu is displayed; otherwise the menu will just be superimposed on whatever was on the screen previously.

Remember, also, to use **GET** with **PICT** "!" in this sort of menu system, so the user can enter the letters in upper or lower case.

This menu could use a loop with the condition **DO WHILE choice** < > "Q" instead of the infinite **DO WHILE .T.** loop. If you do this, you would have to initialize the value of *choice* twice—once before the loop begins, so the condition is true the first time the program comes to the **DO WHILE** statement, and once within the loop, so *choice* is made a blank each time around. **DO WHILE .T.** saves you a tiny bit of typing. What is much more important, though, is that most people find that the **DO WHILE .T.** loop makes the program easier to follow. You can easily see what happens when the user selects Q, because it is right there next to the other selections in the **DO CASE** statement. There is no need to search for the beginning of the loop to find what choice lets the user get out of it—and this can be a significant advantage if you are trying to understand a long program.

It is also possible to use the commands following **ENDDO** within the **DO CASE** statement, following **CASE choice** = "Q". The program uses the command **EXIT** if the user selects Q, in order to break out of the loop and get to the commands that follow **ENDDO**. But why not save a line of code by putting those commands right in the **DO CASE**, where **EXIT** is now? The reason is, studies of structured programming have found that programs are easier to understand if control terminates at the end of each module. Though there may be cases where it is best to put **RETURN** or **QUIT** somewhere in the middle of a module, it does make the program harder to understand and maintain.

You can see the advantage in this example. To begin with, the program has an asterisk before **QUIT**, to make it a comment. When you are testing and debugging the program, you do not want to quit FoxPro and return to DOS each time you finish running it, because you need to use FoxPro to modify and retest it. When you are done with testing, though, you could delete the asterisk so **QUIT** is executed and the program returns the user to the operating system when it is done, rather than returning to FoxPro. Thus, you could make the program act as a stand-alone program rather than just an application within FoxPro. It obviously will be easier to make this change because **QUIT** is on the last line. Likewise, if you add any other environment settings in the course of developing the program, it is very easy to set them off by adding the commands at the end of the program.

Notice, also, how the SCRNHEAD module is used. Before displaying the menu, the main module of the program uses the command **DO scrnhead WITH "Main Menu"** to run the SCRNHEAD procedure at the end of the program, which displays the first few lines of the menu. After this procedure is done, control returns to the next lines in the main module, which display the menu choices further down on the screen.

It is always a temptation to include a bit of code that is this short in the module itself, rather than writing a separate module for it. Given how easy it is to use the editor to copy code from one module to another, it seems easier to write out the screen header four or five times rather than doing the little bit of thinking that is needed to put it in a separate procedure. You might believe that at first, but when you write a prototype of the program, and the client says that it is very good *but* that it would be nice to have the time as well as the date at the top of each menu screen, you will have to go back and modify the code in five different places. When you modify code in this way, it is very hard to make all five screen headers identical: the first time you do it, you will probably make a typographical error and put the date in the wrong place in one of the screen headers. When you get them all right, the client might ask for more changes in the header. By this time, you will have learned the hard way that your job would have been much easier if you had put the screen header in a separate module in the first place.

As you can see, then, this old-fashioned sort of menu illustrates many basic principles of structured programming. What you learn here about control flow and modular programming will be useful to you in virtually any program you ever write.

STUB TESTING

Just as it is difficult to write a program all at once, it is also difficult to test a program all at once. If you wait until all of your modules are written before doing any testing, you will probably spend more time than you would like wondering which module has the bug that is making it come out wrong.

MAINMENU.PRG calls four submenu programs. To test it without actually writing all the submenu programs (and all the programs that *they* call), it is common to write *stubs*. A stub is a "placeholder" program that does something trivial to let you test the program without having to write the entire module it substitutes for. For our testing purposes we will write stubs which have the same names as the submenus but which just clear the screen and ask you to press any key. After you make sure the main menu works properly, you will replace the stubs with the actual programs that are needed. Then, in the next sections, we will stub test the routines the submenu programs call.

First, you must create the database and index files that this program needs. To avoid confusion, you should create a new subdirectory to hold your work.

1. If necessary, start FoxPro; if you want, enter **CLEAR** to clear the screen. To create a new subdirectory, enter the command **RUN MD \MAILPOW**. To make that into the current directory, enter the command **RUN CD \MAILPOW**. Now, new files you create will be in the MAILPOW directory.

2. Select New from the File menu. Select the Database radio button and select OK. Use the Structure dialog box to create a new database file with the structure shown in Figure 11.4. When you are sure the structure is correct, select OK.

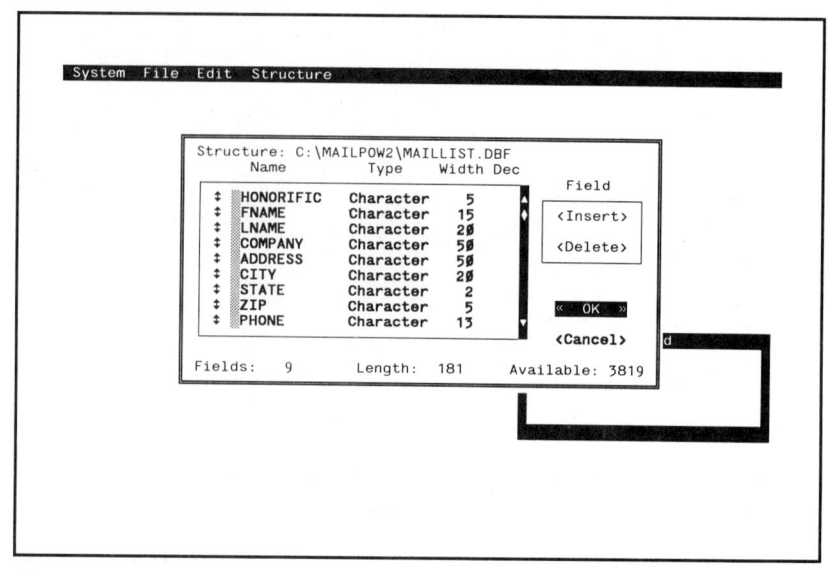

```
┌─────────────────────────────────────────────────────────┐
│ System  File  Edit  Structure                           │
├─────────────────────────────────────────────────────────┤
│                                                         │
│         ┌─────────────────────────────────────┐         │
│         │ Structure: C:\MAILPOW2\MAILLIST.DBF │         │
│         │   Name         Type     Width Dec   │         │
│         │ ↕ HONORIFIC   Character    5      │ Field   │
│         │ ↕ FNAME       Character   15      │ <Insert>│
│         │ ↕ LNAME       Character   20      │         │
│         │ ↕ COMPANY     Character   50      │ <Delete>│
│         │ ↕ ADDRESS     Character   50      │         │
│         │ ↕ CITY        Character   20      │         │
│         │ ↕ STATE       Character    2      │         │
│         │ ↕ ZIP         Character    5      │ « OK » │
│         │ ↕ PHONE       Character   13      │         │
│         │                                     │<Cancel>│
│         │ Fields:   9    Length:  181  Available: 3819 │
│         └─────────────────────────────────────┘         │
│                                                         │
└─────────────────────────────────────────────────────────┘
```

Figure 11.4: The structure of the Mail Power! database file

3. Create the two indexes you need: Enter the commands

   INDEX ON ZIP TAG ZIPS

   and then enter the command

   INDEX ON LNAME + FNAME TAG NAMES

   If you prefer, you can use the menu system to create the same indexes. Notice that it is not necessary to use UPPER (LNAME + FNAME) as the key to your index: because data entry will only be done through this program, you can make sure that all data will be entered in uppercase.

4. Create the main menu program. Select New from the File menu. Select the Program radio button, and select OK. Type in the entire listing of MAILPOW.PRG shown in Figure 11.3, in the previous section. When you are done, select Save As from the File menu. Name the program MAILPOW.

5. Add the stub procedures, shown in Figure 11.5, to the end of MAILPOW.PRG.

```
*****************************************************
* DATAMENU PROCEDURE
* stub for testing
* called by the main menu
*****************************************************

PROCEDURE DATAMENU

CLEAR
? "STUB OF DATA MENU FOR TESTING"
WAIT


*****************************************************
* REPTMENU PROCEDURE
* stub for testing
* called by the main menu
*****************************************************

PROCEDURE REPTMENU

CLEAR
? "STUB OF REPORT MENU FOR TESTING"
WAIT

*****************************************************
* LABLMENU PROCEDURE
* stub for testing
* called by the main menu
*****************************************************

PROCEDURE LABLMENU

CLEAR
? "STUB OF LABEL MENU FOR TESTING"
WAIT

*****************************************************
* EXPTMENU PROCEDURE
* stub for testing
* called by the main menu
*****************************************************

PROCEDURE EXPTMENU

CLEAR
? "STUB OF EXPORT MENU FOR TESTING"
WAIT
```

Figure 11.5: Stubs for testing

6. Now you are ready for testing. Enter **DO MAILPOW**. The Main Menu screen should appear, as shown in Figure 11.6. (If you have a mouse, just move the pointer to the side during testing.) Try all the menu choices. Try some invalid choices also to see if the program beeps. If there are errors, select Cancel to stop execution of the program (if necessary, press Esc), and edit the program file to correct the error. Once you have made the correction, enter **DO MAILPOW** again. After each correction, redo all your testing, as if you were starting from scratch. When you are done, press Q to quit.

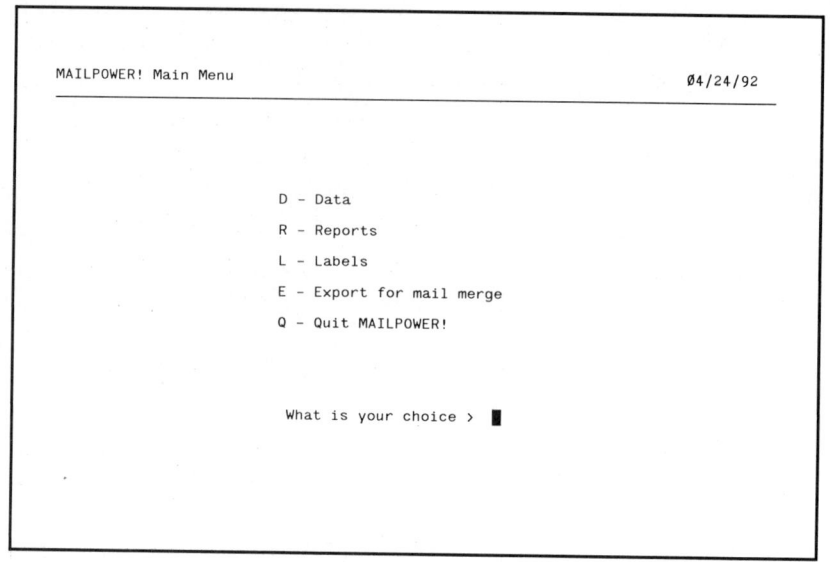

```
MAILPOWER! Main Menu                                      04/24/92
_____


                    D - Data
                    R - Reports
                    L - Labels
                    E - Export for mail merge
                    Q - Quit MAILPOWER!



                    What is your choice > ▮
```

Figure 11.6: The Mail Power! Main Menu screen

Keep testing the program until you are sure this module runs correctly. Since you are testing just one module, and its logic is quite straightforward, it should be easy for you to correct any bugs.

REPORTS AND MAILING LABELS

To add the report and label menus, you will just use FoxPro's report and label generators to create the forms you need, and you will write two simple menu programs to tie them together. As you will see, these programs are very similar to the main menu program, so they will solidify your understanding of the principles that program illustrates. In a professional program, you would add error checking to make sure the printer is on before printing, but this introductory exercise will omit this feature.

THE REPORT MENU

The Mail Power! Report menu will let the user print a complete report that contains all the data in the mailing list, and (since the user might find it handy) a report with just names and telephone numbers. Since there are standard FoxPro label forms that let you print out the data on 3" × 5" (index card size) Rolodex cards or on smaller 4" × 2¼" Rolodex cards, you can also give the user these options on the Report menu.

When you save these forms, there is no need to save the environment. The program itself makes sure that the proper database file and index is in use when the report or labels are produced, so the **REPORT FORM** and **LABEL FORM** commands that the program uses to produce them will not have to include the ENVIRONMENT option that makes them use these saved environments.

1. You must create the first two reports by using the report layout window. The database file should already be in use from the program testing; if it is not, enter **USE MAILLIST**. Select New from the File menu. Select the Report radio button, and select OK.

2. Select Page Layout from the Report menu. Make the top margin 6, the bottom margin 6, the printer indent 5, and the right margin column 75. Then select OK.

3. Move the cursor to the second line of the page header band. Type **MAILPOWER! Complete Report**. Press Enter to stop editing the text and the space bar to select the text object. Select Center from the Report menu to center it, and press Enter to deselect it.

4. Move the cursor to the second line of the detail band. Select Add Line from the Report menu to add a line to the detail band.

5. Begin entering expressions in the detail band. Select Field from the Report menu. In the text box to the right of the Expression text button, enter **PROPER(LNAME)**. Move the cursor so the width is entered automatically. Then select OK.

6. Move the cursor down a line; if necessary, move it to the left margin. Press the right arrow key five times. Select Field from the Report menu, and, in the text box, enter the expression **PROPER(FNAME)** and place it as in Step 5.

7. Move the cursor down a line and to the left margin. Place the field expression **PHONE**, as in Step 5.

8. Move the cursor up one line and right to column 21. Use the menu to place the expression **PROPER(COMPANY)** as above.

9. Move the cursor to immediately below the P of PROPER (COMPANY). Place the expression **PROPER(ADDRESS)**, as above.

10. Move the cursor immediately below the P of PROPER (ADDRESS). Place the expression **PROPER(CITY)**. Move the cursor to column 43, and place the expression **STATE**. Move the cursor to column 48, and place the expression **ZIP**.

11. Move the cursor to the footer band. Select Remove Line from the Report menu to remove one line. Move the cursor to the second line of the three in the page footer band and to the left margin.

12. Now, since the report may be long, you should add page numbers. Select Field from the Report menu, then select the Expression text button to call up the expression builder. In the text box, type "**Page Number** " (do not forget the quotation marks). Select the String popup control and select +, select the String popup control again and select LTRIM( ), then select the String popup control once more and select STR( ). From the scrollable list of memory variables, select _PAGENO. Delete the two commas in the STR( ) function, since you do not need to add numbers to specify the width of the string or the number of decimal places. If you want, select the Verify text button to make sure the expression is valid. The expression should look like Figure 11.7. Select the OK text button to return to the Report Expression dialog box, and select the OK text button to place the expression. Press the space bar to select the expression and then select Center from the Report menu to center it. Press Enter to deselect it.

13. You now have the complete report form, which is shown in Figure 11.8. Select Save As from the File menu and, when the Save Report As dialog box appears, type the name **COMPLETE**, and then select the Save text button to save the file, and select No so the environment is not saved.

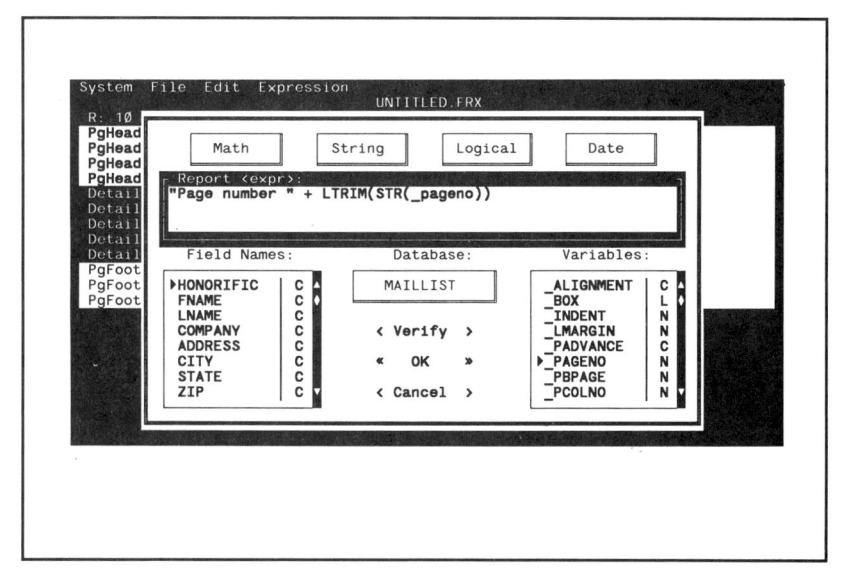

Figure 11.7: The expression to display the page number

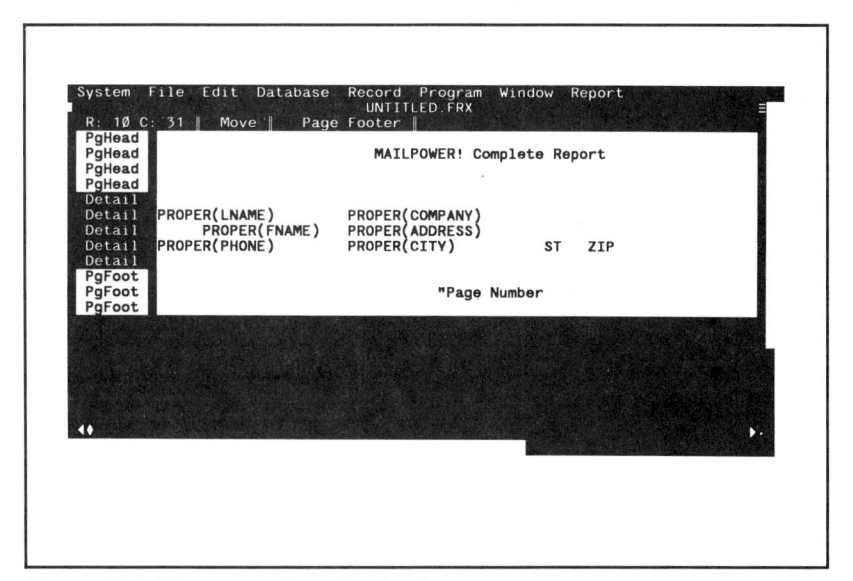

Figure 11.8: The report form for the first report

14. Now, to create the second report, alter this form so it produces a report with just names and telephone numbers. Remove the second and third lines of text in the detail band

by putting the cursor on them, selecting Remove Line from the Report menu, and entering **Y** to confirm that you want to remove the objects on the lines. Move the cursor to PROPER(COMPANY) and then select and delete this expression. With the cursor on column 22, place the expression PROPER(FNAME). With the cursor on column 40, place the expression PHONE. Move the cursor to the title, select Text from the Report menu so you can edit the title, and change it to **MAILPOWER! Phone Report**. When you are done editing, select this text object and select Center from the Report menu to center it. Then deselect it.

15. Select Save As from the File menu. When the Save Report As dialog box appears, type **PHONES** in the text box, make sure the Environment check box is not checked, and select Save to save the report under this name. The final form of this report is shown in Figure 11.9. Then close the report layout window.

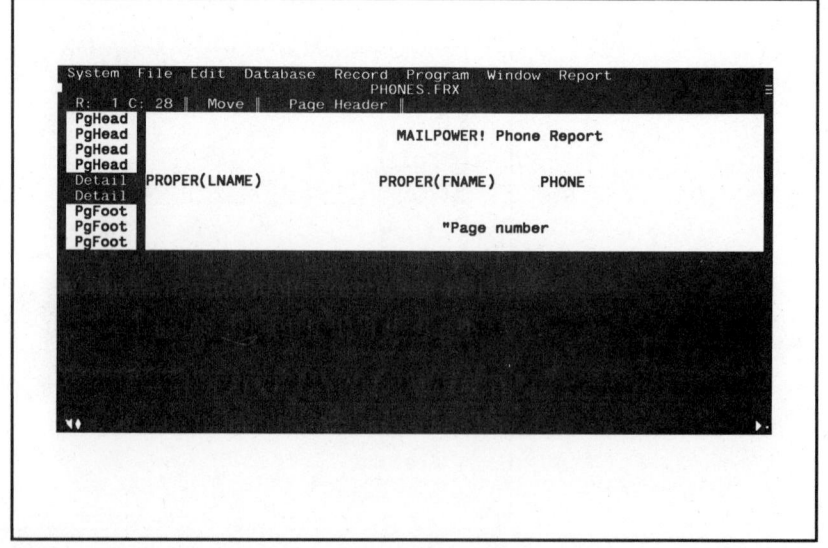

Figure 11.9: The report form for the second report

USING SUBSTR( ) FOR FINE-TUNING

The other two reports are created by using the label layout window. No doubt, you noticed that your first report just barely fit into the width of the report layout window. This is because some fields of this database are very long. Since Label forms are generally narrower, you should shorten some of these fields when you fill out these forms.

You can do this by using the function SUBSTR( ), which lets you use a substring of any character expression. This function has the following form:

SUBSTR(<*char exp, num exp1*>[<, *num exp2*>])

Char exp represents the character expression that you want to use a substring of. *Num exp1* is a numeric expression that you use to specify which character you want the substring to begin with. *Num exp2* is an optional numeric expression that you use to specify the length of the substring; if this expression is omitted, the substring continues until the end of the string.

For example, the function

SUBSTR("abcdefghijkl",1,3)

would return the value *abc*. This substring starts with the first character of the string specified and is three characters long. To give another example, the function

SUBSTR("abcdefghijkl",10)

would return the value *jkl,* since this substring starts with the tenth character of the string specified and continues to the end.

In the exercises below, you will use this function to make a field fit in the width of the label form. For example, if the label form is 40 characters wide, you will use the function

SUBSTR(PROPER(ADDRESS),1,40)

to enter its address. This function returns a substring that begins with the first character of PROPER(ADDRESS) and includes 40 characters.

If the address field is more than 40 characters wide, this function will simply cut off its final characters, so it fits in the label form.

REPORTS USING LABEL FORMS

The first label form you will use to create a report is wide enough for all the fields of your database. The second is narrower, though, so you will need to use SUBSTR( ) with it.

In order to center the fields on these label forms, we want to skip a few lines. Some releases of FoxPro require you to put characters on the first lines of label forms, and they display an alert saying there is an error if you try to save the form when these fields are blank. To avoid this potential problem, the forms will have " " on the first line, a string consisting of the blank character: FoxPro will be satisfied that you are printing something on that line, even if you are just printing a blank space.

1. To create the next "report," select New from the File menu. Select the Label radio button, and select OK. When the label layout screen appears, select Layout from the Label menu and select 3" × 5" Rolodex. Then fill out the label layout screen as illustrated in Figure 11.10. Select Save As from the File menu, select the Environment check box so it is not checked, and save the label form, using the name INDEX.

2. To create the next "report," select 4" × 2¼" Rolodex from the Label menu. The new label layout will keep the fields that were there, and you can edit them so they they look like the form shown in Figure 11.11. Then select Save As from the File menu, make sure the Environment check box is not checked, and save the label form using the name ROLODEX.

3. To tie these forms together, create the menu using the code shown in Figure 11.12, which is very similar to the menu programs you created earlier. (It is probably easiest to create it by editing an earlier menu program and saving it under a new name.) Select Save As from the File menu and save it under the name REPTMENU.PRG, overwriting the file you created earlier to hold the stub of that program. The menu screen it will create is shown in Figure 11.13.

To save time and effort in testing, you can type **&&** before the words TO PRINT to make them comments for now, as they are in the listing in Figure 11.12, since you do not want the reports printed each time you test the program. It is easy to delete these ampersands later.

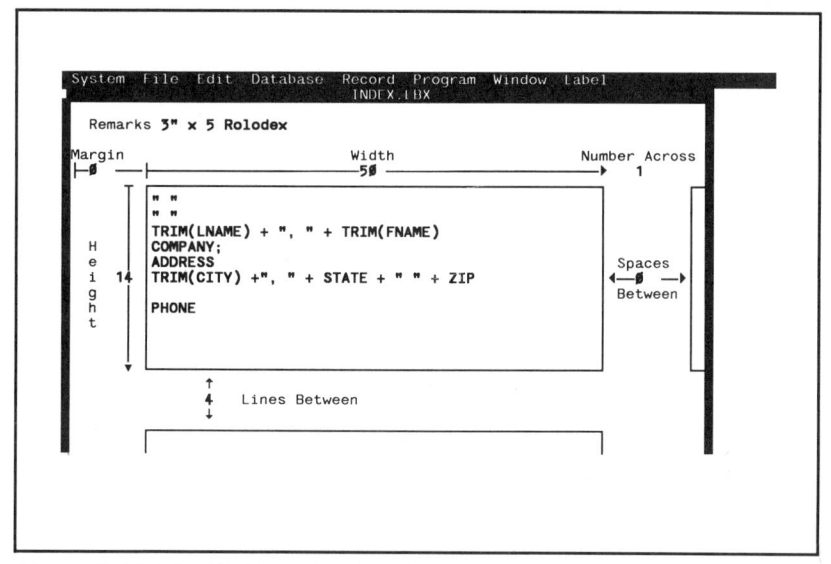

Figure 11.10: The label form for the third report

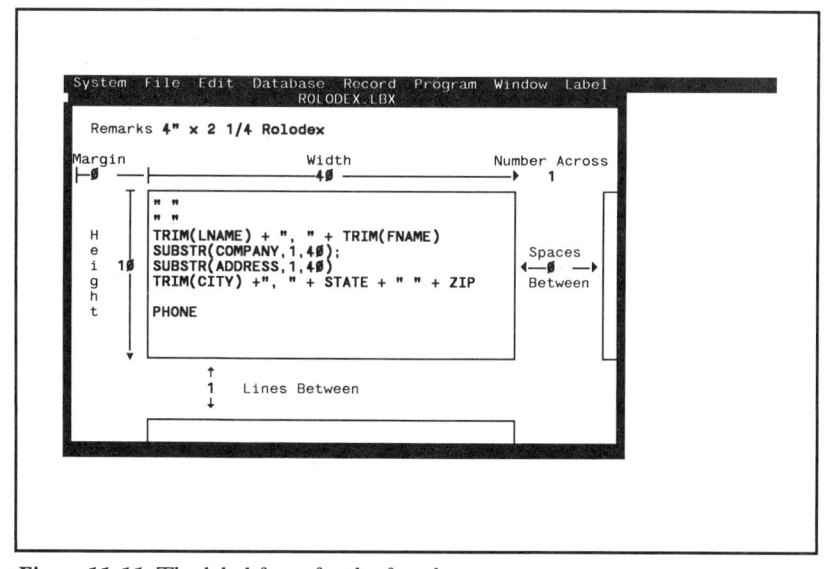

Figure 11.11: The label form for the fourth report

```
******************************************************
*REPTMENU procedure
*The report submenu for Mail Power
*called by the main module
******************************************************

PROCEDURE reptmenu

*------create the main loop, to repeat the menu indefinitely

DO WHILE .T.

    *------create a variable to hold the user's choice
    choice = " "

    *------display main menu and get user's choice
    DO scrnhead WITH "Report Submenu"
    @ 8,25 SAY "C - Complete Report"
    @ 10,25 SAY "P - Phone Numbers and Names"
    @ 12,25 SAY "3 - 3 x 5 Rolodex Cards"
    @ 14,25 SAY "4 - 4 x 2 1/2 Rolodex Cards"
    @ 16,25 SAY "R - Return to the Main Menu"
    @ 22,26 SAY "What is your choice > " GET choice PICT "!"
    READ

    *------perform option that user chose
    *------or beep if choice was invalid
    DO CASE
        CASE choice = "C"
            REPORT FORM complete     &&TO PRINT
            WAIT
        CASE choice = "P"
            REPORT FORM phones       &&TO PRINT
            WAIT
        CASE choice = "3"
            LABEL FORM index         &&TO PRINT
            WAIT
        CASE choice = "4"
            LABEL FORM rolodex       &&TO PRINT
            WAIT
        CASE choice = "R"
            EXIT
        OTHERWISE
            ? CHR(7)
    ENDCASE

ENDDO
RETURN
```

Figure 11.12: The Mail Power! Report menu program

4. In the Command window, Enter **DO MAINMENU** and test all the new options you have just added.

THE LABEL MENU

After you have finished testing your Report menu, you can create the Mail Power! Label menu in much the same way. The easiest way is to

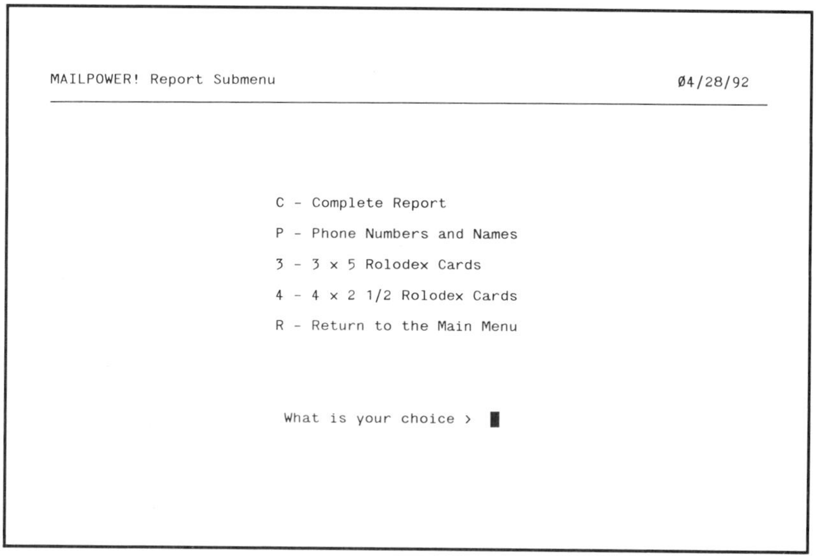

```
MAILPOWER! Report Submenu                                    04/28/92
_____



                      C - Complete Report
                      P - Phone Numbers and Names
                      3 - 3 x 5 Rolodex Cards
                      4 - 4 x 2 1/2 Rolodex Cards
                      R - Return to the Main Menu



                      What is your choice >  ▮
```

Figure 11.13: The Mail Power! Report menu screen

create the new label forms by modifying an existing form, removing what you do not need:

1. Enter **MODI LABEL ROLODEX** to use the previous form. Put the cursor on the T of TRIM(LNAME), and press the Backspace key to delete the previous lines, until the line with the name is the first line of the form. At this point, Backspace will no longer have any effect. Then delete the line that says PHONE, and press Backspace to delete this field name and to move the cursor until it is on the same line as City, State, and Zip, but be careful not to delete any of the field names on this line. Move the cursor back to the line that has the name, and edit it so it reads

   TRIM(FNAME) + " " + TRIM(LNAME)

2. Select Layout from the Label menu and select the first standard format on the list, $3^{1}/_{2}'' \times {}^{15}/_{16}'' \times 1$. The fields all remain on this new form. Since the width of this column is 35, change the name line to

   SUBSTR(TRIM(FNAME),1,14) + " " + TRIM(LNAME)

Likewise, edit the company and address line, so they read

SUBSTR(COMPANY,1,35);

and

SUBSTR(ADDRESS,1,35)

3. Select Save As from the File menu and save this under the name **ONE-COL** (since it produces one-column labels). Make sure not to save the environment.

Notice that the name line was altered so that the first name is truncated if the name is too long to fit in the label: at most, the name can consist of 14 characters from the first name, one blank, and twenty characters from the last name, for a total of 35 characters.

Now, you should continue to produce labels with all the other default layouts on the label menu. Produce them as you did above, by selecting the layouts listed below, editing the character expressions where needed, and selecting Save As from the File menu to rename them. (The first few will not need editing, as they use the same size labels in a two-column and three-column format.)

Use the following names and field expressions:

Layout	3½″ × 15/16″ × 2
Name	TWO-COL
Fields	SUBSTR(TRIM(FNAME),1,14) + " " + TRIM(LNAME)
	SUBSTR(COMPANY,1,35)
	SUBSTR(ADDRESS,1,35)
	TRIM(CITY) + " " + STATE + ", " + ZIP

Layout	3½″ × 15/16″ × 3
Name	THRE-COL
Fields	SUBSTR(TRIM(FNAME),1,14) + " " + TRIM(LNAME)
	SUBSTR(COMPANY,1,35)

SUBSTR(ADDRESS,1,35)

TRIM(CITY) + " " + STATE + ", " + ZIP

Layout $4'' \times 1^{7}/_{16}'' \times 1$

Name LARGE

Fields SUBSTR(TRIM(FNAME)1,11) + " " + TRIM(LNAME)

SUBSTR(COMPANY,1,32)

SUBSTR(ADDRESS,1,32)

TRIM(CITY) + " " + STATE + ", " + ZIP

Layout $3^{2}/_{10}'' \times {}^{11}/_{12}'' \times 3$

Name CHESHIRE

Fields TRIM(FNAME) + " " + TRIM(LNAME)

SUBSTR(COMPANY,1,40)

SUBSTR(ADDRESS,1,40)

TRIM(CITY) + " " + STATE + ", " + ZIP

Layout $6^{1}/_{2}'' \times 3^{5}/_{8}$ ENVELOPE

Name SMALLENV

Fields " "

" "

" "

" "

" "

SPACE(15) + TRIM(FNAME) + " " + TRIM(LNAME)

SPACE(15) + COMPANY;

SPACE(15) + ADDRESS

SPACE(15) + TRIM(CITY) + " " + STATE + ", " + ZIP

Layout	9⅞″ × 7⅛ ENVELOPE
Name	LARGEENV
Fields	" "
	" "
	" "
	" "
	" "

SPACE(25) + TRIM(FNAME) + " " + TRIM(LNAME)

SPACE(25) + COMPANY;

SPACE(25) + ADDRESS

SPACE(25) + TRIM(CITY) + " " + STATE + ", " + ZIP

Once you are done creating all the label forms, write the Label menu program to tie them together, using the code shown in Figure 11.14, which will display the menu screen shown in Figure 11.15. Test all the new options you just added.

```
****************************************************
*LABLMENU procedure
*The label submenu for Mail Power
*called by the main module
****************************************************

PROCEDURE lablmenu

*------create the main loop, to repeat the menu indefinitely
SET ORDER TO ZIPS
```

Figure 11.14: The Mail Power! Label menu program

```
DO WHILE .T.
    *------create a variable to hold the user's choice
        choice = " "

    *------display main menu and get user's choice
        DO scrnhead WITH "Label Submenu"
        @ 6,25 SAY "1 - One-column labels"
        @ 8,25 SAY "2 - Two-column labels"
        @ 10,25 SAY "3 - Three-column labels"
        @ 12,25 SAY "L - Large one-column labels"
        @ 14,25 SAY "C - Cheshire labels"
        @ 16,25 SAY "S - Small Envelopes"
        @ 18,25 SAY "W - Wide Envelopes"
        @ 20,25 SAY "R - Return to Main Menu"
        @ 22,26 SAY "What is your choice > " GET choice PICT "!"
        READ

    *------perform option that user chose
    *------or beep if choice was invalid
        DO CASE
            CASE choice = "1"
                LABEL FORM one-col        &&TO PRINT
                WAIT
            CASE choice = "2"
                LABEL FORM two-col        &&TO PRINT
                WAIT
            CASE choice = "3"
                LABEL FORM thre-col       &&TO PRINT
                WAIT
            CASE choice = "L"
                LABEL FORM large          &&TO PRINT
                WAIT
            CASE choice = "C"
                LABEL FORM cheshire       &&TO PRINT
                WAIT
            CASE choice = "S"
                LABEL FORM smallenv       &&TO PRINT
                WAIT
            CASE choice = "W"
                LABEL FORM largeenv       &&TO PRINT
                WAIT
            CASE choice = "R"
                EXIT
            OTHERWISE
                ? CHR(7)
        ENDCASE

ENDDO

SET ORDER TO NAMES

RETURN
```

Figure 11.14: The Mail Power! Label menu program (continued)

The only thing new about this menu is that it begins with the command **SET ORDER TO ZIPS**, so the labels are produced in zip code order, and it ends with the command **SET ORDER TO NAMES**, so the records are in alphabetical order again when control returns from this menu to the rest of the program.

```
MAILPOWER! Label Submenu                                04/28/92



                    1 - One-column labels
                    2 - Two-column labels
                    3 - Three-column labels
                    L - Large one-column labels
                    C - Cheshire labels
                    S - Small Envelopes
                    W - Wide Envelopes
                    R - Return to Main Menu
                    What is your choice >  ■
```

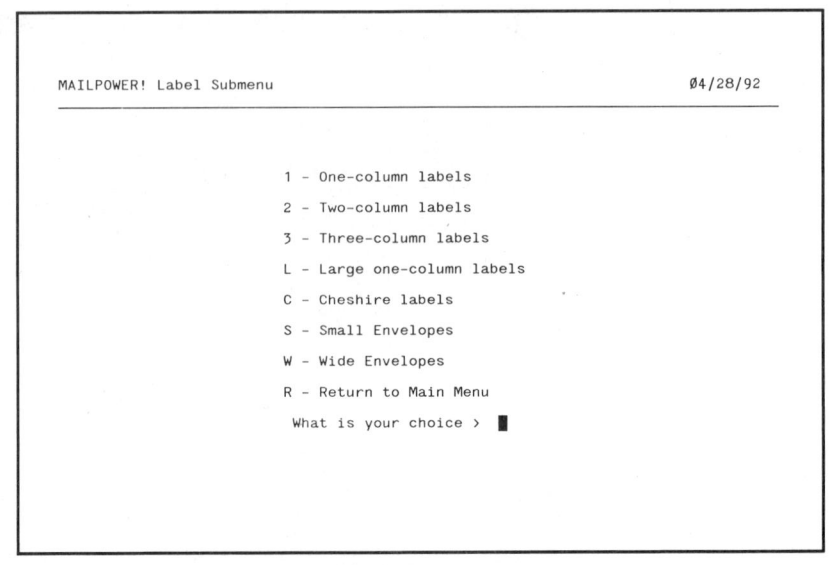

Figure 11.15: The Mail Power! Label menu screen

EXPORTING FOR MAIL-MERGE

You have one more simple menu to write to let the user export the data to a text file to use in mail-merge. It uses a conventional menu system, like the ones you have already created, to let the user choose among the options of the **COPY** command that export the data to different types of files. The command **COPY TO** includes optional clauses that let you copy to Multiplan, Lotus 1-2-3, Symphony, and Excel as well as to other file formats. For complete details, see COPY TO in the help window.

This exercise will just export data to three formats, using the following commands:

- **COPY TO** <*file name*> **TYPE SDF** creates a system data format file, an ASCII text file where records have a fixed length and there is a new line at the end of each record. Fields are not delimited, and leading or trailing blanks are retained so the fields have a uniform length in all records.

- **COPY TO** <*file name*> **TYPE DELIMITED** creates a delimited file, an ASCII text file where character fields are surrounded by quotation marks and fields are separated by commas. There is a new line at the end of each record.

- **COPY TO** <*file name*> **TYPE DELIMITED WITH TAB** is like TYPE DELIMITED except that fields are separated with tabs rather than with commas.

You can use other variations on **COPY TO** to add other options if you want.

This module of the MAILPOWER program is shown in Figure 11.16, and the menu it produces is shown in Figure 11.17. After entering it, you should test all its options. The only thing new about this menu is the command **SET SAFETY OFF** at the beginning. This command lets the program overwrite existing files without displaying a FoxPro alert and getting confirmation from the user. The program can continue to export data to the file named EXPORT.TXT without getting confirmation each time in order to overwrite the last version of that file. At the end of this module, Safety is set on once again.

```
****************************************************
*EXPTMENU procedure
*The export submenu for Mail Power
*called by the main module
****************************************************

PROCEDURE exptmenu

*------create the main loop, to repeat the menu indefinitely

SET SAFETY OFF

DO WHILE .T.
    *------create a variable to hold the user's choice
    choice = " "

    *------display main menu and get user's choice
    DO scrnhead WITH "Export Submenu"
    @ 8,25 SAY "S - Export to SDF File"
    @ 10,25 SAY "C - Export to Comma Delimited File"
    @ 12,25 SAY "T - Export to Tab Delimited File"
    @ 14,25 SAY "R - Return to the Main Menu"
    @ 22,26 SAY "What is your choice > " GET choice PICT "!"
    READ
```

Figure 11.16: The program to export data for mail-merge

```
       *------perform option that user chose
       *------or beep if choice was invalid
       DO CASE
           CASE choice = "S"
               COPY TO export.txt TYPE SDF
           CASE choice = "C"
               COPY TO export.txt TYPE DELIMITED
           CASE choice = "T"
               COPY TO export.txt TYPE DELIMITED WITH TAB
           CASE choice = "R"
               EXIT
           OTHERWISE
               ? CHR(7)
       ENDCASE
       IF choice = "S" .OR. choice = "C" .OR. choice = "T"
           CLEAR
           dummy = " "
           @ 10,10 SAY "The data has been copied to a file";
                                   + " named EXPORT.TXT"
           @ 12,20 SAY "Press any key to continue... " GET dummy
           READ
       ENDIF
ENDDO

SET SAFETY ON

RETURN
```

Figure 11.16: The program to export data for mail-merge (continued)

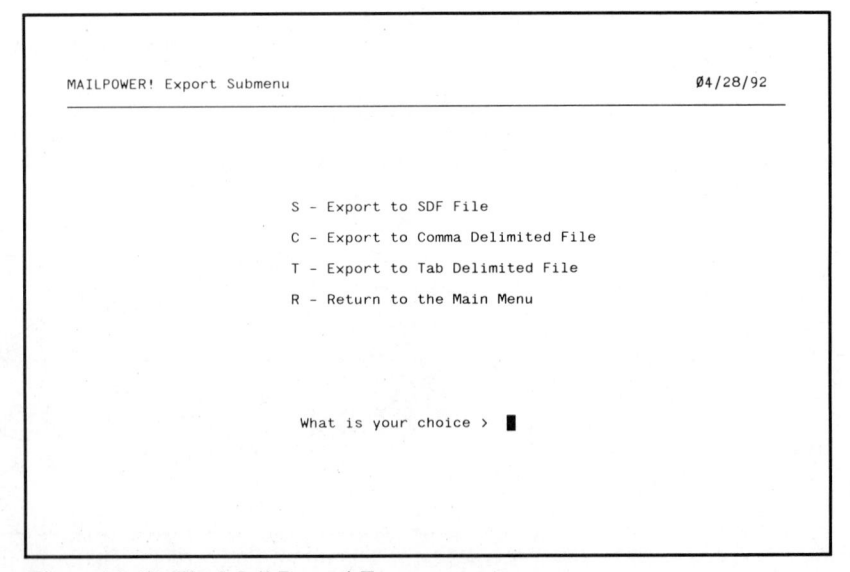

```
MAILPOWER! Export Submenu                                    04/28/92
_____




                       S - Export to SDF File

                       C - Export to Comma Delimited File

                       T - Export to Tab Delimited File

                       R - Return to the Main Menu




                              What is your choice >  ■
```

Figure 11.17: The Mail Power! Export menu screen

THE DATA SUBMENU

You still have to create the most complex part of the program—the data menu and the modules that it calls to let the user edit, append, look up, and delete records. The menu module itself should be easy for you to do, involving two main steps:

1. Leave the procedure heading, but delete the stub of code you wrote under the DATAMENU procedure earlier.
2. Instead, type in the code for the data submenu as it is listed in Figure 11.18. The menu screen is shown in Figure 11.19. As you can see, this menu is very similar to the menus you created previously.

```
****************************************************
*DATAMENU PROCEDURE
*The Data submenu for Mail Power
*called by the main module
****************************************************


*------create the main loop, to repeat the menu indefinitely
DO WHILE .T.

    *------create a variable to hold the user's choice
    choice = " "

    *------display the menu and get user's choice
    DO scrnhead WITH "Data Submenu"
    @ 8,25 SAY "A - Add a new entry"
    @ 10,25 SAY "E - Edit an entry"
    @ 12,25 SAY "D - Delete an entry"
    @ 14,25 SAY "L - Look up an entry"
    @ 16,25 SAY "F - Finalize deletions"
    @ 18,25 SAY "R - Return to the Main Menu"
    @ 22,26 SAY "What is your choice > " GET choice PICT "!"

    READ

    *------perform option that user chose
    *------or beep if choice was invalid
    DO CASE
        CASE choice = "A"
              *------append using custom screen
                 APPEND BLANK
                 SET BELL ON
                 DO apndscrn.spr
                 SET BELL OFF
        CASE choice = "E"
              *------find record user wants and edit
              *------using format screen if found
                 mfound = .F.
                 DO LOOKUP
```

Figure 11.18: The code for the Data menu

```
                    IF .NOT. EOF()
                       SET BELL ON
                       DO editscrn.spr
                       SET BELL OFF
                    ENDIF
               CASE choice = "D"
                    DO LOOKUP
                    IF .NOT. EOF()
                       DELETE
                    ENDIF
               CASE choice = "L"
                    *------use LOOKUP to look up and display the entry
                    DO LOOKUP
               CASE choice = "F"
                    *------use screen program to tell user to wait
                    *------and to PACK
                    DO waitmesg.spr
               CASE choice = "R"
                    EXIT
               OTHERWISE
                    ? CHR(7)
          ENDCASE

ENDDO
RETURN
```

Figure 11.18: The code for the Data menu (continued)

```
MAILPOWER! Data Submenu                                      04/24/92
_____




                       A - Add a new entry

                       E - Edit an entry

                       D - Delete an entry

                       L - Look up an entry

                       F - Finalize deletions

                       R - Return to the Main Menu


                       What is your choice >  ▮
```

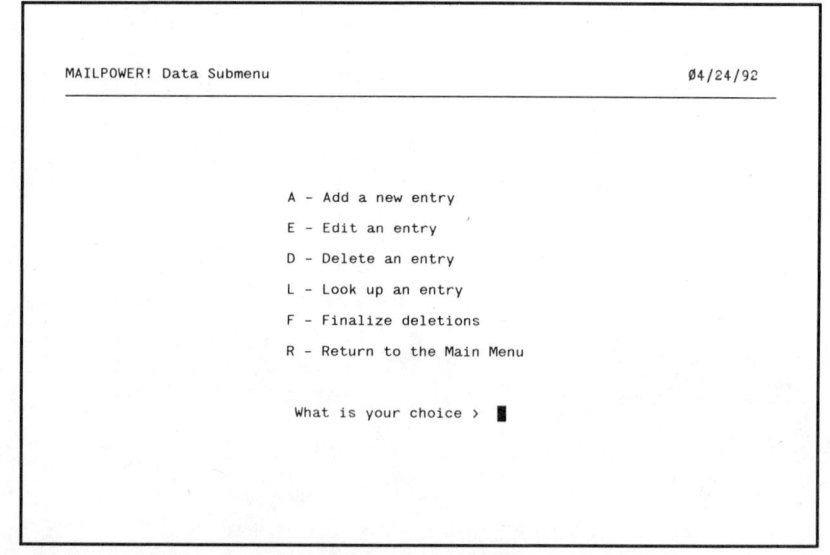

Figure 11.19: The screen displayed by the Data menu code

STUBS FOR TESTING

To test this menu, you need to create stubs of the LOOKUP procedure and of the screens APNDSCRN.SPR, EDITSCRN.SPR, and WAITMESG.SPR which it calls.

The actual LOOKUP procedure will let the user enter a name and will search for it in the database file. If it is not found, it will make EOF( ) true. EOF( ), the end-of-file function, becomes true if a SEEK or LOCATE FOR command is unsuccessful in finding any record that matches the search criterion, and it also becomes true if you try to move the pointer beyond the last record of the database file.

After doing LOOKUP, the DATAMENU procedure deletes or lets the user edit or delete the record if EOF( ) is not true. For testing, you can create a stub of the LOOKUP procedure that simply makes sure that EOF( ) is not true by executing the command GO TOP, to move the pointer to the first record. The stubs of the screen programs must be in separate files, with the names APNDSCRN.SPR, EDITSCRN.SPR and WAITMESG.SPR: they cannot be in procedures. These stubs just get a keystroke from the user and then return to the calling program.

Notice that stubs of some of the screen programs are not needed for testing. For example, the stub of LOOKUP always makes EOF( ) false, so NOTFOUND.SPR, which displays a message when EOF( ) is true, is never used, and no stub of it is needed.

Test the DATAMENU procedure:

1. Enter the program stubs shown in Figure 11.20. Remember that the LOOKUP procedure goes in the MAILPOW.PRG file but that APNDSCRN.SPR, EDITSCRN.SPR, and WAITMESG.SPR must go in separate files with those names.

2. Enter **DO MAILPOW**. Press *D* at the main menu to use the Data menu, and try the menu options. Try making an error also, to make sure the program beeps. When you have finished testing, press *R* to return to the main menu and *Q* to quit.

```
*****************************************************
*LOOKUP PROCEDURE
*stub for testing
*called by DATAMENU procedure
*****************************************************


PROCEDURE LOOKUP

GO TOP

CLEAR
? "STUB OF LOOKUP PROCEDURE FOR TESTING"
WAIT




*****************************************************
*EDITSCRN.SPR
*stub for testing
*called by DATAMENU procedure
*****************************************************


CLEAR
? "STUB OF EDITSCRN.SPR FOR TESTING"
WAIT




*****************************************************
*APNDSCRN.SPR
*stub for testing
*called by DATAMENU procedure
*****************************************************

m_again = 2
m_save = .F.

CLEAR
? "STUB OF APNDSCRN.SPR FOR TESTING"
WAIT


*****************************************************
*WAITMESG.SPR
*stub for testing
*called by DATAMENU procedure
*****************************************************

CLEAR
? "STUB OF WAITMESG.SPR FOR TESTING"
WAIT
```

Figure 11.20: Stubs for testing

THE EDIT SCREEN PROGRAM

Once you have finished testing the DATAMENU procedure, you can begin writing the actual programs to replace the stubs you used for testing.

You can begin with the EDITSCRN.SPR screen program, because FoxPro provides a part of the screen design that you need. The subdirectory \FOXPRO2\GOODIES\LASER\SCREENS created when you installed FoxPro includes the file named CONTROL1.SCX, which is a basic control panel that lets you move through a file—a window that includes pushbuttons and associated code to move the pointer to the next record, the previous record, the top of the file, or the bottom of the file.

Remember you learned in Chapter 10 that you can combine screen files when you generate a screen program. To create an edit screen program, you will first create a screen file with a window that displays all of the fields of the database file. Then you will modify the CONTROL1 screen file a bit, so it fits on the screen with the window you created. Then you will combine them when you generate the program.

Later, you will also combine this fields window with another control panel to create the screen for appending records, and you will modify it a bit and use it again for looking up records:

1. To have the database fields ready to place in the screen design window, enter **USE MAILLIST**. Get rid of the stub of this screen program that you created for testing by entering **RUN DEL EDITSCRN.SPR**. Then, to begin designing the screen, select New from the File menu, select the Screen radio button, and select OK.

2. Select *Quick Screen* from the Screens menu to place all the fields in the screen design window. Make sure *By Row Layout* is selected in the Quick Screen dialog box. Then select OK.

3. When you return to the screen design window, delete the field names Honorific, Fname, and Lname, and type **Name** where Honorific was. Then use one of the techniques you learned in the last chapter to rearrange the fields so they look like Figure 11.21. (Note that the "N" of name is on row 2, column 9.)

4. Now, specify the general features of the screen. Select *Screen Layout* from the Screen menu. Select the Window radio button. To determine the features of the window, select the Type pushbutton: select the Double radio button in the Border box, and select OK to return to the Screen Layout dialog box. In the Name

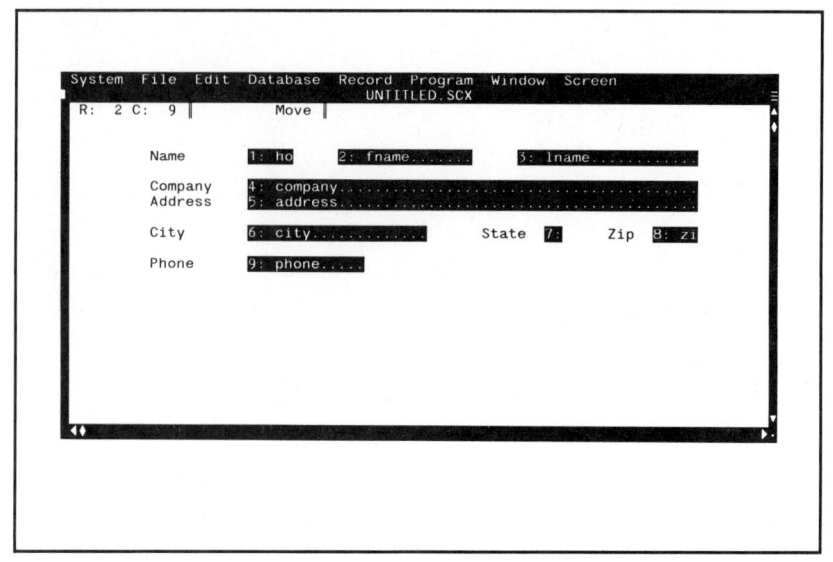

Figure 11.21: The new locations of the fields

    text box, enter **ALLFIELD**. In the Title text box, enter **Mail Power!**. As the height, enter **14**. As the width, enter **78**. Select the Center check box to remove the check from it. Then enter **4** as the row and **1** as the column.

5. Add picture templates and functions. Call up the dialog boxes of the Honorific, Fname, Lname, Company, Address, City, and State fields; select the Format pushbutton; select the To Upper Case check box; and select OK to generate the picture function @!. Then select OK to return to the screen design window. Do this for all these fields—or just type @! to the right of the Format pushbutton rather than selecting the pushbutton and generating that picture function. The Zip and Phone fields should have picture templates. In the dialog box for the Zip field, enter **99999** in the text box to the right of the Format pushbutton. For the Phone field, enter **(999)999-9999** in that text box.

6. Check *Setup* to open an editing window behind the dialog box. Select OK to close the dialog box and save your entry. Type **CLEAR** in the SETUP editing window, and then close

it, saving the changes. This setup code will clear the screen before displaying this window and fields. The fields are now in a window with a border and titles, as in Figure 11.22.

7. Select *Save As* from the File menu. Type **ALLFIELD** as the file name and select the Save pushbutton. When the Save Environment dialog box appears, select No, since you will be setting up the environment in the program itself. Press Esc to close the screen design window.

8. Now, you can modify the CONTROL1.SCX file distributed with FoxPro. Select *Open* from the File menu. Use the scrollable list (and, if necessary, the drive and directory popups) to select the \FOXPRO2\GOODIES\LASER\SCREENS directory. Select CONTROL1.SCX from the scrollable list, and select Open. Initially, this screen looks like Figure 11.23: the panel is vertical, but you want to make it a horizontal panel so that it can be displayed at the bottom of the screen, underneath the ALLFIELDS panel you created.

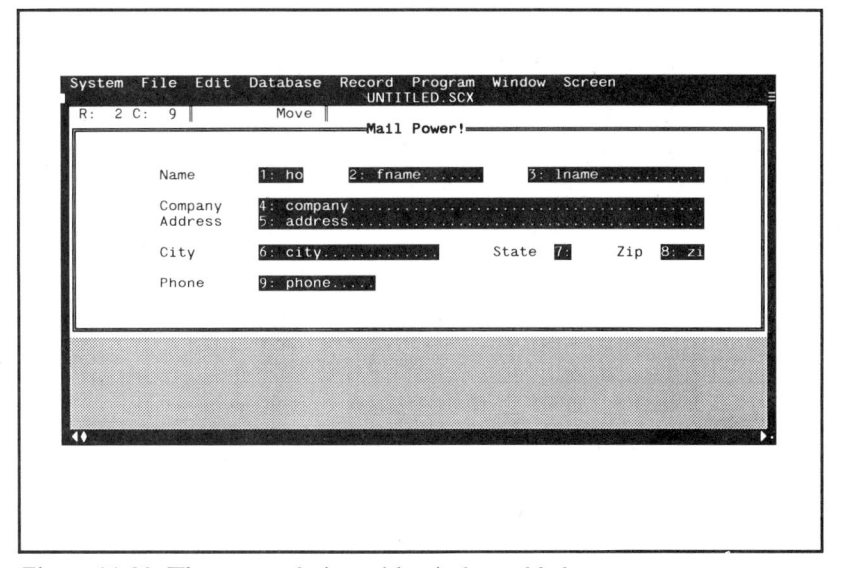

Figure 11.22: The screen design with window added

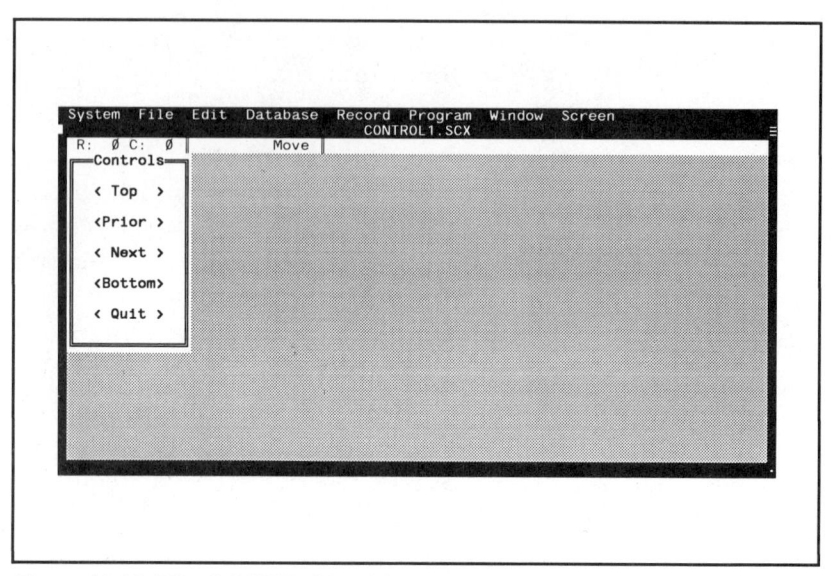

Figure 11.23: The CONTROL1.SCX panel distributed with FoxPro

9. Use the Push Buttons dialog box (by double-clicking on one of the pushbuttons or by moving the cursor to one and pressing enter) and select the Horizontal radio button. Then select OK.

10. Select *Screen Layout* from the Screen menu. As the Height, enter **5**. As the Width, enter **78**. Select OK.

11. Now, select and move the pushbuttons so they are centered in the control panel. The Next pushbutton should be under the title, as in Figure 11.24.

12. Select *Save As* from the File menu. Use the scrollable list (and, if necessary, the drive and directory popups) to select the **MAILPOW** directory as the current directory. Enter **ED_CNTRL** as the name of the file, and select Save.

13. Now generate the code. Select *Generate* from the Program menu, and select the Add pushbutton. Select ALLFIELD.SCX as the file to add, then select the Arrange pushbutton. Move the Mail

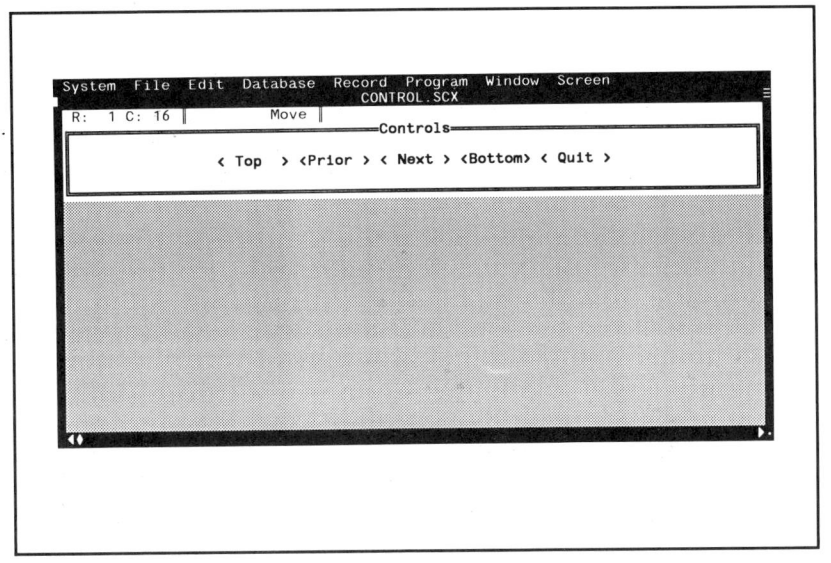

```
┌─────────────────────────────────────────────────────────────┐
│  System  File  Edit  Database  Record  Program  Window  Screen │
│                         CONTROL.SCX                           │
│  R:  1 C: 16        Move                                      │
│                    ═══Controls═══                             │
│            < Top  > <Prior > < Next > <Bottom> < Quit >       │
│                                                               │
│                                                               │
│                                                               │
│                                                               │
└─────────────────────────────────────────────────────────────┘
```

Figure 11.24: The control panel in its altered form

Power! window one space to the left and down two lines, and put the Controls panel two lines below it, as shown in Figure 11.25. Select *Save* from the Arrange menu.

14. In the text box under the Output File pushbutton, enter **EDITSCRN.SPR** as the name of the output file. Select the Generate pushbutton. When FoxPro has finished generating code, close the screen design window.

Now, to test the screen program, enter **DO MAILLIST**. At the main menu, press *D* to use the Data menu, press *E* to edit, and press any key to bypass the LOOKUP stub. The program should display the screen in Figure 11.26 (though, of course, the sample data displayed on your screen will be different). Try editing the fields, and try using the pushbuttons to move around the records. Remember that the LOOKUP stub you are using now always moves you to the first record before you use the edit screen. When you are done, select the Quit pushbutton to return to the Data menu. Press *R* to return to the Main menu, and press *Q* to quit Mail Power.

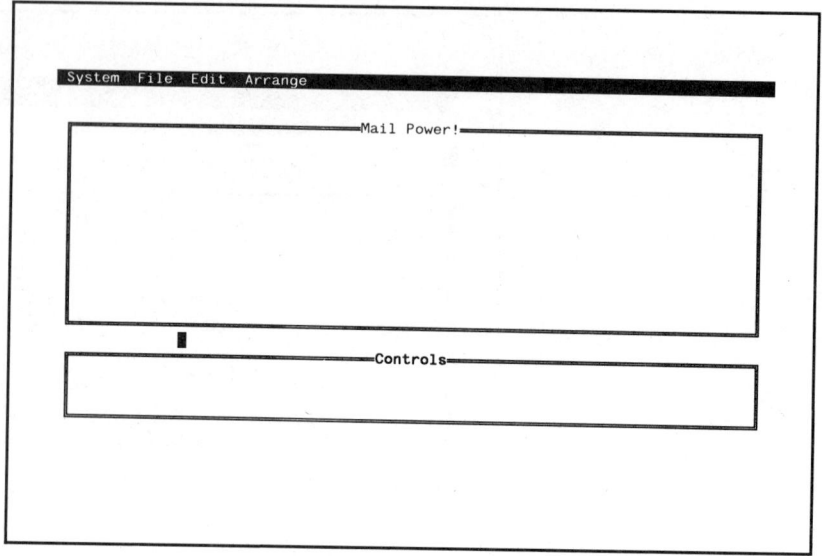

Figure 11.25: Arranging the windows

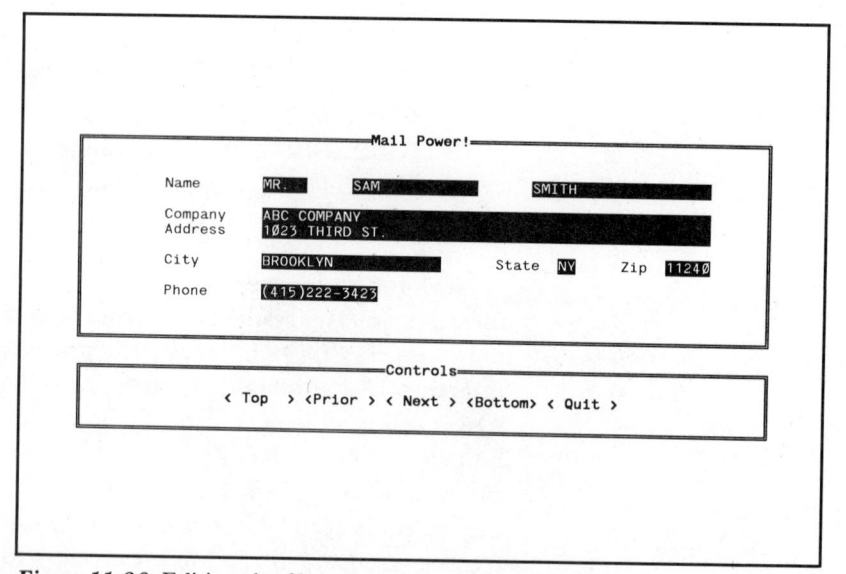

Figure 11.26: Editing the file using the screen you created

> If you cancel the program while a window is still open, enter **DEACTIVATE WINDOWS ALL** in the Command window to get rid of it.

If there are any errors, FoxPro will display an editing window with the error in generated code: select Cancel, and look for key words that you recognize to get a general idea of which window and which clause the error is in. Then close the editing window, open the screen design file that has the error, and use the screen design window to correct the error. Then generate the code again, combining screens as you did above.

THE LOOKUP MODULE

You can now write the procedure to look up a record in order to give the user the ability to actually find a particular record to edit. Instead of the stub you wrote earlier for testing, you will use the procedure shown in Figure 11.27.

```
****************************************************
* LOOKUP PROCEDURE
* a general purpose procedure to look up a record
* leaves pointer on record if found or on EOF() if not found
* called from DATAMENU module
****************************************************


PROCEDURE LOOKUP

m_name = SPACE(20)
m_found = 0

DO getname.spr

m_name = TRIM(m_name)
LOCATE FOR LNAME + FNAME = m_name
IF EOF()
    DO notfound.spr
ELSE
    DO WHILE .T.
        DO confirm.spr
        DO CASE
            CASE m_found = 1
                EXIT
            CASE m_found = 2
                SKIP
                IF lname <> m_name
                    GO BOTTOM
                    SKIP
                    DO notfound.spr
                    EXIT
                ENDIF
            CASE m_found = 3
                GO BOTTOM
                SKIP
                EXIT
        ENDCASE
    ENDDO
ENDIF
```

Figure 11.27: The procedure for looking up a record

Though it is a bit complex, this procedure is not difficult to understand. It must search for the name that the user enters; if the name is not in the file, it must make sure that EOF( ) is true, so that the program that calls it can check EOF( ) to see whether the name has been found.

The added complication, though, is that there might be a number of people with the same last name. Moreover, the person the user wants might not even be in the file, even if there are a number of people with the same name in the file.

First, this module uses a screen program, GETNAME.SPR, to retrieve the name the user wants to find. After getting the name, it uses the command **m_name = TRIM(m_name)** to trim blanks from it, in order to allow inexact matches. For example, if the user typed **SMITH**, m_name would be equal to SMITH followed by fifteen blank spaces, and this would not match SMITHSON or SMITHFIELD. By trimming off the trailing blanks, we allow the user to enter just part of the name being searched for.

After getting the name, the program uses the LOCATE FOR command to search for a record with this name. Notice that the program searches for LNAME + FNAME. Though the user enters only the last name, it searches for the entire index expression; therefore *Rushmore* is used.

If the search fails, there is no problem: the person is not in the file, and EOF( ) has automatically been made true, because the search failed. The command following **IF EOF( )** then executes, displaying a screen that says the record was not found.

If the search succeeded in finding a match, though, then you have the problem of seeing if it really succeeded in finding the record the user is looking for. This is the job of the code following **ELSE**, which is executed if EOF( ) is not true. This code is executed repeatedly, because it is in a **DO WHILE .T.** loop.

If there is a match, the code in this loop uses the CONFIRM.SPR screen program to display the current record and ask the user if it is the one that is needed. The screen program uses the user's response to determine the value of the variable **m_found**. As you will see, if the user selects the Yes pushbutton, m_found equals 1; selecting the No pushbutton makes m_found equal 2; and selecting the Cancel pushbutton makes m_found equal 3.

If m_found is 1, the command **EXIT** breaks the program out of this loop, leaving the pointer on the current record, the record that the user wanted.

If m_found is not true, the command **SKIP** moves the pointer to the next record. Remember that the NAMES index tag is the controlling index, so any other matching records would be immediately after the first matching record. If there is no other matching record, the code following **IF lname < > m_name** is executed: **GO BOTTOM** and **SKIP** make EOF( ) true, so the calling program knows there is no match; NOTFOUND.SPR displays a message telling the user there was no match; and **EXIT** breaks the user out of the loop. On the other hand, if LNAME is still equal to m_name, none of this happens: the program simply repeats the loop once again, and (as long as the user selects No) keeps repeating the loop until LNAME does not equal m_name.

If m_found is equal to 3, the commands **GO BOTTOM** and **SKIP** make EOF( ) true, and **EXIT** breaks the user out of the loop without displaying a message that there was no match. Since EOF( ) is true, the calling program does nothing, and both LOOKUP and the command that called it are effectively canceled.

The logic should be clear now. Note that this procedure calls three screen programs: GETNAME.SPR to get the name from the user; CONFIRM.SPR if a matching name is found, to see if it is the one the user wants; and NOTFOUND.SPR to display a message saying the record was not found. Try producing and testing these three screen programs.

GETNAME.SPR

1. Note, from looking at the code above, that the LOOKUP procedure uses GETNAME.SPR to get the contents of the variable m_name. To have this variable available when you design the screen, enter **M_NAME = SPACE(20)** at the Command window. Then enter **MODI SCREEN GETNAME** to design the screen file.

2. Select *Screen Layout* from the Screen menu. Select the Window radio button. As the name, enter **GETNAME**. As the height,

enter **7**; as the width, enter **60**. Leave Center checked as the position, and leave the default settings for Type. Select OK to return to the screen design window.

3. At row 1, col 9, type **Enter the last name:**. Move the cursor to row 3, column 9. Select *Field* from the Screen menu, then the Get pushbutton; select M_NAME from the scrollable list of memory variables; and select OK to return to the Field dialog box. Select the Format pushbutton, then the Alpha Only and the To Upper Case check boxes. Select OK to return to the Field dialog box, generating the Picture functions **@A!**. Select OK to return to the screen design window, placing the field.

4. Move the cursor to row 2, column 46. Select *Push Button* from the Screen menu, to call up the Push Button dialog box. As the prompts, enter **\!OK**. In the text box to the right of the Get pushbutton, type **DUMMY** as the variable name. Select the Terminating check box, then select OK to return to the screen design window, placing the pushbutton, as shown in Figure 11.28.

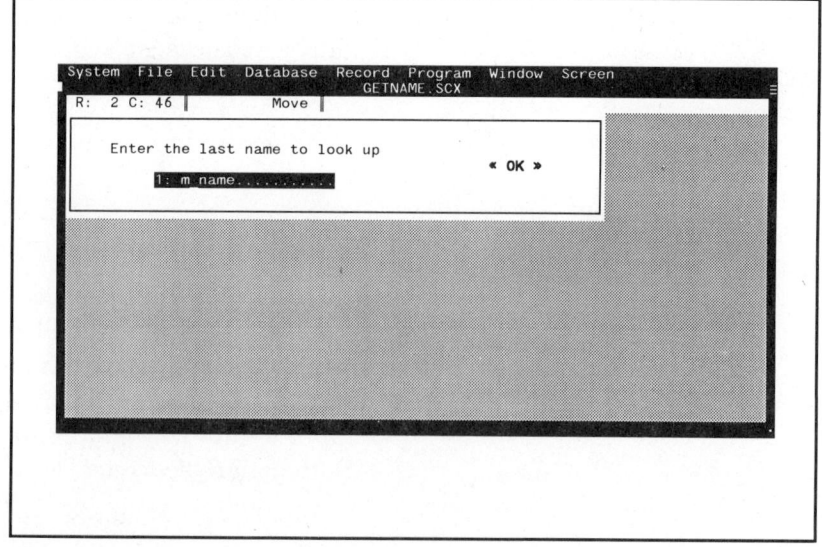

Figure 11.28: The design of the GETNAME screen

5. Select *Save* from the File menu, and press *N* so the environment is not saved. Select *Generate* from the Program menu, and select the Generate pushbutton in the dialog box. When program generation is done, close the screen design window.

To test the screen, enter **DO GETNAME.SPR** in the Command window. When the dialog box appears, enter a name and select OK to return to the Command window. Then enter **? m_name** to make sure that the variable is what it should be. Also, try using Ctrl-Enter to select the OK pushbutton.

CONFIRM.SPR

1. You need to display a record without letting the user edit it, and you can do this by modifying the ALLFIELD screen and saving it under a different name. Enter **MODI SCREEN ALLFIELD**. When the screen design window is displayed, select Save As from the File menu, enter **SHOFIELD** as the name to save the screen under, and select Save. Then call up the dialog box for each of the fields of the screen, and select the Say radio button and check the Refresh check box for each. Make sure you have done this for all the fields, and then press Ctrl-W to save your work and return to the Command window.

   Although the Refresh check box will not be needed in the way that SHOFIELD will be used here (because the pointer is not moved while this screen is displayed), checking it does make this screen more versatile. For example, you can combine SHOFIELD with ED_CNTRL, and the fields displayed will change as you move the pointer.

2. Now you can modify the GETNAME screen to create a window for the user to confirm whether the record displayed is the correct record. Enter **MODI SCREEN GETNAME**. Select *Save As* from the File menu, enter **CONFIRM** as the name to save the file under, and select Save.

3. To alter the dialog box, delete the text object that says "Enter the name to look up." Move the cursor to row 2, column 8, and type **Is this the record you want**. Then move the pushbutton up to row 0, and call up the dialog box for the pushbuttons. As the list of prompts, type \<**Yes** and \<**No** and \?**Cancel**—making *Y* and *N* the hot keys for Yes and No (since it does not make sense to make one of these keys the default), and assigning Esc to Cancel. Edit the variable name

so it is **m_found**. Then select OK to return to the screen design window. The final design of the screen is shown in Figure 11.29. Select *Save* from the File menu to save the changes.

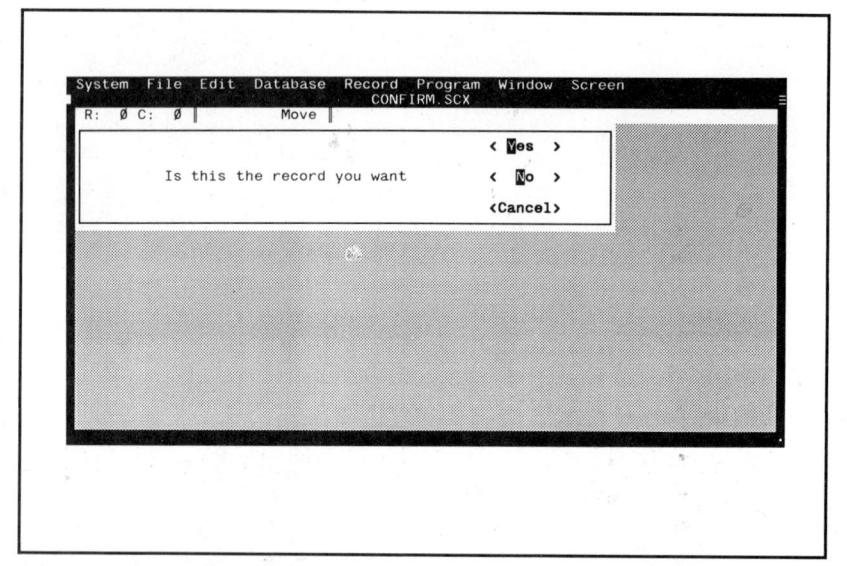

Figure 11.29: The confirm screen design

    4. Select *Generate* from the Program menu. Select the Add pushbutton. Select SHOFIELD.SCX as the screen to add. Then select Arrange, and move the windows so SHOFIELD is where ALLFIELD was in previous screens, and CONFIRM is centered under it, as in Figure 11.30. Then select Save from the Arrange menu. Leave the name of the Output file as CONFIRM.SPR, and select Generate. When code generation is finished, press Esc to return to the Command window.

To test this screen, first enter **USE MAILLIST**. Then enter **DO CONFIRM.SPR**. The screen program displays the fields of the current record and the Confirm window, and it terminates when you select one of the pushbuttons.

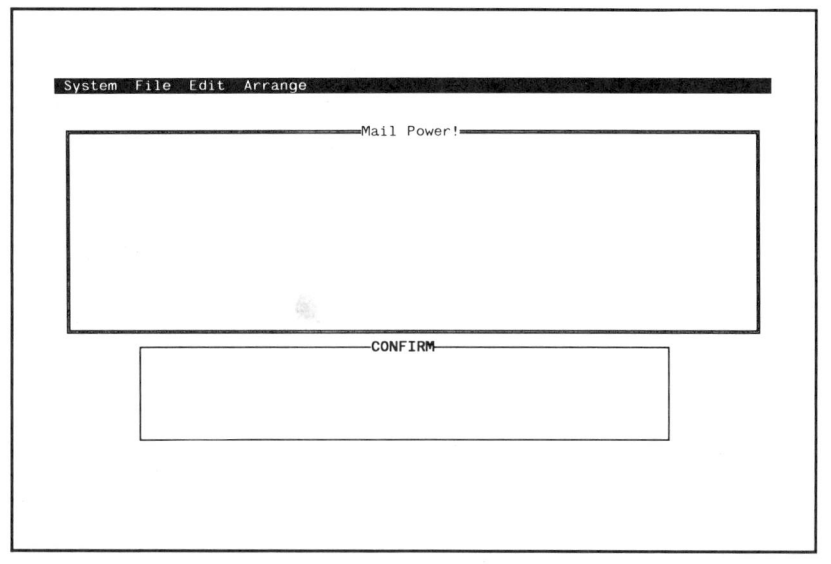

Figure 11.30: Arranging the windows

NOTFOUND

1. Enter **MODI SCREEN CONFIRM**. Select *Save As* from the File menu, enter **NOTFOUND** as the new name of the file, and select Save.

2. Delete the text object. Type, beginning at row 2, column 3, **The record you want is not in the file**.

3. Delete the pushbuttons. Move the cursor to row 2, column 48. Select *Push Button* from the Screen menu. As the prompt, enter **\! OK** , with a blank space before the O and another after the K. Check the Terminating check box. As the variable, enter **dummy** in the text box to the right of the Choose pushbutton. Select OK to return to the screen design window.

4. Select *Save* from the File menu, and then select Generate from the Program menu, and select the Generate pushbutton. After the code is generated, press Ctrl-W to close the window and save your changes. To test the screen program, enter **DO NOTFOUND.SPR**. It should display the message

in the center of the screen, as in Figure 11.31, and terminate when you select OK.

TESTING LOOKUP

Now you can finally test the entire LOOKUP procedure.

If you have not already done so, enter the LOOKUP procedure listed above instead of the stub of LOOKUP you used for testing.

```
┌─────────────────────────────────────────────────────────────┐
│                                                             │
│                                                             │
│         ┌─────────────────────────────────────────┐         │
│         │  The record you want is not in the file    « OK » │
│         └─────────────────────────────────────────┘         │
│                                                             │
│                                                             │
└─────────────────────────────────────────────────────────────┘
```

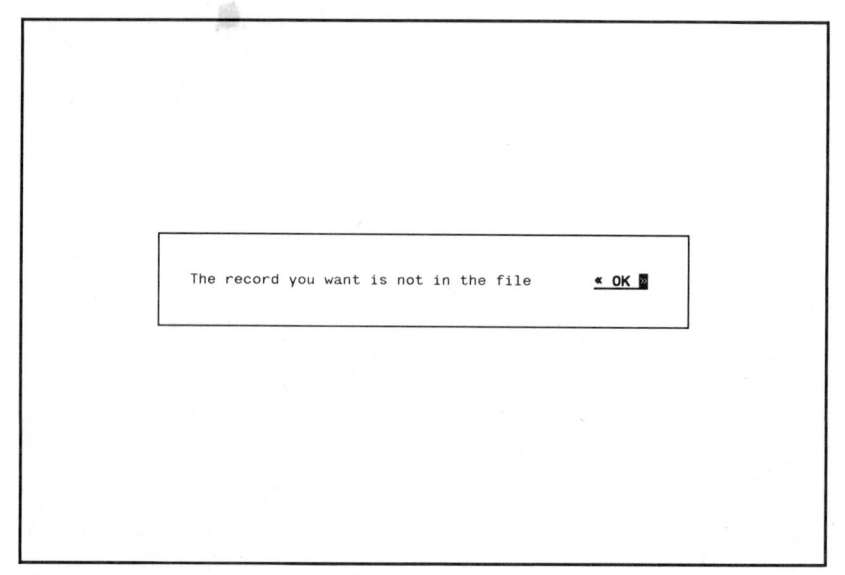

Figure 11.31: The notfound screen

Then run the Mail Power! program, select Edit from the Data menu, test all the features of the LOOKUP procedure. For example, try entering names that do not match as well as ones that match names in your database file. Enter a name that matches multiple names in the file, and do not confirm that any of them is the name you were searching for. A typical screen is shown in Figure 11.32.

THE APPEND SCREEN PROGRAM

So far, you have just used screen programs to display screens and get input to be used by the calling program. Now you can move to a

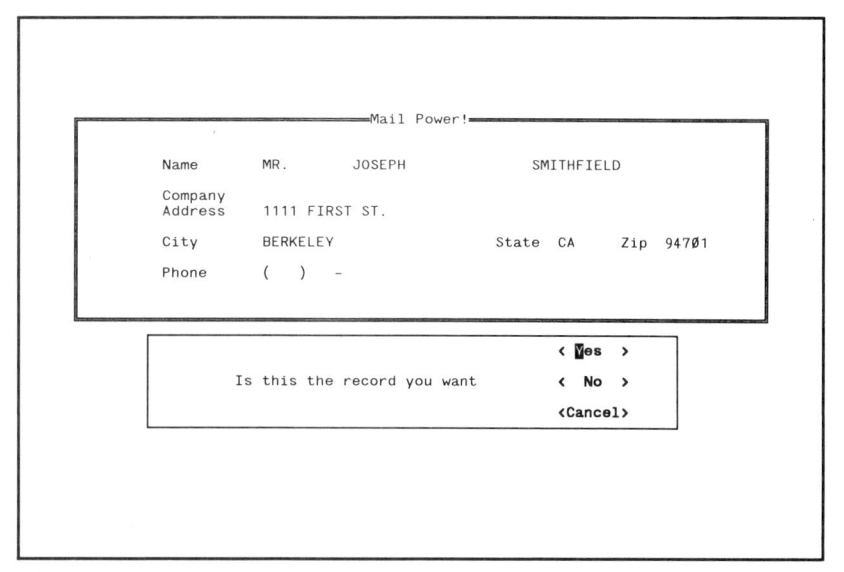

```
                    ═══Mail Power!═══
    Name        MR.        JOSEPH              SMITHFIELD
    Company
    Address     1111 FIRST ST.
    City        BERKELEY                State  CA    Zip  94701
    Phone       (   )   -


                                              <  Yes  >
              Is this the record you want     <  No   >
                                              <Cancel>
```

Figure 11.32: Searching for a name to edit

more advanced screen program, which includes code snippets. You will create a control panel for appending data. This control panel should work like the control panel that comes with FoxPro, the one you used for editing the database file.

The Append control panel needs to do only two things:

- It should give the user the option of appending another record or returning to the main menu. Since it is usual to append a number of records at once, appending another record can be the default choice.

- It should also give the user the option of saving or discarding the current record. Usually, of course, the user would want to save the record, but there are times when the data entered is garbled enough that it is easiest to just discard the record and start over.

Deleting the record is easy. You simply need to create a check box with the prompt **Save this record**, which is checked by default. This check box determines the value of the variable **m_save**: remember that this check box assigns 0 to a variable if it is not checked. Thus, the VALID clause of this object simply needs the code snippet:

```
IF m_save = 0
   DELETE
ENDIF
RETURN 0
```

This VALID clause is executed whenever the READ command is executed, and it deletes the current record if the box is not checked, but it does nothing if the box is checked. Since we SET DELETED ON at the beginning of the program, the command **DELETE** is enough to make the record seem to disappear from the file: there is no need to take the time to PACK the file.

The pushbuttons will give the user the option to append another record or to quit, and they will assign the choice to the variable **m_again**. They will have this code snippet in their VALID clause:

```
IF m_again = 1
   APPEND BLANK
   SHOW GETS
ELSE
   CLEAR READ
ENDIF
RETURN 0
```

If the user selects Yes, the snippet executes the command **APPEND BLANK**, which adds a new blank record to the file and makes it the current record, and the command **SHOW GETS**, which refreshes all of the GET fields, displaying the value in the current record. (If SHOW GETS were not used, each field would not be refreshed until the cursor moved to it.)

Otherwise, if the user selects Quit, the snippet executes the command **CLEAR READ**, which terminates the current-level READ command and returns control to the previous level READ. This command is a more powerful alternative to checking the Terminating check box. That check box terminates the current READ when any pushbutton is selected, but CLEAR READ lets you control which pushbutton terminates the READ. The screen program is executed until that pushbutton is selected.

Now that you have seen the logic that they are based on, you should have no trouble creating your first screen controls:

1. For consistency of size and window type, use the control panel you already created for editing and modify it to create the new control panel: enter **MODI SCREEN ED_CNTRL**. Then select and delete the pushbuttons. Select *Save As* from the File menu, then enter **AP_CNTRL** as the new file name and select the Save pushbutton. Now you have a window of the same size and with the same border as the one with the editing controls, and you can add controls to it.

2. Move the cursor to row 1, column 42. Select *Check Box* from the Screen menu. In the Check Box Prompt text box, type **Save This Record**. In the text box to the right of the Choose button, type **m_save** as the variable, then select the Initially Checked check box. Select the Valid check box, and in the text-editing area, enter the snippet discussed earlier:

   ```
   IF m_save = 0
      DELETE
   ENDIF
   RETURN 0
   ```

3. When you have entered this, select OK to return to the dialog box, and select OK to place the check box and prompt.

4. Move the cursor to row 1, column 10. Select *Push Button* from the Screen menu. As the prompts, enter **\!Append** on the first line and **\?Quit** on the second line. Select the Spacing pushbutton; enter **3** as the number of characters for spacing, and select OK. As the variable, type **m_again** in the text box to the right of the Choose pushbutton. Make sure the Horizontal radio button is selected and the Terminating check box is not selected. Select *Valid*, and, in the text-editing area, enter the other code snippet discussed earlier:

   ```
   IF m_again = 1
      APPEND BLANK
      SHOW GETS
   ELSE
   ```

```
CLEAR READ
  ENDIF
RETURN 0
```

5. Select OK to return to the dialog box, and select OK to return to the screen design window, placing the pushbuttons, as shown in Figure 11.33.

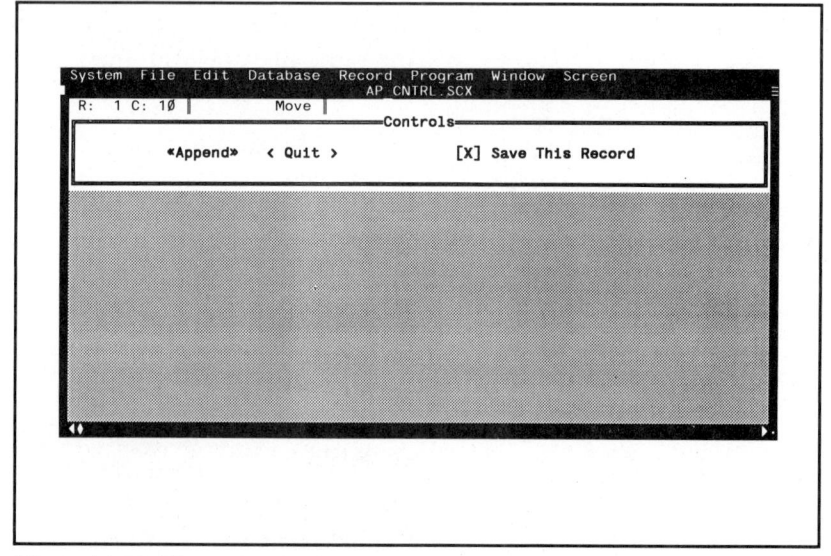

```
┌─────────────────────────────────────────────────────────────┐
│ System  File  Edit  Database  Record  Program  Window  Screen │
│                         AP_CNTRL.SCX                         │
│ R:  1 C: 10          Move                                    │
│ ═══════════════════════════Controls══════════════════════════│
│       «Append»    < Quit >        [X] Save This Record       │
│                                                              │
└─────────────────────────────────────────────────────────────┘
```

Figure 11.33: The append control panel

That is all it takes to create this control panel. Press Ctrl-W to save the changes and return to the Command window. Now let's combine this control panel with the ALLFIELD panel and generate the code:

1. From the Command window, enter **MODI FILE ALLFIELD**. Select *Generate* from the Program menu. Select the Add pushbutton, then select AP_CNTRL.SCX from the scrollable list as the file to add. Select the Arrange pushbutton, and arrange the windows as you did when you added the Edit control panel. Select *Save* from the Arrange menu to return to the Generate dialog box.

2. As the name of the Output file, enter **APNDSCRN.SPR**. Select *Generate*. FoxPro warns you that APNDSCRN.SPR already exists: this is the stub you created earlier. Press *Y* to overwrite it. When program generation is complete, close the screen design window, and test the program as you did earlier:

3. Enter **DO MAILPOW**. Enter *D* at the Main menu to use the Data menu. Enter *A* at the Data menu to append; the screen should look like Figure 11.34.

4. Add several records. In some cases, select the Save This Record check box that you created, so the appended record is deleted. Then select Quit to return to the Data menu.

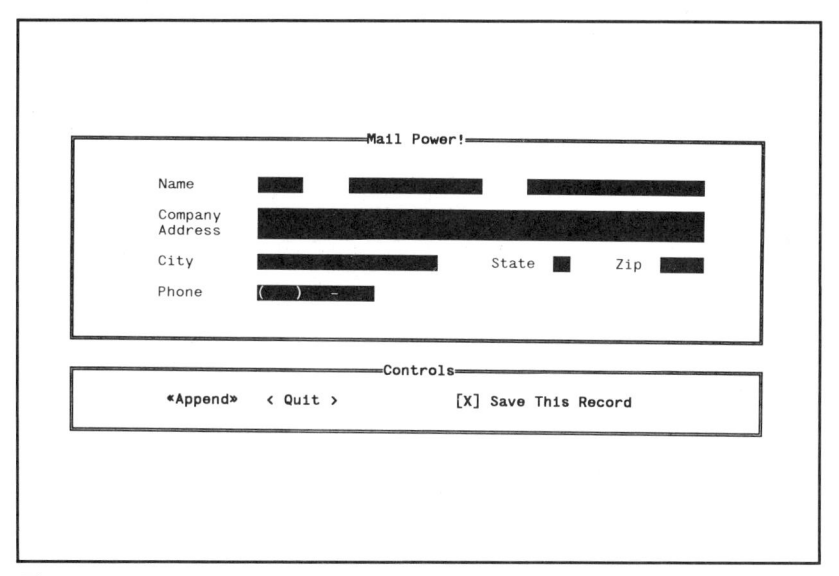

Figure 11.34: Using the append screen

You might want to select Edit from the data menu, and use the edit controls to move through the entire list, to make sure the records you added are there, and the records you deleted are not. After you quit Mail Power, you should enter **USE MAILLIST** and **LIST FOR**

DELETED( ) in the Command window, to make sure that the records you did not opt to save have indeed been deleted.

OTHER FEATURES OF THE DATA MENU

You now have the program to the point where it is almost ready to run, at least as an initial prototype, since the LOOKUP procedure you wrote earlier, to be used for editing, also lets the user look up and delete records. In an actual program, you would want to add more bells and whistles than you have here. For example, you would probably want to get an additional keystroke before removing the screen when the user is looking up a record, and you would want to get confirmation from the user before deleting a record. You might also want to add a message to tell the user to turn the printer on before labels and reports are printed, and to convert the message displayed after data is exported into a screen program. This sample program will omit these features for the sake of brevity; you might want to go back and add them as an exercise after finishing this book.

The one module that must be added before the entire program can be run is the WAITMESG procedure, which displays a message and packs records. This happens to be a very interesting procedure, because you can go into the program file generated by the screen generator and change its code in order to produce it.

You want a message to be displayed on the screen only for as long as the database is being searched or used, and then you want it to disappear without the user having to press a key. The screen generator, however, by adding the command **READ CYCLE** (or just **READ** if the READ CYCLE check box is not checked), makes the user enter a keystroke before the program continues, even if there are no GET statements pending. To get around this problem, you can use the screen generator to create a screen message, and then edit the program that is generated to eliminate the READ and add the command **PACK** instead.

1. Enter **MODI SCREEN NOTFOUND**. Select *Save As* from the File menu, enter **WAITMESG** as the new file name, and select the Save pushbutton to return to the screen design window.

2. Delete the text object and pushbutton that are in this screen design. Then move the cursor to row 2, column 17 and type **Please wait a moment....** Select *Screen Layout* from the Screen menu, and as the window name, enter **NOTFOUND**.

3. Select *Generate* from the Program menu. Press *Y* to save the changes you made in the screen design. Then select the Generate pushbutton to generate the program, and press *Y* to overwrite the stub you created earlier. When program generation is complete, press Esc to close the screen design window. Before you edit the program, you might want to run Mail Power and test this module to confirm that it makes you enter a keystroke.

Now edit the program you generated. Enter **MODI COMM NOTFOUND.SPR**. Zoom the edit window, and scroll down through this short program until you have gotten beyond the comment that says **WAITMESG Screen Layout**. A few lines below it, you will see the code

```
ACTIVATE WINDOW getname
READ CYCLE
RELEASE WINDOW getname
```

The command **READ CYCLE** is what makes the program wait for a keystroke. Delete it and enter the command **PACK** instead, so the code now reads

```
ACTIVATE WINDOW getname
PACK
RELEASE WINDOW getname
```

Then save the code and test the program.

As you can see, the new version of the code activates the window to display the message, then packs the database file to remove deleted records, and, as soon as it is done packing, releases the window. If you have a small file, the message will just be displayed for an instant, since packing only takes that long; but with a longer file this message is a necessity to reassure the user that the program has not simply stopped.

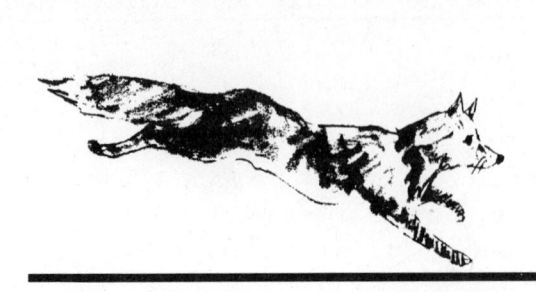

Chapter 12

Using the Menu Builder

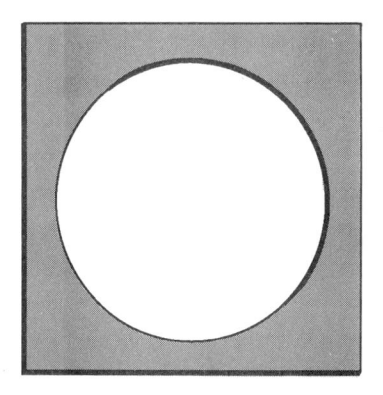

BY THE END OF THE LAST CHAPTER, YOUR SAMPLE program had a split personality. It began by using an old-fashioned menu system without mouse support, which illustrated some basic principles of programming. Then it used the screen generator to add a more up-to-date interface, with windows, controls, and mouse support.

In this section, you will bring the program's menu system up to date also, by using the menu builder to create popup menus for it.

THE MENU DESIGN WINDOW

You use the menu design window, shown in Figure 12.1, in much the same way that you use other features of FoxPro. To use the menu builder to create a new menu, select New from the File menu, select the Menu radio button, and select OK; name the menu later by selecting Save As from the File menu. Alternatively, simply enter the command **CREATE MENU** <*menu name*>.

Likewise, to use the menu design window to modify an existing menu, select Open from the File menu and use the Open dialog box in the usual way to open the menu file you want. Alternatively, enter

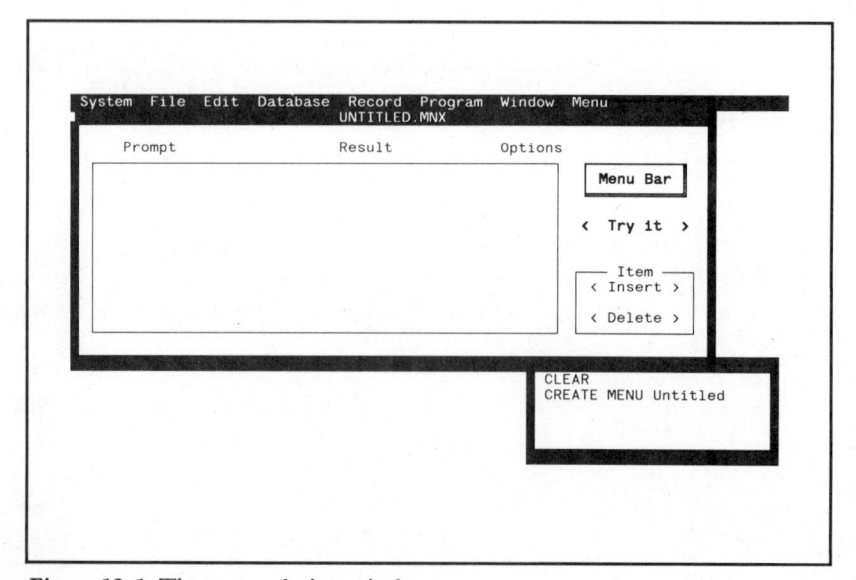

Figure 12.1: The menu design window

the command **MODIFY MENU** <*menu name*>. When you use the menu design window, a Menu menu pad is added to the FoxPro system menu.

When you save the design you created in the menu design window, the specifications for the menu are kept in an ordinary database file with the extension MNX.

You generate menu code in the same way you generated code when you used the screen builder, by selecting Generate from the Program menu. The code that is generated is kept in a program with the extension MPR, so that you must use the entire name of the program, including its extension, in order to run it, as you did when you ran screen programs.

The menu builder is easy to use. You type the prompts of the main menu bar in the left column. Once you enter a prompt, a popup control and pushbutton appear in the Result column. For the main menu bar, as you can see in the Figure 12.2, the options on the popup control are Command, Pad Name, Submenu, and Proc. (an abbreviation for procedure).

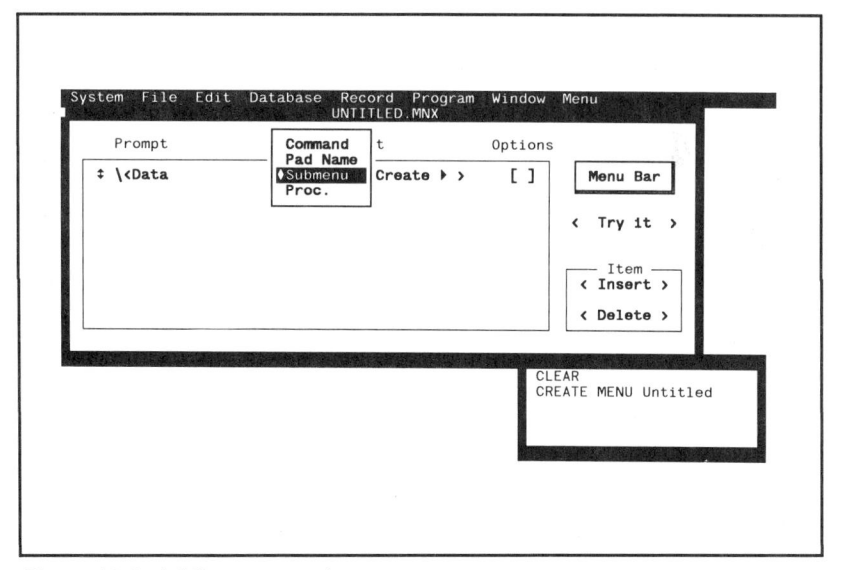

Figure 12.2: Adding a menu item

> To assign FoxPro system menu pads to the pads you are defining, use the names _MSM_SYSTM for the System menu, _MSM_FILE for the File menu, _MSM_EDIT for the Edit menu, _MSM_DATA for the Database menu, _MSM_RECRD for the Record menu, _MSM_PROG for the Program menu, and _MSM_WINDO for the Window menu.

> To see the names of all the menu bars of the FoxPro system menu, select Quick Menu from the Menu menu. This option creates a menu with pads and popup options that are the same as the FoxPro system menu. Each popup submenu item uses **Bar #** to assign it the same action as the equivalent item on the FoxPro menu, as discussed below in the section on Quick menus.

If you select Command or Pad Name a data-entry area appears to the right of this popup. You can enter a single command that will be executed when the user selects this menu pad, or you can enter the name of a menu pad—either one you defined yourself or one of the FoxPro system menu pads—to assign this menu pad all of its features.

If you select Submenu or Proc, a Create pushbutton appears to the right of this popup. Selecting it lets you create a submenu (in a way that you will look at in a moment), or opens an editing window where you can enter a procedure to be executed whenever this popup is selected. You should not use the PROCEDURE command to name this procedure, as FoxPro will generate the procedure name when it generates the program. Once you create the submenu or procedure, this pushbutton changes from Create to Edit, and you can select it to modify the submenu or procedure you created earlier.

When you are working on the main menu bar, the default setting of the popup control is Submenu, since you most often want to activate a popup (which is a submenu) when a pad of the main menu bar is selected. As soon as you enter a prompt name, the popup is set on Submenu, and you just need to select the Create pushbutton to create a menu popup.

When you create a submenu, you use a panel that is just like the panel you use to enter the main menu bar. Simply enter the prompts to be displayed by the popup in the left column, and enter the result for each in the Result column. The only difference, as you can see in Figure 12.3, is that, when you are working on submenus, the default result is Command and the options on the Result popup are Command, Bar #, Submenu, and Proc. Rather than assigning an item a pad as its result, you can assign it a bar number of your own or the name of one of the bars of the FoxPro system menu. As with the main menu, do not use the PROCEDURE command to name procedures you enter here, as FoxPro will generate a name when it creates the program.

You can see how easy it is to create a main menu bar and submenu popups. Notice that you can create a submenu under a submenu—that is, a popup that appears when one of the bars on a popup is selected—with no extra effort.

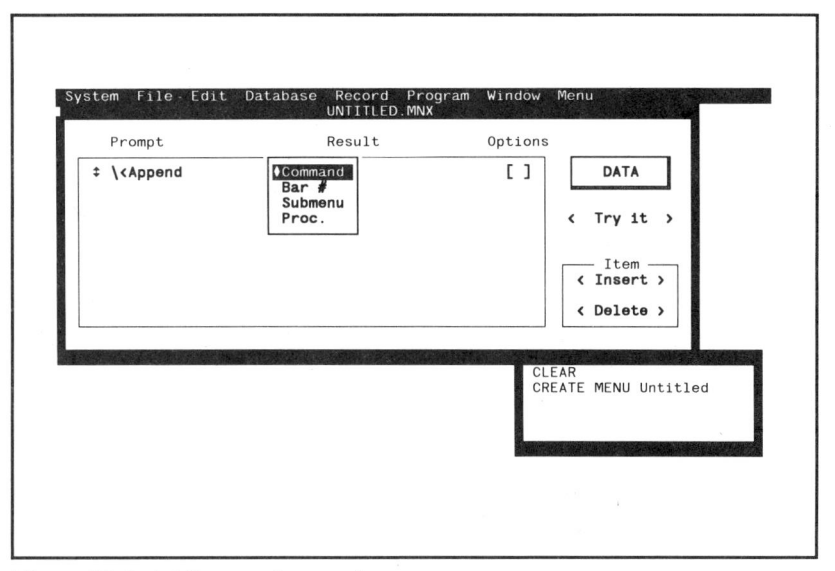

Figure 12.3: Adding a submenu item

To work on a submenu, as you know, you select the appropriate Create or Edit button of its parent menu. To move back up to the parent menu from a submenu, select the popup control in the upper right corner of the menu design window, shown in Figure 12.4. This popup has the name of the current menu on it, whether it is the main menu bar or a submenu. To move up the menu system, select it and select the name of the parent menu that you want to work on.

Select the Delete pushbutton to delete the currently selected menu item. Select the Insert pushbutton to insert a new menu item above the currently selected menu item. You can also select Delete Item or Insert Item from the Menu menu to do the same thing.

Select the Try It pushbutton to try using the menu system without taking time for code generation. When you select this pushbutton, the menu bar you defined appears at the top of the screen, and popups appear when you select pads. The program is not executed, however; instead, a text dialog box displays the code that would be executed when you chose an option.

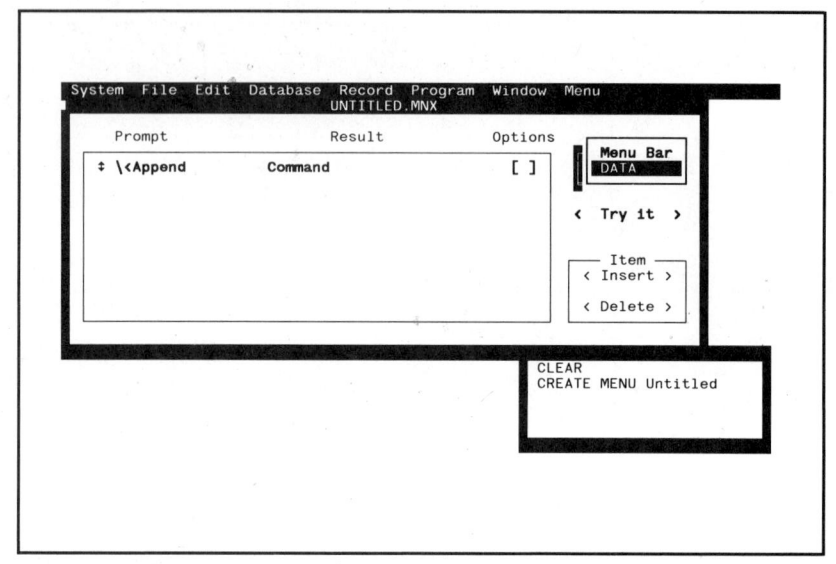

Figure 12.4: Moving up the menu tree

HOT KEYS

You can specify hot keys for menu options as you did when you were defining screen controls: add the characters \< before the character you want to use as the hot key.

Another special character is used when you are defining menus. Many FoxPro menu popups have their options grouped, with groups separated by lines. If you want to group choices in this way, you can add this sort of line by using the characters \- as a prompt. Hot keys in menus you create in this way work the same way as hot keys in the FoxPro system menu. If one of the menu pads is already highlighted (for example, because you pressed Alt or F10), then you can select any menu pad simply by pressing its hot key. If a popup is already displayed, then you can select any of its options simply by pressing its hot key.

On the other hand, FoxPro also has shortcut key combinations for many menu choices, which can be used at any time. In the case of the main menu pad, the shortcut key combination is Alt plus the hot key. For example, if one of the menu pads is already highlighted, you can use the Database menu by pressing the hot key *D*. At any other time, you can use the Database menu by pressing the shortcut key combination *Alt-D*. In the case of menu bars, the shortcut key combination is generally Ctrl plus some key. For example, you can select Paste from the Edit menu at any time by pressing *Ctrl-V*.

You must use the Options check box to implement shortcut key combinations.

THE OPTIONS CHECK BOX

Selecting the Options check box for any menu item displays the dialog box shown in Figure 12.5. Select the Shortcut check box to specify a key combination shortcut (as described above) for that menu item. FoxPro displays a dialog box that prompts you to press the key that you want to use as the shortcut. If you want to follow the same conventions as the FoxPro system menu, press *Alt* plus the hot key as the shortcut for main menu pads.

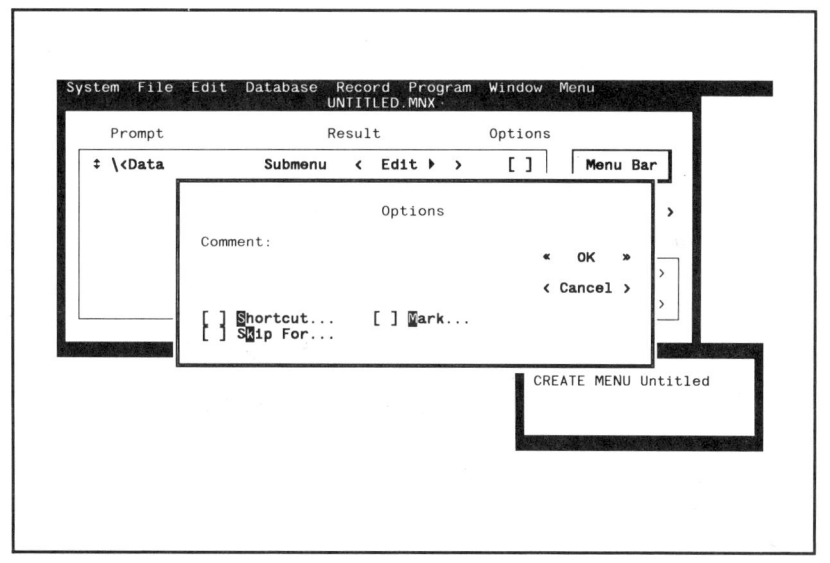

Figure 12.5: The Options dialog box

Select the Skip For check box to disable this menu item under certain conditions. FoxPro displays the expression builder, and you must create or enter a logical expression. The menu option will be disabled when this expression evaluates to .F.

Selecting Mark specifies that a checkmark character be placed before options to indicate if they are toggled on or off—or to indicate some other condition. FoxPro displays a scrollable list of the ASCII characters for you to choose among. This just specifies the check character to be used; you must write the code that displays this character.

Use the Comment text-editing area to enter comments for your own use.

THE MENU MENU

When you use the menu design window, a Menu menu pad, shown in Figure 12.6, is added to the FoxPro System menu. As you learned earlier, the Insert Item and Delete Item options are equivalent to the Insert and Delete pushbuttons in the menu design window. They let you insert a new menu item above the currently selected item and delete the currently selected item.

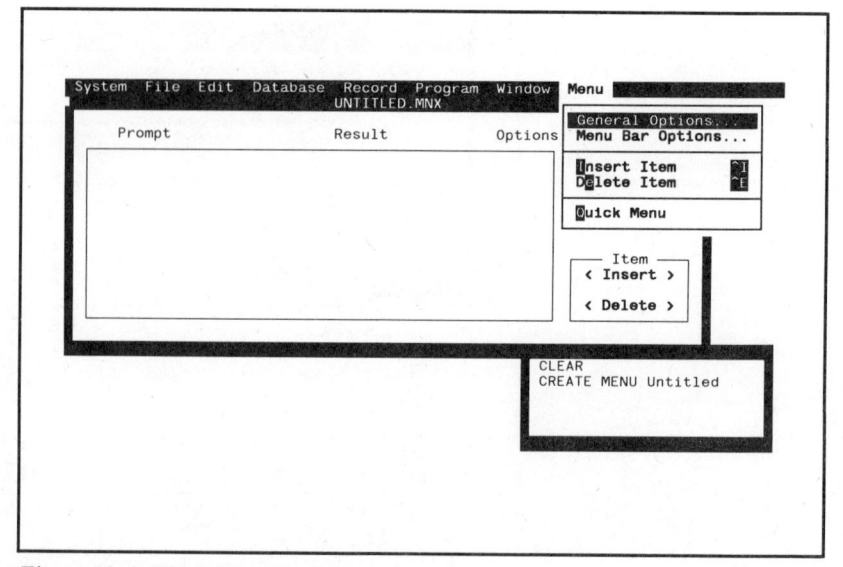

Figure 12.6: The Menu menu

GENERAL OPTIONS

Selecting General Options from the Menu menu calls up the dialog box shown in Figure 12.7. The most important features of this dialog box are the Setup and Cleanup check boxes. Select these to call up text-editing windows where you can enter setup code to be executed before the menu definition commands of the generated program, and cleanup code to be executed after the menu definition commands of the generated program.

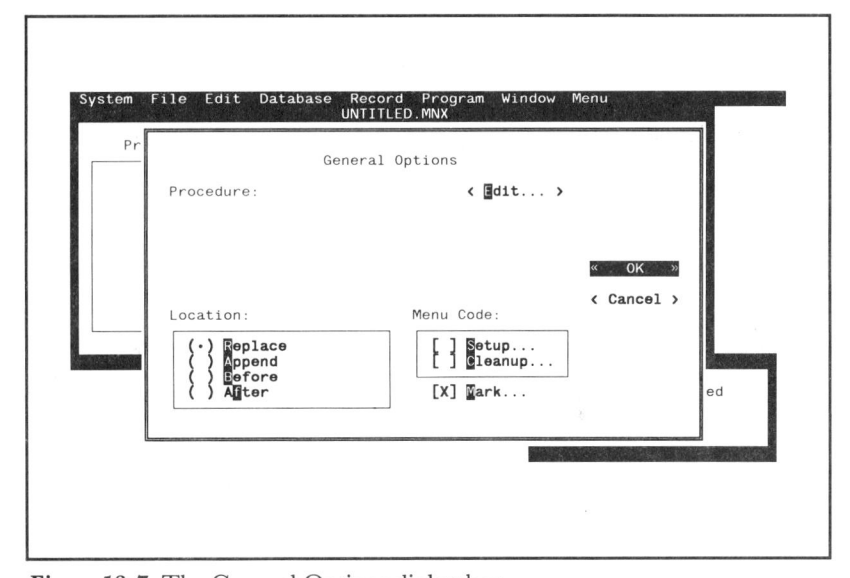

Figure 12.7: The General Options dialog box

You can also use the Cleanup text-editing window to enter general-purpose procedures that are called by various options of the menu system—like the LOOKUP procedure in your MailPower! system. Unlike procedures entered as the results of menu items, these procedures must include the **PROCEDURE** command to name them. Since you call them elsewhere in the program, you must know their names, and so their names cannot be generated by FoxPro. Simply type the procedure after the cleanup code: when the program is generated, cleanup code will be at the end of the main module, and the procedure will appear immediately after it, just where you would put it if you were writing out the program by hand.

Select the Mark check box to enter a global mark character. This works like the mark you enter for a specific item, described above, but it applies to all the items of the menu. If a different mark is specified for a submenu or for a specific item, it overrides the global mark.

Select one of the Location radio buttons to specify how the menu system you are defining is placed with respect to the active menu. By default, Replace is selected, so the new menu system replaces the active menu. You can select Append to add the new menu system to the right of the active menu. If you select Before or After, a popup appears to let you select among the prompts of the active menu: the new menu system will be inserted before or after the prompt you select.

Use the Procedure text-editing area to enter a procedure for the entire menu system (or, for a longer procedure, select the Edit pushbutton to open an editing window). This procedure will be executed when any menu pad is selected. If you have created a procedure for a specific menu pad, however, it will be executed instead. The procedure entered in this text-editing area is executed only if no other procedure exists for the menu pad.

MENU OPTIONS

Selecting <*menu name*> Options from the Menu menu calls up the dialog box shown in Figure 12.8, which lets you add options for just the main menu bar or for just a specific submenu popup. If you are working on the main menu bar, the option on the Menu menu will read Menu Bar Options; if you are working on a submenu (such as the Data menu popup) it will include the name of that submenu (for example, Data Options).

Use the Color Scheme popup to select a color scheme for the main menu bar or for that submenu popup.

Mark selects a mark character for the menu bar or popup, as described above. Marks specified here override marks specified by selecting General Options from the Menu menu, and they are overridden by marks specified by selecting the Options check box for an individual menu item.

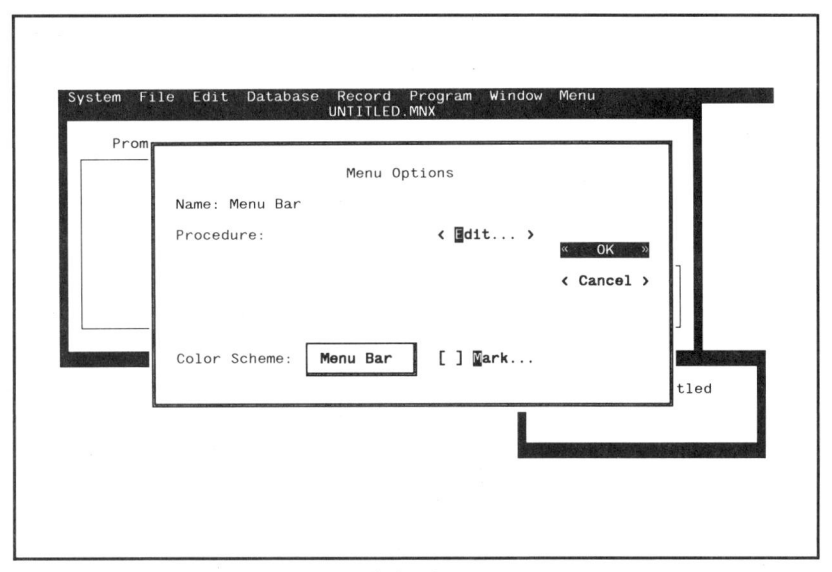

Figure 12.8: The Menu Options dialog box

Use the Procedure text-editing area or select the Edit pushbutton to enter a procedure to be used by all the menu options. If this procedure is entered when you are working on the menu bar, it will be executed when any option on any menu popup is selected. If it is entered when you are working on a popup, it will be executed when any option from that popup is selected. In any case, the procedure at the lowest level takes precedence, and the procedure entered here is executed only when there is no other procedure defined for the menu option.

QUICK MENUS

The Quick Menu option of the Menu menu is active only if nothing has been entered in the Menu definition window. Select it to create a quick menu that works identically to the FoxPro system menu.

As you can see in Figure 12.9, the Quick Menu main menu bar has the same options as the system menu, and each calls a submenu. Figure 12.10 shows its System submenu, which has the same items as FoxPro's System submenu popup. Each of these items uses the Bar # option of the Result popup to assign it the same result as the equivalent item in the FoxPro system menu.

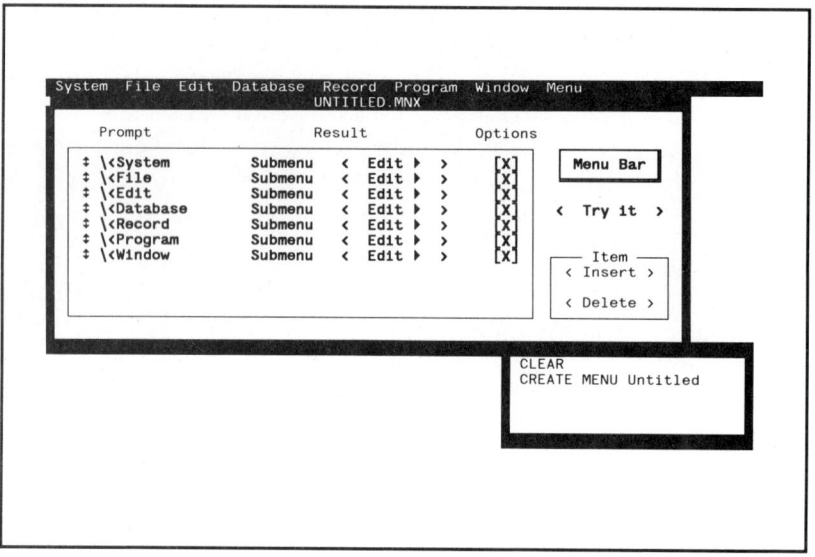

Figure 12.9: The Quick Menu main menu bar

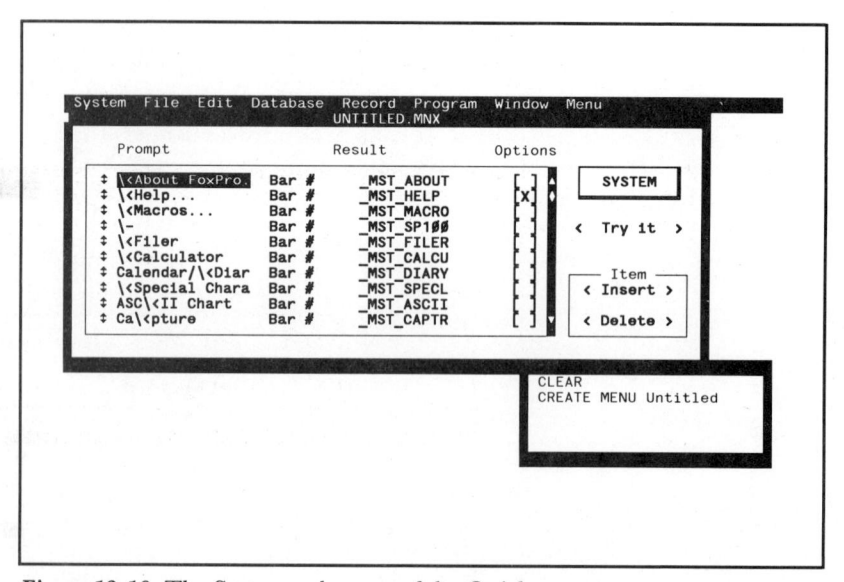

Figure 12.10: The System submenu of the Quick menu

Note the names used to refer to the items of the FoxPro System menu popup. Though it is difficult to see, because they are underlined, each begins with an underscore character and has a second underscore character after MST. Results are assigned to all the submenus of the quick menu in the same way. As you know, you can use the Bar # option of the Result popup plus one of these names to define the result of any submenu item on any menu you create.

You can begin with this Quick menu and alter it in any way you want to create variations on the FoxPro system menu. For example, if you want to be able to execute the MailPower! program from your FoxPro system menu, just add a prompt for it to one of these submenus, and enter the command **DO MAILPOW** as its result.

GENERATING CODE

Once you have finished designing the menu system, produce the code by selecting Generate from the Program menu to call up the dialog box shown in Figure 12.11. As you can see, this dialog box has features that are familiar from the dialog box you used to generate screen code, but it is much simpler.

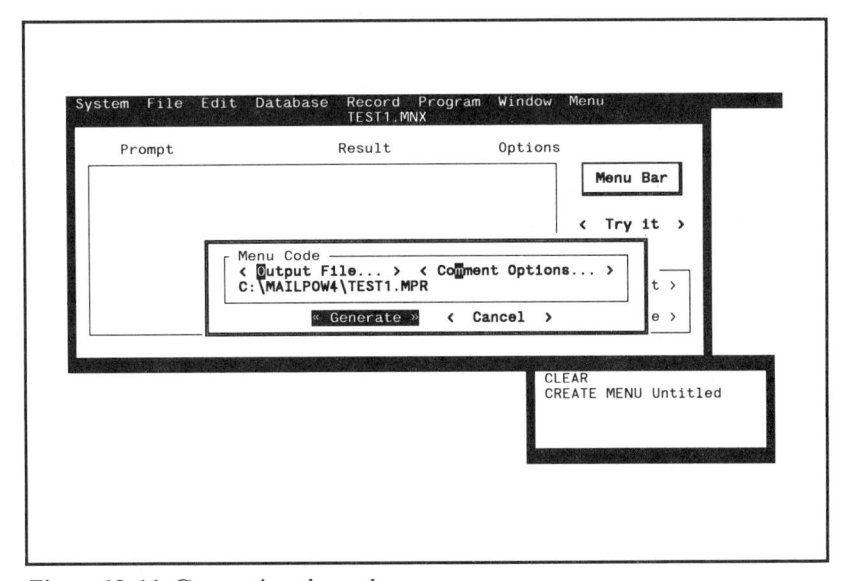

Figure 12.11: Generating the code

Indicate the name of the file that the code goes in by selecting the Output File pushbutton or simply by entering the file name below that pushbutton. Select the Comment Options pushbutton to call up a Comment Options dialog box similar to the one used with screen files. This box enables you to enter your name and company name, and lets you choose whether comments should be surrounded by boxes or asterisks.

MENUING COMMANDS

It might seem strange that the Quick Menu option lets you create menus that are variations of the FoxPro system menu, since it is very unlikely that any program you ever write will have a menu similar to FoxPro's menu. However, FoxPro actually lets you use menus in two different ways:

- You can define menus to use in your own programs. The most common way to do this is to give the menu a unique name when you define it and to use the command **ACTIVATE MENU** <*menu name*> in your program.

- You can define menus to use as substitutes for the FoxPro system menu. One way of doing this is to give the menu the name _MSYSMENU when you define it. Another is to use the command **SET SYSMENU TO**.

As an example of the substitute method, **SET SYSMENU TO** <*popup list*> will limit the system menu to the popups in the list. To set up FoxPro so that it is easy for a beginner to use, you can enter

```
SET SYSMENU TO _MSM_FILE, _MSM_DATA,
_MSM_RECORD, _MSM_WINDO
```

to eliminate some advanced menu features and to leave the essentials. **SET SYSMENU TO** by itself displays a system menu bar with no pads. Finally, **SET SYSMENU TO DEFAULT** displays the normal FoxPro system menu once again.

Rather than using the ACTIVATE MENU command, the FoxPro menu builder makes the menu that you define the system menu.

Note the names used to refer to the items of the FoxPro System menu popup. Though it is difficult to see, because they are underlined, each begins with an underscore character and has a second underscore character after MST. Results are assigned to all the submenus of the quick menu in the same way. As you know, you can use the Bar # option of the Result popup plus one of these names to define the result of any submenu item on any menu you create.

You can begin with this Quick menu and alter it in any way you want to create variations on the FoxPro system menu. For example, if you want to be able to execute the MailPower! program from your FoxPro system menu, just add a prompt for it to one of these submenus, and enter the command **DO MAILPOW** as its result.

GENERATING CODE

Once you have finished designing the menu system, produce the code by selecting Generate from the Program menu to call up the dialog box shown in Figure 12.11. As you can see, this dialog box has features that are familiar from the dialog box you used to generate screen code, but it is much simpler.

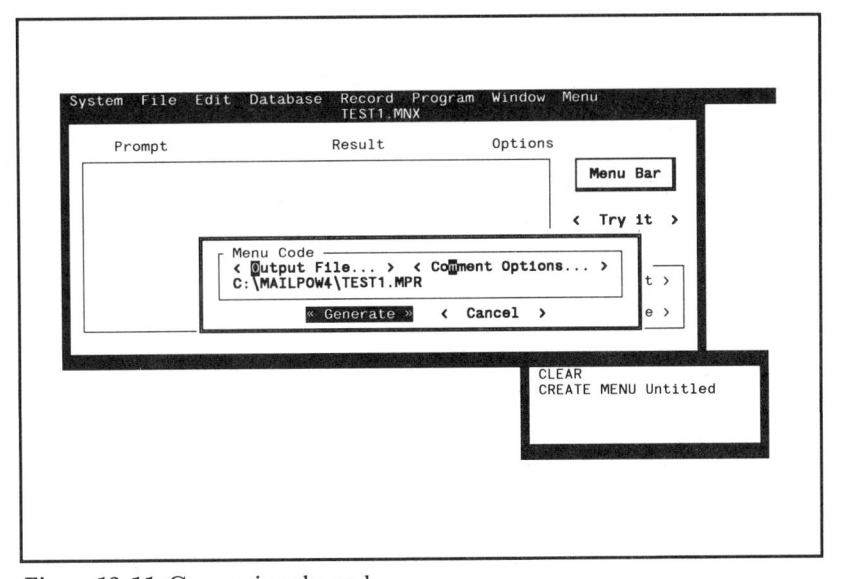

Figure 12.11: Generating the code

Indicate the name of the file that the code goes in by selecting the Output File pushbutton or simply by entering the file name below that pushbutton. Select the Comment Options pushbutton to call up a Comment Options dialog box similar to the one used with screen files. This box enables you to enter your name and company name, and lets you choose whether comments should be surrounded by boxes or asterisks.

MENUING COMMANDS

It might seem strange that the Quick Menu option lets you create menus that are variations of the FoxPro system menu, since it is very unlikely that any program you ever write will have a menu similar to FoxPro's menu. However, FoxPro actually lets you use menus in two different ways:

- You can define menus to use in your own programs. The most common way to do this is to give the menu a unique name when you define it and to use the command **ACTIVATE MENU** <*menu name*> in your program.
- You can define menus to use as substitutes for the FoxPro system menu. One way of doing this is to give the menu the name _MSYSMENU when you define it. Another is to use the command **SET SYSMENU TO**.

As an example of the substitute method, **SET SYSMENU TO** <*popup list*> will limit the system menu to the popups in the list. To set up FoxPro so that it is easy for a beginner to use, you can enter

```
SET SYSMENU TO _MSM_FILE, _MSM_DATA,
_MSM_RECORD, _MSM_WINDO
```

to eliminate some advanced menu features and to leave the essentials. **SET SYSMENU TO** by itself displays a system menu bar with no pads. Finally, **SET SYSMENU TO DEFAULT** displays the normal FoxPro system menu once again.

Rather than using the ACTIVATE MENU command, the FoxPro menu builder makes the menu that you define the system menu.

> If a program that includes a menu is interrupted—for example, because it includes an error—the program's menu will still be the system menu. Remember that you can enter **SET SYSMENU TO DEFAULT** to return to the ordinary FoxPro menu.

Unless you write code to prevent it, FoxPro goes through the entire program when you execute the menu program, including setup and cleanup code, and returns you to the FoxPro Command window with the menu that you defined as the system menu.

It is not difficult to add code to your menu definition to prevent this from happening. First, though, take a brief look at the menu definition commands that FoxPro generates.

DEFINING A MENU

Before the menu builder was added to FoxPro, you had to type out a tedious and repetitive set of commands to define a menu system. The descriptions that follow are intended mainly to help you understand the code that the menu builder generates, not to let you write menu code. For more details, see the individual commands and cross references in the Help window.

First, you had to use the command **DEFINE MENU** <*menu name*> to specify the name of the main menu bar. Then, you had to use a series of commands in the form **DEFINE PAD** <*pad name*> **OF** <*menu name*> **PROMPT** <*char exp*> to specify the names and prompts of all the pads of this menu bar.

You also had to use a series of commands in the form **DEFINE POPUP** <*popup name*> **FROM** <*row, col*> to specify the names and locations of the popups. And, for each of the popups, you had to use a series of commands in the form **DEFINE BAR** <*num exp*> **OF** <*popup name*> **PROMPT** <*char exp*> to specify all of its options.

For each pad, you also had to use the command **ON PAD** <*pad name*> **OF** <*menu name*> **ACTIVATE POPUP** <*popup name*> to "install" the popups in the appropriate pads, so the popup is activated when the pad is selected.

And you had to write a series of commands in the form **ON SELECTION POPUP** <*popup name*> <*command*> to specify the command that would be executed when a selection was made from each popup. This is just an outline of the commands used for defining a menu, but it is enough to let you look through the code generated by the menu builder without being totally lost, and it is enough to let you see how unwieldy these commands are and how much easier it is to use the menu builder than to type them in by hand.

USING THE MENU BUILDER
TO CREATE NON-SYSTEM MENUS

As you learned above, the menu generator is designed to create a system menu. Generated code begins with the command **SET SYSMENU TO** to eliminate the ordinary system menu. Then, rather than specifying a unique name for the menu that is being defined, it uses commands in the form of **DEFINE PAD** <*pad name*> **OF _MSYSMENU PROMPT** <*char exp*>, generating a name for each pad you defined and using the prompt you specified for it as the character expression of the command. Note that it defines the pads that it creates as pads of _MSYSMENU, the system menu.

The code also does not include an **ACTIVATE MENU** command. After executing your setup code, defining the menu that you designed as a new FoxPro system menu, and executing your cleanup code, it returns you to the FoxPro Command window, with the menu you designed as the main menu.

In some menu programs, particularly if they were part of a complex system, you might want to go into the generated code and change it. You could change the name of the menu by adding the command **DEFINE MENU** <*menu name*> and, whenever it occurs in the code, changing _MSYSMENU to the menu name that you specified; it would not be difficult to do this using the editor. Finally, you could add the command **ACTIVATE MENU** <*menu name*> as appropriate.

In our sample program, though, we will use a much simpler method that does not require editing the generated code. The menu's cleanup code will include the commands shown in Figure 12.12. That is, we will leave the menu name as _MSYSMENU, and we will put the command

```
m_again = .T.
DO WHILE m_again
    ACTIVATE MENU _MSYSMENU
ENDDO

USE
SET TALK ON
SET BELL ON
SET DELETED OFF
SET SYSMENU TO DEFAULT
```

Figure 12.12: Cleanup code for a new system menu

ACTIVATE MENU _MSYSMENU in a DO WHILE loop, so that the program keeps displaying this menu and getting choices from the user rather than finishing the program and returning to the FoxPro Command window.

Selecting the menu pad Quit, however, will execute the command **m_again = .F.** When it is selected, the condition of the DO WHILE LOOP will no longer be true, and rather than continuing to get menu choices from the user, the program will execute the remaining code, to close the MAILLIST database file and set the environment back to its default values. In addition to the SET commands from the end of the original version of this program, we need the command **SET SYSMENU TO DEFAULT** to return the FoxPro menu to normal.

Remember that if the program is interrupted because of an error and you return to the Command window with the MailPower! menu bar displayed instead of the FoxPro menu, you should enter **SET SYSMENU TO DEFAULT** to restore the normal FoxPro system menu.

A SAMPLE MENU SYSTEM

You now know enough about the menu builder and the code that it generates to create popup menus for the MailPower! system that you wrote in the last chapter.

The main menu module that you created in the last chapter is equivalent to the menu bar: one pad of this menu will simply exit from the program, and the other four will activate popups with the same options as the four submenus you wrote in the previous chapter.

After filling in the menu builder with these menu items, all you will need is to add their results, which are similar to the procedures or commands that the equivalent menu choices execute in the first version of the program. In some cases, you will have to make minor changes in the original code. For example, the original program clears the screen before displaying a menu screen, but a popup menu does not, so you will have to add the command **CLEAR** after printing reports and labels. Apart from a few exceptions such as these, though, you will be able to edit the original version of the program and simply copy the procedures executed by the original menu choices into the editing area the menu builder provides for the results of popup menu choices.

Of course, you will also have to use the code described above in order to activate the menu. You can call the new menu program MAILMENU in order to avoid confusion with the MAILPOW program you have been working with so far.

1. In the Command window, enter **MODI MENU MAILMENU** to call up the menu design screen. First enter all the prompts for the menu bar: enter \<**Data** on the first line, under the heading Prompt, and enter \<**Reports**, \<**Labels**, \<**Export**, and \<**Quit** on the four lines below it, as shown in Figure 12.13.

2. You defined the hot keys when you entered these prompts, but you should also define shortcut keys using *Alt* and the same letter in combination. Select the Options check box for the Data prompt, and select the Shortcut check box of the Options dialog box. The Key Definition dialog box prompts you to press the key: press *Alt-D*, and that combination appears in the dialog box, as shown in Figure 12.14. Select

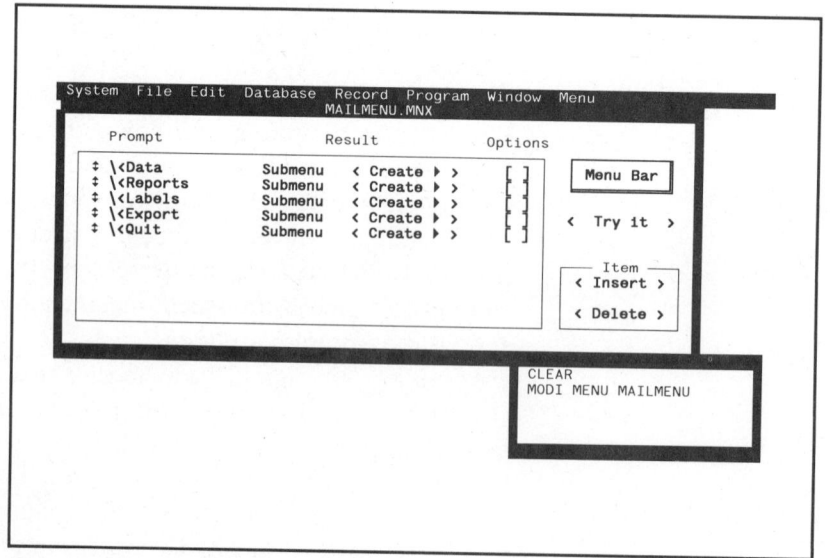

Figure 12.13: The menu bar prompts

USING THE MENU BUILDER 505

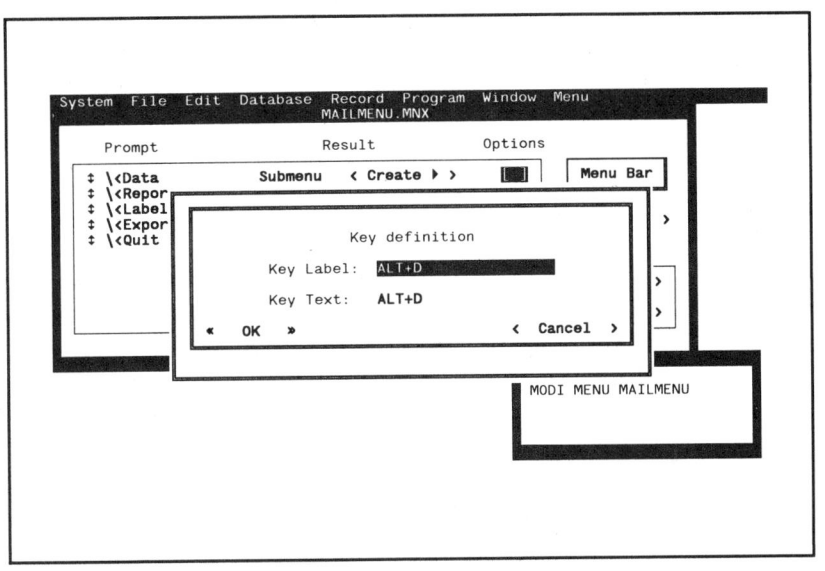

Figure 12.14: Defining a shortcut key combination

OK to return to the Options dialog box and OK to return to the menu definition window. Now, select the Options check box for all the other menu items, and repeat the same process to define Alt-R as the shortcut for Reports, Alt-L as the shortcut for Labels, Alt-E as the shortcut for Export, and Alt-Q as the shortcut for Quit.

3. Before defining submenus, define the command for the Quit pad, since it is the simplest result of all the menu items. Select the Result popup control for the Quit item, which sets to the default option Submenu, and select Command from the popup. The Create pushbutton is replaced by a text entry area: enter the command that this menu choice executes: **m_again = .F.**

4. Now, you might want to copy code from the DATAMENU procedure of the original program to use as the result for options on the Data submenu popup. If so, move the cursor to the Command window (by selecting Cycle from the Window menu or by clicking it with the mouse) and enter **MODI COMM MAILPOW**. Move the Edit window for this

program to the bottom of the screen and cycle back to the Menu definition window.

5. Select the Create pushbutton for the Data item in order to create the Data submenu popup. As the prompts, type **\<Append**, **\<Edit**, **\<Delete**, **\<Look Up**, and **\<Finalize**.

6. To enter the result for the Append item, first select the popup, which now says Command (the default for a submenu), and select Proc from the popup control. Select the Create pushbutton that appears to its right. An editing window appears with the heading MAILMENU Append Procedure. Enter the code shown in Figure 12.15. You can copy this code from the DATAMENU procedure of the MAILPOW program, or you can simply type it into this editing window. (If you do copy it, you will probably want to delete the tab characters that you used to indent it in the original program.) When you are done, close the editing window, saving the code.

7. In the same way, select the popup control for the Edit item, select Proc from the popup, select the Create pushbutton, and enter the code shown in Figure 12.16.

```
*------append using custom screen
APPEND BLANK
SET BELL ON
DO apndscrn.spr
SET BELL OFF
```

Figure 12.15: Code for the Append result

```
*------find record user wants and edit if found
DO lookup
IF .NOT. EOF()
    SET BELL ON
    DO editscrn.spr
    SET BELL OFF
ENDIF
```

Figure 12.16: Code for the Edit result

> The LOOKUP procedure, because it is called by several items on the Data submenu, will be entered as a separate procedure in the Cleanup editing box.

8. Select the popup control for the Delete item, select Proc from the popup, select the Create pushbutton, and enter the code shown in Figure 12.17.

9. For the Lookup item, leave the popup control on the default setting, Command, and simply enter the command **DO LOOKUP**. Likewise, for the Finalize item, simply enter the command **DO WAITMESG.SPR**. When you are done, select the Data popup control in the upper right corner of the dialog box, and select Menu Bar from the popup to return to the main menu.

```
DO lookup
IF .NOT. EOF()
     DELETE
ENDIF
```

Figure 12.17: Code for the Delete result

10. Now, add the features of the Reports menu. As the Result of the Reports item, leave the popup set on Submenu and select the Create pushbutton. As the first prompt, enter \<**Complete**. Use the Result popup for this item to select Proc, and then select the Create pushbutton to use an editing window headed MAILMENU Complete Procedure. Assuming that you still do not want to send the report to the printer while you are testing the program, enter

REPORT FORM complete   && TO PRINT

Remember that you must add **CLEAR** after this, because there is no longer a full-screen menu that begins with CLEAR, as there was in the original program. Now, enter other prompts similar to those you used in the first version of the program—but abbreviate them, perhaps to **Phone**, **3 x 5**, and **4 x 2 1/2**, so the popup is not too large, and designate a hot key for each one. As the Result for each item, select Proc, select the Create pushbutton, and enter the appropriate procedure: **REPORT FORM phones**, **LABEL FORM index**, and

LABEL FORM rolodex, each followed by the command **CLEAR**. When you are done, use the popup control on the upper right to move back to the main menu.

11. Likewise, select the Create pushbutton for the Labels item. To define the submenu, enter prompts similar to the ones you used in the earlier version of the program: One-Column, Two-Column, Three-Column, and so on, designating a hot key for each. Then select Proc from the Results popup, select the Create pushbutton, and enter the appropriate procedure for each—for example:

    SET ORDER TO zips
    LABEL FORM one-col   && TO PRINT
    CLEAR
    SET ORDER TO names

    for the One-Column prompt, and similar procedures using the other label forms for the other prompts.

12. As the prompts for the submenu of the Export pad, enter \<SDF, \<Comma Delimited, and \<Tab Delimited. As the first procedure, assuming that you are still using the message from the original program, enter the code shown in Figure 12.18. Of course, if you have designed a screen program to display this message, use it instead. Enter similar procedures for the other prompts, using the **COPY** command with the optional clauses TYPE DELIMITED and TYPE DELIMITED WITH TAB.

13. Now, prepare to enter the setup and cleanup code for the entire program. Select *General Options* from the Menu menu,

```
SET SAFETY OFF
COPY TO export.txt TYPE SDF
dummy = " "
@ 10,10 SAY "The data has been copied to a file named EXPORT.TXT"
@ 12,10 SAY "Press any key to continue..." GET dummy
READ
SET SAFETY ON
CLEAR
```

Figure 12.18: The first procedure

■ **SET SYSMENU AUTOMATIC**, a new command in FoxPro version 2, sets the system menu on and automatically makes the menu and individual pads accessible and inaccessible as appropriate. For more information, see the Help window.

select the Setup and Cleanup check boxes, and select OK to use a MAILMENU Setup and a MAILMENU Cleanup editing window.

14. Enter the code shown in Figure 12.19 in the Setup editing window: If you are copying this from the earlier version of the program, notice that the command **SET SYSMENU OFF** has been removed. Since the generated code creates a system menu and uses **SET SYSMENU AUTOMATIC** to activate it, this command is superfluous. When you finish, close the edit window, saving the changes.

15. Now, enter the code shown in Figure 12.20 in the Cleanup window (and do not close the window when you are done).

```
*------display the title screen
CLEAR
@ 11,34 SAY 'MAILPOWER!"
@ 14,14 SAY "copyright: Advanced Technology Development Systems"
*------use database and set environment
SET TALK OFF
SET BELL OFF
SET DELETED ON
USE MAILLIST ORDER names

*------delay to let user read screen
counter = 0
DO WHILE counter < 1000
    counter = counter + 1
ENDDO
CLEAR
```

Figure 12.19: The setup code

```
m_again = .T.
DO WHILE m_again
    ACTIVATE MENU _MSYSMENU
ENDDO

USE
SET TALK ON
SET BELL ON
SET DELETED OFF
SET SYSMENU TO DEFAULT
*QUIT
```

Figure 12.20: The cleanup code

Remember that the command you entered for the Quit pad of the main menu bar was **m_again = .F.** This cleanup code appears after the menu definition code, and the DO WHILE loop continues to execute the ACTIVATE MENU command and to remain in the program until the user selects Quit and makes the loop's condition untrue.

16. In this Cleanup editing window, after the cleanup code of the main module of the program, which you just entered, you must also enter the LOOKUP procedure, which is called by the Data menu. In the generated program, it will come after the main module, just where you would put it if you were writing the entire program by hand. Enter the code shown in Figure 12.21 below what you just entered (or copy it from the earlier version

```
**************************************************
* LOOKUP PROCEDURE
* a general purpose procedure to look up a record
* leaves pointer on the record if found or on EOF() if not found
* called from Data Menu
**************************************************
PROCEDURE LOOKUP

m_name = SPACE(20)
m_found = 0

DO getname.spr

m_name = TRIM(m_name)
LOCATE FOR LNAME + FNAME = m_name
IF EOF()
    DO notfound.spr
ELSE
    DO WHILE .T.
        DO confirm.spr
        DO CASE
            CASE m_found = 1
                EXIT
            CASE m_found = 2
                SKIP
                IF lname <> m_name
                    GO BOTTOM
                    SKIP
                    DO notfound.spr
                    EXIT
                ENDIF
            CASE m_found = 3
                GO BOTTOM
                SKIP
                EXIT
        ENDCASE
    ENDDO
ENDIF
```

Figure 12.21: The Lookup procedure

of the program). When you finish, close the window, saving the changes.

17. Now, select Save from the File menu to save your menu design. Then select Generate from the Program menu and select the Generate pushbutton, leaving the name of the generated file as MAILMENU.MPR. When program generation is complete, close the menu design window. To test the program, enter **DO MAILMENU.MPR** in the Command window. The main menu bar and Data popup are shown in Figure 12.22.

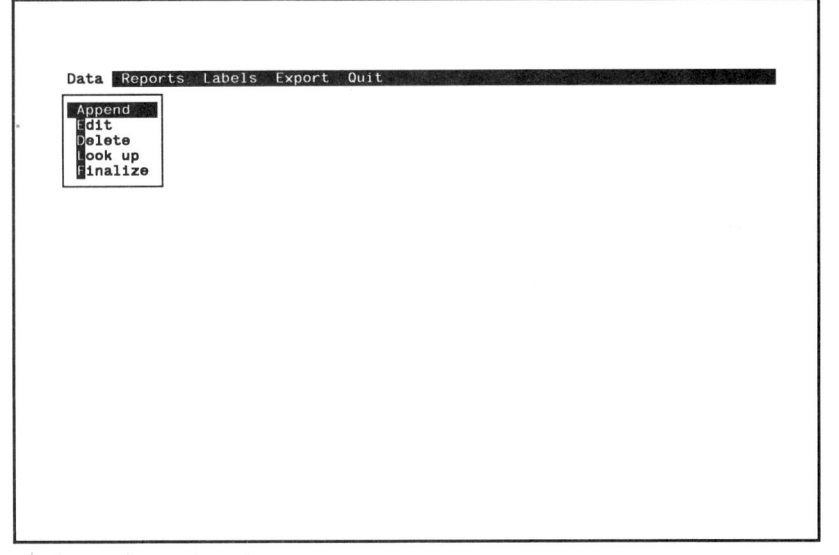

```
Data Reports Labels Export Quit
┌─────────┐
│Append   │
│Edit     │
│Delete   │
│Look up  │
│Finalize │
└─────────┘
```

Figure 12.22: Using the new menu system

Test the program thoroughly. It might have bugs if you made a typographical error—for example, if you left out one of the " delimiters of a character string. If there are bugs, FoxPro behaves as it does when there are bugs in any program: it displays the location of the bug in the code and gives you the options Cancel, Suspend, and Ignore. You should cancel the program and look at the generated code to see what the bug is, then close the editing window, modify the menu design in the menu builder in order to correct the bug, and generate the menu code again.

Appendix A

Installing FoxPro on Your PC

INSTALLING FOXPRO IS A VERY SIMPLE PROCESS. After you enter the **INSTALL** command, it is essentially done for you. After the main program is installed, you will be asked to decide which of FoxPro's optional features you want to install. In addition, you must make a simple alteration to your AUTOEXEC.BAT file in order to use FoxPro from any subdirectory.

You may install either the standard or extended version of FoxPro or FoxPro/LAN. The standard version runs on any IBM-PC or compatible with 512 kilobytes of RAM. The extended version, which takes full advantage of the 32-bit memory addressing capability of the 80386 microprocessor for faster performance, requires an 80386 or better microprocessor and at least 1.5 additional megabytes of RAM. If you have any doubts about which of these to use, install the standard version.

FoxPro is distributed on high-density (1.2 megabyte) $5\frac{1}{4}$" disks. In general, the disk drive needed to read these disks is available on computers that are IBM-AT compatible or better—that is, computers with an 80286 or better microprocessor. If you have an older IBM-PC or IBM-XT compatible computer, it probably has a floppy disk drive that reads only 360-kilobyte $5\frac{1}{4}$" disks. This disk drive cannot be used to install the disks that are distributed with FoxPro, but if you contact Fox Software, they will provide you with a copy of the program on disks that your computer can use. If your floppy disk drive uses $3\frac{1}{2}$" disks, you must also call Fox Software to get them.

Before installing FoxPro, you must make sure you have enough hard disk space to hold it. The base program requires about 6 megabytes of hard disk space. Of this, the Help file requires about $1\frac{1}{2}$ megabytes, so you can install the base product with just $4\frac{1}{2}$ megabytes of free space on your hard disk if you omit the help file. This book does refer you to the Help file for more information, however, so you should install it if at all possible.

Installing all the optional components of FoxPro requires an additional 6 megabytes of hard disk space, but you do not need most of these to use this book. The one set of optional files used in this book requires 649 kilobytes of disk space. The installation program indicates the amount of disk space needed by the optional files that you select and the amount of free space on your hard disk.

If you want to find out how much free disk space you have before you begin installation, just use the DIR command. Virtually all IBM compatible microcomputers use **C:** (the letter C followed by a colon) to refer to the hard disk drive; unless you have some special hardware configuration (such as a hard drive that is partitioned and referred to by either **C:** or **D:**) you may assume that **C:** is the hard drive and follow these instructions:

1. Make sure your DOS prompt indicates that you are using your hard disk. If it does not, enter the command **C:** (do not forget to include the colon). You can be in any subdirectory of the hard disk.

2. Type the command **DIR** and press Enter. The directory of files will scroll by and the number of bytes free on the disk will be at the bottom of the listing.

Before installing FoxPro, you need two things that came with the program:

- four 5¼" high-density distribution disks that came with the program (or the disks sent specially by Fox Software if you have another type of floppy disk drive)
- the envelope with your activation key and serial number

The envelope includes a "demonstration" activation key on the outside and a "live" activation key on the inside. If you want to install a demonstration version of FoxPro—just to try the program out, for up to thirty days—DO NOT OPEN THE ENVELOPE; just use the key printed on the outside to install a demo version of FoxPro. Note that this version cannot hold more than 120 records. Once you open the envelope to use the inside key, you accept the FoxPro licensing agreement; be sure you read this agreement before opening the envelope. You can upgrade from the demo to the live version of FoxPro at any time by reinstalling the program using the inside key.

With this background information, you are ready to install FoxPro:

1. First enter **C:** to make sure you are in the C drive (or another appropriate letter, such as **D:** if you want to install it in another drive). Then insert FoxPro distribution disk 1 into your **A:** floppy disk drive, and enter **A:INSTALL**.

2. After reading the initial screen, press any key to continue. FoxPro asks which products you want to install, as shown in Figure A.1. Enter **Y** or **N** to indicate yes or no for the standard or extended version; enter **Y** to select the help file unless you do not have enough disk space for it.

3. FoxPro asks you to confirm that the program should be installed in the default directory C:\FOXPRO2\ (which it will create automatically). Unless you have some special reason to use another directory, enter **Y**.

4. After reading the next screen, press any key to continue. When you are prompted, enter your serial number, and then enter either the demo or "live" activation key. FoxPro displays messages to inform you that it is copying files to your hard disk. When instructions appear on the screen, telling

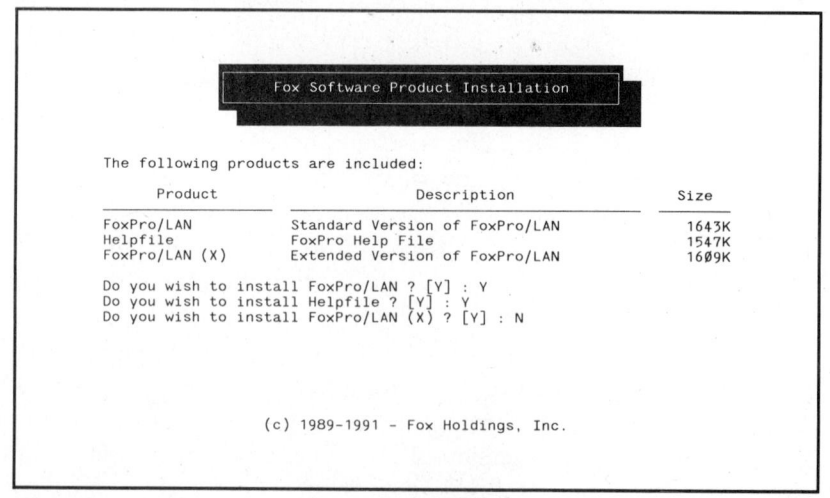

```
                    Fox Software Product Installation


The following products are included:

        Product                Description                    Size

FoxPro/LAN             Standard Version of FoxPro/LAN        1643K
Helpfile               FoxPro Help File                      1547K
FoxPro/LAN (X)         Extended Version of FoxPro/LAN        1609K

Do you wish to install FoxPro/LAN ? [Y] : Y
Do you wish to install Helpfile ? [Y] : Y
Do you wish to install FoxPro/LAN (X) ? [Y] : N



                    (c) 1989-1991 - Fox Holdings, Inc.
```

Figure A.1: Selecting the product to be installed

you to insert a new disk and to press any key to continue, follow them. When the basic installation is done, FoxPro prompts you to press any key to continue installing optional components of the program.

5. FoxPro displays the screen shown in Figure A.2 so you can select monitor type. If you know you have one of the specific monitors listed, select it. Otherwise, just select Generic Color if you have a color monitor or Generic Monochrome if you do not have color. Choose an option by moving the highlight to it using the arrow keys and then pressing Enter or simply by double-clicking it with the mouse.

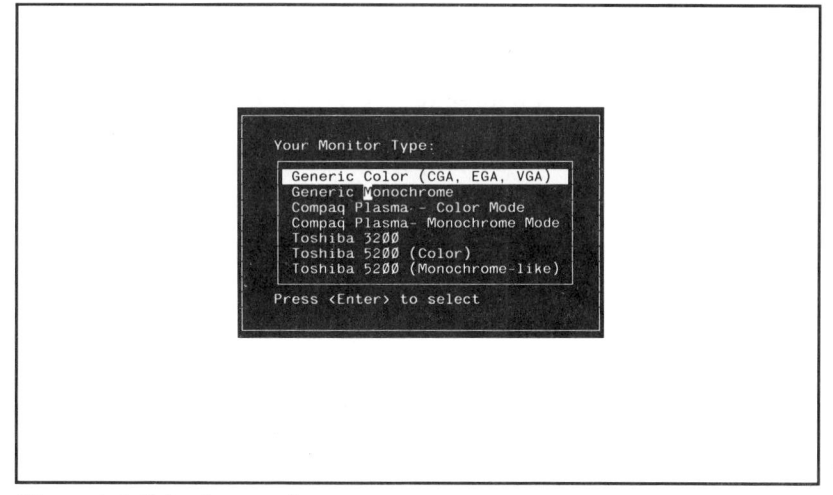

```
Your Monitor Type:
Generic Color (CGA, EGA, VGA)
Generic Monochrome
Compaq Plasma - Color Mode
Compaq Plasma - Monochrome Mode
Toshiba 3200
Toshiba 5200 (Color)
Toshiba 5200 (Monochrome-like)

Press <Enter> to select
```

Figure A.2: Selecting monitor type

A screen appears displaying the supplemental programs and files available. This screen includes a scrollable list of all the available optional features at the top of the screen and a description of the currently highlighted feature in the bottom half of the screen. When you select one of the features, a check appears to its left in the scrollable list. Note the box at the very bottom of the screen, which gives statistics on the amount of free space available on your floppy disk and the total amount of space that the selected files require. Of course, you should check these figures to make sure that the files you have selected do not take up more disk space than you can spare.

You can select supplemental features in three ways:

- Use the arrow keys to highlight the feature that you want in the scrollable list, and then press Enter.
- Double-click the feature with your mouse.
- Move the highlight to the feature and then select the Check pushbutton.

In addition to Check, the pushbuttons on the right of the screen include Un-Check, Check All, and Un-Check All. To remove a feature from those selected for installation, move the highlight to it and select the Un-Check pushbutton. To select all the optional features for installation, select the Check All pushbutton. To undo all your selections and start over, select the Un-Check All pushbutton.

To select any of these pushbuttons using a mouse, simply click it. To select them using the keyboard, press Tab until the pushbutton that you want is highlighted, then press Enter.

Take a moment to consider which of these features you want to install before you continue; move the highlight through them and read the description of each. You must select **Simple Application** to do the exercises in Chapter 11 of this book.

1. Select **Simple Application** and any other optional features that you want to install. Check the figures on the bottom of the screen for available disk space and the amount of disk space needed for the features you have selected.
2. After you have selected all the features you want, press Ctrl-Enter or click the Install pushbutton with your mouse. While it is installing the optional features, FoxPro may ask you to insert other disks; simply follow its instructions.

When installation is complete, FoxPro prompts you to press any key to continue. Pressing a key returns you to the DOS prompt.

SETTING THE PATH

Finally, before using FoxPro, you should change the **PATH** command in your AUTOEXEC.BAT file, which is found in your root directory. This file contains a list of commands that DOS automatically executes whenever you start your computer.

A PATH command determines which directories the system looks in when you enter a command at the DOS prompt. DOS always looks first in the current directory, and then in the directories listed in the PATH command. For example, consider this typical PATH command:

PATH C: ;C: \DOS;C: \UTIL;C: \WP51;C: \FOXPRO 2

Notice that a semicolon is used to separate directory names, but it is not used after the final directory name.

After this command is executed, DOS looks not only in the current directory, but also in the root directory, in a directory named C:\DOS which contains DOS commands, in a directory named C:\UTIL which contains utility programs, in a directory named C:\WP51 which contains a word processing program, and in a directory named C:\FOXPRO 2 which contains FoxPro. Once you have entered this command, you can execute any of these programs from any directory; you do not have to be in the directory that contains them to use them.

Follow these instructions to add the new directory you created to hold FoxPro to the directories already listed in your PATH command, so you can use FoxPro from any directory in your hard disk:

1. Enter **CD ** to make the root directory the current directory. Enter **TYPE AUTOEXEC.BAT** to display the contents of this file on the screen.

2. Your AUTOEXEC.BAT file probably contains a line that begins with the word PATH and looks something like the PATH command listed above. Use any word processor or text editor that can edit plain ASCII files (which some word processors call DOS files) to add the directory you just created to hold FoxPro. (Add it to the end of the list.) Add a semicolon before but not after the directory name, and use the full name, beginning with the letter of the disk, followed by a colon, followed by a backslash, followed by the subdirectory name—**C:\FOXPRO 2**. If you are using a word processor, be sure to save it as an ASCII file.

3. If you do not have a PATH command in your AUTOEXEC-
.BAT file, add one on a separate line from the other commands. If you do not have an AUTOEXEC.BAT file, you can create one with just the PATH command. If you want to add other directories to the search path, just remember to place semicolons between directory names but not after the last directory name.

4. Save the file as AUTOEXEC.BAT. When you start your computer again, the AUTOEXEC.BAT command will be executed, including the **PATH** command that you added.

Appendix B

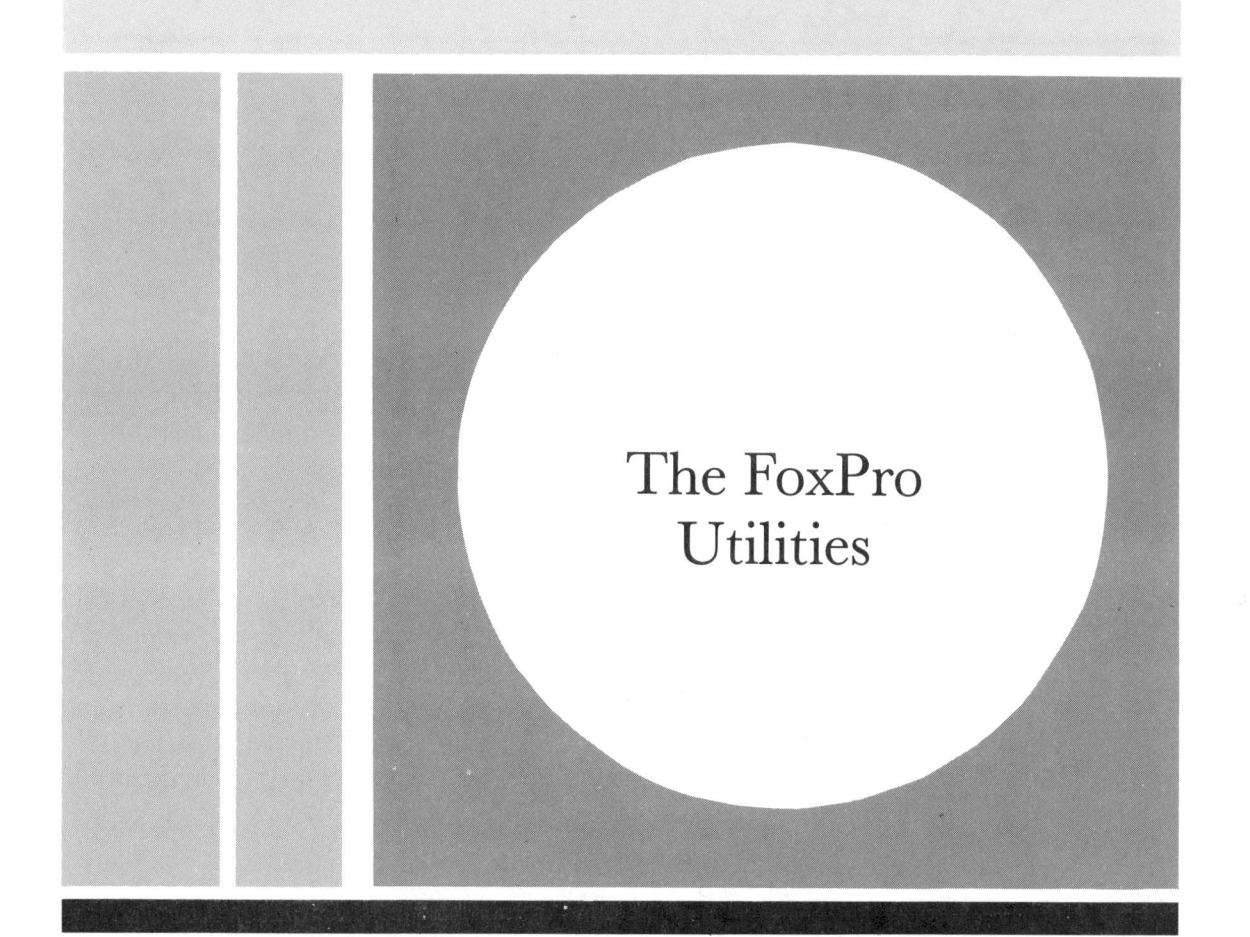

The FoxPro Utilities

YOU CAN USE FOXPRO'S SYSTEM MENU POPUP TO access the filer and a number of other desktop utilities, including a calculator, a calendar/diary, an ASCII chart, a screen capture utility, and a utility that lets you use DOS special characters.

These menu options were not discussed in the main body of this book because they are not directly related to the main purpose of FoxPro—database management. As utilities, they are useful (by definition), but they are not of the essence of the program, so it did not make sense to interrupt learning the main functions of FoxPro to learn about them. Now that you have finished the main portion of this book, though, you will find that it is worth your while to learn the capacities of these added utilities.

THE FILER

The filer is a file management utility that can perform most of the functions of the DOS operating sytems. Because DOS is based on procedural commands that are difficult to learn, many commercial programs have been developed that act as menu-driven substitutes for it. The filer replaces DOS with a system that uses pushbuttons, text boxes, scrollable lists, and the other interface features that you should be very comfortable with after having used FoxPro. It is also much more powerful than DOS.

The filer has two panels. Its Files panel lets you work with individual files. Its Tree panel lets you work with the entire subdirectory system, so you can manipulate all the files in a directory or a group of directories.

When you are using the filer, you can move between these panels in two ways. Each has a pushbutton in its lower right corner that lets you toggle to the other: select the Files or Tree pushbutton of the respective panels to toggle between panels. When you are using the filer, a Filer menu pad is added to the menu bar: the last option on its menu popup lets you move to the panel you are not using. Depending on which panel you are using, select Tree Panel or Filer Panel from the Filer popup in order to toggle between the two.

You can start the filer by selecting Filer from the System menu or by entering **FILER** in the Command window. When you first start it,

THE FILES PANEL

When you start the filer, you use the Files panel, shown in Figure B.1. If you compare the pushbuttons on this panel with the options on the Filer menu bar, shown in Figure B.2, you will see that the selections on the Filer popup are essentially the same as the selections offered by the pushbuttons in the dialog box. (The two menu options that are dimmed, Mkdir and Chdir, are activated when the Tree panel is used and are offered as pushbuttons in that panel.) As with some other features of FoxPro that you have learned, the menu of the filer is meant largely as an alternative to selecting pushbuttons: if you get in the habit of using the Control-key combinations listed on the menu, you will be able to use the filer very quickly even with the keyboard.

MOVING AMONG DIRECTORIES AND FILES

The filer's Files panel contains a scrollable list of files and Drv and Dir popup controls that are very similar to the ones you have seen

the Files panel appears: since this is the default panel of the filer, we will discuss it first.

> The first three files in the scrollable list in the illustration are temporary files created by FoxPro, which FoxPro names using random combinations of letters and numbers. You should never delete or otherwise alter these files while you are using FoxPro, and they are dimmed in the filer's scrollable list, so you cannot access them. If some are not deleted automatically when you quit from FoxPro, you can delete them from the DOS prompt—but do not do this while FoxPro is still running.

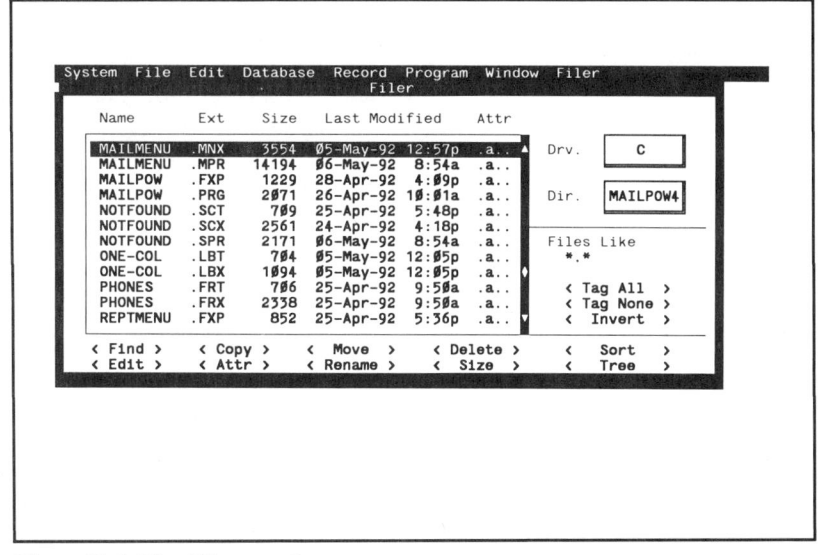

Figure B.1: The Files panel

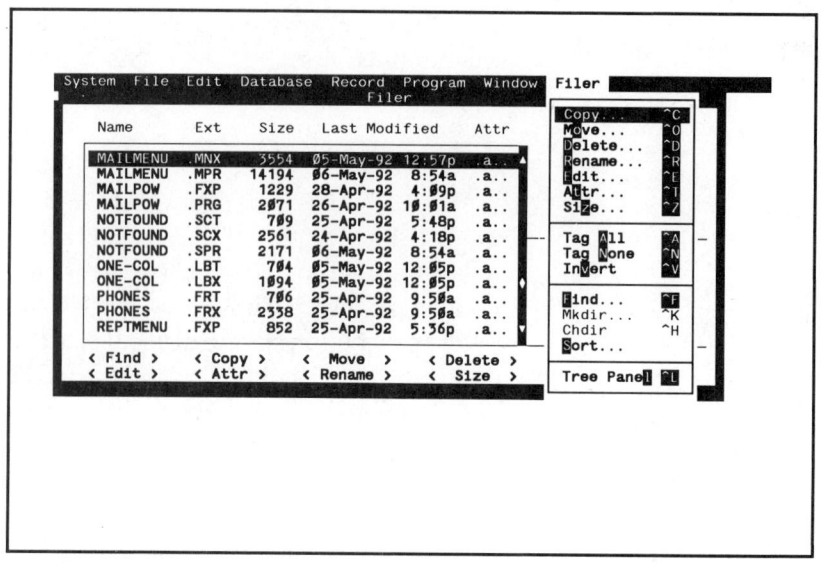

Figure B.2: The Filer menu

> The hierarchical directory structure was explained in Chapter 2. If you need to review the details of how the directory structure is organized, see that chapter.

elsewhere in FoxPro, for example, in the Open and the Save As dialog boxes.

As in these other dialog boxes, the scrollable list of files in the filer includes (in addition to the names of the files in the current directory) the names of all the children directories that are under the current directory enclosed in square brackets, and two dots enclosed in square brackets to represent the parent directory of the current directory. By selecting parent or child directories, you can move up and down through the entire hierarchical directory system.

This scrollable list also contains other details about the file, which are included in DOS directories but not in similar scrollable lists of files that you have seen in FoxPro. In addition to a file's name and extension, the filer's scrollable list also includes the file's size (in bytes) and the date and time that it was last modified, as DOS directories do. Finally, in the column at its far right, the filer's scrollable list includes the files' attributes: these determine such things as whether a file can be written to or can be read only. The filer makes it easy to change them using the Attr pushbutton or via a menu selection: attributes will be discussed in detail when these selections are discussed.

The two popup controls in the filer also work like the popup controls that you have seen in the Open and Save As dialog boxes. The Drv popup lets you change the drive—for example, you can select A: to make floppy disk drive A the current drive. The Dir popup control lets you move quickly through a directory structure that is many levels deep, by letting you select any subdirectory, up to the root directory, from the popup rather than repeatedly selecting the parent directory from the scrollable list.

The text box labeled Files Like (under the Dir popup control) lets you use a scrollable list that displays only some of the files in the current directory. The default setting for Files Like is *.*, which displays all files, but you can specify files to be displayed by using literal characters in combination with the two DOS wild-card characters:

- * represents any word
- ? represents any single character

The file name and extension are two different words, so that *.* represents any name followed by any extension. If you wanted to list only your FoxPro database files, you could enter *.**DBF** in this text box, so files with any name followed by the DBF extension would be listed. If you have a group of files that you gave names beginning with the letter J, you could list them all by entering J??????.* in this text box.

You can combine more than one specification in this box if you separate them with semicolons. For example, you could enter *.**DBF**;*.**DBT**;*.**FPT** to list all database files and any associated memo files (including both FoxPro and the older dBASE compatible memo files). Do not leave a space after the semicolon.

TAGGING FILES

The process of tagging files is the key to using the filer. Tagging simply means selecting a file in such a way as to make a triangle marker appear to the left of its file name. Most pushbuttons or menu selections work only on files that are tagged. If no file is tagged when you select them, they will simply display an error message.

Tagging Files Individually with the Keyboard   To tag an individual file using the keyboard, move the highlight to it and press the space bar. A triangle appears to the left of any file that you tag.

Since you generally want to perform commands on a single file, tagging one file normally eliminates any tag you previously put on another file. If you want to tag more than one file while selecting files individually, press Shift and the space bar together, and the tags you created previously will not be eliminated.

If a file is already tagged, moving the highlight to it and pressing Shift and the space bar together will eliminate the tag.

Tagging Files Individually with the Mouse   To tag an individual file using the mouse, point to the file and click. To tag more than one file, hold down the Shift key when you select later files—or hold down the Shift key and drag the mouse to select a number of consecutive files.

To untag a file using the mouse, press Shift while you point to the file and click. If it is already tagged, the tag will disappear.

Tagging Groups of Files   The filer also contains three pushbuttons that let you tag and untag groups of files; there are three menu options that are identical to these pushbuttons.

- **Tag All:** tags all the files that are displayed in the scrollable list. This option is most useful if you use it in combination with the Files Like text box. For example, enter *.**DBF** in the Files Like text box, so that your database files are displayed; then select Tag All to tag all the database files.

- **Tag None:** removes tags from all files in all directories. Unlike Tag All, Tag None does not work only on displayed files—it works on all files in all directories. Use it to make sure that you do not have any files tagged that you do not know about.

- **Invert:** removes tags from all tagged files, and tags all untagged files in the current directory. For example, if you want to delete all except the database files in the current directory, you can tag the database files and then select Invert. The database files will be untagged and all the other files will be tagged, at which point you can then select Delete.

You can also tag more than one file at a time by selecting the Find pushbutton (or menu option), described in the next section.

FIND

Selecting the Find pushbutton or selecting Find from the Filer menu calls up the Find dialog box, shown in Figure B.3.

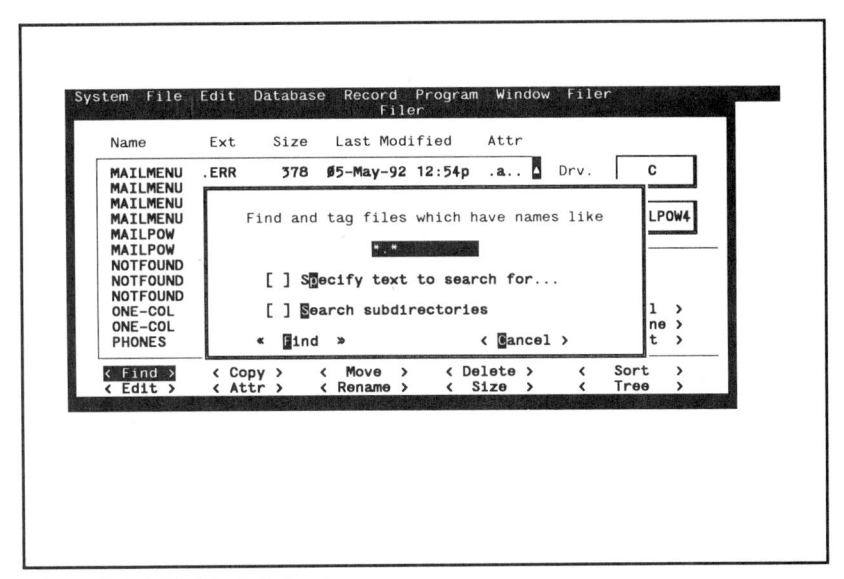

Figure B.3: The Find dialog box

The Find dialog box lets you tag files based either on their names or on their content. It can search in just the current directory or in a number of directories.

The simplest way to use Find is to fill in the text box in the same way that you do the Files Like text box of the Filer dialog box. As you can see in the illustration, this box contains *.* by default, which means it matches all files unless you instruct it to do otherwise. You can fill it out with the wild-card characters (* and ?) and literal characters just as you learned to do with the Files Like text box in the previous section.

Even if you are just searching for file names in this way, though, the Find dialog box does more than the Files Like text box, because you can select its Search Subdirectories check box to find matching files in all subdirectories under the current directory. If you want to search all the directories in the current drive, just make the root directory the current directory before beginning the search. For example, if you make the root directory the current directory, enter *.**DBF** in the text box, and check the Search Subdirectories check box, you can tag all the database files in all the directories of the current disk drive.

You can also use Find to search text files. It will tag those that contain text that you specify. If you select the Specify Text To Search For check box, you will call up the dialog box shown in Figure B.4.

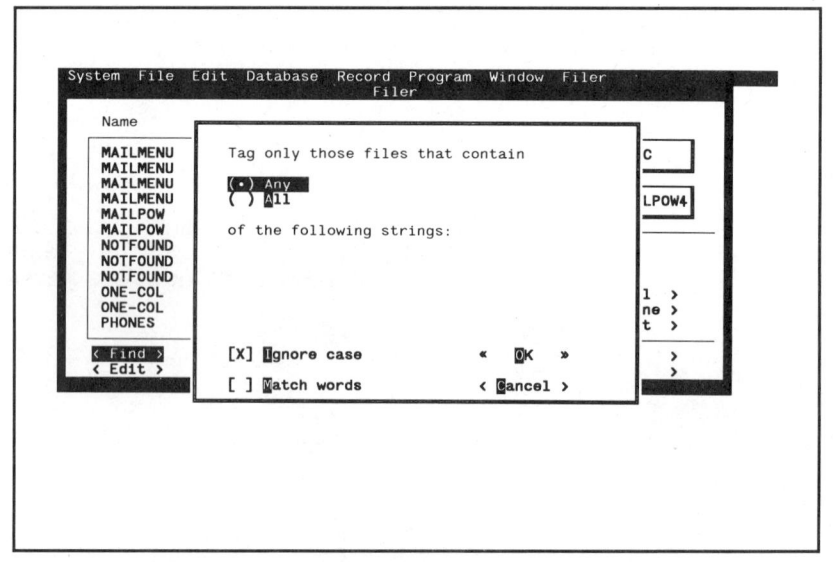

Figure B.4: Dialog box for tagging files based on content

Though you cannot see them in the illustration, there are three text boxes under the words "of the following strings," where you can fill in the character strings that you want to search for.

The Any and All radio buttons are useful if you fill in more than one of these text boxes: they let you specify whether the file or files should be tagged if they contain any of the strings you specified, or whether they should be tagged only if they contain all the strings you specified.

The Ignore Case check box, as you might imagine, lets you determine whether the search will tag a file if the capitalization of the characters in the file is different than in the string you specified. As you can see, the search ignores capitalization by default.

Checking the Match Words check box makes the search tag a file only if the string that matches your specification is a separate word, not embedded in some larger word. If you were looking for the word *id*, for example, you would want to check this check box so that the program does not tag files that contain words such as *slid, idiom,* and *widget*.

Consider an example that combines several capacities of Find: tagging all the FoxPro programs in your hard disk that contain the **LOOP** command. First, you move to the root directory of your hard disk. Then select Find to call up the Find dialog box, and enter ***.PRG** in its text box. Check the Search Subdirectories check box, check the Specify Text to Search For check box to call up the second dialog box, enter **LOOP** in its text box as the string to search for, remove the check from the Ignore Case check box (assuming that you capitalize the key words in your programs), check the Match Words check box, and select OK to return to the Find dialog box. Finally, select Find to tag the matching files.

As you will see, you can use the filer to perform operations on all of these files after they are tagged. For example, you can delete, copy, or even edit all of them at once.

COPY

If there are any files tagged, you can select the Copy pushbutton, or Copy from the Filer menu, to call up the Copy dialog box, shown in Figure B.5.

This dialog box lets you copy tagged files. Copying a file preserves the original file and creates a duplicate of it that either has another name or is in another location.

Remember that the files must be tagged before you call up the Copy dialog box.

The Copy Tagged Files As text box; at the top of this dialog box, lets you specify the name of the file. The default, *.*, keeps the original name of the file. You can change the name by adding literals

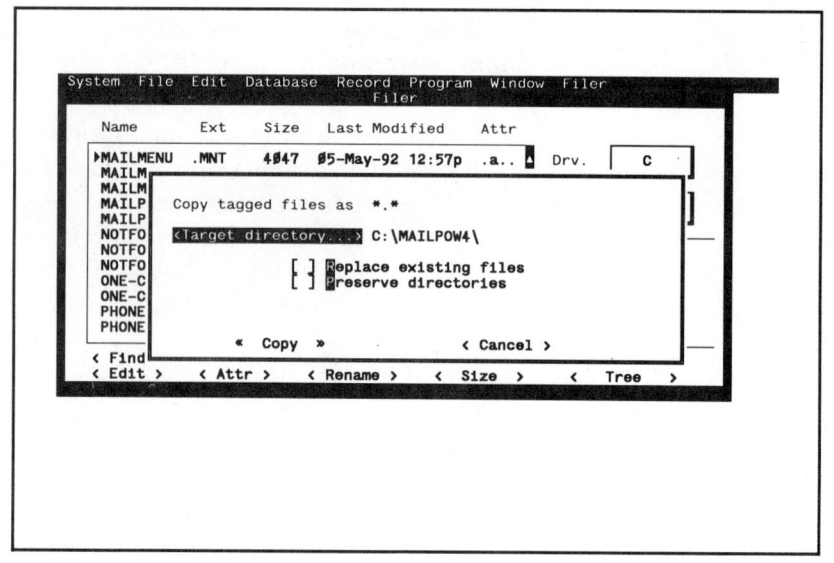

```
System  File  Edit  Database  Record  Program  Window  Filer
                                Filer
        Name        Ext     Size   Last Modified    Attr
       ▶MAILMENU    .MNT    4047   05-May-92 12:57p  .a..    Drv.  [   C   ]
        MAILM
        MAILM
        MAILP    Copy tagged files as  *.*
        MAILP
        NOTFO    <Target directory...> C:\MAILPOW4\
        NOTFO
        NOTFO              [ ] Replace existing files
        ONE-C              [ ] Preserve directories
        ONE-C
        PHONE
        PHONE              «  Copy  »         < Cancel >
       < Find
       < Edit >   < Attr >   < Rename >   < Size >   < Tree >
```

Figure B.5: The Copy dialog box

instead of the wild-card characters. For example, if you want to make backups of tagged files, you can enter ***.BAK** in this text box: all the tagged files will be copied to files with the same name except for the .BAK extension.

The target directory pushbutton and text box let you specify the directory that you want the copies of the file to be in. If you select this pushbutton, you will call up the Select Target Directory dialog box, shown in Figure B.6. As you can see, this dialog box works like the Open or Save As dialog box: it lets you use a scrollable list to move to the parent or children directories of the current directory; the Directory popup control lets you move quickly up and down the subdirectory tree; and the Drive popup control lets you select the disk drive. Alternately, you can just type the disk and directory in the text box to the right of this pushbutton.

Notice that the default target directory is the current directory; you have also seen that the default is for the copies to have the original files' names. You must change one of these defaults. You can copy files to another directory or disk while keeping their current names, or you can copy files in the current directory with different names, but you cannot have two files with the same name in the same directory.

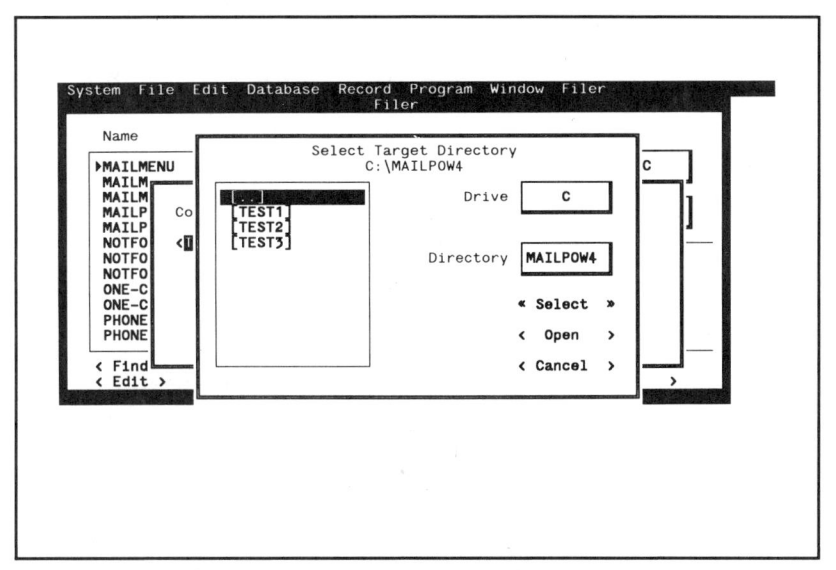

Figure B.6: The Select Target Directory dialog box

If you check the Replace Existing Files check box of this dialog box, the files produced by the **COPY** command will overwrite existing files with the same names without giving you any warning. If you do not check this check box, the command will display an alert before it overwrites a file. After you select Yes or No to determine whether that file will be overwritten, the command will go on and copy the rest of the tagged files.

If you check the Preserve Directories check box, the command will copy the directory structure as well as the files that are tagged. If this check box is not checked, tagged files from various subdirectories will all be copied into a single subdirectory. This feature will be explained in the discussion of the filer's Tree panel.

MOVE

Selecting the Move pushbutton, or Move from the Filer menu, calls up the Move dialog box, shown in Figure B.7.

Move is like Copy, except for one point. Copy creates a duplicate file and preserves the original; Move creates a duplicate file and eliminates the original.

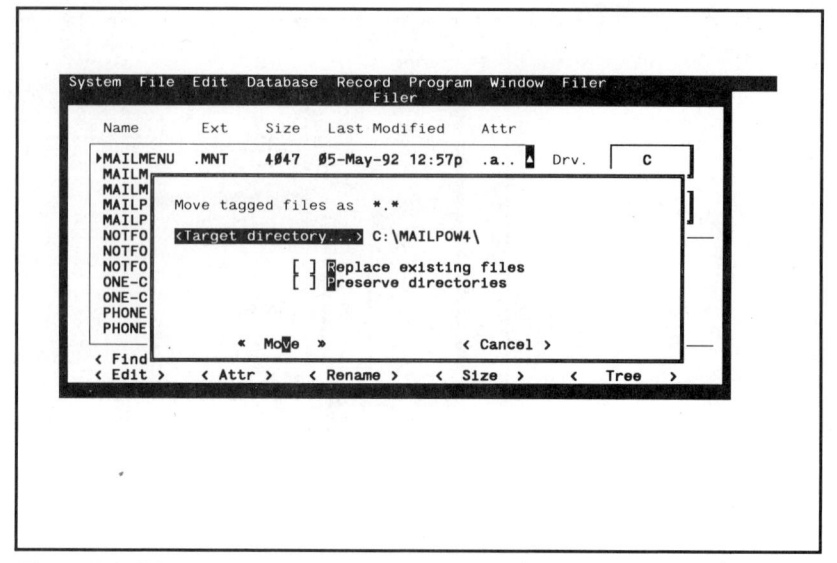

```
System  File  Edit  Database  Record  Program  Window  Filer
                              Filer
    Name     Ext    Size    Last Modified   Attr
  ▶MAILMENU  .MNT   4047    05-May-92 12:57p  .a..      Drv.    C
   MAILM
   MAILM
   MAILP    Move tagged files as   *.*
   MAILP
   NOTFO    <Target directory...>  C:\MAILPOW4\
   NOTFO
   NOTFO              [ ] Replace existing files
   ONE-C              [ ] Preserve directories
   ONE-C
   PHONE
   PHONE          «  Move  »              < Cancel >
  < Find
  < Edit >   < Attr >   < Rename >   < Size >   < Tree >
```

Figure B:7: The Move dialog box

As you can see, the Move dialog box looks exactly like the Copy dialog box, and all of its features function in the same way. The only difference is that, after you enter all of the specifications and select Move, the original file is eliminated. The effect is that the file is moved from its current location to the specified location; it is not just copied at the specified location.

DELETE

Selecting the Delete pushbutton, or Delete from the Filer menu, calls up the Delete dialog box, shown in Figure B.8.

This dialog box asks you to confirm that you want to delete each of the tagged files. Select Delete to delete the one file whose name is displayed. Select Skip to retain the file whose name is displayed; the dialog box will go on and ask you about deleting any other tagged files. Select Delete All to avoid this file-by-file confirmation process and delete all tagged files immediately. Needless to say, you should use Delete All with caution.

SORT

Selecting the Sort pushbutton or Sort from the Filer menu calls up the Sort dialog box, shown in Figure B.9.

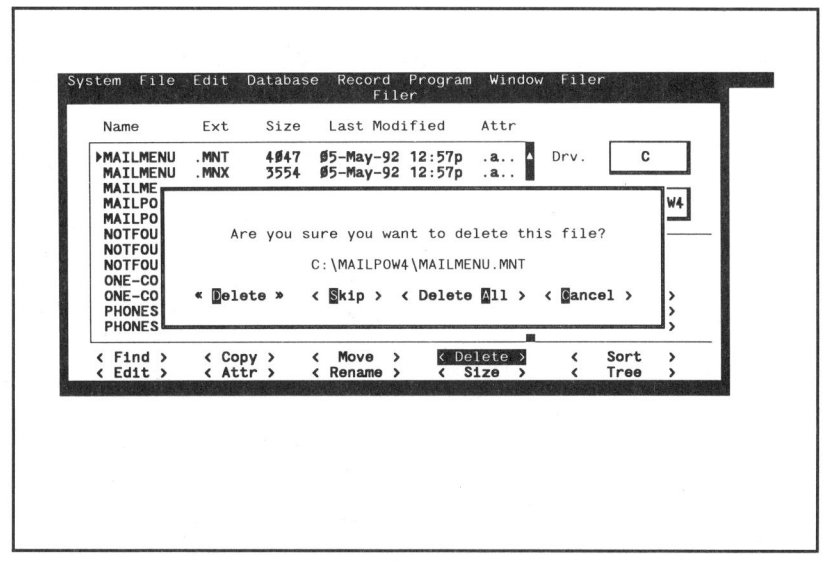

Figure B.8: The Delete dialog box

Figure B.9: The Sort dialog box

This dialog box lets you change the order in which files are displayed in the filer's scrollable list. As you can see, the radio buttons Name and Ascending are checked by default, so that the files are displayed alphabetically by name.

You can also select radio buttons to display the files in the order determined by their extension, size, date, or attributes. (Attributes will be discussed later in this appendix.) The most useful of these is Extension: it is often handy to sort by extension so that files of the same type (database files, index files, program files, and so on) are grouped together.

The other two radio buttons let you choose ascending or descending order. You might want to choose Descending in order to have the most recent dates come first, or to have the largest files come first.

EDIT

Selecting Edit opens edit windows for all tagged files.

You might find this useful, for example, if you want to open edit windows for all your program files. You could enter ***.PRG** in the Files Like text box and then select Tag All to tag all program files, then simply select Edit to open edit windows for all these files. The edit windows will appear to be stacked, and you can call any one forward to work on it.

ATTR

Selecting the Attr pushbutton, or Attr from the Filer menu, calls up the Attributes dialog box, shown in Figure B.10.

These attributes are represented by letters in the Attr column of the file list.

An **h** in this column means that the file is a hidden file, which does not appear in an ordinary DOS directory. DOS includes two hidden files in the root directory, IBMBIO.COM and IBMDOS.COM; you have not seen these in your root directory, but you can see them, with the h attribute, if you use the filer to look at your root directory.

An **s** in this column means that the file is a system file. There are several key DOS files that are protected with this attribute, because they must have a specific location on the disk. The filer does not let you move, delete, rename, or overwrite a file with this attribute.

You can alter any of these attributes by selecting the appropriate check box. Then, if you select the Change pushbutton, FoxPro will ask you to confirm that you want to make this change to each of the

> Changing the system or the hidden attribute can let you create later errors that prevent your operating system from working.

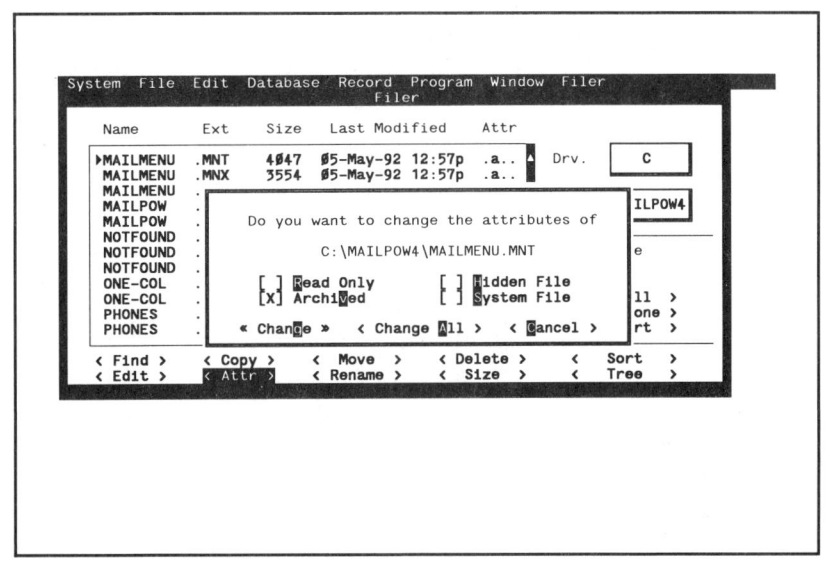

Figure B.10: The Attributes dialog box

tagged files. If you select Change All, FoxPro will change all tagged files without this confirmation process.

RENAME

Selecting the Rename pushbutton, or Rename from the Filer menu, calls up the Rename dialog box, shown in Figure B.11.

To rename a file, simply fill in the new name in the text box of this dialog box and select Rename. The current file name appears in the dialog box by default, in case you want to give the new file a similar name. The dialog box lets you rename all of the tagged files in turn.

If another file already has the new name you want to give to a file, an alert will appear, saying you have made an error: You cannot use Rename to give a file a name that is already used. The alert asks you to choose Yes if you want to continue renaming other tagged files or No if you want to cancel the process and return to the Files panel.

SIZE

Selecting the Size pushbutton, or Size from the Filer menu, calls up the Size dialog box, shown in Figure B.12.

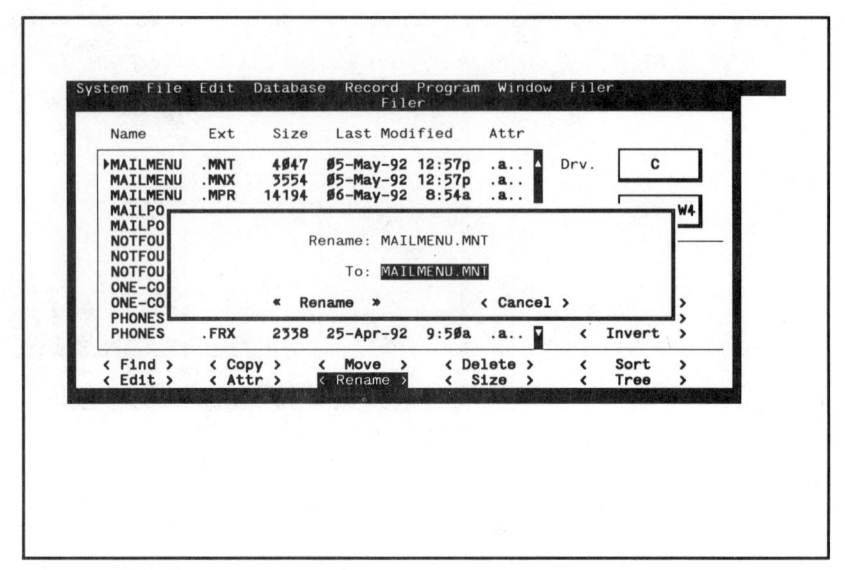

Figure B.11: The Rename dialog box

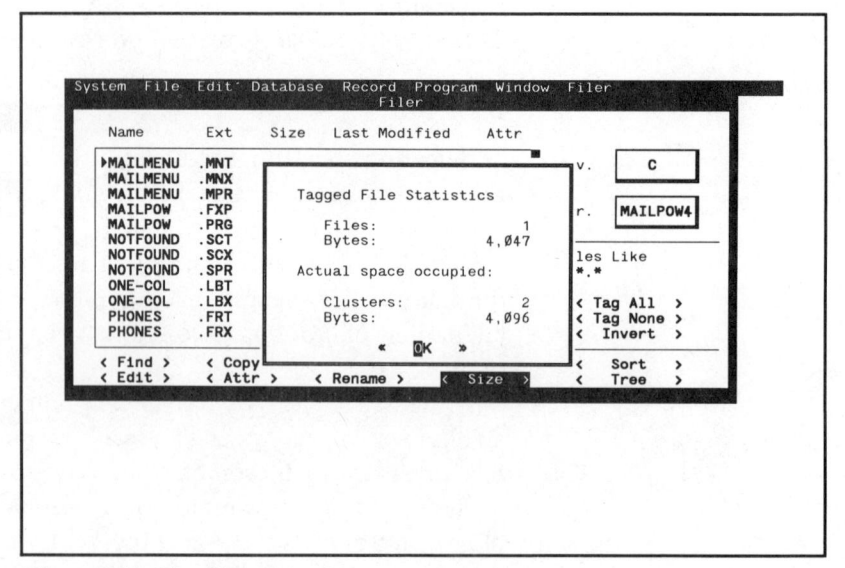

Figure B.12: The Size dialog box

THE FOXPRO UTILITIES 537

This dialog box simply displays information about tagged files, including the number of files currently tagged, their total size in bytes, and the amount of space they occupy on the disk in clusters and bytes.

The number of bytes the files occupy on the disk is greater than the number of bytes in the files themselves, because disk space is broken up into clusters, and files must be allocated some whole number of clusters. You can see in the illustration that although the file occupies 4,047 bytes, it has been allocated one cluster—of 4,096 bytes. Therefore, this 4,047-byte file takes up 4,096 bytes of space on the disk.

THE TREE PANEL

Selecting Tree, the final pushbutton on the lower right of the Files panel, or selecting Tree Panel from the Filer menu, lets you use the filer's Tree panel, shown in Figure B.13.

First, FoxPro will take a moment to scan your entire directory structure, because it uses this panel to work with entire subdirectories

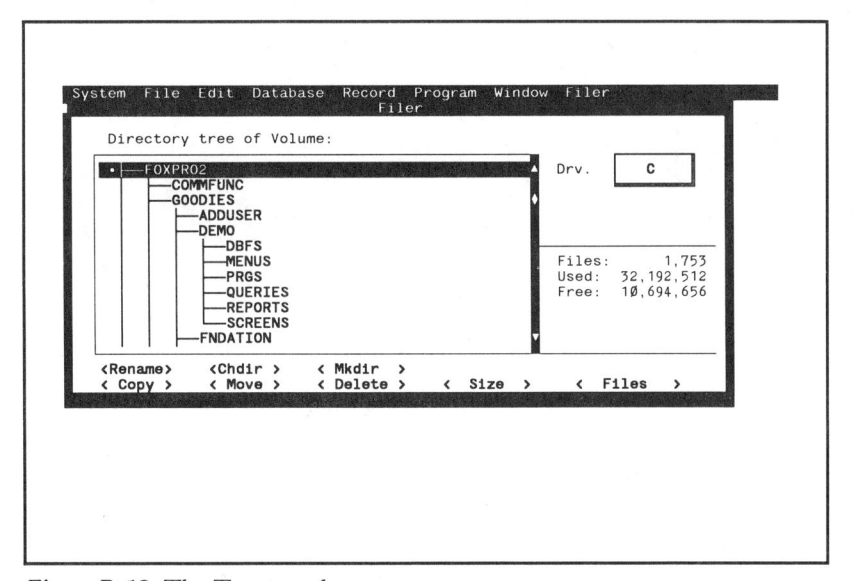

Figure B.13: The Tree panel

and all the files they contain (rather than just with files in the current subdirectory, as the Files panel does).

As you can see from the illustration, this panel displays a graphic representation of the hierarchical directory structure. The letter C: at the top represents the root directory. All of the subdirectories connected directly with it by lines are directly under the root. You can see that API, FIXIT, and FOXAPP are subdirectories of the FOXPRO subdirectory, and that FOXAPP has a subdirectory named MENUS. The current directory (in the illustration, this is the current directory) has a bullet to its left.

All these directories are in a scrollable list, and you can move the highlight among them as you do in any scrollable list. This panel also has a popup control that lets you select the drive, and some basic data on the number of files on the disk, the amount of space they use, and the amount of space free.

TAGGING DIRECTORIES

You must tag the directories that you manipulate with the Tree panel just as you tag the files that you manipulate with the Files panel. As with the Files panel, a triangle appears to the left of a directory that is tagged in the Tree panel.

RENAME

Selecting the Rename pushbutton or selecting Rename from the Filer menu calls up the Rename dialog box, shown in Figure B.14.

This dialog box renames the tagged directories, and works just like the dialog box that is used for renaming files. Fill in the new name in its text box: the current name appears as the default, in case you want to use a similar name. If multiple subdirectories are tagged, the filer lets you rename them all in sequence.

CHDIR

Selecting the Chdir pushbutton or selecting Chdir from the Filer menu lets you change the current directory. Simply tag the directory that you want as the current directory, and make this selection. The

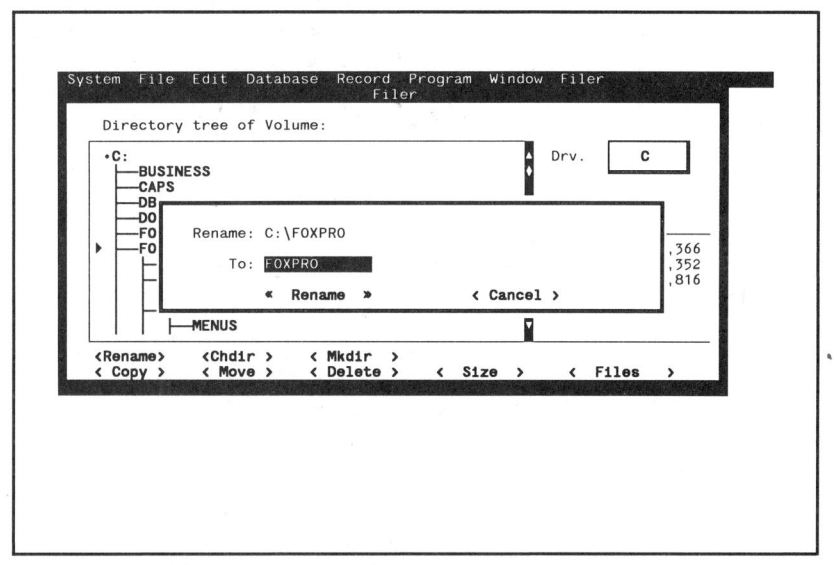

```
┌─────────────────────────────────────────────────────────────┐
│  System  File  Edit  Database  Record  Program  Window  Filer│
│                           Filer                              │
│    Directory tree of Volume:                                 │
│   ┌─────────────────────────────────────────┐                │
│   │ •C:                                  ▲  │   Drv.  ┌───┐  │
│   │   ├─BUSINESS                            │         │ C │  │
│   │   ├─CAPS                                │         └───┘  │
│   │   ├─DB                                  │                │
│   │   ├─DO                                  │                │
│   │   ├─FO ┌──────────────────────────────┐ │         ,366   │
│   │ ▶ ├─FO │ Rename: C:\FOXPRO            │ │         ,352   │
│   │   │    │    To: [FOXPRO          ]    │ │         ,816   │
│   │   │    │      « Rename »   < Cancel > │ │                │
│   │   │    └──────────────────────────────┘ │                │
│   │   └─MENUS                            ▼  │                │
│   └─────────────────────────────────────────┘                │
│   <Rename>  <Chdir >   < Mkdir  >                            │
│   < Copy >  < Move >   < Delete >  < Size >   < Files >      │
└─────────────────────────────────────────────────────────────┘
```

Figure B.14: The Rename dialog box

bullet that shows which directory is the current directory will move to indicate the change.

MKDIR

Selecting the Mkdir pushbutton or selecting Mkdir from the Filer menu calls up the Mkdir dialog box, shown in Figure B.15.

To create a new subdirectory under the current directory, simply enter the name you want to give it and select Mkdir.

COPY

Selecting the Copy pushbutton, or Copy from the Filer menu, calls up the Copy dialog box, shown in Figure B.16.

This dialog box is like the one that you use to copy files, and it is used the same way, except that it copies all the files of the *directories* that are tagged when you use it from the Tree panel.

The Preserve Directories check box becomes useful in this panel. If you do not check it, all the files in tagged directories will be copied

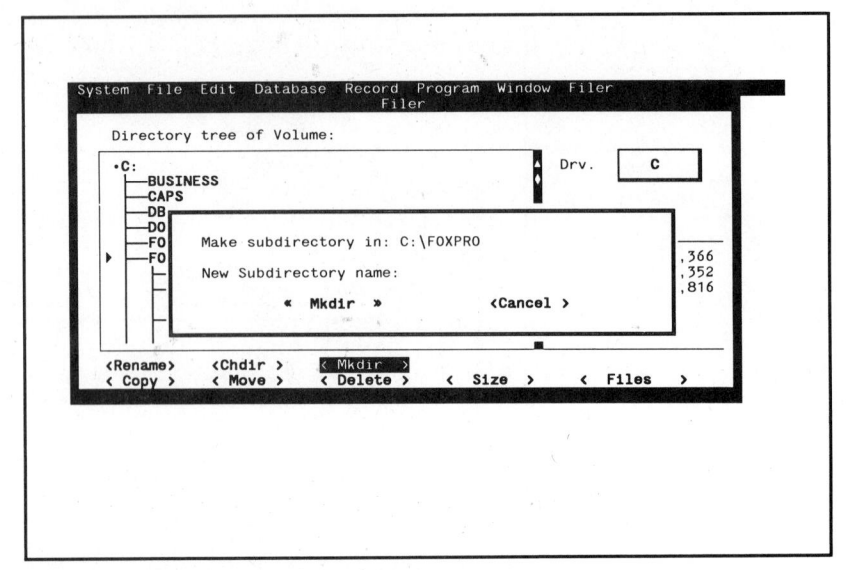

Figure B.15: The Mkdir dialog box

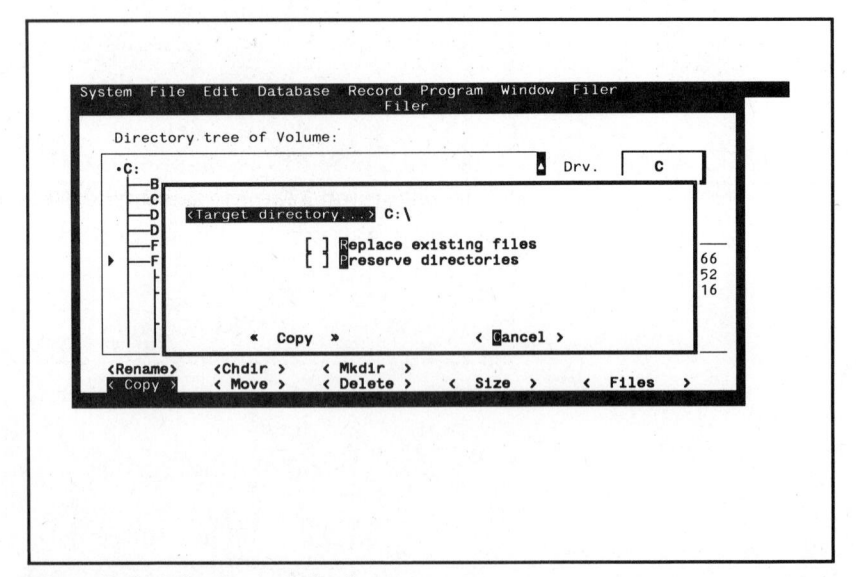

Figure B.16: The Copy dialog box

into a single target directory. If you do check it, the filer will create a subdirectory structure under the target directory that corresponds to the structure of tagged subdirectories under the highest tagged directory. The files in the highest tagged directory will be copied into the target directory, but files in the directories under it will be copied into separate, newly created subdirectories with the same names as their original directories.

MOVE

Selecting the Move pushbutton, or Move from the Filer menu, calls up the Move dialog box, shown in Figure B.17.

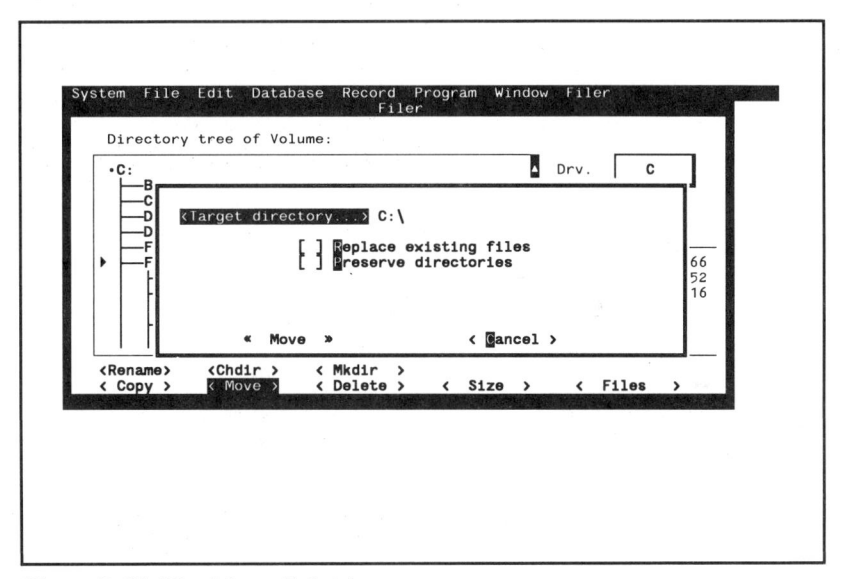

Figure B.17: The Move dialog box

As in the Files panel, the Move option of the Tree panel is identical to the Copy option, except that the original files are deleted and only the copies in the new locations are left.

DELETE

Selecting the Delete pushbutton, or Delete from the Filer menu, calls up the Delete dialog box, shown in Figure B.18.

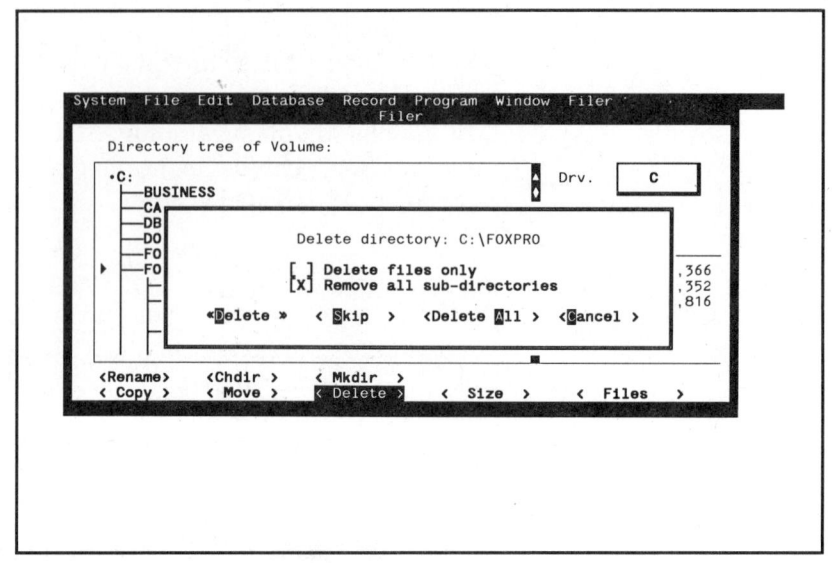

```
┌─────────────────────────────────────────────────────────┐
│ System  File  Edit  Database  Record  Program  Window  Filer │
│                              Filer                       │
│   Directory tree of Volume:                              │
│  •C:                                          ▲   Drv. ┌──┐│
│    ├─BUSINESS                                 ▓        │ C││
│    ├─CA                                       ▽        └──┘│
│    ├─DB  ┌───────────────────────────────────┐            │
│    ├─DO  │     Delete directory: C:\FOXPRO   │            │
│  ► ├─FO  │  [ ] Delete files only            │     ,366   │
│    └─FO  │  [X] Remove all sub-directories   │     ,352   │
│          │                                   │     ,816   │
│          │ «Delete»  < Skip >  <Delete All>  <Cancel> │    │
│          └───────────────────────────────────┘            │
│                                                          │
│   <Rename>    <Chdir>    < Mkdir >                       │
│   < Copy >    < Move >   < Delete >   < Size >  < Files >│
└─────────────────────────────────────────────────────────┘
```

Figure B.18: The Delete dialog box

⊙ Use this feature with extreme caution, as you cannot see the names of the files in the directories that you are deleting.

This dialog box looks like the one that the Files panel uses to delete files, but there is one vital difference. The one in the Files panel lets you confirm the deletion of each file that is tagged; this one only lets you confirm the deletion of each *directory* that is tagged. Select Delete to confirm the deletion of the directory, or Skip to skip it and make the filer continue with the next directory.

You can also delete all tagged directories without confirmation by selecting Delete All.

If the Delete Files Only check box is checked, the files in the specified directories will be deleted, but the directories themselves will remain (though, of course, they will be empty). The default state of the Delete Files Only check box is *not checked*; unless you check it, the files will be deleted *and* the directories themselves removed.

If the Remove All Subdirectories check box is checked, not only the tagged directory but all the subdirectories under it will be deleted. You do not need to tag the subdirectories individually: just tag the single directory at the top of the group that you want to delete and use this check box.

The fact that this check box is checked by default makes it very dangerous. If you mistakenly tag your root directory and then select Delete All without changing the default setting of the check boxes, the filer can delete every file and every directory of your hard disk.

SIZE

Selecting the Size pushbutton or selecting Size from the Filer menu calls up the Size dialog box, shown in Figure B.19.

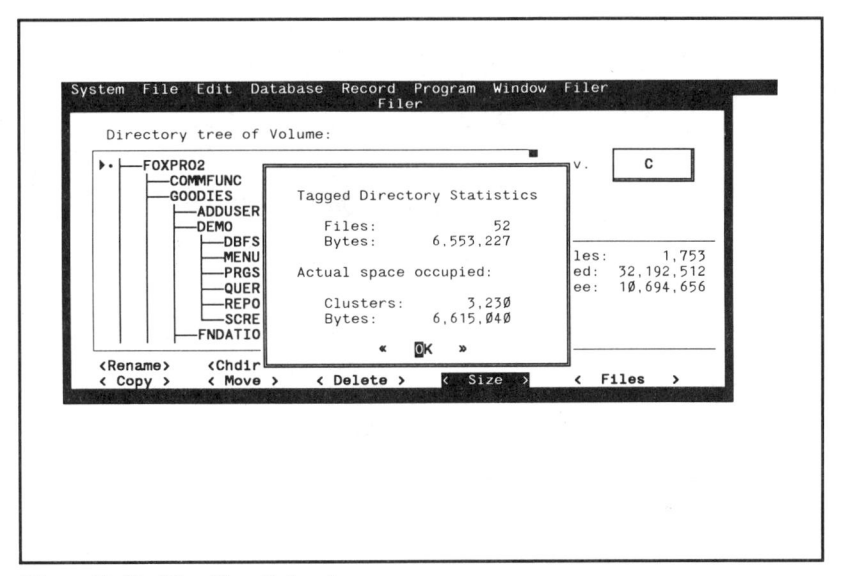

Figure B.19: The Size dialog box

As you can see, this dialog box is gives you basic statistics about the number of files in the tagged directories, their size, and the number of clusters and actual disk space they occupy, just like the dialog box that appears when you select Size from the Files panel.

FILES

Selecting the Files pushbutton on the lower right, or selecting Files Panel from the Filer menu, brings you back to the Files panel.

THE DESKTOP UTILITIES

The filer is the most elaborate utility included with FoxPro, but the System menu also includes a number of desktop utilities similar to the ones included in other popular programs. These utilities are meant to replace items that ordinarily clutter up your desk, such as a calculator and an appointment calendar.

THE CALCULATOR

Selecting Calculator from the System menu calls up the calculator, shown in Figure B.20.

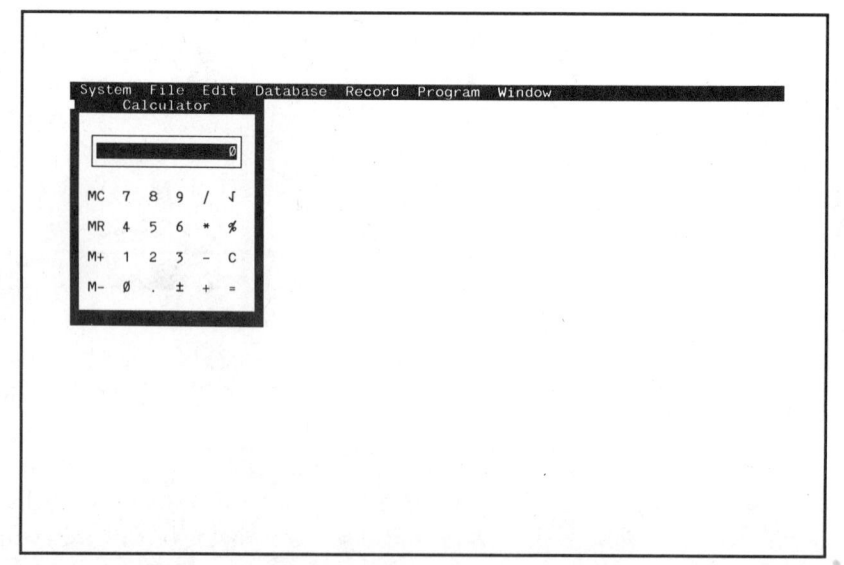

Figure B.20: The calculator

The calculator is used like many pocket calculators, so it is easy to learn. If you are using the mouse, you simply click the numbers or operators you want to use, just as you would press the buttons of a calculator. If you are using the keyboard, you just press the key of any number or operator that is represented on your keyboard; for functions that are not represented by a single key on the keyboard, use the keys shown in Table B.1.

Table B.1: Special Keys for Using the FoxPro Calculator with the Keyboard

KEY	FUNCTION	CALCULATOR EQUIVALENT
Q	square root	$\sqrt{}$
N	plus or minus	±
A	add to memory value	M+
S	subtract from memory value	M−
R	recall memory	MR
Z	clear memory	MC

The discussion below talks about typing and using numbers, operators, and calculator functions. In every case, this means either selecting them with the mouse or typing them using the keyboard and the special keys listed in the table.

The functions of the calculator keys will probably be familiar to you.

The number keys and the decimal point are, of course, used to enter numbers. Simply type in the number and it will appear on the display panel on the top of the calculator.

The arithmetic operator keys +, −, *, and / are used to indicate addition, subtraction, multiplication, and division. To perform these operations, type the first number, then type the operator (when you type the operator, the first number that you typed will be highlighted in the display panel to indicate that it is fully entered, and the operator that you typed will appear to its right), then type the second number. Once the second number is on the display panel, type = to complete the calculation.

To find a square root, first type the number. When it is displayed correctly, use the square root operator. The result will be displayed in the display panel immediately.

The percent operator lets you perform operations that use some percentage of the number in the display panel. For example, to find a number 10 percent larger than a given number, first type the given number, and when it is in the display panel, type +, then type **10**, then use %. A number 10 percent larger than the original number is displayed.

The ± *(plus/minus)* operator changes the sign of the number that is displayed: it is equivalent to multiplying the number by −1. Just use this operator, and the sign of the value that is displayed will change instantly.

C clears the value from the display area. If you have pressed an operator key and there is an operator displayed to the right of the value, then you must use C twice to remove the operator as well as the number.

MC, **MR**, **M+** and **M−** let you temporarily store values in the calculator's memory and work with those values. When a value is stored in memory, an M appears to the left of the display panel.

To store the value that is currently displayed in the display panel, simply use **M+**. An M will appear to the left of the display panel to indicate that there is a number stored in memory. To recall the number from memory, use **MR**. The value in memory will appear in the display panel, overwriting any value that is currently displayed. To clear the value that is in memory, use **MC**. The value will be cleared and the M to the left of the display panel will disappear.

The **M+** and **M−** keys are used to add or subtract from the number that is in memory. For example, if you want to make the value in memory 10 less than it is, enter **10**, then use **M−**. Then when you press **MR**, you will recall a number that is 10 less than the number that was previously in memory.

If you select Preferences from the Edit menu popup while you are using the calculator, you can use the Calculator Preferences dialog box to alter the default settings of the calculator. This dialog box contains just two sets of radio buttons.

The first set lets you determine the way in which the calculator affects the NumLock key of your computer. As you know, you can use the numeric keypad on the right of your computer keyboard either to enter numbers or to move the cursor (using the arrow keys, PgUp, PgDn, Home, and End). You toggle between these two functions of the numeric keypad by pressing the NumLock key. In its default mode, the calculator does not affect the current setting of the NumLock key; if you find it more convenient, though, you can choose one of the preferences to automatically make the numbers on the keypad available to you whenever you use the calculator. You can make your choice from three radio buttons:

- **Don't Alter NumLock:** When the calculator is used, the status of NumLock remains what it was. This is the default setting.
- **Remember NumLock State:** The calculator remembers what the NumLock status was the last time it was used and reverts to that status automatically when you use it.
- **Force NumLock On:** NumLock is turned on automatically when you use the calculator, so that you can use the numeric keypad to enter numbers.

The other set of radio buttons lets you adjust how decimals are displayed. It also includes three choices:

- **Automatic:** The number of decimal places the calculator displays in the results of calculations depends on the number of decimal places in the numbers that are entered and on the operations that are performed. This is the default setting.
- **Floating:** displays numbers with as many decimal places as are needed to show the entire number as precisely as possible. Unnecessary trailing zeros are eliminated.
- **Fixed:** displays numbers with a fixed number of decimal places. When you make this selection, a text box appears that lets you enter the number of decimal places you want displayed. All numbers are displayed with this number of decimal places, with trailing zeros added if necessary.

THE CALENDAR/DIARY

Selecting Calendar/Diary from the System menu calls up the Calendar/Diary window, which is shown in Figure B.21 along with the related Diary menu popup.

Whenever you select the calendar/diary, the calendar is on the current date, and any entry for that date in the diary is shown in the Diary panel (the right half of the window). Selecting dates on the calendar lets you see existing diary entries and make entries in

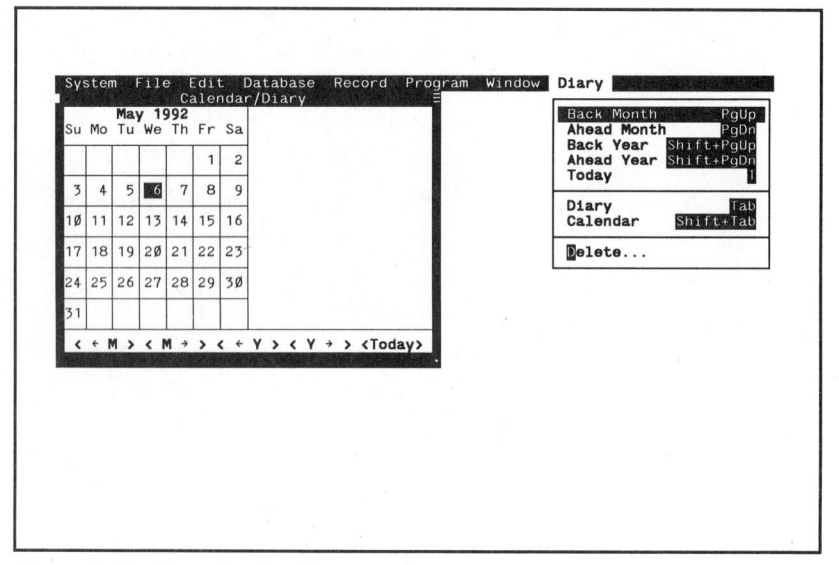

Figure B.21: The calendar/diary

the diary for those dates. The diary entry is thus associated with the calendar date and is displayed when that date is selected. If there is an entry for a given day, that date appears on the calendar in enhanced display.

When you begin, the calendar is selected. The name of the month is underlined in the Calendar panel when the calendar is active, and the cursor appears in the Diary panel when the diary is active. You can move between the two in several ways:

- press Tab to move to the Diary panel and Shift-Tab to move to the Calendar panel
- select Diary or Calendar from the Diary menu popup to move to the corresponding panel
- using the mouse, simply click on the panel that you want to move to

When the Diary panel is active, use the usual editing techniques to make diary entries. They may be of any length, and you can scroll through them in the usual ways or resize or zoom the Calendar/Diary window to see more of an entry.

When the Calendar panel is active, move among the days of the current month by using the arrow keys or (if you have a mouse) simply by clicking the day that you want. To move to a different month, either use the pushbuttons at the bottom of the Calendar panel, the corresponding options on the Diary menu, or the hot keys, as follows:

- The ←M pushbutton, the Back Month option on the Diary menu, or the PgUp key moves you back a month.
- The M→ pushbutton, the Ahead Month option on the Diary menu, or the PgDn key moves you forward a month.
- The ←Y pushbutton, the Back Year option on the Diary menu, or the Shift-PgUp key combination moves you back a year.
- The Y→ pushbutton, the Ahead Year option on the Diary menu, or the Shift-PgDn key combination moves you forward a year.

In addition, the Today pushbutton, the Today option on the Diary menu, or the T key moves you back to the current date, no matter where you are in the calendar when you select it.

The Delete option of the Diary menu lets you delete all entries in the Diary *prior to* the date selected on the Calendar. It presents you with a warning before deleting this data, and the No pushbutton is the default choice. These should help you to avoid deleting data by mistake. Select the Yes pushbutton to confirm that you want to delete all entries prior to the date selected on the calendar.

Use the usual editing techniques to delete the entry for a single day.

SPECIAL CHARACTERS

Selecting Special Characters from the System menu calls up the Special Characters window, shown in Figure B.22.

This utility gives you an easy way of using the special characters that are available in the extended ASCII character set. You can add any of these characters to any text that you are creating using the FoxPro editor—for example, if you are using a foreign name and want to include a letter with an accent mark.

> Not all printers handle all these special characters. Before using them in a document you want to print, make sure that they will work with your printer by checking its documentation or by creating and printing a short test document with the special characters you want to use.

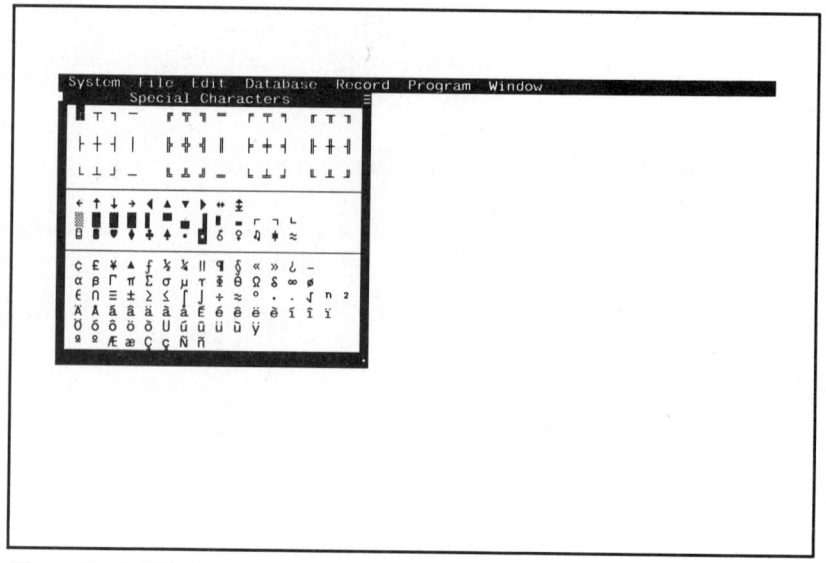

Figure B.22: The Special Characters window

Notice that the top third of this panel includes box-drawing characters, the middle includes special graphic characters, and the bottom third includes special symbols and foreign letters.

To use one of these characters, simply place the cursor on it and select it. It is pasted in the place where the cursor was in the last window that was active.

For example, if you are typing a document and come to a point where you need a foreign character, simply leave the cursor at that point, select Special Characters from the System menu, and select the character you want. When you close the Special Characters window and return to the document, the character will be there.

For this process to work, the window where you are placing the character must be open and must be a type of window where you can normally use the Paste option of the Edit menu. If you have trouble making the special character appear, try holding down the Shift key while you select it from the Special Characters window.

THE ASCII CHART

Selecting ASCII Chart from the System menu calls up the ASCII chart shown in Figure B.23.

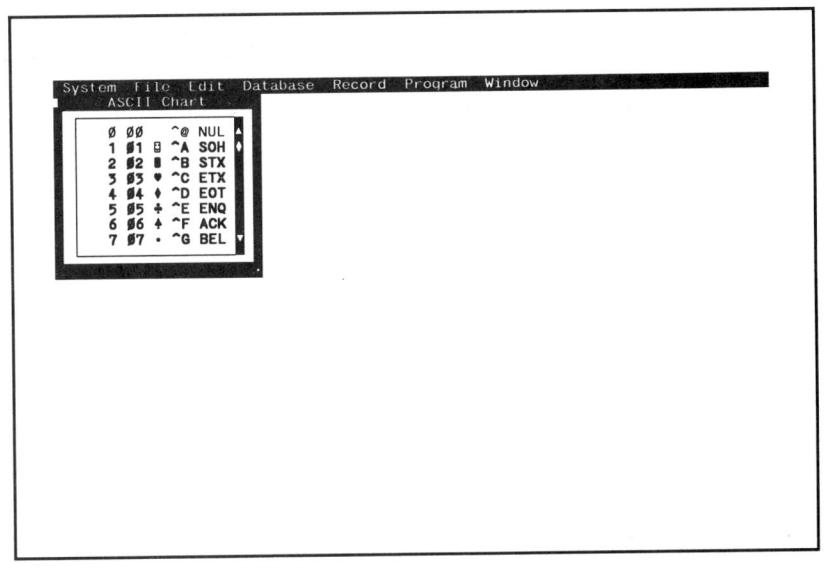

Figure B.23: The ASCII chart

The first column shows the ASCII number of the character in decimal notation. The second column shows the same ASCII number in hexadecimal (base 16) notation: if you do not know hexadecimal notation, you can simply ignore this column, as it is not needed for FoxPro programming. The third column shows the graphic representation of the character. (Most characters are shown as they are printed, but the lower-number ASCII characters are control characters, which are not printed, so they are represented by graphics—such as a face.) The fourth column shows the Control-key combination (if there is one) for the character. The fifth column represents the meaning of control characters (lower-number ASCII characters) in an abbreviated form: for example, you learned that ASCII character 7 makes the computer beep, and you can see that its name is BEL.

If you select an ASCII character from this chart, its graphic representation from column three is pasted in the location where the cursor was before you opened the ASCII chart window—just as characters from the Special Characters window are.

THE CAPTURE UTILITY

Selecting Capture from the System menu lets you use the Capture utility to copy text from all or a part of the screen into the clipboard, so that you can paste it into an editing window. Graphic characters, such as the borders of windows, cannot be captured.

After you select Capture from the menu, a message appears telling you to select the top left corner. You then begin to select the text that you want to capture. Thus, using the mouse, move the pointer to the upper left corner of the area you want to select, and press the mouse button. A message appears saying that you should select the bottom right corner. Drag to the lower right corner of the area you want to select and release the mouse button to capture the text in the selected area.

If you are using the keyboard, use the arrow keys to move the cursor to the upper left corner of the area you want to select, and press Enter. A message appears saying that you should select the bottom right corner. Move the cursor to the lower right corner of the area you want to select and press Enter to capture the text in the selected area.

A message saying "Captured and placed on the clipboard" appears when you have finished capturing the text. Once it is on the clipboard, you can select Paste from the Edit menu to paste it in a document.

Appendix C

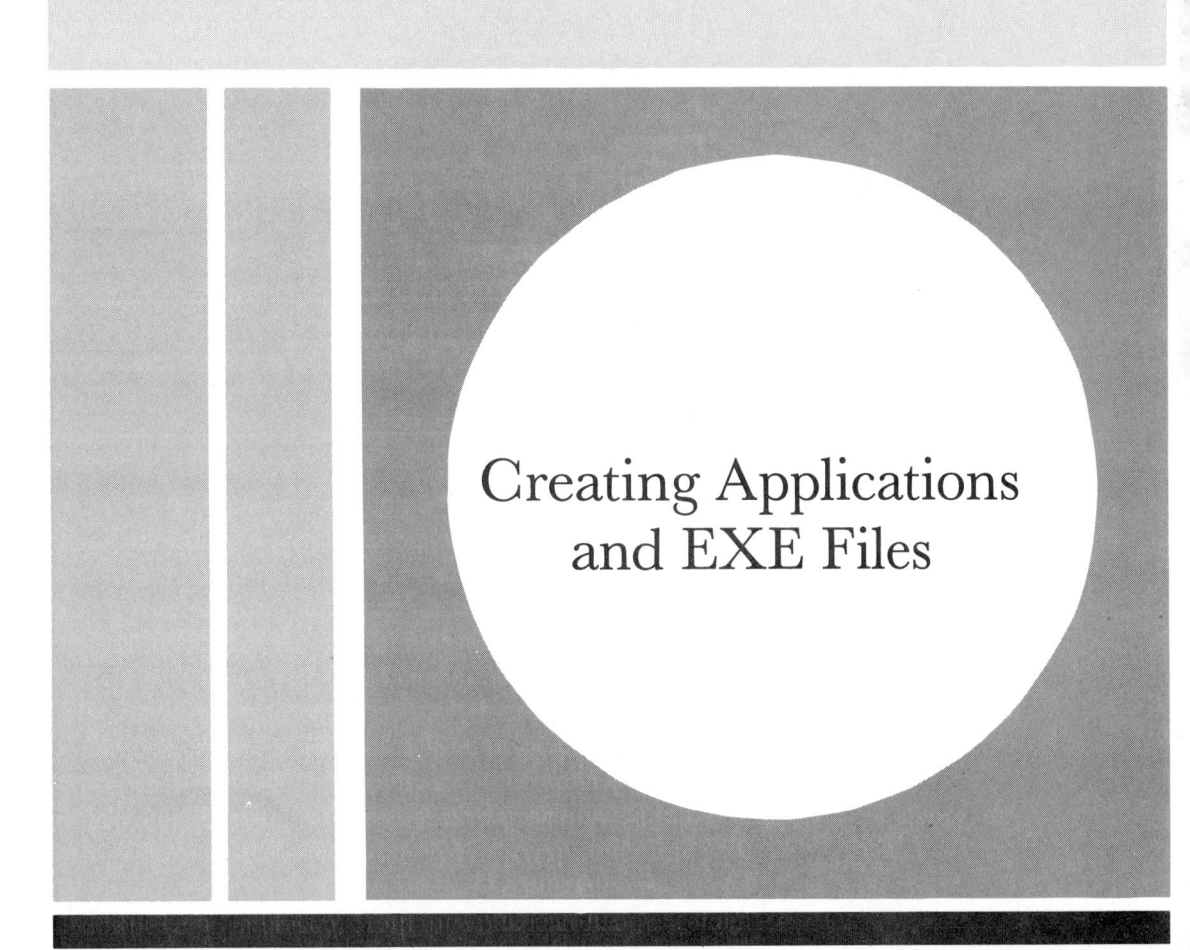

Creating Applications
and EXE Files

THE PROJECT MANAGER ALLOWS DEVELOPERS to combine all the files of an application into a single file for commercial distribution. It is also useful for keeping track of all the files involved when developing a complex program within FoxPro, but it is meant primarily for developers creating applications for distribution. In order to use the Project Manager in this way, however, you must first purchase FoxPro's distribution kit, which lets you create stand-alone applications (with an APP extension) and several types of EXE files, the type of file used for most commercial programs. All of these can be run by users who do not have FoxPro.

Programs (ordinary PRG files and also the SPR and MPR files generated by the screen and menu builder), report forms, and label forms can all be combined in this single file. Even database files and indexes can be included in this file if they are read-only. If the program simply uses the database file and index as a look-up table, they can be included in the APP or EXE file, but if the user modifies a database file, that file and its indexes must be kept as separate files.

THE PROJECT MANAGER

> You can also specify the files to be included in the project by using the command **BUILD PROJECT** <*project file*> **FROM** <*file list*>. For more details, see this command in the Help Window.

You create a project in the familiar way. Select New from the File menu, select the Project radio button, and select OK to use the Project Window; name the project later by selecting Save As from the file menu. Alternatively, enter the command **CREATE PROJECT** <*project name*>.

Likewise, you can modify an existing project in the familiar ways. Select Open from the File menu, select Project from the popup control, select the name of the project you want to modify from the scrollable list, and select Open. Alternatively, just enter the command **MODIFY PROJECT** <*project name*>.

When you work on a project in any of these ways, FoxPro opens the Project window and adds a Project pad to the menu. The Project window and menu are shown in Figure C.1.

FoxPro keeps the information about a project in a database file with the extension PJX and an associated memo file with the extension PJT.

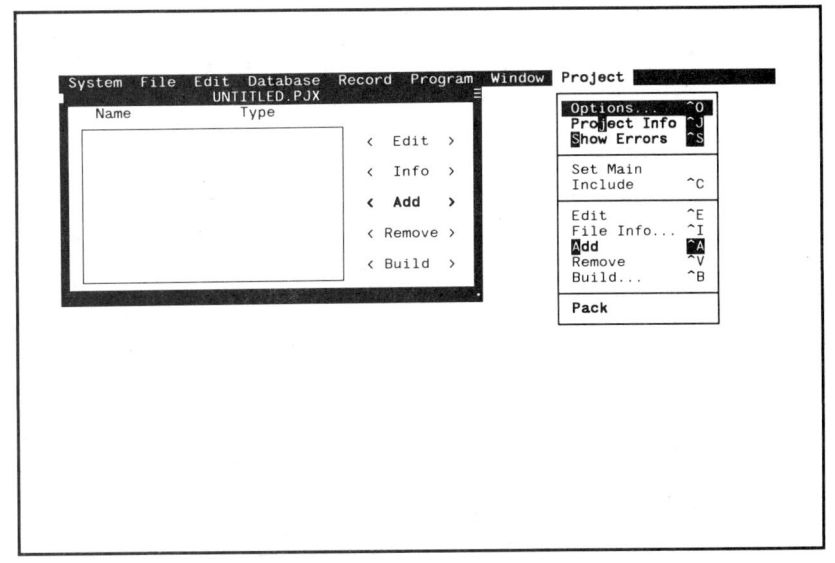

Figure C.1: The Project window and menu

USING THE PROJECT WINDOW

As you can see from the illustration, the third group of options on the Project menu is the same as the options offered by the pushbuttons of the Project window.

In addition to these buttons, the Project window consists of a scrollable list of files that are part of the project, including the name and type of each.

Select Add to add a file to this list. FoxPro displays a dialog box (shown in Figure C.2) to let you select among existing files. As you can see in the illustration, the type popup lets you choose the file type displayed in the scrollable list. Selecting Program displays SPR and MPR files as well as PRG files. Selecting Screen or Menu displays SCX and MNX files. You should be familiar with all of the file types on this popup except for two: Format refers to an older type of screen format file (with an FMT extension), which has been supplanted by the SPR file in version 2 of FoxPro, and Library refers to libraries of routines written in C language (which you can create if you purchase the FoxPro library construction kit).

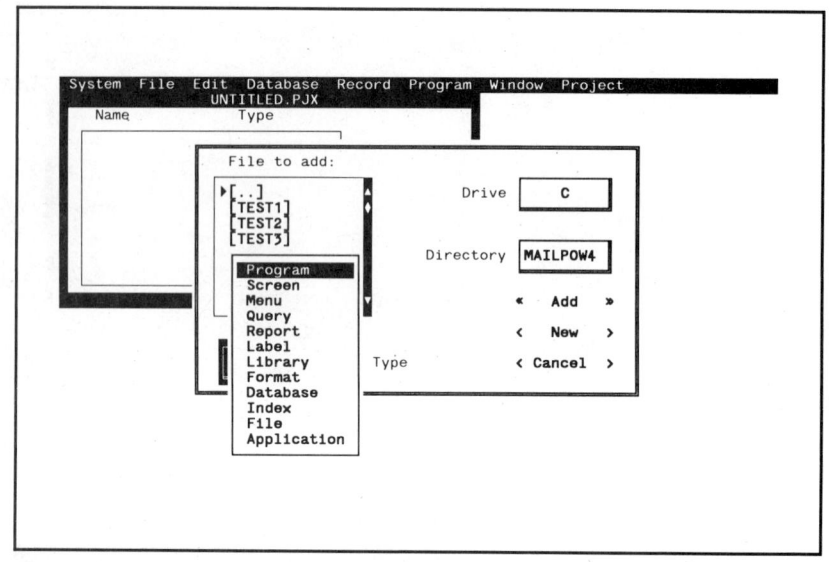

Figure C.2: Adding a file to the application

By default, the first file that you add is used as the main module of the application. It has a bullet to the left of the file type in the scrollable list within the Project window to indicate this fact.

Select Remove in the Project window to remove the currently selected file from the list.

Select Edit to edit the currently selected file on the list. This selection opens whichever window is needed to work on the currently selected file, for example, the menu builder window if it is an MPX file, the screen builder, report layout, or label layout windows for their respective files, or an editing window for a program or text file.

Selecting Build displays the dialog box shown in Figure C.3, which is the key to using the Project Manager. As you can see, the three radio buttons give you these options:

- **Rebuild Project:** Update the project: add any new files that are called by the programs in the project, and generate new code if screen or menu design has been altered since the last build.

- **Build Application:** Update the project and create a stand-alone APP file.

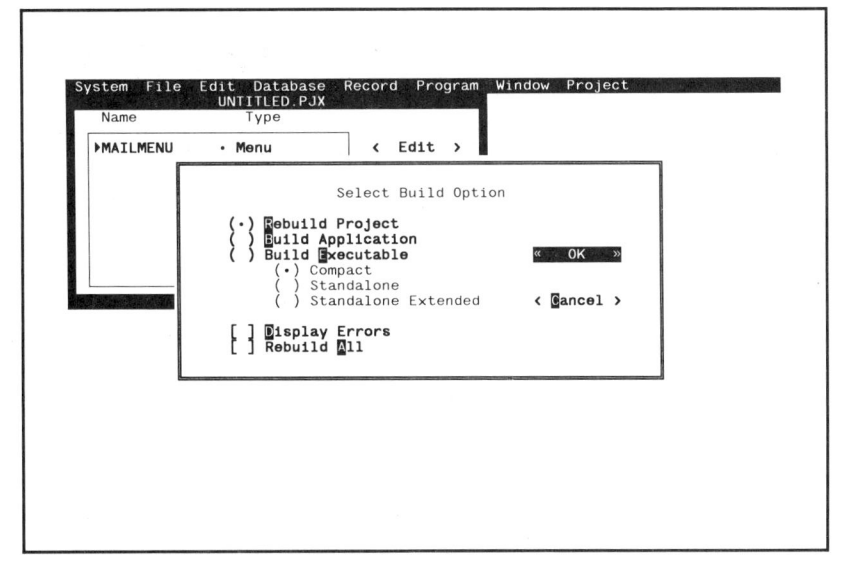

```
System  File  Edit  Database  Record  Program  Window  Project
                    UNTITLED.PJX
     Name              Type
  ▶MAILMENU         • Menu           <  Edit  >

                    Select Build Option
              (•) Rebuild Project
              ( ) Build Application
              ( ) Build Executable           «   OK   »
                    (•) Compact
                    ( ) Standalone
                    ( ) Standalone Extended  <  Cancel  >
              [ ] Display Errors
              [ ] Rebuild All
```

Figure C.3: The Select Build Option dialog box

- **Build Executable:** Update the project and create an EXE file. The three radio buttons under this button give you the options of building a compact EXE file (which requires the FoxPro EXE support library to run), stand-alone (which creates a completely self-contained EXE file), or stand-alone extended (which creates a self-contained EXE file with features of the extended version of FoxPro).

By default, these options update the project by refreshing files whose source file has a time stamp that is more recent than that in the project file. If the Rebuild All check box is checked, however, it will refresh all files in the project.

One of the most convenient features of the Project Manager is that, if you add a file to the list, selecting any of these Build options automatically adds all the files that are called by that file. Rather than adding files individually, you can simply add the main menu and then select Build to add all the files that it calls. The most important exceptions are database and index files—generally, you do not want to build these into the application—and screens based on SCX files that do not have the same name as the SPR file that was generated from them.

APP. C

> Most report and label forms have been removed from this application so you can see all the important files in this list. If there are more files in the application than can be displayed in the list, a scroll bar is added to its right.

For example, if you add only MAILMENU.MPX to the list and you select one of the Build Options, FoxPro will add all the files shown in Figure C.4 to the project, but, as it is generating the project, it will display a dialog box such as the one show in Figure C.5 to indicate that it cannot find APNDSCRN or EDITSCRN, though there are references to them in the code. This dialog box gives you the options:

- **Locate:** Lets you use a dialog box to search through other subdirectories to find the missing file
- **Ignore:** Ignores the fact that this file is missing and continues the build
- **Ignore all:** Ignores all files that are missing and continues the build.
- **Cancel:** Cancels the build

If the Display Errors check box of the Select Build Options dialog box is checked when you do the build, FoxPro automatically displays the error file over the project window when the build is complete, as in Figure C.6. As you can see, errors are kept in a file with the same

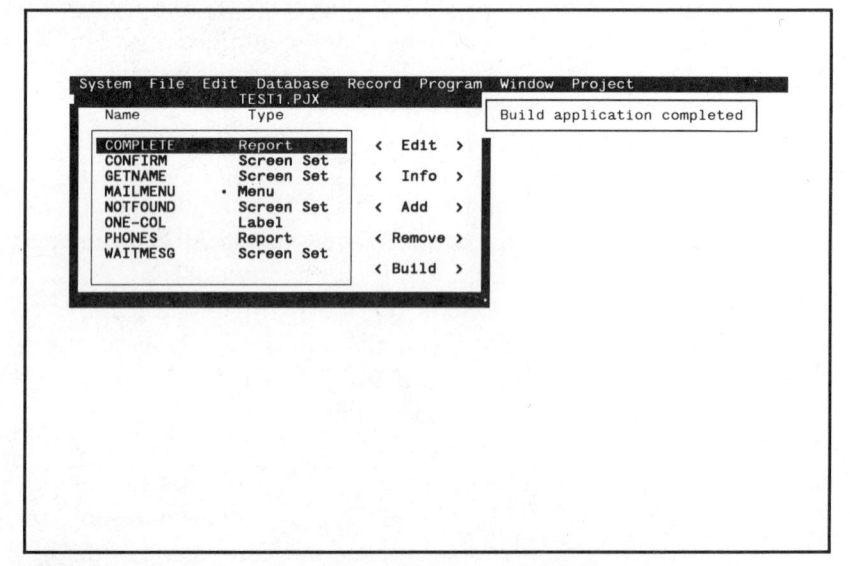

Figure C.4: Files are added to the project automatically

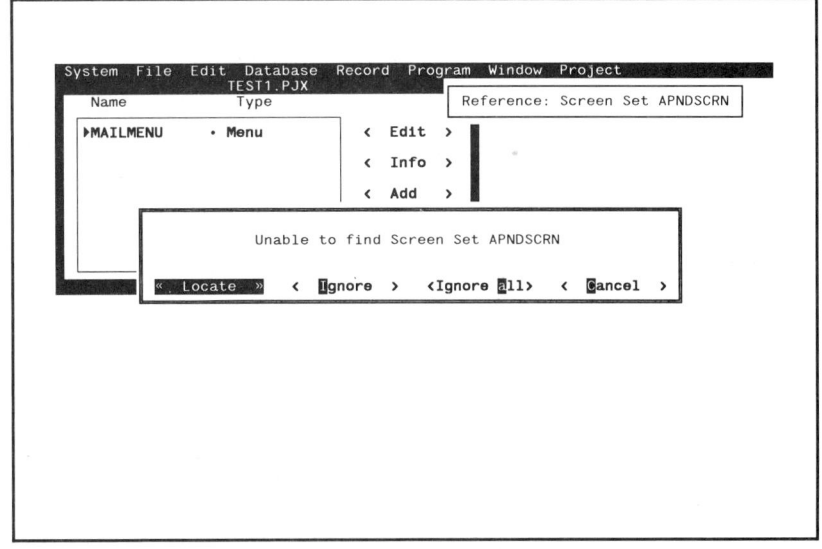

Figure C.5: A dialog box indicates that a file cannot be found

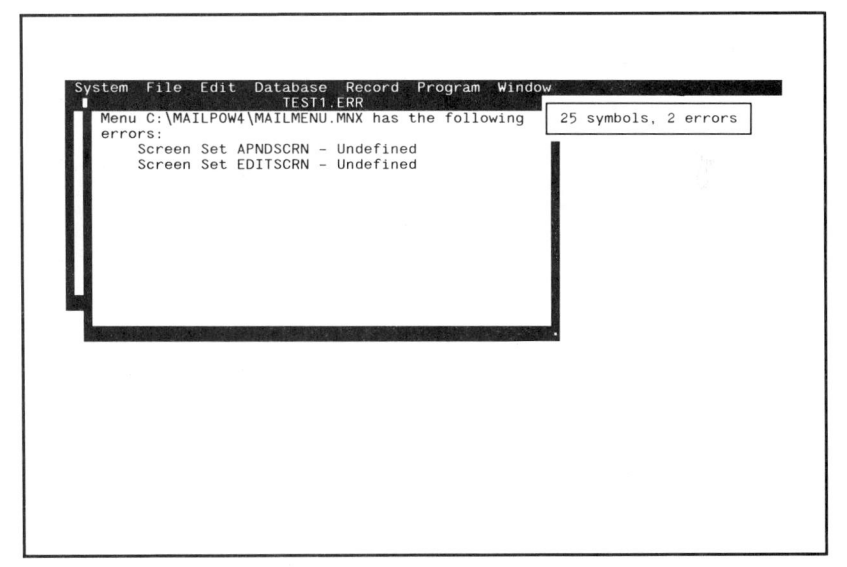

Figure C.6: The Error file

name as the project and with the extension ERR. You can also look at this file by selecting Show Errors from the Project menu (or by using the command **MODI FILE** <*project name*>.ERR).

You add complex screen sets such as APNDSCRN or EDITSCRN to the project in the same way that you created them earlier in this book. After selecting the Add pushbutton, select Screen from the popup control, and select the name of one of the files of the screen set (such as ALLFIELD) to display the dialog box shown in Figure C.7. Select the Add and Arrange pushbutton to add and arrange the other SCX files that are needed, and enter the name for the combined screen set in the text-editing area below, exactly as you did when you were creating screens in Chapter 11; finally, select OK to add the screen set to the scrollable list in the Project window under that name.

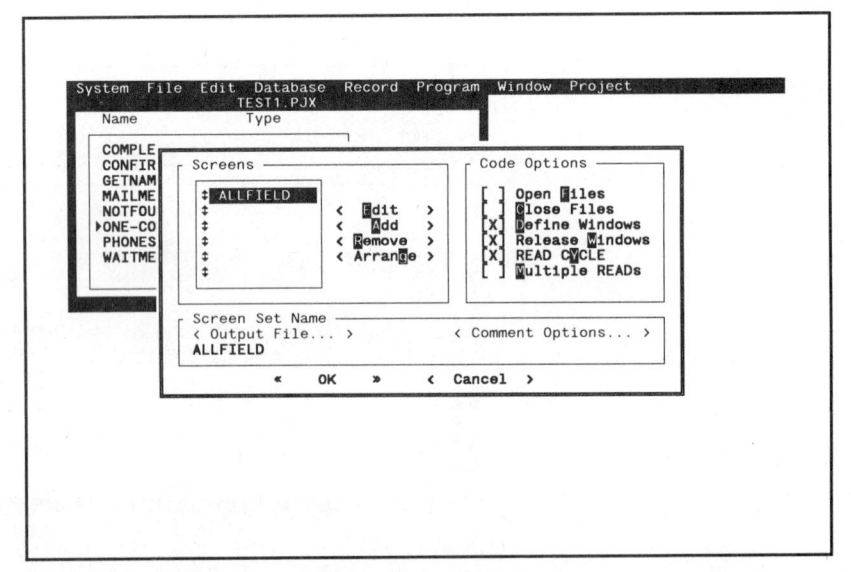

Figure C.7: Adding a screen set to the project

If you select Info, FoxPro displays the dialog box shown in Figure C.8, with information on the files that make up the project. As you can see from the examples in this illustration, this dialog box contains the file name and type at the top. Next, it gives the date and time that the current version of the file was created (and when the version of the file last included in a build was created), so that you can see if the current version of the file is included in the application as it now stands; the date of the last build is also listed here.

The scrollable list in this dialog box includes all of the files defined or referenced by this file. As you can see from this illustration, this list can be as short as one element or it can be very long. The list for the

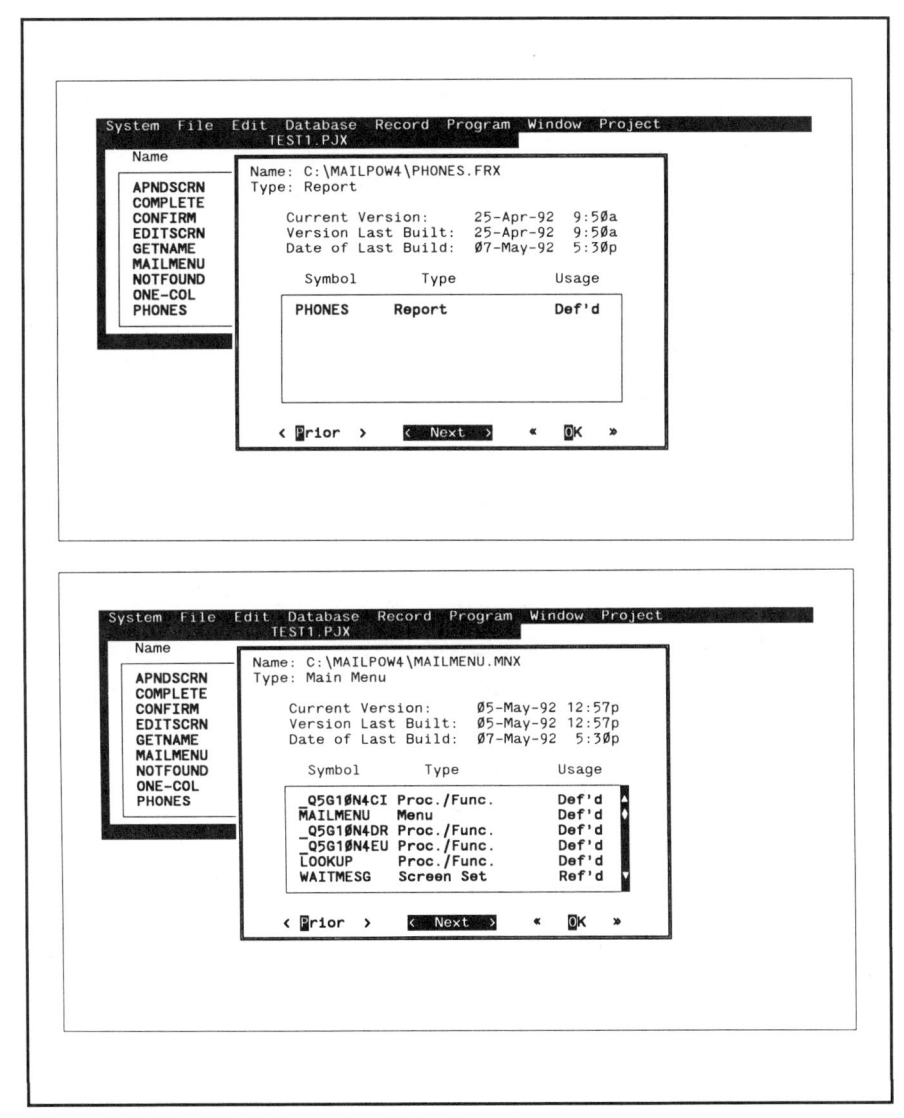

Figure C.8: The File Information dialog box

Phones file just includes the Phones report itself, which is defined in that file. The list for the MAILMENU file included all the procedures that are defined in that file (such as the LOOKUP procedure you added in the Cleanup code, as well as the procedures generated by FoxPro), and all the files that are referenced by that file (such as all the screen sets that are used when you make menu selections).

Use the Prior and Next pushbuttons of this dialog box to page through the information for all the files in the project. When you have finished, select OK to return to the Project window.

THE PROJECT MENU

Select *Options* from the Project menu to display the dialog box shown in Figure C.9, which lets you select options used in generated code and other build options. This dialog box is similar to the Options dialog boxes you can use with the screen and menu builder.

Select Project Info from the Project menu to use the dialog box shown in Figure C.10. To supplement the File Information dialog box, discussed above, which gives detailed information on each file,

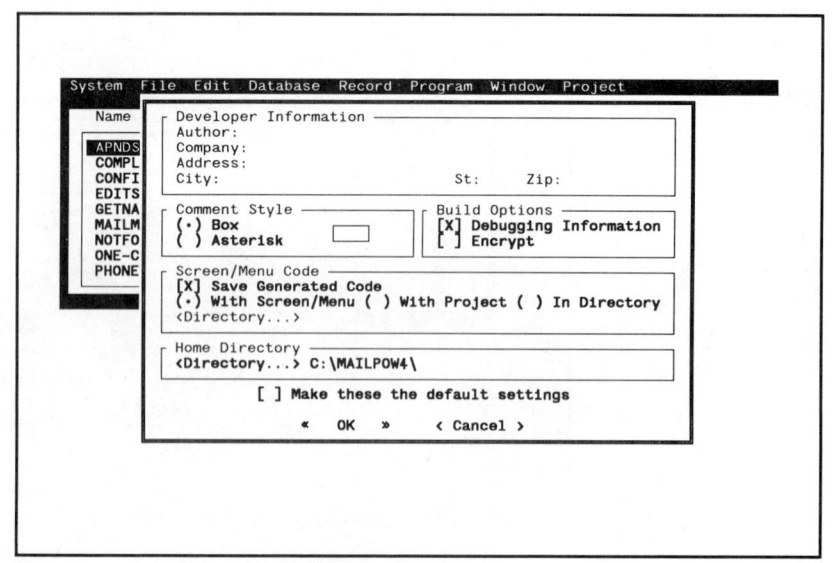

Figure C.9: The Options dialog box

this dialog box gives a general overview of all the files in the project: the total number of files of each type in the project, how many are included in the current build of the project, and for how many the current build is out of date.

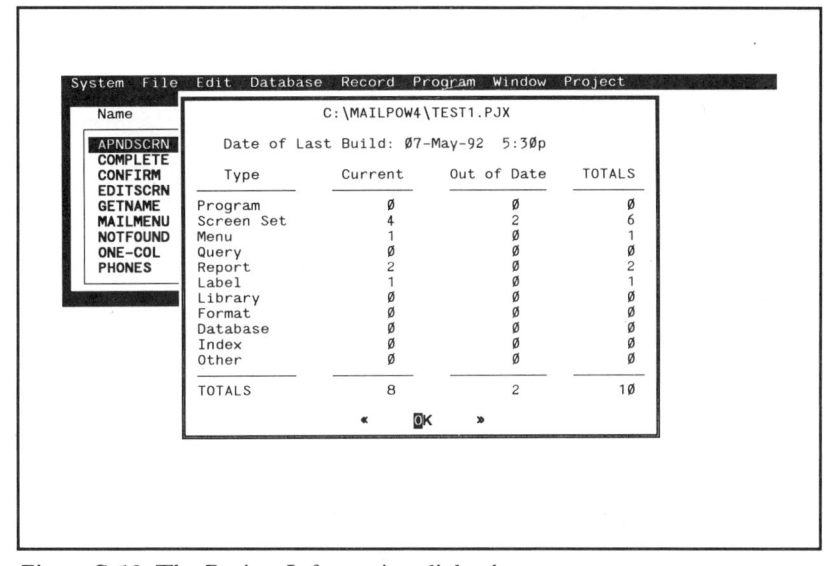

Figure C.10: The Project Information dialog box

> The Set Main option is disabled if the file selected in the scrollable list of the Project window cannot be the main module of a program: for example, if it is a Label or Report form.

Select *Set Main* from the Project menu to make the currently selected file the main module of the generated program. As you know, the first file you add to the project is the main module by default. This menu option can be used to change the main module. The main module is indicated by a bullet in the scrollable list.

Select *Exclude* from the Project menu to exclude the currently selected file from the APP or EXE file that is built. This option lets you use the Project Manager to keep track of files in the project without their being included in the EXE or APP file that the Project Manager creates. As you know, database files and indexes should not be included in these files unless they are read-only, but you can add them to the scrollable list, highlight them, and select Exclude in order to use the Project Manager to help you keep track of them without including them in the EXE or APP file that it creates. In Figure C.11, the MAILLIST database and index files have been added to the scrollable list and excluded from the application file that is created: notice the symbol next to them to indicate that they are excluded. When an excluded file is highlighted, this menu option toggles from Exclude to Include, and you can select it to include the currently selected file in the build, removing the symbol next to it.

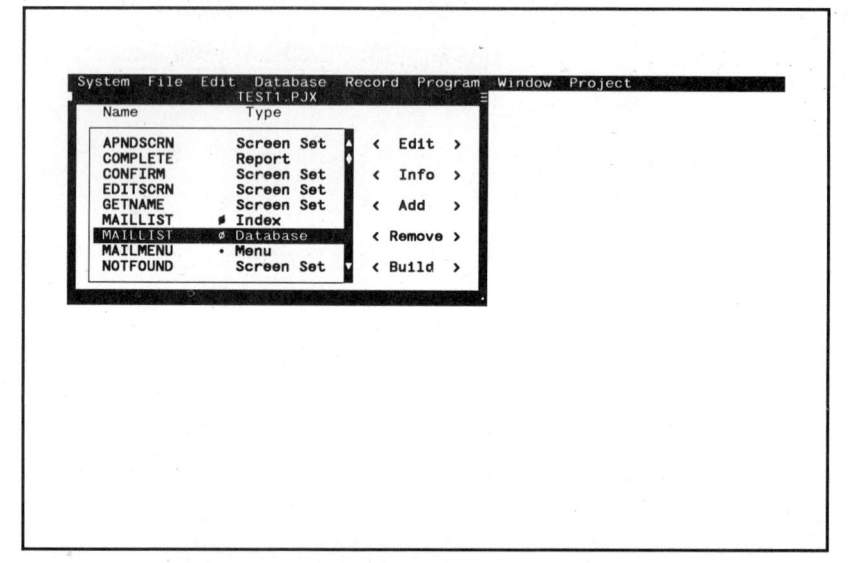

Figure C.11: The database and index file are excluded

The next group of options in the menu is identical to the pushbuttons in the Project window, discussed above.

Select *Pack* from the Project menu to pack the entire project. Remember that the project is stored in an ordinary database file with the extension PJX. When you remove a file from the project, the associated record in the PJX file is marked for deletion. Selecting Pack removes this record permanently.

Index

SPECIAL CHARACTERS

(number symbol)
    as picture template symbol, 403
    as relational operator, 164, 174
$ (dollar sign)
    as picture function/template symbol,
        403, 405
    as relational operator, 163-164, 188
^ (caret)
    as exponentiation operator, 134
    as picture function symbol, 405
    for popups, 415
& (ampersand), for scrollable lists, 416
&& (double ampersands), as program comment
        indicator, 347
* (asterisk)
    as DOS wildcard character, 70, 201, 525
    as multiplication operator, 133
    as picture template symbol, 403
    as program comment indicator, 347
    as pushbutton symbol, 409
*C (asterisk-C), for check boxes, 413
*I (asterisk-I), for invisible pushbuttons, 417
*R (asterisk-R), for radio buttons, 412
_ (underscore)
    in field names, 44-45
    for System menu item names, 499
+ (plus sign)
    as addition operator, 133, 136
    for string concatenation, 136-137
; (semicolon)
    with invisible buttons, 418
    within character strings, 347
< > (angle brackets)
    in discussions of FoxPro commands, 42
    with pushbuttons, 17
    as relational operators, 164, 174, 188
> > (double arrow head), as empty record indicator,
        79-80
-> (arrow operator), 263
= (equals sign), as relational operator, 162-166, 188
= = (double equals sign), as relational operator,
        163-165

{} (curly brackets)
    for date constants, 122, 129
    for special keys in macros, 311
? (question mark)
    as command, 123, 125, 348-351
    as DOS wildcard character, 201, 525
@ (at sign)
    as command, 357-360
    as picture function, 402
/ (slash)
    in dates, 47
    as division operator, 133
\ (backslash)
    in directory designations, 56
    with directory names, 41
    for grouping of menu options, 492
    for hot keys and pushbuttons, 409-410
, (comma), in FIELDS clause, 200
! (exclamation point)
    as picture template/function symbol,
        402-403, 405
    as relational operator, 164, 166, 174
- (minus sign)
    for string concatenation, 136-137, 140
    as subtraction operator, 133
( ) (parentheses)
    for array index numbers, 349
    with functions, 123, 132, 140
    for grouping logical operations, 166, 168
    as grouping operator, 134
    as picture function symbol, 404
    with radio buttons, 17
. (periods), as logical expression delimiters, 162
.. (two consecutive periods), as current directory parent
        indicator, 57-59, 524
... (ellipsis), to indicate subsequent dialog box, 6, 15
" (quotation marks), for character constants, 122, 137
' (single quotation mark), for character constants, 122
[ ] (square brackets)
    for array index numbers, 349
    for character constants, 122
    for check boxes, 17
    for subdirectories in scrollable lists, 58, 524

A

abbreviating, FoxPro commands, 62
ACCEPT command, 355-356
Activate dialog box, 396-397
ACTIVATE MENU command, 503
ACTIVATE WINDOWS command, 395
Add Alias (report printing option), 218
addition operator, 133
Add Line (Report menu option), 233
alerts, 32
    upon file overwrite attempts, 146
    upon mismatched data types, 138, 164
    upon program errors, 348, 353-354
aliases for file names, 263, 281
ALL (Scope clause setting), 198-199
ALLTRIM( ) function, 127
Alt-key combinations
    Alt-D, 493
    for menu selections, 7
    permissible in macros, 305, 312
ampersand (&), for scrollable lists, 416
ampersands (&&), as program comment indicator, 347
.AND. logical operator, 166-168
angle brackets (< >)
    in discussions of FoxPro commands, 42
    as empty record indicator, 79-80
    with pushbuttons, 17
    as relational operators, 164, 188
APPEND BLANK command, 89-90
APPEND command, 76
APPEND FROM command, 326
Append From dialog box, 324-326
Append mode, 76
.APP extensions, 554
application creation, 554
appointment diary/calendar (desktop utility), 547-549
arithmetic mean, 330
arithmetic operations. *See also* calculations
    with calculator (desktop utility), 544-547
    performing for reports, 229-231
arithmetic operators, 133-135
Arrange menu, 424
arrays, 349
arrow keys
    in FoxPro editor, 24
    for repositioning dialog boxes, 20
arrow operator (->), 263
ASCENDING command, 118
ASC( ) function, 131
ASCII chart (desktop utility), 550-551

ASCII format
    converting date data to, 128-129
    converting to, 103, 550-551
    for dates, 47
    explained, 120
    exporting files in, 458-459
    outputting reports in, 203-204
    program files in, 346
    returning for characters, 131, 418
    sorting records and characters by, 117, 140, 143
assembly language, 343
asterisk (*)
    as DOS wildcard character, 70, 201, 525
    as multiplication operator, 133
    as picture template symbol, 403
    as program comment indicator, 347
    as pushbutton symbol, 409
asterisk-C (*C), for check boxes, 413
asterisk-I (*I), for invisible pushbuttons, 417
asterisk-R (*R), for radio buttons, 412
at sign (@)
    as command, 357-360
    as picture function, 402
    @...EDIT command, 401
    @...GET command, 400
    @...SAY command, 401
    @...SAY...GET command, 357-360, 395
Attributes dialog box, 534-535
attributes of files, 524
AUTOEXEC.BAT file, 514, 518-519
AVERAGE command, 331
Average dialog box, 330-331
averages, 230, 330-331, 335
AVG( ) function, 330, 335

B

background processing, for databases, 60-64
backslash (\)
    in directory designations, 56
    with directory names, 41
    and exclamation sign (\!), for default pushbuttons, 410
    and hyphen (\-), for grouping of menu options, 492
    and less-than sign (\<), for hot keys, 409
    and question mark (\?), for Esc-key-selectable pushbuttons, 410

Backspace key, 24
backups, automatic, 321-322
.BAK extensions, 69, 321
bands, on reports, 212
BASIC, versus FoxPro, 343
basic optimizable expressions, 174
beeps
    adjusting pitch of, 290
    with NOEDIT option, 106
    silencing, 286
    upon data type entry, 79
    upon error entry, 350
    upon filled fields, 79, 436
bell. *See* beeps
blanks
    in FoxPro programs, 347
    inserting in character data, 137, 200
    with mathematical operators, 135
    in records, 80, 89
    trimming from character data, 126-127, 136-137
blink, 339
boldface
    adding to report objects, 215
    specifying for reports, 228-230
borders. *See also* lines
    for windows, 394
Box dialog box, 223-224, 398-400
boxes. *See also* dialog boxes; lines
    on reports, 213
    on screens, 398-400
Box (Report menu option), 223-225
braces { }
    for date constants, 122, 129
    for special keys in macros, 311
brackets. *See* angle brackets; square brackets
Bring to Front
    Report menu option, 233-234
    Screen menu option, 419
BROWSE command, 75
Browse display
    altering, 91-95
    appending data with, 84-86
    searching for text from, 319
BROWSE FIELDS command, 271, 282
Browse mode, 74-76, 90
BUILD PROJECT command, 554
bullets, 323
buttons. *See* pushbuttons, radio buttons

C

CALCULATE command, 335
Calculate dialog box, 229-231, 333-335
calculations. *See also* arithmetical operations
    with memory variables, 328-335
    performing for reports, 229-231
    performing on all fields, 336-337
calculator (desktop utility), 544-547
calendar/diary (desktop utility), 547-549
Cancel option, 31
capitalization. *See also* case
    conventions for program listings in this book, 437
    routine for, 378-379
CapsLock indicator, 323
Capture utility, 551-552
caret (^)
    as picture function symbol, 405
    for popups, 415
case
    of FoxPro program code, 352
    functions for converting, 123, 125
    ignoring in searches, 319, 529
    problems in queries, 190
    sensitivity to, 80-81
CDAY( ) function, 131
CD (Change Directory DOS command), 57
CDOW( ) function, 131
.CDX extensions, 111
centering
    report objects, 234
    screen objects, 419
Center (Report menu option), 234
century formatting, 289
CHANGE command, 75-76, 88
Change display, 78-84
Change mode, 74-76
changing (editing) data, 86-90
character constants, 122
character data type
    converting to/from dates, 128-129
    converting to/from numeric, 128-129
    described, 46
Chdir (Tree panel option), 538-539
Check Box dialog box, 414
check boxes, 17, 413-414
child directories, 56
child files, 264
choice = variable, 439

Choose a Field or Variable dialog box, 401
CHR( ) function, 131, 418, 436
cleanup code, 495, 502, 509
CLEAR command, 29-30, 350, 439
CLEAR GETS command, 359-360
Clear (Environment button in Page Layout dialog box), 218
clipboard
    copying text to, 551-552
    printing from, 316
clock, 289-290
CLOSE ALL command, 280
close box, 22
Close (Window menu option), 23-24
closing
    Command window, 28
    databases, 61
    views, 280
    windows, 22
CMONTH( ) function, 131
CNT( ) function, 335
COBOL, 344
code. *See also* comments; programming; programs
    adding for screen handling, 395-396, 421-425
    and assembly language, 343
    compiling, 323
    and high-level languages, 344
    and machine language, 343
    and pseudocode, 435
code snippets, 397-398
color picker dialog boxes, 338, 420
colors, on screen, 337-339
columns, moving among, 50
COM1/COM2/COM3, 315
comma (,), in FIELDS clause, 200
comma-delimited files, 325-326, 459
commands. *See also individual commands by name*
    abbreviating, 62
    reissuing, 28
    and use of Enter key, 139
Command window, 4-5, 28-31
comments
    adding to labels, 246
    adding to pushbuttons, 411
    adding to report objects, 215
    in FoxPro programs, 347-348, 408
    specifying for reports, 232
COMPACT command, 118
compact indexes, 112

compiling programs, 323
compound index files, 111, 151
computations. *See* calculations
Console On/Off radio buttons, 211
constants, 122
CONTINUE command, 177, 179-180
control flow, 345-346
Control-key shortcuts, 6, 18. *See also* Ctrl-key combinations
controlling file, 264
controlling index, 147-149
control panels, 390
controls, in dialog boxes, 15-18
CONTROL.SCX file, 390, 465, 467-468
copy-and-paste operations, 27, 214
    from Help window to Command window, 35-36
COPY command, 182-184
Copy dialog box, 529-530, 539-541
copying
    database structure, 65-70, 186-188
    directory structure, 531, 539, 541
    files, 529-530
    records, 188
    text to clipboard, 551-552
COPY STRUCTURE command, 65
COPY TO command, 458-459
Copy (Tree panel option), 539-541
COUNT command, 332
Count dialog box, 331-332
CREATE command, 42
CREATE MENU command, 488
CREATE PROJECT command, 554
CREATE QUERY command, 291
CREATE SCREEN command, 388-389
credit numbers, 228
CTOD( ) function, 128-129
Ctrl-key combinations
    as shortcuts, 6
    in FoxPro editor, 24-25
    permissible in macros, 305
    Ctrl-Backspace, 25
    Ctrl-D hot key, 68
    Ctrl-End, 87
    Ctrl-Enter, 18
    Ctrl-I hot key, 68
    Ctrl-PgDn, 88
    Ctrl-Q, 87
    Ctrl-W, 87
    Ctrl-Z for end of file, 323

curly brackets {}
    for date constants, 122, 129
    for special keys in macros, 311
currency formats, 289
current directory, 538
cursor
    column/line indication for, 323
    moving in FoxPro editor, 24
    moving to menu bar, 7
cut-and-paste operations, 27, 214

D

data. *See also* databases; data types; files; queries;
    records; text
    appending, 76–78
    browsing through, 90–95
    and case sensitivity, 80–81
    changing (editing), 86–90
    normalization of, 260
    verifying upon data entry, 407
Database menu popup, 11–12
    Append From option, 324–326
    Average option, 330–331
    Calculate option, 333–335
    Count option, 331–332
    Sum option, 332–333
    Total option, 326–328
databases. *See also* data; files; queries; relational
    databases
    accessing open, 156
    background operation of, 60–61
    copying and modifying structure of,
        65–70
    creating, 40–43
    defining structure of, 43–54
    naming, 42
    opening and closing, 61–64
    saving, 55–60
    sorting, 155–157
data dictionary, 428
Data Grouping (Report menu option), 219–221
data types
    converting to and from, 128–130
    defaults for, 45
    described, 46–49
date constants, 122

date data type
    converting to/from character data,
        128–129
    described, 47
DATE( ) function, 123, 130
date operators, 136
Date popup, 124
dates
    European format for, 47, 227, 288
    formatting in reports, 227–228
    formatting with View window, 288–289
DAY( ) function, 131
.DBF extensions, 42, 48, 201
.DBT extensions, 48
Deactivate dialog box, 396–397
DEACTIVATE WINDOWS command, 395, 471
debit numbers, 228
debugging. *See* testing
decimal places
    allowing spaces for, 46
    defaults by data type, 45
    on Calculator utility, 547
    with STR( ) function, 129
DECLARE command, 350
DEFAULT.FKY file, 306, 314
default macros, 306
defaults
    for calculations, 230
    for data types, 45
    for decimal places, 135
    for drives, 286
    for fields by data type, 51
    for file format preferences, 321–323
    for macros, 313–314
    for pushbuttons, 410
    for SET...ON/OFF commands, 284–285
DEFINE BAR command, 501
DEFINE MENU command, 501
DEFINE PAD command, 501
DEFINE POPUP command, 501
DEFINE WINDOW command, 394–395, 424
DELETE ALL command, 199
DELETED( ) function, 191
Delete dialog box, 97, 532–533, 541–543
Delete (Tree panel option), 541–543
deleting
    files, 532–533
    records, 95–99, 430
    text, 26

delimited files, 325-326, 458-459
Del key, 24
DESCENDING command, 118
Desktop radio button, 391-392
desktop utilities
    ASCII chart, 550-551
    calculator, 544-547
    calendar/diary, 547-549
    Capture utility, 551-552
    special characters, 549-550
dialog boxes
    ellipsis as indicator for, 6
    how to use, 18-20
    types of, 15-18
dialogs. *See* dialog boxes
diary/calendar (desktop utility), 547-549
.DIF extensions, 325
DIMENSION command, 350
directories
    copying structure of, 531, 539, 541
    current, 538
    for databases, 41
    FoxPro utilities for handling, 537-543
    specifying for file copies, 530-531
DISABLE clause, 412
disks, required for FoxPro, 514
DISPLAY command, 102, 199
DISPLAY STRUCTURE command, 61-63
division operator, 133
DO CASE...ENDCASE command, 367, 371-372
DO command, 348, 376
dollar sign ($)
    as picture function/template symbol, 403, 405
    as relational operator, 163-164, 188
DOS, directory structure in, 55-58
DOS commands
    MD (Make Directory), 57
    PATH, 518-519
    RD (Remove Directory), 57
    substitutes for, 522
DOS files, programs as, 346
double ampersands (&&), as program comment indicator, 347
double arrow head (>>), as empty record indicator, 79-80
double equal sign (= =), as relational operator, 163-165
DOW( ) function, 131

DO WHILE...ENDDO command, 361-366, 372-376
drives, changing current, 525
DTOC( ) function, 128
DTOS( ) function, 128-129

E

EDIT command, 75, 88
editing
    data, 86-90
    procedures and expressions, 396-397
Edit menu popup, 10-11, 27, 317-323
ejecting pages, 211, 217, 317
ellipsis (...), in dialog box controls, 6, 15
ENDDO command, 361-362, 364, 366
End key
    in FoxPro editor, 24
    for repositioning dialog boxes, 20
End Of File (EOF), 162
Enter key, as entry confirmation, 436
environment settings
    for reports, 218
    saving, 398
    from View window, 258, 284-291
EOF( ) function, 162, 463
equals sign (=), as relational operator, 162-166, 188
.ERR extensions, 558, 560
ERROR clause, 407-408
Error file, 558-560
Esc (Escape) key
    for closing windows, 22, 88
    interrupt function of, 31-32, 348
    for selecting default option, 18
Establish 1-To-Many Relationship dialog box, 281
European date formats, 47, 227, 288
EXACTLY LIKE join condition, 293
Excel
    appending files from, 325
    exporting files to, 458
exclamation point (!)
    as picture template/function symbol, 402-403, 405
    as relational operator, 164, 166
.EXE extensions, 557
EXIT command, 372-375
exiting FoxPro, 36
exponentiation operator, 134
exporting files, 458-460

expression builder dialog box, 140-147, 334
expressions
    basic optimizable, 174
    and constants, 122
    described, 120-121
    editing, 396-397
    for fields on reports, 225-232
    and functions, 122-133
    logical, 161-170
    and operators, 122, 133-140
    using in indexes, 140-147
    using substrings of, 449-450
extensions, sorting on, 534

F

Field dialog box, 400-408
field names, 121
field picker dialog boxes, 201, 277, 421
Field (Report menu option), 225-232
fields
    changing order or size of, 91-92
    data types for, 46-50
    entering field names and types into, 50-54
    filling automatically, 336
    formatting for reports, 225-232
    formatting for screens, 400-408, 419
    key, 260, 271
    naming, 44-45
    preventing user edits of, 408
    restricting for command execution, 200-202
    specifying for LIST operations, 103-104
    as variables, 349
    width determination for, 51, 53, 91-92
FIELDS clause, 200-202
fifth-generation languages, 346
File Information dialog box, 560-561
File menu popup, 8-10, 314-317
filename extensions. *See* extensions
Filer utility. *See also* Files panel (of Filer); Tree panel (of Filer)
    described, 522
    as System menu option, 41
files. *See also* databases; records
    aliases for, 263, 281
    attributes of, 524
    child, 264

    closing with USE command, 61-62
    compound index, 111
    copying, 529-530
    deleting, 532-533
    delimited, 325
    FoxPro's temporary, 523
    FoxPro utilities for handling, 523-537
    hidden, 534
    moving, 531-532
    packing, 98-99
    parent or controlling, 264
    printing, 315-317
    program, 314
    renaming, 535
    resource, 288
    saving, 58-59
    sorting in scrollable lists, 532-534
    specifying for help text, 287-288
    system, 534
    tagging, 525-527
    text, 314
Files panel (of Filer)
    how to use, 523-527
    Attr option of, 534-535
    Copy option of, 529-531
    Delete option of, 532
    Edit option of, 534
    Find option of, 527-529
    Move option of, 531-532
    Rename option of, 535
    Size option of, 535-537
    Sort option of, 532-534
Files panel (of View window), 286-288
Files (Tree panel option), 543
Filter check box, 155, 193
filters, 160, 192-194
Find dialog box, 318-320, 527
Find (Edit menu option), 318-320
.FKY extensions, 313
float data type, 46
.FMT extensions, 555
fonts, proportional, 203
footers
    printing on reports, 212
    for report groups, 211
    for windows, 393
For check box, 97
FOR clauses
    with COPY command, 183-184
    indexing with, 195-196

with LIST command, 202-203
with LOCATE command, 176-178
with logical expressions, 171
foreign language characters, 549-550
Format check box, 155
Format dialog box, 226-228
formatted input/output, 348-349, 357-361
fourth-generation languages, 346
FoxPro library construction kit, 555
.FPT extensions, 48, 201
Framework II, appending files from, 326
.FRM extensions, 210
FROM clause, 415
.FRT extensions, 210
.FRX extensions, 210
FUNCTION clause, 409
FUNCTION command, 380-381
function keys, 305-306
functions
    described, 123-125
    logical, 162
    picture, 401-405
    types of, 125-133
    user-defined, 380-382
    within functions, 132

G

General options dialog box, 495-496
Generate dialog box, 390, 421-425
global mark character, 496
GO BOTTOM command, 102
GO RECORD command, 102
GOTO commands, limitations of, 344-345
Goto dialog box, 100, 318
Goto Line (Edit menu option), 318
Goto option, 96, 100
GO TOP command, 102
greater than/less than symbols (< >). *See* angle brackets
Grid Off option, 95
Group dialog box, 219-220
Group Info dialog box, 219-221
grouping
    of data on reports, 212, 219-221
    files by tagging, 526-527
    of menu options, 492
    operator for, 134

report objects, 234
screen objects, 419
Group (Report menu option), 234

H

hard disk space requirements, 514-515
headers
    printing on reports, 212
    for report groups, 221
    suppressing on reports, 211
Heading (report printing option), 211
headings on reports, 211
Help
    how to request, 33-36
    specifying files for, 287-288
    using with expression builder, 147
hidden files, 534
HIDE WINDOWS command, 395
high-level languages, 344
highlighting
    of dialog box options, 19
    of menu options, 7
Home key
    in FoxPro editor, 24
    for repositioning dialog boxes, 20
horizontal arrangement of controls, 410, 412, 418
hot keys, 19, 409, 413, 492-493
    Ctrl-D, 68
    Ctrl-I, 68
hyphen. *See* minus sign (-)

I

.IDX extensions, 110-111
IF/ELSE commands, 345
IF...ELSE...ENDIF command, 367-371
Ignore option, 31
indentation, 321-322
    on reports, 217
independent compound indexes, 111, 151
indexes
    adding, 150-151
    of arrays, 349
    controlling, 147-149
    creating with Index On dialog box, 112-118, 442

creating with Structure dialog box, 118-120
described, 110
naming, 114, 118
opening, 150-151
and reindexing, 151-153
types of, 110-112
using expressions in, 140-147
warning on modification of, 283-284
whether to use with queries, 170-175
INDEX ON command, 117-118
Index On dialog box, 154
creating indexes with, 112-116
other features of, 116-117
index tags, 111
INPUT command, 351-356
insert mode, 24, 323
Ins key, 24
installing FoxPro, 514-519
instruction sets, 343
invisible pushbuttons, 417-418
italic
adding to report objects, 215
specifying for reports, 228-230
iteration. *See* looping

J

join conditions, 293
justification
of report fields, 227
of text, 323

K

keyboard. *See also* Alt-key combinations; Ctrl-key combinations; macros; Shift-key combinations
for changing field size or order, 92
controlling windows with, 23-24
for dialog box selections, 19
in FoxPro, editor, 24-25
and function keys, 306
handling report objects with, 213-214
and hot keys, 19
for menu selections, 7-8
partitioning windows with, 94-95
tagging files with, 526

Keyboard Macros dialog box, 306
key fields, 260, 271
warning on modification of, 271, 273, 283-284

L

label form, 243
Label menu popup, 247
labels
creating, 243-251
creating from related databases, 279
and Rolodex cards, 314, 433-434, 444-445
last names
entering in caps, 80
naming fields for, 51
searching for, 172
leading blanks, 126
leading zeroes, 228
LESS THAN join condition, 293
LIKE join condition, 293
line feeds, 321-323
lines
adding/removing on report bands, 233
numbering when printing, 317
printed per page, 217
seeking by line number, 318
skipping after report headers, 221
lines (as grids)
for field separation, 95
on reports, 213, 223
on screens, 398-400
linking, of window partitions, 93, 95
LIST command, 102-103, 199, 202-204
literals (constants), 122
Locate dialog box, 176
LOCATE FOR command, 175-180
logical data type, 46-47
logical expressions, 161-170
logical functions, 162
logical operators, 166-168
LOOP command, 373-376
looping
described, 345, 361-364
with nested loops, 364-367, 372-376
Lotus 1-2-3
appending files from, 326
exporting files to, 458

LOWER( ) function, 126
LPT1/LPT2/LPT3, 315
LTRIM( ) function, 127

M

machine language, 343
Macro Edit dialog box, 311–312
Macro Key Definition dialog box, 307–308
macros
 described, 305–306
 editing, 311–312
 pausing execution of, 309–310
 recording, 307–311
 saving, 313
 using, 312–314
Macros menu popup, 307
mail-merge operations, exporting files for, 458–460
Mailpower! programming exercise
 label operations, 452–458
 mail-merge operations, 458–460
 main menu, 435
 reports operations, 444–452
 sample popup menu system, 503–511
 stub testing techniques, 441–444
 task description, 430–434
main menus, 431
many-to-many relationships, 260–261
margins, 217
Mark check box, 496
marking records for deletion, 96–98, 190–192
matching words (in searches), 529
Math popup, 124
MAX( ) function, 335
MD (Make Directory DOS command), 57
memo data type, 47
memo fields
 described, 47–48
 excluded from sorts, 155
 querying on, 188–190
 when empty, 88
memory
 required for FoxPro, 514
 and typeahead buffer, 290
memory variables
 calculations with, 328–335
 creating, 351, 355, 421
 naming, 349, 357

 public versus private, 377
 scope of, 377
 selecting, 121
 storing calculation results in, 331, 333
 using in reports, 223
menu bar, 6–7
menu builder
 code generation, 499–500
 Menu design window, 488–494
 menuing commands, 500–503
 Menu menu, 494–499
 sample menu system, 503–511
Menu design window, 488–494
Menu menu, 494–499
menu options, 6
Menu Options dialog box, 496–497
menu pad, 6–7
menu popups, 6–7
menus. *See also* menu builder
 creating, 488–489
 saving, 488
 selecting from, 6–8
 structure of, 4–6, 15
MESSAGE clause, 407, 411
messages
 creating, 407–408
 from the system, 32
MIN( ) function, 335
minus sign (–)
 for string concatenation, 136–137, 140
 as subtraction operator, 133
Misc panel (of View window), 288–291
Mkdir dialog box, 539–540
Mkdir (Tree panel option), 539
.MNX extensions, 489
.MOD extensions, 325
MODIFY COMMAND command, 314
MODIFY FILE command, 314
MODIFY MENU command, 489
MODIFY QUERY command, 291
MODIFY REPORT command, 210
MODIFY SCREEN command, 389
modules, independent within programs, 376–377, 432, 439–440
MONTH( ) function, 131
MORE THAN join condition, 293
mouse
 adjusting tracking sensitivity of, 290
 for changing field size or order, 92
 controlling windows with, 21–23

for data type selection, 52
for dialog box selections, 18
in FoxPro editor, 26
handling report objects with, 213-214
for menu selections, 6-7
partitioning windows with, 93-94
tagging files with, 526
Move
    dialog box, 531-532, 541
    Tree panel option, 541
    Window menu option, 23
moving files, 531-532
.MPR extensions, 489
Multiplan
    appending files from, 325
    exporting files to, 458
multiplication operator, 133

N

naming
    databases, 42
    fields, 44-45
    index files, 114, 118
    memory variables, 349, 357
    procedures, 490
    reports, 208
    windows, 392
negative numbers, 228
nested loops, 364-366
net present value, 335
New dialog box, 314-315
NEXT (Scope clause setting), 198-199
NOEDIT option, 105-106
No Eject (report printing option), 211
NOOPTIMIZE clause, 175
No Order pushbutton, 148, 154
normalization of data, 260
NOTE, as program comment indicator, 347
.NOT. logical operator, 166, 168
NPV( ) function, 335
number constants, 122
numbers. *See also* calculations
    changing sign of, 546
    and decimals, 45-46, 129, 547
    and float data type, 46
    and numeric data type, 46, 128-129

number symbol (#)
    as picture template symbol, 403
    as relational operator, 164, 174
numeric data type
    converting to/from character data, 128-129
    described, 46
    and float data type, 46
NumLock indicator, 323, 546-547

O

objects
    boxes and lines as, 225
    in report layouts, 213
    in screen design, 391
one-to-many relationships, 260, 263-264, 280-283
one-to-one relationships, 261
On/Off panel (of View window), 284-286
ON PAD command, 501
ON SELECTION POPUP command, 501
Open All Snippets option, 397
opening
    databases, 61-64
    indexes, 150-151
    views, 275
operators
    arithmetic, 133-135
    date, 136
    logical, 166-168
    relational, 162-166
    string, 136-140
    types of, 133-140
optimizable expressions, 174
Options dialog box, 493, 562
.OR. logical operator, 166-167
Overwrite dialog box, 308-309
overwrite mode indicator, 323

P

PACK command, 98-99, 485
packing of files
    described, 98-99
    for projects, 564
    and rebuilding of indexes, 111

page eject, 211, 217, 317
Page Layout
    dialog box, 216
    Report menu option, 215–218
Page Preview (Report menu option), 218–219
Paradox, appending files from, 326
PARAMETER command, 378
parent directories, 56
parent files, 264
parentheses
    for array index numbers, 349
    with functions, 123, 132, 140
    for grouping arithmetic operations, 134
    for grouping logical operations, 166, 168
    with radio buttons, 17
parenthesis (left), as picture function symbol, 404
partitions, of windows, linking, 93, 95
paste (cut-and-paste operations), 27, 214
PATH (DOS command), 518–519
paths
    specifying for FoxPro, 518–519
    specifying for searches, 286
    as used in DOS, 55–58
pausing
    before display of main menu, 435
    execution of macros, 309–310
    execution of programs, 348
    for user input, 356–357
pending GETs, 359
percent (calculator operation), 545–546
periods
    as logical expression delimiters, 162
    three consecutive (. . .), to indicate dialog box, 6, 15
    two consecutive (..), as current directory parent indicator, 57–59, 524
PgUp/PgDn keys
    in FoxPro editor, 24
    for repositioning dialog boxes, 20
PICTURE clause, 401–405, 409–410
picture functions, 401–405
picture templates, 401–402
.PJT extensions, 554
.PJX extensions, 554, 564
Plain (report printing option), 211, 218
plus sign (+)
    as addition operator, 133, 136
    for string concatenation, 136–137
pointer, 87, 99–102
popup controls, 17, 415–416

Popup dialog box, 415–416
popup menus. *See* menu popups
pound sign. *See* number symbol
precedence
    in logical operations, 168–170
    in mathematical operations, 134
Preferences dialog box
    for Calculator utility, 546
    for Edit menu, 321–323
previewing report layouts, 218–219
.PRG extensions, 355
Print dialog box, 316–317
printer, listing database files on, 103
Printer Setup dialog box, 315–316
printing
    files, 315–317
    labels, 244–245
    with LIST TO PRINT command, 103
    suppressing for repeated values, 231
PRIVATE command, 377
PRN (default printer), 315
procedure files, 287
procedures
    creating, 489–490
    editing, 396–397
    naming, 490
    value of separate, 376–377
    versus user-defined functions, 380–382
program files, 314
programming. *See also* structured programming
    diagraming structure, 430–434
    task analysis, 428–430
    tutorial. *See* Mailpower! programming exercise
Program popup, 13–14
programs
    compiling, 323
    independent modules of, 376–377, 432, 439–440
    sample. *See* Mailpower! programming exercise
Project Information dialog box, 562–564
Project Manager, described, 554
projects
    creating, 554
    saving, 554
Project window and menu, 554–555
prompts
    creating with INPUT or ACCEPT commands, 354–355

waiting for, 356-357
PROPER( ) function, 126
proportional fonts, 203
pseudocode, 435
PUBLIC command, 377
Push Button dialog box, 411
pushbuttons
    creating, 409-412
    described, 17
    Esc-key-selectable, 410
    invisible, 417-418

Q

queries
    and CREATE QUERY command, 291, 296-298
    described, 160
    with filters, 192-194
    and indexes, 170-175
    in indexes, 194-197
    and logical expressions, 161-170
    for multiple records, 182-192
    reports from, 202-204
    restricting, 197-202
    and Rushmore technology, 170, 173-175
    and searches with Find (Edit menu option), 318-320
    with SELECT command of SQL, 291, 298-300
    for single records, 175-182
question mark (?)
    as command, 123, 125, 348-351
    as DOS wildcard character, 201, 525
Quick Menu (Menu menu option), 497-499
Quick Report (Report menu option), 234-235
Quick Screen dialog box, 389, 420-421
quitting FoxPro, 36
quotation marks (' and "), for character constants, 122, 137

R

Radio Button dialog box, 413
radio buttons
    creating, 412-413
    described, 17
RANGE clause, 406-407

RapidFile, appending files from, 326
RD (Remove Directory DOS command), 57
READ command, 358-359, 425
READ CYCLE command, 424
RECALL ALL command, 199
Record menu popup, 12-13, 335-337
record numbers, 100
records. *See also* data; files; queries
    copying, 188
    counting number of, 331-332, 335
    deleting, 95-99, 430
    empty versus unused, 80, 89
    hiding those marked for deletion, 191
    marked for deletion, 96-98, 190-192
    restricting for command execution, 198-200
RECORD (Scope clause setting), 198
Redo feature (Edit menu option), 27
reindexing, 151-153
reissuing commands, 28
relational databases. *See also* View window
    browsing in, 270-275
    choosing fields in, 275-277
    creating, 261-270
    described, 258-261
    an exercise for creating, 264-270
    and one-to-many relations, 263-264, 280-283
    reports from, 277-280
    and RQBE (Relational Query By Example), 291-298
    and SQL SELECT command, 298-300
relational operators, 162-166, 174
RELEASE WINDOWS command, 395, 424
Remove Line (Report menu option), 233
Rename dialog box, 535-536, 538-539
Rename (Tree panel option), 538
renaming files, 535
REPLACE command, 335-337, 360
Replace dialog box, 335-337
replacing text, 320
Report dialog box, 210-211, 242
Report Expression dialog box, 225-226, 228-232
report form, 208, 210
REPORT FORM command, 211
report layout window, 208-209, 212-215
Report menu pad, 209
Report menu popup, 215-235
reports
    creating, 208-211
    layout window for, 212-215

naming, 208
number openable, 215
proportional fonts for, 203
from relational databases, 277-280
Report menu popup, 215-235
sample, 235-243
saving, 218
using Quick Report option, 234-235
resource files, 288
Restore (Page Layout dialog box environment button), 218
REST (Scope clause setting), 198
RESUME command, 348
RETURN command, 376-377, 397-398
RETURN TO MASTER command, 376
Rolodex cards, 433-434, 444-445
root directory, 56, 538
rounding, 46
RQBE (Relational Query By Example), 291-298
RQBE Display Options dialog box, 296
RUN command, 28-30
Rushmore technology, 170, 173-175

S

sample program. *See* Mailpower! programming exercise
Save View As dialog box, 274
saving
    databases, 55-60
    environment settings, 398
    files, 58-59
    label formats, 244
    macros, 313
    menus, 488
    projects, 554
    reports, 218
SCAN WHILE command, 366
scientific calculations, 46
scientific notation operator, 134
Scope clause, 197-200
Scope dialog box, 200
scope of variables, 377
screen. *See also* screen builder
    and blink, 339
    designing for data-entry, 360
    disabling storage of output of, 287
screen builder
    advantages of, 388
    Box dialog box, 398-400

creating controls, 409-418
creating screens, 388-390
entering text, 408
Field dialog box, 400-408
Generate dialog box, 390, 421-425
manipulating objects, 419
Quick Screen dialog box, 389, 420-421
Screen Layout dialog box, 389, 391-398
window and menu, 389
Screen Color Picker dialog box, 420
Screen Layout dialog box, 389, 391-398
Scrollable List dialog box, 416-417
scrollable lists, 16-17, 416-417
scroll bars, 16-17, 22-23
Scroll (Window menu option), 23-24
.SCX extensions, 390
SDF files, 325, 458
searches. *See also* queries
    with Find (Edit menu option), 318-320
    repeating, 320
SEEK command, 180-182, 192, 285
Seek option, 96
Select a Character dialog box, 224
Select Build Option dialog box, 556-557
SELECT command (of SQL), 291, 298-300
selection control flow, 345, 367-372
selection marquee, 214
Select Target Directory dialog box, 530-531
semicolon (;)
    with invisible buttons, 418
    within character strings, 347
Send to Back
    Report menu option, 233-234
    Screen menu option, 419
sequential control flow, 345, 361
SET ALTERNATE ON/OFF command, 287
SET ALTERNATE TO command, 286-287
SET BELL ON/OFF command, 290, 436
SET BELL TO command, 290
SET CONFIRM ON/OFF command, 436
SET CONSOLE ON/OFF command, 351
SET DEFAULT TO command, 286
SET DELETED ON/OFF command, 191, 332, 430
SET ESCAPE ON/OFF command, 348
SET EXACT ON/OFF command, 165
Set Fields check box, 155, 276
SET FIELDS ON/OFF command, 202
SET FIELDS TO command, 202
SET FILTER TO command, 192-194
SET HELP TO command, 288

SET NEAR ON/OFF command, 180
SET ODOMETER TO command, 290
SET OPTIMIZE ON/OFF command, 175
Set Order pushbutton, 148, 154
SET ORDER TO command, 149, 457
SET PATH TO command, 286
SET PRINT ON/OFF command, 350
SET PROCEDURE TO command, 287
SET RELATION command, 263, 268
SET SAFETY ON/OFF command, 99, 286, 459
SET SKIP TO command, 282
SET SYSMENU AUTOMATIC, 509
SET SYSMENU ON/OFF command, 435
SET SYSMENU TO command, 500
SET SYSMENU TO DEFAULT command, 500–501
SET TALK ON/OFF command, 436
SET TYPEAHEAD command, 290
setup code, 509
Setup dialog box, 66–67, 147–150, 153–155, 258
shadows
    behind features, 339
    behind windows, 393
Shift-key combinations
    for marking text, 24–25
    permissible in macros, 305
    Shift-F10, 307, 309
shortcuts
    defining, 504–505
    described, 6, 18
    with Esc key, 18, 20
    specifying in menu design, 492–493
Show dialog box, 396–397
SHOW GETS command, 480
SHOW WINDOWS command, 395
single quotes ('), for character constants, 122
size control, for windows, 22
Size
    dialog box, 535–537, 543
    Tree panel option, 543
    Window menu option, 23
sizing
    box cursor, 223–225
    boxes, 399
    fields, 91–92
    report objects, 214
    windows, 393
SKIP command, 102
slash (/)
    in dates, 47
    as division operator, 133

snippets, of code, 397–398
Social Security numbers
    formatting in reports, 228
    formatting upon data entry, 402–403, 405
Sort Destination File dialog box, 156–157
Sort dialog box, 155–157, 532–534
sorting
    databases, 155–157
    files in scrollable lists, 532–534
SORT TO < > ON command, 157
space bar, 19
spaces. *See* blanks
special character (desktop utility), 549–550
spreadsheets, appending files from, 325–326
.SPR extensions, 390, 423
SQL (Structured Query Language) SELECT command, 291, 298–300
square brackets [ ]
    for array index numbers, 349
    for character constants, 122
    for check boxes, 17
    for subdirectories in scrollable lists, 58, 524
square roots, 335, 545
standard deviation, 230, 335
starting FoxPro, 5, 31
state names
    in logical expressions, 161, 171
    in logical operations, 167–168
    querying records by, 194–195
statistical calculations, 230
status line, 322–323
STD( ) function, 335
Stop Recording dialog box, 309–310
STORE TO command, 329
STR( ) function, 128–129
string data. *See* character data type
string operators, 136–140
String popup, 124
structural compound indexes, 111, 151
structure
    copying for databases, 65–70, 186–188
    copying for directories, 531, 539, 541
    defining for databases, 43–54
structure diagrams, 428, 430–434
Structure dialog box, 118–120
structured programming
    and control flow considerations, 343–348, 361

and input/output considerations, 348-361
and looping, 345, 361-367, 372-376
and procedures and parameters, 376-382
and selection control flow, 345, 367-372
and sequential control flow, 345, 361
stub testing techniques, 441-444
Style dialog box, 228-230
styles
    adding to report objects, 215
    specifying for reports, 228-229
subdirectories
    creating, 441
    for databases, 41
submenus, 490-491
subscripts
    adding to report objects, 215
    specifying for reports, 228-230
SUBSTR( ) function, 449-450
subtraction, operator for, 133
SUM command, 332-333
SUM( ) function, 335
Summary (report printing option), 211, 218
superscripts
    adding to report objects, 215
    specifying for reports, 228-230
Suspend option, 31
SYLK files, 325
symbols. *See also Special Characters Index*
    used in picture functions, 404-405
    used in picture templates, 403
Symphony
    appending files from, 325-326
    exporting files to, 458
system clock, 289-290
system date, 130
system files, 534
system menu pads, 490
System menu popup, 8-9
system messages, 32
system variables, 121

T

tab-delimited files, 459
Tab key, 19, 323
TAG command, 117-118
tagging of files, 525-527

talk feature, 31, 99, 290, 332
    disabling, 32, 286
.TBK extensions, 69
templates, 226, 228-229
    picture, 401-402
temporary files, 523
testing
    menu systems, 491
    sample program, 511
    and stub testing techniques, 441-444
text. *See also* data
    copying to clipboard, 551-552
    deleting, 26
    entering with screen builder, 408
    formatting for reports, 232-233
    marking with keystrokes, 24-25
    marking with mouse, 26
    replacing, 320
text boxes, 18
Text dialog box, 232-233
TEXT...ENDTEXT command, 350-351
text files, 314
Text (Report menu option), 232-233
thumb, in scroll bar, 23
tie-breakers
    for sorting fields, 155
    for sorting last names, 140
titles
    on reports, 212, 222
    of windows, 21-22, 392
Title/Summary dialog box, 222
.TMP extensions, 29
Toggle Delete option, 96-97
TO PRINT command, 350
Total On dialog box, 326-328
totals. *See also* calculations; grouping
    computing, 326-328, 332-333
trailing blanks, 126
Tree panel (of Filer)
    how to use, 537-538
    Chdir option of, 538-539
    Copy option of, 539-541
    Delete option of, 541-543
    Files option of, 543
    Mkdir option of, 539
    Move option of, 541
    Rename option of, 538
    Size option of, 543
TRIM( ) function, 127, 140
true/false condition checking (logical expressions), 161-170

true/false data type, 46-47
Try It pushbutton, 491
tutorial. *See under* programming
typeahead buffer, 290
Type dialog box, 393-394
typeover mode, 24

U

underlining
    of report objects, 215
    specifying for reports, 228-230
underscore (_)
    in field names, 44-45
    for System menu item names, 499
Undo feature (Edit menu option), 27
unformatted input/output, 348, 350-357
Ungroup (Report menu option), 234
Unlink Partitions option, 95
UPPER( ) function, 125-126
USE command, 61-62
user, and input/output issues, 348-361
utilities. *See* desktop utilities; Filer utility

V

VAL( ) function, 128
VALID clause, 407, 411
Valid dialog box, 396-397
VAR( ) function, 335
variables. *See also* arrays; memory variables
    described, 349
    formatting, 402-405
    scope of, 377
    selecting initial values for, 412
Variables (Report menu option), 223
variance, 230
versions of FoxPro, standard versus extended, 514
vertical arrangement of controls, 410, 412, 418
views
    closing, 280
    opening, 275
View window. *See also* relational databases
    closing views, 280
    described, 258-259
    environment settings of, 284-291
    for relational database setup, 261-270
.VUE extensions, 291

W

WAIT command, 356-357
warnings. *See* alerts
WHEN clause, 407, 411
When dialog box, 396-397
While check box, 97
WHILE clauses
    with COPY command, 184-186
    with LOCATE command, 176
    with logical expressions, 171-173
wildcard characters, 70, 201, 525, 527
Window popup, 14
windows. *See also* dialog boxes
    closing, 22
    controlling with keyboard, 23-24
    controlling with mouse, 21-23
    creating, 392-395
    cutting/copying and pasting from, 214-215
    how to use, 20-21
    partitioning, 93-95
.WK3 extensions, 326
.WKS extensions, 326
word-wrap feature, 82-83, 314-315, 321
    in programs, 347
.WR1 extensions, 326
wrap around feature (in searches), 320
wrap words feature, 82-83, 314-315, 321, 347
.WRK extensions, 325

X

.XLS extensions, 325

Y

YEAR( ) function, 131

Z

ZAP command, 99
zeroes, leading, 228
Zip codes, 433, 457
zoom control, 22

Selections from The SYBEX Library

SPREADSHEETS AND INTEGRATED SOFTWARE

1-2-3 for Scientists and Engineers
William J. Orvis
341pp. Ref. 407-0

Fast, elegant solutions to common problems in science and engineering, using Lotus 1-2-3. Tables and plotting, curve fitting, statistics, derivatives, integrals and differentials, solving systems of equations, and more.

The ABC's of 1-2-3 (Second Edition)
Chris Gilbert
Laurie Williams
245pp. Ref. 355-4

Online Today recommends it as "an easy and comfortable way to get started with the program." An essential tutorial for novices, it will remain on your desk as a valuable source of ongoing reference and support. For Release 2.

The ABC's of 1-2-3 Release 2.2
Chris Gilbert
Laurie Williams
340pp. Ref. 623-5

New Lotus 1-2-3 users delight in this book's step-by-step approach to building trouble-free spreadsheets, displaying graphs, and efficiently building databases. The authors cover the ins and outs of the latest version including easier calculations, file linking, and better graphic presentation.

The ABC's of 1-2-3 Release 3
Judd Robbins
290pp. Ref. 519-0

The ideal book for beginners who are new to Lotus or new to Release 3. This step-by-step approach to the 1-2-3 spreadsheet software gets the reader up and running with spreadsheet, database, graphics, and macro functions.

The ABC's of Excel on the IBM PC
Douglas Hergert
326pp. Ref. 567-0

This book is a brisk and friendly introduction to the most important features of Microsoft Excel for PC's. This beginner's book discusses worksheets, charts, database operations, and macros, all with hands-on examples. Written for all versions through Version 2.

The ABC's of Quattro
Alan Simpson
Douglas J. Wolf
286pp. Ref. 560-3

Especially for users new to spreadsheets, this is an introduction to the basic concepts and a guide to instant productivity through editing and using spreadsheet formulas and functions. Includes how to print out graphs and data for presentation. For Quattro 1.1.

The Complete Lotus 1-2-3 Release 2.2 Handbook
Greg Harvey
750pp. Ref. 625-1

This comprehensive handbook discusses every 1-2-3 operating with clear instructions and practical tips. This volume especially emphasizes the new improved graphics, high-speed recalculation techniques, and spreadsheet linking available with Release 2.2.

The Complete Lotus 1-2-3 Release 3 Handbook
Greg Harvey
700pp. Ref. 600-6

Everything you ever wanted to know about 1-2-3 is in this definitive handbook.

As a Release 3 guide, it features the design and use of 3D worksheets, and improved graphics, along with using Lotus under DOS or OS/2. Problems, exercises, and helpful insights are included.

Lotus 1-2-3 2.2 On-Line Advisor Version 1.1
SYBAR, Software Division of SYBEX, Inc.
Ref. 935-8

Need Help fast? With a touch of a key, the Advisor pops up right on top of your Lotus 1-2-3 program to answer your spreadsheet questions. With over 4000 index citations and 1600 pre-linked cross-references, help has never been so easy to find. Just start typing your topic and the Lotus 1-2-3 Advisor does all the look-up for you. Covers versions 2.01 and 2.2. Software package comes with 3½" and 5¼" disks. **System Requirements:** IBM compatible with DOS 2.0 or higher, runs with Windows 3.0, uses 90K of RAM.

Lotus 1-2-3 Desktop Companion
SYBEX Ready Reference Series
Greg Harvey
976pp. Ref. 501-8

A full-time consultant, right on your desk. Hundreds of self-contained entries cover every 1-2-3 feature, organized by topic, indexed and cross-referenced, and supplemented by tips, macros and working examples. For Release 2.

Lotus 1-2-3 Instant Reference Release 2.2
SYBEX Prompter Series
Greg Harvey
Kay Yarborough Nelson
254pp. Ref. 635-9, 4 ¾" × 8"

The reader gets quick and easy access to any operation in 1-2-3 Version 2.2 in this handy pocket-sized encyclopedia. Organized by menu function, each command and function has a summary description, the exact key sequence, and a discussion of the options.

Lotus 1-2-3 Tips and Tricks (2nd edition)
Gene Weisskopf
425pp. Ref. 668-5

This outstanding collection of tips, shortcuts and cautions for longtime Lotus users is in an expanded new edition covering Release 2.2. Topics include macros, range names, spreadsheet design, hardware and operating system tips, data analysis, printing, data interchange, applications development, and more.

Mastering 1-2-3 (Second Edition)
Carolyn Jorgensen
702pp. Ref. 528-X

Get the most from 1-2-3 Release 2.01 with this step-by-step guide emphasizing advanced features and practical uses. Topics include data sharing, macros, spreadsheet security, expanded memory, and graphics enhancements.

Mastering 1-2-3 Release 3
Carolyn Jorgensen
682pp. Ref. 517-4

For new Release 3 and experienced Release 2 users, "Mastering" starts with a basic spreadsheet, then introduces spreadsheet and database commands, functions, and macros, and then tells how to analyze 3D spreadsheets and make high-impact reports and graphs. Lotus add-ons are discussed and Fast Tracks are included.

Mastering Enable/OA
Christopher Van Buren
Robert Bixby
540pp. Ref 637-5

This is a structured, hands-on guide to integrated business computing, for users who want to achieve productivity in the shortest possible time. Separate in-depth sections cover word processing, spreadsheets, databases, telecommunications, task integration and macros.

Mastering Excel on the IBM PC
Carl Townsend
628pp. Ref. 403-8

A complete Excel handbook with step-by-step tutorials, sample applications and an extensive reference section. Topics include worksheet fundamentals, formulas and windows, graphics, database techniques, special features, macros and more.

Mastering Framework III
Douglas Hergert
Jonathan Kamin
613pp. Ref. 513-1

Thorough, hands-on treatment of the latest Framework release. An outstanding introduction to integrated software applications, with examples for outlining, spreadsheets, word processing, databases, and more; plus an introduction to FRED programming.

Mastering Quattro Pro 2
Gene Weisskopf
575pp, Ref. 792-4

This hands-on guide and reference takes readers from basic spreadsheets to creating three-dimensional graphs, spreadsheet databases, macros and advanced data analysis. Also covers Paradox Access and translating Lotus 1-2-3 2.2 work sheets. A great tutorial for beginning and intermediate users, this book also serves as a reference for users at all levels.

Mastering SuperCalc5
Greg Harvey
Mary Beth Andrasak
500pp. Ref. 624-3

This book offers a complete and unintimidating guided tour through each feature. With step-by-step lessons, readers learn about the full capabilities of spreadsheet, graphics, and data management functions. Multiple spreadsheets, linked spreadsheets, 3D graphics, and macros are also discussed.

Mastering Symphony (Fourth Edition)
Douglas Cobb
857pp. Ref. 494-1

Thoroughly revised to cover all aspects of the major upgrade of Symphony Version 2, this Fourth Edition of Doug Cobb's classic is still "the Symphony bible" to this complex but even more powerful package. All the new features are discussed and placed in context with prior versions so that both new and previous users will benefit from Cobb's insights.

Teach Yourself Lotus 1-2-3 Release 2.2
Jeff Woodward
250pp. Ref. 641-3

Readers match what they see on the screen with the book's screen-by-screen action sequences. For new Lotus users, topics include computer fundamentals, opening and editing a worksheet, using graphs, macros, and printing typeset-quality reports. For Release 2.2.

Understanding PFS: First Choice
Gerry Litton
489pp. Ref. 568-9

From basic commands to complex features, this complete guide to the popular integrated package is loaded with step-by-step instructions. Lessons cover creating attractive documents, setting up easy-to-use databases, working with spreadsheets and graphics, and smoothly integrating tasks from different First Choice modules. For Version 3.0.

OPERATING SYSTEMS

The ABC's of DOS 4
Alan R. Miller
275pp. Ref. 583-2

This step-by-step introduction to using DOS 4 is written especially for beginners.

Filled with simple examples, *The ABC's of DOS 4* covers the basics of hardware, software, disks, the system editor EDLIN, DOS commands, and more.

ABC's of MS-DOS (Second Edition)
Alan R. Miller
233pp. Ref. 493-3

This handy guide to MS-DOS is all many PC users need to manage their computer files, organize floppy and hard disks, use EDLIN, and keep their computers organized. Additional information is given about utilities like Sidekick, and there is a DOS command and program summary. The second edition is fully updated for Version 3.3.

DOS Assembly Language Programming
Alan R. Miller
365pp. Ref. 487-9

This book covers PC-DOS through 3.3, and gives clear explanations of how to assemble, link, and debug 8086, 8088, 80286, and 80386 programs. The example assembly language routines are valuable for students and programmers alike.

DOS 3.3 On-Line Advisor Version 1.1
SYBAR, Software Division of SYBEX, Inc.
Ref. 933-1

The answer to all your DOS problems. The DOS On-Line Advisor is an on-screen reference that explains over 200 DOS error messages. 2300 other citations cover all you ever needed to know about DOS. The DOS On-Line Advisor pops up on top of your working program to give you quick, easy help when you need it, and disappears when you don't. Covers thru version 3.3. Software package comes with 3½" and 5¼" disks. **System Requirements:** IBM compatible with DOS 2.0 or higher, runs with Windows 3.0, uses 90K of RAM.

DOS Instant Reference SYBEX Prompter Series
Greg Harvey
Kay Yarborough Nelson
220pp. Ref. 477-1, 4 ¾" × 8"

A complete fingertip reference for fast, easy on-line help:command summaries, syntax, usage and error messages. Organized by function—system commands, file commands, disk management, directories, batch files, I/O, networking, programming, and more. Through Version 3.3.

Encyclopedia DOS
Judd Robbins
1030pp. Ref. 699-5

A comprehensive reference and user's guide to all versions of DOS through 4.0. Offers complete information on every DOS command, with all possible switches and parameters—plus examples of effective usage. An invaluable tool.

Essential OS/2 (Second Edition)
Judd Robbins
445pp. Ref. 609-X

Written by an OS/2 expert, this is the guide to the powerful new resources of the OS/2 operating system standard edition 1.1 with presentation manager. Robbins introduces the standard edition, and details multitasking under OS/2, and the range of commands for installing, starting up, configuring, and running applications. For Version 1.1 Standard Edition.

Essential PC-DOS (Second Edition)
Myril Clement Shaw
Susan Soltis Shaw
332pp. Ref. 413-5

An authoritative guide to PC-DOS, including version 3.2. Designed to make experts out of beginners, it explores everything from disk management to batch file programming. Includes an 85-page command summary. Through Version 3.2.

Graphics Programming Under Windows
Brian Myers
Chris Doner
646pp. Ref. 448-8

Straightforward discussion, abundant examples, and a concise reference guide to graphics commands make this book a must for Windows programmers. Topics range from how Windows works to programming for business, animation, CAD, and desktop publishing. For Version 2.

Hard Disk Instant Reference
SYBEX Prompter Series
Judd Robbins
256pp. Ref. 587-5, 4 ¾" × 8"

Compact yet comprehensive, this pocket-sized reference presents the essential information on DOS commands used in managing directories and files, and in optimizing disk configuration. Includes a survey of third-party utility capabilities. Through DOS 4.0.

Inside DOS: A Programmer's Guide
Michael J. Young
490pp. Ref. 710-X

A collection of practical techniques (with source code listings) designed to help you take advantage of the rich resources intrinsic to MS-DOS machines. Designed for the experienced programmer with a basic understanding of C and 8086 assembly language, and DOS fundamentals.

Mastering DOS (Second Edition)
Judd Robbins
722pp. Ref. 555-7

"The most useful DOS book." This seven-part, in-depth tutorial addresses the needs of users at all levels. Topics range from running applications, to managing files and directories, configuring the system, batch file programming, and techniques for system developers. Through Version 4.

MS-DOS Power User's Guide, Volume I (Second Edition)
Jonathan Kamin
482pp. Ref. 473-9

A fully revised, expanded edition of our best-selling guide to high-performance DOS techniques and utilities—with details on Version 3.3. Configuration, I/O, directory structures, hard disks, RAM disks, batch file programming, the ANSI.SYS device driver, more. Through Version 3.3.

Understanding DOS 3.3
Judd Robbins
678pp. Ref. 648-0

This best selling, in-depth tutorial addresses the needs of users at all levels with many examples and hands-on exercises. Robbins discusses the fundamentals of DOS, then covers manipulating files and directories, using the DOS editor, printing, communicating, and finishes with a full section on batch files.

Understanding Hard Disk Management on the PC
Jonathan Kamin
500pp. Ref. 561-1

This title is a key productivity tool for all hard disk users who want efficient, error-free file management and organization. Includes details on the best ways to conserve hard disk space when using several memory-guzzling programs. Through DOS 4.

Up & Running with Your Hard Disk
Klaus M Rubsam
140pp. Ref. 666-9

A far-sighted, compact introduction to hard disk installation and basic DOS use. Perfect for PC users who want the practical essentials in the shortest possible time. In 20 basic steps, learn to choose your hard disk, work with accessories, back up data, use DOS utilities to save time, and more.

Up & Running with Windows 286/386
Gabriele Wentges
132pp. Ref. 691-X

This handy 20-step overview gives PC users all the essentials of using Windows—whether for evaluating the software, or getting a fast start. Each self-contained lesson takes just 15 minutes to one hour to complete.

NETWORKS

The ABC's of Local Area Networks
Michael Dortch
212pp. Ref. 664-2

This jargon-free introduction to LANs is for current and prospective users who see general information, comparative options, a look at the future, and tips for effective LANs use today. With comparisons of Token-Ring, PC Network, Novell, and others.

The ABC's of Novell Netware
Jeff Woodward
282pp. Ref. 614-6

For users who are new to PC's or networks, this entry-level tutorial outlines each basic element and operation of Novell. The ABC's introduces computer hardware and software, DOS, network organization and security, and printing and communicating over the netware system.

Mastering Novell Netware
Cheryl C. Currid
Craig A. Gillett
500pp. Ref. 630-8

This book is a thorough guide for System Administrators to installing and operating a microcomputer network using Novell Netware. Mastering covers actually setting up a network from start to finish, design, administration, maintenance, and troubleshooting.

UTILITIES

Mastering the Norton Utilities 5
Peter Dyson
400pp. Ref. 725-8

This complete guide to installing and using the Norton Utilities 5 is a must for beginning and experienced users alike. It offers a clear, detailed description of each utility, with options, uses and examples—so users can quickly identify the programs they need and put Norton right to work. Includes valuable coverage of the newest Norton enhancements.

Mastering PC Tools Deluxe 6
For Versions 5.5 and 6.0
425pp. Ref. 700-2

An up-to-date guide to the lifesaving utilities in PC Tools Deluxe version 6.0 from installation, to high-speed back-ups, data recovery, file encryption, desktop applications, and more. Includes detailed background on DOS and hardware such as floppies, hard disks, modems and fax cards.

Mastering SideKick Plus
Gene Weisskopf
394pp. Ref. 558-1

Employ all of Sidekick's powerful and expanded features with this hands-on guide to the popular utility. Features include comprehensive and detailed coverage of time management, note taking, outlining, auto dialing, DOS file management, math, and copy-and-paste functions.

Up & Running with Norton Utilities
Rainer Bartel
140pp. Ref. 659-6

Get up and running in the shortest possible time in just 20 lessons or "steps." Learn to restore disks and files, use UnErase, edit your floppy disks, retrieve lost data and more. Or use the book to evaluate the software before you purchase. Through Version 4.2.

every dBASE command, with step-by-step instructions and exact keystroke sequences. Commands are grouped by function in twenty precise categories.

dBASE III PLUS Programmer's Reference Guide
SYBEX Ready Reference Series
Alan Simpson
1056pp. Ref. 508-5

Programmers will save untold hours and effort using this comprehensive, well-organized dBASE encyclopedia. Complete technical details on commands and functions, plus scores of often-needed algorithms.

dBASE IV 1.1 Programmer's Instant Reference (Second Edition)
Alan Simpson
555pp, Ref. 764-9

Enjoy fast, easy access to information often hidden in cumbersome documentation. This handy pocket-sized reference presents information on each command and function in the dBASE IV programming language. Commands are grouped according to their purpose, so readers can locate the correct command for any task—quickly and easily.

dBASE IV User's Instant Reference (Second Edition)
Alan Simpson
356pp, Ref. 786-X

Completely revised to cover the new 1.1 version of dBASE IV, this handy reference guide presents information on every dBASE operation a user can perform. Exact keystroke sequences are presented, and complex tasks are explained step-by-step. It's a great way for newer users to look up the basics, while experienced users will find it a fast way to locate information on specialized tasks.

Mastering dBASE III PLUS: A Structured Approach
Carl Townsend
342pp. Ref. 372-4

In-depth treatment of structured programming for custom dBASE solutions. An ideal study and reference guide for applications developers, new and experienced users with an interest in efficient programming.

Mastering dBASE IV Programming
Carl Townsend
496pp. Ref. 540-9

This task-oriented book introduces structured dBASE IV programming and commands by setting up a general ledger system, an invoice system, and a quotation management system. The author carefully explores the unique character of dBASE IV based on his in-depth understanding of the program.

Mastering FoxPro
Charles Seigel
639pp. Ref. 671-5

This guide to the powerful FoxPro DBMS offers a tutorial on database basics, then enables the reader to master new skills and features as needed—with many examples from business. An in-depth tutorial guides users through the development of a complete mailing list system.

Mastering Paradox 3.5
Alan Simpson
650pp, Ref. 677-4

This indispensable, in-depth guide has again been updated for the latest Paradox release, offering the same comprehensive, hands-on treatment featured in highly praised previous editions. It covers everything from database basics to PAL programming—including complex queries and reports, and multi-table applications.

Mastering Q & A (Second Edition)
Greg Harvey
540pp. Ref. 452-6

This hands-on tutorial explores the Q & A Write, File, and Report modules, and the Intelligent Assistant. English-language command processor, macro creation, interfacing with other software, and more, using practical business examples.

Up & Running with PC Tools Deluxe 6
Thomas Holste
180pp. Ref.678-2

Learn to use this software program in just 20 basic steps. Readers get a quick, inexpensive introduction to using the Tools for disaster recovery, disk and file management, and more.

COMMUNICATIONS

Mastering Crosstalk XVI (Second Edition)
Peter W. Gofton
225pp. Ref. 642-1

Introducing the communications program Crosstalk XVI for the IBM PC. As well as providing extensive examples of command and script files for programming Crosstalk, this book includes a detailed description of how to use the program's more advanced features, such as windows, talking to mini or mainframe, customizing the keyboard and answering calls and background mode.

Mastering PROCOMM PLUS
Bob Campbell
400pp. Ref. 657-X

Learn all about communications and information retrieval as you master and use PROCOMM PLUS. Topics include choosing and using a modem; automatic dialing; using on-line services (featuring CompuServe) and more. Through Version 1.1b; also covers PROCOMM, the "shareware" version.

Mastering Serial Communications
Peter W. Gofton
289pp. Ref. 180-2

The software side of communications, with details on the IBM PC's serial programming, the XMODEM and Kermit protocols, non-ASCII data transfer, interrupt-level programming and more. Sample programs in C, assembly language and BASIC.

DATABASES

The ABC's of dBASE III PLUS
Robert Cowart
264pp. Ref. 379-1

The most efficient way to get beginners up and running with dBASE. Every 'how' and 'why' of database management is demonstrated through tutorials and practical dBASE III PLUS applications.

The ABC's of dBASE IV 1.1
Robert Cowart
350pp. Ref. 632-4

The latest version of dBASE IV is featured in this hands-on introduction. It assumes no previous experience with computers or database management, and uses easy-to-follow lessons to introduce the concepts, build basic skills, and set up some practical applications. Includes report writing and Query by Example.

The ABC's of Paradox 3.5 (Second Edition)
Charles Siegel
334pp, Ref. 785-1

This easy-to-follow, hands-on tutorial is a must for beginning users of Paradox 3.0 and 3.5. Even if you've never used a computer before, you'll be doing useful work in just a few short lessons. A clear introduction to database management and valuable business examples make this a "right-to-work" guide for the practical-minded.

Advanced Techniques in dBASE III PLUS
Alan Simpson
454pp. Ref. 369-4

A full course in database design and structured programming, with routines for inventory control, accounts receivable, system management, and integrated databases.

dBASE Instant Reference
SYBEX Prompter Series
Alan Simpson
471pp. Ref. 484-4; 4 ¾" × 8"

Comprehensive information at a glance: a brief explanation of syntax and usage for

Power User's Guide to R:BASE
Alan Simpson
Cheryl Currid
Craig Gillett
446pp. Ref. 354-6

Supercharge your R:BASE applications with this straightforward tutorial that covers system design, structured programming, managing multiple data tables, and more. Sample applications include ready-to-run mailing, inventory and accounts receivable systems. Through Version 2.11.

Understanding dBASE III
Alan Simpson
300pp. Ref. 267-1

dBASE commands and concepts are illustrated throughout with practical, business oriented examples—for mailing list handling, accounts receivable, and inventory design. Contains scores of tips and techniques for maximizing efficiency and meeting special needs.

Understanding dBASE III PLUS
Alan Simpson
415pp. Ref. 349-X

A solid sourcebook of training and ongoing support. Everything from creating a first database to command file programming is presented in working examples, with tips and techniques you won't find anywhere else.

Understanding dBASE IV 1.1
Alan Simpson
900pp, Ref. 633-2

Simpson's outstanding introduction to dBASE—brought up to date for version 1.1—uses tutorials and practical examples to build effective, and increasingly sophisticated, database management skills. Advanced topics include custom reporting, managing multiple databases, and designing custom applications.

Understanding Oracle
James T. Perry
Joseph G. Lateer
634pp. Ref. 534-4

A comprehensive guide to the Oracle database management system for administrators, users, and applications developers. Covers everything in Version 5 from database basics to multi-user systems, performance, and development tools including SQL*Forms, SQL*Report, and SQL*Calc. Includes Fast Track speed notes.

Understanding Professional File
Gerry Litton
463pp. Re. 669-3

Build practical data management skills in an orderly fashion with this complete step-by-step tutorial—from creating a simple database, to building customized business applications.

Understanding R:BASE
Alan Simpson
Karen Watterson
609pp. Ref. 503-4

This is the definitive R:BASE tutorial, for use with either OS/2 or DOS. Hands-on lessons cover every aspect of the software, from creating and using a database, to custom systems. Includes Fast Track speed notes.

Understanding SQL
Martin Gruber
400pp. Ref. 644-8

This comprehensive tutorial in Structured Query Language (SQL) is suitable for beginners, and for SQL users wishing to increase their skills. From basic principles to complex SQL applications, the text builds fluency and confidence using concise hands-on lessons and easy-to-follow examples.

Up & Running with Q&A
Ranier Bartel
140pp. Ref. 645-6

Obtain practical results with Q&A in the shortest possible time. Learn to design and program forms, use macros, format text, use utilities, and more. Or use the book to help you decide whether to purchase the program.

DESKTOP PRESENTATION

Mastering Harvard Graphics (Second Edition)
Glenn H. Larsen
375pp. Ref. 673-1

"The clearest course to begin mastering Harvard Graphics," according to *Computer Currents*. Readers master essential principles of effective graphic communication, as they follow step-by-step instructions to create dozens of charts and graphs; automate and customize the charting process; create slide shows; and more.

Understanding WordStar 2000
David Kolodney
Thomas Blackadar
275pp. Ref. 554-9

This engaging, fast-paced series of tutorials covers everything from moving the cursor to print enhancements, format files, key glossaries, windows and MailMerge. With practical examples, and notes for former WordStar users.

Visual Guide to WordPerfect
Jeff Woodward
457pp. Ref. 591-3

This is a visual hands-on guide which is ideal for brand new users as the book shows each activity keystroke-by-keystroke. Clear illustrations of computer screen menus are included at every stage. Covers basic editing, formatting lines, paragraphs, and pages, using the block feature, footnotes, search and replace, and more. Through Version 5.

WordPerfect 5 Desktop Companion
SYBEX Ready Reference Series
Greg Harvey
Kay Yarborough Nelson
1006pp. Ref. 522-0

Desktop publishing features have been added to this compact encyclopedia. This title offers more detailed, cross-referenced entries on every software feature including page formatting and layout, laser printing and word processing macros. New users of WordPerfect, and those new to Version 5 and desktop publishing will find this easy to use for on-the-job help.

WordPerfect 5 Instant Reference
SYBEX Prompter Series
Greg Harvey
Kay Yarborough Nelson
316pp. Ref. 535-2, 4 ¾" × 8"

This pocket-sized reference has all the program commands for the powerful WordPerfect 5 organized alphabetically for quick access. Each command entry has the exact key sequence, any reveal codes, a list of available options, and option-by-option discussions.

WordPerfect 5.1 Instant Reference
Greg Harvey
Kay Yarborough Nelson
252pp. Ref. 674-X

Instant access to all features and commands of WordPerfect 5.0 and 5.1, highlighting the newest software features. Complete, alphabetical entries provide exact key sequences, codes and options, and step-by-step instructions for many important tasks.

WordPerfect 5.1 Macro Handbook
Kay Yarborough Nelson
532pp, Ref. 687-1

Help yourself to over 150 ready-made macros for WordPerfect versions 5.0 and 5.1. This complete tutorial guide to creating and using work-saving macros is a must for every serious WordPerfect user. Hands-on lessons show you exactly how to record and use your first simple macros—then build to sophisticated skills.

WordPerfect 5.1 Tips and Tricks (Fourth Edition)
Alan R. Neibauer
675pp. Ref. 681-2

This new edition is a real timesaver. For on-the-job guidance and creative new uses, this title covers all versions of WordPerfect up to and including 5.1—streamlining documents, automating with macros, new print enhancements, and more.

SYBEX®

FREE CATALOG!

Mail us this form today, and we'll send you a full-color catalog of Sybex books.

Name _____

Street _____

City/State/Zip _____

Phone _____

Please supply the name of the Sybex book purchased.

_____

How would you rate it?

_____ Excellent   _____ Very Good   _____ Average   _____ Poor

Why did you select this particular book?

_____ Recommended to me by a friend
_____ Recommended to me by store personnel
_____ Saw an advertisement in _____
_____ Author's reputation
_____ Saw in Sybex catalog
_____ Required textbook
_____ Sybex reputation
_____ Read book review in _____
_____ In-store display
_____ Other _____

Where did you buy it?

_____ Bookstore
_____ Computer Store or Software Store
_____ Catalog (name: _____)
_____ Direct from Sybex
_____ Other: _____

Did you buy this book with your personal funds?

_____ Yes   _____ No

About how many computer books do you buy each year?

_____ 1-3   _____ 3-5   _____ 5-7   _____ 7-9   _____ 10+

About how many Sybex books do you own?

_____ 1-3   _____ 3-5   _____ 5-7   _____ 7-9   _____ 10+

Please indicate your level of experience with the software covered in this book:

_____ Beginner   _____ Intermediate   _____ Advanced

Which types of software packages do you use regularly?

_____ Accounting	_____ Databases	_____ Networks
_____ Amiga	_____ Desktop Publishing	_____ Operating Systems
_____ Apple/Mac	_____ File Utilities	_____ Spreadsheets
_____ CAD	_____ Money Management	_____ Word Processing
_____ Communications	_____ Languages	_____ Other _____
		(please specify)

Which of the following best describes your job title?

_____ Administrative/Secretarial	_____ President/CEO
_____ Director	_____ Manager/Supervisor
_____ Engineer/Technician	_____ Other _____
	(please specify)

Comments on the weaknesses/strengths of this book: _____

_____
_____
_____
_____

PLEASE FOLD, SEAL, AND MAIL TO SYBEX

- -

SYBEX, INC.
Department M
2021 CHALLENGER DR.
ALAMEDA, CALIFORNIA USA
94501

SYBEX ®

SEAL

PRINCIPAL DATABASE MANAGEMENT OPERATIONS USING FOXPRO

(continues from first page)

Setting Up the Current Work Area

The Setup dialog box lets you control the database file that is open in the currently active work area. You can change the actual structure of the database, and you can create, open, or modify indexes to control the order in which the database, fields, and records are displayed and used.

The Setup dialog box

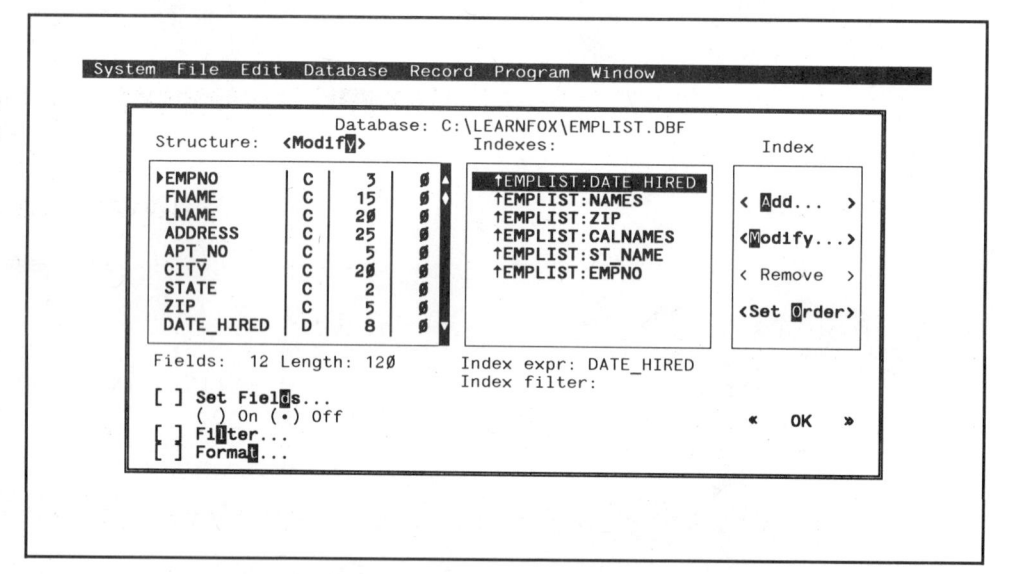

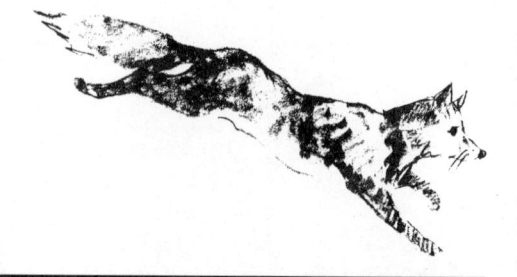